Handbook of Brand Relationships

Handbook of Brand Relationships

Deborah J. MacInnis

C. Whan Park

Joseph R. Priester

Editors

Society for Consumer Psychology

M.E.Sharpe
Armonk, New York
London, England

Library of Congress Cataloging-in-Publication Data

Handbook of brand relationships / edited by Deborah J. MacInnis, C. Whan Park, and Joseph R. Priester.
   p. cm.
Includes bibliographical references and index.
ISBN 978-0-7656-2357-7 (cloth : alk. paper)
1. Relationship marketing. 2. Brand choice. 3. Branding (Marketing) 4. Customer relations.
I. MacInnis, Deborah J. II. Park, C. Whan. III. Priester, Joseph R., 1960–

HF5415.55.H357 2009
658.8′27—dc22   2008053551

Printed in the United States of America

The paper used in this publication meets the minimum requirements of
American National Standard for Information Sciences
Permanence of Paper for Printed Library Materials,
ANSI Z 39.48-1984.

CW (c)   10   9   8   7   6   5   4   3   2   1

CONTENTS

Introduction

Why Brand Relationships?

Deborah J. MacInnis, C. Whan Park, and Joseph Priester

Researchers and marketing practitioners maintain a keen interest in brand relationships: what they are, why they are formed, how they evolve, what effects they have on consumers and the marketplace, and when and why they cease to exist. The chapters in this volume provide a state-of-the-art perspective on what is known about this fast-growing area and chart directions for future research on this topic. This study of brand relationships is informed by the research topics shown in Figure I.1 and addressed in this book.

BRAND RELATIONSHIPS

As Figure I.1 suggests, the construct of a brand relationship is quite complex. Numerous types of brand relationships can be identified and each of them is associated with different emotions and norms. The types of brand relationships that are characterized by different dimensions can evolve via various processes. Although marketers may be interested in developing deep and lasting relationships between consumers and their brands, not all relationships are regarded as "committed partnerships." Some are like best friends, others like causal flings, codependencies, or secret affairs. Brand relationships, much like committed partnerships, take many forms. They may be infused with emotion and involve obsessive thought, or they can be simply habitual and subsequently less emotionally charged and cognitively based. Some brand relationships are regarded as transactional; that is, they are regarded as one-time affairs where the relationship is based on norms of an economic exchange. Others are communal and are based on norms of reciprocity, altruism, and responsiveness to the other's needs. Brand relationships also vary along numerous dimensions, such as whether they are conflict-ridden or conflict-free, permanent or temporary, and interdependent or independent, among others.

CONSUMER AND BRAND RELATIONSHIPS

As Figure I.1 suggests, consumers form these relationships because they serve a purpose. One critical purpose is that they help consumers develop and communicate something about themselves: who they were, who they are, who they want to be, and who they don't want to be. The development of an individual's identity is only one motivation

Figure I.1   **Critical Issues in the Study of Brand Relationships**

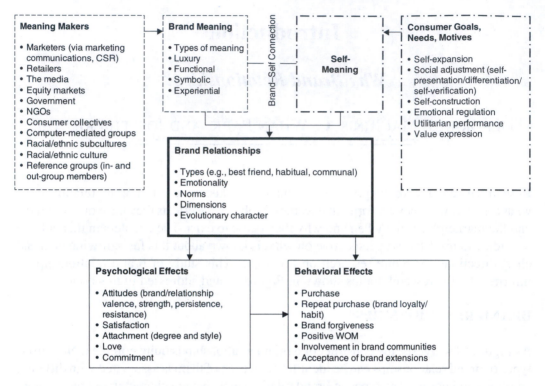

Abbreviations: CSR, corporate social responsibility; NGO, nongovernmental organization; WOM, word of mouth.

for forming brand relationships. Brands also provide utilitarian and emotional benefits to consumers. Brand relationships help consumers to solve problems, feel better, look better, act according to their values, and maintain harmonious relationships with others. In short, brands provide resources to consumers that meet their needs, help them attain goals, and motivate them in their daily lives.

BRAND MEANING AND BRAND-SELF CONNECTIONS

Consumer brand relationships are predicated on a connection between the consumer and the brand. These brand-self connections are based on not just the individual and the meaning that the consumer attaches to the brand. Consumers can impart unique and idiosyncratic meaning to brands through their brand relationships and personal experiences. Moreover, this meaning may evolve over the course of a brand relationship. However, consumers are not the only ones who impart brand meaning. Marketers play a pivotal role in the initial establishment of brand meaning through marketing communications, corporate social responsibility programs, and related activities. Many other individuals also lend a hand in defining a brand, such as marketing-related groups (e.g., retailers, the media), the external public (e.g., equity markets, government, nongovernmental organizations), and consumer groups (e.g., consumer collectives, cultures, subcultures, and reference groups). The extent to which brands possess the meaning intended by the original marketer (e.g., luxury or symbolic status) depends on the input of numerous other parties.

OUTCOMES OF BRAND RELATIONSHIPS

Just as brand relationships have numerous characteristics, meanings, and motivators, they also have varied outcomes. Whether marketers can expect that consumer-brand relationships will evoke behaviors such as brand loyalty, brand forgiveness, positive word-of-mouth, involvement in brand communities, or acceptance of brand extensions depends to a great degree on the psychological implications of a given brand relationship. Some brand relationships are based on positive attitudes that are neither strong or persistent. Such relationships may be transient and vulnerable to competitive activities, brand rumors, or other negative publicity. Other brand relationships are resistant to competitive attacks and negative marketplace news because they are based on strong brand attitudes that have persisted over time and can resist external influence. In addition to strong positive attitudes toward brands, consumers may also have a strong attachment to a brand, which is characterized by strong brand-self connections and prominent brand thoughts. Such strong psychological attachment is related to intense psychological outcomes such as brand love and a psychological commitment to stay in the brand relationship. This psychological commitment can be revealed by the behavioral effects noted in Figure I.1, such as brand forgiveness and acceptance of brand extensions.

ORGANIZATION OF THIS BOOK

The *Handbook of Brand Relationships* describes in detail the issues mentioned here and articulated in Figure I.1. The chapters are organized into four parts. Part I addresses the concept of brand relationships and the various types and dimensions that characterize such relationships. Part II considers the motivation consumers have for developing brand relationships as well as the role of brands in developing self-identity. Part III considers the various meaning-makers that impact the type and nature of the connections that link the consumer with the brand. Finally, Part IV examines the psychological and behavioral effects of brand relationships characterized by varying degrees of strength, attachment, and love.

PART I: FUNDAMENTAL ISSUES IN BRAND RELATIONSHIPS

In Chapter 1, "Lessons Learned about Consumers' Relationships with Their Brands," Susan Fournier, a pioneer in the field of brand relationships, identifies three central tenets on the usefulness of brand relationships, their complexity, and their evolution. These tenets can help to guide research on brand relationships. First, brand relationships are purposive, they provide resources and meaning that help people live their lives. Acknowledging that research on personal and brand identity has contributed much to our understanding of brand relationships, Fournier cautions that a broader lens should be applied to understanding the functions of such relationships. In essence, brand relationships serve as means to higher-level goals (e.g., "getting by," connecting with others, and emotional comfort); goals that include but also go beyond identity. The meaning of brands and brand relationships is thus informed by understanding how the brand "resonates" with those needs and goals. The second principle refers to the complexity of brand relationships, which are characterized by numerous dimensions and take various forms. Fournier identifies over 50 such dimensions. Brand relationships can be characterized as cooperative or competitive, emotional or functional, deep or superficial. They can take forms that are positive (committed partnerships, best friendships), neutral (casual acquaintances), or negative (enslavements). Fournier argues that a contractual lens on the relationship phenomenon can also provide insight into brand relationships, since that lens affords a consideration of the rules and norms that guide the development, maintenance, and dissolution of relationships. This perspective leads to the third tenet, which describes the process of how relationships form and evolve. The evolving nature of brand relationships has been largely unexplored. Fournier concludes with an important point—if work on brand relationships is to advance, we must move beyond mere descriptions of such relationships and offer insight for managers into measuring and impacting these relationships. That insight, she argues, can be realized through the integration of discipline-based perspectives on relationships.

In Chapter 2, "Using Relationship Norms to Understand Consumer-Brand Interactions," Pankaj Aggarwal reviews his program of research on relationship norms. He argues that just as consumers have norms that guide human relationships, they also have norms that guide brand relationships. Two types of brand relationship norms can be identified. Some brand relationships are viewed from a transactional perspective. Such relationships dictate norms such as prompt repayment for specific benefits received, a desire to receive payments for benefits soon after their receipt, and tracking the input and output that relationship partners have traded over the course of the relationship. In contrast, other relationships are viewed from a communal perspective. Such relationships dictate norms such as rendering help when needed (with no expectation of monetary payment), less tracking of the relative inputs and outputs of relationship partners, and considerable leeway with regard to when repayments are expected. Aggarwal's studies show that consumers' evaluations of brands are impacted by whether the brand's (marketer's) behavior is consistent or inconsistent with the norms that guide that type of relationship. Thus, consumers in transactional relationships are more sensitive to monetary repayment and repayment that is immediate (vs. delayed). Aggarwal shows that relationship norms not only impact consumers' reactions to norm violations, they also affect how consumers treat and interact with the brand and its representatives. Consumers in communal relationships are more sensitive to issues of procedural fairness, that is, how these consumers are treated as opposed to consumers in transactional, or exchange, relationships. In contrast, consumers in transactional relationships are more sensitive to issues of distributive justice;

that is, how benefits are allocated to consumers. Consumers in communal relationships also tend to process information about the brand on a more abstract level.

In Chapter 3, "Brand Loyalty Is Not Habitual," Leona Tam, Wendy Wood, and Mindy Ji examine relationships formed through habits. Whereas repeat purchases can suggest a brand relationship based on loyalty, it is important to differentiate between loyalty and habit-based relationships. The authors define a habit-based brand relationship as a "behavioral disposition in which past responses are triggered by associated context cues," as opposed to being driven by goals, attitudes, or intentions. Such cues include time, place, and social context. On the other hand, brand loyalty is regarded as an evaluative tendency that entails either a positive or a negative response. It entails commitment to the brand and involves potentially strong and positive brand attitudes. Whereas habits occur unconsciously, brand-loyal responses involve deliberate processing that involves thoughts, feelings, and beliefs about the brand and its relative performance in comparison with competitive offerings. Whereas habits are cued by context, loyalty is relatively independent of context and unaffected by contextual cues. The authors suggest that brand loyalty can exist on an implicit level, meaning that consumers may be unaware of their relative brand preference. However, while implicit attitudes still impact intentions and can be revealed by a flexible orientation, habits are substantially more rigid. That is, they involve a standardized response when one is confronted with a specific cue. Both habitual and loyalty relationships can lead to positive outcomes for companies. They can also affect consumers (perhaps resembling the dependency relationship types identified by Fournier). In light of these outcomes, Tam and colleagues consider managerial and consumer implications of the management of both types of relationship.

PART II: GOALS, NEEDS, AND MOTIVES THAT FOSTER BRAND RELATIONSHIPS

In Chapter 4, "Self-Expansion Motivation and Inclusion of Brands in Self: Toward a Theory of Brand Relationships," Martin Reimann and Arthur Aron expand on Fournier's first tenet—the purposive nature of brand relationships. The authors suggest that brand relationships are fundamentally motivating because they help consumers fulfill their goals. Aron's self-expansion theory posits that people are (consciously or unconsciously) motivated to expand themselves by enhancing their ability to achieve various higher and lower order goals. Relationships with other people are important mechanisms by which individuals expand the self; through a relationship with a partner, one comes to see the partner's resources, identities, and perspectives as one's own. Although empirical work using self-expansion theory in a *brand* relationship context is limited, Reimann and Aron posit that, like people, *brands afford opportunities for consumers to expand their sense of self;* hence the self-expansion construct may afford a useful mechanism for explaining why consumers become brand loyal. Moreover, consumers may value brands because the resources, identities, and perspectives the brand offers are also seen as part of the self (perhaps fostering a brand-self connection). The authors hypothesize that new brand relationships can be emotionally intense and can create strong potential for self-expansion (although this self-expansion potential may wane as the relationship evolves). This reduction in self-expansion may be particularly acute for low-involvement products.

"Why on Earth Do Consumers Have Relationships with Marketers? Toward Understanding the Function of Brand Relationships," by Laurence Ashworth, Peter Dacin, and Matthew Thomson also delves into Fournier's first tenet as the authors examine the motivations that guide brand relationships. Ashworth and colleagues articulate and develop a scale to assess six potential functions of brand relationships. Specially, they argue that consumers are motivated to develop relationships with brands that (1) help consumers fit into a group, (2) are practical and/or useful, (3) evoke positive feelings, (4) fit with the consumers' values and their sense of self, (5) evoke feelings of closeness and intimacy, and (6) foster an understanding of one's daily world. The authors label these the social adjustment, utilitarian, hedonic, affiliation, value expressions, and knowledge motivations, respectively. All of these, except the knowledge motivations, were found to be positively related to relationship strength. Interestingly, different motivations are related to different relationship outcomes. For example, after controlling for relationship strength, the social adjustment and utilitarian motivations were positively related to perceptions of brand quality, whereas the affiliation and value expression motivations were negatively related to perceived quality.

In Chapter 6, "Self-Brand Connections: The Role of Reference Groups and Celebrity Endorsers in the Creation of Brand Meaning," Jennifer Escalas and James Bettman review their program of research on brand-self connections. They focus on the social motivations consumers have for developing brand-self connections, suggesting that consumers use brands for purposes of self-construction, social integration, self-differentiation, and self-presentation. The process by which consumers develop brand-self connections is also considered. Leveraging prior theory, the authors argue that brands come to hold meaning through their associations with various aspirational, associative, or dissociative reference groups and/or celebrities. When brands have these associations, and when consumers have a desire to emulate the relevant group/celebrity, they develop brand-self connections. Brand-self connections have been observed with regard to brands that are consistent with the image of an ingroup as opposed to those that are associated with an outgroup. Interestingly, the authors' research shows that consumers with a self-enhancement goal (those who want to look good in the eyes of others) are more likely to develop brand-self connections to brands associated with aspirational groups, or groups that they want to emulate. In contrast, consumers with a self-verification goal (those who want verification of their self-image) are more likely to develop brand-self connections with actual reference groups. These effects are particularly strong for brands with symbolic brand meaning.

Chapter 7, "When Brands Are Built from Within: A Social Identity Pathway to Liking and Evaluation," considers that consumers often hold numerous social identifiers (labels they use to express who they are). Americus Reed, Joel Cohen, and Amit Bhattacharjee also postulate that different self-identities may be more or less salient at different points in time. The collective set of identities held by an individual is part of their self-concept, though not all of these identities are salient and part of working memory at all points in time. The authors argue that attitudes based on identity considerations may be formed through a different set of processes than those formed through nonidentity bases. Hence, different communication strategies may be more or less effective depending on whether or not the attitude is identity-based. Prior attitude formation models have considered social influences on attitudes, and focused more on normative and information influences on attitudes rather than identity-based concerns. Moreover, the attitudes toward brands may depend on the particular identity that happens to be salient at the time. Different contexts may cue different identities, which suggests that consumers' evaluations of an advertised brand may depend not only on the brand but also on its relationship to a salient identity. The authors' analysis points to the social adjustment function of consumer-brand relationships. For marketers, the task is to develop brand-self connections by attaching social identities to brands that will resonate with consumers' own personal identities.

In Chapter 8, "Group-Based Brand Relationships and Persuasion: Multiple Roles for Identification and Identification Discrepancies," Monique Fleming discusses how social identities, as forms of brand-self connections, affect consumers' brand attitudes. Starting from the perspective that brand attitudes are typically more favorable when a persuasive message is consistent with a group to which the consumer belongs, the author asks why and how such persuasion occurs. Fleming identifies both thoughtful and nonthoughtful bases for such persuasion among individuals who are highly identified with the group.

PART III: BRAND MEANING AND MEANING MAKERS

The authors of Chapter 9, "Collective Brand Relationships," Thomas O'Guinn and Albert Mūniz, Jr., discuss the importance of focusing on brand meaning in research. Meaning is the most powerful form of competitive differentiation. O'Guinn and Mūniz argue that it is limiting to focus only on brands and consumers. This approach restricts the role of meaning makers to marketers, as opposed to the many parties, institutions, and publics that develop, sustain, and change brand meanings. Besides marketers, meaning makers and modifiers include consumers, consumer collectives (face-to-face groups), computer-mediated groups, institutions such as the media, retailers, equity markets, and government and nongovernmental institutions. The authors point out that meaning occurs through a set of processes, which include accommodation (the marketers' meaning is accepted to a certain degree by consumers); negotiation (where meaning makers bargain over what the brand means and to whom it belongs); cultivation of brand meaning through its integration with the world of consumers; polity (i.e., modification or development through political or revolutionary groups); rumors; and disruption (where brand meaning is impacted by breaks in society's economic, demographic, or other relevant circumstance). The authors reject brands as humans, arguing that brands do not have relationships or personality. But they do acknowledge that brands are makers of social identity. As such, brands gain particular significance during times of transition when reliance on brand meaning eases role transitions. A repeated refrain is that brand meaning is not owned by marketers alone, although marketers can play a role in shaping it. Instead, meaning is held by consumers and shaped through a variety of entities and processes.

Marketers often communicate brand meaning through traditional activities such as advertising and other marketing communications. However, companies can also be meaning makers through their corporate social responsibility (CSR) activities. In Chapter 10, "Building Brand Relationships through Corporate Social Responsibility," Sankar Sen, Shuili Du, and C.B. Bhattacharya review the literature on what is known about the relationship outcomes engendered by CSR activities, why these outcomes occur, and when they are likely to occur. The authors argue that CSR activities are a part of companies' process of changing from a transactional to an exchange-based relationship with consumers. CSR activities can help marketers develop meaningful connections between the company, its brands, and consumers. The authors posit that CSR activities are more effective than traditional marketing activities for triggering rarer, longer-term consumer advocacy behaviors; these relationship outcomes occur because CSR activities humanize the company, creating identification with the company and its brands; and marketers need to be aware of the myriad factors that moderate the relationship between CSR and these activities. Factors driving the success of CSR activities include consumers' awareness of the activities, their beliefs about the effectiveness or efficacy of the CSR program in fostering consumer welfare, and whether they attribute CSR activities to intrinsic motivations as opposed to purely extrinsic motivations. If consumers are aware of the CSR activities and have positive beliefs and positive attributions about the company's CSR activities, they come to identify with the company, creating stronger brand-self connections. These strong brand-self connections create positive outcomes, for example: purchase loyalty, resilience to negative information, and brand advocacy. These positive outcomes are contingent on a host of moderating factors, which include whether consumers see a fit between the company and its CSR activities, whether marketers try to overdo things in terms of self-promoting their CSR activities, whether the company is already considered the socially responsible brand in a particular category, and the proximity of consumers to the benefits of the CSR cause.

Chapter 11, "Ethnicity, Race, and Brand Connections," by David Schumann, Edith Davidson, and Bridget Satinover provides a conceptual distinction between race (classifications based on biological differences) and ethnicity (classifications based on cultural meaning and psychological connections with cultural groups). The authors articulate the size and growth of the Hispanic, African American, and Asian populations in the United States and describe marketers' efforts to segment markets and differentially target these populations over time. Three race-based targeting practices are described: primary market strategy, which involves developing products and brands specific to a racial group; secondary market targeting, which involves varying the message linked to a given product so that it appeals to the population of interest; and subsumed market strategy, which aims to reach various racial and ethnic groups by targeting the public at large. The authors review brand connections to racial groups in marketing communications. The authors also review self-brand connections that are initiated by ethnic consumers' unique use of a product. They further indicate that cultural meanings and symbols move from the culture to the consumer's own identity. The authors identify various types of ethnic-brand connections made through language, religion, music, genres, color schemes, familial representations, traditions, and associations with ethnic organizations. They also consider how the creation of brand-self connections based on race or ethnicity benefits marketers.

In Chapter 12, "Cultural Value Dimensions and Brands: Can a Global Brand Image Exist?" Susan Forquer Gupta, Doan Winkel, and Laura Peracchio consider how culture impacts the meanings that consumers attach to brands. Because culture is learned and is an adaptive system, the meaning of brands within and across cultures is always subject to change. National cultural values affect brand meanings and the importance consumers put on various brand meanings. Values such as individualism and collectivism, power distancing, masculinity/femininity, uncertainty avoidance, and time orientation can all affect whether consumers value various brand meanings. Culture can also impact the brand personality assigned to a brand as well as the outcomes of brand relationships, such as brand attitudes or preferences and acceptance of brand extensions.

When consumer-brand relationships are strong and positive, marketers can leverage the relationship through the use of brand extensions. Research has shown that consumers' evaluations of brand extensions depend, in part, on whether the brand extension seems to "fit," with the parent brand. In Chapter 13, "Understanding Cultural Differences in Brand Extension Evaluation: The Influence of Analytic versus Holistic Thinking," Alokparna (Sonia) Monga and Debbie Roedder John consider the impact of culture on brand meanings assigned by consumers and their acceptance of brand extensions. Specifically, Western consumers are considered to have an analytical processing style, meaning that they focus on the attributes of an object, the categories to which it belongs, and have a preference for rules that dictate category membership. In contrast, Asian consumers have a more holistic processing style, which focuses on relationships among objects and have a preference for explaining and predicting the world based on these relationships. The authors hypothesize (and find) that consumers in Asian cultures are better able to find a fit between a parent brand and a low-similarity extension, and are more favorably disposed to such brands than their counterparts from Western cultures. Monga and John have also found that consumers from the two cultures generate different types of thoughts toward a brand extension, and these thoughts mediated the impact of cultural differences on brand extension evaluation. The results of the authors' research are consistent with the view stated earlier about the differences in Asian and Western consumer processes.

Brands can communicate many symbolic meanings, including those having to do with status and prestige. In Chapter 14, "Luxury Branding," Vanessa Patrick and Henrik Hagtvedt recognize a marketplace shift that is occurring in the luxury market. That shift involves the rise of "new luxury" products consumed by middle-market consumers. Whereas old luxury brands were based on status and prestige, new luxury brands focus on creating pleasurable emotional experiences and connections with consumers. In sum, the new luxury brand represents a movement from symbolism (external focus) to hedonism (internal focus). Back to Fournier's opening chapter, this perspective complements the social-based perspectives evident in several of chapters in this book by focusing on hedonic motivations for brand relationships. In addition, such brands are seen to offer "top-of-category" experiences, which are unique, hedonically special, and emotionally gratifying. Their rare and unique benefits induce a willingness to pay top dollar for their consumption. Individual differences (e.g., trait hedonism, culture of origin) as well as situational factors (e.g., goal priming) can influence susceptibility toward luxury brand consumption. Despite the prevalence of this branding strategic option, Patrick and Hagtvedt note that research on luxury branding is limited and hence rife with opportunities for research advancement. They chart three directions: (1) a reconceptualization of the luxury concept and a better understanding of the source from which consumers derive value in luxury consumption; (2) an analysis of how luxury brands are evaluated—perhaps using a different mechanism from that suggested by Reed et al. for self-identity-based brands; and (3) the study of how luxury brands can be best managed.

PART IV: PSYCHOLOGICAL AND BEHAVIORAL EFFECTS OF STRONG BRAND RELATIONSHIPS

In Chapter 15, "Attitudes as a Basis for Brand Relationships: Contributions of Elaboration, Metacognition, and Bias Correction," Duane Wegener, Vanessa Sawicki, and Richard Petty investigate the correlation between attitudes and behavior as suggested by research on the specificity of measuring attitudes and behaviors, the impact of social others (Theory of Reasoned Action), and the sense of personal control over behavioral enactment (Theory of Planned Behavior). The authors suggest that similar factors may be involved in the relationship between consumers' attitudes toward a brand relationship and their willingness to have a sustained relationship with a brand. Literature on attitude strength is reviewed, noting that strong attitudes are based on thoughtful processing and that they better predict attitude-behavior linkages, and attitude resistance and persistence over time. Properties that go along with strong attitudes include the extent of knowledge about the attitude object, the attitude's accessibility, and the certainty with which the attitude is held. The Elaboration Likelihood Model and the role of persuasion variables in attitude formation and change processes are reviewed, with regard to the level of elaboration (high vs. moderate vs. low) and whether processing is biased or unbiased. The authors assess the role of metacognition (thoughts about thoughts). With respect to attitudes (the primary cognition), consumers can have thoughts (metacognitions) regarding the target of the thought, its origin, its valence, the amount of thought, and whether it is good or bad to hold such an attitude. Assessments of the confidence with which an attitude is held can also be considered as a form of metacognition. Certainty can be affected by direct experience with the attitude object, repeated expression of the attitude, ease of generating attitude-consistent thoughts, and consensual support for one's attitude. When people believe they have resisted a persuasion attempt but realize that they have done so based on weak arguments, the confidence in their attitude can actually decrease. People's confidence can be increased when they are asked to find fault with very strong counterarguments for why a brand is good.

As for Chapter 16, "Putting Context Effects in Context: The Construction and Retrieval as Moderated by Attitude Strength (CARMAS) Model of Evaluative Judgment": While strong brand relationships may be predicated on favorable attitudes, considerable research has debated fundamental processes that govern attitude formation processes. Some research suggests that attitudes are stored, evaluative judgments, based on thoughtful processes that in turn guide behavior. Other research suggests that attitudes are not stored, but are instead constructed online based on contextual information at hand. In a series of studies, Dhananjay Nayakankuppam and Joseph Priester show that the process that best describes attitude formation processes is moderated by attitude strength. Strong attitudes are those that are held with confidence. They are more accessible, persist over time, resist competitive attempts, and are more likely to guide choice than weakly held attitudes. The authors suggest that because strong attitudes are more accessible than weak attitudes and because they are based on effortful thought, they are more likely than weak attitudes to be diagnostic or relevant; they are therefore more likely to create the behavioral effects shown in Figure I.1. Support for the fact that strong attitudes are retrieved while weak attitudes are constructed is found in studies that measure and manipulate attitude strength. Moreover, the results are replicated using different measures of attitude strength.

The construct of attachment is described in Chapter 17, "The Connection-Prominence Attachment Model (CPAM): A Conceptual and Methodological Exploration of Brand Attachment." C. Whan Park, Joseph Priester, Deborah MacInnis, and Zhong Wan characterize attachment as a psychological construct, comparing brand relationships to committed partnerships. The authors articulate two conceptual properties that underlie the attachment construct: brand-self connections and prominent brand thoughts and feelings. In three studies, the authors develop a measure of brand attachment based on these conceptual properties, differentiate it from an alternative measure of attachment, and demonstrate that it has convergent, discriminant, and predictive validity. Interestingly, whereas prior research establishes the importance of brand-self connections as fundamental to strong brand relationships, Priester and colleagues argue that brand attachment is best revealed by a combination of strong brand-self connections and prominent thoughts and feelings about the brand.

In Chapter 18, "Love, Desire and Identity: A Conditional Integration Theory of the Love of Things," Aaron Ahuvia, Rajeev Batra, and Richard Bagozzi describe brand relationships characterized by love. Based on interviews with 69 educated professionals, the authors find that most consumers report possessing loved objects (LOs). The LO is closely related to the self. Respondents used the term *love* to describe objects that affect or express the self, those that are viewed as a physical extension of the self, and those with which they have a shared history. This connection between the self and the LO was reflected in respondents' personification of the LO as an image of their ideal selves, the fact that respondents used self-relevant emotions when describing the LO, and their reported thoughts of separation distress from the object's loss. Ahuvia and colleagues report two processes by which a LO is related to the self. One process resembles Reimann and Aron's self-expansion model, in which passion for the LO lends it various forms of integration with the self (physical, cognitive, and identity). Although relationships formed through this integration process are initially intense, the relationship cools over time, moving from intense passion to less intense warmth. Other LO relationships are formed through a process of emergence from the self. Here, rather than being incorporated into the self, the LO is seen to arise from the self, often because the LO relationship has been created by the user. The intrinsic value ascribed to LOs has been attributed to several factors: they are regarded as outstanding (high in quality); they are intrinsically rewarding; they appeal to higher order needs; and they relate to a variety of consumer meanings and benefits. Finally, the authors indicate that what differentiates real "love" from metaphoric "love" when used to describe an LO is that the LO evokes an intense transforming experience. Like Fournier, Ahuvia and colleagues note that understanding LOs cannot occur in a vacuum. Objects are loved because of their relevance to real world needs and values.

As brand relationships progress over time, there is an increase in opportunities for brand failures or transgressions that threaten the brand relationship. In Chapter 19, "Customer Coping in Response to Relationship Transgressions: An Attachment Theoretic Approach," Marcel Paulssen and Richard Bagozzi suggest that whether consumers react favorably or unfavorably to relationship transgressions may depend on their attachment style. They hypothesize that consumers who have a secure attachment style (e.g., those who we are willing to rely on or trust in businesses and brands and who have a desire for close bonds with the business and its employees) are less vulnerable to relationship transgressions. Indeed, consumers with greater attachment security were less likely to be angered by a relationship transgression and less likely to attribute the transgression to the brand or company. These less extreme negative reactions and attributions made it less likely that consumers would engage in negative word-of-mouth or leave or neglect the relationship. In sum, securely attached consumers coped better and more constructively with relationship transgressions than did consumers who had low attachment security. Since these same kinds of effects have been observed with human relationships, these results suggest similarities between consumer-brand relationships and personal relationships.

PART V: CONCLUSIONS AND RESEARCH DIRECTIONS

Chapter 20, "Research Directions on Strong Brand Relationships," leverages the ideas and research issues noted in earlier chapters and develops a research agenda related to the study of strong brand relationships. C. Whan Park, Deborah MacInnis, and Joseph Priester limit their discussion to the dimension of brand relationships described by Fournier as strong brand relationships, arguing that this dimension has the greatest potential to contribute to consumer happiness and the profit potential of firms. The authors also suggest that these strong relationships are best characterized by consumers' attachment to the brand. As such, they consider relationships that resemble the committed partnership or best-friend relationship type described by Fourier, those for which Aggarwal argues entail a communal relationship perspective, and characterized by Ahuvia and colleagues as involving love. Utilizing the ideas in the measure of attachment described in Chapter 17, the authors argue that brand attachment is characterized by strong brand-self connections as well as prominent brand thoughts. With these conceptual properties in mind, they provide some tentative ideas about how attachment differs conceptually and empirically from potentially related concepts such as strong brand attitudes, commitment, love, and loyalty—ideas that deserve empirical validation. The authors also argue that relationships characterized by strong attachment may exhibit unique behaviors, such as proximity seeking and separation distress. Furthermore, attachment may be more strongly related than strong brand attitudes to the behavioral outcomes noted in Figure I.1. The authors suggest that research on the role of various meaning makers in fostering brand attachment is needed, and that research on the motivations and other drivers of attachment is critical. They also suggest research that relates brand attachment to the equity derived by a firm from brand relationships. Finally, the need for research on how relationships characterized by strong brand attachment evolve, weaken, and eventually terminate is expressed.

CONCLUSION

The domain of brand relationships is extremely complex. There are numerous types of brand relationships and multiple dimensions that characterize them. They involve varying types and intensities of emotions and normative processes. They vary in the motivations that drive them, the strength of the connection bonding the consumer with the brand, and the role of various meaning makers in creating, establishing, and expanding the brand's relationship to the self. Moreover, the psychological and behavioral outcomes of brand relationships are also numerous and complex. This book addresses state-of-the-art research on brand relationships, and we hope it will inform the reader as well as inspire additional work on this highly productive and important research domain.

Handbook of Brand Relationships

PART I

FUNDAMENTAL ISSUES IN BRAND RELATIONSHIPS

CHAPTER 1

LESSONS LEARNED ABOUT CONSUMERS' RELATIONSHIPS WITH THEIR BRANDS

SUSAN FOURNIER

It has been ten years since the publication of "Consumers and their Brands: Developing Relationship Theory in Consumer Research" (Fournier 1998). Over the course of the decade, we have learned a great deal about the nature and functions of consumers' relationships with brands, and the processes whereby they develop at the hands of consumers and marketers. In a broader sense, brand relationship research, grounded as it is in the notion of consumers as active meaning makers, helped pave way for the paradigm of co-creation embraced in brand marketing today (Allen, Fournier, and Miller 2008). Recent research, such as that in this volume, continues to build upon basic relationship fundamentals. Still, not surprisingly, many unresolved issues and conundrums remain. My own thinking about consumer-brand relationality has also evolved a great deal, particularly as important realities unanticipated or underdeveloped in the original theory are brought to the fore. In the sections that follow, I identify lessons I have learned about the relationships consumers form with their brands. These lessons are organized within the broader theoretical framework that guided my original thesis. Where applicable, I have leveraged research that my colleagues and I currently have in progress to inform my points.

TENET 1: PURPOSEFUL RELATIONSHIPS

> Tenet 1: Relationships are purposive, involving at their core the provision of meanings to the persons who engage them.

A core insight from my thesis research emphasizes the purposeful nature of consumer-brand relationships: brand relationships are meaning-laden resources engaged to help people live their lives. According to this tenet, the relationships formed between brand and consumer can be understood only by looking to the broader context of the consumer's life to see exactly what the brand/company relationships serviced. Still, in conducting our research, we have been guilty of reifying brand relationships. We forget that relationships are merely facilitators, not ends in and of themselves. A strong relationship develops not by driving brand involvement, but by supporting people in living their lives.

   Academics and managers alike fall into the trap of assuming that brand relationships are all about identity expression: that the driving need behind people's brand relationships has to do with trying on the identities that the brand enables, or otherwise gaining status through the brand. This logic leads to a natural circumscription of the relationship phenomenon, wherein the perspective is meaningful only in high visibility/high involvement categories where identity risks apply. Brand relationships can serve higher-order identity goals, addressing deeply rooted dialectic identity themes and enabling centrally held life projects and tasks. But they can also address functions lower on the need hierarchy by delivering against very pragmatic current concerns. Karen, our struggling single mother from the original thesis and article, bought Tide, All, and Cheer because one of these reliable mass brands was guaranteed to be on sale when she needed it. Karen's brand portfolio was filled with habitual purchases of otherwise "invisible brands" (Chang Coupland 2005). These relationships allowed Karen to extend her resources and develop the skills and solutions she needed to make it through her day. Karen's basic commercial exchanges can still be understood as brand relationships. Less emotional, surely, and less salient, perhaps; but brand relationships they remain.

Many brand relationships are also functional in that they focus on extracting greater exchange value from the company and the brand. So-called loyal customers often engage relationships not through zealous brand evangelism, but rather through a pragmatic desire for the better deals and special treatments that come with elite relationship status. Here again strong brand relationships emerge as a by-product of meeting functional needs, not a drive to express identity through the brand.

The status of the brand relationship as a means versus an end is nowhere clearer than it is within the context of brand relationships forged at the community level. As seven years of brand community research has taught us, people are often more interested in the social links that come from brand relationships than they are in the brands that allow those links to form (Cova and Cova 2002; see also Chapter 9). People often develop brand relationships to gain new social connections or to level out their connections in some significant way. Brand relationships can also provide venues wherein emotional support, advice, companionship, and camaraderie are provided. As research into so-called Third Place brands (Rosenbaum et al. 2007) has pointed out, these strong brand relationships are a consequence, not a cause; they result from the social connections engendered through the brand relationship. As researchers, we are guilty not just of prioritizing identity needs over those that are more functional, we have also disproportionately focused on idiosyncratic relationships versus collective relationships supporting the brand.

Robust brand relationships are built not on the backs of brands, but on a nuanced understanding of people and their needs, both practical and emotional. The reality is that people have many relational needs in their lives, and effective relationships cast a wide net of support. Table 1.1 provides a sample of the different purposes that brand relationships can serve; in Chapter 5, Ashworth, Dacin, and Thomson provide another perspective on the functions served by people's relationships with their brands. Brand relationship efforts that comprehensively recognize and fulfill the needs of real people—individually and collectively—are those that deliver results.

Solving the "reification problem" also requires qualifying the conditions wherein brand relationships will viably form. When we push the theory too far and imply that all consum-

Table 1.1

A Sampling of Relational Needs and Provisions

Reach beyond my network	Raise the quality of my interactions
Establish roots	Pursue luxuries guilt-free
Preserve moments of privacy	Sustain my passions
Capture the present	Explore different parts of my identity
Get help to get stuff done	Express devotion
Cultivate interests and skills	Deepen bonds through shared ownership
Stay adventurous	Aspire to be my own keeper
Manage expectations of me	Help position myself in the larger picture
Support my unique DNA	Level out my connections
Help resolve nagging tensions about who I am	Distance me from an unwanted self
Enable important role transitions	Provide comfort through routines and rituals
Help me contribute to the "greater good"	Get special treatment from the company
Build legitimacy and overcome fear of stigma	Get more out of my brand investments
Relax within a safe haven	Get technical support and advice
Get emotional support and encouragement	Clarify my values

ers form relationships to the same degree and in all circumstances, we unnecessarily lose supporters. Several researchers have turned to attachment theory and its secure, anxious/ambivalent, and avoidant relationship styles for person moderators of relationship activity (see Chapter 19). In our own research, we have developed an attachment construct specific to commercial relationships that holds promise in predicting brand relationship propensities (Paulssen and Fournier 2008). Consumer manifestations of different relationship styles (independent, discerning, and acquisitive, Matthews 1986), orientations (power versus intimacy, McAdams 1984), and drives (McAdams 1988) should also inform the boundary conditions affecting people's relationships with brands.

To control runaway applications, we also need a way to identify the relationship potential of a given brand. Category involvement serves this purpose for some, but the concept is not consumer-sensitive. Much has also been written about the facility offered through brand anthropomorphization. This factor has proven itself a red herring, or a moot point in the simplest case. We do not need to qualify the "human" quality of the brand character as a means of identifying the brand's relationship potential: all brands—anthropomorphized or not—"act" through the device of marketing mix decisions, which allow relationship inferences to form (Aaker, Fournier, and Brasel 2004; Aggarwal 2004). More useful are screening criteria that build not from product categories and brand characteristics, but from the contexts of people's lives. One such approach builds upon the insight that consumers play active roles as meaning makers in their brand relationships, mutating and adapting the marketers' brand meanings to fit their life projects, concerns, and tasks. The key is to understand how meanings attain significance in the context of the person's lifeworld. In current research (Fournier, Solomon, and Englis 2008), we have come to understand this question as a search for "Meanings that Matter," the answer to which lies in the construct of brand meaning resonance. Figure 1.1 provides a multifaceted model for thinking about the resonance construct and its role as a relationship strength mediator. Resonance forces a shift in our thinking from firm- and competition-centric

Figure 1.1   **Resonance: How Meanings Matter**

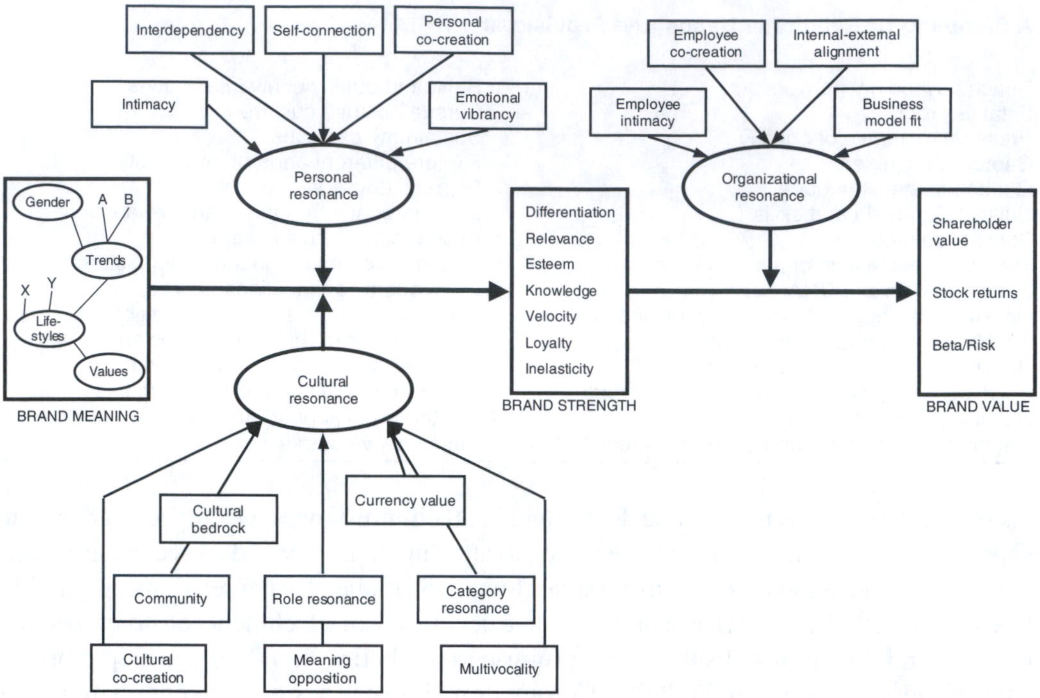

criteria such as the salience, uniqueness, favorability, and dominance of brand meanings to the reverberation and significance of those meanings in the personal and sociocultural world. Resonance focuses not on what brands mean, but rather how they come to mean something to the consumers who use them. It highlights the developmental mechanisms driving the initiation and maintenance of consumers' relationships with brands.

Holt (2004) and others (Chapter 9; Schroeder and Salzer-Mörling 2005; Thompson, Rindfleisch, and Arsel 2006, to name but a few) have contributed greatly to our understanding of the cultural processes that enable brand resonance. This research serves a critical perspective-gaining function by shifting attention from consumers' relationships with brands to brands' relationships with cultures. Predictable psychosocial factors can also trigger relational activity by precipitating a search for resonant brand meanings (Fournier 1998; see also Chapter 9). Events such as coming of age, the transition to parenthood, or a change in marital status serve as self-defining moments wherein identity planes experience tectonic shifts. Companies that anticipate these shifts with meaningful brand bridges add much-needed semantic continuity to consumers' lives; this is rewarded with strong relationship activity. Research can greatly inform these fertile periods wherein the individual's hunger for meanings is exacerbated and explicate the processes involved in the personal birth of relationships with the brand.

Pushed one step further, the notion of resonance and the meaning-based tenet on which it is built have implications for how we think about the strength and quality of a given brand relationship. Again, our metrics suffer from firm-centricity, focusing on evaluation of the person's satisfaction with or depth of commitment to the brand relationship that is formed. But relationships that resonate have a different focal goal: they are engaged to make people's lives easier, better, or happier. The construct of subjective well-being within the domain of positive psychology (Diener, Kesebir, and Lucas 2008) has much to offer in this regard.

TENET 2: RELATIONSHIP DIVERSITY

> Tenet 2: Relationships are multiplex phenomena: they range across several dimensions and take many forms.

The second tenet calls attention to the reality of relationship diversity. As a field, we have always been interested in strong versus weak relationships, with extensive learning generated under the brand loyalty rubric. But relationships can also be meaningfully distinguished as hierarchical versus egalitarian or forced versus voluntary, for example, precipitating many different relationship types and forms (e.g., master-slaves and childhood friendships). Savvy relationship research recognizes that consumer-brand relationships are quite complex, necessitating differential treatment according to their operative terms.

The multiplex phenomenon lends itself well to the development of marketing metrics, both to measure the strength levels of different brand relationships and to qualify various relationship types and forms. Brand attachment (Thomson, MacInnis, and Park 2005) provided one approach to relationship strength measurement; the brand-relationship quality (BRQ) construct (Fournier 1998) served a similar goal. Leveraging ideas from interpersonal relations, BRQ included five relationship facets beyond the commitment and affect (love/passion) levels that typically qualify brand relations: intimacy, partner quality perceptions, behavioral interdependence, attachment, and self-connection. Over the past several years, I have conducted extensive research to develop a reliable and valid scale for measuring BRQ. Table 1.2 provides items for the BRQ scale derived from a survey among 2,250 respondents using a 3 (packaged goods, services, durables) × 2 (product categories) × 3 (brands) research design (Fournier 2000). Results provide preliminary support for the convergent, discriminant, and predictive validity of BRQ, and its distinction from similar concepts of loyalty, satisfaction, and brand attitude. The structure of BRQ is hierarchical, with seven correlated first-order facets and a latent BRQ factor.

Although BRQ was intended to inform questions of relationship complexity by qualifying the strength of any given brand relationship, hindsight reveals it to suffer from a general bias that restricts its application and scope. As a field, we remain myopically fixated on the one type of relationship thought most capable of delivering firm value: the highly committed and affectively laden "marital" relationship ideal. This bias crept into the BRQ measure, where facets such as passion, commitment, intimacy, and overlapping selves dominated. Experience has taught me that metrics must be sensitive to the type of relationship under consideration: you cannot measure relationship strength or vitality independent of the relationship form.

Table 1.2

The Brand Relationship Quality (BRQ) Scale

	R^2	Std Loading	SMC	Alpha
Interdependence				0.89
Need brand and rely on its benefits	0.79	00.89[a]	0.79	
Brand is an integral part of my daily life	0.70	0.84[a]	0.71	
Dependent on brand	0.69	0.83[a]	0.69	
Love/Commitment				0.95
Brand and I are perfect for each other	0.78	0.88[a]	0.77	
Really love the brand	0.76	0.87[a]	0.76	
Thought of not being able to use brand disturbs me	0.72	0.85[a]	0.72	
Very loyal to brand	0.71	0.85[a]	0.72	
Willing to make sacrifices to keep using	0.70	0.83[a]	0.69	
Unique feelings for brand	0.68	0.83[a]	0.69	
No longer keep eye out for alternatives	0.64	0.80[a]	0.64	
Partner Quality				0.91
Brand takes care of me	0.72	0.85[a]	0.72	
Brand listens to me	0.71	0.84[a]	0.71	
Brand makes up for mistakes	0.66	0.82[a]	0.67	
Count on brand to do what's best for me	0.65	0.81[a]	0.66	
Brand is responsive to my concerns	0.64	0.80[a]	0.64	
Self-Connection				0.93
Brand is part of me	0.75	0.86[a]	0.74	
Makes statement about what's important to me	0.74	0.86[a]	0.74	
Connects with part of me that makes me tick	0.73	0.85[a]	0.72	
Fits with life goals or problems	0.68	0.83[a]	0.69	
By using brand I'm part of a shared community	0.68	0.82[a]	0.67	
Develop relationships with others who use brand	0.65	0.80[a]	0.64	
Nostalgic attachment	0.83			
Have sentimental feelings for brand	0.70	0.83[a]	0.69	
Brand reminds me of phase of my life	0.59	0.77[a]	0.59	
Thoughts of brand contain personal memories	0.56	0.74[a]	0.55	
Intimacy (Consumer-Brand)				0.81
Know brand history/background	0.64	0.80	0.64	
Know what brand stands for	0.61	0.78	0.61	
Know more about brand than average consumer	0.54	0.73	0.53	
Intimacy (Brand-Consumer)				0.86
Company understands my needs	0.71	0.84[a]	0.71	
Knows me so well, could design product for me	0.67	0.82[a]	0.68	
Company knows a lot about me as a person	0.62	0.79[a]	0.62	

Source: Fournier (2000).
[a] Significant at p = .001.

In ten years, however, we have progressed very little in our understanding of the complexity of brand-relationship space. Consumer research that demarcates exchange relationships from communal relationships provides one important step in the right direction (Aggarwal 2004). Still, this research taps just the tip of the iceberg of relationship variability, especially when one considers our tendency to relegate exchanges to "nonrelational status" in the end. Preliminary attention has been given to other forms of commercial relationships, for example: friendships (Price and Arnould 1999), secret relationships (Goodwin 1992), and abuse (Hill 1994; Hill and Kozup 2007). But relationship-inspired theory concerning these and other potentially valuable or common consumer relationship forms is deficient. The status of consumer-brand relationship mapping looks much like that observed for business-to-business relationships more than twenty years ago. "Much remains to be done in distinguishing commercial, work, and romantic relationships. Also, the model is presented abstractly. It lacks conceptual detail and obvious ways to operationalize key variables" (Dwyer, Schurr, and Oh 1987, p. 20).

A first step toward a more conscious incorporation of the multiplex criterion involves a comprehensive identification of the relationship dimensions that allow us to map consumer-brand relationship space. Although relationship strength may reign supreme for practical reasons, this is but one of many important dimensions along which relationships vary. I have now inducted 52 facets distinguishing people's brand relationships (see Table 1.3), and have initiated survey research using mapping techniques to identify the structure of people's relationship perceptions. In a recent pilot, 225 MBA students rated perceived normative relationships with 35 strong national and regional brands on the 52 relationship facets using seven-point semantic differential scales. Each subject rated twelve facets; four scales were in common and the remaining items were divided into four parallel survey sets. Another 150 MBA students rated eleven prototypical human relations along these same dimensions, again with facets allocated among respondents in three survey sets to reduce fatigue. Multidimensional scaling using INDSCALE identified seven dimensions accounting for 78 percent of the variance in brand relationship ratings: cooperative and harmonious versus competitive and hostile; emotional and identity-vested versus functionally oriented; strong and deep versus weak and superficial; equal and balanced versus one-sided and hierarchical; long term and enduring versus short term; interactive/interdependent versus independent; and flexible/voluntary versus constrained/imposed. The first four of these dimensions emerged cleanly in the rating of human relations as well, accounting for 58 percent of the variance. The map in Figure 1.2 depicts the brands and human relations plotted on dimensions of strength and type of reward.

A more tractable avenue for descriptive and validation research considers the higher-order relationship models organizing people's perceptions. Fiske's (1991) relational models theory, which proposes communal sharing, authority ranking, equality matching, and market pricing as discrete relational categories offers a useful framework with strong empirical support. A similar empirical exercise considers the above brand-mapping data using factor-analytic methods. Three general forms of consumer-brand relationality manifest: partnerships (harmonious, interactive, and emotive engagements), benign acquaintanceships (harmonious though functional and shallow affiliations), and negative, disjointed relations. To date, negative brand relations have been considered only through postmodern social critique that often lacks managerial application (for exception, see Hill 1994; Hill and Kozup 2007; and Thompson et al. 2006). Managerially sensitive relationship applications tend to focus on positive and strong brand relationships or those that can readily be strengthened. Our mapping reinforces the central role that negative brand relationships play in the commercial marketplace. A fully-enabled perspective on consumer-brand relationship behavior must lose its false optimism and incorporate dysfunctional relationship forms.

Table 1.3

A Compendium of Relationship Dimensions

- Emotionally close/Emotionally distant
- Intimate/Not Intimate
- Deep/Superficial
- Based on mutual liking/Not based on liking
- High sharing of information/Limited
- Long term/Short term
- Regular/Irregular
- Stable/Fleeting
- One-sided/Mutual
- Active/Inactive
- Intense interaction/Superficial interaction
- Interdependent/Independent
- Democratic/Autocratic
- Important to both individuals involved/More important for one than the other
- Equal in power/Unequal in power
- Reciprocating/Nonreciprocating
- Harmonious/Clashing
- High on costs and responsibilities/Low costs and responsibilities
- Warm/Cold
- Trustworthy/Not trustworthy
- Sincere/Insincere
- Supportive/Not supportive
- Committed/Not committed
- Driven by attraction to other/Repulsion-driven
- Utilitarian and task-oriented/Emotional
- Frequent/Infequent
- Helps express who I am/Does not help express who I am
- Intense feelings/Superficial feelings
- Emotional/Not Emotional
- Hierarchical/Not hierarchical
- Formal/Informal
- Fair/Unfair
- Secret/Out in the open
- Hidden/Known to others
- Friendly/Hostile
- Compatible goals and desires/Incompatible
- Productive/Destructive
- Relaxed/Tense
- Flexible/Rigid
- Difficult/Easy to break off
- Interesting/Dull
- Reliable/Unreliable
- Positive feelings/Negative feelings
- Easy/Difficult to resolve conflicts
- Altruistic/Selfish
- Solicited/Unsolicited
- Imposed/Voluntary
- Cooperative/Competitive
- Much at risk/Little at risk
- Choice-driven/Chance-driven
- Easy to enter/Difficult to start
- Temporary/Permanent

Figure 1.2   **Brand Relationship Map**

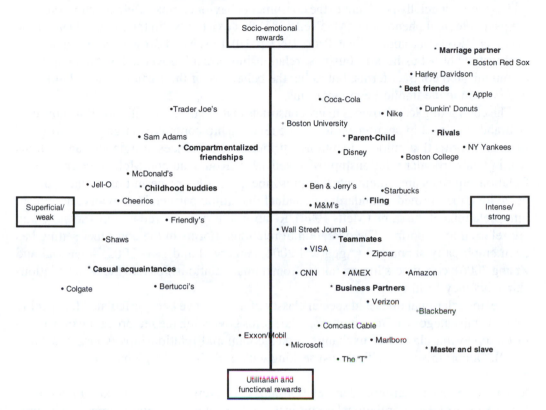

The next logical step in brand relationship space mapping involves the development of thick descriptions of pivotal relationship forms. Building on the insight that emotion profiles usefully distinguish human relations (Guerrero and Andersen 2000; Kayser, Schwinger, and Cohen 1984), Chris Allen, Felicia Miller and I have engaged projective techniques, depth interviewing using Zaltman's Metaphor Elicitation Technique (ZMET), and surveys to identify the characteristic affective profiles for seven prominent brand relationship types. Results support unique emotion constellations for the different brand relationships: people in exchange relationships are pleased and satisfied; true partners experience happiness, appreciation, and fulfillment; adversaries feel anger, irritation, and skepticism in relationships with their brands. Some relationships are uniquely defined by their emotion profiles, as with people's flings and secret affairs with brands.

A third stream of research-in-progress (Fournier, Avery, and Wojnicki 2004) leverages contract theory for insights into relationship phenomenology. The constructs of contracts and relationships are inherently intertwined, as revealed in the etymology of the word "contract," which comes from the Latin *contrahere* meaning "to draw together, to enter into a relationship" (Merriam Webster's Dictionary of Law 1996). Relationships are intrinsically contractual: they are created when two parties come together with the intention of forming a collective understanding of what each party will provide and receive over time (MacNeil 1980). Although contract theory has been applied extensively in business-to-business marketing contexts, the sociopsychological status of contracts also makes them especially pertinent to the consumer behavior context. Relationship contracts are psychological phenomena (MacNeil 1985) that exist only "in the eye and head of the beholder" (Rousseau and McLean Parks 1992, p. 19). Lusch and Brown (1996) empirically demonstrate how business-to-business relationships are not governed by their explicitly communicated contract terms, but rather the behaviors of the parties in the relationship that constitute the implicit contract terms.

The contracting lens provides many constructs that are useful for illuminating consumer-brand relationship phenomenology. The relationship contract is largely comprised of rules and norms that guide perceptions, attributions, inferences, judgments, and actions within that particular relationship (MacNeil 1985; Rousseau and McLean Parks 1992). Relationship rules are statements that prescribe, proscribe, or permit particular types of behaviors; they provide standards of conduct that guide partners' behaviors and inform interpretations of the same (Metts 1994). Relationship rules shared within a social group are referred to as norms. The operation of relational norms in the consumer setting has been empirically supported (Aggarwal 2004; Aggarwal and Law 2005; Aggarwal and Zhang 2006): consumers import norms from human relationships into the brand relationships that they form.

Specific relational rules and special classes of norms have been articulated for specific relationship categories. Best known are the norms governing the reciprocation of benefits in the opposing classes of exchange versus communal relationships (Clark and Mills 1979). Opportunism—"self-interest seeking with guile"—is the global norm governing commercial exchange relations (Williamson 1975); relational norms supersede opportunism to enhance interdependent relationships (MacNeil 1980). Heide and John (1992) identify three classes of relational norms in the context of manufacturer-supplier relations: flexibility, information exchange, and solidarity. Research in psychology supports unique rule sets for particular types of communal relationships, for example: rules of friendship, marriage, kinship, workplace, and marketplace relations (Argyle and Henderson 1984; Davis and Todd 1982; Kayser, Schwinger, and Cohen 1984; O'Connell 1984). Operative relationship templates also dictate a prioritized higher-level norm specific to that type of relationship. For example, an equality norm governs friendships, a need norm governs love relationships, and a contribution norm governs relationships within the workplace (Deutsch 1975; Schwinger 1980). Research-in-progress (Fournier, Avery and Wojnicki 2004) informs an expanded conceptualization of the norms governing consumer-brand relationship contracts. This typology includes not only an extended enumeration of the reward and reciprocity rules familiar to the exchange/communal dichotomy, but also rules sensitive to the relationship marketing context, such as interaction maintenance rules and relational rules governing the expression of intimacy, commitment, and trust.

Content particular to a given relationship contract extends beyond operative rules and norms. Relationship contracts specify the fundamental "gives" and "gets" of the relationship: promises to do something (or to refrain from doing something) in return for a payment-in-kind (Rousseau and McLean Parks 1992). They include operative relationship development goals and primary resource exchanges (Fitzsimons and Bargh 2003;

Kayser, Schwinger, and Cohen 1984), benchmarks for assessing satisfaction (Baucom et al. 1996), prototypical beliefs about relational successes and failures (Baucom et al. 1989), expected risks and rewards (Sabatelli and Pearce 1986), transgression tolerance zones (Rusbult et al. 1991), trust forms and bases (Rousseau et al. 1998), and appropriate assuagement devices in the face of broken rules (Metts 1994). Relationship templates can be usefully thought of as scripts or schemata (Andersen 1993; Baldwin 1992) that offer workable relationship theories-in-use. Research-in-progress informs the multiplex criterion by amplifying the relationship schemata that consumers use (Fournier, Avery, and Wojnicki 2004). The so-called partner template, for example, prioritizes the mutual helping norm. Partners give without getting, exhibit flexibility in company dealings, and accommodate problems with a "let's work together" approach. "Best customers," another prominent template in our research, are governed by norms of privilege. Best customers expect special treatment and "insider status" that sets them apart; they engage in biased equity accounting that allows cashing in without cashing out. Some consumers view themselves as masters in a master-slave engagement, expecting distanced but unquestioning service above all else. Companies in these relationships are expected to anticipate needs, to be seen but not heard, to stick to the rules, and speak (with great formality) only when spoken to. The company slave in this relationship is never intimate, and the boss is always right.

I have applied this thinking in my consulting dealings with Harley-Davidson, Inc., who found value in research identifying Best Friendship as the dominant relationship template for their brand. Harley-Davidson had long operated on the assumption that they were in the business of engaging committed partnerships. Though mapping exercises show that friendships and marriages can occupy the same "upper-right-hand quadrant" ideal space, the contractual differences between these relationships matter significantly. A marriage is a socially supported contract to stay together despite circumstances, both foreseen and unforeseen. Core strength drivers of marital bonds are commitment, love, and passion. Best Friendship, in contrast, is a totally voluntary interdependence between parties intended to facilitate socioemotional goals. The dimensions most characteristic of friendship are reciprocity and intimacy (and the vulnerability that intimacy entails). Buddies are friends too, but their drivers involve interdependence, not intimacy levels. The do's and don'ts of these different relationships contrast sharply, and sometimes conflict in fundamental ways (see Table 1.4).

TENET 3: DYNAMIC RELATIONSHIPS

> Tenet 3: Relationships are process phenomena: they evolve and change over a series of interactions and in response to contextual change.

The third tenet emphasizes the dynamic and interdependent nature of consumer-brand relationships. At a simplified and pragmatic level, relationships unfold through a series of temporal stages including initiation, growth, maintenance, and decline. They manifest characteristic development trajectories such as the biological life cycle, passing fad, cyclical

Table 1.4

Playing by the Rules: Marriage versus Friendships

	Marriage partners	Best friends	Buddies
Do	• Formalize the union • Negotiate the contract • Verbalize need for change • Strive to meet all needs • Add surprises/spark • Erect barriers to exit	• Encourage other friendships • Self disclose • Listen • Ask and reciprocate • Be reliable, predictable	• Compartmentalize per activities • Show only part of the self • Sustain interaction • Make entry/exit easy
Don't	• Breach fidelity pledge • Forget intimate details	• Leak secrets • Discuss implicit contract • Try to change the other • Impose external pressures • Erect barriers to exit	• Establish intimacy, deep or broad • Encourage emotional involvement • Make demands or add responsibility • Drop by uninvited • Use things without permission

resurgence, and approach avoidance. Fluctuations in person, brand, and environmental factors trigger relationship evolution, with entropy and stress factors precipitating decline. Relationships are dynamic, temporal phenomena: they require active management over time.

Despite the fundamental process quality of brand relationships, developmental models that go beyond these broad generalizations have been lacking. Although we have spent decades designing programs to instill customer loyalty, mechanisms beyond commitment through which the consumer advances and maintains brand relationships are just now becoming known. Theories of attitude accessibility (see Chapter 16), attitude change (Chapter 15), self-construction (Chapter 4), and habit (Chapter 3) provide promising avenues for process research.

Another useful approach to process specification is to identify the primary currency driving a given brand relationship, and expose the milestones and mechanisms that represent progress along this path. Research conducted for Harley-Davidson, for example, illuminated the journey of "Becoming a Rider" through a progressive accumulation of status-granting cultural capital of various kinds—knowledge, skills, experiences, and social connections, as well as dispositions concerning what is authentic within the group (see Figure 1.3). Models developed for members of the Harley Owner's Group focused on the accumulation of power and influence in the system, and pivotal experiences providing status credentials in this regard. The point of this example is that relationship development is not always best understood as a process of increasingly deepening relationship bonds; rather, relationships "develop" along foundations critical to the type of engagement at hand.

The relationship contracts perspective also provides a valuable lens on the developmental mechanisms shaping brand relationships. Relationship interruptions that render the contract salient, most notably transgressions, critically affect the relationship trajectory and course. But everything the brand "does" affects the relationship—from the personality-suggestive colors and fonts of the company Web site to the tonality of communications

Figure 1.3   **Cultural Capital Model for the Development of Relationships with the Harley-Davidson Brand**

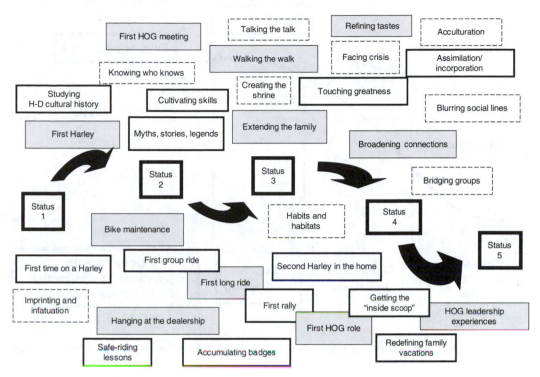

from the brand (Aaker et al. 2004). Findings collectively suggest that consumers make inferences from meaning-laden brand behavioral "signals," so as to interpret and reinterpret the type of relationship contract in play.

Research-in-progress affirms the relevance and value of understanding relationship development as a contract signaling process wherein rules and terms evolve (Fournier, Avery, and Wojnicki 2004). Figure 1.4 presents a working model for the various contract-relevant mechanisms involved in this process. Two subprocesses are particularly interesting for their ability to inform long-standing problems in consumer research. Supracontracting involves extra-role behaviors beyond contract requirements that are engaged voluntarily and purposively on the part of the consumer (or brand) in order to signal a desire to transition the relationship to a new, deeper level. In our data we observed supracontracting in the form of word-of-mouth advocacy, active customer recruitment, brand citizenship behaviors, and employee gifting. Loyalty, as we have come to understand it, can be understood as mutually reinforcing supracontracting on the part of consumers and brands. A second process, contract misalignment, highlights the risks exposed in the inherently interdependent relationship setting. Psychological contracts, though individually interpreted, are assumed to be shared by both parties, who act *as if* their individual contract is aligned with the psychological contract of the relationship other; the concept of the normative contract has been developed to capture this idea (Rousseau 1989). Our

Figure 1.4   **Relationship Contracting Process Mechanisms**

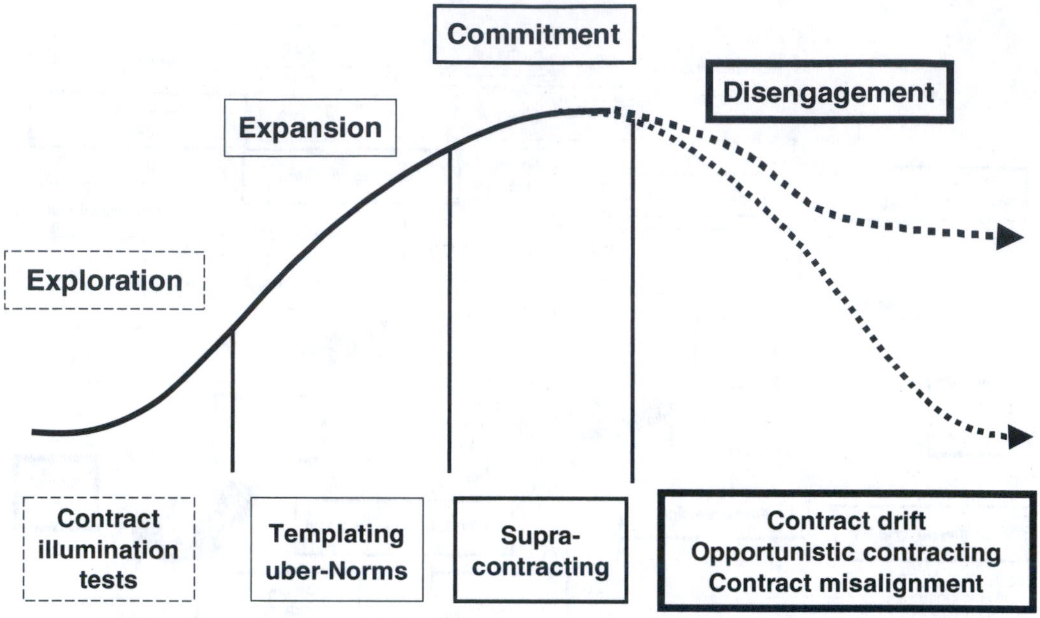

research exposes the frequent presence and consequence of misaligned consumer-firm contracts, particularly in circumstances where the person has been led to believe s/he is a best customer of the firm. Customer Relationship Management (CRM) strategies that are more concerned with the cost versus revenue of a given customer than with delivering on the contracts that have implicitly been put in place exacerbate this disconnect. As the marketing practice of firing customers gains in popularity, it becomes critical that we feel comfortable in our understanding of the relationships that are manifest. Only by stepping backward to fundamental questions of content and process—as informed through the meanings and behaviors that consumers and brands bring to bear in negotiating their relationships—can our relationship theories and practices be informed.

CONCLUDING THOUGHTS

Our move toward a science of consumer-brand relationships presents many challenges. Many doubt that something so idiosyncratic can be brought to the level of generalizability that science requires. But even though relationships may best be revealed by studying individual or collective relationship instantiations, this does not mean that actionable relationship systems cannot result. Individuals and communities manifest relational principles that with dedication can be shown to be generalizable; we just need to apply ourselves to these goals. To have an impact, consumer-brand relationship theory must progress beyond thick description to the provisions of models that not only advance science, but prove to be actionable for firms (see, for example, Chapter 20). These frameworks are essential in order to combat the criticism that consumer-brand relationship research is merely an exercise in metaphor.

Other critics charge that the utility of relationship theory for understanding consumer-brand behavior has diminished and that its application is appropriate only for an egocentric and less socially conscious phase of branding, which no longer exists. This is not a question about applicability, but about analytic perspective. People have relationships with antibrands (Chapter 9) and corporations (see Chapter 10); cultures engage relationships with brands in the marketplace (Holt 2004). Brand relationships can be repellent and negative. Relationships can be purposive at their core. Contemporary brand relationships may be less tied to an image construction view of marketing, but relationships they remain.

As we enter the second phase of brand-relationship research, opportunities for cross-disciplinary and cross-paradigmatic investigation present themselves. Though initially built upon psychological theories, the idiographic notion of brand relationships has matured into a vibrant psycho-socio-cultural construal. Brand relationships are determined by individual factors within a sociocultural context. They manifest within a holistic and reciprocating system wherein the relationship the brand has with the culture affects the relationship the consumer has with the brand, and vice versa. The phenomenon of the brand relationship clearly extends beyond the one-to-one construal that initially fueled the development of the idea in marketing, and includes the one-to-many instantiation of community brand relationships, and the many-to-many relationships that characterize consumer societies as a whole. There is no argument that the sociocultural is a significant part of the consumer-brand relationship equation (see, for example, Chapter 6, 7, and 11). Relationship research that transcends so-called behavioral and consumer culture theory paradigms can integrate the psychosocial aspects of brand relationships in a way that is especially valid and true.

Integration across another common divider can also spark progress in future research. Relationships and the contracts that implicitly and explicitly bind them have a long and rich research tradition in the business-to-business context (cf., Heide 1994; Williamson 1975, 1996) and yet, for one reason or another, we have been reluctant to leverage these published works. Of direct relevance, for example, is Heide and John's (1992) research on the norms of marketing relationships; Heide and Wathne's (2006) probe of the phenomenology of friend and businesspeople relationship roles; and work by Narayandas and Rangan (2004) concerning extracontractual behaviors that fortify and advance relationship bonds.

A third form of integration is also implicated in second-wave brand relationship research: integration across theoretical and substantive planes. While there is no escaping the fact that the notion of brand relationships is fundamentally practical, this nexus has not driven consumer-brand relationship research. Critical in moving research forward is the matter of finding the "so what" in consumer-brand relationships and demonstrating how and why they matter to the firms who engage them. The time has passed for the theoretically-driven among us to shy away from pragmatic relationship applications in a so-called tainted and exploitative marketing world. To have an impact, consumer-brand relationship research must consciously expand its reach into and implications for the substantive marketing domain.

Similarly, those who study brand relationships within the applied perspective of CRM have not leveraged consumer-based relationship theories. To state the case in the extreme, "people" are missing from the CRM relationship equation. Current CRM theory and application, with its focus on segmenting and differentially serving customers based on potential revenues and costs-to-serve, receives its inspiration from the discipline of economics. The error of CRM research lies not in its attention to issues concerning the firm's bottom line, but in an apparent single-minded fixation on economics that ignores and sometimes confounds consideration of the lived experiences of the consumers with whom commercial relationships are engaged. In embracing consumer relationships as business tools that enhance firm profitability, CRM researchers have lost sight of a critical insight pertaining to commercial relationships: relationships provide meanings that help consumers live their lives. Rather than treating consumers as partners in a mutually beneficial, co-creative process of learning and engagement—as relationship marketing theory originally intended (Peppers and Rogers 1993)—the economically centric firm treats consumers as "assets" managed through "good old-fashioned, unsentimental cost/benefit analysis" (Landry 2005, p. 28) for the good of the firm. This lack of customer-centricity is implicated in reports of failed and lagging in-market results for CRM implementations (Boulding et al. 2005; Nelson 2004). To be true to the intended bridging function of marketing, CRM relationship research and strategies must prioritize the people over the firms that benefit from relationship activity (Fournier, Dobscha, and Mick 1998). The lived experiences of consumers' brand and company relations must be more judiciously taken into account, in all their shapes and forms.

As we push to develop substantive consumer-brand relationship theory, we must maintain a focus on and sensitivity to the marketing context in which this theory will be applied. If brand relationship theory is to have an impact, it cannot simply borrow concepts and insights from established interpersonal relationship theories and demonstrate their application to branding. The metaphoric argument for understanding consumer-brand engagements in relationship terms has been made and repeatedly reinforced. To quote Martha Stewart, this is "a good thing." But second-stage contributions require that we do more than prove the manifestation of known relationship principles with a different scale or scope. Substantive contributions such as those contained in this volume advance new theories concerning how people relate to brands.

REFERENCES

Aaker, Jennifer, Susan Fournier, and Adam Brasel (2004). "When Good Brands Do Bad," *Journal of Consumer Research,* 31 (June), 1–25.

Aggarwal, Pankaj (2004). "The Effects of Brand Relationship Norms on Consumer Attitudes and Behavior," *Journal of Consumer Research,* 31 (1), 87–101.

Aggarwal, Pankaj, and Sharmistha Law (2005). "Role of Relationship Norms in Processing Brand Information," *Journal of Consumer Research,* 32 (3), 453–464.

Aggarwal, Pankaj, and Meng Zhang (2006). "The Moderating Effect of Relationship Norm Salience on Consumers' Loss Aversion," *Journal of Consumer Research,* 33 (3), 413–419.

Allen, Chris, Susan Fournier, and Felicia Miller (2008). "Brands and their Meaning Makers." In *Handbook of Consumer Psychology,* ed. Curtis Haugtvedt, Paul Herr, and Frank Kardes. Mahwah, NJ: Lawrence Erlbaum, 781–822.

Andersen, Peter A. (1993). "Cognitive Schemata in Personal Relationships." In *Individuals in Relationships (Understanding Relationship Processes,* volume 1), ed. S. Duck. Newbury Park, CA: Sage Publications, 1–29.

Argyle, Michael, and Monika Henderson (1984). "The Rules of Friendship," *Journal of Social and Personal Relationships,* 1, 211–237.

Baldwin, Mark W. (1992). "Relational Schemas and the Processing of Social Information," *Psychological Bulletin,* 112 (3), 461–84.

Baucom, Donald H., Norman Epstein, Lynn A. Rankin, and Charles K. Burnett (1996). "Assessing Relationship Standards: The Inventory of Specific Relationship Standards," *Journal of Family Psychology,* 10 (1), 72–88.

Baucom, Donald H., Norman Epstein, Steven Sayers, and Tamara Goldman Sher (1989). "The Role of Cognitions in Marital Relationships: Definitional, Methodological, and Conceptual Issues," *Journal of Consulting and Clinical Psychology,* 57 (1), 31–38.

Boulding, William, Richard Staelin, Michael Ehret, and Wesley J. Johnston (2005). "A Customer Relationship Management Roadmap: What is Known, Potential Pitfalls, and Where to Go," *Journal of Marketing,* 69 (4), 155–661.

Chang Coupland, Jennifer (2005). "Invisible Brands: An Ethnography of Households and the Brands in their Kitchen Pantries," *Journal of Consumer Research,* 32 (1), 106–118.

Clark, Margaret S. and Judson Mills (1979). "Interpersonal Attraction in Exchange and Communal Relationships," *Journal of Personality and Social Psychology,* 37 (1), 12–24.

Cova, Bernard, and Veronique Cova (2002). "Tribal Marketing: The Tribalisation of Society and Its Impact on the Conduct of Marketing," *European Journal of Marketing,* 36 (5/6), 595–620.

Davis, Keith E., and Michael J. Todd (1982). "Friendship and Love Relationships," *Advances in Descriptive Psychology,* 2, 79–122.

Deutsch, Morton (1975). "Equity, Equality, and Need: What Determines Which Value Will Be Used as a Basis for Distributive Justice?" *Journal of Social Issues,* 31, 137–50.

Diener, Ed, Pelin Kesebir, and Richard Lucas (2008). "Benefits of Accounts of Well-Being: For Societies and for Psychological Science, "*Applied Psychology,* 57 (July), 37–53.

Dwyer, F. Robert, Paul H. Schurr, and Sejo Oh (1987). "Developing Buyer-Seller Relationships," *Journal of Marketing,* 51 (2), 11–26.

Fiske, Alan Page (1991). *Structures of Social Life: The Four Elementary Forms of Human Relations.* New York, NY: Free Press.

Fitzsimons, Grainne M. and John A. Bargh (2003). "Thinking of You: Non-conscious Pursuit of Interpersonal Goals Associated with Relationship Partners," *Journal of Personality and Social Psychology,* 84 (1), 148–64.

Fournier, Susan (1998). "Consumers and their Brands: Developing Relationship Theory in Consumer Research," *Journal of Consumer Research,* 24 (March), 343–373.

——— (2000). "Dimensionalizing Brand Relationships through Brand Relationship Strength." Presentation at Association for Consumer Research Conference, Salt Lake City, Utah.

Fournier, Susan, Jill Avery, and Andrea Wojnicki (2004). "Contracting for Relationships." Presentation at Association for Consumer Research Conference, Portland, Oregon, October 8.

Fournier, Susan, Susan Dobscha, and David Mick (1998). "Preventing the Premature Death of Relationship Marketing," *Harvard Business Review,* 76 (January), 42–51.

Fournier, Susan, Michael Solomon, and Basil Englis (2008). "When Brands Resonate." In *Handbook of Brand and Experience Management,* eds. Bernd H. Schmitt and D. L. Rogers, Cheltenham, UK and Northampton, MA: Edward Elgar, 35–57.

Goodwin, Cathy (1992). "A Conceptualization of Motives to Seek Privacy for Nondeviant Consumption," *Journal of Consumer Psychology,* 1 (3), 261–284.

Guerrero, Laura K., and Peter A. Anderson (2000). "Emotions in Close Relationships." In *Close Relationships: A Sourcebook,* ed. C. Hendrick and S. Hendrick. Thousand Oaks, CA: Sage Publications, 171–183.

Heide, Jan B. (1994). "Interorganizational Governance in Marketing Channels," *Journal of Marketing,* 58 (1), 71–85

Heide, Jan B., and George John (1992). "Do Norms Matter in Marketing Relationships?" *Journal of Marketing,* 56 (2), 32–44.

Heide, Jan B., and Kenneth H. Wathne (2006). "Friends, Businesspeople, and Relationship Roles: A Conceptual Framework and Research Agenda," *Journal of Marketing,* 70 (July), 90–103.

Hill, Ronald Paul (1994). "Bill Collectors and Consumers: A Troublesome Exchange Relationship," *Journal of Public Policy & Marketing,* 13 (1), 20–35.

Hill, Ronald Paul, and John Kozup (2007). "Consumer Experiences with Predatory Lending Practices," *Journal of Consumer Affairs,* 41 (1), 29–46.

Holt, Douglas B. (2004). *How Brands Become Icons: The Principles of Cultural Branding.* Boston, MA: Harvard Business School Press.

Kayser, Egon, Thomas Schwinger, and Ronald L. Cohen (1984). "Laypersons' Conceptions of Social Relationships: A Test of Contract Theory," *Journal of Social and Personal Relationships,* 1, 433–58.

Landry, John T. (2005). "Reviews," *Harvard Business Review,* 83 (10), 28.

Lusch, Robert F., and James R. Brown (1996). "Interdependency, Contracting, and Relational Behavior in Marketing Channels," *Journal of Marketing,* 60 (4), 19–38.

MacNeil, Ian R. (1980). *The New Social Contract.* New Haven, CT: Yale University Press.

——— (1985). "Relational Contracts: What We Do and Do Not Know," *Wisconsin Law Review,* 483–525.

Matthews, Sarah (1986). *Friendships through the Life Course: Oral Biographies in Old Age,* vol. 161. Beverly Hills, CA: Sage Library of Social Research.

McAdams, Dan P. (1984). "Human Motives and Personal Relationships." In *Communication, Intimacy, and Close Relationships,* ed. V. Derlega. New York, NY: Academic Press, 41–70.

——— (1988). "Personal Needs and Personal Relationships." In *Handbook of Personal Relationships: Theory, Research, Interventions,* ed. S. Duck. New York, NY: Wiley, 7–22.

Merriam Webster's Dictionary of Law (1996). Springfield, MA: Merriam Webster Inc.

Metts, Sandra (1994). "Relational Transgressions." In *The Dark Side of Interpersonal Communication,* ed. W. Cupach and B. Spitzberg. Hillsdale, NJ: Lawrence Erlbaum, 217–239.

Narayandas, Das, and V. Kasturi Rangan (2004). "Building and Sustaining Buyer-Seller Relationships in Mature Industrial Markets," *Journal of Marketing,* 68 (July), 63–77.

Nelson, Scott D. (2004). "CRM Is Dead; Long Live CRM," Stamford, CT: Gartner Group.

O'Connell, Lenahan (1984). "An Exploration of Exchange in Three Social Relationships: Kinship, Friendship, and the Marketplace," *Journal of Social and Personal Relationships,* 1, 333–45.

Paulssen, Marcel, and Susan Fournier (2008). "Attachment Security and the Strength of Commercial Relationships." Working paper, Boston University.

Peppers, Don, and Martha Rogers (1993). *The One to One Future.* New York, NY: Doubleday.

Price, Linda L., and Eric J. Arnould (1999). "Commercial Friendships: Service Provider-Client Relationships in Context," *Journal of Marketing,* 63 (4), 38–56.

Rosenbaum, Mark S., James Ward, Beth A. Walker, and Amy L. Ostom (2007). "A Cup of Coffee with a Dash of Love: An Investigation of Commercial Social Support and Third-Place Attachment," *Journal of Service Research,* 10 (1), 43–59.

Rousseau, Denise M. (1989). "Psychological and Implied Contracts in Organizations," *Employee Responsibilities and Rights Journal,* 2 (2), 121–39.

Rousseau, Denise M., and Judi McLean Parks (1992). "The Contracts of Individuals and Organizations," *Research in Organizational Behavior,* 15, 1–43.

Rousseau, Denise M., Sim B. Sitkin, Ronald S. Burt, and Colin Camerer (1998). "Not So Different After All: A Cross-Discipline View of Trust," *Academy of Management Review,* 23 (3), 393–404.

Rusbult, Caryl E., Julie Verette, Gregory A. Whitney, Linda F. Slovik, and Isaac Lipkus (1991). "Accommodation Processes in Close Relationships: Theory and Preliminary Empirical Evidence," *Journal of Personality and Social Psychology,* 60 (1), 53–78.

Sabatelli, Ronald M., and John Pearce (1986). "Exploring Marital Expectations," *Journal of Social and Personal Relationships,* 3, 307–321.

Schroeder, Jonathan, and Miriam Salzer-Mörling (2005). *Brand Culture.* London: Routledge.

Schwinger, Thomas (1980). "Just Allocations of Goods: Decisions among Three Principles." In *Justice and Social Interaction,* ed. G. Mikula. New York, NY: Springer-Verlag, 95–125.

Thompson, Craig J., Aric Rindfleisch, and Zeynep Arsel (2006). "Emotional Branding and the Strategic Value of Doppelganger Brand Image," *Journal of Marketing,* 70 (January), 50–64.

Thomson, Matthew, Deborah MacInnis, and C. Whan Park (2005). "The Ties that Bind: Measuring the Strength of Consumer's Emotional Attachments to Brands," *Journal of Consumer Psychology,* 15 (1), 77–91.

Williamson, Oliver E. (1996). *The Mechanisms of Governance.* New York, NY: Oxford University Press.

——— (1975). *Markets and Hierarchies.* New York, NY: The Free Press.

CHAPTER 2

USING RELATIONSHIP NORMS TO UNDERSTAND CONSUMER-BRAND INTERACTIONS

PANKAJ AGGARWAL

Even though marketing practitioners have long imbued brands with human traits with the intuitive objective of making their brands more endearing, distinctive, and desirable, marketing researchers have only recently started exploring the brand-as-person metaphor to gain insights into consumer behavior. These insights, drawn largely from social psychology, recast brands not just as passive, economically defined objects to be regarded and judged by consumers, but as partners in socially construed relationships. The concept of consumer-brand relationships as a two-way street, much like any interpersonal relationship, was first more overtly recognized by Fournier (1998). Unlike the passive manner in which consumers were traditionally treated by database marketers, Fournier's seminal work emphasizes the importance of understanding the consumer's perspective, and it generated research examining different aspects of consumer-brand relationships (Aaker, Fournier, and Brasel 2004; Aggarwal 2002; Ji 2002; Swaminathan, Page, and Gurhan-Canli 2007). My own research extends this stream of work by exploring a specific dimension of the complex consumer-brand relationship space with an attempt to develop conceptual tools to better understand the nature of consumer-brand interactions.

My research proposes a theoretical and predictive framework by suggesting that when consumers form relationships with brands, they use norms of behavior underlying these relationships as a guide in their brand interactions in two unique ways: (a) as a lens to evaluate the actions of the brand, and (b) as a tool to guide their own behavior. I find that norms of relationship influence consumer responses, depending upon whether or not the brand's action is seen to be in violation of or in conformity with these norms (Aggarwal 2004), as well as the extent to which consumers are treated unfairly (Aggarwal 2008). Further, relationship norms also influence the type of brand-related information consumers focus on (Aggarwal and Law 2005) and the degree of loss aversion they demonstrate (Aggarwal and Zhang 2006). The main insight of this stream of research is that the key to understanding consumer-brand interactions is a better appreciation of the norms that govern the particular consumer-brand relationship. In my research, I focus not just on examining the effect of relationship norms on consumer attitude and behavior but also on understanding the underlying processes. One specific goal of my research has been to empower marketers with the ability to make predictions about consumer behavior that would not be possible using existing theories of brand personality, brand loyalty, or brand imagery. In this chapter, I summarize the key findings from four different research projects, all of which use the relationship metaphor to better understand consumer-brand interactions.

NORMS OF BEHAVIOR AND THEIR ROLE IN SOCIAL INTERACTION

The key premise underlying all the projects that I discuss here is that social relationships carry with them norms of behavior that each relationship partner is expected to follow. Norms emerge from interactions with others; they may or may not be stated explicitly, and sanctions for deviating from them come from social networks, not the legal system. These norms include general societal expectations for our behavior, our expectations of others' behavior, and our expectations of our own behavior. Cialdini and Trost (1998) have argued that these norms are acquired by people in a social setting over long time periods of the socialization process. As these norms become internalized, they serve as a valuable guide for everyday behavior and allow people to function in situations that may otherwise be new. Thus, when faced with new social situations, people use the norms that are salient at the time to guide them on what is considered the "right" thing to do. In addition, people also use these norms to judge others' behavior. A particular action may therefore be a part of the norms of one relationship and be regarded as appropriate by one person, while the same action may be seen as a serious violation of the norms of another relationship and perceived to be improper by another person. For example, keeping a close tab on how much money one spends on a relationship partner may be considered appropriate in a commercial transaction but inappropriate in interactions with family. It is this adherence to, or violation of, the underlying relationship norms that informs our appraisals when we interact with a relationship partner.

The notion that relationship metaphors can help us to better understand consumer behavior is based on the insight that when consumers see brands as relationship partners they invoke norms that underlie particular social relationships. Depending upon the relationship that they perceive to have formed with the brand, the norms that are salient to the consumers will differ. Consequently, when norms of a particular relationship are salient, consumers use these norms as a lens to view the brand and evaluate the brand's actions. These norms also help consumers guide their own actions, that is, suggest to the consumer what might be the right way to behave. It is this dual role of relational norms in influencing consumer behavior that I explore in my research.

NORMS OF COMMUNAL AND EXCHANGE RELATIONSHIPS

In my research, I have relied on the distinction made in social psychology between *exchange* relationships and *communal* relationships based on the norms governing the giving of benefits to the relationship partner (Clark and Mills 1979). Exchange relationships are

Table 2.1

Exchange Relationships versus Communal Relationships

	Exchange Relationship	Communal Relationship
1.	Prompt repayment for specific benefits received is expected.	Prompt repayment for specific benefits received is not expected.
2.	Desirable to give "comparable" benefits in return for benefits received.	Less desirable to give comparable benefits in return for benefits received.
3.	More likely to ask for repayments for benefits rendered.	Less likely to ask for repayments for benefits rendered.
4.	More likely to keep track of individual inputs and outcomes in a joint task.	Less likely to keep track of individual inputs and outcomes in a joint task.
5.	Less likely to keep track of others' needs.	More likely to keep track of others' needs.
6.	Divide rewards according to each person's inputs and contributions.	Divide rewards according to each person's needs and requirements.
7.	Helping others is less likely.	Helping others is more likely.
8.	Requesting help from others is less likely.	Requesting help from others is more likely.
9.	Accepting help with money is preferred to no payment.	Accepting help with no monetary payment is preferred.
10.	Less responsive to emotional states of others.	More responsive to emotional states of others.

Source: Clark 1981; Clark 1984; Clark and Mills 1979; Clark and Mills 1993; Clark, Mills, and Corcoran 1989; Clark and Taraban 1991; Mills and Clark 1982.

those in which benefits are given to the partner with a specific expectation of receiving a comparable benefit in return; the receipt of a benefit incurs a debt or obligation to return a comparable benefit. In this type of relationship, people are concerned with how much they receive in exchange for how much they give, and with how much is still owed to the partner. Relationships between strangers or those who interact for business purposes often characterize an exchange relationship. In communal relationships, however, the key concern is mutual support by the partners. In such relationships, people give benefits to others to demonstrate a concern for that person and to express attention to their needs. They also expect others to demonstrate a similar concern for their needs. Most family relationships, romantic relationships, and friendships fall into this category. It is important to note here that communal relationships are not completely bereft of a sense of reciprocity and shared giving. Each individual interaction, however, is not scrutinized for balance of the transaction. Instead, the relationship may be evaluated over a longer period of time. The norms of behavior of the two relationships are summarized in Table 2.1 as outlined by Clark and colleagues.

Exchange relationships involve a careful cost-benefit evaluation and the focus is on keeping track of inputs and outputs, while communal relationships focus on mutual support and cooperation and therefore transcend emphasis on self-interest alone. However, these two relationship types are not necessarily mutually exclusive; it is possible to have both a communal *and* an exchange relationship simultaneously with the same person. For example, a business partnership with one's brother is likely to lead to the salience of communal and exchange norms concurrently. One reason why such relationships are difficult to manage in practice is that people may often be uncertain about what norms to use in specific situations. Interestingly, given their commercial nature, arguably all consumer-brand relationships are inherently exchange-like. However, some marketers endeavor to position their brand as focused on the well-being of the consumers rather than on maximizing their own profits. Consequently, such brands are likely to have an overlay of communal norms on top of the exchange norms that inform such commercial transactions. In my research, I have focused on the *relative* salience of exchange versus communal norms in a consumer-brand interaction. Further, in keeping with prior social psychology research, I have treated them as two ends of a scale rather than two orthogonal dimensions. As such, my research examines the influence of relationship types on consumer behavior without compromising the validity of either the concepts or the methodologies.

As mentioned earlier, relationship norms influence consumer behavior in two distinct and crucial ways: (a) in judging others' actions, and (b) in guiding one's own actions. The next section of this chapter explores the influence of relationship norms on consumer evaluation of the brand and its actions in two different contexts. The following section summarizes two projects that look at the role of relationship norms from the other end: how norms guide consumers' own behavior and actions. Together, the four projects summarized here will help us to better understand the ways in which the type of relationships between consumers and brands, or, more specifically, the norms of relationships, influence consumer-brand interactions.

USING RELATIONSHIP NORMS TO EVALUATE THE BRAND

One important role of relationship norms is to act as a lens through which to judge the behavior and actions of the relationship partner. In this role, the norms help consumers to form an initial expectation, and the subsequent actions from the brand and its representatives are gauged in comparison to that norm-based expectation. Depending upon whether or not the actions of the brand are seen to be consistent with the relationship norms, the evaluation of the brand is more or less positive. This overall premise is examined in two uniquely different contexts.

Norm Violation and Its Mediating Effect on Brand Evaluations

The first project examines the influence of consumer-brand relationships on consumers' attitudes and behavior by explicitly testing the mediating role of relationship norm violation (Aggarwal 2002; Aggarwal 2004). The model proposed in this chapter suggests that when consumers form a relationship with a brand, brands too are evaluated as if they are members of a culture and therefore must conform to its norms. If the actions of the brand are in violation of the norms of a relationship then the brand is evaluated negatively, but if the actions conform to the norms of a relationship then the evaluation is positive.

This research uses the context of a request for help (or providing benefits) to test the influence of relationship type on consumers' responses to a particular marketing action. This context was chosen because the key distinction between exchange and communal relationships is based on the motivation for providing benefits to the partner—a request for help captures the essence of that distinction. Three studies were conducted, each examining a very specific aspect of a request for help. Participants were first given a brief scenario description that was a manipulation of norms of communal or exchange relationship. Participants were then presented with a description of request for help. Their reactions to the marketing action and overall brand evaluations were then recorded. The brand's action in all three studies was designed to violate the norms of one relationship and simultaneously conform to the norms of the other relationship. Measures of the participants' evaluation of the brand and its action were finally taken as the main dependent variables.

Study 1 examined participants' reactions to being charged a fee or no fee for a special service rendered by a brand in response to a specific request from the consumer. Help provided for a fee in response to a request conforms to exchange norms since it is in keeping with the principle of quid pro quo. Conversely, providing the service without a fee is in keeping with communal norms of taking care of a partner's needs. To test this premise, the participants were first exposed to a description of a relationship between a consumer and a hypothetical bank aimed at triggering either communal or exchange norms. Next, the scenario described a consumer who sought help from the bank requesting it to write a letter to their utility company who had not received a payment even though it had been cleared by the bank. The participants were subsequently told that the bank informed them a week later that the issue with the utility company had been resolved for no charge, or for a fee of $20.

A demand for a fee by the bank in response to a request for help violates the norms of a communal relationship since the help is being given for the fee rather than out of a concern for the consumer. This action, however, conforms to the norms of an exchange relationship since the fee highlights the quid pro quo nature of the relationship. Hence it was predicted that consumers' reactions to being charged would be different across the two relationship types, with communal consumers evaluating the action negatively relative to exchange consumers. There were two specific dependent variables: a three-item measure of reaction to the brand's action (willingness to pay, action seems appropriate, good business practice) and a three-item measure of brand evaluation (dislike-like, dissatisfied-satisfied, unfavorable-favorable).

As shown in Table 2.2, the results find support for the proposed hypothesis and indicate that, relative to exchange-oriented participants, communal participants evaluate the brand and its actions more positively when the action is in keeping with the communal norms but in violation of exchange norms (no fee was charged) than when the action is in violation of the communal norms but in keeping with the exchange norms (fee was charged).

Table 2.2

Mean Ratings of Communal and Exchange Participants on Reactions to Request for Help

Study 1	Charged		Not Charged	
	Communal	Exchange	Communal	Exchange
Reactions to brand's action	1.37	2.57	5.27	5.30
Brand evaluation	3.33	4.60	6.04	5.27

Study 2	Comparable		Noncomparable	
	Communal	Exchange	Communal	Exchange
Reactions to brand's action	5.57	6.38	6.20	5.53
Brand evaluation	6.67	7.37	6.34	5.60

Study 3	Immediate		Delayed	
	Communal	Exchange	Communal	Exchange
Reactions to brand's action	5.87	6.09	6.08	5.16
Brand evaluation	6.07	6.16	6.17	5.51
Norm violation	3.53	2.98	3.00	3.65

In addition, the twenty-item Postive and Negative Affect Schedule (PANAS) (Watson, Clark, and Tellegen 1988) administered to the participants showed no differences across different conditions, ruling out affect as a potential alternative explanation.

Study 2 examined consumer responses to receiving a comparable or noncomparable benefit from the brand in response to help rendered to a brand. Giving a benefit creates a specific debt and a directly comparable return benefit eliminates this debt owed by the exchange partner more adequately than a noncomparable benefit does since the comparable benefit is in keeping with the quid pro quo norms of an exchange relationship. Conversely, a noncomparable benefit acknowledges that the partner's needs are unique and giving such a benefit conforms to the norms of a communal relationship in which the underlying motivation is to take care of the partner's needs. This study thus explores a different aspect of the helping norm.

As in the first study, participants in study 2 were exposed to a brief description about a health club that was aimed at triggering norms of either a communal or an exchange relationship. Then, the health club requested the consumer to help them develop a Web site on healthy living by responding to a questionnaire that required about an hour of the consumer's time (nonmonetary help) or by donating $15 toward Web site development (monetary help). In return, the brand promised to give the consumer either a coupon for free use of the facility for one hour (nonmonetary reward), which was comparable to the request for time but noncomparable to the monetary help, or a $15-discount coupon (monetary reward) that was noncomparable to the request for time but was comparable to the monetary help. The participants then filled out two sets of dependent variables: a three-item measure of reactions to the brand's action (agree to help, enthusiastic about helping, support such programs in the future), and a three-item measure of brand evaluation (dislike-like, dissatisfied-satisfied, unfavorable-favorable).

Results of study 2 support the main hypothesis about a significant interaction between relationship and comparability of reciprocal benefit. The results suggest that a brand's action elicits different consumer evaluations depending on whether the brand's actions violate or conform to the norms of the underlying consumer-brand relationship (see Table 2.2). Since in an exchange relationship benefits are given with an expectation of getting comparable benefits in return, any such offer, cash or otherwise, would be considered in keeping with the relationship norms. Conversely, in a communal relationship, help is given to show concern for the partner's needs. A comparable benefit violates the underlying communal norms by transforming the relationship into a tit for tat relationship, while a noncomparable benefit would conform to communal norms by de-linking the benefit given from the benefit received and emphasizing the unique needs of the partner.

Study 3 was conducted not just to explore yet another aspect of the helping norm but also to overtly examine the mediating role of relationship norm violation. For this purpose, a direct measure of participants' perceived norm violation was taken, and a mediation analysis was done to explore whether the brand evaluations were in fact influenced by the degree of norm violation experienced by the participants. This study examined how the length of time between help given and help sought causes participants to respond across the two relationships. If a request for help by a partner is immediately countered with a return request, the debt created by the original help is paid off right away, the return request being seen as a quid pro quo would be in keeping with the norms of exchange relationship. However, a return request that is delayed in time is less likely to be connected to the original request and would be seen as a way to extract free help by the partner and would therefore be in violation of the exchange norms. Thus, exchange-oriented consumers would prefer return requests to be made immediately rather than with a time lag.

On the other hand, an immediate return request is likely to be seen as a repayment for the original help and would thus be in violation of communal norms. A delayed return request, in contrast, would be unconnected to the original request, and is likely to be seen as an expression of a genuine need of the partner and consequently be in keeping with the communal relationship norms. Thus, communally oriented consumers should prefer requests that are delayed in time over those made immediately following an original request.

As before, the participants read about a hypothetical coffee shop brand to manipulate either norms of a communal or an exchange relationship; then, the participants read about a situation in which the brand asked the consumer to post promotional materials on campus in response to the customer's request to make a fresh cup of coffee. This request from the brand was made either immediately afterward, or a week after the original request from the consumer. It was expected that relative to participants in a communal relationship, those in an exchange relationship would evaluate the brand's request negatively when it was delayed as compared to when it was immediate. The dependent variables were (a) a measure of likelihood to agree to a request; (b) a three-item brand evaluation score as before; and (c) a six-item measure of norm violation [felt cornered, felt irritated, felt exploited, care about them (reversed), happy to help (reversed), request was appropriate (reversed)].

As expected, the results show that consumer responses depend on the type of relationship norms salient at the time of brand interaction (see Table 2.2). Specifically, the results show that in keeping with the principles of norm violation, exchange consumers evaluate the brand less positively for a delayed request but more positively for an immediate request compared to the communal consumers. Further, the results of this study find that the perceived level of norm violation completely mediates the effects on consumers' assessment of a brand and its actions.

Since communal relationships are likely to be more emotionally laden (Chapter 17), it was important to examine whether emotional attachment rather than the relational norms might have driven these results. To rule this out, the three studies used the PANAS scale (Watson et al. 1988) to take measures of perceived affect. Further, the key hypotheses in all three studies were based on an interaction effect—main effect of relationship was neither expected nor found. Finally, if either attachment or affect was the main driving factor, the results of study 3, in particular, should have been reversed. Overall, results of all three studies support the theory that a violation of or adherence to relationship norms influences consumers' evaluation of a brand. In addition, the studies also ruled out uniqueness of monetary benefits and differences in quality perceptions across the two relationships as two supplemental alternative explanations.

Relationship Norms and Consumer Responses to Interactional Fairness

The second project that examines the effect of relationship norms on consumers' evaluations of a brand and its actions explores issues of fairness in the context of a consumer-brand interaction (Aggarwal 2008). Researchers in organizational behavior have noted that when people assess overall fairness of an action, they first look at aspects of distributive fairness, or the allocation of the final outcome. This aspect of fairness relates to distribution of benefits versus costs. In addition, people also care about issues of interactional fairness, or how people are treated during conflict resolution. This type of fairness relates to whether others exhibit respectful, sensitive, and justifiable behavior. It has been noted in prior research that the extent to which people care about the final allocation depends on how the final allocation is arrived at. That is to say that there is an interactive effect between distributive fairness and interactional fairness: the way people are treated has a greater influence on their attitudes and behavior when the outcome itself is unfair than when the outcome is fair. This project directly tests for the influence of norms in a context of an interaction between a consumer and a marketer, and examines the moderating effect of relationship norms on the interactive effect of distributive and interactional fairness. It is useful to note that although conceptually distinct, distributive fairness is often highly correlated with favorability of outcome and interactional fairness with a superior service orientation.

When faced with low distributive fairness, the type of relationship norms salient at the time of interaction with a brand—communal versus exchange—influence how consumers respond to aspects of interactional fairness (or, how people are treated by others) (Aggarwal 2008). The underlying premise of this research is that since a communal relationship is based on mutual care and concern, low interactional fairness (i.e., being treated shabbily) by the brand, especially if accompanied by low distributive fairness, will be seen as a lack of concern for the consumer, and thus a breach of the underlying relationship norms. However, high interactional fairness would provide reassurance of the genuine concern underlying a communal relationship, and thus would conform to communal norms even in the face of low distributive fairness. In contrast, exchange relationships are quid pro quo: people are concerned first and foremost about what they get for what they give to their partner. Low distributive fairness reflects that the one thing exchange consumers care most about is not forthcoming, and that the underlying norms of exchange relationship have been violated. As a result, whether the accompanying level of interactional fairness is high or low may be of little consequence to such consumers. Thus, under conditions of low distributive fairness, relative to exchange, communal consumers would evaluate the brand more positively when faced with high interactional fairness.

Two studies test this premise. Since the effects are predicted only for low but not for high distributive fairness conditions, the first study examines the three-way interaction of relationship type, distributive fairness, and interactional fairness using a hypothetical consumer-marketer scenario. The second study uses the context of a real brand and a different operationalization of interactional fairness to replicate the main findings of study 1. Study 2 also specifically tests for the mediating role of perceived violation of the underlying relationship norms for these effects.

In study 1, participants were first exposed to a brief description of a hypothetical takeout restaurant designed to make communal or exchange relationship norms salient. Participants then read about an interaction with the restaurant aimed at eliciting perceptions of distributive and interactional (un)fairness. The scenario described a consumer who had ordered food from the restaurant but received something that was too spicy to be eaten. The consumer complained to the restaurant manager, and either got a full refund or no compensation, which was the manipulation of high- and low-distributive fairness. In addition, to manipulate high- and low-interactional fairness the response from the restaurant was communicated either very politely and respectfully or very rudely and disrespectfully. It was expected that relative to participants in the exchange condition, those in the communal condition would evaluate the brand more positively when treated with politeness and respect, especially when they did not receive a refund (low distributive fairness).

The main dependent variables were (a) a four-item measure of brand evaluation (dislike-like, dissatisfied-satisfied, unfavorable-favorable, and extent of trust for the brand), and (b) a three-item measure of future intentions [use the brand again, praise the brand, complain about the brand (reversed)]. In addition, checks were performed for assessing the effectiveness of the relationship, distributive fairness, and interactional fairness manipulations. The results found support for the hypothesized three-way interaction between relationship norms, distributive fairness, and interactional fairness (see Table 2.3). Specifically, the results showed that under conditions of low distributive fairness,

Table 2.3

Mean Ratings of Communal and Exchange Participants on Responses to Interactional and Distributive Fairness

	Communal				Exchange			
	Hi Dist.		Lo Dist.		Hi Dist.		Lo Dist.	
Study 1	Hi Inter	Lo Inter	Hi Inter	Lo Inter	Hi Inter	Lo Inter	Hi Inter	Lo Inter
Brand evaluation	6.26	4.25	5.87	3.39	6.35	4.18	5.25	3.83
Future intention	6.11	4.15	5.65	3.12	6.25	3.84	4.79	3.59

	Communal		Exchange	
Study 2	Hi Inter	Lo Inter	Hi Inter	Lo Inter
Brand evaluation	4.03	3.09	2.22	2.53
Future intention	3.40	2.64	2.02	2.63

Abbreviations: Hi dist, high distributive fairness; lo dist, low distributive fairness; hi inter, high interactional fairness; lo inter, low interactional fairness.

consumers primed with communal norms show a more positive brand evaluation and future intentions compared to those primed with exchange norms when faced with high rather than low interactional fairness.

To replicate the main findings of study 1 in a more realistic context, study 2 used a real brand—Starbucks—and subsequently, measured rather than manipulated communal and exchange norms. Further, study 2 examined the role of a perceived breach of relationship norms as the underlying process variable. Finally, interactional fairness was operationalized differently: by the amount of effort put in to resolve the conflict rather than the politeness shown by the brand.

In study 2, participants were exposed to the Starbucks brand name, a visual of a Starbucks branded coffee cup, and were encouraged to think of their own interactions, feelings, and associations with Starbucks. Participants then responded to some questions about Starbucks that were later used to categorize them into communal- or exchange-oriented consumers. Participants then read about a consumer who had ordered a decaf latte but received regular coffee that was not even hot. When the consumer complained, there was either no effort made to resolve the issue (low interactional fairness), or the salesperson tried with utmost sincerity to resolve it (high interactional fairness). For all consumers the final outcome was the same—the consumer had to pay for the stale regular coffee and did not get a refund. The main dependent variables were the same as in study 1: (a) a four-item measure of brand evaluation, and (b) a three-item measure of future intention. A three-item measure of perceived breach of relationship norms was also administered (violated principles, broke promise, violated rules). Manipulation checks of relationship norms and interactional fairness were administered.

Results replicated those of study 1, showing that under conditions of low distributive fairness, consumers who perceive a communal relationship with the brand are likely to have a more positive brand evaluation and future intention scores than those who perceive an exchange relationship when facing high rather than low interactional fairness (see Table 2.3). The results of study 2 are significant because they are observed in the context of a real brand and a real relationship. More importantly, this study shows that the interactive effects of relationship type and interactional fairness on consumer evaluations are fully mediated by the extent to which consumers perceive a breach of the relationship norms.

Together, the two projects—responses to request for help and issues of fairness—highlight the crucial role of relationship norms in how consumers assess the actions and behavior of a brand and/or its representatives. Findings from these two projects suggest that actions of a brand that are seen to be in violation of the norms of the underlying relationship between the consumer and the brand are likely to lead to a less positive evaluation of the brand compared to actions that are seen as upholding the norms of that relationship. Significantly, the same action is evaluated differently depending upon whether or not it is perceived to be consistent with the relationship norms. This suggests that it is not the action per se but whether or not that action is in keeping with what is expected in the particular relationship that determines the evaluation of that action and the brand. Interestingly, the results of these two projects are consistent with what is suggested by prior work on consumer satisfaction based on expectation confirmation (Oliver 1980). It is reasonable to think of relationship norms as setting consumers' expectations, and the subsequent action of the brand being judged good or not based on whether the expectation is subsequently confirmed or not, that is, in conformity or in violation of the relationship norms. Thus, the norm-based thesis of a consumer-brand relationship also provides insight into the degree of consumer satisfaction in a specific consumer-brand interaction.

USING RELATIONSHIP NORMS AS A GUIDE FOR OWN BEHAVIOR

The second crucial role of relationship norms is to help consumers guide their own behavior when interacting with a brand or its representatives. When in a relationship, the norms of that relationship suggest to the consumer the "right" way to behave. As a consequence, how consumers behave in one particular relationship might be very distinct from how they behave in another relationship. The following section summarizes two projects that examine how the norms of relationship are used as a guide for consumers' own actions and behavior in interactions with a brand.

Role of Relationship Norms in Processing Brand Information

This project examined differences in consumer strategies in processing brand-related information (Aggarwal and Law 2005). In particular, this research suggests that norms of a communal relationship, relative to those of an exchange relationship, make individuals more likely to process brand information at a higher level of abstraction. Prior research suggests that people in an exchange relationship focus on different aspects of information than people in a communal relationship do; more specifically, they are more likely to keep track of their partners' input rather than their partners' needs (Clark 1984). In a consumer-brand context, we expect this focus on the input of others in an exchange relationship to translate into attention to nitty-gritty details about the brand, which allows consumers to track the balance of what they receive for what they pay. In contrast, since consumers primed with communal norms do not look for immediate quid pro quo (Clark and Mills 1993), they are more likely to evaluate brands holistically, that is, to attend to overall brand attributes at a higher level of abstraction. Further, this research argues that it is not even necessary for consumers to form a relationship with the brand to show this effect. Rather, the effect of relationship norms can also work if the norms are made salient in one context and the effect is assessed in a subsequent unrelated behavior.

Three studies were used to test the effects of relationship types on the level of abstraction of brand information. The studies used very different operationalizations of level of abstraction to provide strong converging evidence for the moderating role of relationship norms on consumers' information-processing strategies. Study 1 built upon prior work on categorization to manipulate the level of abstraction by varying the similarity of a proposed extension to the original product; study 2 used memory measures such as recognition and response latency for brand features that vary in their level of abstraction; and study 3 used participants' open-ended responses to examine whether the brand features listed by participants varied by level of abstraction.

In study 1, the context of a near-versus-far product extension was used to examine the level of abstraction at which consumers processed the proposed extension. The logic was that in a communal relationship people process information at a higher level of abstraction, perceive even the far extensions as being similar to the original product category, and evaluate these extensions relatively positively. Conversely, in an exchange relationship, people process brand information at a lower level of abstraction, perceive greater differences between the proposed far product extension and the original category, and are less likely than their communal counterparts to evaluate far product extensions positively. However, when the proposed extension is similar to the original product, no differences across relationships were expected since both sets of consumers were likely to see the similarities between the two.

Scenario descriptions of a hypothetical relationship between two people were used to manipulate communal and exchange relationship norms. Manipulation checks and PANAS scales (Watson et al. 1988) were administered to ensure that the manipulation was effective and that affect was not driving any effects. In a presumably unrelated task, participants then evaluated a proposed extension for a product. Iced tea and toffee were the near and far extensions of a cola product, but the far and near extensions of a chewing gum product. The other pair of extensions was calculator (near/far) and fashion accessories (far/near) for a pen/jean manufacturer. The extensions were evaluated on a four-item scale (dislike-like, bad-good, low quality-high quality, unpleasant-pleasant).

Results showed that the norms of relationships moderate the degree to which far product extensions are seen as similar to the original product, as revealed by the differences in the evaluations of the product extensions: people evaluate the far extensions more posi-

Table 2.4

Mean Ratings of Communal and Exchange Participants on Assessing Abstract versus Concrete Information

Study 1	Communal		Exchange	
Evaluation of near extensions	4.10		4.56	
Evaluation of far extensions	3.48		2.88	
	Proportion of Responses		Response Time	
Study 2	Communal	Exchange	Communal	Exchange
Concrete information				
Correct	.61	.76	4,959	5,802
Incorrect	.39	.24	6,803	7,438
Abstract information				
Correct	.53	.63	9,375	11,314
Plausible	.40	.31	9,859	13,350
Incorrect	.07	.07	8,474	10,494
Study 3	Communal		Exchange	
Average abstractness of features	4.87		4.32	

tively when the norms of a communal rather than an exchange relationship are salient (see Table 2.4). Since a communal relationship leads to information being processed at a higher level of abstraction, participants are able to see the similarities in extensions that are relatively far from the original product category. Conversely, when the norms of an exchange relationship are salient, people attend to the specific/concrete features of a product; hence they are less likely to see similarities beyond the obvious. These results support the premise of differences in processing strategies adopted by consumers across the two relationship types. Interestingly, these results are consistent with those found by Monga and John (Chapter 13), who report differences in processing styles of consumers across independent and interdependent cultures. Since people from interdependent cultures are more concerned about others, their processing strategy is akin to consumers who have a communal orientation. Conversely, people from an independent culture focus on their own well-being quite like those who have an exchange orientation. Although not directly examined, results from study 1 thus suggest that the processing style of consumers who have a communal relationship is similar to those from an interdependent culture while that of those who have an exchange relationship is similar to those from an independent culture. Some interesting research examining issues relating to different relationship types across the two cultural orientations could be conducted by future investigators.

Study 2 employed memory measures to more directly examine the differences induced by relationship types in information processing. It was reasoned that if communal relationship norms more than exchange norms make individuals process abstract or general brand information, then these encoding differences would be reflected in later memory measures. Accordingly, when presented with both abstract as well as more specific (or concrete) brand information, individuals in a communal relationship would overwhelmingly encode the abstract information, whereas those in an exchange relationship condition would attend more to the concrete brand information.

Participants were presented with a description of a new clothing store brand that contained concrete as well as abstract brand information. A memory test was later administered on the participants. The memory test gauged accurate and inaccurate memory for concrete brand information, accurate memory for the more abstract brand information, and memory for information that, although not presented, was nonetheless a plausible inference. It was expected that consumers in an exchange relationship condition would be more likely to correctly recognize such concrete brand information and to accurately detect inaccuracies. However, the impact of relationship type on memory for abstract brand information and plausible inferences as measured by recognition performance was more complex. It was expected that there would be no differences across the communal and exchange relationship groups for accurate recognition since communal participants would simply recall such information from memory while the exchange participants would use their memory of concrete information to generate this information. However, because exchange-oriented consumers are assumed to rely on generating the abstract and plausible information, they would be slower than communal consumers at identifying this information as shown by the response latencies.

Participants were first presented with a relationship manipulation identical to that used in study 1. Next, participants read a 450-word description about a hypothetical clothing store that contained both concrete and abstract brand information (e.g., "stores in thirty-nine countries" vs. "it is an international brand"). Later, following a filler exercise, the participants completed a computer-based, multiple-choice recognition task. A total of fourteen questions were asked, the first two being practice questions. Six of the twelve critical questions tested the participants' memory for the concrete brand information presented earlier; the other six tested their memory for the abstract information. Each question had four possible responses. The six questions on concrete brand information had one accurate and three inaccurate response options. The six questions on abstract brand information had one accurate, one inaccurate, and two plausible inferences as options. Participants were required to select only one of the four responses for each of the twelve questions, and were instructed to do so as quickly and accurately as possible.

The results showed that, as expected, participants in the exchange condition had a higher likelihood of accepting correct concrete brand information and a lower likelihood of accepting incorrect concrete brand information relative to participants in the communal condition (see Table 2.4). Further, there were no differences in the proportion of accurate, inaccurate, or plausible responses for abstract information across conditions. However, participants in a communal condition, relative to those in an exchange condition, had faster access to both correct abstract brand information and plausible inferences, suggesting that they particularly attend to brand information presented at a higher level of abstraction. On the other hand, participants in the exchange condition needed the extra time presumably to construct the abstract brand information from the concrete information. Even though communal and exchange participants show no reliable differences in the amount of time needed to recognize concrete brand information, their levels of accuracy are significantly different. This suggests that at the time of encoding, participants in the exchange condition attend to the concrete brand information relatively more than their communal counterparts and, at retrieval, are able to access more of the relevant information. Together, these findings support the overall premise that brand-related information is processed at a higher level of abstraction in a communal relationship than in an exchange relationship.

The premise of study 3 is the following: if the type of consumer-brand relationship influences the level of abstraction at which the brand's features are processed, then similar differences in abstraction will be revealed in the way in which a consumer describes that brand to a third party. The study used a scenario description to first manipulate communal or exchange relationships with a hypothetical pen brand. Next, each participant was asked to describe the features of the pen to a friend. It was predicted that, relative to those with an exchange relationship, consumers with a communal relationship would list features at a higher level of abstraction. As in studies 1 and 2, participants were first exposed to the relationship-type manipulation, which involved reading a scenario. Unlike the previous two studies, however, the scenario descriptions in this study described interactions between an individual and a product, a fictitious brand of pen. The main dependent variable was the different features of the pen as reported by the participants.

In order to focus on the most important features, the analysis was limited to the first three features mentioned by each participant. Two independent judges rated each feature for each participant on a seven-point, concreteness-abstractness scale, with the higher score indicating a higher level of abstraction. For example, a feature such as "color of the pen" or "ink flow" got a lower rating (1, 2, or 3), but a feature such as "classy" or "style" received a higher rating (5, 6, or 7). For each of the three features, the ratings for each participant were averaged and the average rating for the two judges estimated. This average score was compared across the two relationship conditions. Results showed that, as expected, participants in the communal condition listed brand features at a higher level of abstraction compared to those in the exchange condition (see Table 2.4). Control groups ruled out alternative explanations based on affect, differences in abstractness of the descriptions, perceived quality, amount of effort, and potential demand effects.

These three studies provide converging evidence in support of the hypothesis that communal norms lead consumers to process brand-related information at a higher level of abstraction compared to exchange norms. This research highlights the effect of relationship norms not on how consumers evaluate the brand but on how the norms guide them and suggest to them the proper way to conduct themselves in their interactions with the brand. Finally, as was demonstrated by the methodology adopted in studies 1 and 2, this research also shows that the effect of relationship norms extends beyond the context in which the norms are made salient. The norms of relationship affect consumer behavior even if they have been made salient in a context that is unrelated to the subsequent interaction with the brand.

Relationship Norms and Consumers' Loss Aversion

Following the research that found evidence of the effect of the mere salience of relationship norms on consumers' processing strategies, another study (Aggarwal and Zhang 2006) replicated the important carryover effect of relationship norms beyond the priming context through a task that assessed consumers' loss aversion. In particular, this research argued that communal relationship norms would lead consumers to be more loss averse relative to exchange relationship norms for two key reasons. First, given that consumers' underlying intentions for interaction with the brand are different in the two relationships, relationship norms are expected to change consumers' cognitive perspective, resulting in crucial differences in how gains and losses are treated. Because exchange relationships are quid pro quo—what is received is evaluated in terms of what one gives up—people in an exchange relationship are more concerned with the net balance of inputs and outcomes (Clark and Mills 1993). In other words, people are more likely to compute the net of gains and losses from a transaction rather than evaluating them separately as gains versus losses. And since the value function of losses is steeper than that of gains, aggregating losses with gains would result in a weaker degree of loss aversion. However, matching specific inputs with subsequent outcomes violates the norms of a communal relationship. People avoid linking what they get to what they give up and shun calculating the net of gains and losses. Hence, communal norms would lead to losses being evaluated separately from gains (rather than being aggregated), resulting in consumer behavior that is consistent with a stronger degree of loss aversion.

Second, relationship norms are likely to result in differences in the emotional attachment to the endowed object, engendering different experiences of the loss itself for the two sets of consumers. In particular, communal relationship norms, relative to exchange norms, are likely to inflate the level of perceived loss. When the norms of a communal relationship are salient, consumers see their partners as close friends or family members, suggesting that a much higher value would be required by them to break away from this relationship. Thus, when communal norms are salient, consumers will show an increased fondness for and commitment to their current option and a greater resistance to giving it up—demonstrating the relatively stronger degree of loss aversion. Conversely, exchange norms suggest that the endowed option should be valued primarily for what it can fetch. Giving up such an item may not be all that painful, which results in a lower degree of loss aversion. This suggests that the experience of the loss itself will be greater in a communal than in an exchange relationship, contributing to the differences in consumers' loss aversion.

It is also suggested that the effect of relationship norms is likely to be stronger when consumers have had some opportunity to interact with the product (i.e., they already own a product) than when they have not had this opportunity (i.e., they do not own it): the differences in loss aversion across different relationship types are expected to be driven by the selling rather than the buying prices. Furthermore, given that buying and selling is likely to be seen more as a commercial transaction, the participants in a control group who are not exposed to any relationship manipulation are likely to be similar to the exchange rather than the communal group. Put differently, it is expected that the higher willingness to accept (WTA) in the communal relative to the exchange condition suggested earlier is driven by an enhanced loss aversion caused by the communal norms rather than by a dampened loss aversion caused by the exchange norms.

The study used scenario descriptions to manipulate communal or exchange relationship norms, or no manipulation for the control group. Participants then assumed the role of a buyer or seller of a plain coffee mug, similar to a typical endowment effect study. The coffee mug was bought from a discount store for 99 cents. Buying and selling prices were elicited for each of twenty-four prices ranging from $0.25 to $6.00 (in 25-cent increments). At the end of the study a randomly generated price was chosen and all qualifying transactions conducted. The dependent variable was the buying and selling price indicated by the seller and the buyer groups respectively.

The results suggest that communal norms increase consumers' degree of loss aversion as revealed by a higher WTA. Participants in the control group behaved no differently from those in the exchange group—both showed a lower WTA than the communal group (communal = $5.32; exchange = $3.60; control = $3.42). The willingness to pay (WTP), however, was no different across the three groups (communal = $1.88; exchange = $2.02; control = $2.23). These results suggest that differences across communal and exchange norms are driven by consumers behaving differently from the "average" when primed with communal rather than exchange relationship norms. Also, communal norms do not merely lead to a higher overall valuation of the product because there were differences in WTA but not in WTP. Finally, this research highlights the contextual effect of relationship norms since the experience of loss is affected even when the item of evaluation and relationship are unrelated. This study together with the one on processing strategies highlights the important role of relationship norms in helping consumers determine the appropriate way to behave in their brand interactions.

CONCLUSIONS

The four projects summarized in this chapter examine the interpersonal relationship metaphor in the context of consumer-brand interactions to gain insight into different aspects of consumer behavior. The insight guiding all these projects is that each relationship carries with it a distinct set of norms that are unique to that relationship, and when consumers perceive a certain relationship with a brand they are, in fact, invoking the norms of that particular relationship to guide their own behavior and evaluate that of the brand, their relationship partner. The first two projects (request for help, fairness) highlight the effect of norm salience on the consumers' evaluation of the brand. The other two (processing strategy, loss aversion) emphasize the role of norm salience in guiding consumers' own behavior. Together, this research underscores the value of using the relationship metaphor to better understand consumer-brand interactions. The framework of relationship norms provides a key tool not just for understanding but also for making predictions about consumer behavior that would not be possible otherwise.

Many important questions may be asked, such as how norms are created in the first place, and why some consumers may form communal relationships while others form exchange relationships with the same brand. Clearly, there are different person, product, and context-specific factors that cause particular relationships to develop between a consumer and a brand. Some consumers may be intrinsically more communal-minded while others may never see a commercial exchange as anything more than a quid pro quo. Some product categories may be inherently more communal, such as the commercial exchanges between a doctor and a patient, or those between a school and a student. Aside from these obvious examples, brands that have people as the representatives, such as for most services (e.g., hotels, airlines, etc.), brands that have a combination of product and service as their core offering (e.g., restaurants and some online stores), and brands that require one-on-one personal selling may all be more amenable to being seen as communal relationship partners. Clearly, marketers have a variety of tools available to develop the kind of relationship that they wish to pursue with their consumers. The most important tool for determining which type of relationship might eventually emerge with the consumer is how the brand is positioned in the mind of the consumer. In addition, the dynamic and repeated interactions pursued by marketers in the form of ads, interactive media, direct mail, and telemarketing as well as the use of brand mascots and spokespersons strengthen the type of ongoing relationship that is formed between the brand and the consumer.

The communal-exchange relationship framework is but one framework that could potentially be used in the consumer-brand context. Other frameworks, such as that proposed by Fiske (1992), offer a somewhat more complex model of relationship types. This or some other framework of relationship types could potentially be used in future research to examine more nuanced hypotheses about the research questions relating to issues of consumer behavior. More importantly, as the diverse nature of the four research projects highlighted here suggest, the metaphor of interpersonal relationships is such a versatile framework that future research avenues relating to consumer-brand interactions are only limited by the imagination of the investigating researchers.

ACKNOWLEDGMENTS

I thank my dissertation advisor Ann L. McGill for her guidance on my various projects on consumer-brand relationships and for her comments on this chapter. I also acknowledge the contributions of my co-authors on two of the four projects discussed in this chapter.

REFERENCES

Aaker, Jennifer L., Susan Fournier, and Adam Brasel (2004). "When Good Brands Go Bad: The Effects of Brand Personality and Transgressions on Consumer-Brand Relationships," *Journal of Consumer Research*, 31 (June), 1–16.

Aggarwal, Pankaj (2002). "The Effects of Brand Relationship Norms on Consumer Attitudes and Behavior." Doctoral dissertation, Graduate School of Business, University of Chicago.

———— (2004). "The Effects of Brand Relationship Norms on Consumer Attitudes and Behavior," *Journal of Consumer Research*, 31 (June), 87–101.

——— (2008). "Interactional Fairness and Consumer Responses: The Moderating Role of Relationship Norms." Working paper, University of Toronto.

Aggarwal, Pankaj, and Sharmistha Law (2005). "Role of Relationship Norms in Processing Brand Information," *Journal of Consumer Research,* 32 (December), 453–464.

Aggarwal, Pankaj, and Meng Zhang (2006). "The Moderating Effect of Relationship Norm Salience on Consumers' Loss Aversion," *Journal of Consumer Research,* 33 (December), 413–419.

Cialdini, Robert B., and Melanie R. Trost (1998). "Social Influence: Social Norms, Conformity and Compliance." In *The Handbook of Social Psychology,* vol. 2 (4th ed.), ed. Daniel T. Gilbert and Susan T. Fiske. New York, NY: McGraw-Hill, 151–192.

Clark, Margaret S., (1981). "Noncomparability of Benefits Given and Received: A Cue to the Existence of Friendship" *Social Psychology Quarterly,* 44 (4) December, 375–381.

——— (1984). "Record Keeping in Two Types of Relationships," *Journal of Personality and Social Psychology,* 47(3) September, 549–557.

Clark, Margaret S. and Judson Mills (1979). "Interpersonal Attraction in Exchange and Communal Relationships" *Journal of Personality and Social Psychology,* 37 (1), 12–24.

——— (1993). "The Difference Between Communal and Exchange Relationships: What It Is and Is Not," *Personality and Social Psychology Bulletin,* 19 (6), 684–691.

Clark, Margaret S., Judson Mills, and David M. Corcoran (1989). "Keeping Track of Needs and Inputs of Friends and Strangers," *Personality and Social Psychology Bulletin,* 15 (4), 553–542.

Clark, Margaret S., and Carolyn Taraban (1991). "Reactions to and Willingness to Express Emotion in Communal and Exchange Relationships," *Journal of Experimental Social Psychology,* 27 (4), 324–336.

Fiske, Alan Page (1992). "The Four Elementary Forms of Sociality: Framework for a Unified Theory of Social Relations" *Psychological Review,* 99 (4), 689–723.

Fournier, Susan (1998). "Consumers and Their Brands: Developing Relationship Theory in Consumer Research," *Journal of Consumer Research,* 24 (March), 343–373.

Ji, Mindy F. (2002). "Children's Relationships with Brands," *Psychology and Marketing,* 19 (4), 369–387.

Mills, Judson, and Margaret S. Clark (1982). "Communal and Exchange Relationships." In *Review of Personality and Social Psychology,* ed. Ladd Wheeler. Beverly Hills, CA: Sage, 121–144.

Oliver, Richard L. (1980). "A Cognitive Model of the Antecedents and Consequences of Satisfaction Decision," *Journal of Marketing Research,* 17 (4), 460–469.

Swaminathan, Vanitha, Karen L. Page, and Zeynep Gurhan-Canli (2007). "'My' Brand or 'Our' Brand: The Effects of Brand Relationship Dimensions and Self-Construal on Brand Evaluations," *Journal of Consumer Research,* 34 (2), 248–259.

Watson, David, Lee A. Clark, and Auke Tellegen (1988). "Development and Validation of Brief Measures of Positive and Negative Affect: The PANAS scales," *Journal of Personality and Social Psychology,* 54 (6), 1063–1070.

CHAPTER 3

BRAND LOYALTY IS NOT HABITUAL

LEONA TAM, WENDY WOOD, AND MINDY F. JI

Repeat customers are valued customers. And much of consumer behavior is repetitive. Panel data investigations have identified periodic patterns in consumer purchase and consumption (e.g., Ehrenberg 1991; Khare and Inman 2006). For example, considerable inertia-like repeated purchases of the same brands are evident across different shopping episodes (e.g., Seetharaman 2004). Self-report studies of the items consumers purchase reveal a similar pattern of repetition (e.g., Bettman and Zins 1977). By estimates from these studies, a substantial proportion of consumer purchases are repetitive.

The importance of understanding repeated patronage is illustrated by brand performance data. Market researchers have noted that repeated patronage has long-term financial and brand performance advantages, including increases in market share for a brand, customer lifetime value, and share of wallet (Baumann, Burton, and Elliott 2005; Ehrenberg, Goodhardt, and Barwise 1990; Wirtz, Mattila, and Lwin 2007). These relationships between repeated purchasing and marketing outcomes highlight the importance of understanding the psychological factors that promote repeated purchasing. By understanding these psychological processes, marketers may leverage important brand outcomes.

What is the psychology behind the repeated purchase or consumption of a particular brand? The traditional answer invokes brand loyalty or some other positive brand relationship. When people develop a fondness for particular brands and form attachments to them, these favorable evaluations lead to repeated purchase and consumption. In this chapter, we argue that not all repetition is based on such preferences. Often, people repeatedly purchase and consume out of habit. We explain how understanding the psychology of habits helps marketers to manage consumer behavior.

The distinction between habit and brand loyalty is illustrated by the fast food purchasing profiles of two college students who participated in our research (Ji and Wood 2007). "Holly" reported eating lunch at the Subway shop on campus almost every day after class by herself. She repeatedly purchased fast food in the same location as part of her afternoon routine. In contrast, "Zach" was much more variable in his fast food purchase and consumption. He sometimes bought a sandwich at the Subway when he was on his way to work and other times he stopped by the Subway on campus for a meal after class. Both of these students were valued Subway repeated customers, but they showed strikingly different patterns of repeated patronage.

Given that Holly was regularly repeating a response in a stable context, she was likely to have formed a habit of purchasing and consuming Subway fast food. Brand habits are associations that form in memory between responses of purchasing and consuming a brand and recurring contextual cues (e.g., Holly's routine following morning classes, a Subway shop on campus). Such associations develop slowly in procedural memory over repeated experience (Neal, Wood, and Quinn 2006; Wood and Neal 2007). Zach's responses were more variable in that he did not purchase or eat fast food in any particular context or as part of a routine. Thus, despite frequent repetition, he was not likely to have developed a patronage habit. His continued purchase of the brand instead should have depended on the activation of a preference for Subway fast food over other brands.

Once habits have formed, the simple perception of the context in which the action has been performed in the past can activate the associated response in memory. To the extent that eating at Subway was embedded in Holly's noontime routine, it was activated automatically in memory at the appropriate point in her daily activities. In contrast, Zach's repeated patronage resulted as a function of brand preference or loyalty. This evaluation could guide eating choices through careful, deliberative judgment processes (e.g., carefully evaluating fat content of various brands) or through more efficient processes (e.g., relying on preference rules such as, "Subway is my brand"; having a positive evaluation of Subway triggered with minimal awareness). Thus, Holly and Zach's similar repeated patronage represent different psychological processes, namely, habits and brand loyalty.

DEFINITIONS OF HABITS AND BRAND LOYALTY

In this chapter, we build a theory of repeated patronage based on recent developments in psychological theories of action control and response repetition (Neal et al. 2006; Wood and Neal 2007). In our analysis, repeated purchase and consumption can reflect a habit, defined as a behavioral disposition in which past responses are triggered directly by associated context cues, or brand loyalty, defined as a psychological disposition to evaluate a brand favorably (see Figure 3.1). As we explain, repeated patronage can reflect strong habits and be cued by stable features of purchase and consumption contexts or it can reflect brand loyalty and be influenced by strongly held, favorable brand evaluations that direct repurchase and consumption intentions.

The determinants of repeated patronage in our model build on existing ideas in marketing. Most generally, in line with our focus on behavior repetition, models of scanner panel data estimate the proportion or sequence of consumers' repeated brand purchases across shopping trips (e.g., Seetharaman 2004). However, such models do not identify any particular set of psychological factors that promote repeated responding. Marketing as a field has not yet reached a consensus on the dispositions that drive repeated purchases in scanner data, and individual researchers differ in the specific dispositions they believe are indicated by repetition. Thus, repeated purchases in scanner panel data have been interpreted variously as habit (e.g., Seetharaman 2004) and as brand loyalty (e.g., Raj 1985).

Our definition of habits reflects and refines existing marketing approaches. In the most common definition, habits reflect repeated past purchases (Seetharaman 2004). Thus,

Figure 3.1   **Two Determinants of Repeated Patronage: Habits and Brand Loyalty**

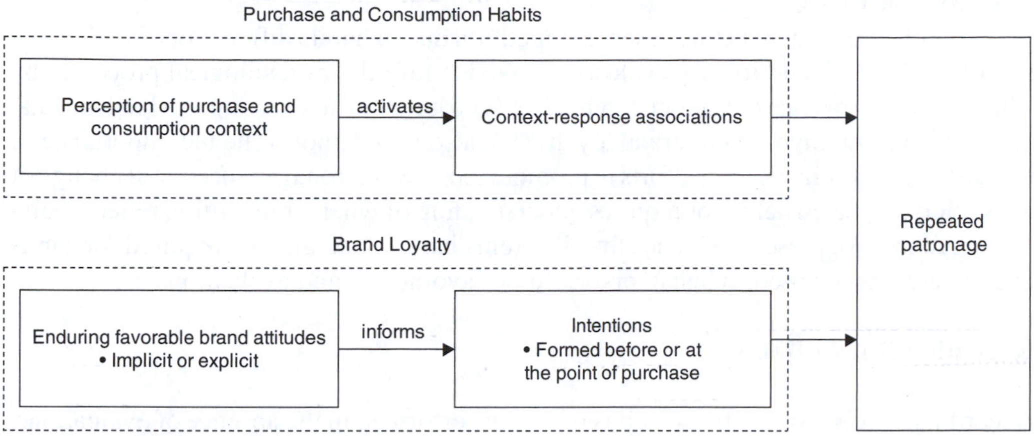

habits have been measured through past purchase frequency (e.g., Kaas 1982), prior brand choice (e.g., Roy, Chintagunta, and Haldar 1996), consecutive brand purchase (Seetharaman 2004), and number of brands purchased (Chaudhuri 1995). Sometimes habits have been defined additionally as a kind of simple decision heuristic (e.g., "I buy the best known brand") that consumers use for unimportant, not highly motivating purchases (MacDonald and Sharp 2000). However, there is reason to believe that heuristic rules used by consumers to make decisions are not equivalent to habits. Specifically, research in cognitive psychology has shown that simple rules and habits rely on qualitatively distinct learning systems and even have distinct neural substrates (Ashby and Maddox 2005). Closer to our perspective, Beatty and Kahle (1988) defined habit as a well-learned schema with a behavioral component. They highlighted the mental association that develops between responses and elements in the purchase and consumption process. When these associations reflect habits, they function outside of awareness to cue performance of repeated responses.

Our definition of brand loyalty builds on established approaches in marketing. Researchers generally agree that brand loyalty has two aspects. One is purchase loyalty, which is a behavioral construct representing willingness to repurchase a brand. Another is attitudinal loyalty, which captures consumers' preference toward a brand. Many researchers treat behavioral and attitudinal loyalty as part of a broader loyalty construct (e.g., Chaudhuri and Holbrook 2001; Dick and Basu 1994; Jacoby and Chestnut 1978; Kim, Morris, and Swait 2008). Especially influential is Oliver's (1997) definition of loyalty as "a deeply held commitment to re-buy or re-patronize a preferred product or service consistently in the future, despite situational influences and marketing efforts having the potential to cause switching behavior" (p. 392). The idea that loyalty is a preference aligns with our definition, but as we will explain, the strength of this preference is not only bolstered by commitment but also by other aspects of attitude strength such as the accessibility of the attitude or its importance. The strength of consumers' brand evaluation determines whether it guides repeated purchase or consumption and whether it resists change (Petty and Krosnick 1995).

In this chapter, we make the case that repetition due to habits differs importantly from repetition due to brand loyalty evaluations. We identify the psychological processes by which habits perpetuate consumer purchase and consumption and distinguish habit mechanisms from those involved in brand loyalty. We also will demonstrate the importance of this distinction for marketing efforts to promote repeated patronage. Successful change of consumers' repeated behavior requires understanding of whether repetition reflects habit or preference. We present evidence that different change strategies are required for habits to be altered as opposed to behaviors based on favorable brand evaluations.

Repetition Due to Habits

According to folk explanations, habits often are performed in the absence of evaluations, intentions, and goals. "I can't help it, it's just a habit," is an excuse that people might offer for their bad habits (e.g., chronic overeating) and for action slips of inadvertent habit performance (e.g., accidentally driving to work when intending to go to the store). Empirical evidence is accumulating in support of this view (Wood and Neal 2007). Once habits have formed, responses are triggered by context cues and require little guidance from attitudes, goals, and behavioral intentions. The independence of habits from motivational constructs is a consistent finding in behavior prediction research, but one that might seem surprising without an understanding of the psychological factors that promote habit-based repetition. In this section, we present evidence that habits are cued directly by contexts without requiring supporting attitudes, goals, or intentions.

In a standard behavior prediction study, people are asked, for example, about their intentions to purchase fast food during the next week and the strength of their purchase habits (based on frequency of past performance in stable contexts). At the end of the week, they are asked how frequently they actually purchased fast food. When researchers use the initial measures of intentions and habits to predict subsequent performance frequency, the classic finding is that intentions (and associated attitudes) are predictive only for people who have not developed strong habits, as people who have strong habits seem to repeat performance at past levels regardless of their intentions (Danner, Aarts, and de Vries 2008; Ferguson and Bibby 2002; Ji and Wood 2007; Wood, Tam, and Guerrero Witt 2005). Thus, brand evaluations and associated intentions predict the repeated purchase and consumption activities of customers who have not formed strong patronage habits. However, evaluations and intentions do not drive the frequency of purchase and consumption activities of habitual customers. Instead, their responses appear to be triggered repeatedly without reference to attitudes and intentions.

Behavior prediction studies provide only correlational evidence that habit repetition does not depend on preferences and associated purchase intentions. Thus, the prediction findings might seem open to a number of alternative interpretations. Our recent work has ruled out a number of these other explanations for habit effects. In particular, we have found that the predictive effects of habits are *not* due to the following factors:

- Shared method variance between the habit predictor (past behavior) and the performance criterion (future behavior; Ajzen 2002; Sheeran 2002). This artifact could account for a main effect of past behavior in the prediction of future behavior but not for the obtained interaction between habits and intentions in which intentions only predict when habits are weak.
- Restriction of range of variation in intentions or behaviors for people who repeat actions frequently. The variation on these measures for those with strong habits does not differ systematically from those with weaker habits (Ji and Wood 2007).
- Additional factors that might be correlated with behavior repetition. Behavior prediction research routinely controls for the effects of intentions in predicting future performance. In addition, Ouellette and Wood (1998, study 2) reported that habits predicted future performance after controlling for (a) self-concept as someone who performs a behavior, (b) perceived behavioral control and efficacy, and (c) attitude accessibility in terms of reaction time to give judgments.
- Weakness in the measure of intentions (Ajzen 2002). Directly contradicting this possibility, people with strong habits report being highly certain of their intentions, despite the fact that these intentions do not predict future behavior (Ji and Wood 2007).
- Phrasing of intentions in specific or abstract ways. When people repeat actions, they come to think less about specific performance details and more about abstract goals and outcomes of the behavior (Vallacher and Wegner 1987). However, the effects of habits do not emerge because intention measures are phrased too specifically. Thus, habits are significant predictors of future behavior whether intentions are measured specifically, abstractly, or in personally idiosyncratic ways (Ji and Wood 2007).

Thus, people with habits tend to repeat past purchase and consumption activities without consulting their intentions, and this finding does not appear to be an artifact of the research methodology in behavior prediction studies.

The decreased reliance on behavioral intentions in prediction research echoes a pattern found in cognitive neuroscience of decreased involvement of goal-related brain areas as responses are repeated, becoming habits. In a typical neuroimaging study of habit formation, the neural correlates of task performance are monitored as participants repeat a motor task until it becomes habitual according to some behavioral criterion (e.g., absence of dual-task interference effects). Repetition and the consequent development of habitual control typically are associated with reduced activation in the prefrontal cortex, an area of the brain associated with goal selection and pursuit, along with increased reliance on subcortical structures including the basal ganglia and cerebellum (see reviews in Jonides 2004; Kelly and Garavan 2005). Thus, the disengagement of the prefrontal cortex during habit formation is consistent with a shift away from behavioral intentions and goals as responses are repeated, becoming habits.

Additional evidence that goals and intentions do not have a causal role in guiding habits comes from a series of experiments by Neal, Wood, and colleagues. For example, Neal, Wood, Lally, and Wu (2009, study 3) demonstrated that a simple behavioral habit (speech intensity) can be triggered by exposure to relevant contexts without activating goals. The measure of habit strength in this study was participants' reports of how often they had visited sports stadiums in the recent past. People who go to stadiums frequently are likely to develop habits for typical behaviors in this context, such as speaking loudly. In evidence, when participants were shown pictures of the stadiums they usually visited, those with stronger habits spoke more loudly. Most importantly, this habit cuing did not depend on the activation of a goal or motivation to speak loudly. That is, participants with stronger stadium habits spoke more loudly despite displaying no changes in goals or motivations related to loudness of speech. Only in a separate experimental condition that directly primed loudness goals outside of participants' awareness (i.e., through a standard scrambled sentence task) did participants report intentions to speak loudly. This experiment demonstrates that the everyday habit of loud speech can be cued directly by the contexts in which it typically occurs and does not require guidance from goals.

Additional evidence that habits do not require guidance from goals comes from a study of popcorn eating habits (Neal et al. 2009, study 4). This research was conducted with theatergoers, who were given a free box of popcorn while they watched movie trailers. The boxes were collected and weighed when the trailers were finished. Unbeknownst to the moviegoers, some received freshly popped popcorn, whereas others received week-old, stale popcorn. When asked later how much they liked it, all indicated that they did not care for the stale popcorn but liked the fresh. The question in this research was whether evaluations of the popcorn would guide eating behavior. Behavior should reflect evaluations only for those who did not report having strong habits of eating popcorn at the cinema. As predicted, moviegoers with weak habits were responsive to taste and ate less of the stale than fresh popcorn. However, moviegoers who had strong habits ate the same amount regardless of its freshness—they ate lots of the stale popcorn and lots of the fresh popcorn. This study demonstrates that habitual eating can be triggered directly by the contexts in which it typically occurs and does not require a supporting evaluation or behavioral intention. Participants with strong habits reported that they did not like the stale popcorn, but they ate it anyway, as if they were not able to modify their habitual response to the current circumstances. In sum, these studies indicate that habit memory is insulated from people's goals and intentions in the sense that habit performance does not require activation of response goals and that it is not flexibly modified due to changes in evaluations or goals.

Readers might wonder about the value of habit-learning mechanisms, given that they promote repetition of past responses in an inflexible way that is insensitive to changes in people's current goals. Habits are part of the wise unconscious. Their functionality comes in part from their origins in past goal pursuit. Because people tend to repeat responses that are rewarding or in some way meet their goals, habits typically are residues of the chronic pursuit of past goals. The logic of habit cuing is that, when contexts remain stable, responses that have been worth repeating in the past are likely to be worth repeating in the future. Thus, a sports fan with a habit of purchasing Planters peanuts at the ballpark acquires this disposition over multiple repeated experiences. The initial repetition presumably occurred because of the utility of the response—buying and eating the peanuts was perhaps a good accompaniment to drinking beer. The gradual development of habits across repeated experience provides a selection mechanism for habit learning because only those patterns that are consistently and frequently repeated will be encoded in procedural memory in the form of habit associations (Gupta and Cohen 2002).

Another sense in which habits are functional is that they retain the recurring features of past experience. Much important knowledge would be at risk if the information accrued slowly over experience could easily be overwritten by new information (McClelland, McNaughton, and O'Reilly 1995). Thus, habits are useful in that they capture the common features of repeated past experiences, and habit memory ensures that this learning is retained for future use. Habit cuing, by which contexts directly activate associated responses, is only one disposition that promotes repeated patronage. In the next section, we consider how repeated purchase and consumption also can arise from strong brand loyalty.

Repetition Due to Brand Loyalty

Brand loyalty reflects a favorable evaluation that is held with sufficient strength and stability to promote a repeatedly favorable brand response. As shown in Figure 3.1, consumer brand preferences promote repeated purchase and consumption by positively influencing behavioral intentions. Typically, loyalty is treated as a preference toward one particular brand. Additionally, Dick and Basu (1994) suggested that brand loyalty has greater predictive power if it is conceptualized in relative terms as a preference toward one brand compared with other brands in the market. Especially in situations in which consumers are choosing among several favorably evaluated brands, brand loyalty may best be treated as a relative judgment across brands.

A loyal customer has a favorable orientation toward a brand that is reflected in at least one of the three traditional attitude components: cognition, affect, and conation (e.g., Dick and Basu 1994; Oliver 1997). Cognitive loyalty is built on thoughts and ideas about the brand, such as beliefs in favorable product or brand attributes. Affective loyalty concerns consumers' positive brand- and product-related feelings, moods, and emotions and their attachment to the brand (see Chapter 17). Although conative loyalty is sometimes treated as a separate component that reflects consumers' favorable past actions and behavioral expectations, we prefer to treat the conative component as a consequence of cognition and affect (Eagly and Chaiken 1993).

Cognition and affect may not always be equally important. Some researchers have proposed that brand preference is a cognitive judgment that is based primarily on beliefs about the brand (Fournier and Yao 1997), whereas others have found that affective loyalty, as reflected in emotional reactions upon perception or consumption of the brand, also plays a role in promoting repetition (Evanschitzky et al. 2006). Still others have suggested that only consumers whose attitudes reflect favorable cognitive and affective loyalty are likely to form repurchase intentions (Oliver 1997). One source of the differing views is researchers' assessments of whether affective loyalty significantly contributes to consumer preference.

We believe that there is good reason to include affect as well as cognition as a component of loyalty. In particular, affective and cognitive attitudes have been found to contribute independently to overall consumer attitudes (Kim and Morris 2007; Kim, Morris, and Swait 2008). For example, affective and cognitive attitudes significantly influenced overall consumer preference for computer software (Kim and Morris 2007). Also, across a variety of purchase domains, including designer sunglasses, high-fashion watches, doughnuts, and soft drinks, both affective and cognitive evaluations of relevant brands independently influenced repurchase intentions (Kim et al. 2008). Thus, the affective component of brand loyalty cannot be ignored. In general, we suspect that the importance of each loyalty component varies across attitude objects (Eagly and Chaiken 1993). Loyalty toward some objects, especially those associated with hedonic experiences (e.g., brands of coffee), is likely to be based more on affective reactions, whereas loyalty toward others (e.g., brands of spark plugs) is likely to be based more on cognitive beliefs.

Brand loyalty as an attitude promotes repeated purchase. Consumers who are loyal to a particular brand believe that favorable outcomes are likely from purchasing and using the brand, and as a result they are likely to re patronize it. In illustration, Bandyopadhyay and Martell (2007) conducted a six-month longitudinal study of toothpaste purchases after initially measuring the favorability of consumer attitudes toward a number of popular toothpaste brands. Consumers with more favorable initial preferences toward a brand had a higher frequency of repeated brand purchase during the period. That these effects of brand loyalty depend on behavioral intentions is suggested by research indicating the positive impact of brand favorability on intention to use a variety of products and services including cosmetics (Chiou and Droge 2006), computer software (Kim and Morris 2007), designer sunglasses, high-fashion watches, doughnuts, soft drinks (Kim et al. 2008), groceries (Hansen 2006), credit cards (Wirtz, Mattila, and Lwin 2007), and retail banking (Baumann, Burton, and Elliott 2005).

Consumers hold brand attitudes with varying amounts of strength, or potency, and attitude strength is key to understanding when consumers will act on favorable purchase intentions. Attitudes are strong for various reasons, including their cognitive accessibility, high elaboration, high involvement, extensive knowledge base, high commitment, and extreme evaluations (see Chapter 15; for a review, see Krosnick and Petty 1995). Commitment is the component of strength mentioned most often in the brand loyalty literature, and, as we noted in the introduction to this chapter, commitment has even been incorporated into some definitions of loyalty (e.g., Kim et al. 2008; Oliver 1997). However, given the evidence that attitude strength can arise from multiple sources (Krosnick and Petty 1995), commitment is best understood as one of many aspects of brand loyalty.

Why is strength important for understanding brand loyalty? Strong loyalties, like other strong attitudes, have a number of characteristic effects, including that they "will endure, will resist attempts in contrary directions, will exert influence on the formation of related perceptions and beliefs, and will predict behavioral decisions with highest fidelity" (Converse 1995, p. xi). That is, stronger brand loyalties are more stable over time and place, are more resistant to the allure of alternative brands, promote more favorable brand perceptions and beliefs, and are more likely to influence behavior.

Resistance to alternative brands is crucial for marketers because even loyal consumers can be tempted by competing brands that offer coupons, deals, and other incentives for brand switching. In a study of household products that included shampoo, toilet paper, chocolate, coffee, toothpaste, and detergent, Jensen and Hansen (2006) found that the effect of consumers' brand loyalty on actual repeated brand purchases were twofold: (1) a stronger brand preference reduced variety-seeking tendencies to try other brands; the diminished variety-seeking resulted in more favorable behavioral intentions to repurchase the same brand. (2) Stronger brand loyalty increased consumer resistance to purchase and consume alternative brands in tempting situations, including when the favored brand was out of stock and when sales promotions were offered by competing brands. Such resistance to competitive brands resulted in weaker behavioral intentions to purchase different brands. Thus, strength of loyalty may lead to more positive intentions to purchase the favored brand as well as resistance to alternatives.

Brand Loyalty Can Be Implicit

Brand loyalties often are held explicitly, as when people are aware of their preferences or the ways in which these preferences influence purchase and consumption. But people are not always aware of their brand preferences. Loyalty is sometimes implicit. When loyalty is held implicitly, consumers are not aware of their brand preference or they are not aware of its impact on their repeated patronage. Like other implicit attitudes and motives, implicit brand loyalty is triggered automatically by the perception of a product or other input (Dijksterhuis et al. 2005).

Implicit brand loyalty differs from habits. In part, this is because implicit loyalty involves an automatically activated evaluation, whereas habits involve an automatically activated response. When implicit loyalty is triggered (e.g., the implicit evaluation, Ben & Jerry's ice cream tastes good), people can flexibly respond with a variety of brand-related behavioral intentions and behaviors (e.g., eating ice cream, recommending it to friends, buying it from the store). Because of this flexibility, implicit loyalty can trigger intentions to perform novel responses as well as responses practiced in the past. For example, high implicit brand loyalty might motivate someone to try a new brand extension product that was perceived as sharing the brand's positive evaluative associations. Empirical evidence supports the idea that implicit attitudes and other implicit motivations promote behavioral flexibility (e.g., Gollwitzer et al. 2008).

In contrast to the flexible evaluative orientation of implicit loyalty, habits are relatively rigid and involve activation of a particular response to a recurring contextual cue (Neal et al. 2009). Thus, with habits, the same response (e.g., going to Subway for lunch) is activated repeatedly upon perception of the cue (e.g., finishing morning class). The practiced habitual response tends to be repeated in the same way each time. Because habits lack a superordinate evaluative component, the habitual purchase of one product or brand is unlikely to transfer, or generalize, via favorable associations to other products or brands.

The idea that habits and implicit loyalty both can be activated automatically may seem confusing. In modern theories of automaticity, however, automatic responding comes in many forms (Bargh 1994; Moors and De Houwer 2006). The critical distinction between habits and brand loyalty for marketers lies in whether repeated purchase and consumption reflect the repetition of a particular response (habits) or whether they reflect an evaluative disposition that can guide repetition of a variety of brand responses (loyalty). Confusing habits with brand loyalty could lead to ineffective, even counterproductive strategies to manage habitual and loyal customers. In the next section, we discuss different approaches to managing repeated patronage due to brand loyalty and habits.

MANAGING REPEATED PATRONAGE

Given that consumers repeatedly purchase and consume due to habits or to strong brand loyalty, the question for marketers is how to manage these different types of consumers. Would some marketing programs change repeated patronage due to brand loyalty but have no effect on patronage due to habits? Would other programs change consumers' patronage habits but have no impact on patronage due to loyalty? Given the different mechanisms behind repeated patronage, it is not possible to apply the same marketing tools to manage all instances in which consumers repeatedly purchase and consume.

Marketers' goals with respect to consumer repetition are twofold: (1) to increase the repeated patronage of occasional customers and (2) to maintain the repeated patronage of loyal and habitual customers. We propose that different strategies are needed to meet each goal (see Figure 3.2). The standard approach to managing consumer patronage is to establish and maintain consumer loyalty. Because loyal consumers purchase and consume due to strong, favorable brand evaluations, marketers have focused on changing or maintaining these evaluations. However, habitual consumers purchase and consume due to perception of the triggering cue. Thus, managing habitual customers requires different programs than those that are typically used to manage loyalty. Managing habits involves changing or maintaining the cue or the response to a cue.

For Brand Loyalty, Manage Brand Attitudes

Given the power of brand loyalty to guide repeated purchase and consumption, the standard approach for marketers has been to change and maintain loyalty. They do so largely through variations on the classic marketing mix variables—the 4 P's of product, price, place, and promotion (Keller and Lehmann 2006; Kumar and Shah 2004). As we noted in the discussion on brand loyalty, consumers who hold strong, favorable brand preferences are likely to hold behavioral intentions to purchase that brand and to act on such intentions. Thus, marketers have reason to improve and maintain brand preference with marketing tools. For example, using celebrity endorsement in advertising can transfer the positive effect of the celebrity's association to a brand (e.g., Till, Stanley, and Priluck 2008). Such positive attitude change caused by pairing of positive stimuli with a brand builds up a favorable brand preference in younger brands (e.g., Kim, Allen, and Kardes 1996) and maintains brand loyalty of mature brands for which consumers have already formed a solid brand preference (Gibson 2008).

Figure 3.2   **Managing Habits and Brand Loyalty**

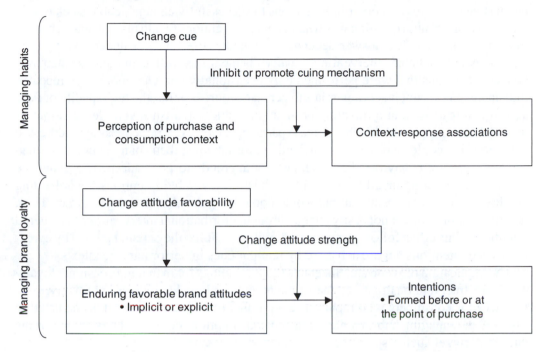

In addition to promoting brand favorability, marketing programs need to ensure that loyalty is held with sufficient strength to exert an effect on re-patronage. Several marketing mix variables influence the strength of brand loyalty, in particular the accessibility of the evaluation and the elaboration of the information underlying the attitude. For example, sales promotion offers made at the point of purchase can increase the accessibility of favorable brand associations and thereby foster the brand preference of nonloyal consumers and maintain that of loyal customers. In illustration, different incentives offered to consumers in a marketing promotion (e.g., drink insulator, towel) influenced the retrieval of brand associations and promoted repeated purchase behavior for packaged goods such as soda (Roehm, Bolman Pullins, and Roehm 2002). Product differentiation also strengthens consumer brand preference and thereby promotes repeated purchase intention (Jensen and Hansen 2006).

Through such interventions, marketers have attempted to increase repurchase intentions by improving brand preferences in terms of favorability and strength. This approach is the standard in the field and central to promoting repeated patronage. In short, it involves improving nonloyal consumers' brand preferences while maintaining those of loyal customers.

Despite the success of marketers in instilling and maintaining loyalty, such programs do not always work. In fact, there is good evidence that programs to change intentions do not work to change certain types of behaviors, especially those that are repeated in stable contexts and thereby formed into habits. Evidence for this pattern comes from a meta-analytic review by Webb and Sheeran (2006). All of the studies in the review used persuasive messages and other interventions to successfully change people's behavioral intentions. The central question was whether the interventions would also generate changes in actual behaviors. The answer depended on whether the behavior under investigation was likely to be a habit. Interventions changed behavior as well as intentions when they concerned actions that were performed only occasionally and were not easily repeated into habits. For example, commercials to persuade tourists about the high quality of food served at a restaurant at a traveling destination would establish favorable intentions to dine at the restaurant and thereby increase patronage. However, if the messages addressed behaviors that could be repeated sufficiently to form habits, then changed intentions had limited effect on behaviors. For example, commercials to persuade people about the importance of eating healthfully might establish unfavorable intentions toward eating at a favorite fast food restaurant but would not affect patronage at that restaurant. Thus, habitual responses were not easily altered through informational interventions that altered intentions. This effect follows from our definition of habits: they are not guided by evaluations and intentions but are activated by familiar cues in performance contexts.

The implication of Webb and Sheeran's (2006) findings for managing consumer loyalty are clear: Interventions that change or maintain brand evaluations are not likely to be effective for consumers who repatronize a product out of habit. Instead, as depicted in Figure 3.2, managing habitual purchase and consumption requires understanding of the cues that trigger such responses.

For Habits, Manage the Context Cues and Behavior

Habits can be triggered by a wide array of cues in performance contexts, including physical settings, presence of others, mood, time of day, and actions that immediately precede a habitual response (Ji and Wood, 2007; Wood and Neal, 2007). Thus, the office environment at midmorning may trigger a trip to Starbucks, or a visit from family around dinnertime might trigger a trip to Olive Garden. When habits have formed, perception of the familiar cues activates a representation of the practiced, habitual response in memory (Neal et al. 2009). Given this reliance on cues, consumer habits are maintained when cues in the performance context remain stable. Habits change when the cues are altered or when consumers are motivated and able to inhibit their automatic responses to the cues. These implications can be adapted by marketers who want to maintain their current customers' habits or to change consumers' habits with competitive brands.

Changing Context Cues

Even when consumers intend to try new brands and thereby change their established brand habits, they may continue to repeat past purchase and consumption activities when those responses are cued automatically by stable features of the environment. Recall the habitual customer Holly who ate lunch at the Subway shop on campus every day after class by herself. Her routinized response of eating at Subway apparently was triggered by cues involving time of day (noon), location (on campus), and the preceding actions in her morning routine (end of class). Given the finding from behavior prediction research that people continue habitual behavior relatively independently of their intentions (e.g., Ji and Wood 2007; Danner et al. 2008), Holly's desire to try brands other than Subway will not always be translated into a change in her lunch choices. Because habits are automatically brought to mind in the appropriate circumstances, they tend to be repeated unless people are willing and able to exert effortful control to inhibit the activated response and to select a new one (Pascoe, Neal, Toner, and Wood 2009).

If consumers' habits do not necessarily change through altering behavioral intentions, what can marketers do to bring about this change? One possibility is to take advantage of the *habit discontinuity effect,* or the disruption in habits that naturally occurs when people change life contexts. With changes in performance contexts, the habitual behavior may no longer be automatically brought to mind, and people may be released to act in ways consistent with their intentions. Accordingly, Verplanken and Wood (2006) proposed that marketers should target behavior change interventions for times when people undergo naturally occurring changes in performance contexts.

Empirical evidence for habit discontinuity comes from Wood, Tam, and Guerrero Witt's (2005) study of college students transferring to a new university. Transfer students are of special interest because the move between schools can disrupt the circumstances that support everyday habits. One month before the transfer and one month after, students reported their intentions to exercise, their typical exercise frequency, and their typical exercise locations. The focus of the study was to identify when exercising at the new university would be guided by intentions and when it would conform to habits (if any) students established at their old university. Some of the students had established strong exercise-related habits at their old school (e.g., working out in the gym). For these students, old exercise habits maintained across the transfer when the performance location was stable from the old to the new university. Exercise habits were disrupted when locations shifted (e.g., students could not work out in a gym). Notably, when locations shifted, the students' behaviors came under intentional control and were predicted by their intentions. Students exercised at the new university if they wanted to, and quit if they did not. Presumably, without the old context cues to trigger automatically the well-practiced behavior, students were spurred to make decisions about exercising. These findings suggest that change in performance contexts can shift consumer habits out of an automatic mode so that purchase and consumption become more deliberate and guided by consumer intentions.

Additional evidence of habit discontinuity comes from a study by Verplanken et al. (2008) on the relationship between environmental values and car driving habits. Some of the participants in the study had recently relocated and thus the cues for their driving had changed. With this change, driving behavior was released from context control, and participants were able to act on their environmental values. Specifically, among those who had moved, greater environmental concern prompted less use of their cars for commuting to work. However, the driving patterns of participants who had not moved were less dependent on their environmental values.

To take advantage of habit discontinuity, marketers might target interventions to change consumers' habits to use competing brands for the times when consumers relocate and may not have access to old retail outlets and associated brands. Illustrating this approach, some metropolitan transit services attempt to increase bus ridership by providing free passes and route information to new residents, a group that is open to such influence because they have yet to establish relevant driving habits given their recent relocation. Additionally, in the hope of promoting brand loyalty and habitual purchase, Home Depot and Bed Bath and Beyond offer discounts as incentives to encourage patronage of consumers who have recently relocated. This strategy should effectively attract habitual consumers of competitor's brands whose habits are disrupted due to relocation.

Controlling Cuing Effects on Behavior

Habitual consumers are not simply at the mercy of contexts. They also can undertake to change their responses to context cues. For example, consumers with strong motivation to change unhealthful eating habits might deliberately choose not to respond to the triggers that have maintained these habits. They might be motivated to find a healthier restaurant than the fast food outlets at which they frequently eat. To bring about this change, consumers would need to control their reactions to the cues that trigger the unwanted habit.

The idea that habits can be changed through individual control of responses to stimuli is a central component of some behavior modification therapies (Follette and Hayes 2000). Especially when habits are strongly held, cue control involves effortful inhibition of the triggered response (Wood and Neal 2007). That is, control of habit cues involves suppression of the unwanted response that is triggered automatically and then selection and performance of an alternative response (or no response).

Consumers need to be motivated to exert the self-control required to inhibit unwanted habits. Marketers can bolster motivation by, for example, providing brand associations that are valued by consumers. Thus, brands positioning themselves as ecologically sensitive, or "green," provide motivation to the growing consumer population that is concerned with the environment. Nonetheless, positive motivation is not sufficient; the inhibition of strong habits requires that consumers have sufficient self-control resources and that they use self-control strategies that are optimal to inhibit habit cuing.

Sufficient Self-Control Resources. To exert self-control or willpower and inhibit responses, people draw on a limited-capacity psychological resource that functions like muscle, in that it is expended with use and regenerates with rest (Muraven and Baumeister 2000). Evidence that habit inhibition requires self-control resources comes from experiments in which participants first performed a task that required strong self-control (e.g., not laughing at a funny movie) and subsequently were less able to inhibit a strong habit (e.g., a habitual mode of self-presentation) (Vohs, Baumeister, and Ciarocco 2005). That is, after self-control resources had been reduced, people did not have sufficient self-control to inhibit habits in the second task. Additional evidence that habit inhibition requires self-control resources comes from Pascoe et al.'s (2009) four-day diary study of the regulation of everyday behaviors. When participants' self-control capacity was reduced, they were unable to inhibit unwanted habits such as buying a candy bar when they were supposed to be studying. Thus, the inhibition of strong habits appears to depend upon the availability of sufficient self-control capacity. Based on these findings, it would be especially difficult for a consumer to change a habit of going to a fast food restaurant for dinner after a day of self-control-depleting events (e.g., biting one's tongue in office meetings, inhibiting distractions to meet a deadline).

Given that self-control resources are required to inhibit unwanted habits, consumer efforts to alter established patterns of brand purchase and consumption might be most successful at times when such resources are available. Thus, consumers may be able to switch from an old, habitually used brand to a new one when they are not undergoing other resource-depleting events in their daily lives, as occurs on weekday mornings when they must rush to work.

In another implication of the self-control required for habit inhibition, marketers may wish to set up promotions and other sales events so that consumers repeatedly purchase and use their brand in ways that foster habit formation. Once formed, habits persist because they require self-control effort to inhibit. Illustrating such a promotion, one of the authors recently received in the mail six $10 coupons for a new grocery store. Each coupon was valid for one week, and the coupon promotion was held over a period of six consecutive weeks. In order to use the coupons, she went to that grocery store every week, despite that there was another store she preferred. After six weeks, when all the coupons were used, she found herself automatically going to the new grocery store for her next shopping trip. She had formed a habit to frequent the new store, and, especially after a depleting day at work, it was easier to follow that habit than to inhibit it and choose another store.

Using the Right Strategy. In addition to having sufficient regulatory strength to inhibit unwanted habitual responses, consumers can be encouraged to use effective inhibitory strategies. Some control strategies appear to be more successful than others in inhibiting habits.

Quinn, Pascoe, Neal, and Wood (2009) examined the effectiveness of a number of habit-control strategies, including distracting oneself from the behavior by thinking about something else. Participants who tried to distract themselves from habit performance were not especially successful at controlling habits. Although thinking about something other than the stimulus can help to delay gratification in responding to temptations (Metcalfe and Mischel, 1999), focusing attention away from habit cues will not necessarily mute their impact. Consider, for example, that a consumer is trying to limit sweet food intake by eating only half of the dessert ordered at a restaurant. If this consumer talks to others or watches TV while eating, then she or he is not attending to how much is being consumed, and old clean-plate habits are likely to be cued by the food remaining on the plate. In fact, action slips of unwanted habit performance are especially likely when people are distracted and not attending to what they are doing (Reason 1990). Thus, distraction is not likely to be an effective habit-control strategy.

The most successful strategy for controlling habits proved to be vigilant monitoring to ensure that the cue did not inadvertently activate the unwanted response (Quinn et al.

2009). Monitoring is effective because this form of willpower ensures that the unwanted response is not triggered inadvertently. In both a diary study assessing the strategies that people spontaneously used to control habits in daily life and in an experiment in which participants were instructed to vigilantly monitor for errors, monitoring was the only consistently successful way for participants to control their unwanted habits.

In summary, in contrast to the common belief that habits can be overcome with sufficient motivation and desire to act in an alternative way, research evidence demonstrates that the self-control resource to carry out this motivation and inhibit unwanted habit cuing is crucial to successful habit change. People are more likely to be able to inhibit strongly habitual responses when they have sufficient self-control strength and when they use a control strategy of vigilantly monitoring to ensure nonperformance of the unwanted response.

In general, different approaches are required to manage consumers' repeated patronage due to brand loyalty and habits. The standard marketing approach of changing the favorability and strength of consumer preferences and associated behavioral intentions is appropriate when consumers' patronage is due to brand loyalty. However, preference favorability and strength have only minimal influence on habitual purchase and consumption. Instead, habits are best managed by maintaining or altering contextual cues and the response triggered by the cues. Marketers can take advantage of changing cues in order to attract habitual customers from their competitors, and they will want to ensure the stability of cues that maintain the habits of their current customers. Stable cues for purchase and consumption can minimize attrition of habitual consumers to competitor products and services.

CONCLUSION

In this chapter, we examined two determinants of repeated patronage. Although habit and brand loyalty both yield repeated purchase and consumption, the different psychological processes behind these two forms of repetition highlight the importance of distinguishing repeated patronage due to habits from patronage due to loyalty. When marketers fail to differentiate between habitual and loyal customers, they do not use optimal strategies to manage consumer behavior and the marketplace.

Repeated purchase due to brand loyalty is maintained or changed through consumers' attitudes toward the brand. To improve brand loyalty, marketers can use standard programs that involve advertising and promotion to change the favorability and strength of brand evaluations and their relation to purchase and consumption intentions. In contrast, repeated purchase due to habits is maintained or changed through the contexts that trigger consumers' brand purchases and consumption. Maintaining the stability of those circumstances will promote the persistence of habitual repeated consumers. On the flip side, by changing the contexts of habitual customers of competitive brands, marketers open up the opportunity to attract new customers to their own brand and product.

We urge marketers to recognize consumer habits when they manage customer relationship programs as well as when they adjust marketing mix variables such as pricing, distribution, advertising, and promotion. Habitual customers do not appear to be sensitive to these types of variables, which are designed to influence brand preferences and purchase/consumption intentions. In support, habitual consumers seem to be less price sensitive than others (Farley, Lehmann, and Winer 1987). Thus, when prices changed, habitual consumers were likely to make less adjustments in the frequency with which they repeated their purchases.

Despite our focus on brand loyalty and habit as determinants of repeated patronage, other factors also may be important in maintaining repeated purchase and consumption. For example, *switching costs* can keep people using the same services or products as in the past. When people repeatedly purchase and consume a brand, they establish structural and psychological factors that maintain their brand patronage and deter change due to the costs they would incur by brand or product switching (Murray and Häubl 2007). Deterrents on change include physical costs, such as search costs (Stigler and Becker 1977), financial costs (Shapiro and Varian 1999), and artificial costs such as discounts offered for repeated purchase (Klemperer 1987). Additional deterrents to change are the cognitive costs that develop as people increase personal experience with a product, brand, or store and thus develop user skills. Illustrating cognitive costs, Johnson, Bellman, and Lohse (2003) found that increases in knowledge of the purchase environment enhanced the attractiveness of prior consumer choices. Switching costs provides another reason, in addition to habits and brand loyalty, to expect that brand patronage will repeat what people have done in the past (Fornell, Robinson, and Wernerfelt 1985).

This chapter discussed the differences in repeated purchase and consumption due to habit and brand loyalty and proposed strategies to manage the repetition that arises from these two dispositions. Despite the considerable interest already in consumer repetition, the unique roles of habits and brand loyalty in promoting repeated purchase and consumption generally have not been recognized. Marketing tools such as loyalty programs aimed at promoting brand loyalty may encourage initial repeated purchase but may disrupt the repurchase behavior of consumers with habits. By understanding consumer habits, marketers will be empowered to better manage these multiple types of repeated customers.

REFERENCES

Ajzen, Icek (2002). "Residual Effects of Past on Later Behavior: Habituation and Reasoned Action Perspectives," *Personality and Social Psychology Review,* 6 (2), 107–122.

Ashby, F. Gregory, and W. Todd Maddox (2005). "Human Category Learning," *Annual Review of Psychology,* 56, 149–178.

Bandyopadhyay, Subir, and Michael Martell (2007). "Does Attitudinal Loyalty Influence Behavioral Loyalty? A Theoretical and Empirical Study," *Journal of Retailing and Consumer Services,* 14 (1), 35–44.

Bargh, John A. (1994). "The Four Horsemen of Automaticity: Awareness, Intention, Efficiency, and Control in Social Cognition." In *Handbook of Social Cognition,* ed. Robert S. Wyer Jr. and Thomas K. Skull. Hillsdale, NJ: Lawrence Erlbaum, 1–40.

Baumann, Chris, Suzan Burton, and Greg Elliott (2005). "Determinants of Customer Loyalty and Share of Wallet in Banking," *Journal of Financial Services Marketing,* 9 (3), 231–248.

Beatty, Sharon E., and Lynn R. Kahle (1988). "Alternative Hierarchies of the Attitude-Behavior Relationship: The Impact of Brand Commitment and Habit," *Journal of the Academy of Marketing Science,* 16 (2), 1–10.

Bettman, James R., and Michel A. Zins (1977). "Constructive Processes in Consumer Choice," *Journal of Consumer Research,* 4 (2), 75–85.

Chaudhuri, Arjun (1995). "Brand Equity or Double Jeopardy?" *Journal of Product and Brand Management,* 4 (1), 26–32.

Chaudhuri, Arjun, and Morris B. Holbrook (2001). "The Chain of Effects from Brand Trust and Brand Affect to Brand Performance: The Role of Brand Loyalty," *Journal of Marketing,* 65 (2), 81–93.

Chiou, Jyh-Shen, and Cornelia Droge (2006). "Service Quality, Trust, Specific Asset Investment, and Expertise: Direct and Indirect Effects in a Satisfaction-Loyalty Framework," *Journal of the Academy of Marketing Science,* 34 (4), 613–627.

Converse, Philip E. (1995). "Foreword." In *Attitude Strength: Antecedents and Consequences,* ed. Richard E. Petty and Jon A. Kronsnick. Mahwah, NJ: Lawrence Erlbaum, xi–xvii.

Danner, Unna, Henk Aarts, and Nanne K. de Vries (2008). "Habit vs. Intention in the Prediction of Future Behavior: The Role of Frequency, Context Stability and Mental Accessibility of Past Behavior," *British Journal of Social Psychology,* 47 (2), 245–265.

Dick, Alan S., and Kunal Basu (1994). "Customer Loyalty: Toward an Integrated Conceptual Frameworklink," *Journal of the Academy of Marketing Science,* 22 (2), 99–113.

Dijksterhuis, Ap, Pamela K. Smith, Rick B. van Baaren, and Daniel H. J. Wigboldus (2005). "The Unconscious Consumer: Effects of Environment on Consumer Behavior," *Journal of Consumer Psychology,* 15 (3), 193–202.

Eagly, Alice H., and Shelly Chaiken (1993). *The Psychology of Attitudes.* Philadelphia, PA: Harcourt Brace Jovanovich.

Ehrenberg, Andrew S.C. (1991). "New Brands and the Existing Market," *Journal of the Market Research Society,* 33 (4), 285–99.

Ehrenberg, Andrew S.C., Gerald J. Goodhardt, and T. Patrick Barwise (1990). "Double Jeopardy Revisited," *Journal of Marketing,* 54 (2), 82–91.

Evanschitzky, Heiner, R. Iyer Gopalkrishnan, Hilke Plassmann, Joerg Niessing, and Heribert Meffert (2006). "The Relative Strength of Affective Commitment in Securing Loyalty in Service Relationships," *Journal of Business Research,* 59, 1207–1213.

Farley, John U., Donald R. Lehmann, and Russell S. Winer (1987). "Stability of Membership in Market Segments Identified with a Disaggregate Consumption Model," *Journal of Business Research,* 15 (4), 313–328.

Ferguson, Eamonn, and Peter A. Bibby (2002). "Predicting Future Blood Donor Returns: Past Behavior, Intentions, and Observer Effects," *Health Psychology,* 21 (5), 513–518.

Follette, William C., and Steven C. Hayes (2000). "Contemporary Behavior Therapy." In *Handbook of Psychological Change: Psychotherapy Processes and Practices for the 21st Century,* ed C. R. Snyder and R. E. Ingram. New York, NY: Wiley, 381–408.

Fornell, Claes, William T. Robinson, and Birger Wernerfelt (1985). "Consumption Experience and Sales Promotion Expenditure," *Management Science,* 31 (9), 1084–1105.

Fournier, Susan, and Julie L. Yao (1997). "Reviving Brand Loyalty: A Reconceptualization within the Framework of Consumer-Brand Relationships," *International Journal of Research in Marketing,* 14 (5), 451–472.

Gibson, Bryan (2008). "Can Evaluative Conditioning Change Attitudes toward Mature Brands? New Evidence from the Implicit Association Test," *Journal of Consumer Research,* 35 (1), 178–188.

Gollwitzer, Peter M., Elizabeth J. Parks-Stamm, A. Jaudas, and Pascal Sheeran (2008). "Flexible Tenacity in Goal Pursuit." In *Handbook of Motivation Science,* ed. James Shah and W. Gardner. New York, NY: Guilford, 325–341.

Gupta, Prahlad, and Neal J. Cohen (2002). "Theoretical and Computational Analysis of Skill Learning, Repetition Priming, and Procedural Memory," *Psychological Review,* 109, 401–448.

Hansen, Torben (2006). "Determinants of Consumers' Repeat Online Buying of Groceries," *International Review of Retail, Distribution, and Consumer Research,* 16 (1), 93–114.

Jacoby, Jacob, and Robert W. Chestnut (1978). *Brand Loyalty: Measurement and Management.* New York, NY: Wiley.

Jensen, Fan Moller, and Torben Hansen (2006). "An Empirical Examination of Brand Loyalty," *Journal of Product and Brand Management,* 15 (7), 442–449.

Ji, Mindy F., and Wendy Wood (2007). "Purchase and Consumption Habits: Not Necessarily What You Intend," *Journal of Consumer Psychology,* 17 (4), 261–276.

Johnson, Eric J., Steven Bellman, and Gerald L. Lohse (2003). "Cognitive Lock-In and the Power Law of Practice," *Journal of Marketing,* 67 (2), 62–75.

Jonides, John (2004). "How Does Practice Make Perfect?" *Nature Neuroscience,* 7 (1), 75–79.

Kaas, Klaus Peter (1982). "Consumer Habit Forming, Information Acquisition, and Buying Behavior," *Journal of Business Research,* 10 (1), 3–15.

Keller, Kevin Lane, and Donald R. Lehmann (2006). "Brands and Branding: Research Findings and Future Priorities," *Marketing Science,* 25 (6), 740–760.

Kelly, A.M. Clare, and Hugh Garavan (2005). "Human Functional Neuroimaging of Brain Changes Associated with Practice," *Cerebral Cortex,* 15 (8), 1089–1102.

Khare, Adwait, and J. Jeffrey Inman (2006). "Habitual Behavior in American Eating Patterns: The Role of Meal Occasions-link," *Journal of Consumer Research,* 32 (4), 567–575.

Kim, John, Chris T. Allen, and Frank R. Kardes (1996). "An Investigation of the Mediational Mechanisms Underlying Attitudinal Conditioning," *Journal of Marketing Research,* 33 (3), 318–328.

Kim, Jooyoung, and Jon D. Morris (2007). "The Power of Affective Response and Cognitive Structure in Product-Trial Attitude Formation," *Journal of Advertising,* 36 (1), 95–106.

King, Jooyoung, Jon D. Morris, and Joffre Swait (2008). "Antecedents of True Brand Loyalty," *Journal of Advertising,* 37 (2), 99–117.

Klemperer, Paul (1987). "Markets with Consumer Switching Costs," *The Quarterly Journal of Economics,* 102 (2), 375–394.

Krosnick, Jon A., and Richard E. Petty (1995). "Attitude Strength: An Overview." In *Attitude Strength: Antecedents and Consequences,* ed. Richard E. Petty and Jon A. Krosnick. Mahwah, NJ: Lawrence Erlbaum, 1–24.

Kumar, V., and Denish Shah (2004). "Building and Sustaining Profitable Customer Loyalty for the 21st Century," *Journal of Retailing,* 80 (4), 317–329.

MacDonald, Emma K., and Byron M. Sharp (2000). "Brand Awareness Effects on Consumer Decision Making for a Common, Repeat Purchase Product: A Replication," *Journal of Business Research,* 48 (1), 5–15.

McClelland, James L., Bruce L. McNaughton, and Randall C. O'Reilly (1995). "Why There are Complementary Learning Systems in the Hippocampus and Neocortex: Insights from the Successes and Failures of Connectionist Models of Learning and Memory," *Psychological Review,* 102, 419–457.

Metcalfe, Janet, and Walter Mischel (1999). "A Hot/Cool-System Analysis of Delay of Gratification: Dynamics of Willpower," *Psychological Review, 106,* 3–19.

Moors, Agnes, and Jan De Houwer (2006). "Automatic Processing of Dominance and Submissiveness," *Experimental Psychology,* 52 (4), 296–302.

Muraven, Mark, and Roy F. Baumeister (2000). "Self-Regulation and Depletion of Limited Resources: Does Self-Control Resemble a Muscle?" *Psychological Bulletin,* 125 (2), 247–259.

Murray, Kyle B., and Gerald Häubl (2007). "Explaining Cognitive Lock-In: The Role of Skill-Based Habits of Use in Consumer Choice," *Journal of Consumer Research,* 34, 77–88.

Neal, David T., and Wendy Wood (2008). "Automaticity in situ and in the Lab: Direct Context Cuing of Habits in Daily Life." In *The Psychology of Action,* vol. 2, *Mechanisms of Human Action,* ed. E. Morsella, John A. Bargh, and Peter M. Gollwitzer. New York, NY: Oxford University Press.

Neal, David T., Wendy Wood, Philippa Lally, and Mengju Wu (2009). "Do Habits Depend on Goals? Perceived versus Actual Role of Goals in Habit Performance" manuscript under review.

Neal, David T., Wendy Wood, and Jeffrey M. Quinn (2006). "Habits: A Repeat Performance," *Current Directions in Psychological Science,* 15 (4), 198–202.

Oliver, Richard L. (1997). *Satisfaction: A Behavioral Perspective on the Consumer.* New York, NY: McGraw Hill.

Ouellette, Judith A., and Wendy Wood (1998). "Habit and Intention in Everyday Life: The Multiple Processes by which Past Behavior Predicts Future Behavior," *Psychological Bulletin,* 124 (1), 54–74.

Pascoe, Anthony T., David T. Neal, Kaitlin Toner, and Wendy Wood (2009). "Habits as External Self-Regulation," manuscript under review.

Petty, Richard E., and Jon A. Krosnick (1995). *Attitude Strength: Antecedents and Consequences.* Mahwah, NJ: Lawrence Erlbaum.

Poldrack, Russell A., J. Clark, J. Paré-Blagoev, D. Shohamy, J. Creso Moyano, C. Myers, and M.A. Gluck (2001). "Interactive Memory Systems in the Human Brain," *Nature,* 414, 546–550.

Quinn, Jeffrey M., Anthony Pascoe, David Neal, and Wendy Wood (2009). "Think You Can't Control Yourself? Monitor those Bad Habits," manuscript under review.

Raj, S.P. (1985). "Striking a Balance between Brand 'Popularity' and Brand Loyalty," *Journal of Marketing,* 49 (1), 53–59.

Reason, James T. (1990). *Human Error.* Cambridge, UK: Cambridge University Press.

Roehm, Michelle L., Ellan Bolman Pullins, and Harper A. Roehm (2002). "Designing Loyalty-Building Programs for Packaged Goods Brands," *Journal of Marketing Research,* 39 (2), 202–213.

Roy, Rishin, Pradeep K. Chintagunta, and Sudeep Halder (1996). "A Framework for Investigating Habits, 'The Hand of the Past,' and Heterogeneity in Dynamic Brand Choice," *Marketing Science,* 15 (3), 280–299.

Seetharaman, P.B. (2004). "Modeling Multiple Sources of State Dependence in Random Utility Models: A Distributed Lag Approach," *Marketing Science,* 23 (2), 263–271.

Shapiro, Carl, and Hal R. Varian (1999). "The Art of Standard Wars," *California Management Review,* 41 (2), 8–32.

Sheeran, P. (2002). "Intention-Behavior Relations: A Conceptual and Empirical Review." In *European Review of Social Psychology,* ed. W. Stroebe and M. Hewstone, 12, 1–36.

Stigler, George J., and Gary S. Becker (1977). "De gustibus non est disputandum," *The American Economic Review,* 67 (2), 76–90.

Till, Brian D., Sarah M. Stanley, and Randi Priluck (2008). "Classical Conditioning and Celebrity Endorsers: An Examination of Belongingness and Resistance to Extinction," *Psychology and Marketing,* 25 (2), 179–196.

Vallacher, Robin R., and Daniel M. Wegner (1987). "What Do People Think They're Doing? Action Identification and Human Behavior," *Psychological Review,* 94, 3–15.

Verplanken, Bas, Ian Walker, Adrian Davis, and Michaela Jurasek (2008). "Context Change and Travel Mode Choice: Combining the Habit Discontinuity and Self-activation Hypotheses," *Journal of Environmental Psychology,* 28 (2), 121–127.

Verplanken, Bas, and Wendy Wood (2006). "Interventions to Break and Create Consumer Habits," *Journal of Public Policy and Marketing,* 25 (1), 90–103.

Vohs, Kathleen D., Roy F. Baumeister, and Natalie J. Ciarocco (2005). "Self-Regulation and Self-Presentation: Regulatory Resource Depletion Impairs Impression Management and Effortful Self-Presentation Depletes Regulatory Resources," *Journal of Personality and Social Psychology,* 88 (4), 632–657.

Webb, Thomas L., and Paschal Sheeran (2006). "Does Changing Behavioral Intentions Engender Behavior Change? A Meta-Analysis of the Experimental Evidence," *Psychological Bulletin,* 132 (2), 249–268.

Wirtz, Jochen, Anna S. Mattila, and May Oo Lwin (2007). "How Effective Are Loyalty Reward Programs in Driving Share of Wallet?" *Journal of Service Research,* 9 (4), 327–334.

Wood, Wendy, and David T. Neal (2007). "A New Look at Habits and the Habit-Goal Interface," *Psychological Review,* 114 (4), 843–863.

Wood, Wendy, Jeffrey Quinn, and Deborah Kashy (2002). "Habits in Everyday Life: Thought, Emotion, and Action," *Journal of Personality and Social Psychology,* 83, 1281–129.

Wood, Wendy, Leona Tam, and Melissa Guerrero Witt (2005). "Changing Circumstances, Disrupting Habit," *Journal of Personality and Social Psychology,* 88 (6), 918–933.

PART II

GOALS, NEEDS, AND MOTIVES THAT FOSTER BRAND RELATIONSHIPS

CHAPTER 4

SELF-EXPANSION MOTIVATION AND INCLUSION OF BRANDS IN SELF

Toward a Theory of Brand Relationships

MARTIN REIMANN AND ARTHUR ARON

Much like relationships between people, relationships between consumers and brands are a central part of life. Similar to processes between persons, it has been argued that consumers purchase brands to construct their self-concepts and, in so doing, create self-brand relationships (Escalas and Bettman 2005). To advance knowledge of the underlying processes, considerable research has concentrated on understanding and describing the different relationships that consumers have with brands (Aaker, Fournier, and Brasel 2004; Carroll and Ahuvia 2006; Escalas and Bettman 2005; Fournier 1998). Several consumer-brand relationship concepts and related measures exist in the marketing and consumer research literature, which can be used to categorize consumers based on the intensity of those relationships (Fournier 1998). These concepts include brand attachment (Thomson, MacInnis, and Park 2005), brand commitment (Warrington and Shim 2000), brand connectedness (Winterich 2007), brand evangelism (Matzler, Pichler, and Hemetsberger 2007), brand love (Ahuvia 2005; Albert, Merunka, and Valette-Florence 2007; Carroll and Ahuvia 2006; Fournier 1998), brand loyalty (Chaudhuri and Holbrook 2001; Jacoby and Chestnut 1978), brand passion (Bauer, Heinrich, and Martin 2007), and brand trust (Chaudhuri and Holbrook 2001), among others. Further, this volume offers a broad assessment of brand relationship, for example in terms of person-object love (Chapter 18) or attachment (Chapter 17).

All of these concepts have a relationship component, yet researchers argue that they are distinct constructs. For example, it has been suggested that brand love drives brand loyalty (Carroll and Ahuvia 2006). Others posit that brand commitment reflects the degree to which a brand is the only acceptable choice within a product category, while brand loyalty is the repeated purchase of a single brand over time (Warrington and Shim 2000).

Despite the richness of different brand relationship facets presented in the marketing and consumer research literature, prior research has not yet identified a theory that unifies previous thought on brand relationships. Describing, however, the underlying processes of consumer-brand relationships provides a better understanding of how consumers relate to brands. In this chapter, we aim to bring to this topic a new perspective—the self-expansion model—that may account for central aspects of brand relationships not previously considered, as well as integrating some diverse findings. Some prior work has related the self-expansion model to relationships with brands (Carroll and Ahuvia 2006); while we think that the application of the model was quite useful, the presented chapter goes beyond the earlier work, which focused on one aspect, to applying the model to a wide range of aspects of consumer-brand relationships.

Besides being of theoretical interest, we believe this approach provides insight into important aspects of brand management and can guide firms on how to promote intensive relationships between particular brands and consumers. Although our focus is on brands, the proposals we develop in this chapter may also have application in related domains in which there are significant person-object relationships, such as political psychology (e.g., relations of persons with political entities), health psychology (e.g., relations of persons with health behaviors and procedures), and environmental psychology (e.g., the relation of persons with nature and with particular natural locales).

This chapter is organized into four sections. First, we discuss the self-expansion model as it has been developed in the context of the social psychology of close relationships between humans (person-person relationships). Second, we consider applications of the basic concepts and findings related to the model for understanding the development and maintenance of brand relationships (person-object relationships). This will lead to the third section, which presents several research propositions on brand relationships based on the self-expansion model. Finally, we conclude with implications for further research and brand management.

THEORETICAL BACKGROUND: THE SELF-EXPANSION MODEL

The self-expansion model is a conceptual framework that attempts to describe how people think, feel, and act in the context of close relationships. It was originally proposed by Aron and Aron (1986) and integrates Eastern psychology's views on the evolution of the self and the nature of love with contemporary Western psychological work on motivation and cognition. The self-expansion model offers two fundamental ideas: (1) a general motivation to expand the self and (2) inclusion of close others in the self.

Self-Expansion Motivation

People seek to expand themselves by enhancing their ability to accomplish goals, leading to ever greater goals or life purposes. This basic motive has been described in Western psychology as exploration, effectance, curiosity, competence, or self-improvement (Bandura 1977; Deci and Ryan 2000; Gecas 1989; Taylor, Neter, and Wayment 1995; White 1959). The self-expansion model emphasizes the central human motive of the desire to expand the self by acquiring resources, perspectives, and identities that enhance one's ability to accomplish goals (Aron, Aron, and Norman 2003; Aron, Norman, and Aron 1998; Aron et al. 2000). Like other self-related motives, self-expansion is a mix of conscious and unconscious processes. People may often be aware of feelings that could be described as "expanded" and of seeking specific goals that facilitate self-expansion; however, expanding the self is generally not a conscious goal. Further, rapid expansion of the self, as often occurs when forming a new romantic relationship or experiencing the birth of a new child, is posited to result in high levels of excited positive affect, consistent with prior findings about the impact on affective state of rapid movement toward a goal (Carver and Scheier 1990).

These abstract ideas can be made more concrete by considering Lewandowski and Aron's the self-expansion questionnaire (2002), which assesses the degree to which a person experiences a relationship partner as a facilitator of increased knowledge, skill, abilities, mate value, positive life changes, and novel experiences. For example, representative items are "How much does your partner provide a source of exciting experiences?," "How much has knowing your partner made you a better person?," and "How much do you see your partner as a way to expand your own capabilities?"

Several research programs lend support to hypotheses generated from the motivational aspect of the self-expansion model. For example, one implication relates to initial attraction. A classic finding in the interpersonal attraction literature is that "similars attract" (Byrne 1971). From the perspective of the self-expansion model, this is due in part to the fact that any relationship expands the self, and people are aware that it is easiest to develop a relationship with someone who is similar to oneself (Aron et al. 2006).

Another implication of the model is that developing a new relationship expands the self. Thus, Aron, Paris, and Aron (1995) tested 325 students five times, once every two-and-a-half weeks over a ten-week period. At each testing, participants answered a number of questions, including items indicating whether they had fallen in love since the last testing, plus an open listing of "who are you today?" As predicted, there was a significantly greater increase in the number of self-content domains in the self-descriptions from before falling in love to after falling in love, as compared to the average changes from before to after other testing sessions for those who fell in love, or as compared to typical between-test changes for participants who did not fall in love. Based on this same line of thinking, through a series of surveys and experiments, other research found that the more expansion provided by a relationship before its dissolution, the greater the contraction of the working self-concept after its dissolution (Lewandowski et al. 2006).

Another important implication of the motivational aspect of the model, which has generated a number of studies, is based on the idea that the *process* of rapid expansion is affectively positive (Strong and Aron 2006). The major line of work developed from this idea has focused on a predicted increase in satisfaction with long-term relationships as a result of joint participation in self-expanding activities. This work emerged from a consideration of the well-documented typical decline in relationship satisfaction after the "honeymoon period" in a romantic relationship, a lowered level that is typically maintained over subsequent years (Tucker and Aron 1993). When two people first enter a relationship, there is usually an initial, exhilarating period in which the couple spends hours talking, engaging in intense risk taking and self-disclosure. From the perspective of the self-expansion model, this initial exhilarating period is one in which the partners are expanding their selves at a rapid rate by virtue of the intense exchange. Once they know each other fairly well, opportunities for further rapid expansion of this sort inevitably decrease.

When rapid expansion occurs, there is a high degree of satisfaction; when expansion is slow or nonexistent, there is little emotion, or perhaps even boredom. If slow expansion follows a period of rapid expansion, the loss of enjoyable emotion may be disappointing and attributed to deficiencies in the relationship. Indeed, this pattern has been demonstrated in previous research such as studies of diaries as well as in field and lab experiments (Aron et al. 2000). For example, in one series of three laboratory experiments, couples in long-term relationships attended what they believed was an assessment session, which involved filling out questionnaires and being videotaped while interacting. The participants completed questionnaires, participated together in a task that was videotaped, and then completed more questionnaires. However, the questionnaires completed before the task served as a pretest and those after as a posttest. The task itself was experimentally manipulated so that some couples engaged in an expanding activity (one that was novel and challenging) and those in the control condition engaged in a more mundane activity. In all three experiments, as predicted, there was a significantly greater increase in relationship satisfaction for the couples in the expanding condition, whether measured by self-report or by blind analysis of content of pre and post verbal interactions between the couples (Aron et al. 2000).

In sum, the motivational aspect of the self-expansion model proposes that a major human motive, which occurs in diverse contexts including close relationships, is the desire to expand one's ability to accomplish goals.

Inclusion of Close Others in the Self

Perhaps the most important way in which people expand themselves is by including others in themselves, through close relationships. According to the model, in a close relationship, the resources, perspectives, and identities of a close other are experienced, to some extent, as one's own.

The *resources* of the other that are potentially included in the self contain material, knowledge-related assets (i.e., conceptual, informational, and procedural assets), as well as social assets (e.g., social status and roles) that can facilitate the achievement of goals. To include a relationship partner's resources means to perceive oneself as having access to or possessing the other's resources; that is, to some extent, that the other's resources are perceived as one's own (e.g., "I can do this because my partner will show me how" or "I have high status because my partner does"). The perceived inclusion of another's resources is particularly important from a motivational point of view because it means that the outcomes (i.e., rewards and costs) incurred by the others are to some extent experienced as one's own. This also implies that the other's acquisition and loss of resources are experienced to some extent as if they were happening to one's own resources (Aron and Aron 1986; Aron et al. 2003). Thus, for example, in game experiments in which people's allocation decisions will be unknown to recipients, people will allocate similar amounts to close others, but not to nonclose others (Aron et al. 1991).

Other examples show that people spontaneously experience the gains and losses of close others as if they were their own. A study of couples in romantic relationships found a standard equity effect (greatest satisfaction for those who are neither under- nor over-benefited), but this pattern was significantly weaker for those who perceived their relationship as having high levels of interconnectedness (Medvene, Teal, and Slavich 2000). That is, the authors predicted this pattern based on the idea that if the partner is part of the self, the partner's benefits are one's own, and if partners do not distinguish between their own and others' outcomes, the meaning of over- or under-benefited in relation to the partner is undermined. Similarly, several studies have found that social comparison processes are dramatically altered to be more like self-comparisons when the other is either already close to the self or closeness is created by a priming manipulation (Beach et al. 1998; McFarland, Buehler, and MacKay 2001; O'Mahen, Beach, and Tesser 2000; Stapel and Koomen 2001). For example, priming inclusion of others in the self completely undermined the negative effect of a partner outperforming the self and the degree of celebration in the close partner's success is correlated with the degree of including the other in the self (Gardner, Gabriel, and Hochschild 2002).

Including the other's *perspective* in the self refers to consciously or unconsciously experiencing the world to some extent from the included other's point of view. This implies that when another is included in the self, various self-related attributional and cognitive biases should also apply to that other person. For example, the usual actor-observer difference in the tendency to make situational versus dispositional attributions (Jones and Nisbett 1971) is smaller when the other is someone close to the self, such as a best friend or romantic partner (Aron et al. 1991; Aron and Fraley 1999; Sande, Goethals, and Radloff 1988). Other studies using memory recall methods have found that items imaged with close others, like items imaged with the self, are less vividly recalled than items imaged with non-close others (Aron et al. 1991). These studies suggest that just as one's own perspective is a background to experience, one's perspective gained through close others is also experienced as a background to experience; and the closer the others are, the more this is the case.

Taking another approach to this point, researchers examined whether people would extend to close others the usual effect found for the self in which past successes are re-called as more recent and past failures as more distant than they actually were. Consistent with the notion of including a close other's perspectives, this same effect was found when participants recalled past events for romantic partners, but only when those partners were close and not when they were distant (Konrath and Ross 2003).

Identity refers to features that differentiate one person from other people and objects primarily in terms of characteristics, memories, and other features that locate the person in social and physical space. Thus, when including a close other's identities in the self, people may easily confuse their own traits or memories with those of the other. In relation to the cognitive aspects in general (i.e., perspectives and identities), the self-expansion model implies shared cognitive elements of self and close others (Aron and Fraley 1999). Thus, for example, one may consider the consistent finding in the long-standing line of work on the "self-reference effect" of an advantage in terms of memory and response time for self-relevant versus other-relevant processing. However, a meta-analysis of the effect found significantly smaller differences in the memory effect between self-reference and other-reference when the other was someone who was close to the self (Symons and Johnson 1997).

The self-expansion model specifically suggests that in a close relationship, the very structure of the self changes in that the self includes the other in its very makeup—that the knowledge structures of close others actually share elements (or activation potentials) with the knowledge structures of the self (Aron et al. 1991). For example, one paradigm to examine this idea focuses on patterns of response latencies in making me/not me decisions (i.e., does the trait describe me?) about traits previously rated for their descriptiveness of self and of a close other. Across multiple studies, traits on which the self matches a close partner (the trait is true of both or false of both), me/not me-responses are faster than when a trait was mismatched for self and partner (true for one but false for the other) (Aron et al. 1991; Aron and Fraley 1999; Smith, Coats, and Walling 1999). Moreover, the magnitude of the effect correlates substantially with self-report measures of closeness and in one study predicted increases in self-reported closeness over a three-month period.

Using a different paradigm, another study had participants rate one set of traits for self, a different set of traits for a close other, and still other traits for one or more nonclose others, such as media personalities (Mashek, Aron, and Boncimino 2003). Participants were then given a surprise recognition task in which they were presented each trait and asked to indicate to which person they had rated it. The analysis focused on confusions; that is, traits that the participant remembered having rated for one person when the participant had actually rated it for a different person. Results were consistent with predictions. For example, if participants did not correctly recognize a trait as having been originally rated for the self, they were more likely to remember it as having been rated for the partner than as having been rated for the media personality. Similarly, if participants did not correctly recognize a trait as having been originally rated for the partner, they were more likely to remember it as having been rated for the self than as having been rated for the media personality.

In summary, the self-expansion model's aspect of "inclusion of close others in the self" posits that in a close relationship each treats the other's resources, perspectives, and identities to some extent as one's own.

APPLICATION TO BRAND RELATIONSHIPS

In this section, we apply key ideas of the self-expansion model, which was developed in the context of the formation and maintenance of close relationships between persons, to the relationships between consumers and brands. We are therefore looking at typical self-expansion processes of consumers, which are intended to lead to an improved theoretical basis of brand relationships. We would like to note that there are also relatively direct ways in which person-person relationships facilitate brand relationships, such as when close friends or admired persons (as in advertisement testimonials) are known to prefer a particular brand. In such cases, the brand may be seen as expanding the self or may be included in the self by extension from the personal relationship. Such vicarious processes have been shown to occur in the context of group identities in which a number of studies of the "extended contact effect" demonstrate that knowledge of a member of one's group having a close friend in another group creates more positive attitudes toward the other group (Wright et al. 1997). However, in this chapter our main focus is on direct person-brand relationships.

Brands and Self-Expansion Motivation

Rapid Self-Expansion with Newly Acquired Brands

Between persons, rapid expansion of the self, as often occurs when forming a new romantic relationship, is posited to result in high levels of excited positive affect. As noted earlier, this idea is consistent with prior analysis of the impact on the affective state of rapid movement toward a goal (Carver and Scheier 1990). This notion also implies a correspondingly intense negative affect when there is rapid "de-expansion" of the self; that is, when there is a rapid loss of perceived potential efficacy, as might occur with the sudden death of a spouse. We argue that between consumers and brands, rapid expansion takes place for newly acquired brands. For example, if a consumer buys a Rolex watch—which is now part of the relevant and actual sets of exclusive watch brands—the purchase and ownership of that watch can result in high levels of excited positive affect. This purchase can also lead to the formation of a new, close relationship between brand and consumer. If the owner loses the watch, this can lead to a rapid de-expansion of the self.

We posit that this takes place not only in high-priced, high-prestige product categories, but also for mundane, everyday brands. That is, if a consumer just changed from buying a no-name instant coffee to buying Nescafé's Taster's Choice brand, owning and using this product may also result in some self-expansion. And, if the brand is no longer available at the consumer's supplier, there may be disappointment. Of course, as the examples suggest, the intensity of the expansion may be smaller for mundane, low-involvement products (e.g., instant coffee) than for exclusive, high-involvement products (e.g., Swiss wristwatches).

As a brief excursion, we define involvement with brands by following the lead of previous research (Zaichkowsky 1985), which characterizes involvement as a person's perceived relevance of an object such as a brand based on inherent needs, values, and interests. Early research on involvement distinguishes between enduring involvement (i.e., represents an ongoing concern with an object that transcends situational influences) and situational involvement (i.e., involvement that occurs only in specific situations) (Houston and Rothschild 1978). Both represent a state of arousal and interest in the object, but they differ in their motivations and in the temporal pattern of their occurrence. Besides this categorization in enduring and situational involvement, the involvement construct may be differentiated into low versus high (Howard and Kerin 2006; Zaichkowsky 1985, 1994). Highly involved consumers are motivated to study information, such as quality, more extensively. However, less involved consumers are more likely to apply simple heuristics or judgment-relevant cues, which are more easily understood (Chen and Chaiken 1999), when processing information (Howard and Kerin 2006; Meyers-Levy and Peracchio 1996).

Pertaining to brand and self-expansion motivation, we focus on enduring involvement toward a brand (Houston and Rothschild 1978), which we further categorize into low and high involvement (Howard and Kerin 2006). Research summarized earlier finds that when doing exciting activities with a person, one comes to value the person more (Aron et al. 2000). This may also apply to relationships with brands on both high- and low-involvement levels. That is, if one is able to do something exciting (i.e., novel and challenging) with a brand, one is likely to feel more positively about it. For example, Omega, another exclusive watch manufacturer, positions its Seamaster brand as the ultimate instrument for the challenging sport of sailing. Brands of products that actually are used in novel and challenging situations are also likely to show this effect; for example, brands of tools or of musical instruments. We posit that having a novel and challenging experience with a brand—even strong associations of the brand with vicariously or imaginably having such experiences—is over and above just having good or positive experiences with the brand. In summary, these arguments lead to the following proposition:

P$_1$: For newly acquired brands, consumers may rapidly self-expand; thus enlarging the content of self-definitions, increasing self-efficacy, and experiencing positive affect. This effect is stronger for brands of high-involvement products and weaker for brands of low-involvement products.

Decreasing Self-Expansion with Well-Known Brands over Time

We also argue that the rate of self-expansion, and therefore positive affect and value associated with the brand, decreases over time with brands that have been repeatedly purchased, owned, and used. Starting from a state of rapid self-expansion with new brands, we posit that ordinarily (i.e., unless the brand is involved in ongoing novel and challenging activities), the amount of self-expansion decreases steadily. To use the previous Rolex example again, a Rolex that has been owned for years might still excite positive affect because of its timelessness; however, it will do so to a lesser extent than the latest, more beautiful, more technologically advanced Rolex model, or even for a newly acquired older model. For mundane, lower-involvement products, this decline starts at a lower level of self-expansion at the start of the brand relationship and may be even more rapid than for high-involvement products. Here, re purchasing this brand may lead to the least self-expansion; that is, it becomes a routine purchase. Thus, we propose:

P$_2$: The longer the relationship with the brand lasts, the less self-expanding the brand is. This effect across time is stronger for brands of low-involvement products and weaker for brands of high-involvement products.

Figure 4.1   **Brands and Self-Expansion Motivation**

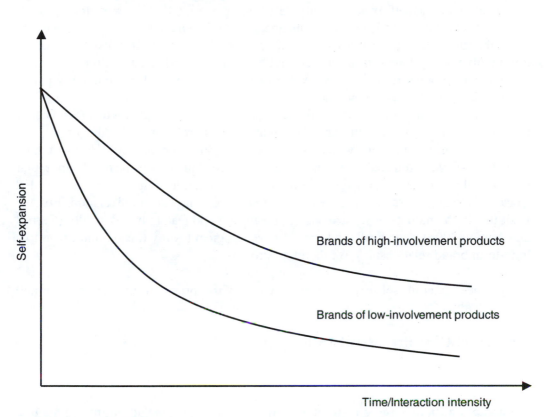

We also posit, however, that it is not just the relationship length that matters but also the intensity of the interaction with the brand. That is, the habituation process (i.e., routine purchase or long-term possession) that arises from relationship length is just one aspect of habituation. For human relationships, relationship length is one of the least important determinants of relationship closeness; more important is how many different things one does with a person and how much time one spends with them from day to day (Berscheid, Snyder, and Omoto 1989). Applied to brand relationships, we argue that the interaction intensity with a brand also reduces the rate of rapid self-expansion. Interaction intensity could, thus, function as an accelerator of the relationship-length effect posited earlier. We therefore offer the following proposition:

P₃: The higher the interaction intensity with the brand, the more decrease in self-expansion will be associated with the brand over time. This effect is stronger for brands of low-involvement products and weaker for brands of high-involvement products.

Figure 4.1 illustrates our idea of high self-expansion levels for relationships with new brands (i.e., rapid self-expansion) and decreasing levels of self-expansion with these brands over time and interaction intensity. It also provides an illustration for our argument that rapid self-expansion entry levels are generally higher for exclusive, high-involvement products and lower for mundane, low-involvement products. Here, we also argue that the link between self-expansion, time, and interaction intensity is steeper for low-involvement products than for high-involvement products. That is, a brand of a low involvement-product results in low levels of self-expansion much more quickly than a brand of a high-involvement product.

Yet, in line with prior human relationship research, we argue that when a consumer provides a high amount of self-expansion in a long-term relationship with a brand, it is more upsetting to "break up" with that brand (Lewandowski et al. 2006). For example, when Coca-Cola introduced New Coke, brand-loyal consumers became highly upset that the original brand was taken away and even boycotted the sale of the new brand. This led Coca-Cola to quickly reintroduce the original brand. Pertaining to brand relationships, we posit that high amounts of self-expansion toward a brand lead to brand loyalty (Carroll and Ahuvia 2006), specifically in terms of psychological loyalty (i.e., commitment to a long-term brand relationship). We therefore propose:

P_4: The greater the self-expansion experienced with a brand, the greater will be brand loyalty.

Inclusion of Close Brands in the Self

Brands as Resources

We argue that brands serve as resources, which consumers include in the self. First, for brands having reached the level of status symbol—such as the famous Polo Ralph Lauren polo player embroidered on shirts or the Montblanc Meisterstück fountain pen—consumers draw from these materialistic resources and eventually include them in the self once they own the branded product. Observational evidence suggests that consumers that include these close brands in the self literally wear the brands with pride and show them to others. Typing on a slim Apple MacBook, quickly responding to an e-mail via the latest Blackberry model, or noting appointments in a leather-bound Filofax in a meeting signals to others that the brand and its user have bonded. Through signaling this bond to others, the brand's resources are perceived as one's own resources. That is, part of the identity of the brand is matched and enclosed with its user's identity. A sudden loss of the close brand may thus be experienced as a loss of one's own resource. Although brand relationships may generally not disappear as suddenly as human relationships (e.g., through death or divorce), automobile enthusiasts have reported a deep cut in their own identity if their beloved car—their own branded product—was lost in an accident. Second, brands literally provide resources for accomplishing goals to the extent they are useful. Therefore, brands that are perceived to be of higher quality (i.e., offer greater utility) may especially expand the self.

In summary, brands offer at least two types of resources, which consumers may include in the self: (1) the social status or role availability that comes from people knowing that one owns the brand (respectively, one's perception of being the kind of person that has that brand) and (2) the actual benefits (e.g., utility) one has by owning that brand. Thus, we propose:

P5: Brands can function as resources. Consumers include these resources in the self and perceive them as their own resources.

Moreover, if brands provide resources that are included in the self, then losses to the brand mean losses to the self and benefits to the brand mean benefits to the self. Thus, consumers who have purchased a brand are likely to promote the brand to others and also to resist arguments from others that the brand has problems. Indeed, in the context of competing brands, there may be devaluation of the competing brand. We therefore offer the following proposition:

P6: Brands function as resources. The more a consumer perceives a brand's resources as the consumer's own resources (i.e., the more the brand is included in the consumer's self), the more the consumer will act on its behalf.

Brands as Perspectives

Further, we argue that consumers tend to consciously or unconsciously experience their world from the perspective of brands they possess (and have included in the self). A consumer would be subject to several attributional and cognitive biases in relation to the brand. For example, the BMW brand has been positioned as "The Ultimate Driving Machine" for many years. Correspondingly, BMW owners have been reported to drive more aggressively than owners of other automobile brands. Although Mercedes-Benz cars generally feature the same level of state-of-the art technology and design as BMWs, Mercedes-Benz operators are not stereotyped as being as aggressive as BMW drivers. We thus argue that consumers may in part view their world and even act from the perspective of close brands. We posit that this is especially true during the consumption and use of the brand. An observation of a wedding party at an upscale hotel revealed that when dressed in expensive Armani and Prada suits, dresses, and shoes, people behaved quite differently than when they had checked into the hotel a few hours earlier, wearing Abercrombie shorts and flip-flops. The relaxed behavior at check-in was exchanged with formal behavior once people changed outfits, even among close relatives. Another example is that those who purchase brands associated with valuing the environment (e.g., Prius hybrid automobile or Ecover dishwasher soap) may take on pro-environmental attitudes. This leads to the following proposition:

P7: Brands function as perspectives. Consumers' view their world from the perspective of brands they have included in the self, in the sense that they see the world from the perspective of perceived owners of the brand.

Brand as Identity

Previous research has argued for the importance of identity when considering consumer-brand relationships (Reed II 2004). It has been further argued that a brand relationship can be looked upon as an expression of consumer identities (Escalas and Bettman 2005). For example, a consumer's relationship with a Mercedes-Benz could build on the need to express individual-level unique identity, while a relationship with a local brand such as a Ford may relate to a group-level patriotic national identity (Swaminathan, Page, and Gürhan-Canli 2007). Other findings in brand relationship research suggest that the greater the fit between human traits that consistently describe and distinguish an individual and those traits that describe and distinguish a brand, the greater the preference will be for that brand (Malhotra 1988; Sirgy 1982; Swaminathan et al. 2007). In the context of person-person relationships, the self-expansion model proposes that the identity of a close other is "included in the self," in the sense that the cognitive representation of the close other actually becomes part the cognitive representation of the self. As a result, the close other functions like the self in terms of recognition, memory, and distinguishing qualities. As summarized earlier, people are faster at identifying a trait as their own when that trait is not also true of the close other (Aron et al. 1991). Similarly, people make source memory confusions between the self and close others (Mashek et al. 2003) and are slower at recognizing themselves when their photo is morphed with that of a close other than when it is morphed with a nonclose other (Riela et al. 2008). Extending this idea to brands, we suggest the following:

P_8: Brands function as identity. When there is a close relationship with a brand, the brand's identity becomes part of the cognitive structure of the self.

In summary, the main difference between the three facets of inclusion of close brands in the self is that a close brand's *resources* can be viewed as part of the owner's self, while *perspective* means seeing the world from the brand's point of view and *identity* refers to a brand's identity becoming part of the cognitive structure of the owner's self.

We also posit that the effect of increasing inclusion in the self is steeper for brands of high-involvement products than for brands of low-involvement products. However, the increase in inclusion in the self continues at a decreasing rate over time. One reason for this effect is that the included brand provides only marginal additional utility to its owner's self. As such, the brand resources will mostly be included in the owner's self over time. Moreover, the perspectives and identity of a brand will merge with the owner's perspectives and identity over time. We also argue that the decreasing rate of inclusion in the self is higher for brands of low-involvement products than for brands of high-involvement products. That is, a close brand of a low-involvement product (e.g., Nescafé instant coffee) will be included much faster than a brand of a high-involvement product (e.g., Rolex wristwatch). Thus, a brand of a high-involvement product results in additional utility for a longer time than a low-involvement product's brand would. We propose that:

Figure 4.2 **Inclusion of Brands in the Self**

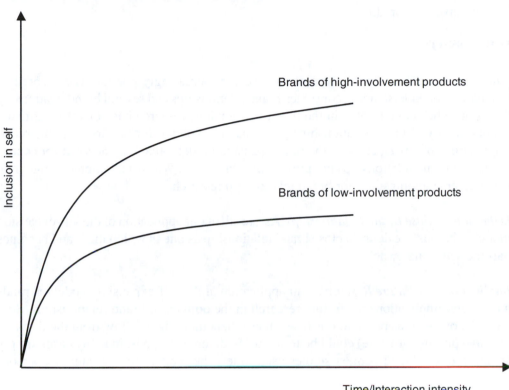

P$_9$: The longer the relationship with the brand over time lasts, the more the brand will be included in the self, although at a decreasing rate. While the effect of inclusion in the self will be stronger overall for brands of high-involvement products and weaker for brands of low-involvement products over time, the decreasing rate of additional inclusion in the self will be stronger for brands of low-involvement products.

We also posit that it is not just the relationship length that matters with respect to inclusion in the self but also the intensity of the interaction with the brand. This, we offer the following proposition:

P$_{10}$: The higher the interaction intensity with the brand, the more the brand will be included in the self, although at a decreasing rate. While the effect of inclusion in the self will be stronger overall for brands of high-involvement products and weaker for brands of low-involvement products, the decreasing rate of additional inclusion in the self will be stronger for brands of low-involvement products.

Figure 4.2 illustrates our idea of increasing inclusion of the close brand in the self over time and interaction intensity. Moreover, we illustrate that the rate at which there will be additional inclusion in the self will decrease more for brands of low- than of high-involvement products.

DISCUSSION

Although the relationship viewpoint has become increasingly popular as a theoretical foundation for understanding consumer-brand relationships and several brand relationship facets have been highlighted in the literature, previous research has not yet identified a general theory of brand relationships. This chapter explored for the first time the broad implications of a perspective—the self-expansion model—that may account for central aspects of brand relationships not previously considered. We also attempted to integrate some diverse findings in prior brand relationship research.

Definition of Close Brand Relationships. As a result of our application of the self-expansion model to brands, we define a close brand relationship as one in which the brand becomes part the self of its owner.

Implications for Future Research. Our application of the self-expansion model to brands has several implications for further research in the domain of brand relationships. Specifically, our various propositions (as well as others that might follow from the thinking we have put forward here) could be tested using diverse methods, in many cases simply adapting to the brand context studies used to test the model in the context of person-person relationships.

Implications for Brand Management. The proposals of this chapter also have some implications for practitioners. Brand managers often emphasize the role of brands in conveying human identities (Swaminathan et al. 2007). However, based on our theoretical assessment, we find that brands may also function as resources and perspectives, which are important aspects to consider when building and managing brands. Our line of argumentation also suggests that there is a difference between brands of high- and low-involvement products. That is, consumers tend to expand themselves more with brands of high- than of low-involvement products. Further, the inclusion in the self also differs between involvement categories. While the overall rate of inclusion in self for brands of high-involvement products is steeper over time than for low-involvement products, the additional utility from inclusion is smaller for low- than for high-involvement products. Particularly for brands of low-involvement products, managers should identify strategies to maintain higher levels of self-expansion and a slower decrease of additional utility when consumers include close brands in their selves. This, for example, could be managed by regularly launching new offers or additional product features before old products expansion levels fall too far.

Conclusion. In sum, we hope that our speculations regarding the application of the self-expansion model to brand relationships will prove sufficiently beneficial in expanding the scope and depth of work on brands, and will lead to including the model in the resources, perspectives, and identities of the field.

REFERENCES

Aaker, Jennifer L., Susan Fournier, and S. Adam Brasel (2004). "When Good Brands Do Bad," *Journal of Consumer Research,* 31 (1), 1–16.

Ahuvia, Aaron C. (2005). "Beyond the Extended Self: Loved Objects and Consumers' Identity Narratives," *Journal of Consumer Research,* 32 (1), 171–184.

Albert, Noël, Dwight Merunka, and Pierre Valette-Florence (2007). "When Consumers Love Their Brands: Exploring the Concept and Its Dimensions," *Journal of Business Research,* 61 (10), 1062–1075.

Aron, Arthur and Elaine N. Aron (1986). *Love and the Expansion of Self: Understanding Attraction and Satisfaction.* New York, NY: Hemisphere.

Aron, Arthur, Elaine N. Aron, and Christina C. Norman (2003). "Self-Expansion Model of Motivation and Cognition in Close Relationships and Beyond." In *Self and Social Identity,* ed. Marilynn B. Brewer and Miles Hewstone. Oxford, UK: Blackwell, 100–123.

Aron, Arthur, and Barbara Fraley (1999). "Relationship Closeness as Including Other in the Self: Cognitive Underpinnings and Measures," *Social Cognition,* 17 (2), 140–160.

Aron, Arthur, Christina C. Norman, and Elaine N. Aron (1998). "The Self-Expansion Model and Motivation," *Representative Research in Social Psychology,* 22, 1–13.

Aron, Arthur, Christina C. Norman, Elaine N. Aron, Colin McKenna, and Richard E. Heyman (2000). "Couples' Shared Participation in Novel and Arousing Activities and Experienced Relationship Quality," *Journal of Personality and Social Psychology,* 78 (2), 273–284.

Aron, Arthur, Meg Paris, and Elaine N. Aron (1995). "Falling in Love: Prospective Studies of Self-Concept Change," *Journal of Personality and Social Psychology,* 69 (6), 1102–1112.

Aron, Arthur, Jodie L. Steele, Todd B. Kashdan, and Max Perez (2006). "When Similars Do Not Attract: Tests of a Prediction from the Self-Expansion Model," *Personal Relationships,* 13 (4), 387–396.

Aron, Arthur, Michael Tudor, and Greg Nelson (1991). "Close Relationships as Including Other in the Self," *Journal of Personality and Social Psychology,* 60, 241–253.

Bandura, Albert (1977). "Self-Efficacy: Toward a Unifying Theory of Behavioral Change," *Psychological Review,* 84 (2), 191–215.

Bauer, Hans H., Daniel Heinrich, and Isabel Martin (2007). "How to Create High Emotional Consumer-Brand Relationships? The Causalities of Brand Passion." In *Australian and New Zealand Marketing Academy,* Dunedin, New Zealand, 2189–2198.

Beach, Steven R.H., Abraham Tesser, Frank D. Fincham, Deborah J. Jones, Debra Johnson, and Daniel J. Whitaker (1998). "Pleasure and Pain in Doing Well, Together: An Investigation of Performance-Related Affect in Close Relationships," *Journal of Personality and Social Psychology,* 74 (4), 923–938.

Berscheid, Ellen, Mark Snyder, and Allen M. Omoto (1989). "The Relationship Closeness Inventory: Assessing the Closeness of Interpersonal Relationships," *Journal of Personality and Social Psychology,* 57 (5), 792–807.

Byrne, Donn E. (1971). *The Attraction Paradigm.* New York, NY: Academic Press.

Carroll, Barbara A., and Aaron C. Ahuvia (2006). "Some Antecedents and Outcomes of Brand Love," *Marketing Letters,* 17 (2), 79–89.

Carver, Charles S., and Michael F. Scheier (1990). "Origins and Functions of Positive and Negative Affect: A Control-Process View," *Psychological Review,* 97 (1), 19–35.

Chaudhuri, Arjun, and Morris B. Holbrook (2001). "The Chain of Effects from Brand Trust and Brand Affect to Brand Performance: The Role of Brand Loyalty," *Journal of Marketing,* 65 (2), 81–93.

Chen, Serena, and Shelley Chaiken (1999). "The Heuristic-Systematic Model in Its Broader Context." In *Dual-Process Theories in Social Psychology,* ed. Shelley Chaiken and Yaacov Trope. New York, NY: Guilford Press, 73–96.

Deci, Edward L. and Richard M. Ryan (2000). "The "What" and "Why" of Goal Pursuits: Human Needs and the Self-Determination of Behavior," *Psychological Inquiry,* 11 (4), 227–268.

Escalas, Jennifer E. and James R. Bettman (2005). "Self-Construal, Reference Groups, and Brand Meaning," *Journal of Consumer Research,* 32 (3), 378–389.

Fournier, Susan (1998). "Consumers and Their Brands: Developing Relationship Theory in Consumer Research," *Journal of Consumer Research,* 24 (4), 343–353.

Gardner, Wendi L., Shira Gabriel, and Laura Hochschild (2002). "When You and I Are We, You Are Not Threatening: The Role of Self-Expansion in Social Comparison," *Journal of Personality and Social Psychology,* 82 (2), 239–251.

Gecas, Viktor (1989). "The Social Psychology of Self-Efficacy," *Annual Reviews in Sociology,* 15 (1), 291–316.

Houston, Michael J., and Michael L. Rothschild (1978). "Conceptual and Methodological Perspectives on Involvement." In *Research Frontiers in Marketing: Dialogues and Directions.* Chicago, IL, 184–187.

Howard, Daniel J., and Roger A. Kerin (2006). "Broadening the Scope of Reference Price Advertising Research: A Field Study of Consumer Shopping Involvement," *Journal of Marketing,* 70 (4), 185–204.

Jacoby, Jacob, and Robert W. Chestnut (1978). *Brand Loyalty: Measurement and Management.* New York, NY: Wiley.

Jones, Edward E., and Richard E. Nisbett (1971). "The Actor and the Observer: Divergent Perceptions of the Causes of Behavior." In *Attribution: Perceiving the Causes of Behavior,* ed. Edward E. Jones. Morristown, NJ: General Learning Press, 79–94.

Konrath, S.H., and M. Ross (2003). "Our Glories, Our Shames: Expanding the Self in Temporal Self Appraisal Theory." *American Psychological Society Conference,* Atlanta, GA.

Lewandowski Jr., Gary W., and Arthur Aron (2002). "The Self-Expansion Scale: Construction and Validation." *Third Annual Meeting of the Society of Personality and Social Psychology,* Savannah, GA.

Lewandowski Jr., Gary W., Sharon Bassis, and Johnna Kunak (2006). "Losing a Self-Expanding Relationship: Implications for the Self-Concept," *Personal Relationships,* 13 (3), 317–331.

Malhotra, Naresh K. (1988). "Self Concept and Product Choice: An Integrated Perspective," *Journal of Economic Psychology,* 9 (1), 1–28.

Mashek, Debra J., Arthur Aron, and Maria Boncimino (2003). "Confusions of Self with Close Others," *Personality and Social Psychology Bulletin,* 29 (3), 382–392.

Matzler, Kurt, Elisabeth A. Pichler, and Andrea Hemetsberger (2007). "Who Is Spreading the Word? The Positive Influence of Extraversion on Consumer Passion and Brand Evangelism." In *2007 AMA Winter Educators' Conference,* San Diego, CA, 25–32.

McFarland, Cathy, Roger Buehler, and Laura MacKay (2001). "Affective Responses to Social Comparisons with Extremely Close Others," *Social Cognition,* 19 (5), 547–586.

Medvene, Louis J., Cayla R. Teal, and Susan Slavich (2000). "Including the Other in Self: Implications for Judgments of Equity and Satisfaction in Close Relationships," *Journal of Social and Clinical Psychology,* 19 (3), 396–419.

Meyers-Levy, Joan, and Laura A. Peracchio (1996). "Moderators of the Impact of Self-Reference on Persuasion," *Journal of Consumer Research,* 22 (4), 408–423.

O'Mahen, Heather A., Steven R.H. Beach, and Abraham Tesser (2000). "Relationship Ecology and Negative Communication in Romantic Relationships: A Self-Evaluation Maintenance Perspective," *Personality and Social Psychology Bulletin,* 26 (11), 1343–1352.

Reed II, Americus (2004). "Activating the Self-Importance of Consumer Selves: Exploring Identity Salience Effects on Judgments," *Journal of Consumer Research,* 31 (2), 286–295.

Riela, Suzanne, Sarah Ketay, Arthur Aron, and Julian P. Keenan (2008). "Including a Close Other's Face in the Self: A Morphing Experiment." In *Society for Personality and Social Psychology Annual Meeting.*

Sande, Gerald N., George R. Goethals, and Christine E. Radloff (1988). "Perceiving One's Own Traits and Others': The Multifaceted Self," *Journal of Personality and Social Psychology,* 54 (1), 13–20.

Sirgy, M. Joseph (1982). "Self-Concept in Consumer Behavior: A Critical Review," *Journal of Consumer Research,* 9 (3), 287–300.

Smith, Eliot R., Susan Coats, and Dustin Walling (1999). "Overlapping Mental Representations of Self, In-Group, and Partner: Further Response Time Evidence and a Connectionist Model," *Personality and Social Psychology Bulletin,* 25 (7), 873–882.

Stapel, Diederik A., and Willem Koomen (2001). "I, We, and the Effects of Others on Me: How Self-Construal Level Moderates Social Comparison Effects," *Journal of Personality and Social Psychology,* 80 (5), 766–781.

Strong, Greg, and Arthur Aron (2006). "The Effect of Shared Participation in Novel and Challenging Activities on Experienced Relationship Quality: Is It Mediated by High Positive Affect?" In *Intrapersonal Processes in Interpersonal Relationships,* ed. Kathleen D. Vohs and Eli J. Finkel. New York, NY: Guilford, 342–359.

Swaminathan, Vanitha, Karen L. Page, and Zeynep Gürhan-Canli (2007). "'My' Brand or 'Our' Brand: The Effects of Brand Relationship Dimensions and Self-Construal on Brand Evaluations," *Journal of Consumer Research,* 34 (2), 248–259.

Symons, Cynthia S., and Blair T. Johnson (1997). "The Self-Reference Effect in Memory: A Meta-Analysis," *Psychological Bulletin,* 121 (3), 371–394.

Taylor, Shelley E., Efrat Neter, and Heidi A. Wayment (1995). "Self-Evaluation Processes," *Personality and Social Psychology Bulletin,* 21 (12), 1278–1287.

Thomson, Matthew, Deborah J. MacInnis, and C. Whan Park (2005). "The Ties That Bind: Measuring the Strength of Consumers' Emotional Attachments to Brands," *Journal of Consumer Psychology,* 15 (1), 77–91.

Tucker, Paula, and Arthur Aron (1993). "Passionate Love and Marital Satisfaction at Key Transition Points in the Family Life Cycle," *Journal of Social and Clinical Psychology,* 12 (2), 135–147.

Warrington, Patti, and Soyeon Shim (2000). "An Empirical Investigation of the Relationship between Product Involvement and Brand Commitment," *Psychology and Marketing,* 17 (9), 761–782.

White, Robert W. (1959). "Motivation Reconsidered: The Concept of Competence," *Psychological Review,* 66, 297–333.

Winterich, Karen P. (2007). "Self-Other Connectedness in Consumer Affect, Judgments, and Action." Dissertation, University of Pittsburgh, Joseph M. Katz Graduate School of Business, Pittsburgh, PA.

Wright, Stephen C., Arthur Aron, Tracy McLaughlin-Volpe, and Stacy A. Ropp (1997). "The Extended Contact Effect: Knowledge of Cross-Group Friendships and Prejudice," *Journal of Personality and Social Psychology,* 73 (1), 73–90.

Zaichkowsky, Judith L. (1985). "Measuring the Involvement Construct," *Journal of Consumer Research,* 12 (3), 341–352.

———. (1994). "The Personal Involvement Inventory: Reduction, Revision, and Application to Advertising," *Journal of Advertising,* 23 (4), 59–70.

CHAPTER 5

WHY ON EARTH DO CONSUMERS HAVE RELATIONSHIPS WITH MARKETERS?

Toward Understanding the Functions of Brand Relationships

LAURENCE ASHWORTH, PETER DACIN, AND MATTHEW THOMSON

The relationship between consumers and brands has garnered considerable attention in the marketing and the consumer behavior literature. In recent years researchers have investigated not only the general nature of the phenomenon of consumer-brand relationships, but also important marketing-related outcomes of this relationship. For example, research in marketing suggests that consumer-brand relationships have sizeable effects on important marketing-related outcomes including repeat purchase, word-of-mouth (WOM) and willingness to pay (see Stern 1997; Sheth and Parvatiyar 1995).

In addition to examining the effects of consumer-brand relationships on these outcomes, academic research has identified additional constructs that are emerging as important aspects of consumer-brand relationships. These constructs include relationship strength and relationship quality, and are fundamental to our understanding of the link between consumers and brands (Fournier 1998).

However, despite the strong interest in consumer-brand relationships, however, there is little understanding of the reasons why consumers develop and maintain relationships with brands. This is somewhat surprising given the insights that market researchers have gleaned by addressing underlying motivations in such areas as attitude research. In this field of research, the study of attitude functions (i.e., why consumers hold attitudes) has provided a deeper understanding of topics such as attitude formation and persuasion (e.g., Katz 1960; Shavitt 1990).

In the human relationship literature, studies of why individuals form and maintain relationships have advanced researchers' knowledge of relationships far beyond what could be gained by simply identifying the outcomes of relationships. It is interesting, therefore, that researchers in marketing and consumer behavior have yet to approach consumer-brand relationships from the perspective of understanding the functions that these relationships provide to consumers (for an exception, see Chapter 4). As the literature continues to develop in the area of consumer-brand relationships it becomes apparent that understanding consumer motivation for entering into these relationships is a logical next step in advancing the field.

Understanding the potential functions that consumer-brand relationships perform would also be important for providing further insights into important concepts such as relationship strength and quality. In consumer-brand relationship research as with attitude research, answering the question, "What function does a given consumer-brand relationship perform in a given consumers' life?" appears to be interwoven with our understanding of the nature, strength, and quality of that relationship.

In light of this, our research undertakes the preliminary step of trying to identify and measure various reasons for consumers to form and maintain relationships with brands. We do this by proposing and empirically examining an approach to consumer-brand relationships that suggests that consumers develop and maintain relationships, in part, because relationships provide a mechanism that enables consumers to address and achieve several higher level goals.

We begin with a brief overview of what is meant by consumer-brand relationships and then discuss the general concept of consumer-brand relationship functions, including some important outcomes of these functions. Based on this discussion, we borrow from a variety of literatures to conceptually identify potential consumer-brand relationship functions as well as a battery of items that tap into these potential functions.

We then describe the procedures we followed in developing measures of these consumer-brand relationship functions and present the results of various psychometric tests used to refine these measures and our conceptualization of consumer-brand relationship functions. We also present the results of exploratory research that suggests consumer-brand relationship functions provide important insights into our understanding of the building and maintaining of these relationships. The chapter concludes with a discussion of several implications for marketing practice and the study of consumer-based relationships in marketing.

CONSUMER-BRAND RELATIONSHIPS

Research in marketing and consumer behavior suggests that some consumers form relationships with brands in much the same way that they form relationships with other individuals, and that the nature of these relationships can differ across consumers (Fournier 1998; Muniz and O'Guinn 2001). In her research, Fournier argues that meaningful relationships exist between consumers and a variety of daily-use products (Fournier 1998; Fournier and Mick 1999; Fournier and Yao 1997). The nature of these relationships can take on a spectrum of intensity including the formation of a very intimate bond with brands and, in some extreme cases, a passion that is often associated only with a close circle of friends and family (Aggarwal 2004).

The relationship concept has become an increasingly important research topic, partly because of the economical advantages that firms are assumed to enjoy as a result of strong consumer-brand relationships. These advantages include reduced marketing costs, ease of access, acquisition of new customers, customer retention, brand equity and, ultimately, increased profits (Blackston 2000; Dowling 2002; Reichheld 1996; Winer 2001). In addition to research investigating outcomes associated with consumer-brand relationships, the nature and properties of different types of person-brand relationships (Aaker and Fournier 1995; Aggarwal 2004) and factors responsible for the dissolution of these relationships (Aaker, Fournier, and Brasel, 2004; Fajer and Schouten, 1995) have also been examined.

Contemplating relationships is important because they are among the "most reliable sources of future revenues and profits" for companies (Lemon, Rust, and Zeithaml 2001, p. 21). Relationships are thought to improve the position of firms by enhancing cash flows, lowering volatility, establishing entry barriers, and offering the possibility of increased prices and market share (Srivastava, Shervani, and Fahey 1998). Similarly, "when available brands are viewed as being similar on substantive product features, any competitive advantage in terms of CRM efforts will affect choice" (Barone et al. 2000, p. 258). Thus the strength of consumer relationships is a commercial asset that is likely predictive of performance and resilience to competition.

Despite the importance of relationships and the volume of research and rhetoric that has gone into promoting their benefits, there has been little consensus on how to conceptualize or measure their strength. Perhaps the most basic means of thinking about strength is how often a person buys a particular brand, either in terms of frequency or as a proportion of category purchases; but this relatively impoverished view ignores the psychological underpinnings of the relationship, which may be more meaningful or predictive.

One dimension of relationships that has received considerable attention and does attempt to capture the psychological experience of consumer-brand relationships is Brand Relationship Quality (BRQ; Fournier 1998). Under this conceptualization, stronger, more meaningful relationships are characterized by feelings such as love and passion, intimacy, commitment, and so on (see Fournier 1998). Other researchers have measured the strength of relationships using complementary approaches, such as by using a composite of satisfaction, trust, and commitment (see for example Gregoire and Fisher 2008), though it should be noted that each of these has implicitly or explicitly been advanced as sole indicators of strength too (e.g., Fournier, 1998; Oliver, 1999). While these views have advanced the field, none seems adequate on its own. For example, it seems possible that consumers can form a strong relationship with a brand, without necessarily developing feelings of intimacy or passion. It is also possible that consumers may be satisfied with a brand but switch when the opportunity arises (Liljander and Roos 2002). Further, consumers do not have to enjoy a strong relationship with a brand in order to be satisfied with it (Barnes 1997).

Other approaches have also been explored. Some researchers have characterized relationships primarily using notions of identification and attachment. *Identification* has been used to refer to the sense of connection between a consumer and some entity and reflects the degree to which consumers define themselves by the same attributes they believe define the entity (e.g., Aqueveque 2005; Einwiller et al. 2006; Brown, Bradley and Lang 2006; Smith, Morgan, and White 2005; Losier and Koestner 1999). Identification represents "the primary psychological substrate for the kind of deep, committed, and meaningful relationships that marketers are increasingly seeking to build with their customers" (Bhattacharya and Sen 2003, p. 76). *Attachment* has been used to describe a person's emotional bond with a particular person or object that he or she perceives as special and irreplaceable (Bowlby 1979; Kleine and Baker 2004). It has been proposed that consumers form attachments to brands and that the strength of these attachments may be a good indicator of strong relationships (see Keller 2001; Thomson, MacInnis, and Park 2005; Thomson 2006; Ball and Tasaki 1992). Strong relationships have also been explained using terms such as involvement (e.g., Park and McClung 1986; Zaichkowsky 1985), affective commitment (e.g., Bergami and Bagozzi 2000), brand commitment (e.g., Ahluwalia, Burnkrant, and Unnava 2000; Beatty, Kahle, and Homer 1988), feelings of loyalty (Rust et al. 2004), trust (e.g., Delgado-Ballester and Munuera-Aleman, 2001), attitudinal loyalty or strength (e.g., Ahluwalia, Burnkrant. and Unnava 2000; Bizer and Krosnick, 2001), self-relevance (e.g., Chung and Darke 2006; see also Chapter 6), and love (see Chapter 18).

Whereas some of these terms, such as identification, tend to be regarded principally as cognitive constructs implicating values and beliefs and leading to affective bonds (see Ahearne et al. 2005), others such as attachment and affective involvement are primarily emotional and tap feelings such as love, fondness, affection, and belonging (Bergami and Bagozzi 2000). Both types of constructs have been mentioned in proposals to establish superior measures of the strength of brands (Lassar, Mittal, and Sharma 1995) and could also serve as indicators of strong relationships because they assess the strength of internalized linkage between a person and a brand (see also Ashmore, Deaux, and Mclaughlin-Volpe 2004; Kyle and Mowen 2005; Kim and Kaplan 2005). There has been no shortage of views on what is the best way to measure the strength of relationships, but advances in the field may be slow until there is some rationalization of these constructs and an examination of their various predictors, effects, measures, and so on.

Overall, relationships have been characterized in a number of different ways that capture various components and possibly different antecedents of the relationship itself. An implicit assumption in most of the work that has examined consumer-brand relationships is that relationships serve some function or goal for the consumer or possibly that the relationship is formed as a result of the brand consistently fulfilling a specific set of goals that the consumer possesses. Looking across the different characterizations of relationships it is apparent that these goals might be quite diverse. For example, the notion of brand identification suggests that one reason a consumer is likely to foster a relationship with a brand is because of the ability of that brand to contribute to the identity the consumer wishes to develop or maintain.

Similarly, the notion of attachment and intimacy suggests that certain consumers may look to brands to fulfill important affiliation needs (as they sometimes look to celebrities—see Thomson 2006). We argue that a more complete understanding of consumers' relationships with brands requires a grasp of the purpose or function underlying the relationship. Specifically, we suggest that relationships can serve a variety of higher-order goals and that the nature of these goals is likely to impact the nature of the relationship and its effect on important marketing outcomes. In the next section we attempt to outline a series of goals that we believe are likely to be particularly important in the context of consumer-brand relationships. The notion of higher-level goals is not uncommon in marketing (for example see Shavitt 1990 in the context of attitudes). Consistent with much of this work, we borrow primarily from the work on attitude functions (e.g., Katz 1960; Shavitt, 1990) as well as from more general work on fundamental human motivations (e.g., Baumeister and Leary 1995).

CONSUMER-BRAND RELATIONSHIP FUNCTIONS

The idea that consumer attitudes and beliefs can serve a function in achieving higher-level goals is widely accepted in psychology and marketing. Originally conceptualized by Smith, Bruner, and White (1956) and Katz (1960), the functional approach to attitudes addresses the motivational bases of people's attitudes (i.e., the functional underpinnings of their attitudes). Over the years, several authors in these fields have written about the functions of attitudes and the insights they provide in understanding why individuals form and maintain certain attitudes and beliefs (e.g., Bhat and Reddy 1998; Chitturi, Raghunathan, and Mahajan 2007; Deci and Ryan 2000; Katz 1960; Maio and Olson 1995a,b; Okada 2005; Park, MacInnis, and Jaworski 1986; Shavitt 1990; Shavitt and Nelson 2002; Sheldon et al. 2001; Voss, Spangenberg, and Grohmann 2003). For example, Shavitt (1990) showed that marketing communications that matched the function of consumers' attitudes toward particular products were more effective at changing the attitude than communications that did not. In other words, an understanding of the function underlying a particular attitude provided insights into how best to change that attitude beyond other characteristics of the attitude (e.g., valence, strength, extremity, etc.)—something we argue is also likely to apply to relationships.

Smith et al. (1956) initially proposed three attitude functions: object appraisal, externalization, and social adjustment. Katz (1960) later proposed four somewhat different functions: utilitarian, knowledge, ego-defensive, and value-expressive. There is, however, considerable overlap and a number of similarities between the two taxonomies, so, for the purpose of this chapter, we focus initially on the four functions proposed by Katz.

Katz suggested that attitudes serve one or more of four basic underlying functions: they serve as an indication of the extent to which an object is associated with rewards or punishment (the utilitarian function; Shavitt 1989); can function to protect an individual from "basic truths" about himself or from "harsh realities of the external world" (Katz 1960; the ego-defensive function); can allow individuals to express personal values and aspects of their self-concept that they find satisfying (the value-expressive function); and finally, can be associated with a basic need to attain a meaningful, stable, and organized view of one's environment (the knowledge function).

As Fazio (1989) pointed out, to some extent all attitudes serve a knowledge function. That is, it could be argued that all attitudes are designed in part to help individuals summarize information in a meaningful and psychologically useful format. As such, this function of attitudes would not appear to be immediately applicable to relationships. It should, however, be noted that this broad interpretation of the knowledge function is perhaps somewhat different than Katz's original formulation. His argument was that attitudes can be specifically motivated by a need to understand, to seek meaning, and to achieve consistency across attitudes. In the context of more current work, we might argue that this function relates to a number of different underlying psychological needs, including a need to understand causes and make sense of situations (Stevens and Fiske 1995), for consistency (Festinger 1957), cognition (Cacioppo and Petty 1982), curiosity and exploration (Kashdan, Rose, and Fincham 2004), and so on. In other words, a somewhat more restrictive, and therefore usable, interpretation of the knowledge function of attitudes could outline the specific knowledge-related motivations that are responsible for the attitude, rather than referring to the general summary function of all attitudes. In the context of relationships, we believe the most applicable of these related needs is that of understanding and making sense of situations. That is, a consumer-brand relationship may exist because it helps a consumer make sense of his or her situation. Although we are uncertain as to whether such a function will necessarily prove important in explaining the basis of consumer-brand relationships, we nevertheless examine a knowledge function as one possible basis of such relationships.

The utilitarian function of attitudes outlined by Katz suggests that attitudes toward certain objects exist due to the rewarding or punishing consequences of interacting with those objects. Like the knowledge function, it could be argued that this function is sufficiently broad to encompass most, if not all, attitudes. In a relationship context, a utilitarian function would suggest that a relationship is fostered (or terminated) based on rewarding (or punishing) consequences of that relationship. Of course, relationships, like attitude objects, can be rewarding (or punishing) for a wide variety of reasons—because they bolster self-esteem for example, or because the partner in the relationship is fun to interact with, or because they are relevant to one's self-concept. In other words, the nature of the consequences of interacting with an object is not sufficient to distinguish this function from more specific functions that relationships might serve.

That is not to say that there is no role for such a function, but rather that it needs refinement to be usable. Here, we draw from work that has distinguished between hedonic and so-called utilitarian products. Hirschman and Holbrook (1982) defined hedonic consumption as consumption involving "multisensory, fantasy, and emotive aspects of product usage experience." Similarly, Chitturi, Raghunathan, and Mahajan (2008) recently defined hedonic product benefits as those that are "aesthetic, experiential, and enjoyment-related," in contrast to utilitarian benefits that are "functional, instrumental, and practical." Despite the fact that much work has used similar distinctions (e.g., Dhar and Wertenbroch 2000; Kivetz and Simonson 2002; Okada 2005; Voss, Spangenberg, and Grohmann 2003) and that the hedonic aspects of consumption are reasonably clear—features that directly lead to positive affective reactions—it is less clear precisely what constitutes a "utilitarian" feature or product. "Practical" and "functional" imply the product or feature is useful in achieving a particular goal; something that could also be used to describe a product where the goal is hedonic (or indeed any other goal). "Instrumental" implies in the service of some other goal—a means, as opposed to the end itself. Such a characterization provides perhaps a better distinction from hedonic features of consumption. Hedonic features are those that directly lead to the end goal of affect, whereas utilitarian features are those that allow a consumer to achieve some other goal, affective or otherwise.

The point is that the utilitarian features of the product are not directly affect-inspiring, but enable the pursuit of other goals. Practically speaking, the utilitarian aspects of a brand refer to the core function of the product as it was designed (not, it is worth noting, the primary function ascribed to product by the consumer). For example, while an automobile may have been purchased because of the thrilling ride it provides (a hedonic motivation that, in this case, is the primary function of the product for the consumer), the core function by design, and therefore, the utilitarian basis of the purchase, is transport—an enabler of other goals. Such a definition also distinguishes relationships founded on a utilitarian basis from other relationships, all based on the ability of the product to directly fulfill a variety of other goals. As such, we define a utilitarian relationship as one in which the basis of the relationship with the brand is due to the ability of the brand to consistently and reliably aid in the achievement of other goals.

Raising the distinction between hedonic and utilitarian features and products suggests certain consumer-brand relationships may be predicated on the ability of a brand to fulfill consumers' hedonic needs directly—their needs for pleasure, fun, excitement, and even calm and relaxation (all of which we would classify as positively valenced affective reactions that represent rewarding end-states, despite differing in arousal). Consequently, we argue that consumer-brand relationships might also serve a hedonic function. That is, the relationship exists because of the ability of the product to reliably and consistently inspire a positive affective reaction in the consumer.

As Katz and others suggest (e.g., Schlosser 1998; Shavitt 1990), attitudes toward particular objects can be in the service of the development and maintenance of the individual's self-concept (see also Chapter 4). Katz called this function value-expression and argued that the attitude exists because it represents or is consistent with an individual's personal values and self-identity. It is worth distinguishing this function from impression-management goals, where the attitude is one cue among others designed to create or avoid particular impressions. Indeed, Katz specifically argued that this was not what his value-expressive function was supposed to capture: "The reward to the person in these instances is not so much a matter of gaining social recognition or monetary rewards as of establishing his self-identity and confirming his notion of the sort of person he sees himself to be" (Katz 1960). Applying this in the context of relationships, we believe that one reason a consumer-brand relationship can exist is because of the fit between the values associated with the brand and the consumer's own values and identity. Consistent with the label used by Katz, we refer to this as a value-expressive function of the relationship.

In contrast to an internally motivated identity fit function (the value-expressive function), consumers may well be externally motivated to form relationships with brands for other reasons, including the social acceptance that comes from creating an image that others value and respect (see also Chapter 9). Such goals have been studied under the rubric of self-presentation and impression management (e.g., Leary 1995; Schlenker 1980). In the literature on attitude functions, impression-management goals have typically been bundled with identity-congruence goals. Smith et al. (1956), for example, labeled both types of goals a social-adjustment function, and Shavitt (1990) referred to public and private identity goals as a broad social identity function. Such goals can clearly be closely related.

Work on the development of the self has demonstrated that others' views of an individual shape that individual's self-concept (Shrauger and Schoeneman 1979). The very notion of an "ought self" (Higgins 1987) implies we are motivated in part to be what others want us to be. Moreover, the "ideal self" can consist of states individuals believe are inherently important (consistent with Maslow's notion of self-actualization; 1954) and states for which they believe will garner the respect of others. In short, the motivation to adhere to and express certain values (through both attitudes and relationships) can be in the service of both self-related and other-related goals. Distinguishing between such goals is awkward because the very values to which individuals subscribe are likely to exist, at least initially, because of others' approval of those values. Despite the difficulties in distinguishing between self- and other-motivated behavior, we believe that there are examples of consumer-brand relationships that are likely to exist primarily because that relationship allows an individual to fit in to an important group or otherwise receive social approval (in contrast to relationships that exist because of a perceived fit with internalized values). Note that we do not distinguish between group membership motives and general social approval motives. In the context of relationships, the important point is that the function of the relationship is to affect the way in which consumers are viewed by others as a consequence of their association with the brand. We refer to this function as a social-adjustive function, consistent with the term DeBono (1987) used to separate this function from the value-expressive function.

Inspired in part by Freudian conceptions of conflict between the needs and values of the id and the superego, Katz described his final function as ego-defensive. He proposed this function because he believed that certain attitudes existed primarily to protect individuals from undesirable truths about themselves or from harsh realities of the external world. Based on this function, Shavitt (1990) described a self-esteem maintenance function of attitudes in which attitudes serve not only to protect individuals' self-esteem, but also to bolster it through, for example, affiliation with certain social groups. In short, certain attitudes may exist as a mechanism to protect and bolster self-esteem. The problem with this conceptualization in the context of relationships is that relationships can impact self-esteem through a variety of different mechanisms, including some of the functions we have previously outlined. For example, consumer-brand relationships that exist because of the ability of the brand to satisfy social-adjustive (i.e., impression-management) goals are likely to be a source of self-esteem; as are consumer-brand relationships that serve a value-expressive (or identity fit) function. In other words, self-esteem can be conceptualized as a broad need that can be satisfied by a number of more specific, presumably adaptive, behaviors and outcomes. This conceptualization is consistent with current research on self-esteem that points to a variety of factors that appear to serve self-esteem needs (e.g., Crocker and Wolfe 2001; Heatherton and Polivy 1991; Leary et al. 1995; Lemay and Ashmore 2006). Rather than positing a broad self-esteem maintenance function of consumer-brand relationships, we argue that such a goal is satisfied through a variety of other, lower-order goals, especially value-expressive and social-adjustive goals. However, we also believe that relationships can more directly serve self-esteem needs in the form of affiliation.

In the context of human relationships, one clear motivation underlying the development and maintenance of such relationships is affiliation (Bowlby 1969). Group living is generally considered a necessary condition for human survival (Stevens and Fiske 1995) and, as such, ongoing acceptance and belonging in the form of relationships should be rewarding. Along these lines, Baumeister and Leary (1995) provide a compelling argument, that humans possess a fundamental need to belong, and a number of researchers (Baumeister, Twenge, and Nuss 2002; Downey et al. 1998; Leary et al. 1995) have demonstrated powerful negative psychological reactions to rejection. This suggests that one reason relationships can be rewarding is because they make individuals in the relationship feel like they belong. Thus, we hypothesize that another, perhaps fundamental function of relationships is that they fulfill affiliation needs. Although such a function is likely to have powerful implications for self-esteem, we do not equate this function with self-esteem maintenance given the likelihood that other functions also contribute to consumer self-esteem. Instead, we argue that certain consumer-brand relationships are primarily motivated by the feelings of affiliation and friendship that are derived from interacting with the brand.

In summary, we believe that as there are attitude functions, there are also consumer-brand relationship functions. That is, consumers are motivated to develop and maintain relationships with brands for a variety of reasons. Understanding these reasons will help us to see clearly the nature of consumer-brand relationships as well as constructs associated with these relationships, such as relationship quality and strength. Specifically, we propose six possible relationship functions: *knowledge*—a relationship that exists because of the inherent understanding it provides the consumer about his or her situation; *utilitarian*—a relationship based on the ability of the brand to consistently and reliably aid in the achievement of other goals; *hedonic*—a relationship based on the ability of the brand to directly inspire a variety of positive affective responses; *value-expressive*—a relationship based on the consistency of the values associated with the brand and the values central to the consumer (similar to the construct, "identification," as it has been conceptualized in the relationship literature); *social-adjustive*—a relationship that exists because consumers' association with the brand creates a desired impression; and finally, *affiliation*—a relationship that serves individuals' basic needs for friendship and belonging. Clearly, this list of functions is not intended to be exhaustive, but rather builds on the work on attitudes functions and existing conceptualizations of relationships. In the next section, we discuss our approach to developing measures of consumer-brand relationship functions and then present the results of the study to illustrate the usefulness of this concept.

Measures of Consumer-Brand Relationship Functions

To develop and examine the potential contribution of the concept of consumer-brand relationship functions to the marketing literature, it was necessary to develop and refine measures of each of these functions. We gathered, adapted, and created items from a variety of previous conceptual and empirical work on brands, attitudes, and forms of consumption that we cite in a previous section of this chapter (e.g., Maio and Olson

1995a,b; Shavitt 1990; Shavitt and Nelson 2002; Chitturi, Raghunathan, and Mahajan 2007; Bhat and Reddy 1998; Katz 1960; Okada 2005; Park, MacInnis, and Jaworski 1986; Voss, Spangenberg, and Grohmann 2003; Deci and Ryan 2000; Sheldon et al. 2001).

The various items relating to potential consumer-brand relationship functions were included in a survey that we administered using an online panel managed by a large Canadian market research firm. In order to ensure that respondents had experience with the subject of the survey, the directions at the outset asked respondents to think about and list the name of a brand that they currently or recently owned. Further, respondents were instructed that "based on your experience with this brand, it might be said that you have some sort of 'relationship' with it." Following these directions, respondents were asked questions that tapped the various functions of their relationship with the brand. The final sample was composed of 515 respondents, approximately evenly split in gender and heterogeneous in terms of age, education level, and geographic dispersion.

The challenges concerning the relationship functions were to ensure each function represented a separable idea and that the measure for each was reliable. Accordingly, we conducted a series of factor analyses with items for the six functions. While we initially included many more items than we ultimately used in the measures for each construct, our goal was to build a reliable, valid, and parsimonious measure consisting of approximately five items per function. For expediency, we provide only the final factor solution in Table 5.1.

The first factor ($\alpha = 0.94$, $M = 2.65$, $SV = 1.65$), labeled social-adjustive, captures social reasons for a consumer's relationship with a brand, namely that the brand facilitates social interaction with other people. Sample items include "It helps me fit in with my friends" and "This brand helps me in fitting into important social situations." Second, utilitarian refers to a factor that captures the practical, functional aspect of a brand ($\alpha = 0.96$, $M = 5.92$, $SV = 1.26$) and includes such items as "This brand is handy and works very well" and "This brand has a practical purpose." The next factor, hedonic ($\alpha = 0.96$, $M = 4.65$, $SV = 1.76$), refers to the positive feelings associated with owning or using a particular brand and includes such items as "This brand makes me feel really good when I use it" and "This brand is truly enjoyable to use."

The fourth factor is value-expression and captures the alignment between a person and his or her brand in terms of reflecting identity and values ($\alpha = 0.95$, $M = 4.00$, $SV = 1.78$). Sample items include "There is a good fit between who I am and this brand" and "This brand really reflects the kind of person I am." Affiliation ($\alpha = 0.96$, $M = 3.09$, $SV = 1.90$) concerns the intimate partnership between a person and the brand directly and includes such items as "This brand is like a friend to me" and "I get satisfaction from the close personal tie I have to this brand." Finally, knowledge ($\alpha = 0.90$, $M = 3.14$, $SV = 1.76$) refers to the understanding the relationship provides the consumer about his or her situation and frees the respondent from uncertainty. It includes such items as "This brand helps to make my world more predictable" and "This brand helps make it easier for me to structure and organize my daily life."

92

Table 5.1

Relationship Functions Factor Scores, Summary Statistics

Item: "The reasons I have a relationship with this brand are because . . ."	Component*					
	Social Adj.	Utilitarian	Hedonic	Value Exp.	Affiliation	Knowledge
It is relevant to the people I socialize with.	0.98					
My friends like the brand.	0.93					
It helps me fit in with my friends.	0.93					
It is an important part of my group identity.	0.89					
This brand helps me in fitting into important social situations.	0.75					
This brand is handy and works very well.		0.94				
It functions very well.		0.94				
It is a very practical brand.		0.92				
This brand has a practical purpose.		0.91				
This brand does what it is supposed to do well.		0.91				
Using this brand gives me a lot of pleasure.			0.94			
This brand makes me feel really good when I use it.			0.92			
This brand is truly enjoyable to use.			0.87			
I really like the positive feelings I get from using this brand.			0.86			
I consistently have a positive reaction to using this brand.			0.84			
This brand is consistent with "my true self."				0.92		
This brand really reflects the kind of person I am.				0.89		
This brand is closely related to values that I think are important.				0.89		
There is a good fit between who I am and this brand.				0.82		
I feel like this brand has the same characteristics that I also have.				0.82		
This brand is like a close personal friend to me.					0.97	
I feel like this brand and I are partners.					0.96	
I feel close to this brand.					0.92	
I get satisfaction from the close personal tie I have to this brand.					0.87	
I feel a sense of intimacy with this brand.					0.78	
This brand helps make it easier for me to structure and organize my daily life.						0.99
This brand helps to make my world more predictable.						0.93
This brand facilitates my understanding of what happens in everyday life.						0.71
This brand makes me feel secure and safe in an uncertain world.						0.50
a	0.94	0.96	0.96	0.95	0.96	0.90
M	2.65	5.92	4.65	4.00	3.09	3.14
SV	1.65	1.26	1.76	1.78	1.90	1.76

*Principal components, Promax rotation; n = 515; all loadings > 0.4 reported.

Table 5.2

Summary Statistics for Outcome Measures (n = 515)

Variable	No. items	Reliability	Mean	St. Dev.
Perceived quality	3	0.91	6.05	1.14
Attitude favorability	3	0.97	6.11	1.24
WOM, passive	2	0.74	5.53	1.38
WOM, active	7	0.93	3.07	1.54
Socially responsible	6	0.83	4.99	1.10
Willingness to defend	2	0.80	4.47	1.56

The Effects of Consumer-Brand Relationship Functions

In addition to items relating to consumer-brand relationships, we included a variety of dependent measures, most of which are conventional outcomes that are popular with marketing researchers. These outcomes included perceived quality, attitude favorability, word-of-mouth behavior, perceptions of social responsibility, and willingness to defend the brand. We asked respondents about the perceived quality of the focal brand using three items: low quality–high quality; inferior product–superior product; very bad quality–very good quality (see Keller and Aaker 1992; Agarwal and Teas 2001). We measured attitude favorability with three items: bad–good; unfavorable–favorable; negative–positive (see Batra and Stayman 1990).

We assessed word-of-mouth (WOM) behavior two ways. The first was to assess whether consumers would demonstrate a subdued or passive form of WOM (WOM$_p$), capturing a state of readiness to say positive things about the brand. However, as opposed to an active form, the passive form does not capture specific WOM-related actions. The consumer who demonstrates this state of readiness may, in fact, not actively promote the brand but would likely speak positively about the brand if asked. We used two items to capture this form of WOM: "I have only good things to say about this brand" and "I would recommend this brand to other people."

The second assessment of WOM captured the more active form of recommendation (WOM$_A$). We used seven items to assess this form of WOM. The items focused on a variety of active WOM behaviors and the frequency and extent of detail of these behaviors. Items for the active form of WOM included, "When I tell others about this brand, I tend to talk about it in great detail," "I go out of my way to mention this brand to other people," and "I mention the name of this brand frequently." Summary statistics for outcome measures appear in Table 5.2.

We also wanted to assess the extent to which respondents saw the focal brand as socially responsible. To measure this, we asked respondents to report their perceptions using six items harvested or adapted from previous research (e.g., Sen and Bhattacharya 2001; Bhattacharya and Sen 2003), including "This is a socially responsible brand/company" and "The brand/company is more beneficial to society's welfare than other brands/companies."

Finally, with respect to outcomes, respondents indicated their willingness to defend the brand by responding to a question posing a hypothetical ("Suppose you heard someone you know saying some negative things about this brand?") and then asking the extent to which respondents would "defend the brand by saying positive things about it" "agree with this person about the negative aspects of the brand," and "stand up for the brand by arguing that what this person is saying is not true."

In order to demonstrate the potential contributions of introducing the functional bases of a consumer-brand relationship to marketing, we felt that it was important to demonstrate this contribution while also accounting for the strength or intensity of a relationship, consequently, we had to obtain an effective and fairly broad measure of the latter. Given that there have been many different tactics advanced in the literature to assess the strength of relationships, we include seven of them in our study to ensure that we captured a broad and fair representation of relationship strength. All the items as well as summary statistics are provided in Appendix 5.1.

Specifically, we included new items and items adapted from previous work on involvement (e.g., Zaichkowsky 1985) to assess directly both the existence of a relationship (relationship), as viewed by the consumer, and the strength of that relationship (importance). Items included, "How important is this brand to you?" and "To what extent would you say you have a relationship with this brand?" We also assessed purchase ("purchase") and use ("use") information with items such as, "How often do you purchase this brand?" and "To what extent would you say you use this brand a lot?" We also captured emotional and behavioral components of relationship strength three ways. First, we assessed how committed or loyal consumers were to the brand (commitment; see Aaker, Fournier, and Brasel 2004; Beatty, Kahle, and Homer 1988; Washburn and Plank 2002), how much they trusted the brand ("trust"; Chaudhuri and Holbrook 2001, 2002; Fletcher, Simpson, and Thomas 2000), and how attached they were to the brand ("attachment"; Thomson, MacInnis, and Park, 2005). Our goal with respect to these efforts is not to suggest each of these constructs or components is the same; indeed, in light of previous research, there are important differences between them. Nor are we proposing that one way is better than another—that is clearly beyond the scope of this chapter. However, each does represent a means of assessing the strength of the relationship, whether in terms of buying inertia, experience, cognitions, affect, or behavior and so we include all of them in our analysis. By using such a broad metric of relationship strength, this step also represents a fairly conservative test of the potential contribution of the functions of consumer-brand relationships.

Next, we constructed a measurement model using structural equation modeling in AMOS that would reflect all the consumer-brand relationship functions as well as the outcomes outlined earlier. Our primary aim was to examine the contribution of each relationship function in explaining variance in the six outcomes, while controlling for relationship strength. However, the model we used could also be interpreted as a meditational model with both direct paths between each function and each outcome and indirect paths through relationship strength (see Figure 5.1). All variables with the exception of the dependent measures were modeled as latents reflecting the items corresponding to Table 5.1. The error terms of each predictor were modeled as correlated, and relationship strength was indicated by relationship, importance, purchase, use, trust, commitment,

Figure 5.1   **Conceptual Model**

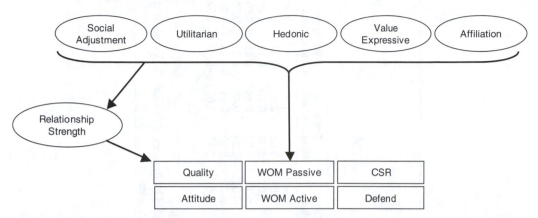

and attachment. The results of the structural equation model appear in Table 5.3. Since all the items loaded significantly on the appropriate latent variables, we shall focus our discussion on the linkages between variables. Also, because the path between knowledge and relationship strength was insignificant, knowledge was dropped from the analysis.

The remaining five functions were all significant predictors of relationship strength (= RS). Specifically, social adjustment negatively predicted RS ($\gamma = -0.19$, $p < .01$) while utilitarian ($\gamma = 0.47$, $p < 0.01$), hedonic ($\gamma = 0.13$, $p < 0.01$), affiliation ($\gamma = 0.41$, $p < 0.01$), and value-expression ($\gamma = 0.38$, $p < 0.01$) all positively predicted RS. In turn, RS was a good predictor of perceptions of quality ($\gamma = 0.87$, $p < 0.01$), attitude favorability ($\gamma = 0.82$, $p < 0.01$), $\mathrm{WOM_P}$ ($\gamma = 0.81$, $p < 0.01$), $\mathrm{WOM_A}$ ($\gamma = 0.32$, $p < 0.01$), social responsibility ($\gamma = 0.58$, $p < 0.01$), and willingness to defend ($\gamma = 0.81$, $p < 0.01$). This result is essentially a replication of a well-established stream of research that jointly reinforces the power of strong consumer-brand relationships (e.g., Fournier 1998; Sheth and Parvatiyar 1995).

While controlling for the effect of RS on the outcomes, the functional bases of these relationships had significant effects on the outcomes. Another way of saying this is that RS does not fully mediate the impact of the functions; there is still substantial unexplained variance in the outcomes that the functions address directly. Specifically, the utilitarian function is a good predictor of consumers' perceived quality ($\gamma = 0.15$, $p < 0.01$) while both affiliation ($\gamma = -0.38$, $p < 0.01$) and value-expression ($\gamma = -0.31$, $p < 0.01$) are significant but negative predictors. Similarly, attitude is negatively influenced by affiliation ($\gamma = -0.36$, $p < 0.01$) and value-expression ($\gamma = -0.29$, $p < 0.01$). With respect to both forms of WOM, there are mixed results. Passive WOM ($\mathrm{WOM_P}$) is predicted positively by utilitarian ($\gamma = 0.17$, $p < 0.01$) and hedonic ($\gamma = 0.11$, $p < 0.04$) functions, but negatively predicted by affiliation ($\gamma = -0.20$, $p < 0.01$) and value-expression functions ($\gamma = -0.24$, $p < 0.01$). The more active form of WOM ($\mathrm{WOM_A}$) is positively predicted by the social adjustment ($\gamma = 0.30$, $p < 0.01$), hedonic ($\gamma = 0.13$, $p < 0.01$), and affiliation ($\gamma = 0.15$, $p < 0.02$) functions. Views of the brand as socially responsible are predicted only by the value-expression function ($\gamma = 0.15$, $p < 0.02$). Finally, a consumer is more willing to

Table 5.3

Key Structural Equation Model Results

From path	Relationship Strength		Perceived Quality		Attitude Favorability		WOM, Passive		WOM, Active		Social Responsibility		Willingness to Defend	
	γ	p <	γ	p <	γ	p <	γ	p <	γ	p <	γ	p <	γ	p <
Relationship strength	—	—	0.87	0.01	0.82	0.01	0.81	0.01	0.32	0.01	0.58	0.01	0.81	0.01
Social adjustment	-0.19	0.01	0.09	0.11	0.04	0.50	-0.01	0.82	0.30	0.01	0.08	0.16	0.19	0.01
Utilitarian	0.47	0.01	0.15	0.01	0.07	0.21	0.17	0.01	-0.07	0.15	0.07	0.18	-0.11	0.05
Hedonic	0.13	0.01	0.05	0.35	0.09	0.16	0.11	0.04	0.13	0.01	-0.04	0.49	0.08	0.18
Affiliation	0.41	0.01	-0.38	0.01	-0.36	0.01	-0.24	0.01	0.15	0.02	-0.12	0.11	-0.14	0.07
Value expression	0.38	0.01	-0.31	0.01	-0.29	0.01	-0.20	0.01	0.03	0.61	0.15	0.02	-0.16	0.02

Chi-square = 2928.71; DF = 621; CMIN/DF = 4.72; NFI = .87; RFI = .84; CFI = .89; RMSEA = .085.

WOM = word of mouth; DF = degrees of freedom; CMIN/DF = minimum sample discrepancy divided by degrees of freedom; NFI = normed fit index; RFI = relative fit index; CFI = comparative fit index; RMSEA = root mean square error of approximation.

defend a brand when his or her relationship with it is based on the social-adjustive ($\gamma = 0.19$, $p < 0.01$) function, but less likely when the relationship is utilitarian ($\gamma = -0.11$, $p < 0.05$) and value-expression-driven ($\gamma = -0.16$, $p < 0.02$). The path between affiliation and willingness to defend is negative but not significant ($\gamma = -0.14$, $p < 0.07$).

DISCUSSION

Fundamentally, our data suggest that the basis of a consumer-brand relationship has an impact on important marketing outcomes, notwithstanding the strength of that relationship, as measured by a series of well-established marketing metrics. Further, strong relationships exist according to a variety of functions and in the pursuit of various consumer-relevant goals. One of the first interesting findings in our data is that relationships that are strong can apparently be based on purely utilitarian goals or functions. That is, the establishment of a strong relationship may follow if a product works really well and in the absence of serving social, value-expression, and other needs. In the marketing literature, there has been much discussion of how brands should facilitate self-expression or service social needs and so on, and it has been suggested that objective performance may be a precondition for the creation of strong bonds (see Fournier 1998), but this result is one of the first to demonstrate that meaningful consumer-brand bonds can be premised on nothing but a brand working really well. Also, using the term "functional" to talk about a brand is challenging because all brands serve some function, goal, or need. The term function may be too broad in the same sense that the knowledge function did not predict strong relationships: the terms probably capture aspects of other functions that, when included in the predictive model, nullify the contribution of the general function. However, when limited to specific aspects such as "handy" and "practical," the utilitarian function indeed plays an important role. Thus, going forward, understanding specific subgoals and being very specific with terminology may better advance our understanding of how relationships operate.

Buying Access

Impression-management concerns negatively predicted strong relationships when other relationship functions were controlled for. On its face, this makes sense from the perspective that a person who uses or buys such a brand may resent it and use it only because it enables more important things—namely acceptance by friends or interaction with other groups. That is, the social adjustment may represent a comparatively shallow goal fraught with both positive and negative emotions. The brand is the ticket that gives the consumer access to certain social benefits, but the consumer may regret the need for that brand as opposed to having access to these benefits directly.

Building a Reputation for Quality

A company that wants to improve the perception of its brand as high in quality appears to be better off simply promoting its utilitarian benefits and actively avoiding efforts to sell the brand's affiliation and value-expression benefits. Consumers who see a brand that is positioning itself in terms of affiliation or value expression may also see these things as a red herring or a smokescreen. This highlights that the marketing profession has in many respects pursued strong relationships on the basis of emotional ties, but has forgotten that so much positioning, advertising, and other tactics amount to secondary window dressing. The heart of marketing is to provide a product or service that works at least modestly well—that is, a product or service that is at least moderately utilitarian or that provides a direct hedonic experience. To be perceived as high quality, firms should first establish or repair objective performance and only later move onto winning friends, managing images, and so on.

Consumers' Selling

If a firm is interested in improving how much and how often consumers talk about its brands (in a positive way), there are several routes it can take. The firm can promote the brand as social-adjustive, hedonistic, or affiliative. Each of these functions has relatively intense, mostly public associations that go very well with more active forms of word of mouth. In some sense, based on our results, the social-adjustive function especially, and to a lesser degree the affiliation function, appear to be best fulfilled by talking about a brand (hence the strong relationship). Furthermore, the hedonic function seems related because positive experiences associated with hedonic features are more likely to lead to an outcome of delight (Chitturi et al. 2007). As such, individuals often like to talk about things that are delightful, more so than just satisfying.

Conversely, value-expression and utilitarian functions do not appear to be effective facilitators. Though it does not have to be, as value-expression is often quite private, a fact that runs counter to the likelihood that a consumer will engage in publicly promoting and selling a brand. It may also be hard for a consumer to become highly enthusiastic about a brand that simply performs its core function well—that is, fulfills a utilitarian function. Chitturi et al. (2007) found that utilitarian features were more likely to lead to satisfaction than delight and that satisfaction was not as good a predictor of WOM as delight was. Consequently, our findings of a positive association between hedonic relationships and WOM and not between utilitarian and WOM are consistent with this perspective. In sum, the main finding was that social-adjustment, hedonic, and affiliation functions associated with a brand greatly assist in setting up consumers to be positive and effusive about that brand.

How to "Be Good"

There are two ways to interpret the finding related to corporate social responsibility. On the one hand, if a firm wants to drive perceptions of its brands as socially responsible, then a major result of our study is that it may be effective to link the brand to consumers' identity. In this case, a brand that expresses the values espoused by a consumer will be perceived as good. No other function seems to work directly in this fashion. If a company wants its brands to be known or seen as ethical, then it would appear to help to associate it with values that the consumer relates to—perhaps because consumers can reaffirm their own values by asserting the ethical nature of the firm, or perhaps because those values are sufficiently important to the consumer that anyone or thing seen to possess those values is regarded positively. While this clearly underscores the need to conduct benefit segmentation and to understand consumer values, it also raises the possibility of some sort of matching hypothesis as far as consumer-brand relationships go. Brands that gain socially responsible reputations are those aligned with identities that match the consumer. On the other hand, it may be that consumers are simply attracted to brands that are socially responsible (as opposed to the relationships themselves providing a biased view of the brand). Either way, this issue is ripe for future research.

CONCLUSION

The objective of this chapter was to undertake the preliminary step of trying to identify and measure various reasons for why consumers form and maintain relationships with brands. Given evidence in other literature, we believed that this understanding was a key missing component of our understanding of consumer-brand relationships. Based on the assumption that consumers develop and maintain relationships, in part, because relationships provide a mechanism that enables consumers to address and achieve several higher-level goals, we were able to identify and develop measures of potential reasons for why consumers formed and maintained relationships with brands. We labeled these reasons as underlying consumer-brand relationship functions.

Given the preliminary nature of our study, our identified consumer-brand relationship functions are clearly not exhaustive. Yet, even in light of this limitation, our preliminary evidence suggests that consumer-brand relationship functions help to provide additional insights concerning important market-related outcomes of the relationships that consumers form with brands. Highlighting the strength of this contribution is that these insights emerge even after accounting for the strength of a consumer-brand relationship.

Clearly, more research is required with respect to consumer-brand relationship functions, especially with respect to refining these functions and their effects on important marketing-related outcomes. While this chapter is only a first step, it serves to demonstrate the extent of the potential contributions that consumer-brand relationship functions bring to marketing. We hope others are just as encouraged by the potential contributions of following this path of research.

Appendix 5.1

Relationship Strength Indicators, Summary Statistics

Component	Item	Statistics*			Correlations**							
		α	M	SV	(1)	(2)	(3)	(4)	(5)	(6)	(7)	(8)
(1) Importance	How important is this brand to you?	0.90	4.86	1.37	—	0.36	0.54	0.58	0.76	0.63	0.48	0.45
	How much do you think about this brand?											
	To what extent would you say this brand is relevant to you?											
	To what extent would you say this brand means a lot to you?											
(2) Purchase	How often do you purchase this brand?	0.90	5.18	1.88	0.36	—	0.46	0.18	0.41	0.43	0.31	0.13
	How many times would you say you have purchased this brand?											
(3) Use	How often do you use this brand?	0.93	5.93	1.36	0.54	0.46	—	0.30	0.50	0.44	0.43	0.16
	To what extent would you say you use this brand a lot?											
(4) Other benefits	To what extent would you say you like this brand for reasons that go beyond its core functional purpose?	0.92	4.61	1.76	0.58	0.18	0.30	—	0.55	0.45	0.32	0.45
	To what extent does this brand provide you with benefits that go beyond it core practical purposes?											
(5) Relationship	To what extent would you say you have a relationship with this brand?	0.95	4.78	1.63	0.76	0.41	0.50	0.55	—	0.61	0.50	0.45
	How strong would you say this relationship is?											

	Items		M	SD	1	2	3	4	5	6	7	8
(6) Commitment	Overall, how important is this relationship to you?	0.89	4.78	1.48	0.63	0.43	0.44	0.45	0.61	—	0.66	0.50
	I am dedicated to this brand.											
	I am committed to this brand.											
	I am devoted to this brand.											
	I consider myself to be highly loyal to this brand.											
	I am very loyal to this brand.											
	I am willing to make small sacrifices in order to keep using this brand.											
	I would be willing to postpone my purchase of this brand if it was temporarily available.											
	I would stick with this brand if it let me down once or twice.											
	I am so happy with this brand that I no longer feel the need to watch out for competitors' alternatives.											
	I am likely to be using this brand one year from now.											
(7) Trust	This brand is trustworthy.	0.97	5.89	1.13	0.48	0.31	0.43	0.32	0.50	0.66	—	0.29
	I can count on this brand.											
	This brand is dependable.											
	This brand is reliable.											
	This brand is credible.											
(8) Attachment	Affectionate, loved, friendly, peaceful, attached, connected, bonded, captivated, passionate, delighted	0.97	3.15	1.77	0.45	0.13	0.16	0.45	0.50	0.45	0.29	—

*n = 515; **all $ps < .01$

REFERENCES

Aaker, Jennifer L., and Susan Fournier (1995). "The Brand as a Character, a Partner and a Person: Three Perspectives on the Question of Brand Personality." In *Advances in Consumer Research,* ed. Frank R. Kardes and Mita Sujan. Provo, UT: Association for Consumer Research, 391–396.

Aaker, Jennifer L., Susan Fournier, and S. Adam Brasel (2004). "When Good Brands Do Bad," *Journal of Consumer Research,* 31 (June), 1–18.

Agarwal, Sanjeev, and R. Kenneth Teas (2001). "Perceived Value: Mediating Role of Perceived Risk," *Journal of Marketing Theory and Practice,* 9 (Fall), 1–14.

Aggarwal, Pankaj (2004). "The Effects of Brand Relationship Norms on Consumer Attitudes and Behavior," *Journal of Consumer Research,* 31 (June), 87–101.

Ahearne, Michael, C.B. Bhattacharya, and Thomas Gruen (2005). "Antecedents and Consequences of Customer-Company Identification: Expanding the Role of Relationship Marketing," *Journal of Applied Psychology,* 90 (3), 574–585.

Ahluwalia, Rohini, Robert E. Burnkrant, and H. Rao Unnava (2000). "Consumer Response to Negative Publicity: The Moderating Role of Commitment," *Journal of Marketing Research,* 37 (May), 203–214.

Aqueveque, Claudio (2005). "Marketing and Market Development: Signaling Corporate Values: Consumers' Suspicious Minds," *Corporate Governance,* 5 (3), 70–81.

Ashmore, R.D., K. Deaux, and T. McLaughlin-Volpe (2004). "An Organizing Framework for Collective Identity: Articulation and Significance of Multidimensionality," *Psychological Bulletin,* 130, 80–114.

Ball, A. Dwayne, and Lori H. Tasaki (1992). "The Role and Measurement of Attachment in Consumer Behavior," *Journal of Consumer Psychology,"* 2, 155–172.

Barnes, James G. (1997). "Closeness, Strength, and Satisfaction: Examining the Nature of Relationships between Providers of Financial Services and Their Retail Customers," *Psychology & Marketing,* 14 (December), 765–791.

Barone, Michael J., Anthony D. Miyazaki, and Kimberly A. Taylor (2000). "The Influence of Cause-Related Marketing on Consumer Choice: Does One Good Turn Deserve Another?" *Journal of the Academy of Marketing Science,* 28 (2), 248–262.

Batra, Rajeev, and Douglas. M. Stayman (1990). "The Role of Mood in Advertising Effectiveness," *Journal of Consumer Research,* 17, 203–214.

Baumeister, Roy F., and Mark R. Leary (1995). "The Need to Belong: Desire for Interpersonal Attachments as a Fundamental Human Motivation," *Psychological Bulletin,* 117 (3), 497–529.

Baumeister, Roy F., J.M. Twenge, and C.K. Nuss (2002). "Effects of Social Exclusion on Cognitive Processes: Anticipated Aloneness Reduces Intelligent Thought," *Journal of Personality and Social Psychology,* 83, 817–27.

Beatty, Sharon E., Lynn R. Kahle, and Pamela Homer (1988). "The Involvement-Commitment Model: Theory and Implications," *Journal of Business Research,* 16 (2), 149–167.

Bergami, Massimo, and Richard P. Bagozzi (2000). "Self-Categorization, Affective Commitment and Group Self-Esteem as Distinct Aspects of Social Identity in the Organization," *British Journal of Social Psychology,* 39, 555–577.

Bhat, Subodh, and Srinivas K. Reddy (1998). "Symbolic and Functional Positioning of Brands," *Journal of Consumer Marketing,* 15 (1), 32–43.

Bhattacharya, C.B., and Sankar Sen (2003). "Consumer-Company Identification: A Framework for Understanding Consumers' Relationships with Companies," *Journal of Marketing,* 67 (April), 76–88.

Bizer, G.Y., and J.A. Krosnick (2001). "Exploring the Structure of Strength-related Attitude Features: the Relation between Attitude Importance and Attitude Accessibility," *Journal of Personality and Social Psychology,* 81, 566–586.

Blackston, Max (2000). "Observations: Building Brand Equity by Managing the Brand's Relationships," *Journal of Advertising Research,* 32 (3), 79–84.

Bowlby, John (1969). *Attachment*. New York, NY: Basic Books.

———— (1979). *The Making and Breaking of Affectional Bonds*. London: Tavistock.

Brown, Lisa M., M.M. Bradley, and P.J. Lang (2006). "Affective Reactions to Pictures of Ingroup and Outgroup Members," *Biological Psychology*, 71, 303–311.

Cacioppo, John T., and Richard E. Petty (1982). "The Need for Cognition," *Journal of Personality and Social Psychology*, 42 (1), 116–31.

Chaudhuri, Arjun, and Morris B. Holbrook (2001). "The Chain of Effects from Brand Trust and Brand Affect to Brand Performance: The Role of Brand Loyalty," *Journal of Marketing*, 65 (2), 81–93.

———— (2002). "Product-class Effects on Brand Commitment and Brand Outcomes: The Role of Brand Trust and Brand Affect," *Journal of Brand Management*, 10 (Sept), 33–58.

Chitturi, Ravindra, Rajagopal Raghunathan, and Vijay Mahajan (2007). "Form Versus Function: How the Intensities of Specific Emotions Evoked in Functional Versus Hedonic Trade-Offs Mediate Product Preferences," *Journal of Marketing Research*, 44 (4), 702–714.

———— (2008). "Delight by Design: The Role of Hedonic Versus Utilitarian Benefits," *Journal of Marketing*, 72 (3), 48–63.

Chung, C.M.Y., and P.R. Darke (2006). "The Consumer as Advocate: Self-Relevance, Culture, and Word-of-Mouth," *Marketing Letters*, 17 (4), 269–279.

Crocker, Jennifer, and Connie T. Wolfe (2001). "Contingencies of Self-Worth," *Psychological Review*, 108 (3), 593–623.

DeBono, Kenneth G. (1987). "Investigating the Social-Adjustive and Value-Expressive Functions of Attitudes: Implications for Persuasion Processes," *Journal of Personality and Social Psychology*, 52 (2), 279–287.

Deci, Edward L., and Richard M. Ryan (2000). "The 'What' and 'Why' of Goal Pursuits: Human Needs and the Self-Determination of Behavior," *Psychological Inquiry*, 11 (4), 227–268.

Delgado-Ballester, Elena, and Jose Luis Munuera-Aleman (2001). "Brand Trust in the Context of Consumer Loyalty," *European Journal of Marketing*, 35 (11/12), 1238–1258.

Dhar, Ravi, and Klaus Wertenbroch (2000). "Consumer Choice between Hedonic and Utilitarian Goods," *Journal of Marketing Research*, 37 (February), 60–71.

Dowling, Graham (2002). "Customer Relationship Management: In B2C Markets, Often Less Is More," *California Management Review*, 44 (3) 87–106.

Downey, Geraldine, Antonio Freitas, Benjamin Michaelis, and Hala Khouri (1998). "The Self-Fulfilling Prophecy in Close Relationships: Rejection Sensitivity and Rejection by Romantic Partners," *Journal of Personality and Social Psychology*, 75 (2), 545–560.

Einwiller, Sabine A., Alexander Fedorikhin, Allison R. Johnson, and Michael A. Kamins (2006). "Enough Is Enough! When Identification No Longer Prevents Negative Corporate Associations," *Journal of the Academy of Marketing Science*, 34 (2), 185–194.

Fajer, Mary T., and John W. Schouten (1995). "Breakdown and Dissolution of Person-Brand Relationships." In *Advances in Consumer Research*, ed. Frank R. Kardes and Mita Sujan. Provo, UT: Association for Consumer Research, 663–667.

Fazio, Russell H. (1989). "On the Power and Functionality of Attitudes: The Role of Attitude Accessibility." In *Attitude Structure and Function*, ed. Anthony R. Pratkanis, Steven J. Breckler, and Anthony G. Greenwald. Hillsdale, NJ: Lawrence Erlbaum, 153–179.

Festinger, Leon (1957). *A Theory of Cognitive Dissonance*. Evanston, IL: Row Peterson.

Fletcher, Garth J.O., Jeffrey A. Simpson, and Geoff Thomas (2000). "The Measurement of Perceived Relationship Quality Components: a Confirmatory Factor Analytic Approach," *Personality and Social Psychology Bulletin*, 26 (3), 340–354.

Fournier, Susan (1998). "Consumers and Their Brands: Developing Relationship Theory in Consumer Research," *Journal of Consumer Research*, 24 (4), 343–373.

Fournier, Susan, and David Glen Mick (1999). "Rediscovering Satisfaction," *Journal of Marketing*, 63 (4), 5–23.

Fournier, Susan, and Julie L. Yao (1997). "Reviving Brand Loyalty: a Reconceptualization within the Framework of Consumer-Brand Relationships," *International Journal of Research in Marketing,* 15 (4), 451–473.

Gregoire, Yany, and Robert J. Fisher (2008). "Customer Betrayal and Retaliation: When Your Best Customers Become Your Worst Enemies," *Journal of the Academy of Marketing Science,* 36 (2), 247–261.

Heatherton, Todd F., and Janet Polivy (1991). "Development and Validation of a Scale for Measuring State Self-Esteem," *Journal of Personality and Social Psychology,* 60 (6), 895–910.

Higgins, E. Tory (1987). "Self-Discrepancy: a Theory Relating Self and Affect," *Psychological Review,* 94 (3), 319–340.

Hirschman, Elizabeth C., and Morris B. Holbrook (1982). "Hedonic Consumption: Emerging Concepts, Methods and Propositions," *Journal of Marketing,* 46 (3), 92–101.

Kashdan, Todd B., Paul Rose, and Frank D. Fincham (2004). "Curiosity and Exploration: Facilitating Positive Subjective Experiences and Personal Growth Opportunities," *Journal of Personality Assessment,* 82 (3), 291–305.

Katz, D. (1960). "The Functional Approach to the Study of Attitudes," *Public Opinion Quarterly,* 24 (2), 163–204.

Keller, Kevin Lane (2001). "Building Customer-Based Equity," *Marketing Management,* 10 (July/August), 14–19.

Keller, Kevin Lane, and David A. Aaker (1992). "The Effects of Sequential Introduction of Brand Extensions," *Journal of Marketing Research,* 29 (1), 35–50.

Kim, Joongsub, and Rachel Kaplan (2005). "Physical and Psychological Factors in Sense of Community," *Environment and Behavior,* 36 (3), 313–340.

Kivetz, Ran, and Itamar Simonson (2002), "Earning the Right to Indulge: Effort as a Determinant of Customer Preferences toward Frequency Program Rewards," *Journal of Marketing Research,* 39 (May), 155–170.

Kleine, Susan Schultz, and Stacey Menzel Baker (2004). "An Integrative Review of Material Possession Attachment," *Academy of Marketing Science Review,* 1, 1–39.

Kyle, Gerard T., and Andrew J. Mowen (2005). "An examination of the Leisure Involvement-Agency Commitment Relationship," *Journal of Leisure Research,* 37 (3), 342–363.

Lassar, Alfried, Banwari Mittal, and Arun Sharma (1995). "Measuring Customer-based Brand Equity," *The Journal of Consumer Marketing,* 12 (4), 11–19.

Leary, Mark R. (1995). *Self-Presentation: Impression Management and Interpersonal Behavior.* Madison, WI: Brown and Benchmark Publishers.

Leary, Mark R., Ellen S. Tambor, Sonja K. Terdal, and Deborah L. Downs (1995). "Self-Esteem as an Interpersonal Monitor: the Sociometer Hypothesis," *Journal of Personality and Social Psychology,* 68 (3), 518–530.

Lemay, Edward P. Jr., and Richard D. Ashmore (2006). "The Relationship of Social Approval Contingency to Trait Self-Esteem: Cause, Consequence, or Moderator?" *Journal of Research in Personality,* 40, 121–139.

Lemon, Katherine N., Roland T. Rust, and Valerie A. Zeithaml (2001). "What Drives Customer Equity," *Marketing Management,* 10 (Spring), 20–25.

Liljander, Veronica, and Inger Roos (2002). "Customer-Relationship Levels—From Spurious to True Relationships," *Journal of Services Marketing,* 16 (7), 593–614.

Losier, G.F., and R. Koestner (1999). "Intrinsic Versus Identified Regulation in Distinct Political Campaigns: the Consequences of Following Politics for Pleasure versus Personal Meaningfulness," *Personality and Social Psychology Bulletin,* 25, 287–298.

Maio, G.R., and J.M. Olson (1995). "Involvement and Persuasion: Evidence for Different Kinds of Involvement," *Canadian Journal of Behavioural Science,* 27, 64–78.

——— (1995b). "Relations Between Values, Attitudes and Behavioral Intentions: The Moderating Role of Attitude Function," *Journal of Experimental Social Psychology,* 31, 266–285.

Maslow, Abraham H. (1954). *Motivation and Personality*. Oxford, UK: Harpers.

Muniz, Albert M., Jr. and Thomas C. O'Guinn (2001), "Brand Community," *Journal of Consumer Research,* 27 (4), 412–431.

Okada, Erica Mina (2005). "Justification Effects on Consumer Choice of Hedonic and Utilitarian Goods," *Journal of Marketing Research,* 42 (1), 43–53.

Oliver, R. (1999). "Whence Consumer Loyalty?" *Journal of Marketing,* 63 (Special Issue), 33–44.

Park, C. Whan, Deborah J. MacInnis, and Bernard J. Jaworski (1986). "Strategic Brand Concept-Image Management," *Journal of Marketing,* 53 (4), 1–23.

Park, C.Whan, and G.W. McClung (1986). "The Effect of TV Program Involvement on Involvement with Commercials." In *Advances in Consumer Research,* ed. Richard Lutz. Provo, UT: Association for Consumer Research, 544–548.

Reichheld, Frederick (1996). "Learning from Customer Defections," *Harvard Business Review,* 74 (2), 56–68.

Rust, Roland T., Tim Ambler, Gregory S. Carpenter, V. Kumar, and Rajendra K. Srivastava (2004). "Measuring Marketing Productivity: Current Knowledge and Future Directions," *Journal of Marketing,* 68 (October), 76–89.

Schlenker, Barry R. (1980). *Impression Management: The Self-Concept, Social Identity, and Interpersonal Relations*. Monterey, CA: Brooks/Cole.

Schlosser, Ann E. (1998). "Applying the Functional Theory of Attitudes to Understanding the Influence of Store Atmosphere on Store Inferences," *Journal of Consumer Psychology,* 7 (4), 345–369.

Sen, Sankar, and C.B. Bhattacharya (2001). "Does Doing Good Always Lead to Doing Better? Consumer Reactions to Corporate Social Responsibility," *Journal of Marketing Research,* 38(2), 225–243.

Sen, Sankar, C.B. Bhattacharya, and Daniel Korschun (2008). "The Role of Corporate Social Responsibility in Strengthening Multiple Stakeholder Relationships: A Field Experiment," *Journal of the Academy of Marketing Science,* 34 (2), 158–166.

Shavitt, Sharon (1989). "Products, Personalities and Situations in Attitude Functions: Implications for Consumer Behavior." In *Advances in Consumer Research,* ed. Thomas K. Srull. Provo, UT: Association for Consumer Research, 300–305.

——— (1990). "The Role of Attitude Objects in Attitude Functions," *Journal of Experimental Social Psychology,* 26, 124–148.

Shavitt, Sharon, and Michelle R. Nelson (2002). "The Role of Attitude Functions in Persuasion and Social Judgment." In *The Persuasion Handbook: Theory and Practice,* ed. J.P. Dillard and M. Pfau. Thousand Oaks, CA: Sage, 137–153.

Sheldon, Kennon M., Andrew J. Elliot, Youngmee Kim, and Tim Kasser (2001). "What Is Satisfying about Satisfying Events? Testing 10 Candidate Psychological Needs," *Journal of Personality and Social Psychology,* 80 (2), 325–339.

Sheth, Jagdish N., and Atul Parvatiyar (1995). "Relationship Marketing in Consumer Markets: Antecedents and Consequences," *Journal of the Academy of Marketing Science,* 23 (4), 255–271.

Shrauger, J. Sidney, and Thomas J. Schoeneman (1979). "Symbolic Interactionist View of Self-Concept: Through the Looking Glass Darkly," *Psychological Bulletin,* 86 (3), 549–573.

Smith, Jessi L., C.L. Morgan, and P.H. White (2005). "Investigating a Measure of Computer Technology Domain Identification: a Tool for Understanding Gender-Differences and Stereotypes," *Educational and Psychological Measurement,* 65, 336–355.

Smith, M. Brewster, Jerome S. Bruner, and Robert W. White (1956). *Opinions and Personality*. Oxford, UK: John Wiley and Sons.

Srivastava, Rajendra K., Tsadduq A. Shervani, and Liam Fahey (1998). "Market-Based Assets and Shareholder Value: A Framework for Analysis," *Journal of Marketing,* 62 (January), 2–18.

Stern, Barbara B. (1997). "Advertising Intimacy: Relationship Marketing and the Services Consumer," *Journal of Advertising,* 26 (4), 7–20.

Stevens, Laura E., and Susan T. Fiske (1995). "Motivation and Cognition in Social Life: A Social Survival Perspective," *Social Cognition,* 13 (3), 189–224.

Thomson, Matthew (2006). "Human Brands: Investigating Antecedents to Consumers' Strong Attachments to Celebrities," *Journal of Marketing,* 70 (July), 104–119.

Thomson, Matthew, Deborah J. MacInnis, and C. Whan Park (2005). "The Ties That Bind: Measuring the Strength of Consumers' Emotional Attachments to Brands," *Journal of Consumer Psychology,* 15 (1), 77–91.

Voss, Kevin E., Eric R. Spangenberg, and Bianca Grohmann (2003). "Measuring the Hedonic and Utilitarian Dimensions of Consumer Attitude," *Journal of Marketing Research,* 40 (3), 310–320.

Washburn, Judith H., and Richard E. Plank (2002). "Measuring Brand Equity: An Evaluation of a Consumer-Based Brand Equity Scale," *Journal of Marketing,* 10 (1), 46–62.

Winer, Russell S. (2001). "A Framework for Customer Relationship Management," *California Management Review,* 43 (4), 89–108.

Zaichkowsky, Judith L. (1985). "Measuring the Involvement Construct," *Journal of Consumer Research,* 12, 341–352.

CHAPTER 6

SELF-BRAND CONNECTIONS

The Role of Reference Groups and Celebrity Endorsers in the Creation of Brand Meaning

JENNIFER EDSON ESCALAS AND JAMES R. BETTMAN

People use products and brands in part to create and represent desired self-images and to present these images to others or to themselves. That is, consumers value psychological and symbolic brand benefits because these benefits can help them construct their self-identity and/or present themselves to others. Brands can be used to construct and cultivate one's self-concept as well as expressing it, either publicly or privately. Brands can be used as tools for social integration or to connect us to the past. Brands act as symbols of personal accomplishment, provide self-esteem, allow one to differentiate oneself and express individuality, and help people through life transitions. In the process of using brands to construct self-identities, the set of brand associations may become linked to the consumer's mental representation of self. We conceptualize and operationalize this linkage at the aggregate level as self-brand connections, the extent to which individuals have incorporated specific brands into their self-concepts. In this chapter, we review the construct of self-brand connections and highlight a series of findings related to the development of self-brand connections.

Our framework is based on the idea that people engage in consumption behavior partly to construct their self-concepts and to create their personal identities (Richins 1994; McCracken 1989; Belk 1988). We examine self-brand connections based on McCracken's (1989) perspective: as consumers construct their self-concept by using brands, they appropriate the symbolic meanings of brands derived in part from cultural sources of meaning, such as celebrities and reference groups. According to McCracken's (1986) theory of meaning movement, symbolic properties of the reference group or celebrity first become associated with the brands they use or endorse. Next, these symbolic meanings are transferred to consumers as they select brands with meanings congruent with their self-concept. When the symbolic properties associated with brands are used to construct the self or to communicate the self-concept to others, a self-brand connection is formed. We provide the first empirical test of the latter implication of McCracken's view.

As shown in Figure 6.1, our research stream examines two cultural sources of brand symbolism: reference groups and celebrity endorsers. In our first series of studies, we focused on different types of reference groups (member groups or ingroups, to which

Figure 6.1   **Cultural Meaning and Self-Brand Connections**

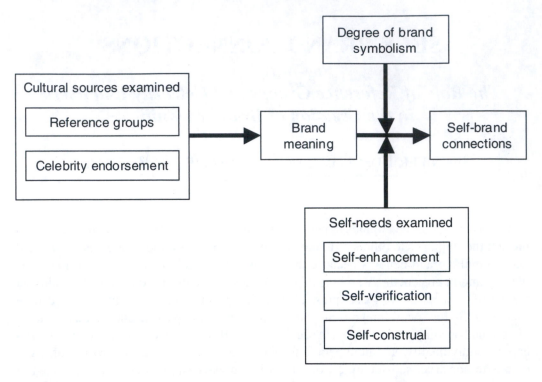

a consumer belongs, aspirational groups, to which a consumer *wishes* to belong, and outgroups, to which a consumer does *not* wish to belong). We find that consumers are more likely to develop a self-brand connection when there is a strong usage association between a reference group and the brand *and* there is a strong connection between the reference group and the consumer's self-concept. When this scenario exists, the consumer may appropriate user imagery and psychological benefit associations of the brand to meet a self-need, leading to a self-brand connection. Further, we find that self-brand connections are lower for brands with images that are consistent with the image of an outgroup compared to brands with images that are inconsistent with an outgroup. We show that these effects are moderated by self-verification, self-enhancement, and self-construal (independent vs. interdependent). We also find that our effects are moderated by degree of brand symbolism, such that brands that communicate something about the user yield stronger effects than brands that do not.

In a second series of studies, we explored the role of celebrity endorsement in the creation of brand meaning and self-brand connections. We found that brands endorsed by celebrities become connected to consumers' self-concepts as they use these brands to define and create themselves. However, the degree to which celebrity usage influences self-brand connections is contingent on an individual's perceived similarity with (or aspiration to be more like) a celebrity. This effect is more pronounced when we threaten participants' self-esteem: they appropriate aspirational celebrity symbolism to bolster their self-esteem after the threat. Our effects are again moderated by degree of brand symbolism, with more symbolic brands having greater effects than less symbolic brands. Taken together, our research provides evidence that consumers use brands to communicate their self-concept, appropriating brand associations that characterize reference groups and celebrities and forming self-brand connections as a result of this process.

SELF-BRAND CONNECTIONS

For a particular individual, there are at least two aspects of what a brand means. First, there's the brand's image, which is primarily a function of marketers' actions and other external influences, such as culture. McCracken's (1986) model of meaning transfer asserts that meanings "get into" a brand through advertising, the fashion system, and other cultural influences. Second, what a brand means to a particular consumer is influenced by his or her personal experiences with the brand. Consumers bring their own life experiences with them to every encounter with a brand or communication about a brand. While theoretically difficult to capture, idiosyncratic aspects of brand meaning are important. Hirschman (1980) found that roughly one-fourth of meaning was idiosyncratic (see also Richins 1994). Rather than approaching "meaning" as a set of specific associations with a brand, the self-brand connection concept allows consumers to ascribe their own meanings to brands and examines the intensity of the relationship between the brand and the consumer's self-concept.

Consumers value products and brands for different reasons. One reason is for a product's instrumental features or attributes, which provide tangible benefits. For example, cars provide transportation, and salt adds flavor to food. On the other hand, sometimes consumers form a special, self-brand connection with products or brands. These brands come to signify more than just the sum of their features. Consumers ascribe these brands with an intrinsic meaning that makes them worth more than the value of their features or instrumental benefits. As an example of special meaning, many people become particularly attached to their first brand of car. The car provides freedom and independence; it is part of a rite of passage into adulthood. Important memories become associated with the car, such as going to the prom or high school graduation. The car may be a used, second-hand vehicle, but if purchased with money from one's first job, it can symbolize accomplishment. Based on any or all of these factors, the consumer may come to associate positive feelings and memories with this brand of automobile. Obviously, the car's functional performance needs to be strong as well, but while many other brands of car may perform well, this particular brand has become incorporated into the consumer's sense of self. It represents a part of who he is and can be used to communicate who he is to others.

How does this meaning become associated with the brand? In order to understand this process, we must recognize that brands have symbolic properties that extend beyond their functional benefits (Levy 1959). As such, brands can be used to meet higher order, psychological needs, such as self-construction, social integration, self-differentiation, and self-presentation (e.g., Kleine, Kleine, and Allen 1995; Richins 1994; Ball and Tasaki

1992; Schultz, Kleine, and Kernan 1989; McCracken 1989; Belk 1988). Aaker (1991) asserts that brands generate value by providing functional, emotional, and self-expressive benefits. Much of consumer research under the information processing paradigm has focused on the functional benefits of brands. The focus of this chapter is on the emotional and self-expressive benefits of brands. Levy (1959) claims that brands, as symbols, take on meaning when they join with, add to, and reinforce the way consumers think about themselves. Thus, in order to study the symbolic benefits of brands, we must be able to measure the relationship between the brand and the consumer's sense of self. This relationship between consumers' self-concepts and brands is referred to as self-brand connections because these brands become associated with, or connected to, consumers' mental representations of self.

Early on, consumer research spent a good deal of effort in examining the congruency between consumer and brand personality; however, the results were disappointing (see Kassarjian 1971; although see Aaker 1997 for more nuanced results). However, consumer researchers have pointed out the connection between brands and self-concepts many times (e.g., Krugman 1965; Csikszentmihalyi and Rochberg-Halton 1981; Belk 1988; Hirschman and LaBarbera 1990; Schultz et al. 1989; Myers 1985). In particular, much consumer research has examined the connection between products and the self through in-depth interviews that examine idiosyncratic relationships between people and things (e.g., Fournier 1998; Zaltman and Higie 1993, Belk, Wallendorf, and Sherry 1989; Wallendorf and Arnould 1988). These studies demonstrate that people become connected to possessions and brands. This chapter extends that body of work by utilizing a scale that measures self-brand connections, which allows us to experimentally examine the nature of these connections.

We propose that the set of brand associations can be more meaningful the more closely it is linked to the self. We conceptualize and operationalize this linkage at the aggregate level of self-brand connections, using the seven-item scale provided in Table 6.1 (Escalas 2004). To achieve their identity goals (Huffman, Ratneshwar, and Mick 2000), people use products and brands to create and represent self-images and to present these images to others or to themselves. As a result of this process, a link bridges the brand and the self. We focus on self-brand connections, rather than specific brand associations, because we believe that brand meaning is most often dependent upon the entire constellation, or gestalt, or the set of brand associations. In sum, the self-brand connection scale comprehensively examines the link between brands and consumers' self-concepts, treating consumers' interactions with brands as a constructive, active process.

We distinguish self-brand connection from the brand relationship research conducted by Susan Fournier (Chapter 1). Fournier identifies six dimensions of brand relationship quality (BRQ). The self-brand connection concept is most similar to the BRQ dimension entitled "self-concept connections" and could be considered a subset of BRQ. However, the major difference between our notion of self-brand connections and the brand relationship approach is that brands in our framework are not construed as active relationship partners. In our approach, brands are vessels of symbolic meaning, with this meaning appropriated by consumers as they use brands' symbolic properties

Table 6.1

Self-Brand Connection Scale Items

1. This brand reflects who I am.
2. I can identify with this brand.
3. I feel a personal connection to this brand.
4. I use this brand to communicate who I am to other people.
5. I think this brand will help me become the type of person I want to be.
6. I consider this brand to be "me" (it reflects who I consider myself to be or the way that I want to present myself to others).
7. This brand suits me well.

Note: Anchored by strongly disagree (0) to strongly agree (100).

to meet self-needs. There is no active role for brands; they are passive instruments. To extend the "life is a stage" metaphor of Goffman (1959), in this chapter brands are considered to be props used by actors for character development rather than as fellow actors. We believe both approaches are valid and worthy of research by academics as well as marketing practitioners.

RESEARCH ON SELF-BRAND CONNECTIONS

McCracken's (1986) model of meaning transfer asserts that meaning originates in the culturally constituted world, moving into goods via the fashion system, word of mouth, reference groups, subcultural groups, celebrities, and the media. For example, meanings can be ascribed to a brand through advertising because ads reference the general cultural symbols needed to provide meaning. Next, meaning moves from goods to consumers, as consumers construct themselves through their brand choices based on congruency between brand image and self-image. Thus, the meaning and value of a brand is not just its ability to express the self, but also its role in helping consumers create and build their self-identities (McCracken 1989).

In a series of studies, our research has provided the first empirical demonstration of McCracken's (1989) ideas by demonstrating that reference group brand usage and celebrity endorsement are sources of symbolic brand meaning. Consumers connect the symbolism associated with the reference group or celebrity and the brands they use or endorse, transferring these meanings from the brand to themselves as they actively construct themselves by selecting brands with meanings relevant to an aspect of their self-concept. Consumers form connections to brands that become meaningful through this process, and self-brand connections measure the extent to which individuals have incorporated such brands into their self-concept (Escalas 2004). We believe that the self-brand connection approach is uniquely well suited to explore how consumers use culturally constituted brand symbolism to construct and communicate their self-concepts. We first review our research on brand symbolism derived from reference groups, followed by our research on celebrity endorsement.

Reference Groups

Reference groups can be a critical source of brand meanings. Consumers use others as a source of information for arriving at and evaluating their beliefs about the world, particularly others who share beliefs and are similar on relevant dimensions. Consumer research on reference groups has demonstrated congruency between group membership and brand usage (e.g., Bearden and Etzel 1982; Bearden, Netemeyer, and Teel 1989; Burnkrant and Cousineau 1975; Childers and Rao 1992; Moschis 1985) and has defined several types of social influence (e.g., Bearden and Etzel 1982; Park and Lessig 1977). Our research explores value-expressive reference group influences, characterized by the need for psychological association with a group either to resemble the group or due to a liking for the group. Our studies demonstrate that brand use by reference groups is a source of brand meaning. Consumers form associations between reference groups and the brands they use and transfer these meanings from brand to self by selecting brands with meanings relevant to an aspect of their current self-concept, or possible self, which is whom they would like to become or whom they are afraid of becoming (Markus and Nurius 1986).

A critical distinction in terms of such self-construction processes is that between the use of brand associations deriving from one's own group (an ingroup) versus groups to which one does not belong (an outgroup). Consumers are likely to accept meanings from brands associated or consistent with an ingroup and reject meanings associated or consistent with an outgroup. For example, if I consider myself to be an intellectual and my member group of intellectuals tends to drive Volvos, I also may choose to drive a Volvo as a symbol of how intellectual I am. As a result, consumers may form self-brand connections to the brands used by reference groups to which they belong (ingroup or member group). On the other hand, consumers may avoid associations derived from groups to which they do not belong (White and Dahl 2006; Berger and Heath 2007).

When outgroup members use a brand, consumers may form associations about the brand that they would not like to have transferred to themselves. Nevertheless, the brand becomes meaningful through the process of avoiding the outgroup symbolism in constructing one's possible self. For example, if I am not a member of a fraternity (and do not desire to be a member) and see fraternity members wearing Polo clothing, I may specifically choose not to wear Polo clothing in an attempt to distance myself from the fraternity symbolism of the Polo brand.

However, if a brand is not typically associated with an ingroup (e.g., its image is incongruent with the group), this may negatively affect self-brand connections. The same identification processes that lead to a connection with a brand associated with an ingroup may lead to rejection of a brand with an image incongruent with the ingroup. On the other hand, if a brand's image does not match an outgroup, the lack of match may actually be viewed favorably, thus leading to enhanced self-brand connections. Thus, continuing with the fraternity example, if a fraternity member would never wear Birkenstocks, I might be more likely to adopt Birkenstocks to distance myself from the fraternity image.

Similarly, consumers may utilize the associations derived from groups to which they would like to belong, that is, aspiration groups. When aspiration groups use a brand, consumers may form associations about the brand that they attempt to transfer to themselves, despite the fact that they are not yet members of the aspiration group. Nevertheless, the brand becomes meaningful in the process of being used to construct one's possible self. For example, if a consumer wishes to be more hip and sees hip people wearing Versace clothing, he or she may choose to wear Versace clothing in an attempt to appropriate the hip associations of that brand.

In one of our earliest experiments (Escalas and Bettman 2003), we instructed student participants to identify both member groups and aspiration groups on their university campus. Participants also rated a series of brands for the extent to which they were likely to be used by each group, as well as completed the self-brand connection items in Table 6.1. Our results demonstrate that consumers are more likely to develop a self-brand connection when there is a strong perceived usage association between the member group and the brand *and* there is a strong connection between the member group and the consumer's self-concept or possible self. The same relationships exist between aspiration groups, brands, and self-brand connections. We believe that consumers are appropriating the meaning of the brand derived from reference group usage in order to meet a self-need, which results in a self-brand connection. Thus, these results provide preliminary support for the theory that consumers use brand symbolism in self-construction processes.

Self-Motivations: Self-Enhancement and Self-Verification

In our model, consumers appropriate symbolic brand associations in order to achieve goals that are motivated by the self, and these associations are linked or connected to the self as a result of this process. Thus, our framework is based on the premise that people are motivated to create a favorable and consistent self-identity and use brands to do so. In order to verify our theoretical framework, we begin by examining the role of two different self-motives that guide behavior to achieve the realization of personal goals: self-enhancement and self-verification.

People are often motivated to create a favorable self-identity and are heavily influenced by the need to maintain and enhance self-esteem (Crocker and Park 2004; Tesser 2000; Greenwald, Bellezza, and Banaji 1988). People are motivated to create a good impression to gain social approval and for the intrinsic satisfaction of projecting a positive self-image, even to oneself (Schlenker 1980). Heine, Proulx, and Vohs (2006) assert that maintenance of self-esteem helps individuals make their lives meaningful. If an individual is guided by self-enhancement goals, that is, seeking feedback that is favorable and creating favorable impressions on others, then we would expect a greater influence of aspiration groups. Self-enhancement would be achieved by creating/projecting an image consistent with groups to which the individual wishes he or she belonged.

In addition to the need for self-enhancement, people often have needs for self-knowledge, including self-verification. In general, people seek out and interpret situations and adopt behavioral strategies that are consistent with their existing self-conceptions. Similarly, they avoid situations and behaviors that yield information contradictory to their existing self-conceptions. If an individual is guided by self-verification goals, that is, seeking accurate feedback regardless of its favorability, then we would expect that he or she would strive to create and/or project a realistic image of himself or herself. An accurate self-image would reflect membership in reference groups to which the individual belongs (i.e., member groups or ingroups).

In a second study (Escalas and Bettman 2003), we asked participants to identify reference groups and rate brands for how likely the groups are to use a particular brand. Participants then rated their self-brand connections to the same set of brands. We also asked participants the extent to which they were motivated to self-enhance and self-verify. The results of this study demonstrate that self-motives play an important role in the self-construction processes used by consumers. Participants motivated to enhance their self-concept reported stronger connections to brands that were used by groups they aspired to belong to, while people motivated to verify their self-concept reported stronger connections to brands used by groups to which they already belonged. By differentiating self-enhancement goals from self-verification goals, we provide some support for the idea that brand symbolism is appropriated from certain reference groups by individuals who construct their self-concepts in a manner consistent with their predominant self-motivations. Individuals with different types of goals appear to be differentially influenced by the member groups versus aspiration groups that provide images with which to create their self-concept. Specifically, self-enhancers can form connections to brands used by aspiration groups to achieve their need to look better to themselves and others, while self-verifiers can form connections to brands used by groups to which they actually belong in order to achieve their goal of verifying or maintaining consistency with their existing self-concept.

Self-Motivation: Self-Construal

Our next set of studies examined how self-construction goals differ depending upon a consumer's self-construal. We proposed that the influence of ingroup and outgroup brand usage differs depending upon whether the consumer has a primarily independent or interdependent self-construal. Although the self-concept often is considered to be distinct from other people's self-concepts, recent cross-cultural evidence suggests that individuals' mental representations of self may depend on social aspects of self, such as relationships with others and membership in social groups (Brewer and Gardner 1996; Markus and Kitayama 1991; Triandis 1989). Such research indicates that on average, Western cultures tend to focus on the personal self, thinking of themselves in terms of unique personal traits and attributes and de-emphasizing others (independent self-construal), whereas Eastern cultures tend to focus on the social self and how the self is related to other people (interdependent self-construal; Markus and Kitayama 1991). These two aspects of self can also coexist within the individual (Aaker and Lee 2001; Brewer and Gardner 1996) and can vary across ethnocultural background within Western society. That is, individuals may have both independent and interdependent aspects of self but may differ in the relative strength of those aspects on a chronic basis, leading to individual differences in self-construal that can be assessed (Singelis 1994).

These differences are important because independent self-construals can lead to different motivations from interdependent self-construals. Independent self-construal goals include both independence (i.e., self-determination) and differentiation (i.e., distinctiveness), whereas interdependent self-construal goals focus on aspects of self shared with some subset of others, enhancing maintenance of relationships (Aaker and Schmitt 2001; Kampmeier and Simon 2001). Kampmeier and Simon (2001) have shown that when the focus is on a comparison to an outgroup, the differentiation aspect of the individual self is emphasized. Thus, for more independent individuals, comparison to the outgroup should lead to a heightened need to differentiate from the outgroup to create a unique self-concept. On the other hand, people with more interdependent self-construals should be more immune to outgroup brand associations, as their primary motivation stems from forming relationships within the ingroup. This implies that a brand associated with the outgroup should lead to lower self-brand connections for more independent individuals than for more interdependent individuals.

In a third study (Escalas and Bettman 2005), we examined the influence of ingroups and outgroups on self-brand connections due to differences in independent and interdependent selves that arise from ethnocultural background differences within the United States. Specifically, we compared Asian and Hispanic consumers to white consumers, based on previous research that showed that Asian- and Hispanic-Americans generally have more interdependent self-construals, while white Americans have more independent self-construals (Aaker and Schmitt 2001; Lee et al. 2000; Markus and Kitayama 1991; Triandis 1989). In this study, we asked participants to identify an ingroup and an outgroup, as well as a brand that was consistent with the image of each group and a brand that was inconsistent with the image of each group. For example, if a participant entered "fraternity members" as a group, he might indicate "Polo" as a consistent brand and "Birkenstock" as an inconsistent brand. Participants also reported their self-brand connections to all four brands entered.

Our results showed that all participants reported stronger self-brand connections for brands with images that are consistent with the image of an ingroup compared to brands with images that are not consistent with an ingroup. The positive effect of ingroup brand associations on self-brand connections was consistent with both assimilation goals for individuals with interdependent self-construals and self-determination goals for those with independent self-construals. We also found that brands consistent with an outgroup were less likely to show a self-brand connection than brands with images inconsistent with the outgroup. This negative effect of outgroup brand associations on self-brand connections was stronger for independent consumers than for interdependent consumers. As Kampmeier and Simon (2001) argue, differentiation needs are more predominant for the independent self when outgroups are the focus. Thus, different self-construals lead to differences in how consumers appropriate brand symbolism from reference groups (in this case, rejection of outgroup images) and form self-brand connections.

Degree of Brand Symbolism

Our basic premise is that consumers appropriate the meaning of brands as they construct their self-identities. However, some brands are better able than others to communicate something about the person using them. For example, prior consumer research proposes that publicly consumed (vs. privately consumed) and luxury (vs. necessity) products are better able to convey symbolic meaning about an individual (Bearden and Etzel 1982). Additionally, a brand that is very popular and used by many different types of people (e.g., a Honda Accord automobile) may not communicate specific associations about the person who uses it. Consumers will be more likely to form self-brand connections to symbolic brands with appropriate associations as they construct their self-identities than with brands that do not communicate much about the self-identity of the user. Conversely, consumers will be more likely to *reject* forming a self-brand connection with symbolic brands with inappropriate associations than with nonsymbolic brands.

In a fourth study (Escalas and Bettman 2005), we used the same methodology as the third study, described above. However, we examined independent-interdependent differences independently of ethnicity by measuring chronic tendencies toward independent and interdependent self-construals (Singelis 1994), and we also asked participants to rate the degree to which the brands they listed were able to communicate something about self-identity as a measure of degree of brand symbolism. Again, we found that consumers reported higher self-brand connections for brands with associations that are congruent with an ingroup compared to those that are incongruent. Additionally, brands that were associated with the image of an outgroup were less likely to show a self-brand connection than brands with images not associated with an outgroup. The negative effect of outgroup brand associations on self-brand connections only occurs for independent consumers and not for interdependent consumers, which replicates the findings from our third study.

Furthermore, differences in self-construal were more pronounced with symbolic brands compared to nonsymbolic brands. In the case of ingroup brand associations, the positive effect of ingroup brand usage on self-brand connections was more pronounced for those brands that were perceived to communicate something about the brand's user, compared to brands that were not. Furthermore, the negative effect of outgroup brand usage on self-brand connections was driven entirely by symbolic brands. Only symbolic brands were used to differentiate the individual from an outgroup: brands that were not perceived as communicating much about the brand's user did not show a negative effect from outgroup associations. The finding that the degree of symbolism moderates the effect of reference group usage on self-brand connections provides additional evidence that consumers use brands to communicate their self-concepts to others.

Celebrity Endorsement

Another source of brand symbolism is celebrity endorsements (McCracken 1989). Our framework proposes that consumers may also appropriate the brand symbolism arising from celebrity endorsement to construct and communicate their self-concepts. There is a critical distinction, in terms of self-construction processes, between brand associations derived from celebrities with whom consumers identify or feel an affinity and associations derived from celebrities that consumers do not like or do not perceive as being similar to themselves. Consumers are likely to accept meanings from brands associated or consistent with a celebrity whom they perceive as similar to themselves or whom they aspire to emulate and to reject meanings associated or consistent with a celebrity who does not represent who they are or whom they would like to become.

For example, a consumer may consider himself to be athletic and hip, like David Beckham, who currently endorses many brands, including Adidas and Police sunglasses. Due to his aspiration to be more like Beckham (i.e., to appropriate Beckham's "meanings" for use in constructing himself), the consumer may choose to play soccer in Adidas gear and wear Police sunglasses when not on the field. As a result, he may form a self-brand connection to these brands endorsed by Beckham, which helps construct his self-concept around the images of being athletic and hip and communicates that self-image to others.

On the other hand, consumers may avoid associations derived from celebrities with images they do not aspire to obtain. When such a celebrity endorses a brand, consumers may form associations about the brand that they would not like to have transferred to themselves. Nevertheless, the brand becomes meaningful through the process of avoiding the celebrity symbolism in constructing one's possible self. For example, if a consumer rejects the associations of Paris Hilton and she endorses Carl's Jr., that consumer may specifically choose not to eat at Carl's Jr. in an attempt to reject (distance himself from) the symbolism associated with Paris Hilton. Thus, the specific symbolism associated with a celebrity will have an impact on the effectiveness of the celebrity's endorsement. Consumers will be motivated to appropriate the symbolic associations of celebrities they aspire to emulate, but reject the symbolic associations of celebrities they do not.

McCracken's (1989) view also suggests that a symbolic "match" should exist between the celebrity image and the brand image in order for the celebrity endorsement to be effective. A generic, well-liked celebrity endorsement will not have the same "punch" as a celebrity endorsement in which the image of the celebrity matches the image of the brand. For example, if David Beckham were to endorse Sears, or Paris Hilton to endorse Saturn, the symbolic mismatch would dampen the endorsement's favorable or unfavorable effect. Even if a consumer aspires to be like David Beckham or rejects Paris Hilton, the effect of a mismatched celebrity-brand endorsement will be less powerful than a matched celebrity-brand endorsement.

Our first celebrity study (Escalas and Bettman 2008) used a methodology similar to that used to study reference groups. Respondents were members of the eLab online panel; they entered their most and least favorite celebrities, along with one brand each celebrity endorsed in an Internet-based survey. We found that consumers reported higher self-brand connections for brands with images that were consistent with the image of a celebrity that they aspired to be like, but lower self-brand connections when consumers did not aspire to be like the celebrity. This effect was more pronounced when the brand image was congruent with the celebrity's image; that is, when there was a symbolic "match" between the celebrity and the brand, the effect of a favorable celebrity endorsement was more positive (however, the effect of an unfavorable celebrity endorsement only directionally more negative).

Degree of Brand Symbolism

In this same study, we also looked again at the idea that consumers will be more likely to form self-brand connections to symbolic brands than to brands that do not communicate much about the self-identity of the user. Conversely, we predict that consumers will be more likely to *reject* forming a self-brand connection with symbolic brands associated with a disliked celebrity than with nonsymbolic brands. Our study results find that the effects of celebrity endorsement were moderated by the degree to which the brand was perceived to communicate something about the brand's user. When a well-liked celebrity's image matched the brand image being endorsed, the endorsement was *most* beneficial for a brand that was perceived as being able to communicate the brand user's image to others. On the other hand, the negative effect of a disliked celebrity is more negative in the cases where a symbolic brand is endorsed. Thus, celebrity endorsements can be an effective marketing strategy when the celebrity image, brand image, and consumer aspirations are taken into consideration, particularly for symbolic brands.

Self Motivation: Threat to Self-Esteem

In our framework, celebrity-based brand associations can help consumers achieve goals that are motivated by the self, such as self-construction and self-enhancement. Consumers construct their self-concepts in a manner consistent with their predominant or currently activated self-motivations. Thus, our theory implies that celebrity endorsement effects will be stronger when self-needs relevant to constructing one's self-identity are high. In our final study, we once again explore self-enhancement needs. We've already shown that consumers with strong self-enhancement goals tend to form self-brand connections to brands used by aspiration groups. We believe a similar process is at work with celebrity endorsement. A consumer may appropriate symbolic brand meaning derived from a celebrity who has characteristics that the consumer aspires to possess in order to self-enhance.

Research shows that self-enhancement is particularly desired after a threat to the self (Leary et al. 1995; Tesser and Cornell 1991; Steele 1988): people engage in self-enhancement in response to a threat to the self as they attempt to repair their self-esteem (Steele 1988). Therefore, the activation of self-enhancement goals by a threat to the self should increase the extent to which celebrity endorsement influences self-brand connections. We expect that consumers who have active self-enhancement motives will be more likely to form self-brand connections to brands that are endorsed by a celebrity that they aspire to be like. On the other hand, self-enhancers will be more likely to reject brand associations created by a celebrity endorsement where the celebrity associations are rejected (e.g., the Paris Hilton example), compared to consumers who do not have active self-enhancement goals.

Our final study was also conducted online with the eLab panel (Escalas and Bettman 2008). Participants rated six celebrities from most favorite to least favorite; half then saw their second most versus second least favorite celebrity in a print ad endorsing a fictitious watch brand. Self-esteem was threatened for participants high in U.S. national identity by having them read a negative article about America. We found that the effect of celebrity endorsement on self-brand connections was augmented when consumers' self-esteem was threatened, in both the positive aspirational celebrity condition and the negative nonaspirational celebrity condition, compared to consumers who did not have active self-enhancement goals. Thus, consumers self-enhance by building connections to favorable celebrity images or distancing themselves from unfavorable celebrity images. This finding demonstrates that consumers are motivated by their self-needs to utilize brand associations derived from celebrity endorsement in a contingent fashion to construct and present their self-identities.

CONCLUSION

In this chapter, we developed a conceptual framework that highlights why people develop a personal connection to certain brands. The basic premise is that brands can become incorporated into one's mental representation of self by serving some purpose, such as creating a certain self-image, representing a part of the self that one wishes to communicate to others, establishing a social tie, and so on. Our empirical research tested this process of symbolic meaning movement from two cultural sources of meaning, reference groups and celebrities, to the brand and to the consumer, resulting in a self-brand connection.

Summary of Research Findings

In our reference group research, we found that consumers are more likely to develop a self-brand connection when there is a strong usage association between a reference group and the brand *and* there is a strong connection between the reference group and the consumer's self-concept. When this scenario exists, the consumer may appropriate user imagery and psychological benefit associations of the brand to meet a self-need, such as self-enhancement or self-verification. In the case of self-verifiers, member groups have a larger effect on self-brand connections, while for self-enhancers, the effect of aspiration groups on self-brand connections is greater. We believe that this finding is an important demonstration that consumers are motivated by their self-needs to utilize brand associations derived from different types of groups to construct their self-concepts: consumers behave consistently with their predominant self-motivations.

Our studies also show that consumers report higher self-brand connections for brands with images that are consistent with the image of an ingroup compared to brands with images that are inconsistent with the image of an ingroup. Further, we find that self-brand connections are lower for brands with images that are consistent with the image of an outgroup compared to brands with images that are inconsistent with an outgroup. In these studies, we also find that independent versus interdependent self-construals interact with our congruency findings to determine the level of self-brand connections: the negative effect of outgroup brand associations on self-brand connections is stronger for independent consumers than for interdependent consumers, due to the stronger needs of more independent consumers to differentiate themselves from outgroups (Kampmeier and Simon 2001). We also find that our effects are moderated by degree of brand symbolism, such that brands that communicate something about the user yield stronger effects than brands that do not.

Finally, in our research on celebrity endorsement, we argue that consumers appropriate brand meanings from celebrity endorsement to construct their self-concepts. Our studies show that consumers report higher self-brand connections for brands with images that are consistent with the image of a celebrity that they aspire to be like, particularly in the case when the image of the celebrity and the brand match. We also find that our celebrity endorsement effects are moderated by brand symbolism, such that brands that communicate something about the user yield stronger effects than brands that do not. Finally, we find that for consumers with active self-enhancement goals, the effect of celebrity endorsement on self-brand connections is stronger, both more positive in the aspirational celebrity condition and more negative in the nonaspirational celebrity condition, compared to consumers who do not have active self-enhancement goals. Thus, our research stream empirically demonstrates McCracken's (1986) theory of meaning movement. In particular, we study the effects of two cultural sources of meaning, reference groups and celebrities, on self-brand connections and show important moderators of those effects. These studies begin to capture the complex and important relationship between brands and consumers' conception of self (see Figure 6.1).

Directions for Future Research

We have focused on the antecedents of self-brand connections, but it is also important to study the consequences of self-brand connections. For example, to the degree that a self-brand connection is formed, a consumer's attitude toward the target brand will likely be affected. If a consumer's first car was a Honda and he has formed a positive self-brand connection to Honda, then he will have a very favorable and robust attitude toward Honda automobiles. This connection may also have an impact on behavioral intentions. When his Honda Civic wears out, the consumer may plan on buying a Honda Accord. Other forms of consumer behavior may also be affected by a self-brand connection. The consumer connected to Honda may pay more attention to Honda advertisements and new product introductions. He may interpret the performance of his Civic more favorably because Honda means so much to him. And he may tell all his friends about how great his experience with Honda has been. Future research could explore the consequences of self-brand connections, which include effects on attitudes toward the brand, behavioral intentions toward the brand, and actual behavior toward the brand.

Additionally, the set of associations consumers have about a brand is an important component of brand equity (Keller 1993), and we believe that forming a self-brand connection is a psychological manifestation of such equity at the consumer level. For example, future research can explore the idea that self-brand connections may lead to robust brand attitudes, that is, attitudes that are not very susceptible to change. Consumers who have used brand associations to construct their self-identities may be more forgiving of marketer blunders, such as a poor advertising campaign or a temporary product quality problem. They may also be more brand loyal and less likely to switch to competitors' brands in response to price cuts, special displays, bundling tactics, and coupons. Therefore, the notion that consumers form a link to a brand as they use the brand's associations for self-construction is important to marketing managers. When consumers' self-concepts are linked to a brand, then the company behind the brand may be able to gain an enduring competitive advantage, because this type of connection is difficult for competitors to imitate.

The self-brand connection framework has implications for marketing managers. The attitudinal, intentional, and behavioral implications of a positive self-brand connection to their brand are very favorable. Therefore, marketers should try to build self-brand connections. In order to do so, they must know if their brand meets any psychological needs. This implies a thorough understanding of the target consumer. While it may be more difficult for marketers to measure the immediate effectiveness of marketing tactics on a long-term construct such as self-brand connections, the rewards of making the effort to do so are great because self-brand connections lead to committed consumers. When consumers have a self-brand connection, then the company behind the brand can gain an enduring competitive advantage. Although competitors may easily copy a positively regarded product attribute or feature, a self-brand connection creates a bond that may be difficult to break. Thus, research demonstrating these effects would have an important impact on both marketing theory and practice.

REFERENCES

Aaker, David A. (1991). *Managing Brand Equity: Capitalizing on the Value of a Brand Name.* New York, NY: The Free Press.

Aaker, Jennifer L. (1997). "Dimensions of Brand Personality," *Journal of Marketing Research,* 34 (3), 347–356.

Aaker, Jennifer L., and Bernd Schmitt (2001). "Culture-Dependent Assimilation and Differentiation of the Self: Preferences for Consumption Symbols in the United States and China," *Journal of Cross-Cultural Psychology,* 32 (September), 561–576.

Aaker, Jennifer L., and Angela Y. Lee (2001). "'I' Seek Pleasures and 'We' Avoid Pains: The Role of Self-Regulatory Goals in Information Processing and Persuasion," *Journal of Consumer Research,* 28 (June), 33–49.

Ball, A. Dwayne, and Lori H. Tasaki (1992). "The Role and Measurement of Attachment in Consumer Behavior," *Journal of Consumer Psychology,* 1 (2), 155–172.

Bearden, William O., and Michael J. Etzel (1982). "Reference Group Influence on Product and Brand Purchase Decisions," *Journal of Consumer Research,* 9 (September), 183–194.

Bearden, William O., Richard G. Netemeyer, and Jesse E. Teel (1989). "Measurement of Consumer Susceptibility to Interpersonal Influence," *Journal of Consumer Research,* 15 (March), 473–481.

Belk, Russell W. (1988). "Possessions and the Extended Self," *Journal of Consumer Research,* 15 (September), 139–168.

Belk, Russell W., Melanie Wallendorf, and John F. Sherry Jr. (1989). "The Sacred and the Profane in Consumer Behavior: Theodicy on the Odyssey," *Journal of Consumer Research,* 16 (March), 1–38.

Berger, Jonah, and Chip Heath (2007). "Where Consumers Diverge from Others: Identity Signaling and Product Domains," *Journal of Consumer Research,* 34 (2), 121–134.

Brewer, Marilynn B., and Wendi Gardner (1996). "Who Is This 'We'? Levels of Collective Identity and Self Representations," *Journal of Personality and Social Psychology,* 71 (July), 83–93.

Burnkrant, Robert E., and Alain Cousineau (1975). "Informational and Normative Social Influence in Buyer Behavior," *Journal of Consumer Research,* 2 (December), 206–215.

Childers, Terry L., and Akshay R. Rao (1992). "The Influence of Familial and Peer-based Reference Groups on Consumer Decisions," *Journal of Consumer Research,* 19 (September), 198–211.

Crocker, Jennifer, and Lora E. Park (2004). "The Costly Pursuit of Self-Esteem," *Psychological Bulletin,* 130, 392–414.

Csikszentmihalyi, Mihaly, and Eugene Rochberg-Halton (1981). *The Meaning of Things: Domestic Symbols and the Self,* Cambridge, UK: Cambridge University Press.

Escalas, Jennifer Edson (2004). "Narrative Processing: Building Consumer Connections to Brands," *Journal of Consumer Psychology,* 14 (1 and 2), 168–179.

Escalas, Jennifer Edson and James R. Bettman (2003). "You Are What They Eat: The Influence of Reference Groups on Consumer Connections to Brands," *Journal of Consumer Psychology,* 13 (3), 339–348.

——— (2005). "Self-Construal, Reference Groups, and Brand Meaning," *Journal of Consumer Research,* 32 (December), 378–389.

——— (2008). "Connecting with Celebrities: Celebrity Endorsement, Brand Meaning, and Self-Brand Connections." Working paper.

Fournier, Susan (1998). "Consumers and Their Brands: Developing Relationship Theory in Consumer Research," *Journal of Consumer Research,* 24 (March), 343–373.

Goffman, Erving (1959). *The Presentation of Self in Everyday Life.* Garden City, NY: Doubleday & Company, Inc.

Greenwald, Athony G., Felipe S. Belleza, and Mahzarin R. Banaji (1988). "Is Self-Esteem a Central Ingredient of the Self-Concept?" *Personality and Social Psychology Bulletin,* 14, 34–45.

Heine, Steven J., Travis Proulx, and Kathleen D. Vohs (2006). "The Meaning Maintenance Model: On the Coherence of Social Motivation," *Personality and Social Psychology Review,* 10 (2), 88–110.

Hirschman, Elizabeth C. (1980). "Commonality and Idiosyncrasy in Popular Culture: An Empirical Examination of the 'Layers of Meaning' Concept." In *Symbolic Consumer Behavior: Proceedings of the Conference on Consumer Esthetics and Symbolic Consumption,* ed. Elizabeth C. Hirschman and Morris B. Holbrook. Provo, UT: Association for Consumer Research.

Hirschman, Elizabeth C., and Priscilla A. LaBarbera (1990) "Dimensions of Possession Importance," *Psychology & Marketing,* 7 (3), 215–233.

Huffman, Cynthia, S. Ratneshwar, and David G. Mick (2000). "Consumer Goal Structures and Goal-Determination Processes: An Integrative Framework." In *The Why of Consumption: Perspectives on Consumer Motives, Goals, and Desires,* ed. R. Ratneshwar, D.G. Mick, and C. Huffman. New York, NY: Routledge Press, 9–35.

Kampmeier, Claudia, and Bernd Simon (2001). "Individuality and Group Formation: The Role of Independence and Differentiation," *Journal of Personality and Social Psychology,* 81 (September), 448–462.

Kassarjian, Harold H. (1971). "Personality and Consumer Behavior: A Review," *Journal of Marketing Research,* 8 (November), 146–153.

Keller, Kevin Lane (1993). "Conceptualizing, Measuring, and Managing Customer-Based Brand Equity," *Journal of Marketing,* 57 (January), 1–22.

Kleine, Susan Schultz, Robert E. Kleine III, and Chris T. Allen (1995). "How Is a Possession 'Me' or 'Not Me'? Characterizing Types and Antecedents of Material Possession Attachment," *Journal of Consumer Research,* 22 (December), 327–343.

Krugman, Herbert E. (1965). "The Impact of Television Advertising: Learning without Involvement," *Public Opinion Quarterly,* 30, 349–356.

Leary, Mark R., Ellen S. Tambor, Sonja K. Terdal, and Deborah L. Downs (1995). "Self-Esteem as a Interpersonal Moniter: The Sociometer Hypothesis," *Journal of Personality and Social Psychology,* 68 (3), 518–530.

Lee, Angela Y., Jennifer L. Aaker, and Wendi L. Gardner (2000). "The Pleasures and Pains of Distinct Self-Construals: The Role of Interdependence in Regulatory Focus," *Journal of Personality and Social Psychology,* 78 (June), 1122–1134.

Levy, Sidney J. (1959). "Symbols for Sale," *Harvard Business Review,* 37 (July-August), 117–24.

Markus, Hazel, and Shinobu Kitayama (1991). "Culture and the Self: Implications for Cognition, Emotion, and Motivation," *Psychological Review,* 98 (April), 224–253.

Markus, Hazel, and Paula Nurius (1986). "Possible Selves," *American Psychologist,* 41 (September), 954–969.

McCracken, Grant (1986). "Culture and Consumption: A Theoretical Account of the Structure and Movement of the Cultural Meaning of Consumer Goods," *Journal of Consumer Research,* 13 (June), 71–84.

———(1989). "Who Is the Celebrity Endorser? Cultural Foundations of the Endorsement Process," *Journal of Consumer Research,* 16 (December), 310–321.

Moschis, George P. (1985). "The Role of Family Communication in Consumer Socialization of Children and Adolescents," *Journal of Consumer Research,* 11 (March), 898–913.

Myers, Elizabeth (1985). "Phenomenological Analysis of the Importance of Special Possessions: An Exploratory Study," *Advances in Consumer Research,* 12, 560–565.

Park, C. Whan, and V. Parker Lessig (1977). "Students and Housewives: Differences in Susceptibility to Reference Group Influence," *Journal of Consumer Research,* 4 (September), 102–210.

Richins, Marsha L. (1994). "Valuing Things: The Public and Private Meanings of Possessions," *Journal of Consumer Research,* 21 (December), 504–521.

Schlenker, Barry R. (1980). *Impression Management: The Self-Concept, Social Identity, and Interpersonal Relations.* Monterey, CA: Brooks/Cole.

Schultz, Susan E., Robert E. Kleine III, and Jerome B. Kernan (1989). "'These Are a Few of My Favorite Things': Toward an Explication of Attachment as a Consumer Behavior Construct," *Advances in Consumer Research,* 16, 359–366.

Singelis, Theodore M. (1994). "The Measurement of Independent and Interdependent Self-Construals," *Personality and Social Psychology Bulletin,* 20 (October), 580–591.

Steele, Claude M. (1988). "The Psychology of Self-Affirmation: Sustaining the Integrity of the Self." In *Advances in Experimental Social Psychology,* ed. L. Berkowitz. New York, NY: Academic Press, 21, 261–302.

Tesser, Abraham (2000). "On the Confluence of Self-Esteem Maintenance Mechanisms," *Personality and Social Psychology Review,* 4, 290–299.

Tesser, Abraham, and David P. Cornell (1991). "On the Confluence of Self Processes," *Journal of Experimental Social Psychology,* 27 (6), 501–526.

Triandis, Harry C. (1989). "The Self and Behavior in Differing Cultural Contexts," *Psychological Review,* 96 (July), 506–520.

Wallendorf, Melanie, and Eric J. Arnould (1988). "'My Favorite Things': A Cross-Cultural Inquiry into Object Attachment, Possessiveness, and Social Linkage," *Journal of Consumer Research,* 14 (March), 531–547.

White, Katherine, and Darren W. Dahl (2006). "To Be or Not Be? The Influence of Dissociative Reference Groups on Consumer Preferences" *Journal of Consumer Psychology,* 16 (4), 404–414.

Zaltman, Gerald, and Robin A. Higie (1993). "Seeing the Voice of the Consumer: The Zaltman Metaphor Elicitation Technique." Marketing Science Institute Working Paper, report no. 93–114.

CHAPTER 7

WHEN BRANDS ARE BUILT FROM WITHIN

A Social Identity Pathway to Liking and Evaluation

AMERICUS REED II, JOEL B. COHEN, AND AMIT BHATTACHARJEE

Social identity is represented by the collection of labels that consumers use to express who they are. These labels are numerous and fluid, varying over a consumer's lifetime and across consumption situations. From demographics (e.g., African American), social roles (e.g., parent), and shared consumption patterns (e.g., dieters), to identifiers created by marketers (e.g., Pepsi generation), there are a multitude of ways in which consumers can express their identities and distinguish themselves from others. Consumers are attracted to products and brands that are linked to actual and, particularly, desired social identities (Reed 2004; Forehand, Deshpande, and Reed 2002; Stayman and Deshpande 1989). This happens for many reasons. For example, the brand or product may symbolize the consumer's personality traits (Aaker 1997), may reflect or support a desirable self-image, or may embody the "type" of person that the consumer aspires to think, feel, and be like (Belk, Bahn, and Mayer 1982; cf. Levy 1959). Products and brands can even boost esteem through self-enhancement (Sedikides and Strube 1997) and self-verification (Kleine, Kleine, and Allen 1995).

The outcome of symbolic, social identity-based preferences is often observed in marketing practice and frequently attributed at least partially to the success of many flagship brands and category leaders (e.g., Nike, Harley Davidson, Starbucks, Apple, Marlboro, Budweiser, Ikea, Jeep, MTV, Facebook). Strategists position brands and products to reflect a particular social identity–oriented lifestyle[1] in order to prompt more favorable judgments from consumers who either possess or identify with that social identity (Reed 2004) and to create a "deeper" sense of loyalty (Oliver 1999).

Underlying deeply loyal behavioral responses toward these brands is a systematic evaluative response—that is, a positive attitude. We posit that these positive attitudes stem from a markedly different formation and recruitment process, based on a consideration of the attitude object in relation to the self rather than object-based associations such as attributes or brand similarities (e.g., Cohen and Reed, 2006a). If these attitudes are "different" in any appreciable way from object/brand-based attitudes, and if marketers wish to encourage consumers to form strong, positive attitudes on the basis of a belief about who they are or want to become, then it will be important to understand this process and to consider its implications for marketing and brand management.

The idea that a consumer's sense of who they are should relate to purchase decisions has been widely discussed. It is well established that a consumer's identity sometimes motivates the formation and expression of identity-oriented beliefs, and, more importantly, the selection (avoidance) (see Berger and Heath 2008) of constellations of products and services that reinforce the desired (undesired) identity (Kleine, Kleine, and Kernan 1993; Laverie, Kleine, and Kleine 2002; Forehand et al. 2002; Reed 2004). How and why social identity plays a substantial role in brand evaluations in some cases and not others is less well understood. Shavitt (1990) insightfully linked certain brand attitudes to a "value-expressive" function earlier identified by attitude theorists (Katz 1960; Smith, Bruner, and White 1956). Perhaps such identity-based judgments are "socially anchored" (McGarty et al. 1994; Pilkington and Lydon 1997), thereby leading to further reinforcement within social networks comprising others who also share that attitude (Visser and Mirabile 2004); this would make them particularly resistant to change (Bolton and Reed 2004).

However, very little research in marketing has systematically examined the process of how social identity–based attitudes are formed and the potential advantages that may accrue to these kinds of evaluative judgments (for exceptions see Forehand et al. 2002; Reed 2004; Bolton and Reed 2004). Moreover, little work has addressed the *strategic implications* of when and how brand judgments are impacted by identity processes. This is an important area in marketing because *product positioning* can occur around attributes and key features, versus being positioned around a social identity–based lifestyle (see Reed and Bolton 2005).

The purpose of this chapter is to set forth a more detailed conceptual analysis of how attitudes come to be formed "based on" social identity, and what the implications of this pathway to evaluation are for branding and marketing. The first part of this chapter describes how attitudes, once generated, are assessed for behavioral reliance (Cohen and Reed 2006a). We focus on particular factors that affect how social identity–based attitudes accrue (1) clarity and coherence through an initial metacognitive assessment we term *representational sufficiency* and (2) appropriateness for particular behavioral applications through a subsequent assessment we term *functional sufficiency* (see Cohen and Reed 2006a). The second part of this chapter relies on recent work in social identity theory (Bolton and Reed 2004; Forehand et al. 2002; Reed 2004) to describe and illustrate a social identity pathway to liking and evaluation. The last portion of this chapter focuses on implications for brand managers who either seek to position start-up brands or reposition existing brands. We conclude with the special case of co-branding alliances (see Verrochi and Reed 2008) in which two brand identities must be simultaneously managed to create favorable evaluations toward the co-branded effort. Along the way, we illustrate our points by summarizing past research and also by referring to and describing our own ongoing preliminary work in this area.

A MODEL OF ATTITUDE GENERATION AND RECRUITMENT

Cohen and Reed's (2006a) Multiple Pathway Anchoring and Adjustment (MPAA) model discusses alternative pathways to attitude formation and the process by which consumers rely on attitudes (or don't) when they decide to act in a particular way. A long-standing tradition in marketing has assumed that consumer attitudes toward branded products typically result from an assessment of each product's attributes, derived benefits, positive reaction to associated advertising, spokespeople, and so on. The "raw material" for such evaluations (i.e., the object itself) lies outside the person. Cohen and Reed (2006a) make the case that attitudes can also be formed based primarily on "inside-out" social identity–based evaluations of people, issues, and objects, such as branded products. In the second part of their model they explain that subsequent behavior does not follow directly from retrieval of attitudes, regardless of how they were formed. Their MPAA model lays out a process through which consumers rely on retrieved attitudes that may be formed on the basis of social identity, modify those attitudes by integrating other relevant information into them, or reject those attitudes in favor of a more context-driven evaluation of perceived alternatives.

The Prevailing View

The correspondence principle (Fishbein and Ajzen 1975; Ajzen and Fishbein 2005) for predicting behavior (i.e., predictive attitudes should fully correspond to the details of the behavior—donating $100 to a presidential candidate within the next thirty days, versus general attitudes toward that politician) provides very helpful measurement advice. However, it is difficult to imagine consumers storing and retrieving an almost infinite array of such action-specific attitudes. So, current process-oriented models that intend to describe how and when attitudes guide behavior and promote resistance to persuasion have moved in a different direction. Despite nuances of meaning and preferences for particular measures and manipulations, a consensus has emerged that strong and favorable attitudes, held with sufficient certainty, not only confer resistance to attitude change attempts but also produce attitude-consistent behavior. Tormala and Rucker (2007) define attitude certainty as follows:

> Whereas an attitude refers to one's evaluation of something (e.g., the extent to which one likes a person, favors a brand, or supports a policy), attitude certainty refers to the subjective sense of conviction one has about one's attitude, or the extent to which one is confident or sure of one's attitude (p. 469, citations deleted).

They add:

> Attitude certainty is considered to be a dimension of attitude strength, where attitude strength is defined as the durability and impactfulness of an attitude. In general, strong attitudes are more durable and impactful than are weak attitudes. Compared to weak attitudes, then, strong attitudes are more likely to guide behavior, more likely to resist influence attempts, and more likely to persist across time (pp. 469–470, citations deleted).

Discussion of this "subjective sense of conviction" has recently given rise to a focus on certain types of metacognitive assessments of consumer attitudes. Metacognitive assessments represent secondary thoughts about internal states and knowledge (in this case attitudes) that allow people to monitor their meaning and relevance, and to direct subsequent thought and action (see Petty, Brinol, Tormala, and Wegener 2007 for an extended discussion). Attitude certainty, a pivotal dimension of attitudes under the prevailing view, has been associated with subjective assessments of clarity and correctness (Petrocelli, Tormala, and Rucker 2007).

But what is it, exactly, that consumers need to be certain about before relying on their attitudes for purchases and related consumer behaviors? Will a subjective assessment of an attitude's inherent (i.e., self-contained) clarity and correctness be sufficient to lead consumers to rely on it in making decisions? Furthermore, is the underlying assumption that attitude strength (however well measured) provides a firm basis for behavioral predictions correct? Some evidence calls this bedrock assumption into question: models highlighting intrinsic (i.e., apart from a behavioral context) attitude assessment alone are not sufficient. Specifically, studies have shown substantial self-correction of even strongly held attitudes (i.e., to overcome the effects of bias, prejudice, temporary moods, and heightened accessibility of a partial subset of attitude-relevant beliefs) when consumers are motivated to make good decisions and/or be accountable for them (Wegener and Petty 1997; Dunton and Fazio 1997; Dovidio et al., 1997; Cohen, Belyavsky, and Silk 2008) or when reduced self-efficacy or perceived behavioral control (Bandura 1982; Ajzen and Madden 1986; Ajzen and Fishbein 2005) diminishes willingness to rely on such attitudes.

MPAA's View of Metacognitive Assessments

We believe a more complete and accurate depiction of the self-interrogation process through which consumers make judgments regarding the adequacy of their attitudes cannot terminate when consumers assess an attitude as being held with a high degree of certainty, conviction, or strength. Instead, we argue that consumers sequentially make two very different assessments of a retrieved attitude (Cohen and Reed 2006a). The first, representational sufficiency (RS), overlaps with clarity and correctness dimensions identified in the previously mentioned stream of research and with the aligned notion of metacognitive "validity tags," as advanced by Petty and colleagues (Petty 2006; Petty et al. 2007). However, RS also includes the subjective assessment of personal ownership of the attitude, which will be discussed further.

The implicit decision to *rely* on one's attitude is more a question of its appropriateness for the specific behavior in question (or diagnosticity; see Lynch 2006; Cohen and Reed 2006b) than its inherent correctness. Cohen and Reed (2006a) term this assessment *functional sufficiency* (FS). One fairly general factor influencing functional sufficiency that may not be reflected in attitude certainty or correctness was investigated by Fabrigar, Petty, Smith, and Crites (2006). They showed that people were more likely to use their attitudes to guide behavior when these attitudes were based on multiple and consistent dimensions of knowledge rather than a single basis even though there were no differences in attitude certainty. When attitudes have multiple bases, they seem more widely applicable to a variety of contexts, thereby suggesting a metacognitive link to functional sufficiency (Petty 2006).

A recent study further clarifies the separate role of functional sufficiency in MPAA. Cohen, Belyavsky, and Silk (2008) found that attitudes toward purchasing a product accompanied by a rebate were primarily associated with the desirability of the downstream savings. This is because people focused more on benefits than on the feasibility of carrying out steps necessary to redeem the rebate, even though these steps were not exceptional and should have been anticipated. Among those subsequently asked to visualize each of the rebate redemption steps, however, the balance between desirability and feasibility changed. Initial attitudes proved to be a poor predictor of whether people would again choose the rebate option relative to an initial (but less compelling) purchase price. Thus, intrinsic assessments of attitude clarity, correctness, certainty, and strength appear to miss the subsequent and behavioral context-focused assessment that Cohen and Reed (2006a) refer to as functional sufficiency.

The position advocated by Cohen and Reed (2006a) notes that previous conceptions of the attitude-behavior relationship were remarkably static: essentially that correctly measured attitudes (i.e., incorporating some aspects of strength) at time one would predict behavior at some subsequent time as long as outside factors did not intervene. Instead, Cohen and Reed (2006a) do not assume that attitudes will predict behavior. They assume that these evaluative assessments will be stored and retrieved just like any other information, but because evaluative assessments of focal objects, other consumers, and other issues are more relevant to action than the individual pieces of information about them, attitudes are more likely than any other information to *guide* behavior. The difference between *predict* and *guide* is extremely important. The model advanced by Cohen and Reed (2006a) assumes that attitudes will guide behavior, but will only predict behavior when people believe they can rely on those attitudes to direct whatever consumer behavior is under consideration.

MPAA and Social Identity–Based Attitudes

As discussed, MPAA asserts that consumers subjectively assess two aspects of their attitudes at different points in time to make a given judgment. First, they assess an attitude's representational sufficiency when it is retrieved from memory and is used to make any judgment (such as liking). Consumers want to be confident that the retrieved attitude is clear and coherent and represents their own point of view. While these first two dimensions correspond to some extent with clarity and correctness, the latter dimension is unique to MPAA. Suppose that a person brings to mind a product evaluation that is recalled as being supplied by some other person or perhaps as inferred from an ad. To the extent that the source of that information is salient, personal ownership may be lacking, and the attitude may be weaker than it originally appears to be. One could argue, however, that this should show up in an assessment of correctness or certainty. While that may be possible, if we are trying to identify the relevant metacognitive assessments people actually make, we should separate those that are clearly different (both substantively and temporally). Consistent with this position, the aforementioned study by Fabrigar and colleagues is an argument against relying on assessments of structural dimensions of attitudes (such as certainty and strength) when examining attitude-behavior relationships. Recall that despite no differences in attitude certainty, attitudes differed in applicability when there was a broader basis for assessments of relevance. Thus, the attitude became a stronger argument for engaging in the behavior (Fabrigar, MacDonald, and Wegener 2005).

MPAA acknowledges that any factor comprising or influencing the content of an attitude that facilitates feelings of certainty will increase the likelihood that the attitude possesses relatively high representational sufficiency. Social identity–based attitudes are not driven by information about the object per se, but rather by information internal to the person about how the object relates to the person's social identity. Because these attitudes are often derived from norms linked to particular social identities, forming a social identity–based attitude is likely to have social consensus properties (beliefs that this attitude is also held by others who share that social identity) and personal ownership (because the social identity–based attitude is more deeply linked to a person's sense of who they are). In addition, forming, holding, and expressing a social identity–based attitude is likely to serve self-enhancement and self-verification goals. Both of these advantages—greater ownership and satisfaction of self goals—imply greater feelings of certainty and commitment.

Based on this reasoning, social identity–based attitudes may, in general, appear to be higher in representational sufficiency than object-based attitudes. However, people occupy multiple roles and think about themselves somewhat differently depending on their social surroundings as well as on thoughts that "prime" different aspects of self (e.g., making family, gender, race, occupation, aspirations more salient). Accordingly, attitudes formed in one context may not generalize as well to other contexts where somewhat different priorities and values are important. If that is the case, social identity–based attitudes should be less "stable" over time than attitudes based on consistent properties of objects, including brands. Such a difference would not be expected whenever the social identity basis for the attitude is highly central to the person, and thus a reasonably permanent aspect of who the person considers himself or herself to be. Though our analysis is speculative in the absence of significant empirical research, it suggests that marketers would be taking greater risks by attempting to link their brands to more transient (and especially "made up") product personalities as a way of forming favorable brand attitudes, as these attitudes might then be unstable and lack representational sufficiency. However, in product categories with accelerated growth, where differentiation must be created quickly and often, such an approach may be less risky if it allows marketers to respond more quickly to market dynamics by repositioning brands to align with more transitory marketer-driven product personalities.

According to MPAA, consumers subsequently assess the attitude's functional sufficiency when the representationally sufficient attitude is brought to mind as a potential guide to some behavior. The question they ask at that point is whether the attitude is an adequate guide to whatever specific behavior is being contemplated. If consumers assess the attitude as functionally sufficient, it will both guide and predict behavior. If consumers are confronted with unanticipated or changed information about the object (often because contextual factors make other issues, such as attitudes toward risk or interpersonal implications, salient), that additional information (whether perception- or memory-based) will be integrated into the retrieved attitude and used to guide behavior. Cohen and Reed (2006a) describe this in terms of an anchoring and adjustment process in which the amount of adjustment (i.e., from a further search for and integration of information) is a function of the perceived importance/riskiness of the behavior, in keeping with concepts common to Fazio's MODE model (Motivation and Opportunity as Determinants of attitude-behavior consistency; Fazio and Towles-Schwen 1999) and Chen and Chaiken's sufficiency principle (1999).

Another key question is whether social identity–based attitudes are likely to be different in functional sufficiency than object-based attitudes. Attitudes that are likely to "power through" changes in context are likely to be those that truly matter to you. Therefore, more fundamental (in terms of being self-defining) social identity–based attitudes are very likely to have a considerable advantage. Whether and when that advantage is likely to manifest itself in consumer decision making (e.g., how central or self-defining such attitudes are) deserves study. Our next step is to discuss the social identity pathway to attitude formation in greater depth, including when such attitudes are likely to be relevant and important, when they are salient, and how stable they are likely to be (vs. easy to change).

SOCIAL IDENTITY–BASED ATTITUDES: BASIC DEFINITIONS

Attitudes Based on an External (Object) versus Internal (Social Identity) Focus

The separation of the psychological environment into self (person) and object (Lewin 1951) has been a staple of theory and research (Heider 1958; Jones and Davis 1965). For example, causal attributions (Kelley and Michela 1980) are generally categorized as either external (i.e., the salient object, external actor, or situational condition) or internal (i.e., the self). A similar analogy can be made in the domain of attitude formation. For our purposes, an *object-oriented attitude* refers to any attitude whose focal point is external to the consumer, hence strongly associated with some object, issue, or person. Most products have benefits or features that could be used to define them and presumably differentiate them from other potential competitive offerings. When brand managers develop such a product concept they often choose levels of these attributes that are designed to be very close to the ideal points of targeted segments of consumers. Then brand managers attempt to communicate attribute positioning to the end consumer. This is effective presumably because consumers often consider the brand and its product concept in a feature-driven fashion—by thinking about certain attributes that define the product concept and how important those attributes are for that product category. This may happen systematically via an analytical impression formation process, merely through associative linkages forged by product experience or advertising, or even some heuristic, such as product similarity–based inferences. For example, an object-oriented attitude toward a branded product may be based on direct experience with the brand, information from other sources (e.g., *Consumer Reports,* advertising), or inferences from related objects or categorical representations (e.g., a brand extension may be evaluated based on attitude toward the company).

In contrast, a *social identity–oriented* attitude is linked to aspects of one's self-identity, such as personal values, roles, and social identity. For example, a person might develop a favorable attitude toward some particular conservation-related behavior based on thoughts about "being an environmentalist" (see Bolton and Reed 2004). Thus, the beliefs that function as building blocks of such self-oriented attitudes are likely to be different in content than those supporting an object-oriented attitude. In these instances, rather than a focus on the object and its features or attributes per se, the consumer's evaluative processes may be disproportionately driven by thoughts about one's self-concept or one's current or desired social identity. For example, when buying clothing, how often have you thought to yourself, "Is this me?" or "What sort of impression will I make?" Surprisingly, the self-object distinction—although proven to be important in understanding perception and attribution processes—has not been a major focus in the attitude literature. We now turn to a more formal conceptualization that attempts to detail this process: that is, when attitudes come to be formed on the basis of one or more salient social identities. We begin with the definition of social identity as we use it in this chapter.

Social Identity

The analysis begins with the idea that consumers think about themselves in terms of various social identities (cf. Tajfel 1959; Tajfel and Turner 1979; Turner and Oakes 1986) and at any given point in time will have available a subset of social categories that can become a part of the "working" or "spontaneous" self-concept (Markus and Nurius 1988; McGuire, McGuire, and Winton 1979). A consumer may adopt a social category as a social identity in order to think about various actions or judgments (see Reed 2004). For clarity of exposition, a *social category* refers to any of the vast number of potential social constructions that may come from culture, the organization of society, mass media, peer groups, and so on. The term *social identity* refers to the actuated perspective or frame of reference that a consumer possesses as part of the repertoire of who they are or who they want to appear to be. Accordingly, some thought process actuates a social identity that the person is prepared to adopt (based on prior learning and, importantly, a judgment of personal relevance) in order to judge or evaluate some other person, object, or action (see Reed and Forehand 2008).

A Social Identity Pathway to Liking and Evaluation

We now elaborate on the specific process of how a consumer forms an attitude based on social identity. We term this process a social identity pathway to liking and evaluation, and base it on the following premise. As mentioned in the previous section, a consumer has a multitude of social identities that they may adopt. These social identities are more than just labels. They are knowledge structures organized around schema of different information (e.g., the image of the kind of person likely to hold that particular social identity, beliefs, values, and norms that are strongly associated with group members who also share that social identity). The content of the knowledge structure that comes to mind when a social identity is made salient is the basis for responding to (i.e., evaluating) objects and objects of thoughts. To the extent that a social identity is a salient basis for self definition, and that social identity is important to the person and provides a basis for responding to the object, there is an increased likelihood that an individual will base their attitude on that social identity.

It is possible for different social identities to have very different evaluative implications with respect to a particular attitude object. As an example, one of the most important public policy issues we face is likely to involve raising the retirement age for Medicare eligibility. If people think about the issue as "senior citizens" (with their senior citizen hat on, so to speak), then they might be opposed to it and perhaps bring pressure on both political parties. But if they were to think about the issue as "Americans," they might conclude that this type of Medicare reform is good for everyone, and their response to the issue could be totally different. Recent research that we have conducted is consistent with this notion. A study by Aquino and colleagues (Aquino et al. 2007) found significant reduction of the positive relationship between moral disengagement and pro-war–related thoughts, attitudes, and behaviors when people's moral identity was either chronically salient or primed. However, this relationship was *strengthened* whenever American identity was chronically salient or temporarily primed (see Finnel et al. 2008). We interpret these findings as evidence of different evaluative recruitment processes that arise as a person thinks about an attitude object from the perspective of a particular identity that may be salient at the time of attitude formation. It is possible to elicit differential evaluative responses based on particular social identities that may be cued by the environment, and indeed, these different social identities may have completely different evaluative implications for that attitude object. This carries implications for how one might balance these potential different selves and the attitudes recruited from them.

Balancing Social Identity, Brand, and Self-Concept

One may think of the multitude of various possible social identities as akin to viewing an ambiguous attitude object through various phenomenological lenses, with each lens linked to a particular social identity. Each lens would thus represent learned and socialized group norms that reflect collective beliefs and values, which are in turn rooted in those external social categories that may be adopted by the individual consumer as one of many social identities. This readily applies to the case of brands and products and other consumer behaviors. Figure 7.1 illustrates this graphically.[2] One can think about the links between any individual consumer, a social identity, and any object, and identify attitudinal implications derived from a social identity pathway to evaluation. For example, the link between a consumer and a social identity (link 1 in Figure 7.1) represents the strength/likelihood of that social identity coming to mind and being important to that consumers' overall self-definition. This has been discussed in terms of centrality (Deshpande and Stayman 1994; Deshpande, Hoyer, and Donthu 1986) or self-importance (Aquino and Reed

Figure 7.1   **A Social Identity Pathway to Evaluation**

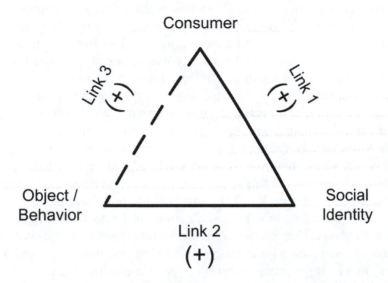

2002), as well as the accessibility of that social identity.[3] With similar reasoning, one can also consider the link between a social identity and a specific object, issue, or behavior (link 2 in Figure 7.1) as identity relevance (Reed 2004), applicability, or "diagnosticity" (Feldman and Lynch 1988). The extent to which link 1 and link 2 are congruent (i.e., balanced and positive) implies the formation of a favorable consumer attitude, as shown in terms of an evaluative response from the consumer toward the object in question (link 3 in Figure 7.1). As per MPAA, such a generated attitude would then be subject to both an RS and FS assessment before it would be recruited as a guide for behavior.

To illustrate this attitude formation logic, consider the social identity of "athlete." A consumer might adopt this social identity and use its associated evaluative content [e.g., perceptions of what an athlete thinks (attitudes) and does (behaviors)] as the basis to form an attitude (e.g., attitude toward Nike sports shoes or attitudes toward exercise). This process is likely to result in a collectively anchored attitude that is formed via identification processes (Kelman 1958) and is held, expressed, or used as a guide for behavior in order to establish, maintain, or even communicate that social identity to others (Shavitt 1990). Existing research corroborates this point and illustrates the balance logic mentioned previously and graphically depicted in Figure 7.1. In the attitude literature, Terry and Hogg (1996) argued that psychological "group membership" should influence people's attitudes. They found that perceived norms linked to a behaviorally relevant reference group ("regular exercisers") influenced intentions to engage in exercise, but only for subjects who identified with the group (Terry and Hogg 1996, experiment 1; see also Ybarra and Trafimow 1998). In the substantive area of biased information scanning, researchers found that, compared to white females, black females who had recently had their ethnic (female) identity made salient had more favorable (unfavorable) perceptions of O.J. Simpson's innocence (Newman et al. 1997). In the stereotype literature, another study demonstrated that when a particular social identity was made salient at an implicit level, performance was altered in the direction predicted by the stereotype associated with the social identity. In this study, Shih, Pittinsky, and Ambady (1999) found that Asian-American women performed better on a math test when their ethnic identity was activated, but worse when their gender identity was activated, compared with a control group who had neither social identity activated. These three studies are consistent with the idea that there is a unit (e.g., ownership, membership) relationship between the person and the group (i.e., the social identity), and that the group's values/beliefs are directionally relevant to the issue, leading the person to adopt the group's attitude.

Although the previously mentioned studies are consistent with the logic inherent in a social identity pathway to liking and evaluation, Reed and Cohen (2009) provide what might be the first direct test of this logic. In their study, they sought to experimentally manipulate the links in Figure 7.1. All participants (women exclusively) in the study first provided their initial attitude toward a number of issues including affirmative action to deal with glass ceiling problems facing women. Then participants engaged in an online chatroom discussion with other group members (actually a computer-driven set of responses) in which the group members in certain conditions gave solid reasons to support an attitude that was opposite to each participant's initial attitude, instantiating the link between the social identity and the issue (link 2 in Figure 7.1). Several days later, participants received a phone call from an ostensibly unrelated national polling agency and were queried about their attitude on the critical issue, among other things. At the outset of this phone call, the social identity that all participants had reflected on in the prior chatroom setting was either made salient or not by a subtle difference in the name of the organization "sponsoring" the survey. Heightening the salience of the particular social identity was intended to instantiate link 1 of Figure 7.1 and was expected to affect the attitudes people recruited; either their initial attitudes *or* their chatroom-based social identity attitudes toward the issue. Only when the chatroom social identity was made salient were attitudes that had been developed in the identity-relevant context, rather than initial attitudes, used to provide survey responses (Reed and Cohen, 2009, study 2). Interestingly, subsequent survey questions showed that both initial attitudes and newly created attitudes (for participants in chatroom contexts where these were formed) were available, thereby implicating some combination of attitude recruitment (probably due to heightened salience) and willingness to rely on the recruited attitude, hence functional sufficiency.

A Different Kind of Social Influence in Attitude Formation

Social identification implies a psychological connection with some other person or group (Deaux 1996). Early in life, identification is considered a largely automatic (as opposed to strategic) process of imitating referent others who serve as models for beliefs, values, and behaviors (as well as many other learned behaviors). In later stages of maturation, the identification process involves conscious choice and discrimination among possible social identities (Higgins, Loeb, and Moretti 1995). For example, Kelman's (1958, 1961,

2006) typology of social influence uses the term *identification* to describe situations where an individual willingly adopts an attitudinal position whether or not the referent other intends this outcome or is even aware of the person's desire to close the psychological distance between them. The motivation for adopting the position is that it establishes or maintains a positive self-defining relationship with the referent other (see also French and Raven 1959). Unlike informational influence, the recipient makes no assessment of the likelihood that the referent's position is in any way "correct," and is not dependent on a context in which social reality is substituted due to the person's inability to determine objective reality. It is important to note that an *identification process* (Kelman 1958) is also very different from a *compliance-based process* in that it is not dependent on the referent other's direct surveillance of the individual's behavior nor rewards and punishments associated with refusal to adopt the referent other's particular attitudinal position.

Normative social influence processes have probably received more attention and are certainly important in some instances. If consumers are made to believe that important others will vehemently disapprove of some behavior, then that behavior is less likely to manifest publicly if the consumer is motivated to comply with that referent. This suggests that marketers who are interested in curtailing potentially harmful behaviors such as smoking and alcohol use or who are interested in facilitating productive behaviors such as recycling and donating blood could make use of compliance-based pressures associated with peer groups or external others who are likely to administer punishments and rewards based on observable behaviors (e.g., only dopes take dope/your grandchildren will thank you for a healthy planet). However, there may be real advantages to considering attitude formation through a social identity pathway, since this leads to actual acceptance of the evaluation and does not depend on a combination of surveillance and reward/punishment power. For example, consumer researchers could follow a strategy that strengthens the link between the individual consumer and some important social identity (link 1 in Figure 7.1). In the recycling example, a persuasive communication might emphasize the "global community" and its importance to the self-definition of the individual consumer. So the emphasis would be on solidifying and reinforcing the extent to which an individual consumer will adopt the perspective, or wear the hat, that is associated with that social identity. Once this is established, then the communications strategy can focus on the link between that social identity and certain behaviors (link 2 in Figure 7.1).

In summary, the consumer researcher would be facilitating the likelihood that a social identity–based consumer attitude will come to mind and guide behavior. This is done by increasing the likelihood that (1) a consumer will possess what Heider (1958) described as a unit relationship between an individual and a behaviorally relevant social identity and (2) the social identity in question (member of the global community) provides a logically consistent basis for a positive attitude toward recycling. Some recent research in our own program further demonstrates the usefulness of this analysis for behavioral change interventions. A study by Finnel, Reed, Volpp, and Armstrong (2008) found that the likelihood of maintaining an ongoing medication protocol in a sample of male hypertension patients was a function of the extent to which a patient's attitudes toward hypertension were related to their social identities. More specifically, the study revealed a positive relationship between the medication's anticipated impact on the self-image and compliance intentions. Unexpectedly, however, this positive relationship was much weaker when patients' prior involvement in sports and athletics was a central part of their social identity and when they believed they currently possessed feelings of strength, power, and independence. Why did this happen, and what can be done to overcome the problem? Applying the logic of Figure 7.1, open-ended protocols with the patients revealed a negative relationship between the concept of "athlete and sports participant" and the behavior of "taking medicine" (link 2 in Figure 7.1). Our data suggested that this relationship emerges because of the inconsistency inherent between the social identity (which represents strength, power, and autonomy) and the act (which represents being sickly and weak). Hence, for those patients who had a strong positive link to that social identity, they resolved the imbalance by not adhering to their medication protocols. In addition to collecting information about patients' objectively verifiable health indicators, practitioners may wish to ask patients about their views of themselves and/or assess the salience and importance of certain social identities that may conflict with certain medical protocols. This kind of information can then be used to determine an appropriate behavioral intervention for each patient. Such insight would have been much less likely to have emerged within the traditional views of social factors within attitude theory. These kinds of intervention-relevant insights (that come from a consideration of social identity–based attitudes) offer some promise when attempting to create favorable consumption behaviors and deter unfavorable ones in important areas of public policy in marketing (Wilkie 2005).

SUBSTANTIVE ISSUES FOR BRAND MANAGERS

Implications for Branding

Though conceptualizations and methods of measuring it vary, brand equity can generally be defined in terms of the portion of marketing outcomes that can be attributed solely to the brand (Keller 1993). Building a strong brand—one that communicates a set of clear, coherent associations that distinguish it from competitive offerings—has a number of financial and strategic advantages, such as enhanced customer loyalty and the ability to charge price premiums (e.g., Aaker 1997; Keller 2003). For brand equity to be meaningful, brand attitudes or consumers' overall summary evaluations of a brand must be recalled and used in guiding consumption behavior. The MPAA perspective raises a number of substantive issues concerning the management of brands and brand attitudes that may be driven by social identity.

A great deal of research has focused on external, tangible, product-related aspects of brands. For example, the literature in consumer behavior on developing and positioning new brands has focused on the way in which new members to a brand or product category are evaluated (see Loken 2006, for a review). Existing categories are seen as sets of both attributes and exemplars, and accessible category information is used to evaluate new entrants based on perceived similarity (e.g., Loken, Joiner, and Peck 2002; Meyvis and Janiszewski 2004). Thus, much attention has been given to positioning new brands with

Figure 7.2 **The Brand-Specific Case of New vs. Existing Social Identities**

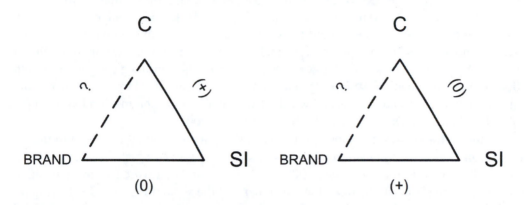

respect to existing competitors and category members, with the focus on brand attributes—in other words, outside-in routes to brand attitude formation. However, MPAA proposes that consideration of inside-out routes to brand attitude formation (i.e., those that rely on internal, psychological aspects of consumers, such as social identity) is equally pivotal, and practitioners as well as researchers may have much to gain from broadening their perspectives (Cohen and Reed 2006a).

Creating a Social Identity–Based Brand Attitude from Scratch

If social identity often serves a social adjustment function for consumers who wish to reinforce their connection to similar (real or imagined) others and create separation from dissimilar (real or imagined) others (Smith et al. 1956, p. 42), then a consumer's social identity facilitates this adjustment by directing the consumer to specific beliefs and behaviors that signal identification externally to society and internally to the self. The connection between the self and a brand is widely regarded as being forged through a matching process, whereby consumers strive for congruity between their self-image and a brand image (e.g., Escalas and Bettman 2003; Sirgy 1982). But how can managers foster this connection with a new brand? Our account underscores the importance of consistency (i.e., cognitive balance) between consumers, a social identity they possess (or want to possess), and an attitude object (in this case, a specific brand or product). The account we have presented provides clear implications for managers attempting to create a social identity–based brand attitude from scratch. From a managerial point of view, in order to foster a positive and accessible social identity–based brand attitude, managers must consider all three links depicted in Figure 7.1. Figure 7.2 is a brand-specific modification of Figure 7.1 that graphically depicts the step-by-step logic associated with facilitating a social identity–based attitude for a new brand.

As part of a market segmentation approach, brand managers should first consider the full market of consumers, and identify individual segments that can be meaningfully grouped in terms of social identities that already exist in society, or who have the potential to be personified because they project personally desired categorical associations and dissociations. Each selected social identity must be clear and differentiated from others that already may be linked to existing competitive brands. Brand managers should link (positively or negatively) their brand to symbolic associations that embody the chosen social identity. These associations might include reference group symbols (Cialdini et al. 1976; Smith and Mackie 1995), symbols related to outgroups (see Berger and Heath 2008; Wilder and Shapiro 1984), outgroup members themselves (Marques, Yzerbyt, and Rijsman 1988), or visual images and words (Hong et al. 2000; Chatman and von Hippel 2001; Forehand and Deshpandé 2001; Forehand et al. 2002).

The most straightforward approach to establishing a social identity–based brand attitude from scratch is to position a brand so that it fits an existing social identity (e.g., Aaker 1997; Belk, Bahn, and Mayer 1982; Sirgy 1982). In other words, a strong positive association already exists between the consumer and the social identity (C → SI; Figure 7.2, left panel), but no association as of yet between that social identity and the brand (SI → BRAND). In this case, the marketer's task is to establish a link between the identity and the brand. To the extent that the brand is representative of the social identity–oriented lifestyle, consumers who possess that identity should develop a positive, accessible attitude toward the brand. If this segment of consumers deems the brand to be expressive of the values associated with their social identity (Shavitt 1990), then they may exhibit a deeper sense of identification and loyalty toward the brand (Oliver 1999; Reed 2004).

For example, Harley Davidson is strongly linked to a social identity of a rebel image. In other words, the existing social identity represents outsider status (Schouten and McAlexander 1995, p. 58), a degree of marginality, and an outlaw culture (Muniz and O'Guinn 2001). Schouten and McAlexander (1995, p. 50) describe the connection of the Harley Davidson brand with its consumer community as so powerful that the brand is "in effect, a religious icon, around which an entire ideology of consumption is articulated." While this may be an extreme example of a brand community, it is a clear demonstration of how brands can resonate with consumers (the BRAND → C link in Figure 7.2), leading to a socially embedded, entrenched sense of brand loyalty that is driven by the consumer connection to others who embrace the social identity represented by the brand.

Given that consumers already possess the social identity and define themselves in terms of it, the marketer's challenge lies in convincing consumers that the social identity is relevant and applicable to the evaluation of the brand. Social identities that are fundamental and deeply held by consumers are likely to guide behavior across a variety of contexts. Adding cues to the external environment (e.g., through media campaigns) that reinforce the connection between the brand and the social identity may make it more salient and accessible to consumers (e.g., Cialdini et al. 1976; Forehand et al. 2002). Furthermore, by adding identity cues to the evaluation or purchase environment, marketers can increase the chances that the social identity will be activated within the purchase context, so that evaluation and behavior are driven by attitudes related to that identity (Reed 2004). For example, retailers such as H&M strive to create a hip, fashionable purchase environment, while Nike and Foot Locker incorporate athletic symbols and equipment, so that the appropriate social identities are cued, driving consumer brand evaluation and behavior.

Alternatively, marketers might encourage interactive activities that embody the social identity–oriented lifestyle in question and involve consumers. For example, Red Bull has built a devoted brand community by sponsoring activities centered on a young, creative, "extreme sports culture" social identity that is closely associated with the brand.

Another possible approach to positioning a new brand is the creation of a new, marketer-defined social identity that is closely aligned with the brand. This represents a scenario in which a positive association exists between the brand and a social identity (SI → BRAND; Figure 7.2, right panel), but none exists between the social identity and the consumer (C → SI; Figure 7.2, right panel). Thus, the marketer's challenge is to foster a connection and sense of personal resonance between a segment of consumers and the identity. To the extent that this link can be established (i.e., that consumers adopt the social identity as important to their self-definitions), consumers should form positive associations toward the brand. Furthermore, given the link between the identity and the brand, once an attitude has been acquired, it seems likely that consumers will bring it to mind when a relevant product decision is being made. Whether they will act on this attitude (i.e., whether it will be functionally sufficient) depends on factors discussed earlier in the chapter, especially the importance of the aspect of self-identity (relative to other aspects) and the degree to which ownership of this brand is viewed as a defining aspect of that self-identity.

The ongoing "Mac vs. PC" advertisements produced by Apple are a good example of a social identity–oriented marketing campaign with social identities essentially created by marketers. The Mac is represented by a laid-back, artistic-looking young man in casual, hip clothing, while the PC is represented by an uptight, nerdy-looking older man in glasses and a conservative suit. Though the advertisements often discuss product attributes, their main thrust is to present these two characters as embodiments of the respective brands. In other words, the advertisements clearly depict the social identity associated with Apple computers—and by extension, Apple consumers—as distinct from the social identity associated with PCs and PC consumers.[4] By associating Apple with a desirable social identity, and evoking an outgroup social identity in presenting PCs, Apple hopes to entice consumers to abandon PCs and adopt Apple computers (Berger and Heath, 2008). In other words, they hope to establish a positive attitude toward Apple through a social identity pathway.

How strong are the associations that become linked to a brand? Recent research has demonstrated that these associations can even impact consumers outside of conscious awareness. Fitzsimons, Chartrand, and Fitzsimons (2008) found that mere exposure to a brand can automatically shape behavior: participants exposed to the Apple brand performed significantly higher on a standard measure of creativity than those exposed to the IBM brand. However, this held only for those participants who reported a preexisting goal to "be creative." Similarly, participants primed with the Disney Channel brand responded more honestly than those primed with E! Channel logos. Thus, just as consumer attitudes toward brands can be influenced via their social identities, consumers with social identities associated with a brand might be influenced by that brand, even outside of conscious awareness (Fitzsimons et al. 2008). As a cautionary note, such studies speak more to the

Figure 7.3   **The Brand-Specific Case of Repositioning**

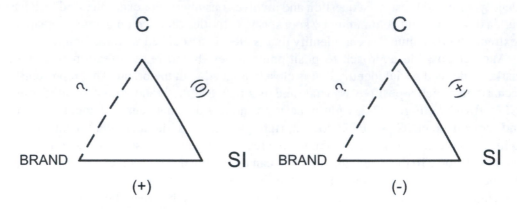

validity of the psychological processes themselves than to their actual impact when other information and sources of influence are present.

As we suggested earlier, from an RS and FS perspective in MPAA, it may be risky for managers to position new brands linked to transient social identities that are not a natural basis for self-definition. Creating an identity with clear and coherent associations that consumers will identify with and internalize presents a substantial hurdle. Consumers may find the identity poorly defined or not truly theirs, decreasing the likelihood that their attitude toward the social identity will be retrieved and subsequently used.

Repositioning Existing Brands

Consumers and brands are not static. Rather, the needs of consumers and the meaning and perception of brands are in a state of flux. Given the changing demands and opportunities of the marketplace, brand managers may reposition brands to adapt and compete (Aaker 1996). Our proposed social identity pathway to brand evaluation also has implications for managers wishing to reposition existing brands across the product life cycle. Figure 7.3 is a brand-specific modification of Figures 7.1 and 7.2 that graphically depicts the stepwise logic at play here for repositioning an existing brand.

One way in which brand managers might reposition a brand is to reach a new social identity–oriented segment of consumers. In this scenario, a positive association may exist between the brand and a particular social identity (SI → BRAND; Figure 7.3, left panel), but consumers may see that social identity as negative (C → SI; Figure 7.3, left panel). For example, in recent years, Coca-Cola experienced difficulty in reaching male consumers with Diet Coke. Though men were becoming more health conscious, and latent demand existed for a low-calorie alternative to sugary regular Coca-Cola, many men held negative attitudes toward Diet Coke. Diet Coke was strongly associated with women (link 2 in Figure 7.3, left panel), a social identity from which men wished to differentiate (link 1 in Figure 7.3, left panel). Hence, Coca-Cola faced the challenge of attempting to foster a more positive attitude between consumers and the identity associated with their diet soft drink (i.e., change the C → SI link in the left panel, Figure 7.3 from negative to positive). Such a strategy can prove exceedingly difficult, as consumers may be predisposed against adopting the identity (e.g., men may be reluctant to be associated with any reduced-calorie soft drink offerings, despite their health concerns). Brand managers may be better served by changing the elements of the brand that are most associated with the prior social identity, thus addressing both the brand-identity connection and the consumer-identity connection (i.e., changing the C → SI and the SI → BRAND links in Figure 7.3).

Similarly, another scenario may involve targeting the same social identity–oriented segment of consumers, but changing the brand itself (Figure 7.3, right panel). Again, altering symbolic aspects of the brand may be essential to fostering a positive evaluative connection between the identity and the brand (i.e., changing the SI → BRAND link in the right panel of Figure 7.3 from negative to positive). As an illustration, in the study involving hypertension patients, a strongly positive athlete identity (link 1 in Figure 7.3, right panel) was incompatible with hypertension medication compliance (link 2 in Figure 7.3, right panel), so patients adopted a negative attitude toward compliance (Finnel et al. 2008). An appropriate intervention might describe medication compliance in terms that are more consistent with an athlete identity (e.g., "following this regimen will improve strength and performance over the course of one's life," "like athletes, one must take appropriate measures to prevent illness and injury"). By repositioning the representation of the brand (or behavior) to fit an existing social identity, practitioners can encourage the formation of positive brand attitudes.

The challenge for marketers in repositioning brands is twofold: existing attitudes must be suppressed as new attitudes are made more accessible. In such cases, achieving adequate clarity, coherence, and differentiation from the prior brand positioning may be quite difficult, especially for identity-relevant attitudes that may be deeply held (Oliver 1999). Existing attitudes are likely to interfere with repositioning efforts: if existing brand symbols are associated with negatively viewed group identities or negatively valenced evaluations, then consumers are likely to avoid the brand (Berger and Heath 2008). Moreover, even if existing associations do not directly offset repositioning efforts, they are likely to hamper the establishment of a clear, coherent set of new brand associations. Thus, utilizing altogether different brand imagery may be more likely to facilitate the development of positive social identity–driven brand evaluations.

For example, Oldsmobile attempted to reposition itself as a youthful brand in the 1980s, with the tagline, "It's not your father's Oldsmobile," and was widely perceived to have failed. Presumably, many young consumers had highly accessible brand attitudes associating Oldsmobile with an older outgroup identity, and were reluctant to adopt the brand. Conversely, Toyota has achieved great success in introducing the Scion line of automobiles, targeted to consumers possessing a young, hip, adventurous identity. Similarly, the resolution to Coca-Cola's dilemma was the introduction of Coke Zero, a calorie-free soft drink differentiated from Diet Coke in name, taste, packaging, and media campaign. Thus, by changing both C → SI and SI → BRAND links at once and managing the symbolic aspects of the transition, Coca-Cola was able to successfully reposition a diet offering as distinct from existing associations.

A crucial goal for marketers is to make the association between the consumer and the created social identity highly accessible. Marketers can employ elements of the marketing mix (e.g., media campaigns) in order to persuade consumers that they possess qualities that match the social identity associated with the brand (e.g., Escalas and Bettman 2003). However, they face an additional challenge: consumers must feel a sense of personal ownership over an attitude (in accordance with RS; see Cohen and Reed 2006a). Thus, marketers must strive to create an identity that resonates with consumers as authentically their own. One way of fostering this sense of ownership might be to associate spokespeople or exemplars who are admired by consumers possessing the created social identity. For instance, our research has revealed the power of social identity–based attitudes when targeted marketing messages are delivered by spokespeople who resonate culturally with consumers. A study by Puntoni and Reed (2008) explored the differential reactions to spokespeople of either Dutch or Chinese descent for first-generation participants (those raised in China, but who had moved to the Netherlands) versus second-generation participants (those born in China, but who had been raised in the Netherlands) after exposure to subtle identity primes that activated either cultural dimension of their social identity. Compared to first-generation participants, second-generation participants should possess two well-developed cultural identities to draw upon (a self-identity rooted in both ethnic-Chinese and mainstream-Dutch culture). One study showed that compared to a control condition, for participants primed with either an ethnic versus mainstream cultural cue, spokespersons are liked more (less) by second-generation participants when the spokesperson's ethnicity corresponds (does not correspond) to the participant's ethnicity. Additionally, the spokesperson liking effect was found to be mediated by a heightened sense of psychological connection (i.e., perceived similarity and identification) that is triggered by the presence of cues that prime ethnicity versus mainstream culture (Puntoni and Reed 2008, study 2). Furthermore, these differences in reactions are more likely to emerge for second-generation participants whose ethnic identity has evolved through a deeper involvement (more contact and consideration) and internalization with their senses of self.

While it is certainly true that consumers bring a variety of social identities with them into consumer contexts, social identities themselves are also shaped by a lifetime of experience, social interaction, cultural influences, and self-expression (Belk 1988; Escalas and Bettman 2003; Fournier 1998; Richins 1994). This logic suggests the possibility that the content of one's social identity may itself shift in response to contextual cues and triggers, thereby fundamentally altering the direction of subsequent identity-driven effects. For example, marketers often try to appeal to consumers by presenting an image of youth via the choice of content and imagery used in ads that promote their product. When viewing such an advertisement featuring young, virile actors, some consumers may feel kinship with those actors and feel more youthful as a result. Alternatively, many consumers may not identify with the actors, instead classifying them as clear "others," which could weaken their own sense of youth. In this situation, the advertising cues not only activate one's identity, as past research has documented, but they may also fundamentally shift the content associated with the activated identity. Therefore, the cues may alter the nature of subsequent identity-based effects (i.e., brand cues may change the $C \rightarrow SI$ connection). A study by Forehand, Perkins, and Reed (2008) provides evidence of this phenomenon. They found that consumer self-youth associations assimilated toward age-based imagery when the discrepancy between the self and the imagery was moderate, but contrasted with the imagery when the discrepancy was extreme. However, these effects occurred only when consumers engaged in explicit comparison with the depicted user imagery. Moreover, the effects of automatic self-other categorization were further tested by directing consumers to evaluate either their similarities or dissimilarities with the user imagery. The effects of extremely discrepant user imagery were eliminated when consumers engaged in similarity assessment, and the effects of moderately discrepant user imagery were eliminated when consumers engaged in dissimilarity assessment (Forehand et al. 2008, study 2). To attest to the power of these shifts on actual marketing responses of interest, a third experiment found that self-youth association activation mediated the relationship between youth cues in advertising and positive response to the advertised products.

The Special Case of Co-Branding Alliances

To position brands around a social identity, marketers must utilize elements of the marketing mix to appeal to consumers who believe that they possess the social identity, utilize actors or endorsers who are clear and unambiguous exemplars of that social identity, or develop other techniques that can foster a psychological connection between a social identity and the brand. As the BRAND $\rightarrow$ SI link becomes stronger, the brand itself can become a powerful retrieval cue that triggers the associations that have been built up over time. These associations embodying a particular social identity also represent at least part of the brand's inherent equity, and may be the basis for target marketing as either explicit or implicit cues.

Many of these considerations also apply to co-branding (i.e., the case of brand alliances), and should be a fruitful future substantive domain in which to apply the aforementioned conceptual analyses. For example, it is well established that the success of such brand alliances depends on the perceived "fit" between the two brands (e.g., Simonin and Ruth 1998). For instance, while Intel and Dell are a natural fit, co-branding between Haagen Dazs and SlimFast would be ill-advised. Thus, the idea of fit between brands is often conceptualized as complementarity between product attributes (Samu, Krishnan, and Smith 1999; Venkatesh and Mahajan 1997). However, if brands are identity–relevant, then the picture is somewhat more complicated. Figure 7.4 is a graphic illustration.

Given our proposed balance theory approach to social identity–based brand attitudes, managers must consider not only the fit between the two brands, but also the link between each brand's consumer base and the social identity associated with its partner brand (i.e., given two allied brands A and B, $C_A \rightarrow SI_B$ and $C_B \rightarrow SI_A$ must be considered), and the link between the social identity associated with each brand and its partner brand (i.e., ($SI_A \rightarrow BRAND_B$ and $SI_B \rightarrow BRAND_A$). Recent research provides preliminary empirical evidence for this account (Verrochi and Reed 2008). Specifically, participants viewed ad-

Figure 7.4   **The Special Case of Co-branding**

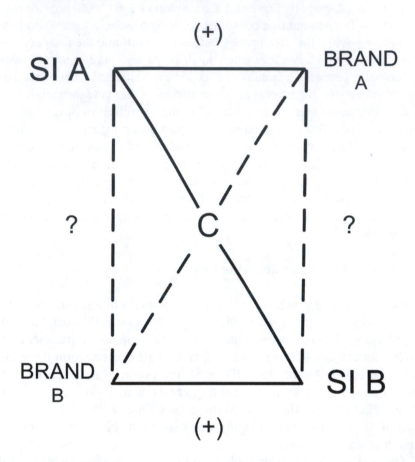

vertisements for the Nike + iPod brand alliance, and were primed in order to activate their athlete, student, or fashionista social identities. Participants whose fashionable identities were activated reported more favorable attitudes toward the brand alliance than those in the other two conditions. Thus, if consumers hold an identity that is incongruent with one of the parent brands, brand attitudes toward the overall alliance will be less positive (Verrochi and Reed 2008, study 1a). In a second study, participants were primed to activate either their runner or fashionista identities, and evaluated brand alliances containing shoe brands that were perceived as either more functional (Mizuno and New Balance) or more fashionable (Adidas and Nike). Results indicated that participants whose runner identities were activated perceived the alliance with functional shoes to be a better fit, while participants whose fashionista identities were activated perceived the alliance with fashionable shoes to be a better fit. These results suggest that attitudes toward brand alliances are driven by consumer social identities, and provide evidence for the importance of taking social identity into account (Verrochi and Reed 2008, study 1b). Thus, marketing managers must be careful to consider consumers and the social identities that they hold as well as brands when evaluating co-branding alliances: perceived complementarity between parent brands and resulting brand attitudes can rely on the activated identities of consumers.

CONCLUSIONS

At any given point in time, consumers have a subset of social identities that they may adopt in order to guide their thoughts and actions. Marketing practitioners certainly understand the value of targeting consumers, segmenting markets, and positioning products based on the evaluative implications of these social identities. From an applied standpoint, if the brand comes to represent the consumer's social identity, such that the brand is connected to deeply engulfing, self-defining aspects of the consumer (Oliver 1999), then the consumer would say that the brand is "part of me" (cf. Kleine, Kleine and Allen 1995). In other words, the brand can become an extension of the self (Belk 1988), such that the consumer cannot conceive of him or herself as whole without it (cf. Oliver 1999). Arguably, the goal of successfully executing such a social identity–oriented marketing strategy can be more effectively met if marketing strategists have a framework that elucidates the key mechanisms of social identity–driven processing and their marketing implications. It is our hope that the analysis presented here is a useful framework that will help serve that purpose.

NOTES

1. Identity-based marketing is not just the repackaging of psychographic segmentation techniques. Psychographic segmentation is based on the assumption of a single self-concept. It assumes that consumers' stable personality traits can be identified and linked to particular broad lifestyle orientations that can then be classified into broad product categories. However, researchers and practitioners are beginning to realize that such approaches are too simplistic because consumers have many selves that cannot be collapsed into just one broad lifestyle category bucket. Identity-based marketing explicitly recognizes this by more fully taking into account the complexity of consumers' self-concepts (Reed and Bolton 2005).

2. This logic is based on principles of balance theory first proposed by Heider (1958) and elaborated on by others (Abelson 1959; Newcomb 1968).

3. At this point, it may be important to point out important similarities and differences in the strength of the connection between a person and a social identity with related constructs such as chronic accessibility (see Higgins 1996; Higgins and Brendl 1995). Higgins and colleagues (see for example Higgins 1989) think of accessibility as a very broad memorial concept critical to understanding basic processes of knowledge activation (Higgins, Rholes, and Jones 1977). For example, Higgins and colleagues apply this construct to all stored knowledge and define it as the "pre-stimulus preparedness for activation" or the "activation potential" of the stored knowledge (Higgins 1996). Second, and more importantly, Higgins and his colleagues conceptualize and operationalize chronic accessibility in a way that intentionally makes no assumption as to the extent to which that stored knowledge is self-defining. Hence, chronic accessibility is a very broad theoretical construct that is useful in explaining the influence of activated knowledge structures in people's heads—but these concepts in their heads need not be a part of who they are.

4. Interestingly, in late 2008, Microsoft began a campaign to counter this series of advertisements by Apple. The thrust of Microsoft's response is to try to convey the negativity associated with stereotyping a particular group. This was done by showing a range of PC enthusiasts from a myriad different

backgrounds, ethnicities, and so on. In this way, Microsoft is trying to undermine the social identity–based associations on which Apple is trying to capitalize.

REFERENCES

Aaker, David (1996). *Building Strong Brands.* New York, NY: Free Press.

Aaker, Jennifer (1997). "Dimensions of Brand Personality," *Journal of Marketing Research,* 34 (August), 347–357.

Abelson, Robert P. (1959). "Modes of Resolution of Belief Dilemmas," *Journal of Conflict Resolution,* 3 (4), 343–352.

Ajzen, Icek, and Martin Fishbein (2005). "The Influence of Attitudes on Behavior." In *The Handbook of Attitudes,* ed. Dolores Albarracin, Blair T. Johnson, and Mark P. Zanna. Mahwah, NJ: Lawrence Erlbaum, 173–221.

Ajzen, Icek, and Thomas J. Madden (1986). "Prediction of Goal-Directed Behavior: Attitudes, Intentions, and Perceived Behavioral Control," *Journal of Experimental Social Psychology,* 22 (5), 453–474.

Aquino, Karl, and Americus Reed II (2002). "The Self-Importance of Moral Identity," *Journal of Personality and Social Psychology,* 83 (6), 1423–1440.

Aquino, Karl, Americus Reed II, Stefan Thau, and Dan Freeman (2007). "A Grotesque and Dark Beauty: How Moral Identity and Mechanisms of Moral Disengagement Influence Cognitive and Emotional Reactions to War," *Journal of Experimental Social Psychology,* 43 (3), 385–392.

Bandura, Albert (1982). "Self-Efficacy Mechanism in Human Agency," *American Psychologist,* 37 (2), 122–147.

Belk, Russell W. (1988). "Possessions and the Extended Self," *Journal of Consumer Research,* 15 (3), 139–168.

Belk, Russell W., Kenneth D. Bahn, and Robert N. Mayer (1982). "Developmental Recognition of Consumption Symbolism," *Journal of Consumer Research,* 9 (June), 4–17.

Berger, Jonah, and Chip Heath (2008). "Who Drives Divergence? Identity-Signaling, Out-Group Similarity, and the Abandonment of Cultural Tastes," *Journal of Personality and Social Psychology,* 95 (3), 593–607.

Bolton, Lisa E., and Americus Reed II (2004). "Sticky Priors: The Perseverance of Identity Effects on Judgment," *Journal of Marketing Research,* 41 (4), November, 397–410.

Chatman, Celina M., and William von Hippel (2001). "Attributional Mediation of In-Group Bias," *Journal of Experimental Social Psychology,* 37 (3), 267–272.

Chen, Serena, and Shelly Chaiken (1999). "The Heuristic-Systematic Model in its Broader Context." In *Dual-Process Theories in Social Psychology,* ed. Shelly Chaiken and Yaacov Trope. New York, NY: Guilford Press, 73–96.

Cialdini, Robert B., Richard J., Borden, Avril Thorne, Marcus R. Walker, Stephen Freeman, and Lloyd R. Sloan (1976). "Basking in Reflected Glory: Three (Football) Field Studies," *Journal of Personality and Social Psychology,* 34, 366–375.

Cohen, Joel B., Julia Belyavsky, and Tim Silk (2008). "Using Visualization to Alter the Balance Between Desirability and Feasibility During Choice." Working paper.

Cohen, Joel B., and Americus Reed II (2006a). "A Multiple Pathway Anchoring and Adjustment (MPAA) Model of Attitude Generation and Recruitment," *Journal of Consumer Research,* 33 (1), 1–15.

Cohen, Joel B., and Americus Reed II (2006b). "Perspectives on Parsimony: How Long Is the Coast of England? A Reply to Park and MacInnis; Schwarz; Petty; and Lynch," *Journal of Consumer Research,* 33 (1), 28–30.

Deaux, Kay (1996). "Social Identification." In *Social Psychology: Handbook of Basic Principles,* ed. E.T. Higgins and A.W. Kruglanski. New York, NY: Guilford Press, 777–798.

Deshpandé, Rohit, Wayne D. Hoyer, and Naveen Donthu (1986). "The Intensity of Ethnic Affiliation: A Study of the Sociology of Hispanic Consumption," *Journal of Consumer Research,* 13 (2), 214–220.

Deshpandé, Rohit, and Douglas M. Stayman (1994). "A Tale of Two Cities: Distinctiveness Theory and Advertising Effectiveness," *Journal of Marketing Research,* 31 (1), 57–64.

Dovidio, John F., Kerry Kawakama, Craig Johnson, Brenda Johnson, and Adaiah Howard (1997). "On the Nature of Prejudice: Automatic and Controlled Processes," *Journal of Experimental Social Psychology,* 33 (5), 510–540.

Dunton, Bridget C., and Russell H. Fazio (1997). "Categorization by Race; the Impact of Automatic and Controlled Components of Racial Prejudice," *Journal of Experimental Social Psychology,* 33 (5), 451–470.

Escalas, Jennifer Edson, and James R. Bettman (2003). "You Are What They Eat: The Influence of Reference Groups on Consumers' Connections to Brands," *Journal of Consumer Psychology,* 13 (3), 339–348.

Fabrigar, Leandre R., Tara K. MacDonald, and Duane T. Wegener (2005). "The Structure of Attitudes." In *The Handbook of Attitudes,* ed. Dolores Albarracin, Blair T. Johnson, and Mark P. Zanna. Mahwah, NJ: Lawrence Erlbaum, 79–125.

Fabrigar, Leandre R., Richard E. Petty, Stephen M. Smith, and Stephen L. Crites Jr. (2006). "Understanding Knowledge Effects on Attitude-Behavior Consistency: The Role of Relevance, Complexity, and Amount of Knowledge," *Journal of Personality and Social Psychology,* 90 (4), 556–577.

Fazio, Russell H., and Tamara Towles-Schwen (1999). "The MODE Model of Attitude-Behavior Processes." In *Dual-Process Theories in Social Psychology,* ed. Shelly Chaiken and Yaacov Trope. New York, NY: Guilford Press, 97–116.

Feldman, Jack M., and John G. Lynch Jr. (1988). "Self-Generated Validity and Other Effects of Measurement on Belief, Attitude, Intention, and Behavior," *Journal of Applied Psychology,* 72 (3), 42–35.

Finnel, Stephanie, Americus Reed II, Karl Aquino, and Stefan Thau (2008). "Marketing War: The Case of Dueling Identities." Under review.

Finnel, Stephanie, Americus Reed II, Kevin Volpp, and Katrina Armstrong (2008). "The Joint Influence of Past, Present and Future Selves on Hypertension Medication Compliance." Under review.

Fishbein, Martin, and Icek Ajzen (1975). *Belief, Attitude, Intention, and Behavior: An Introduction to Theory and Research.* Reading, MA: Addison-Wesley.

Fitzsimons, Grainne M., Tanya L. Chartrand, and Gavan J. Fitzsimons (2008). "Automatic Effects of Brand Exposure on Motivated Behavior: How Apple Makes You 'Think Different,'" *Journal of Consumer Research,* 35 (June), 21–35.

Forehand, Mark R., Rohit Deshpandé (2001). "What We See Makes Us Who We Are: Priming Ethnic Self-Awareness and Advertising Response," *Journal of Marketing Research,* 38 (3), 336–348.

Forehand, Mark R., and Rohit Deshpandé, and Americus Reed II (2002). "Identity Salience and the Influence of Differential Activation of the Social Self-schema on Advertising Response," *Journal of Applied Psychology,* 87(6) 1086–1099.

Forehand, Mark R., Andrew Perkins, and Americus Reed II (2008). "The Shaping of Social Identity: Assimilation/Contrast Responses to Ad Exposure." Under review.

Fournier, Susan (1998). "Consumers and Their Brands: Developing Relationship Theory in Consumer Research," *Journal of Consumer Research,* 24 (4), 343–373.

French, John R.P. Jr., and Bertram H. Raven (1959). "The Bases of Social Power." In *Studies in Social Power,* ed. D. Cartwright. Ann Arbor, MI: Institute for Social Research, 150–167.

Heider, Fritz (1958). *The Psychology of Interpersonal Relations.* New York, NY: Wiley.

Higgins, E. Tory (1989). "Knowledge Accessibility and Activation: Subjectivity and Suffering from Unconscious Sources." In *Unintended Thought,* ed. J.S. Uleman and J.A. Bargh. New York, NY: Guilford Press, 75–123.

——— (1996). "Knowledge Activation: Accessibility, Applicability and Salience." In *Social Psychology: Handbook of Basic Principles,* ed. E.T. Higgins and A.W. Kruglanski. New York, NY: Guilford Press, 133–168.

Higgins, E. Tony, and Miguel Brendl (1995). "Accessibility and Applicability: Some 'Activation Rules' Influencing Judgment," *Journal of Experimental Social Psychology,* 31, 218–243.

Higgins, E. Tony, Israela Loeb, and Marlene Moretti (1995). "Self-Discrepancies and Developmental Shifts in Vulnerability: Life Transitions in the Regulatory Significance of Others." In *Emotion, Cognition, and Representation: Rochester Symposium on Developmental Psychology 6,* ed. D. Cicchetti and S.L. Toth. Rochester, NY: University of Rochester Press, 191–230.

Higgins, E. Tony, W.S. Rholes, and C.R. Jones (1977). "Category Accessibility and Impression Formation," *Journal of Experimental Social Psychology,* 13, 141–154.

Hong, Ying-yi, Michael W. Morris, Chi-yue Chiu, and Veronica Benet-Martínez (2000). "Multicultural Minds: A Dynamic Constructivist Approach to Culture and Cognition," *American Psychologist,* 55 (7), 709–720.

Jones, E.E., and K.E. Davis (1965). "From Acts to Dispositions: The Attribution Process in Person Perception." In *Advances in Experimental Social Psychology,* ed. L. Berkowitz. New York, NY: Academic Press, 219–266.

Katz, Daniel (1960). "The Functional Approach to the Study of Attitudes," *Public Opinion Quarterly,* 24(2), 163–204.

Keller, Kevin L. (1993). "Conceptualizing, Measuring, and Managing Customer-Based Brand Equity," *Journal of Marketing,* 57 (1), 1–22.

——— (2003). "Brand Synthesis: The Multidimensionality of Brand Knowledge," *Journal of Consumer Research,* 29 (March), 595–600.

Kelley, Harold H. and John L. Michela (1980). "Attribution Theory and Research," *Annual Review of Psychology,* 31, 457–501.

Kelman, Herbert C. (1958). "Compliance, Identification, and Internalization: Three Processes of Attitude Change," *Journal of Conflict Resolution,* 2, 51–60.

——— (1961). "Processes of Opinion Change," *Public Opinion Quarterly,* 25, 57–78.

——— (2006). "Interests, Relationships, Identities: Three Central Issues for Individuals and Groups in Negotiating their Social Environment," *Annual Review of Psychology,* 57, 1–26.

Kleine, Robert E. III, Susan Schultz Kleine, and Jerome B. Kernan (1993). "Mundane Consumption and the Self: A Social Identity Perspective," *Journal of Consumer Psychology,* 2 (3), 209–235.

Kleine, Susan Schultz, Robert E. Kleine III, and Chris T. Allen (1995). "How Is a Possession 'Me' or 'Not Me'? Characterizing Types and an Antecedent of Material Possession Attachment," *Journal of Consumer Research,* 3 (December), 327–343.

Laverie, Debra A., Robert E. Kleine III, and Susan Schultz Kleine (2002). "Reexamination and Extension of Kleine, Kliene, and Kernan's Social Identity Model of Mundane Consumption: The Mediating Role of the Appraisal Process," *Journal of Consumer Research,* 28 (4), 659–669.

Levy, Sidney J. (1959). "Symbols for Sale," *Harvard Business Review,* 37(4), 117–124.

Lewin, Kurt (1951). *Field Theory in Social Science.* New York, NY: Harper.

Loken, Barbara (2006). "Consumer Psychology: Categorization, Inferences, Affect, and Persuasion," *Annual Review of Psychology,* 57, 453–485.

Loken, Barbara, Christopher Joiner, and Joann Peck (2002). "Category Attitude Measures: Exemplars as Inputs," *Journal of Consumer Psychology,* 12 (2), 149–161.

Lynch, John G. (2006), "Accessibility-Diagnosticity and the Multiple Pathway Anchoring and Adjustment Model," *Journal of Consumer Research,* 33 (1), 25–27.

Markus, Hazel, and Paula Nurius (1987). "Possible Selves: The Interface Between Motivation and the Self-Concept." In *Self and Identity: Psychosocial Perspectives,* ed. Krysia Yardley and Terry Honess. New York, NY: Wiley, 157–172.

Marques, Jose M., Vincent Y. Yzerbyt, and John B. Rijsman (1988). "Context Effects of Intergroup Discrimination: In-Group Bias as a Function of Experimenter's Provenance," *British Journal of Social Psychology,* 27, 301–318.

McGarty, Craig, S. Alexander Haslam, Karen J. Hutchinson, and John C. Turner (1994). "The Effects of Salient Group Memberships on Persuasion," *Small Group Research,* 25 (2), 267–293.

McGuire, William J., Claire V. McGuire, and Ward Winton (1979). "Effects of Household Sex Composition on the Salience of One's Gender in the Spontaneous Self-Concept," *Journal of Experimental Social Psychology,* 15, 77–90.

Meyvis, Tom, and Chris Janiszewski (2004). "When Are Broader Brands Stronger Brands? An Accessibility Perspective on the Success of Brand Extensions," *Journal of Consumer Research,* 31 (September), 346–357.

Muniz, Albert M. Jr., and Thomas C. O'Guinn (2001). "Brand Community," *Journal of Consumer Research,* 27 (March), 412–432.

Newcomb, Theodore M. (1968). "Interpersonal Balance." In *Theories of Cognitive Consistency: A Sourcebook,* ed. R.P. Abelson, E. Aronson, W.J. McGuire, T.M. Newcomb, M.J. Rosenberg, P.H. Tannenbaum. Chicago, IL: Rand McNally, 28–51.

Newman, Leonard S., Kimberly Duff, Nicole Schnopp-Wyatt, Bradley Brock, and Yonit Hoffman (1997). "Reactions to the O.J. Simpson Verdict: 'Mindless Tribalism' or Motivated Inference Processes," *Journal of Social Issues,* 53 (Special Issue), 547–562.

Oliver, Richard L. (1999). "Whence Consumer Loyalty?" *Journal of Marketing,* 63 (Special Issue), 33–44.

Petrocelli, John V., Zakary L. Tormala, and Derek D. Rucker (2007). "Unpacking Attitude Certainty: Attitude Clarity and Attitude Correctness," *Journal of Personality and Social Psychology,* 92 (1), 30–41.

Petty, Richard E. (2006). "A Metacognitive Model of Attitudes," *Journal of Consumer Research,* 33 (1), 22–24.

Petty, Richard E. Pablo Brinol, Zakary L. Tormala, and Duane T. Wegener (2007). "The Role of Metacognition in Social Judgment." In *Social Psychology: Handbook of Basic Principles* (2nd ed.), ed. E.T. Higgins and A.W. Kruglanski. New York, NY: Guilford Press, 254–284.

Pilkington, Neil W., and John E. Lydon (1997). "The Relative Effect of Attitude Similarity and Attitude Dissimilarity on Interpersonal Attraction: Investigating the Moderating Roles of Prejudice and Group Membership," *Personality and Social Psychology Bulletin,* 23 (2), 107–122.

Puntoni, Stefano, and Americus Reed II (2008). "Generational Influences on Reaction to Ethnic Cues in Advertising." Working paper.

Reed II, Americus (2004). "Activating the Self-Importance of Consumer Selves: Exploring Identity Salience Effects on Judgments," *Journal of Consumer Research,* 31 (2), 286–295.

Reed II, Amencus, and Lisa E. Bolton (2005). "The Complexity of Identity," *Sloan Management Review,* 46 (3), 17–22.

Reed II, Amencus, and Joel B. Cohen (2009). "Chatroom Study." Working paper.

Reed II, Amencus, and Mark. R. Forehand (2008). "Managing Social Identity: Strategies for Creating Brand Identification and Community." Working paper.

Richins, Marsha L. (1994). "Valuing Things: The Public and Private Meanings of Possessions," *Journal of Consumer Research,* 21 (3), 504–521.

Samu, Sridhar, Shanker H. Krishnan, and Robert E. Smith (1999). "Using Advertising Alliances for New Product Introduction: Interactions Between Product Complementarity and Promotional Strategies," *Journal of Marketing,* 63 (1), 57–74.

Schouten, John W., and James H. McAlexander (1995). "Subcultures of Consumption: An Ethnography of New Bikers," *Journal of Consumer Research,* 22 (June), 43–61.

Sedikides, Constantine, and Michael J. Strube (1997). "Self-Evaluation: To Thine Own Self Be Good, to Thine Own Self Be Sure, to Thine Own Self Be True, and to Thine Own Self Be Better," In *Advances in Experimental Social Psychology,* 29, ed. M. P. Zanna. New York, NY: Academic Press, 209–269.

Shavitt, Sharon (1990). "The Role of Attitude Objects in Attitude Functions," *Journal of Experimental Social Psychology,* 26(2), 124–148.

Shih, Margaret, Todd L. Pittinsky, and Nalini Ambady (1999). "Stereotype Susceptibility: Identity Salience and Shifts in Quantitative Performance," *Psychological Science,* 10 (1), 80–83.

Simonin, Bernard L., and Julie A. Ruth (1998). "Is a Company Known by the Company It Keeps? Assessing the Spillover Effects of Brand Alliances on Consumer Brand Attitudes," *Journal of Marketing Research*" 35 (1), 30–42.

Sirgy, M. Joseph (1982). "Self-Concept in Consumer Behavior: A Critical Review," *Journal of Consumer Research,* 9, 287–300.

Smith, Eliot R., and Diane M. Mackie (1995). *Social Psychology.* New York, NY: Worth Publishers.

Smith, M. Brewster, Jerome S. Bruner, and Robert W. White (1956). *Opinions and Personality.* New York, NY: Wiley.

Stayman, Douglas M., and Rohit Deshpandé (1989). "Situational Ethnicity and Consumer Behavior," *Journal of Consumer Research,* 16 (December), 361–371.

Tajfel, Henri (1959). "Quantitative Judgment in Social Perception," *British Journal of Psychology,* 50, 16–59.

Tajfel, Henri, and John C. Turner (1979). "An Integrative Theory of Intergroup Conflict." In *The Social Psychology of Intergroup Relations,* ed. W.G. Austin and S. Worchel. Monterey, CA: Brooks-Cole, 33–47.

Terry, Deborah J., and Michael A. Hogg (1996). "Group Norms and the Attitude Behavior Relationship: A Role for Group Identification," *Personality and Social Psychology Bulletin,* 22, 776–793.

Tormala, Zakary L., and Derek D. Rucker (2007). "Attitude Certainty: A Review of Past Findings and Emerging Perspectives," *Social and Personality Psychology Compass,* 1 (November), 469–492.

Turner, John C., and Penelope J. Oakes (1986). "The Significance of the Social Identity Concept for Social Psychology with Reference to Individualism, Interactionism, and Social Influence," *British Journal of Social Psychology,* 25, 237–252.

Venkatesh, R., and Vijay Mahajan (1997). "Products with Branded Components: An Approach for Premium Pricing and Partner Selection," *Marketing Science,* 16 (2), 146–165.

Verrochi, Nicole M., and Americus Reed II (2008). "Brand Alliances: When Do Consumers (Not) Fit?" Working paper.

Visser, Penny S., and Robert R. Mirabile (2004). "Attitudes in the Social Context: The Impact of Social Network Composition on Individual-Level Attitude Strength," *Journal of Personality and Social Psychology,* 87 (6), 779–795.

Wegener, Duane T., and Richard E. Petty (1997). "The Flexible Correction Model: The Role of Naïve Theories of Bias in Bias Correction." In *Advances in Experimental Social Psychology,* ed. Mark P. Zanna. San Diego, CA: Academic Press, 141–208.

Wilder, David A., and Peter N. Shapiro (1984). "Role of Out-Group Cues in Determining Social Identity," *Journal of Personality and Social Psychology,* 47, 342–348.

Wilkie, William (2005). "Needed: A Larger View of Marketing and Scholarship," *Journal of Marketing,* 69, 4 (October), pp. 8–10.

Ybarra, Oscar, and David Trafimow (1998). "How Priming the Private Self or Collective Self Affects the Relative Weights of Attitudes and Subjective Norms," *Personality and Social Psychology Bulletin,* 24 (4), 362–370.

CHAPTER 8

GROUP-BASED BRAND RELATIONSHIPS AND PERSUASION

Multiple Roles for Identification and Identification Discrepancies

MONIQUE A. FLEMING

Consumer behavior theory and research have increasingly used a relationship perspective to understand consumers' interactions with brands (e.g., Escalas and Bettman 2005; Fournier 1998; Park, MacInnis, and Priester 2006). Interactions of interest have ranged from purchase to loyalty to a willingness to pay a price premium, and it is generally thought that fostering a strong relationship between consumers and a brand will increase these behaviors. One way that a relationship between a consumer and a brand can be established is by associating a brand with a group to which the consumer already belongs to (i.e., an ingroup; e.g., see Chapter 6 and Swaminathan, Page, and Gürhan-Canli 2007 for reviews). What effect does associating a brand with a consumer's ingroup have on attitudes toward the brand, responses to persuasive appeals such as brand advertising, and consumer-brand interactions? This chapter draws on an attitudes and persuasion perspective to answer these questions.

GROUP-BASED RELATIONSHIPS AND PERSUASION

Research suggests that associating a brand or a consumer product with a consumer's ingroup in a persuasive appeal such as an ad generally leads to more positive attitudes (e.g., Gürhan-Canli and Maheswaran 2000; Hong and Wyer 1990; Maheswaran 1994; Reed 2004; Shavitt and Nelson 2000). Thus, group-based brand relationships can have a positive effect on attitudes. More generally, linking any attitude object in a persuasive appeal (e.g., a political or social object, a consumer product) with an ingroup has been found to typically lead to more positive attitudes. For example, persuasion has been found to be greater when the source of a persuasive message about an attitude object is a member of the message recipient's ingroup rather than outgroup (e.g., Cohen 2003; Mackie, Gastardo-Conaco, and Skelly 1992; van Knippenberg and Wilke 1992), when an attitudinal position toward an attitude object is attributed to a message recipient's ingroup rather than outgroup (e.g., Wood, Pool, Leck, and Purvis 1996), or when a persuasive message about an attitude object simply associates the attitude object with a message recipient's ingroup (e.g., Reed 2004). Two questions of interest regarding such group-based persuasion have been: (1) How does it occur? and (2) Why does it occur? The answers to these questions have implications for understanding the conditions under which group-based brand relationships might be expected to guide consumer-brand interactions.

HOW DOES GROUP-BASED PERSUASION OCCUR?

One focus of persuasion research has been to examine the cognitive processes through which a variable changes attitudes. In particular, the Elaboration Likelihood model (ELM; Petty and Cacioppo 1986b) and the Heuristic-Systematic model (HSM; Chaiken, Liberman, and Eagly 1989) propose that variables can lead to persuasion through thoughtful processes that involve consideration of the merits of arguments or information presented in a persuasive appeal, or through relatively nonthoughtful processes, such as relying on a shortcut or cue in the persuasion context (see also Chapter 15). The process through which persuasion occurs has been shown to have consequences for resulting attitudes. Attitudes resulting from a thoughtful process have been found to be stronger such that they persist longer over time, are more resistant to counterattack, and are more predictive of behavior than attitudes resulting from a nonthoughtful process (e.g., see Petty, Haugtvedt, and Smith 1995, for a review).

Thus, from an attitudes perspective, in order to know how consequential a group-based brand relationship will be, it is not only important to know if it has led to a more positive or more negative attitude, but it is also important to know the process(es) through which it has done so. For decades, the traditional view regarding group-based attitude change was largely that such persuasion was the result of relatively nonthoughtful processes that were distinct from influence based on a thoughtful consideration of the viewpoint or merits of arguments presented (e.g., Asch, 1951; Deutsch and Gerard 1955; Festinger 1950; Kelman 1958, 1961; e.g., see Fleming and Petty 2000; Mackie and Queller 2000; Prislin and Wood 2005; van Knippenberg 1999, 2000, for reviews). For example, Kelman (1958, 1961) proposed that ingroup sources likely induced attitude change through *identification,* a process of persuasion involving a desire to establish or maintain a self-defining relationship with the source's group, which he contrasted with *internalization,* a process of persuasion involving the thoughtful and thorough integration of new material into a broad framework of cognitive associations. Were the traditional view to be true, we would not expect group-based persuasion to be very consequential.

The development of new methods to examine the processes through which persuasion occurs (see Chaiken et al. 1989; Petty and Cacioppo 1986b, for reviews) has allowed more recent research on group-based persuasion to directly examine this question. This research suggests that, in contrast to traditional views, group-based persuasion can occur through both nonthoughtful *and* thoughtful processes (e.g., see Fleming and Petty 2000; Mackie and Queller 2000; Prislin and Wood 2005; van Knippenberg 1999, 2000, for reviews).

However, it is unclear precisely when each type of process occurs. Some research has found that ingroup persuasion occurs through a thoughtful process when the topic of the persuasive message is relevant to the ingroup [e.g., SAT exams or oil drilling off of the California coast for ingroup University of California at Santa Barbara (UCSB) students], or the position taken in the persuasive message is not stated until after arguments are presented, but occurs through a nonthoughtful process of relying on the ingroup source's position as a cue when the topic is not relevant to the ingroup and outgroup (e.g., handgun possession or euthanasia for ingroup UCSB students and outgroup University of Manitoba students) and the position is stated before arguments are presented (Mackie, Worth, and Asuncion 1990; Mackie et al. 1992; van Knippenberg, Lossie, and Wilke 1994).

In contrast, other research has found that, under what seem to be the latter conditions, that is, when the topic is not relevant to the ingroup and outgroup and positions are stated first, high-identified individuals show ingroup persuasion through a thoughtful process. Specifically, when given only the counterattitudinal positions held by ingroup (U.S.-born Texas A&M students) and outgroup members (foreign-born Texas A&M students) on topics not particularly relevant to the ingroup or outgroup ("I would not approve of a friend who took illegal drugs," and "Sex of employees should be considered in promotion"), high-identified individuals were more persuaded by an ingroup than an outgroup position because they interpreted the ingroup's position as having an uncommon meaning that allowed them to more easily agree, in what is seemingly a form of positively biased thinking (Wood et al. 1996; see also Asch 1940, 1948). For example, when the position "Sex of employees should be considered in promotion" was attributed to the ingroup rather than the outgroup, high-identified individuals were more likely to interpret the phrase *should be considered* as having the more qualified and palatable interpretation "promote the best person unless the job requires physical skills like strength," and interpretations mediated the effect of group attitudes on participant's attitudes.

GROUP-BASED PERSUASION: WHAT DETERMINES PROCESS?

Prior theorists have proposed a number of interesting hypotheses of when group-based persuasion will be thoughtful rather than nonthoughtful that could plausibly account for these findings. Two theories have predominated, and both implicate identification—the extent to which the ingroup membership is an important part of message recipient's self-concept (Tajfel and Turner 1986).

The first hypothesis is that identification may determine the process through which ingroup persuasion occurs. This hypothesis suggests that high-identified individuals may show ingroup persuasion through a thoughtful process, whereas low-identified individuals may show ingroup persuasion through a nonthoughtful process (e.g., Prislin and Wood 2005; van Knippenberg 1999; see also Cohen and Reed 2006 and Chapter 7). For example, elaborating on tripartite analyses of motives in influence settings that differentiate between the motives of relating, being, and understanding (e.g., Chaiken, Giner-Sorolla, and Chen 1996; Wood 1999, 2000), Prislin and Wood (2005) conceptualize identification as a measure of the strength of the motive of *relating* to others, and propose that strength of motive (identification) may moderate whether ingroup persuasion is thoughtfully or nonthoughtfully mediated. They propose that high-identified individuals may show ingroup persuasion through a thoughtful process, but low-identified individuals may show ingroup persuasion through a nonthoughtful process, because both may be motivated to establish a relationship with the ingroup by agreeing with the ingroup, and stronger motivation may lead to greater cognitive efforts to do so.[1] Similarly, van Knippenberg (1999) proposes that high-identified individuals may be particularly likely to show ingroup persuasion through a thoughtful process (and presumably low-identified individuals would show ingroup persuasion through a nonthoughtful process), because a greater number or range of topics may become group-relevant the more strongly an individual is identified with a group, or because they see ingroup views as particularly informative.

From this perspective, identification may have been higher in the research that found thoughtful (biased interpretation) effects than in the research that found nonthoughtful (cue) effects when the topic is not relevant to the ingroup and outgroup and positions are stated first. As mentioned, biased interpretation of the ingroup's position occurred only for high-identified individuals (Wood et al. 1996). Perhaps the cue effect (Mackie et al. 1992; van Knippenberg et al. 1994) occurred for low-identified individuals. Although ingroup persuasion did not occur for low-identified individuals in the research by Wood and colleagues (1996), as would be expected by this perspective (i.e., ingroup persuasion must occur for low-identified individuals for it to be mediated differently), perhaps that study did not have enough power to detect a difference.

The second hypothesis proposes instead that high-identified individuals may be more likely to show group-based persuasion than low-identified individuals, and that, for high-identified individuals, ingroup persuasion may occur thoughtfully when the likelihood of elaborating the contents of a persuasive message is high in the persuasion context, but may occur nonthoughtfully when the likelihood of elaboration is low (e.g., Fleming and Petty 2000; van Knippenberg 1999, 2000; see also Mackie et al. 1990, 1992, 2000; van Knippenberg et al. 1994). Elaboration likelihood is determined by people's motivation and ability to think about a persuasive message in a particular context. Elaboration likelihood is high when people are both motivated and able to think about a persuasive message, but is low when people are either unmotivated or unable to think, or both. For example, individuals have been found to elaborate when a message topic is personally relevant to them, and thus motivation to think is high (e.g., Petty and Cacioppo 1979), and when there are no distractions present in the persuasion context, and thus ability to think is high (e.g., Petty, Wells, and Brock 1976).

This second perspective would suggest that, as for the biased interpretation effect, the cue effect also occurred for high-identified individuals when the topic was group-irrelevant and positions were stated first (see also Mackie et al. 1992), but elaboration likelihood was higher in the research that found biased interpretation effects than in the research that found cue effects. For example, the group-irrelevant topics used in the research that found biased interpretation effects (i.e., friends using illegal drugs and sex being considered in promotion) may have been of higher *personal* relevance for college student participants than the group-irrelevant topics used in the research that found cue effects (i.e., handgun possession and euthanasia), increasing motivation to think.

A study was conducted to examine these possibilities (Fleming, 2009). A group of

661 undergraduate students, (371 males, 290 females) was recruited for a study to investigate how people felt about new and revived products that were presumably being test-marketed around the country at the time of the study. Participants were either high or low in identification with their gender group as measured by the four-item identity subscale of the collective-esteem scale (Luhtanen and Crocker 1992). An example item of the scale reads: "In general, belonging to the group (males or females) is an important part of my self-image."

Group relevance and position timing were held constant—always using a relatively group-irrelevant topic, and stating the message position before arguments were presented. Specifically, participants were given a purported mock-up advertisement containing two persuasive messages, one positive and one negative, about a group-irrelevant product. The first sentence of each message contained the message position [i.e., "Snickerdoodles are men's (women's) favorite snack food"; "Women (Men) are concerned that Snickerdoodles are unhealthy"), and subsequent sentences contained relatively cogent reasons supporting the message position. For some participants, the ingroup message was positive and the outgroup message was negative, whereas for others, the outgroup message was positive and the ingroup message was negative, and this constituted the manipulation of group appeal.

After the messages, attitudes toward the product, and the valence of thoughts in response to the advertisement (positive, negative, or neutral toward Snickerdoodles) were measured. Elaboration likelihood was also measured, with the need for cognition scale (Cacioppo and Petty 1982), which assesses individual differences in chronic tendencies to thoughtfully elaborate information across contexts (Cacioppo et al. 1996).

Given this design, if group appeal affects attitudes through a thoughtful process in some conditions, as expected, then we would expect more positive thoughts and attitudes when the ingroup message was positive and the outgroup negative, than when the outgroup message was positive and the ingroup negative, and thoughts should mediate the effect of group appeal on participant's attitudes. Use of group positions as a cue would result in more positive attitudes, but not thoughts, when the ingroup message was positive and the outgroup negative, than when the outgroup message was positive and the ingroup negative, and thoughts should not mediate the effect of group appeal on attitudes, indicating instead that the effect of group appeal on attitudes is direct (i.e., nonthoughtful).

Thus, if identification determines the process through which ingroup persuasion occurs, then both high- and low-identified individuals would be expected to show ingroup persuasion, that is, there must be an effect of group appeal on their attitudes to mediate (see Muller, Judd, and Yzerbyt 2005). In addition, we would expect that for high-identified individuals, group appeal affects thoughts, and thoughts mediate the effect of group appeal on attitudes. In contrast, for low-identified individuals, we would expect the effect of group appeal on thoughts to be absent, and thoughts should not mediate the effect of group appeal on attitudes, indicating instead that the effect of group appeal on attitudes is direct (i.e., nonthoughtful).

If instead elaboration likelihood, that is, Need for Cognition (NC), moderates the process through which ingroup persuasion occurs for high-identified individuals, then

Figure 8.1 **Standardized Mean Attitudes as a Function of Identification and Group Appeal**

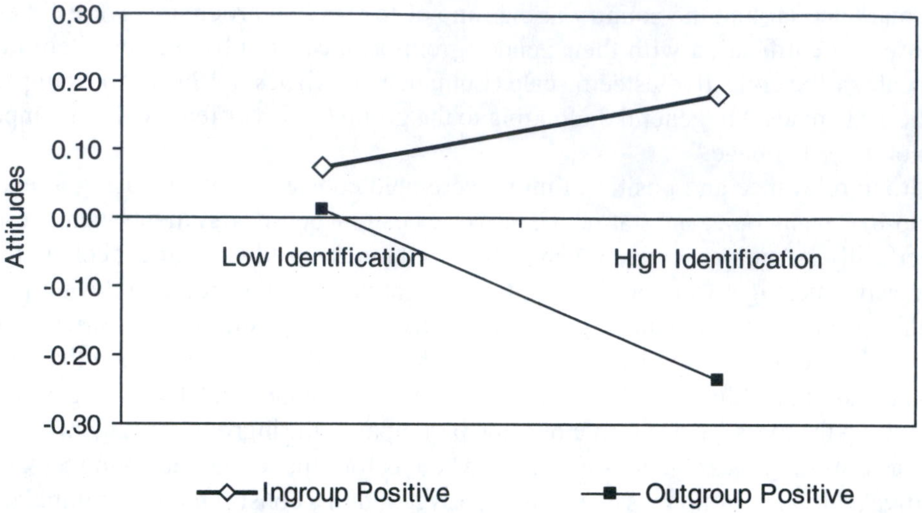

Note: Plotted at +1 and −1 SD for identification.

high-identified individuals would be expected to show ingroup persuasion both when elaboration likelihood was high (high-NC) and when elaboration likelihood was low (low-NC; see Muller et al., 2005). In addition, we would expect that for high-identified high-NC individuals, group appeal affects thoughts, and thoughts mediate the effect of group appeal on attitudes. In contrast, for high-identified low-NC individuals, we would expect the effect of group appeal on thoughts to be absent, and thoughts should not mediate the effect of group appeal on attitudes, indicating instead that the effect of group appeal on attitudes is direct (i.e., nonthoughtful).

A Group Appeal (effect-coded ingroup positive/outgroup negative = 1, outgroup positive/ingroup negative = −1) × Identification with ingroup × NC between-participants simultaneous multiple regression on attitudes (Aiken and West, 1991), revealed an Identification × Group Appeal interaction (see Figure 8.1), indicating that group appeal had an effect on the attitudes of high-identified individuals such that their attitudes were more favorable toward the product when the ingroup was positive and outgroup negative than when the outgroup was positive and ingroup negative. That is, high-identified individuals showed ingroup persuasion. In contrast, for low-identified individuals, group appeal had no effect, indicating that they did not show ingroup persuasion, and replicating the pattern found by Wood and colleagues (1996) Thus, it does not appear that identification determined the process through which ingroup persuasion occurred.

Simple mediation tests for high-identified individuals (those above the median) were conducted for the high-identified high-NC versus high-identified low-NC groups (Baron and Kenny, 1986). These analyses revealed that, for high-identified individuals who were high-NC (see Figure 8.2, top), group appeal had a positive effect on both attitudes and

Figure 8.2   **High-identified: High-NC versus Low-NC**

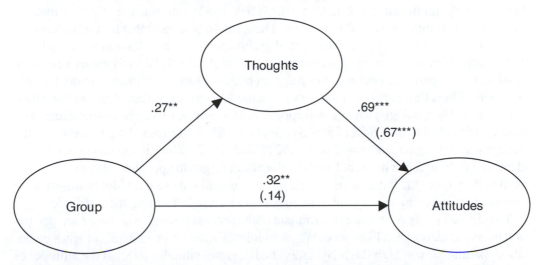

High-identified/High-NC: Unstandardized estimates from regression mediation analyses for those high-identified and high-NC. Estimates in parentheses are for simultaneous model; estimates not in parentheses are previous steps.

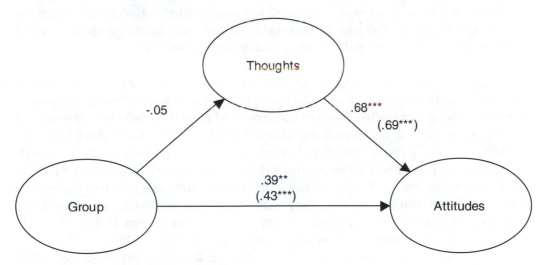

High-identified/Low-NC: Unstandardized estimates from regression mediation analyses for those high-identified and low-NC. Estimates in parentheses are for simultaneous model; estimates not in parentheses are for previous steps.

thought positivity, and thought positivity was related to attitudes. That is, both their attitudes and their thoughts about snickerdoodles in response to the ad were more positive when the ingroup was positive about snickerdoodles and the outgroup was negative than when the outgroup was positive about snickerdoodles and the ingroup was negative. When group appeal and thought positivity were simultaneously placed in the model predicting attitudes, the effect of group appeal on attitudes was no longer significant, and this decrease was significant, $z = 2.80$, $p < .01$ (Sobel, 1982), whereas the effect of thought positivity on attitudes remained significant. These findings suggest that for high-identified individuals who were high-NC, the effect of group appeal on attitudes was fully mediated by thoughts in response to the advertisement. For high-identified individuals who were low-NC (see Figure 8.2, bottom), group appeal had an effect on attitudes, but not thought positivity. Thus, thoughts could not serve as a mediator of the effect of group appeal on attitudes. Not surprisingly, when group appeal and thought positivity were simultaneously placed in the model, the effect of group appeal on attitudes remained significant, and the change was not significant, $z = -.50$, $p = .62$ (Sobel, 1982). Thus, it appears that for high-identified individuals who were low-NC, the effect of group appeal on attitudes was not mediated by thoughts but was instead direct. Presumably, these individuals simply used the positions taken by the ingroup and outgroup as a cue in forming their attitude.

These results suggest that one determinant of the process through which ingroup persuasion occurs is elaboration likelihood. When recipients' motivation to think, and thus elaboration likelihood, was high (high-NC individuals), group attitudes affected the attitudes of high-identified individuals by affecting their thoughts in reaction to an ad. When recipients' motivation to think, and thus elaboration likelihood, was low (low-NC individuals), group attitudes affected the attitudes of high-identified individuals through a relatively nonthoughtful process, relying on group positions as a cue to forming attitudes. Both findings occurred with group relevance and message position held constant, such that the group relevance of the topic was relatively low, and message positions were stated first.

Thus, these findings provide a possible integrative resolution to the seemingly inconsistent findings about the processes through which ingroup appeals affect persuasion when the topic is not group-relevant and positions are stated before message arguments. It appears that elaboration likelihood can determine whether thoughtful or nonthoughtful ingroup persuasion will occur, even under these conditions. Given that elaboration likelihood has also been proposed to explain why group-relevance and position timing moderate the process through which ingroup persuasion occurs (e.g., Mackie et al. 1990, 1992; van Knippenberg et al. 1994), these findings help to organize the research in the ingroup persuasion literature under one conceptual umbrella, suggesting that ingroup persuasion, more generally, occurs through a thoughtful process when elaboration likelihood is high, but through a nonthoughtful process when elaboration likelihood is low.

Group appeals only enhanced persuasion, through these multiple processes, when individuals were highly identified with their ingroup. Thus, two additional points can be made. First, group appeals only served as a cue for those who were highly identified with the ingroup. In contrast, those low in identification did not show ingroup persuasion. These findings support the hypothesis proposed by Mackie and colleagues (1992) that ingroup sources have the power to act as a simple persuasive cue to the extent that message recipients identify as group members.

These results also seem to provide evidence of a mechanism of persuasion similar to what Kelman (1958, 1961) presumably intended by identification: attitude change that arises from a desire to establish or maintain a self-defining relationship with the source's group, a process of persuasion that is distinct from the thoughtful and thorough integration of new material into a broad framework of cognitive associations. Thus, it appears that identification can lead to nonthoughtful group-based persuasion, suggesting that simply knowing if a message recipient is highly identified with the ingroup will not ensure that consequential (i.e., thoughtful) group-based persuasion will occur.

Second, high-identified individuals also showed *thoughtful* ingroup persuasion, whereas low-identified individuals did not. When elaboration likelihood was high, the thoughts of high-identified individuals in response to the ad were more positive toward the product when the identical arguments described why the ingroup was positive and the outgroup negative than when they described why the outgroup was positive and the ingroup negative, and these more positive thoughts resulted in more positive attitudes. Thus, the current results suggest that, unlike Kelman's theory, ingroup identity not only affects attitudes positively by a nonthoughtful process he termed identification (going along simply because of one's identity) but also by a thoughtful process more similar to what he termed internalization (going along because one's identity affects one's thoughtful assessment of the evidence presented). This thinking appears to have been biased, consisting either of biased thinking in which message recipients selectively search for and find the strengths in the arguments in the ingroup message but the flaws in the arguments in the outgroup message, or of increased objective thinking about the ingroup rather than outgroup appeal in which the bias is in the selective attention given to an ingroup message over an equally available outgroup message.

Prior to the current work, it may have appeared that the findings of Wood and colleagues (1996) already ruled out the notion that high-identified individuals would always show nonthoughtful ingroup persuasion. However, in the research by Wood and colleagues, the ingroup was also in the numerical majority, constituting 87 percent of all students at the university, and thus high-identified individuals may have shown thoughtful majority group rather than ingroup persuasion, perhaps due to another mechanism such as surprise at holding an attitude that is discrepant from the valued majority view (Baker and Petty 1994). The thoughtful ingroup persuasion for high-identified individuals found here occurred even though the ingroup was not in the numerical majority, and thus this appears to be the first demonstration of thoughtful ingroup nonmajority persuasion.

In sum, the current findings suggest that identification, that is, one's self-defining relationship with the ingroup, does not lead only to nonthoughtful ingroup persuasion (i.e., the traditional viewpoint, e.g., Kelman 1958, 1961), or to thoughtful ingroup persuasion (more recent views). Instead, identification appears to do both, consistent with the ELM's (Petty and Cacioppo 1986a) notion that variables can serve multiple roles in persuasion depending on elaboration likelihood.

THOUGHTFUL AND NONTHOUGHTFUL GROUP-BASED PERSUASION: WHY DOES IT OCCUR?

These results also speak to the question of why group-based persuasion occurs. Specifically, they suggest that the importance of the ingroup to the self-concept (i.e., the centrality component of identification, see Ashmore, Deaux, and McLaughlin-Volpe 2004) can motivate individuals to adopt the ingroup's attitudes through thoughtful and nonthoughtful processes. A number of more specific reasons why we might expect high-identified individuals to be particularly likely to show ingroup persuasion have been proposed (e.g., see Fleming and Petty 2000, for a review). We will focus here on two explanations, having to do with the function attitudes may play in individuals' management of their relationship to the ingroup.

Thus far, there is no evidence that low-identified individuals show nonthoughtful (or thoughtful) ingroup persuasion. Revisiting Kelman's (1958, 1961) notion that identified individuals may adopt the ingroup's attitudes in order to *establish* or maintain their self-defining relationship with the ingroup (see also the motive of *relating* to others, e.g., Chaiken et al. 1996; Prislin and Wood 2005; Wood 1999, 2000) led to an examination of whether individuals can lack the identification level they want. In other words, loosely building on Higgins's (1989) self-discrepancy theory and its application to social roles (e.g., child) in identity-discrepancy theory (Large and Marcussen 2000; Marcussen 2006), is it possible that *identification discrepancies* exist (Fleming and Petty, 2000)? For example, there may be some individuals who are less identified than they ideally wish to be such that they are *under-identified,* others who are more identified than they ideally want to be such that they are *over-identified,* and still others with no discrepancy who are *satisfied* with their identification level.

If identification discrepancies do exist, they may have consequences for ingroup persuasion that shed light on why it occurs. For example, those who are satisfied with their identification level, whom we may previously have assumed constituted our entire sample, may show the pattern found thus far: those who are highly identified with their ingroup and are satisfied may adopt ingroup attitudes in order to *maintain* their relationship with the ingroup, whereas those who are low in identification with their ingroup and satisfied may choose not to agree with ingroup attitudes in order to maintain their lack of a relationship with the ingroup.

A second reason individuals adopt ingroup attitudes may be that they want to reduce the discrepancy between their actual and ideal level of identification, and become more identified—that is, they want to *establish* a self-defining relationship with the ingroup. This second possibility suggests that under-identified individuals may be more likely to show ingroup persuasion than over-identified individuals, even when they are low in identification.

In combination, these hypotheses predict that the ingroup persuasion previously found for high-identified individuals will be moderated by identification discrepancy, such that ingroup persuasion occurs for high-identified individuals who are satisfied, and high-identified individuals who are under-identified, but is attenuated for high-identified individuals who are over-identified. In addition, ingroup persuasion may emerge for under-identified individuals who are low identified, in which case a Group Appeal × Identification Discrepancy interaction should also emerge for low-identified individuals. Either motive could lead individuals to adopt ingroup attitudes through a thoughtful process when elaboration likelihood is high, and through a nonthoughtful process when elaboration likelihood is low.

In order to examine these questions, we also included a measure of identification discrepancy. Specifically, immediately following the identification measure, participants also completed a measure of their ideal level of identification with their gender ingroup, which consisted of four items that were modified from the (actual) identification measure. These items read: "In general, I would like belonging to the group (males or females) to be an important part of my self-image"; "Overall, ideally I would like my membership in the group (males or females) to have very little to do with how I feel about myself" (reverse-scored); "Ideally, I would like the group I belong to (males or females) to be an important reflection of who I am"; and "Ideally, I would like the group I belong to (males or females) to have nothing to do with my sense of what kind of a person I am" (reverse-scored). Identification discrepancy was calculated by subtracting the ideal score from the (actual) identification score. This calculation revealed that the majority of participants had an identification discrepancy with regard to their gender ingroup, a rather extraordinary finding in itself: 16 percent of the sample ($N = 104$) had identification discrepancy scores of zero and were thus presumably satisfied; 60 percent ($N = 399$) were more identified than they ideally wanted to be and were thus over-identified; and 24 percent ($N = 158$) were less identified than they ideally wanted to be and were thus under-identified.

A Group Appeal (ingroup positive/outgroup negative or outgroup positive/ingroup negative) × Identification with ingroup level (high or low) × Identification Discrepancy level (over-identified or satisfied or under-identified) × NC level (high or low) between-participants ANOVA on attitudes revealed an Identification × Group Appeal × Identification Discrepancy interaction (see Figure 8.3).[2] This interaction indicated that, for high-identified individuals, a Group Appeal × Identification Discrepancy interaction occurred indicating that the effect of group appeal on attitudes did not differ between high-identified individuals who were satisfied and high-identified individuals who were under-identified, and ingroup persuasion was greater for these two groups combined than for high-identified individuals who were over-identified. For low-identified individuals, however, no effects were significant, indicating that ingroup persuasion did not occur, regardless of discrepancy level.

These results suggest that ingroup persuasion occurs because individuals want to maintain or increase the self-defining relationship with the ingroup they already have. That is, high-identified satisfied individuals may have adopted ingroup attitudes because they want to maintain their self-defining relationship with the ingroup (Kelman, 1958, 1961), whereas high-identified under-identified individuals may have adopted ingroup attitudes because they want to maintain or increase the self-defining relationship with the ingroup that they already have. The finding that under-identified individuals who were low-identified did not also show ingroup persuasion suggests that individuals did not adopt the ingroup's attitudes because they were motivated to establish a self-defining relationship with the ingroup that they did not already have (Kelman, 1958, 1961; Chaiken et al., 1996; Prislin and Wood, 2005; Wood, 1999, 2000), or to reduce the discrepancy between their actual and ideal level of identification to become more identified (Fleming and Petty, 2000).

Figure 8.3 **Standardized Mean Attitudes as a Function of Identification, Group Appeal, and Identification Discrepancy Level**

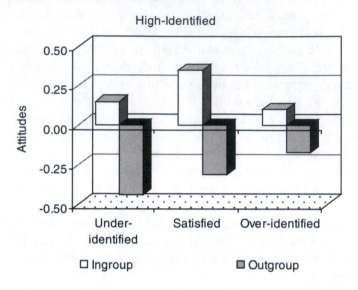

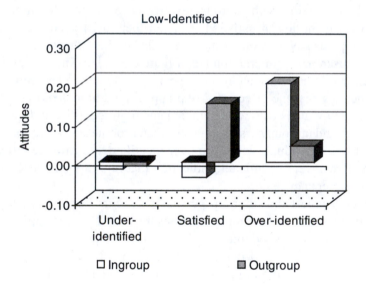

Thoughts were then analyzed to examine whether either motive, or both, leads individuals to adopt ingroup attitudes through a thoughtful process when elaboration likelihood is high, and through a nonthoughtful process when elaboration likelihood is low. Initial analyses of thoughts indicated that identification discrepancy (satisfied versus under-identified) did not moderate results, and thus the two groups—high-identified satisfied and high-identified under-identified individuals—were collapsed. Simple mediation tests revealed that, for high-identified satisfied and high-identified under-identified individuals

Figure 8.4 **High-identified/Satisfied and Under-identified: High-NC vs. Low-NC**

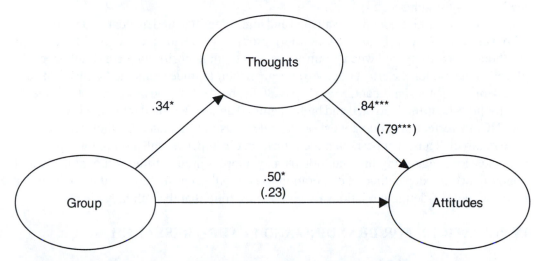

High-identified/Satisfied and Under-identified/High-NC: Unstandardized estimates from regression mediation analyses for those high-identified satisfied and under-identified and high-NC. Estimates in parentheses are for simultaneous model; estimates not in parentheses are previous steps.

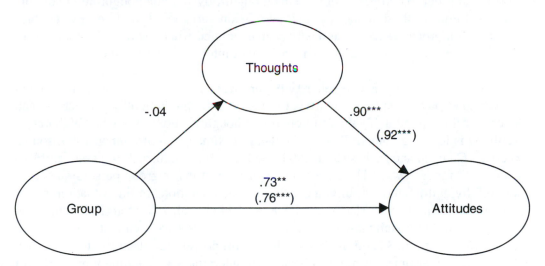

High-identified/Satisfied and Under-identified/Low NC: Unstandardized estimates from regression mediation analyses for those high-identified satisfied and under-identified and low-NC. Estimates in parentheses are for simultaneous model; estimates not in parentheses are for previous steps.

who were high-NC (see Figure 8.4, top), group appeal had an effect on both attitudes and thought positivity. In addition, thought positivity was related to attitudes. When group appeal and thought positivity were simultaneously placed in the model, the effect of group appeal on attitudes was no longer significant, and this decrease was significant, $z = 1.96$, $p < .05$ (Sobel 1982), whereas the effect of thought positivity on attitudes remained significant, suggesting that for high-identified satisfied and high-identified under-identified individuals who were high-NC, the effect of group appeal on their attitudes was fully mediated by thoughts.

In contrast, for high-identified satisfied and high-identified under-identified individuals who were low-NC (see Figure 8.4, bottom), group appeal had an effect on attitudes, but not thought positivity, and when group appeal and thought positivity were simultaneously placed in the model, the effect of group appeal on their attitudes remained significant, and the change was not significant, $z = -.18$, $p = .86$ (Sobel 1982). Thus, in contrast, it appears that for high-identified satisfied and high-identified under-identified individuals who were low-NC, the effect of group appeal on attitudes was not mediated by thoughts but was instead direct. Thus, it appears that identification discrepancies also serve multiple roles in persuasion, suggesting that individuals may adopt ingroup attitudes thoughtfully and nonthoughtfully, depending on elaboration likelihood, because they want to maintain or increase the self-defining relationship with the ingroup that they already have.

IMPLICATIONS FOR BRANDING AND FUTURE RESEARCH

These findings suggest that group-based persuasion is especially likely to occur for high-identified individuals, particularly those who are satisfied or under-identified. They also suggest that group-based persuasion occurs thoughtfully and nonthoughtfully under the same conditions as those found for other persuasion variables. The effects of variables on persuasion processes have classically been examined when the message topic is not particularly relevant to the independent variable of interest, and when the message position is stated before arguments are presented (see Hovland, Janis, and Kelley 1953; Eagly and Chaiken 1993; Petty and Wegener 1998, for reviews). In this situation, other persuasion variables have been found to affect persuasion through thoughtful processes when elaboration likelihood is high, and through nonthoughtful processes when elaboration likelihood is low (e.g., mood: Petty, Schumann, Richman, and Strathman 1993; source expertise: Chaiken and Maheswaran 1994; see Eagly and Chaiken 1993; Petty and Wegener 1998, for reviews).[3] The current findings suggest that ingroup persuasion occurs thoughtfully and nonthoughtfully under these same conditions in this situation, rather than only as a simple cue (Mackie et al. 1990; Mackie et al. 1992; van Knippenberg et al. 1994), or only through biased thinking (Wood et al. 1996). Given that prior research has shown that attitudes resulting from a thoughtful process are stronger such that they persist longer over time, are more resistant to counterattack, and are more predictive of behavior than attitudes resulting from a nonthoughtful process (Petty et al. 1995), these findings suggest that group-based persuasion will be as consequential as persuasion created by other variables, producing stronger (more consequential) attitudes when it occurs under high-elaboration likelihood conditions (through a thoughtful process) than under low-elaboration likelihood conditions (through a nonthoughtful process).

Thus, from an attitudes and persuasion perspective, fostering a brand relationship by associating a brand with a consumer's ingroup in a marketing appeal would be expected to have a positive impact on consumer-brand interactions such as brand purchase, loyalty, and willingness to pay a price premium when the consumer is highly identified with the ingroup—and, in particular, is satisfied that this is the case or is under-identified, and when the consumer has high motivation and ability to elaborate the contents of the appeal. It is not sufficient to know if the consumer is a member of a particular group. Nor, however, is it sufficient to know only if the consumer is highly identified with the ingroup, or has high motivation and ability to elaborate the contents of the appeal. For a group-based appeal to be effective, it seems that one needs to know all three.

One remaining question is whether strong, cogent arguments in favor of the brand (attitude object) are necessary. Some research has found that, when message recipients are elaborating message contents, group-based persuasion is attenuated or even reversed when weak arguments are presented—that is, an ingroup message source leads to attitudes that are as positive or even less positive than an outgroup message source (e.g., Mackie et al. 1990, 1992), because the more one thinks objectively about specious arguments, the weaker they seem and the more negative message recipients are toward the attitude object (see Petty and Cacioppo 1986a). However, other work suggests that high-identified individuals are motivated to interpret information associated with the ingroup in a positively biased fashion (e.g., Wood et al. 1996). In the current work, the thinking under high-elaboration likelihood by high-identified (satisfied and under-identified) individuals consisted either of biased thinking or of increased objective thinking about the ingroup than outgroup appeal. If the latter, then weak arguments would be expected to be ineffective or backfire when ingroup persuasion is thoughtful, in which case fostering a group-based relationship between a consumer and a brand will decrease rather than increase behaviors such as brand purchase, loyalty, and willingness to pay a price premium.

Interestingly, the current perspective may suggest a solution to a recent challenge to the role of strong attitudes in guiding behavior. Recently, it has been suggested that although strong attitudes may guide easier or less complex brand-related behaviors (e.g., one-time purchase), a strong relationship with a brand in the form of attachment instead guides more difficult and complex brand-related behaviors (e.g., postponing purchase, Park, MacInnis, and Priester 2006). By strengthening brand relationships as well as creating strong attitudes, group-based persuasion may belong to a somewhat unique set of persuasion variables that cover the entire spectrum of behaviors.

An interesting related question is whether persuasion that occurs through high elaboration also creates stronger brand relationships than persuasion that occurs through low elaboration, in addition to stronger brand attitudes, or whether merely linking a persuasive appeal to the ingroup (with which the consumer is highly identified) suffices in creating strong brand relationships. Consistent with the former possibility, Wegener and colleagues (Chapter 15) propose that the attitude a consumer has toward a brand *is* the relationship the consumer has with the brand, or is the basis for such a relationship, and that the same processes that lead to the formation of strong brand attitudes lead to the formation of strong brand relationships.

Finally, the Multiple Pathway Anchoring and Adjustment (MPAA) model of attitude generation and recruitment (Cohen and Reed 2006; see also Chapter 7) proposes that when the group is a prominent aspect of one's self-concept, group-based attitude change is likely to occur through an inside-out process consisting of self-related elaboration and evaluating the attitude object from a self-system standpoint, as opposed to an outside-in process consisting of object-centered elaboration and evaluating the attitude object on the basis of its important attributes. In contrast, the current research provides clear evidence for the latter, that group-based persuasion can occur through an outside-in process because identification affects object-centered thoughts.

It would be interesting to examine whether group-based persuasion can occur because identification affects self-related thoughts, and whether object-centered and self-related thought lead equally to the creation of strong attitudes. These possibilities gain credence with the recent finding that consumers primed with an interdependent self-construal (perhaps situationally induced high identification) resisted negative information about a brand from their own country (but not a different country) with country-of-origin-based counterarguments (e.g., "Dell is a reliable American brand, and I don't trust these ratings"), thus maintaining their initial positive attitudes (Swaminathan et al. 2007, p. 253).

In sum, the current perspective advances our understanding of when ingroups' influence is thoughtful versus nonthoughtful, for whom it occurs, and why. This work suggests that attitudes are relevant to the maintenance and possibly development (though not establishment) of relationships with ingroups, in that individuals appear to adopt ingroup attitudes in order to maintain and possibly increase the self-defining relationship with the ingroup that they already have, and do so thoughtfully and nonthoughtfully depending on elaboration likelihood. These insights increase our understanding of when brand relationships based on group membership will be consequential for consumer-brand interactions.

NOTES

1. Prislin and Wood (2005) also propose an alternative conceptualization of identification as a measure of the strength of the motive of *being* oneself, and propose that high-identified individuals may show ingroup persuasion through a thoughtful process, but low-identified individuals may show ingroup persuasion through a nonthoughtful process, because both may be motivated to express themselves as a coherent and favorably evaluated entity by agreeing with the ingroup, and stronger motivation may lead to greater cognitive efforts to do so. Both conceptualizations lead to the same predictions for the present purposes.

2. Results for ANOVA are reported rather than regression because the conceptual difference between scores of 0 versus 1 (satisfied versus over-identified) and 0 versus–1 (satisfied versus under-identified) is larger than the difference between a score of 9 versus 10 (over-identified versus slightly more over-identified), and ANOVA better captures this trichotomous conceptualization. However, results are the same in regression when identification discrepancy is entered as a trichotomous variable using two effects-coded variables (Aiken and West 1991), and identification and need for cognition remain continuous.

3. For example, when a person's mood and the message position were introduced prior to a mood-irrelevant message, mood has been found to lead to persuasion through a thoughtful process, by biasing thinking, when elaboration likelihood is high because recipients are high in need for cognition, and through a nonthoughtful process, by serving as a cue, when elaboration likelihood is low because recipients are low in need for cognition (Petty et al. 1993). The same is true for source expertise (Chaiken and Maheswaran 1994).

REFERENCES

Aiken, L.S., and West, S.G. (1991). *Multiple Regression: Testing and Interpreting Interactions.* Thousand Oaks, CA: Sage.

Asch, S.E. (1940). "Studies in the Principles of Judgments and Attitudes: II. Determination of Judgments by Group and by Ego Standards," *Journal of Social Psychology,* 12, 433–465.

———. (1948). "The Doctrine of Suggestion, Prestige, and Imitation in Social Psychology," *Psychological Review,* 55, 250–276.

———. (1951). "Effects of Group Pressure upon the Modification and Distortion of Judgments." In *Groups, Leadership and Men,* ed. H. Guetzkow. Pittsburgh, PA: Carnegie Press, 177–190.

Ashmore, R.D., K. Deaux, and T. McLaughlin-Volpe (2004). "An Organizing Framework for Collective Identity: Articulation and Significance of Multidimensionality," *Psychological Bulletin,* 130, 80–114.

Baker, S.M., and R.E. Petty (1994). "Majority and Minority Influence: Source Position Imbalance as a Determinant of Message Scrutiny," *Journal of Personality and Social Psychology,* 67, 5–19.

Baron, R.M., and D.A. Kenny (1986). "The Moderator-Mediator Variable Distinction in Social Psychological Research: Conceptual, Strategic, and Statistical Considerations," *Journal of Personality and Social Psychology,* 51, 1173–1182.

Cacioppo, J.T., and R.E. Petty (1982). "The Need for Cognition," *Journal of Personality and Social Psychology,* 42, 116–131.

Cacioppo, J.T., R.E. Petty, J.A. Feinstein, and W.B.G. Jarvis (1996). "Dispositional Differences in Cognitive Motivation: The Life and Times of Individuals Varying in Need for Cognition," *Psychological Bulletin,* 119, 197–253.

Chaiken, S., R. Giner-Sorolla, and S. Chen (1996). "Beyond Accuracy: Defense and Impression Motives in Heuristic and Systematic Information Processing." In *The Psychology of Action: Linking Cognition and Motivation to Behavior,* ed. P.M. Gollwitzer and J.A. Bargh. New York, NY: Guilford, 553–578.

Chaiken, S., A. Liberman, and A.H. Eagly (1989). "Heuristic and Systematic Information Processing within and beyond the Persuasion Context." In *Unintended Thought,* ed. J.S. Uleman and J.A. Bargh. New York, NY: Guilford Press, 212–252.

Chaiken, S., and D. Maheswaran (1994). "Heuristic Processing Can Bias Systematic Processing: Effects of Source Credibility, Argument Ambiguity, and Task Importance on Attitude Judgment," *Journal of Personality and Social Psychology,* 66, 460–473.

Cohen, G.L. (2003). "Party over Policy: The Dominating Impact of Group Influence on Political Beliefs," *Journal of Personality and Social Psychology,* 85, 808–822.

Cohen, J.B., and A. Reed (2006). "A Multiple Pathway Anchoring and Adjustment (MPAA) Model of Attitude Generation and Recruitment," *Journal of Consumer Research,* 33, 1–15.

Deutsch, M., and H.B. Gerard (1955). "A Study of Normative and Informational Influences upon Individual Judgment," *Journal of Abnormal and Social Psychology,* 51, 629–636.

Eagly, A.H., and S. Chaiken (1993). *The Psychology of Attitudes.* Fort Worth, TX: Harcourt, Brace, Jovanovich.

Escalas, J.E., and J.R. Bettman (2005). "Self-construal, Reference Groups, and Brand Meaning," *Journal of Consumer Research,* 32, 378–389.

Festinger, L. (1950). "Informal Social Communication," *Psychological Review,* 57, 271–282.

Fleming, M.A. (2009). "Ingroup and Outgroup Messages and Persuasion: Different Roles for Ingroup Identification and Identification Discrepancies under High- and Low-Elaboration Conditions," working paper, University of Southern California.

Fleming, M.A., and R.E. Petty (2000). "Identity and Persuasion: An Elaboration Likelihood Approach." In *Attitudes, Behavior, and Social Context: The Role of Norms and Group Membership,* ed. D.J. Terry and M.A. Hogg. Mahwah, NJ: Lawrence Erlbaum, 171–199.

Fournier, S. (1998). "Consumers and Their Brands: Developing Relationship Theory in Consumer Research," *Journal of Consumer Research,* 24, 343–373.

Gürhan-Canli, Z., and D. Maheswaran (2000). "Cultural Variations in Country of Origin Effects," *Journal of Marketing Research,* 35, 464–473.

Higgins, E.T. (1989). "Self-Discrepancy Theory: What Patterns of Self-Beliefs Cause People to Suffer?" In *Advances in Experimental Social Psychology* (Vol. 22), ed. L. Berkowitz. New York, NY: Academic Press, 93–136.

Hong, S., and R.S. Wyer (1990). "Determinants of Product Evaluation: Effects of Time Interval between Knowledge of a Product's Country-of-origin and Its Specific Attributes," *Journal of Consumer Research,* 17, 277–288.

Hovland, C.I., I.L. Janis, and H.H. Kelley (1953). *Communication and Persuasion: Psychological Studies of Opinion Change.* New Haven, CT: Yale University Press.

Kelman, H.C. (1958). "Compliance, Identification, and Internalization: Three Processes of Attitude Change," *Journal of Conflict Resolution,* 2, 51–60.

———. (1961). "Processes of Attitude Change," *Public Opinion Quarterly,* 25, 57–78.

Large, M.D., and K. Marcussen (2000). "Extending Identity Theory to Predict Differential Forms and Degrees of Psychological Distress," *Social Psychology Quarterly,* 63 (1), 49–59.

Luhtanen, R., and J. Crocker (1992). "A Collective Self-esteem scale: Self-evaluation of One's Social Identity," *Personality and Social Psychology Bulletin,* 18, 302–318.

Mackie, D.M., M.C. Gastardo-Conaco, and J.J. Skelly (1992). "Knowledge of the Advocated Position and the Processing of In-Group and Out-Group Persuasive Messages," *Personality and Social Psychology Bulletin,* 18, 145–151.

Mackie, D.M., and S. Queller (2000). "The Impact of Group Membership on Persuasion: Revisiting 'Who says what to whom with what effect?'" In *Attitudes, Behavior, and Social Context: The Role of Norms and Group Membership,* ed. D.J. Terry and M.A. Hogg. Mahwah, NJ: Lawrence Erlbaum, 171–199.

Mackie, D.M., L.T. Worth, and A.G. Asuncion (1990). "Processing of Persuasive In-group Messages," *Journal of Personality and Social Psychology,* 58, 812–822.

Maheswaran, D. (1994). "Country of Origin as a Stereotype: Effects of Consumer Expertise and Attribute Strength on Product Evaluations," *Journal of Consumer Research,* 21, 354–365.

Marcussen, K. (2006). "Identities, Self-esteem, and Psychological Distress: An Application of Identity-Discrepancy Theory," *Sociological Perspectives,* 49 (1), 1–24.

Muller, D., C.M. Judd, and V.Y. Yzerbyt (2005). "When Moderation Is Mediated and Mediation Is Moderated," *Journal of Personality and Social Psychology,* 89, 852–863.

Park, C.W., D.J. MacInnis, and J.R. Priester (2006). "Beyond Attitudes: Attachment and Consumer Behavior," *Seoul National Journal,* 12 (2), 3–36.

Petty, R.E., and J.T. Cacioppo (1979). "Issue Involvement Can Increase or Decrease Persuasion by Enhancing Message-Relevant Cognitive Responses," *Journal of Personality and Social Psychology,* 37, 1915–1926.

———. (1986a). *Communication and Persuasion: Central and Peripheral Routes to Attitude Change.* New York, NY: Springer-Verlag.

———. (1986b). "The Elaboration Likelihood Model of Persuasion." In *Advances in Experimental Social Psychology* (Vol. 19), ed. L. Berkowitz. New York, NY: Academic Press, 123–205.

Petty, R.E., C.P. Haugtvedt, and S.M. Smith (1995). "Elaboration as a Determinant of Attitude Strength: Creating Attitudes that Are Persistent, Resistant, and Predictive of Behavior." In *Attitude Strength: Antecedents and Consequences,* ed. R.E. Petty and J.A. Krosnick. Hillsdale, NJ: Lawrence Erlbaum, 93–130.

Petty, R.E., D.W. Schumann, S.A. Richman, and A.J. Strathman (1993). "Positive Mood and Persuasion: Different Roles for Affect Under High- and Low-Elaboration Conditions," *Journal of Personality and Social Psychology,* 64, 5–20.

Petty, R.E., and D.T. Wegener (1998). "Attitude Change: Multiple Roles for Persuasion Variables." In *The Handbook of Social Psychology,* 4th ed. (Vol. 1), ed. D. Gilbert, S. Fiske, and G. Lindzey. New York, NY: McGraw-Hill, 323–390.

Petty, R.E., G.L. Wells, and T.C. Brock (1976). "Distraction Can Enhance or Reduce Yielding to Propaganda," *Journal of Personality and Social Psychology,* 34, 874–884.

Prislin, R., and W. Wood (2005). "Social Influence in Attitudes and Attitude Change." In *The Handbook of Attitudes,* ed. D. Albarracín, B.T. Johnson, and M.P. Zanna. Mahwah, NJ: Lawrence Erlbaum, 671–706.

Reed, A. (2004). "Activating the Self-Importance of Consumer Selves: Exploring Identity Salience Effects on Judgments," *Journal of Consumer Research,* 31, 286–295.

Shavitt, S., and M.R. Nelson (2000). "The Social-identity Function in Person Perception: Communicated Meanings of Product Preferences." In *Why We Evaluate: Functions of Attitudes,* ed. G. Maio and J.M. Olson. Mahwah, NJ: Lawrence Erlbaum, 37–57.

Sobel, M.E. (1982). "Asymptotic Confidence Intervals for Indirect Effects in Structural Equations Models." In *Sociological Methodology 1982,* ed. S. Leinhart. San Francisco, CA: Jossey-Bass.

Swaminathan, V., K.L. Page, and Z. Gürhan-Canli (2007). "'My' Brand or 'Our' Brand: The Effects of Brand Relationship Dimensions and Self-construal on Brand Evaluations," *Journal of Consumer Research,* 34, 248–259.

Tajfel, H., and J.C. Turner (1986). "The Social Identity Theory of Intergroup Behavior." In *Psychology of Intergroup Relations,* ed. S. Worchel and W.G. Austin. Chicago, IL: Nelson-Hall, 7–24.

van Knippenberg, D. (1999). "Social Identity and Persuasion: Reconsidering the Role of Group Membership." In *Social Identity and Social Cognition,* ed. D. Abrams and M.A. Hogg. Oxford, UK: Blackwell, 315–331.

———. (2000). "Group Norms, Prototypicality, and Persuasion." In *Attitudes, Behavior, and Social Context: The Role of Norms and Group Membership,* ed. D.J. Terry and M.A. Hogg. Mahwah, NJ: Lawrence Erlbaum, 157–170.

van Knippenberg, D., N. Lossie, and H. Wilke (1994). "In-group Prototypicality and Persuasion: Determinants of Heuristic and Systematic Message Processing," *British Journal of Social Psychology,* 33, 289–300.

van Knippenberg, D., and H. Wilke (1992). "Prototypicality of Arguments and Conformity to Ingroup Norms," *European Journal of Social Psychology,* 22, 141–155.

Wood, W. (1999). "Motives and Modes of Processing in the Social Influence of Groups." In *Dual Process Theories in Social Psychology,* ed. S. Chaiken and Y. Trope. New York, NY: Guilford, 547–570.

———. (2000). "Attitude Change: Persuasion and Social Influence," *Annual Review of Psychology,* 51, 539–570.

Wood, W., G.J. Pool, K. Leck, and D. Purvis (1996). "Self-Definition, Defensive Processing, and Influence: The Normative Impact of Majority and Minority Groups," *Journal of Personality and Social Psychology,* 71, 1181–1193.

PART III

BRAND MEANING AND
MEANING MAKERS

CHAPTER 9

COLLECTIVE BRAND RELATIONSHIPS

THOMAS C. O'GUINN AND ALBERT M. MUÑIZ, JR.

Fanship, brandship, and relationship are all a part of what the statement "I like this" really means. Your judgment joins a pool of other judgments, a small relationship economy, one of millions that continually coalesce and dissolve, and reform around cultural products-movies, sneakers, jeans, pop songs. Your identity is your investment in these relationship economies.
—*John Seabrook (2000)*

Your judgment joins a pool of other judgments . . .

Yes, it does. There is something to brands beyond the individual consumer. A brand relationship is more than the thoughts and feelings of individual consumers about a brand. There are meaningful collective brand relationships. Further, all "individual" relationships pass through collectives. Brand relationships are made through social forces.

When we were first approached about contributing to this volume we were both flattered and ambivalent. We don't see brand relationships or theorize them as most of these distinguished contributors do. As presently conceived and constituted we are outliers in this sub-area of brand research. To us, brand relationship is an area so thoroughly dominated by psychologists (at least in U.S. business schools) that even the interpretive work (Fournier 1998) in the area is thoroughly individualistic and retro in its 1950s-era projective ethos. There is very little discussion of collective action, thought, memory, or even the role of institutions, society, or collectivity in general. There are just the individual consumers and their minds. Sociology 101 was apparently dropped from the field's brand curriculum. In U.S. academic marketing circles, brand relationships are all about brand-consumer dyads. It even sometimes requires thinking of brands as animate beings, often with personalities (Aaker 1997). So, if the cornflake brand were a human would he/she be friendly/unfriendly, happy-go-lucky, or sullen? Aside from the already noted too-tight focus on the object-person dyad and complete lack of social constructionist thought is the odd (at least to us) reliance on anachronistic 1950s-era neo-Freudian *brand-as-person/pet school* of thought (Bartos 1986). While these formulations may be valuable in creative positioning, an easy-to-get managerial metaphor, and no-doubt entertaining, our own experience, theorizing, and data have led us elsewhere.

Thus the word "relationship" in U.S. academic marketing has typically been used in a very narrow manner. The social world is reduced to brand and consumer, and that's it. Part of the relationship conceit is that these two parties somehow behave toward one another as if both were alive. They both even have personalities despite the fact that one is usually a thing. To state the obvious: brands typically do not have personalities because they do not have predisposition of behavior. Anthropomorphic packaging and mascots aside (Hine 1995; Ludacer 2008), the average Consumer Packaged Good (CPG) does not emote, think, or behave. Marketing departments, ad agencies, media outlets, and any of the myriad other frequently conflicting institutions involved in the production of a brand may do so, but brands do not. We know of no compelling evidence that humans, without being somehow coaxed or demanded to do so, think of brands as humans or even humanlike. While acknowledging brands as the objects of all sorts of human desire, creativity, fantasy, and play (Holbrook and Hirschman 1982), it is humans, human collectives, and institutions that make brands. But this is missing from the brand literature. Where are the discussions of institutions and collectives? Do brand relationships have to be so narrowly conceived?

What we offer instead is an alternative theoretical space for discussing, among other things, brand relationships. It is an attempt to at least change the conversation, even a little. We do this by situating our discussion of brand relationships within an evolving social model of brands that we have been working on for some time. We begin with a definition of brands.

brand (n.) A vessel of popular meaning.

The reader will no doubt note that we use the term *popular* rather than *commercial* or some other narrower mercantile construction. A visit to a contemporary thesaurus shows *popular* as a synonym to *commercial*. This of course makes sense, in that life inside a consumer culture has erased whatever distinction once (if ever) existed between these terms. The popular is the commercial. Commercial culture is popular culture. Just as the U.S. Supreme Court has acknowledged the difficulty in attempting to separately define political and commercial (popular) speech, we cannot say that California Governor Arnold Schwarzenegger is not a brand or that Ben & Jerry's contains no political meaning. Meaning defines brands. This holds true even when that meaning is mundane.

For just a moment, think about how modern brands began. In the late nineteenth century, brands replaced many unmarked commodities. While it is true that there were some branded products prior to this period (such as patent medicines and tobacco), it is during the last two decades of the nineteenth century that the ubiquitous branding we know today began. Between 1875 and 1900, many branded products replaced unbranded commodities (see Figure 9.1). The phenomenal growth first took place in packaged goods. Soap, previously sold by weight from a generally unbranded cake, became Ivory (1882) and Sapolio (circa 1875). Beer, previously drawn from an unnamed keg, became Budweiser (1891) and Pabst (1873). All across the spectrum of goods and services, existing commodities became brands, as did the flood of new things designed for the modern marketplace of 1900.

During the last years of the nineteenth and the first two decades of the twentieth centuries,

Figure 9.1   Number of Brands Registered per Year in the United States, 1870–2006

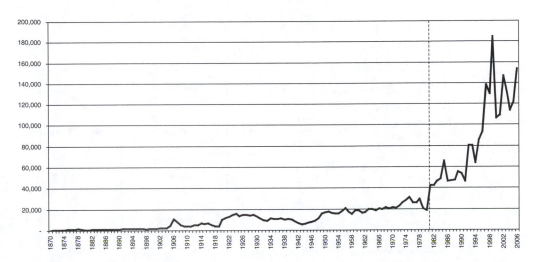

Note: This chart illustrates the dramatic increase in brands in the latter part of the twentieth century.

branding exploded. Advertising and branding pushed marketplace modernity along; they were its engines, its mode. Over the next eight decades, the branding tide rose to cover just about everything. A century later even dirt and water were branded.

THE SOCIAL BRAND

Brands are created by interactions of multiple parties, institutions, publics and social forces. Even the term *co-creation* belies the brand's true nature and is stuck in a fictive dyad: brand/marketer-consumer. Nothing in the material world, the social world, or brand world is that simple or isolated. Thus, we also reject the au courant term, *co-creation,* not because it goes too far, but because it doesn't go far enough. There are more social actors than consumer and marketer in this play. Co-creation, as it is typically used, is thus a critically constrained construct.

Brand managers have for decades spoken in terms of qualitative insights and brand *meaning.* The oft-repeated object lesson of The Coca-Cola Company's confusing attitude assessment of a product with the cultural meaning of a brand is now MBA legend, as it should be (Hays 2004, Pendergrast 1993). Completely consistent with this is the high demand for consultants and brand experts from anthropology, communications, and sociology (Sunderland and Denny 2007).

In the modest hope of improvement we offer a social model of the brand. It is a work in progress. But, it is an honest (if not provocative) attempt to move the brand discourse in a different direction. Brand meaning is plastic and dynamic, continually molded by social forces. We would like to bring some of the sociological imagination (Mills 1959) to the conversation.

Figure 9.2   **A Social Construction Model of Brands**

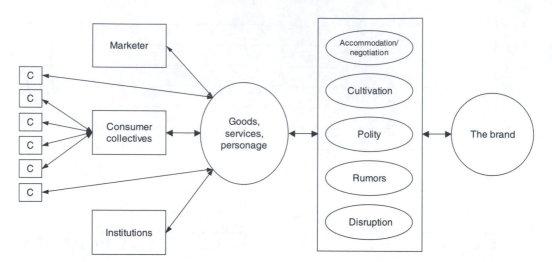

Elsewhere, we have offered the first steps toward a social model of brands (O'Guinn and Muñiz 2009). The basic components (see Figure 9.2) are: the marketer; the good, service, or personage; the individual consumer; consumer collectives; and institutions. Essential processes are accommodation, negotiation, mediated cultivation, collective memory, polity, rumor, and disruption. We will use this model as a platform on which to rest our understanding of brand relationships. Our theory of brands is based on the interplay of several social forces, institutions, consumers, and collectives of consumers. This interplay yields meaning. It yields brands.

The *marketer* is easily conceived. It is the agent who at one time was thought, by some, to own the brand and determine brand meaning. While that was never really true, it is certainly not the case today. Marketers "create" the brand in the sense that they give it initial form, message, packaging, position, and platform. Marketers control a certain amount of monetary capital, means of production, intellectual property, pricing, and distribution authority. The marketer launches the brand and tries to vest it with intended meanings in an attempt to bring about a desired consumer response. But in reality marketers neither own nor control the brand. They do not create the brand: society does. The marketer is a relatively powerful social actor, but by no means the only one.

Even the mighty marketer rarely begins tabula rasa. Marketers are themselves products of social production. Tide is manufactured by Procter & Gamble (P&G). P&G is itself socially formed by various stakeholders, partners, biases, traditions, cultures, social memory, laws, customs, and real and imagined competitors. Interested and vested parties contribute to the birth and launch of brands. The various institutional configurations of P&G's brand management system (and its impact on the general practice of brand management) are well documented (Low and Fullerton 1994). That these differing hierarchies impact the resulting brand offering is taken as a given. Marketers negotiate with engineers, creators, and holders of intellectual property, market researchers, and competitors within and beyond the company and project these things into constructing the "imagined" market for the good or service. For those who have had the opportunity to actually be involved in the launch of a brand, you know about all the backstage politics, expectations, games, test market results, institutional memory and history, imagined target market, and on and on (Rothenberg 1994; Stabiner 1993). All of these, and more, are involved in the social production of the brand before it is ever launched.

The *good, service, or personage* is just that, the physical thing, the material, the actual item offered to the marketplace.

The *consumer* is a focal social actor in the model. This part of the model is where consumer research has labored and produced knowledge about how individuals process brand information, advertising, and other brand communication, and make judgments and decisions.

Consumer Collectives

Sometimes collectives are face-to-face interactions, such as local car clubs or user groups, but more often they are computer-mediated (e.g., online communities), and almost always they are imagined. Other than in face-to-face settings, most community members meet or interact with a fairly small percentage of community members. Most others have to be imagined. The idea of imagined community was notably promoted by sociologist Benedict Anderson (1983) to explain how nation-states (a relatively new phenomenon in human history) came to be. How could hundreds of million people residing in nations covering hundreds or thousands of square miles come to actually think of themselves as Americans, Germans, or Chinese? How can people who never meet one another share such a strong sense of identity, something worth killing and dying for?

In an obviously more trivial sense, how can millions of users of a brand come to think of themselves as loyal Coke drinkers, Blackberry users, or Volvo types? In the imagined brand community is we see admittedly small but meaningful felt affiliations to untold and unseen others. This is not a trivial part of what we call brand equity. As the late Daniel Boorstin, historian and former Librarian of Congress, once noted:

> . . . nearly all the things we consume become thin, but not negligible bonds with thousands of other Americans (Boorstin 1961).

Remember: "thin but not negligible bonds." This is perhaps the hardest notion to get across in thinking about human-brand relationships. These bonds are the thin and typically diaphanous threads that, when combined through the twisting of ubiquitous popular social forces, amount to strong ties to many unseen and unknown others. In modernity most communities are imagined, they are experienced as the soft, comfortable, and sure knowledge of the like-ethos others, whether they involve the other 300 million Americans one does not know directly or the much smaller collective of loyal Pabst Blue Ribbon beer drinkers. We do not know them by name but we know they are there. Brand communities, like most modern communities, depend on the imagined unmet and unremunerated

Figure 9.3   **Brand Community-Invoking In-Store Display**

admirers or users of their brand. It is this understood and imagined notion of other brand users being "just like me" that leads to spontaneous parking lot discussions among drivers of the same brand of car.

If (post)modern society is increasingly noted for a surface orientation, a disconnectedness from neighbors and face-to-face community (Putnam 2000), an ephemeral attachment orientation to all things civic, then would it not make sense that known-in-common commercial referents (brands) would become more, not less, important in social collectivity? For most consumers, that is the level at which the social brand and brand community exist. This is what the sum of our research tells us. True, in our earlier work we highlighted instances where brand communities were active, powerful, and large (Muñiz and O'Guinn 2001). Certainly such communities exist; they have in fact become much more common and widely acknowledged than we first imagined. But we do not want other researchers, managers, or readers to believe that communal brand relationships must always be this strong, or this seemingly fanatical. They do not (see Figure 9.3).

We should not limit brand community discussions to the vanguard, the lead user, or the proudly marginal to engage the larger parent construct: the social brand. For all things there are distributions; the same holds true of brand-person relationships. For most consumers, most of the time, brand relationships are thin (but not negligible), and most collectives or brand communities are imagined and far from fanatical. Unlike people who are weekend Klingons (Kozinets, Stardate June 2001) the typical brand community member has a life that does not require costumes or pilgrimages to the now franchised Burning Man. The typical brand community member merely has to admire collectively and quietly; they do not have to leave town with the circus or find it at a "desert near you." They merely admire and imagine.

The larger point is that in a consumer society brands become non-negligible connections to others. To a relative few, these brand-centered collectives sometimes supplant other social organizing and sanctioning structures. For even fewer, they become truly vital to the consumer and their interface with the social world. Our data reveal this level of brand community commitment as relatively rare, but not completely unimportant, because these highly motivated consumers often figure prominently in social networks. It is, therefore, the entire distribution of brand community affiliation that should be considered. The late CEO of The Coca-Cola Company was not referring to freakish or marginal consumers when he said:

> People around the world are today connected to each other by
> brand-name consumer products as much as by anything else.
> —*Roberto Goizueta, former CEO, The Coca-Cola Company (Pedergrast, 2000)*

The next components in our model are institutions.

Institutions

Institutions include, but are not limited to, media, retailers, equity markets, government, and nongovernmental organizations (NGOs). Institutions also play a role in brand creation. These institutions bring the weight of economics, norms, practice law, and regulation to the ongoing creation of brands. The media, for example, determine what raw materials and modes of meaning creation (e.g., television advertisements, Web pages, branded entertainment, and consumer-generated content) will be available. They determine, as institutions, what demographics can be reached during a certain day-part for a given cost per thousand of eyeballs delivered. They not only define the channels of communication opportunity, but they also define what is not possible, what audiences cannot be delivered for a certain brand for a given price.

Television is bought in the "up-fronts" in a highly institutionalized manner; about $10 billion a year in the United States alone. The parameters of those institutions, their rules, their highly ritualized procedures, their lists of possible and impossible have a significant impact on how a brand comes to have its meaning. The types of programs available are themselves a product of deeply embedded group and cultural processes. For example, the 2007–2008 television season witnessed a pronounced thematic shift, with networks moving way from longtime trusted genres featuring doctors, cops, and lawyers, to shows featuring distinctly spiritual and supernatural themes. Most observers agreed that this shift represented a culturally driven desire for fantasy and escapism. As one network programming director noted, "the real world has become such a horrendous place that people are looking for magic to avoid the tragic" (Brill quoted in Elliott, 2007, p. 5). Has a nation of 200 million or so unaffiliated spiritual seekers become resonant with cultural media production: a genre seeking viewers and generating advertising revenue? These sorts of processes and effects have as much impact on brand meaning as the actions of account managers and advertising creative directors.

The list of institutions is long. Obviously retailers significantly participate in the creation of brands. The almost byzantine structure of retail space negotiation has an enormous impact on what a brand comes to signify through its display in public space. Governmental agencies significantly restrict what a brand can mean. They may bring formal legal action when a company produces what is deemed as an inappropriate brand or a brand that is by its nature monopolistic. Assumptions and estimates of the likelihood of greater regulation, possible class action lawsuits, and more restrictive public policy serve to frame the positioning or repositioning of many brands. The mere presence of regulations and the institutions charged with creating, modifying, and imposing those makes a significant impact on which meanings are allowed for a brand and which are not. Likewise, NGOs exert force in the social construction of brands. Brands recently sanctioned by the Environmental Defense Fund or the Sierra Club mean something different than those without such blessings.

Processes

The primary processes that act to form brands include accommodation, negotiation, and cultivation.

Accommodation is a process through which the marketer's intended meaning is given some degree of acceptance by consumers. Consumers typically accommodate some, but not all, of the marketer's desired meaning. The term *accommodation* explicitly acknowledges that some of the marketer's meaning will likely remain.

Negotiation refers to a social process in which actors actively "bargain" for something, in this case what the brand means and for whom. We are speaking of the shared meaning, the sphere of negotiated commonality. In textual terms, this would be where reader and writer share meaning. Without it, meaningful communication about brands, or anything else, is impossible. Negotiation for meaning occurs with all brands, but at any given moment in the life of a brand the meaning of that brand might be closer to the preferred meaning of the marketer or that of the consumer. Famous instances of brand "hijacks" or "appropriations" by consumers are plentiful in the brand literature (Wipperfurth 2005). More typically however, common ground is found without such theatrics and drastic action (Walker 2008). Radical asymmetries certainly occur and are inherently interesting, but the norm is far subtler, if less entertaining. Relationships around the mode are predictably more stable but still involve various social collectives. In these staid and stable relationships the various agents are content enough to find the status quo desirable. Certain brands, such as Morton Salt or State Farm Insurance, have had essentially the same marketing, and in most places consumer relationships, for decades. In regard to the latter, in states where changes in insurance laws and regulation are in flux, new strategies (including exit) are sometimes attempted by marketers. Consumers and other parties then negotiate the decades-old brand promise, "Like a good neighbor . . . State Farm is there."

When a brand emerges from more organic social roots it is often the case that the marketer (if wise) accommodates organic brand meaning, including the rituals that reify it. Consider an example from the Gatorade brand. Gatorade had been an established, nationally distributed brand for nearly twenty years before one of the brand's most defining elements was created. Moreover, this element was created independently of the marketer. The phenomenon in question, often called "the Gatorade shower" (Rovell 2006), occurs when a team wins an important game and dumps a cooler of Gatorade on their coach's head. Though its origins are contested by at least two different teams and their fans, Rovell (2006) speculates that it most likely originated during a New York Giants victory over the Washington Redskins in 1985, when nose guard Jim Burt dunked his coach, Bill Parcells, at the end of the game. Though the practice was initially considered disrespectful, it quickly came to be seen as a playful sign of affection in subsequent incidents. Once its nature was understood, the media began to expect it with each Giants victory and scrambled to capture and broadcast it. The practice quickly spread, becoming part of the ritual of the game for all kinds of athletes. Rovell (2006) notes that

> . . . a Gatorade dunking probably happens on a football field in every state, and the reporting of the event gives the brand thousands of free media mentions and impressions every year. It has reached a point where coaches in all sports—including tennis, basketball, soccer and baseball—have received the ice cold shower (p. 78).

Yet this ritual originated and developed without any input from Gatorade. Aside from a one-time $1,000 Brooks Brothers' gift certificate to Parcells to cover the damage to his wardrobe, Gatorade never encouraged the practice (in fact, doing so might have robbed it of its legitimacy). Here, the original social actors were professional athletes and the journalists who reported on them. They created the practice, disseminated it, and vested it with meaning, meaning that was then widely embraced by amateurs and professionals alike.

Consumer collectives often assert negotiating power. In their early study of brand communities, Muñiz and O'Guinn (2001) commented on a way in which this happens, referred to as *desired marginality*. Here, brand community members actively try to keep the community ethos one of marginality; they prefer that ethos and actively try to maintain it, sometimes working against the marketer's quest for market share. A brand such as Apple with approximately 6 percent of the U.S. computer market has marginality as part of its core brand meaning. Apple brand communities thrive and celebrate their marginal status (Kahney 2004). Thus, some brand community members actively work against market share growth, or at least the perception of growth. These communities must walk a tricky path between rejecting willing new members and sustaining a large enough market share to keep the brand viable. If the brand gains too much market share or becomes too mainstream then cultural cachet is lost and the brand is no longer as desirable. Here the boundaries of community and brand are upheld by the collective. As Apple moves toward double-digit market share a new, more mainstream brand meaning may have to be negotiated. Clearly, such a new brand meaning will not be the result of unilateral action by the marketer.

Cultivation is another social construction process that affects the social construction of brands. O'Guinn and Shrum (1997) demonstrated that goods and services frequently used in television programming are seen by those who watch more television as systematically more plentiful in the social world. That is, consumption life on television helps to cultivate the belief of a similar world in the minds of those who watch television. This is mass-mediated social construction. Just how much of the social world do we actually directly experience? Surprisingly little. So, the social world outside our direct experience is constructed; built through indirect means. In a nation where the average person watches more than four hours of television a day along with several more hours online, we must know that much of what we think we know about the world is brought to us by commercial media. Do you suppose this colors the picture, helps consumers construct the world outside the one they directly experience, the one they assume and imagine? Brands are an integral part of media world; media world exists because brands exist. It is certainly no coincidence that brands, mass media, and the advertising industry all have parallel histories from the late nineteenth century on.

This is one essential reason that branded entertainment is so incredibly popular at this time. A significant process in the social construction of brands is those brands' appearance within programming content. They become part of mental representations shared by viewing audiences as representing what other people have and use in their daily lives. Given how much television the average person watches, and the branded plentitude found in contemporary programming content (not to mention the ads between the programs), brand meaning can be significantly influenced by what viewers believe about the social world as presented to them via television, films, and other mediated content. This is highly significant in that what is being delivered to viewers/consumers is a representation of the social world and its brands and consumption plentifully and seamlessly integrated within. As sociologist Michael Schudson (1984) has noted, American advertising is "capitalist realism." Media and advertising realities are constructed, not randomly or casually, but carefully. In what Thomas Burrell called *positive realism* an African-American family (see Figure 9.4) is portrayed against a pejorative stereotype: note the emphasis on family, the professional and present father, and the very clearly middle class setting. This ad was created by an agency that specialized in advertising to African Americans. At the center of this social reality construction is a brand, mediated through family, social class, and so on; not driven by U.S. Census Bureau data. Here the sociological and the psychological meaningfully interact.

Polity

Brands and politics were never complete strangers. In the United States, brands have an entanglement with politics that goes to our very founding. The politics of goods and their "branding" were present in the American Revolution (Axtell 1999) and in several, perhaps all, major social movements since. As several historians have noted, this merging of brand and polity has only accelerated, particularly since the end of World War II (Cohen 2000). It hit its stride in the cultural revolution of the 1960s, which was very much

Figure 9.4 **Ad Depicting "Positive Realism" with an African-American Family**

about the "establishment," material existence, and stuff, including brands. It is here, as noted by Frank (1997) and others, that the revolution paradoxically became about what (brands) you bought, not whether or not you bought them. Today, it is easy to point to a slew of brands that have been overtly politicized.

Many so-called revolutionaries now strike blows against the capitalist empire by buying things (Frank 1997; Heath and Potter 2004). As paradoxical as this seems (is), the brands of revolution have been granted community approval. In the new sociopolitical order, revolutionary politics are enacted not through choices of consuming or not consuming, but in identification, group sanctioning, and community championing of brands that are deemed by the collective to be the best vessels of the group's "alternative" politics. Such social processes can be seen in many brands. American Apparel, Apple, Ben & Jerry's, Carhartt, Diesel, MAC cosmetics, REI, The Body Shop, and Tom's of Maine are some good examples.

Politics is all about felt we-ness and politics must have social identity markers: brands are the postmodern campaign button. Recently, the open discussion of the Republican and Democratic brands has made this so thoroughly ordinary as to almost escape comment. The Obama brand is testament to what the savvy harnessing of consumer-generated content and shared construction can do [Trippi (2004) asserts that this tactic started with Howard Dean's 2000 campaign] . When the "Change" brand space became clearly more powerful, the McCain brand managers attempted to crowd that sector with their own "Change You Can Trust" positioning. Since Joe McGinnis's classic book (1968), and Doyle Dayne Bernbach's "Daisy" ad for Lyndon B. Johnson (Kern 1989), branding and polity have become inseparable in modern politics. Forty-something years later politics have found their way firmly into the dry goods aisle.

Rumors also play an important role in the social construction of the brand. Rumors allow the community to express properties of the brand that might not be true, but reflect what the community *wants* to be true. Rumors surrounded the reintroduction of Volkswagen's New Beetle in 1997, as community members looked for reasons to be optimistic that the New Beetle would honor its roots (Muñiz, O'Guinn, and Fine 2005). As a result, rumors about the new model, including the use of the original plans and the re-hiring of retired designers, were rife in the months leading up to the launch of the New Beetle. Long-time community members wanted to believe that the New Beetle would be true to the ethos of the original, despite fearing otherwise. The belief that the New Beetle had become a "chick" car or a "gay car" gave meaning to the brand.

Members of the Apple brand community spent considerable time discussing the introduction of the iPhone as community members looked for evidence that the device would revolutionize the smartphone the same way the iPod revolutionized personal MP3 players. In a reaction, members of the Blackberry brand community spent much time discussing the iPhone introduction along with rumors of the phone Blackberry would introduce to compete with it. We have observed several instances where rumors of an impending line-extension or repositioning have caused sufficient push-back from brand loyalists to get companies to either reconsider or outright abandon their plans. We first saw this in consumer electronics, technology, and automotive categories. Later we saw it spread via the Internet social networking to just about every category. Recently, we saw it in the Mini Cooper community as members discussed the rumors of the new model that eventually became the Clubman.

The brand world is inherently self-reflexive. The social construction of a brand is full of feedback loops and recursive action. Marketers are immersed in feedback from consumers through market research, consumer-generated content, brand blogs, on-line brand community chatter, and so on. They react to one another and perceptions of one another. They "imagine" each other. Consumers perceive the "schemer schema" (Wright 1986) or the persuasive intent and modus operandi of the marketer. Consumers form ideas as to what the marketer is trying to do with a brand. Sometimes they reject that view altogether, other times they embrace it, but they almost always have some reaction. Consumers always leave their mark, their fingerprints, on the brand. Consumers are aware of changes made to their brands and the marketer-preferred meaning, just as they are to the meaning ascribed by social collectives who "appropriate" or "hijack" the brand for their own purposes. In fact, all the institutions and social actors play this role, and respond to others in building the meaning of the brand. This process is not confined to the brand-consumer dyad, no matter how reassuring such simplicity may seem.

Manjoo (2008) provides some excellent examples of other ways in which self-reflexivity plays out in the Apple and Windows brand communities. He relates the experiences of technology reviewers David Pogue (*The New York Times*) and Walt Mossberg (*The Wall Street Journal*). Both strive for balanced, nonbiased reviews, yet both are routinely taken to task by brand fans for what they perceive to be biased reviews. For example, Pogue once wrote a detailed review of the Windows Vista operating system (OS). Manjoo (2008) notes that the review was generally positive toward both Windows (he found several things to like about it) and Apple (he also noted that several of Vista's innovations had been standard for many years in the Mac OS). Despite such strident attempts at reason and balance, members of both communities saw systematic biases against their OS of choice in the review. "The Mac people saw it as a rave review for Windows Vista" while the Windows folks, focusing on two minor criticisms, "saw it as a vicious slam on Windows" (Pogue, quoted in Manjoo 2008, p. 160). Mossberg suggests such disproportionate reactions reflect "the Doctrine of Insufficient Adulation" (Mossberg, quoted in Manjoo 2008, p. 161). It appears that consumer collectives, comprised of a chorus of similarly voiced devotees, creates an understanding of reality that has little room for criticisms from outsiders. This becomes a significant node in the consumer-brand-consumer relationship.

Today, many things from vehicles (Volkswagen), to computers (Macintosh), to soft drinks have a dedicated consumer base (generally small in number but not in communicative properties) that interacts with other consumers. Through their interactions, members of these consumer communities enact consumption practices, influence product development, interpret the meaning of the brand to (users and nonusers alike), and otherwise fold within what used to be the corporate marketing agenda. These consumers are drawn together by a common interest in, and commitment to, the brand and a social desire to bond with like-minded others. New modes of computer-mediated communication facilitate and flavor communal communication. We have observed this many times. Consider the following, posted to a thread entitled "A great Mini summer day":

> On the ride home yesterday, I was smiled at by a nice looking young lady in a Prius, challenged by a slammed blatty Integra, waved at by two smiling little kids in an SUV, and given a flash-and-wave by a fellow Mini. What other car can give you that? It was a GREAT day . . . (just wanted to share . . .)

Drivers like to share these prototypical or iconographic experiences with one another, often including directions and maps on how others can replicate it. In this way, the community continually creates the perfect brand consumption experience. These ideals are typically influenced by the advertising for the brand, but are communally scripted. Their potential to influence the consumption experience and the meaning of the brand is large.

Disruption is a process in which there is a perceptible break in social continuity. This occurs in times of change in a society's circumstance, economics, demography, or along some other social dimension. An early modern historical example is Ivory soap. Ivory,

Figure 9.5 **Ad Focusing on Health**

along with two or three other major competitors, were leaders in turning commodities into the modern CPG industry. When Ivory staked out the "purity space" it was leveraging a major social disruption. Urban modernity had brought enormous disruption to American society. It was a period of enormous in-migration, movement to cities, and massive changes in social character and norms of behavior, not to mention personal hygiene and daily practices of living.

The average life expectancy in the United States in 1900 was 49.2 years (Sullivan 1926). Infant mortality was twice what it would be just twenty-five years later (Sullivan 1926). A concerned public pushed Congress to pass the Pure Food and Drug Act in 1906. *Purity* was more than a word; it was, at that time, one of the few things the public believed might prevent them or their children from dying young. So, Ivory floats. Its purity was demonstrated by a market logic. No one really had to understand the physical mechanism relating purity to floating, it became a marketplace myth. Social context gave meaning to Ivory's branding, its advertising claim, its marketplace logic, and the meaning of a bar of soap that floated. Ivory *meant* something. It was pure, 99 44/100 pure. Ivory was no longer a commodity; its set of acceptable substitutes shriveled. The same was true of countless other branded goods and services.

The early 1920s Lifebuoy ad shown in Figure 9.5 is a good example. While most soap

Figure 9.6   **Virginia Slims Ad**

brands of the day positioned themselves toward women as beauty bars, Lifebuoy positioned itself as a male brand. Ads for beauty soaps told mothers to prepare their daughters for the "beauty contest of life (Marchand 1985) through beautiful skin. Lifebuoy reminded anxious mothers of the odds against their young sons living a long life: the flu epidemic of 1918 and the incredibly brutal trench warfare of World War I.

Likewise, many other brands leveraged social disruption and took their meaning from them. Virginia Slims came to much of its meaning by the resonance of marketers and all the other interested parties with the second wave of American feminism (see Figure 9.6). The brand's social construction was part Philip Morris's and part general cultural resonance. Philip Morris financed some of the more visible second-wave televised moments, such as The Virginia Slims Women's Tennis Series and the rise of women's tennis in general. Remember, the Battle of the Sexes between Bobby Riggs and Billie Jean King was actually significant in the larger acceptance and mainstreaming of the second wave: "You've Come a Long Way Baby."

Other times, a brand came to its meaning through a largely consumer-oriented response or resonance, which was then appropriated from the consumer collective. Wipperfurth (2005) provides examples, such as Pabst Blue Ribbon being rediscovered and appropriated by bike messengers in the Northeastern United States, thereby making the once blue-collar staple the choice for hipsters first and then mainstream consumers in search of status via coolness (Heath and Potter 2004) second. Consumers may appropriate the brand, reject the marketer's

Figure 9.7   **Tommy Hilfiger "Tommy Girl" Ad**

assigned meaning, and collectively reinvent the brand to their own liking. Rather than being random, these consumer appropriations, and then marketer reappropriations, are typically part of a changing set of social props reflecting age-cohort, demographic, economic, political, gender role and other shifting social sands. The cool kids in Chicago's northern suburbs have long been known to appropriate their look from census tracts miles and many dollars of income distant from their origin (Harris 2000). Conversely, do you think Tommy Hilfiger (see Figure 9.7) set out to be the official brand of gangsta rap (Gladwell 1997)? Probably not, but for a period, when that was its appropriated meaning, the company accommodated some of the consumers' brand creation.

Famously, Coke (see Figure 9.8) leveraged the identity crisis of the late 1960s and 1970s with this answer to the ubiquitous question: Is anything real?

Of course, social inequities (stratification) clearly matter in these disruptions. Race, gender, and class are rarely affected or put in play in an egalitarian fashion. Even some-

Figure 9.8   **Coca-Cola Ad: "The Real Thing"**

thing as seemingly benign as a car can be caught up in this. Many long-time members of the Volkswagen community resent the company's continued move up-market. The following member comment makes this clear:

> VWoA [Volkswagen of America] can kiss my ass. Volkswagen literally means "people's car." Modern Volkswagens are one of the furthest things from the original "people's car" in the world. I'm absolutely disgusted with VWoA and think they deserve whatever's coming their way.

These sentiments frequently emerge in discussions of Volkswagen's advertising. Consider the following message from a discussion of ads for the Passat:

> [These ads] stink outloud. Obviously, they reflect VWoA's attempt to take their cars upmarket, and in the process have lost any of the flair and humor which has been a trademark of their ads for years. I personally think it is an extension of how VW has lost its way and is going to end up alienating the very people they need to touch to buy their cars.

Many resent the new drivers being attracted to Volkswagen, as well, labeling them *yuppies* or *white preppy clients*. The relevance of such tendencies is obvious. A new buyer may do an Internet search on Volkswagen and immediately be put into contact with a vision of car and driver that is at odds with the vision management intended.

CONCLUSION

We have offered a discussion of collective brand relationships situated in an attempt at a social model of brands. The model calls into question some of the basic assumptions that have guided marketing theory on brands for fifty years. In their place it offers a new definition of brands and the key social entities and processes involved in their social construction. Importantly, it has asserted a place for the average and ordinary consumer, and thereby mitigating the tendency to conflate fanatical status with social action. Early brand community work was sometimes cast as only important to the freakishly loyal. A decade of "real world" reality by practitioners and consumers has shown this to be too limiting. This model uses the notions of the imagined consumer and marketer to broaden the discourse to the larger formulation of the social brand. We believe all brands are socially constructed; not merely attitude summations, but vessels of popular meaning. We believe the social brand to be a place where disciplines such as psychology and sociology might meaningfully interact.

Brand communities are but one example of consumer collectives. Consumer tribes (Cova and Cova 2002), subcultures of consumption (Schouten and McAlexander 1995), and subcultural communities (Kates 2004) are other examples. Brand communities possess three defining characteristics: consciousness of kind, evidence of rituals and traditions, and a sense of obligation to the community and its members. Muñiz and O'Guinn (2001) and others (Bagozzi and Dholakia 2006; Cova and Pace 2006; Cova, Pace, and Park 2007; Muñiz and Schau 2005) have extended, refined, and better specified brand community. The use of specialized forms of brand creation through community action and the use of consumer-generated media content have quite naturally extended the brand community work into the "co-creation" realm (Etgar 2008; Muñiz and Schau 2007). Perhaps most importantly, we assert that most brand community affiliation is thin, but not negligible.

The big question of brand relationship, at least in collective settings, is, "Why brands?" Why should a brand be at the center of a social organization? Why would brand relationships be defined by this context? For one, as has been noted many times, many traditional Western social institutions are experiencing significant challenges. Also, humans use metaphors, metanarratives, and other social templates for sense making and communication; two of the things that make humans human. As Putnam (2000) and others have noted, traditional social institutions and collectives are disappearing. Our research is centered on what is replacing or co-mingling with them. It has particular social theory significance if they are being replaced by the very same commercial forces that helped to undermine or supplant the traditional forms and structures. What could be more iconic of a consumer society than a brand? What could be more ironic for social thought?

Now, after two centuries or so, we arrive at this moment when three things are true: (1) brands are a ubiquitous aspect of daily life; (2) brands are at some level meaningful to ordinary contemporary citizens; and (3) community was not so easily done away with—the communal urge of humans and the benefits that accrue to collectives and institutions ensured community's adaptive longevity. Community endures in many forms in many

Figure 9.9   **Coca-Cola "Open House" Ad**

places, including the marketplace. Community, of a particular sort, is alive and well in the form of the brand community. Brand communities possess the hallmarks of traditional communities, but have their own unique market logic and expression.

Ultimately, brand communities matter because they look and behave like other forms of community, and community is essential. These are socially embedded and entrenched entities, and thus extremely durable. The increasing embedded-ness of consumer society has changed the world. Like it or not, brands are not just names of marketed things, but increasingly are part of the social fabric and centers of social organization. Our political parties are regularly and unremarkably cast as brands, as are our schools, religious sects, and all manner of ideologies. For this reason, they shape, limit, and inform social discourse and relationships (see Figures 9.8 and 9.9). Our models, our thinking, and our practice need to catch up with this reality.

How should brand relationship research evolve? Clearly, we believe it could benefit by an infusion of sociological conscience. Brand relations are meaningful because they are social. Humans use brands as known-in-common referents, as symbolic markers of collectivity, of social meaning. To the looking-glass self (Cooley 1902) there is no meaning without the social. Basic human relationships (e.g., father-son, mother-daughter) are given meaning and form through social means. So, why would it be different with brands? It isn't. Let us be clear: While we wholeheartedly acknowledge, admire and approve of the contributions made by social cognition brand theorists such as Keller (1993), who attempt to meaningfully connect basic cognitive process to classic social structures, we argue that such has been the exception rather than the rule, and that while this work has moved in the direction of the social, it could move further. We hope we have at least changed the conversation in that direction.

We need to see brands as vessels of popular meaning, where negotiation of the meaning is meaningful. Where consumers bring themselves and a social world to them and thus create them. Brands are not just names of things, but an increasingly important part of the social fabric and centers of social organization. Brands work to bring people together, to divide them, to mark meaningful collectives of identity, to meaningfully define human relationships. When we invoke the phrase "consumer-brand relationship" we are calling forth a lot more than a simple attitude-object dyad. We should be offering more than brand-as-person games, or brand personality. Brand relationship research desperately needs sincere and informed sociological thought.

> This craving for community is the chief misery of every man individually and all humanity from the beginning of time.
> —*Dostoevsky*

REFERENCES

Aaker, Jennifer L. (1997). "Dimensions of Brand Personality," *Journal of Marketing Research,* 44 (August), 347–356.

Anderson, Benedict (1983). *Imagined Community.* London, UK: Verso.

Axtell, J. (1999). "The First Consumer Revolution." In *Consumer Society in American History: A Reader,* ed. Lawrence B. Glickman. Ithaca, NY: Cornell University Press.

Bagozzi, R.P., and U.M. Dholakia (2006). "Antecedents and Purchase Consequences of Customer Participation in Small Group Brand Communities," *International Journal of Research in Marketing,* 23 (March), 45–61.

Bartos, R. (1986). "Ernest Dichter: Motive Interpreter," *Journal of Advertising Research,* 17 (3): 3–9.

Boorstin, D.J. (1961). *The Image: A Guide to Pseudo-Events in America.* New York, NY: Atheneum.

Cohen, L. (2000). "From Town Center to Shopping Center: The Reconfiguration of Community Marketplaces in Postwar America." In *The Gender and Consumer Culture Reader,* ed. Jennifer Scanlon. New York, NY: New York University Press, 243–266.

Cooley, C.H. (1902). *Human Nature and the Social Order.* New York, NY: Scribner.

Cova, B., and V. Cova (2002). "Tribal Marketing: The Tribalisation of Society and Its Impact on the Conduct of Marketing," *European Journal of Marketing,* 36 (5/6), 595–620.

Cova, B. and S. Pace (2006). "Brand Community of Convenience Products: New Forms of Customer Empowerment—The Case 'My Nutella the Community,'" *European Journal of Marketing,* 40 (9–10), 1087–1105.

Cova, B., S. Pace, and D.J. Park (2007). "Global Brand Communities across Borders: The Warhammer Case," *International Marketing Review,* 24 (3), 313–329.

Elliott, S. (2007). "In a Time of High Anxiety, a Sedative of the Occult," *The New York Times,* Section C, Column 1, p. 5.

Etgar, M. (2008). "A Descriptive Model of the Consumer Co-production Process," *Journal of The Academy of Marketing Science,* 36 (March), 97–108.

Fournier, S. (1998). "Customers and Their Brands: Developing Relationship Theory in Consumer Research," *Journal of Consumer Research,* 24 (March), 343–373.

Frank, T. (1997) *The Conquest of Cool: Business Culture, Counterculture, and the Rise of Hip Consumerism.* Chicago, IL: University of Chicago Press.

Gladwell, M. (1997). "The Coolhunt," *The New Yorker,* March 17, 1997, 78–88.

Harris, D. (2000). *Cute, Quaint, Hungry and Romantic.* Cambridge, MA: Da Capo Press.

Hays, C.L. (2004). *The Real Thing: Truth and Power at the Coca-Cola Company.* New York, NY: Random House.

Heath, J., and A. Potter (2004). *Nation of Rebels: Why Counterculture Became Consumer Culture.* New York, NY: HarperCollins.

Hine, T. (1995). *The Total Package: The Secret History and Hidden Meanings of Boxes, Bottles, Cans and Other Persuasive Containers.* Boston, MA: Little, Brown and Company.

Holbrook, M.B., and E.C. Hirschman (1982). "The Experiential Aspects of Consumption: Consumer Fantasies, Feelings and Fun," *Journal of Consumer Research,* 9 (September), 132–140.

Kahney, L. (2004). *The Cult of Mac.* San Francisco, CA: No Starch Press.

Kates, S.M. (2004). "The Dynamics of Brand Legitimacy: An Interpretive Study in the Gay Men's Community," *Journal of Consumer Research,* 31 (2), 455–464.

Keller, K.L. (1993). "Conceptualizing, Measuring, and Managing Customer-Based Brand Equity," *Journal of Marketing,* 57 (January), 1–22.

Kern, M. (1989). *30-Second Politics.* New York, NY: Praeger.

Kozinets, R.V. (2001). "Utopian Enterprise: Articulating the Meanings of Star Trek's Culture of Consumption," *Journal of Consumer Research,* 28 (June), 67–87.

Low, G.S., and R.A. Fullerton (1994). "Brands, Brand Management and the Brand Manager System," *Journal of Marketing Research,* 31 (May), 173–190.

Ludacer, R. (2008). "Anthropomorphic Packaging Mascots," box vox—packaging as content, September 8. Available at http://www.blog.beachpackagingdesign.com/2008/09/anthropomorphic.html (accessed September 23, 2008).

Manjoo, F. (2008). *True Enough: Learning to Live in a Post-Fact Society.* Hoboken, NJ: John Wiley and Sons.

Marchand, R.(1985). *Advertising the American Dream.* Berkeley, CA: University of California Press.

McGinnis, J. (1988; repr., 1968). *The Selling of the President.* New York, NY: Penguin Books.

Mills, C.W. (1959). *The Sociological Imagination.* London, UK: Oxford University Press.

Muñiz, A.M. Jr., and Thomas C. O'Guinn (2001). "Brand Community," *Journal of Consumer Research,* 27 (4) (March), 412–431.

Muñiz, A.M. Jr., Thomas C. O'Guinn, and G.A. Fine (2005). "Rumor in Brand Community." In *Advances in Social and Organizational Psychology: A Tribute to Ralph Rosnow,* ed. Donald A. Hantula. Mahwah, NJ: Lawrence Erlbaum.

Muñiz, A.M. Jr., and H.J. Schau (2005). "Religiosity in the Abandoned Apple Newton Brand Community," *Journal of Consumer Research,* 31 (March), 737–747.

O'Guinn, T.C. and A. M. Muñiz, Jr. (2009). "Towards a Sociological Model of Brands." In *Contemporary Branding Issues: A Research Perspective,* eds. Barbara Loken, Rohini Ahluwalia, and Michael J. Houston. New York, NY: Taylor and Francis.

O'Guinn, T.C. and L.J. Shrum (1997). "The Role of Television in the Construction of Consumer Reality," *Journal of Consumer Research,* (March), 278–294.

Pendergrast, M. (2000). *For God, Country, and Coca-Cola: The Unauthorized History of the Great American Soft Drink and the Company That Makes It.* New York, NY: Scribner.

Putnam, R.D. (2000). *Bowling Alone: The Collapse and Revival of American Community.* New York, NY: Simon and Schuster.

Rothenberg, R. (1994). *Where the Suckers Moon: An Advertising Story.* New York, NY: Alfred A. Knopf.

Rovell, D. (2006). *First in Thirst: How Gatorade Turned the Science of Sweat Into a Cultural Phenomenon.* New York, NY: AMACOM.

Schouten, J.W., and J. McAlexander (1995). "Subcultures of Consumption: An Ethnography of the New Bikers," *Journal of Consumer Research,* 22 (June), 43–61.

Schudson, M. (1984). *Advertising, the Uneasy Persuasion.* New York, NY: Basic Books, 129–146.

Seabrook, J. (2000). *NoBrow: The Culture of Marketing, the Marketing of Culture.* New York, NY: Vintage Books.

Stabiner, K. (1993). *Inventing Desire.* New York, NY: Simon and Schuster.

Sullivan, M. (1926). "Immense Decrease in the Death Rate." In *Visions of Technology: A Century of Debate About Machines, Systems and the Human World,* ed. Richard Rhodes. New York, NY: Touchstone, 88–89.

Sunderland, P.L., and R.M. Denny (2007). *Doing Anthropology in Consumer Research.* New York, NY: Left Coast Press.

Trippi, J. (2004). *The Revolution Will Not Be Televised: Democracy, the Internet and the Overthrow of Everything.* New York, NY: HarperCollins.

Walker, R. (2008). *Buying In: The Secret Dialogue Between What We Buy and Who We Are.* New York, NY: Random House, 21–34.

Wipperfurth, A. (2005). *Brand Hijack.* New York, NY: Portfolio.

Wright, P. (1986). "Schemer Schema." Presidential address, Association for Consumer Research. Provo, UT.

CHAPTER 10

BUILDING BRAND RELATIONSHIPS THROUGH CORPORATE SOCIAL RESPONSIBILITY

SANKAR SEN, SHUILI DU, AND C.B. BHATTACHARYA

As the field of marketing continues to shift from a transactional to a relational paradigm (Palmatier et al. 2006), there has been growing consensus among marketing academics and practitioners that nurturing and maintaining consumer relationships is crucial to a firm's financial performance and long-term survival (Oliver 1999; Reichheld, Markey, and Hopton 2000). Consequently, the marketplace has witnessed a proliferation of relationship marketing programs, such as loyalty programs and direct mailings, which seek to strengthen consumer-company relationships and engender consumer loyalty. However, it appears that consumers cannot be bribed into loyalty (Braum 2002); empirical studies on the impact of relationship marketing programs, most of which are limited to offering economic incentives for repeated purchase, have reported either very small positive effects or even nonsignificant effects (Verhoef 2003; De Wulf, Odekerken-Schröder, and Iacobucci 2001). More dire, recent studies suggest that, contrary to common beliefs, many frequent buyers (i.e., those typically designated as "loyal" customers) are actually more price sensitive, more expensive to serve, and do not market the company at all (e.g., Reinartz and Kumar 2002; Thomas, Reinartz, and Kumar 2004), pointing to fundamental flaws in the traditional relationship marketing programs that aim to retain consumers only via economic incentives.

Reflecting this frustration, Fournier, Dobscha, and Mick (1998) commented that "Relationship marketing as it is currently practiced has not brought us closer to customers. It has sent us farther afield." According to Martin (2005), "Companies have installed customer relationship management systems to forge links with consumers, but the latter feel more manipulated than understood as a result."

Disillusioned with the performance of economic incentives–based loyalty programs, companies continue to search for effective ways to nurture lasting, meaningful relationships with their consumers. Reflecting this trend in the marketplace, the Marketing Science Institute (2006) has listed "connecting customers with the company" as one of its capital research topics, calling for more research that "explores new ways to create and sustain emotional connections with the brand."

In this chapter, we draw on our research on consumer reactions to corporate social responsibility (CSR) to proffer the basic argument that by revealing its values, "soul," or "character" (Brown and Dacin 1997; Sen and Bhattacharya 2001), a company's CSR initiatives can be extremely effective at forging deep meaningful connections with its consumers, transforming them into company/brand[1] champions who are not only loyal, but also actively promote the company within their social networks. While definitions of CSR abound, it can be understood broadly as a company's "status and activities with respect to its perceived societal obligations" (Brown and Dacin 1997) or "a commitment to improve [societal] well-being through discretionary business practices and contributions of corporate resources" (adapted from Kotler and Lee 2005).

Over the last decade, CSR has come to occupy a prominent place on the global corporate agenda, winning over even some of its staunchest detractors (e.g., *Economist* 2007). Today, more than ever before, companies are devoting substantial resources to various social and environmental initiatives ranging from community outreach and neutralizing their carbon footprint to socially responsible business practices in employment, sourcing, product design, and manufacturing. To give but two examples, over the years, Avon has raised more than $500 million in total to fight breast cancer, domestic violence, and disaster relief. As part of its Ecomagination initiative, General Electric invested $1 billion in cleaner technologies (e.g., renewable and hydrogen energy) in 2007, and will grow its Research and Development (R&D) expenditure to $1.5 billion in 2010

These unprecedented CSR efforts are spurred in part by the premise that in today's marketplace, CSR is not only the *right* thing to do, but also the *smart* thing to do (Smith 2003, p. 52). According to a special report in *Fortune* magazine (Ioannou 2003), "91 percent of surveyed CEOs believe CSR management creates shareholder value," and the top ten reasons companies are becoming more socially responsible include "competitive advantage, cost savings, and customer demands." Indeed, findings from both marketplace polls and academic research suggest that consumers are increasingly more likely to take actions to reward good corporate citizens and punish bad corporate citizens. According to a Cone research study (2007), 87 percent of American consumers are likely to switch from one brand to another (price and quality being equal) if the other brand is associated with a good cause, an increase from 66 percent since 1993. On the other hand, 85 percent will consider switching to another company's products or services because of a company's negative corporate responsibility practices and 66 percent will boycott such a company's products or services. Consistent with these findings, a growing body of academic research attests to the generally positive influence of CSR on not only short-term, transactional behaviors such as purchase but also longer-term, more relational behaviors such as consumer loyalty and advocacy (e.g., willingness to pay a price premium, positive word-of-mouth; Lichtenstein, Drumwright and Braig 2004; Du, Bhattacharya, and Sen 2007).

Interestingly, however, the relationship marketing literature has paid scant attention to the power of CSR in building consumer-brand relationships. This chapter advances our understanding of brand relationships by providing insights into not only the nature and extent of such relationships wrought by a company's CSR programs, but also when and why such relationships are likely to occur. In other words, this chapter focuses on three related questions: (1) *What* relationship outcomes does CSR engender? (2) *Why* do these outcomes occur (i.e., what are the psychological processes through which CSR builds relationships)? and (3) *When* are such outcomes most likely to occur (i.e., under what

Figure 10.1   **Effect of CSR on Consumer-Company Relationships**

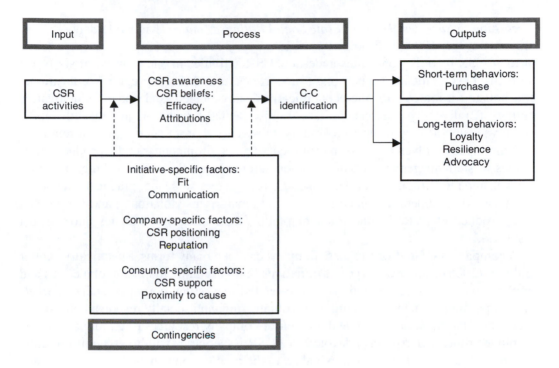

conditions will CSR trigger these outcomes)? In doing so, we paint an individual-level, process-oriented, contingent picture of the relationship-building capabilities of CSR.

To shed light on these questions, we conceptualize the CSR-brand relationships link as a CSR inputs → process → behavioral outputs sequence, as shown in Figure 10.1. Our perspective on the role of CSR in building consumer-brand relationships hinges on three basic premises. First, CSR activities, unlike the more conventional relationship marketing activities, can not only enhance purchase behavior, but also trigger the rarer, longer-term consumer advocacy behaviors that marketers covet. Second, such relationship outcomes occur because CSR activities tend to humanize a company, encouraging consumers to not just like, respect, or admire the company but actually identify with it. Such identification satisfies certain fundamental self-definitional needs that consumers have (i.e., "Who am I?"), aligning their self-interests with those of the company. Third, and perhaps most importantly, CSR initiatives are not a guarantee for strong brand relationships; there exists considerable heterogeneity in CSR's contribution to strong consumer-brand relationships, contingent on a host of companies, initiatives, and consumer-specific factors.

The rest of the chapter fleshes out our CSR-brand relationship framework. After a brief discussion of the CSR inputs, we focus on key elements of the process through which these inputs translate to the outputs. These outputs are discussed next, followed by a discussion of the key contingencies that influence the input-output relationship.

CSR INPUTS

According to *Socrates: The Corporate Social Ratings Monitor* (Kinder, Lydenberg, Domini & Co. Inc. 1999), a database that describes and rates over 600 companies in terms of their CSR records, companies undertake CSR activities in one or more of six broad domains: (1) community support (e.g., support of arts and health programs, educational and housing initiatives for the economically disadvantaged, and generous/innovative giving); (2) diversity (e.g., gender, race, family, sexual orientation, and disability); (3) employee support (e.g., concern for safety, job security, profit-sharing, union relations, and employee involvement); (4) environment (e.g., environment-friendly products, hazardous waste management, use of ozone-depleting chemicals, animal testing, pollution control, and recycling); (5) non-U.S. operations [e.g., overseas labor practices (including sweatshops) and operations in countries with human rights violations]; and (6) product (e.g., product safety, R&D/innovation, marketing/contracting controversies, and antitrust disputes).

A company's CSR efforts in these domains can take many forms. Specifically, Kotler and Lee (2005) catalog six types of initiatives that vary in their specific objectives and implementation: cause promotions, cause-related marketing, corporate social marketing, corporate philanthropy, community volunteering, and socially responsible business practices. Naturally, the nature and amount of company resources (e.g., money, goods, employee time, and expertise) devoted to a CSR issue varies with the type of initiative through which it is implemented. Notably, in the case of companies that do not engage in corporate branding, these programs also vary in the extent to which they are associated with the company (e.g., Procter & Gamble), rather than one or more of its specific brands (e.g., Crest or Tide).

PROCESSES

CSR Awareness and Beliefs

Regardless of the objective inputs into a company's CSR programs, consumer reactions to these are based on their subjective perceptions of not only what a company is doing but also how well it is implementing its CSR programs and why it is engaging in CSR in the first place. In other words, consumers' awareness, favorable perceptions, and interpretations of a company's CSR are key prerequisites to the favorable impact of CSR on consumer-brand relationships. In this regard, a key challenge facing companies is how to increase awareness of their CSR activities among target consumers. Specifically, our research is in line with other data (Dawkins 2004) that reveals consumer awareness and knowledge of companies' CSR activities to be rather low (Sen, Bhattacharya, and Korschun 2006; Du et al. 2007). For example, in a field study involving a real world CSR initiative (Sen et al. 2006), only 17 percent of students were aware of a large charitable gift made by a company to their university despite its extensive communication through various channels, such as e-mails, press releases, and the campus newspaper. Not surprisingly, of the twenty attributes measured in the annual Harris Interactive corporate reputation study published by *The Wall Street Journal,* people are most in the dark about corporate citizenship; questions about whether companies are socially and environmentally responsible consistently elicit the most "don't know" responses (Alsop 2005). In sum, lack of CSR awareness represents a key stumbling block for companies interested in reaping relationship benefits from their CSR initiatives.

CSR Efficacy Beliefs

Once consumers become aware of a company's CSR activities, their beliefs regarding these activities determine their subsequent reactions to the company. As more and more companies engage in CSR, and as consumers become increasingly aware of their power (via marketplace behaviors) in driving social change, it appears it is not enough for companies to merely engage in CSR. Our research suggests that consumers, particularly those most affected by a company's CSR efforts, are attuned to whether or not these efforts are actually making an impact. In other words, a key aspect of consumers' psychological reactions to CSR is their beliefs about the effectiveness, or efficacy, of a specific CSR program in improving community welfare. For example, in the context of a company-sponsored dental hygiene program (Du, Sen, and Bhattacharya 2008b), we found that the program beneficiaries' intention to support the corporate sponsor was tied to their beliefs of the program's effectiveness in improving their (and their children's) oral health. Several reasons underlie this finding. First, high CSR efficacy signals a company's genuine concern for societal/community welfare, therefore reinforcing CSR's ability to strengthen relationships. Second, reciprocity is a powerful social norm that underlies consumer-company relationships (Baggozi 1995). This norm evokes obligation toward others on the basis of their past behavior: people should return good for good, in proportion to what they receive (Goulder 1960). In the context of CSR, when deciding to what extent they want to reciprocate toward the company, the efficacy of CSR in improving the welfare of its intended beneficiaries (Du et al. 2008b) is likely to be a key decision criterion for consumers.

CSR Attributions

Another key aspect of consumers' CSR beliefs pertains to why a company is doing what it is doing (i.e., causal attributions regarding CSR). Prior research has, in general, identified two types of CSR motives: intrinsic (e.g., a genuine concern for societal/community welfare) and extrinsic motives (e.g., a desire to increase sales and profits), and has showed in laboratory settings that consumers will react positively to CSR initiatives when they perceive intrinsic motives, and negatively when they perceive extrinsic motives (Yoon, Gurhan-Canli, and Schwarz 2006). Our research suggests that in the marketplace, however, consumers often perceive mixed (i.e., both intrinsic and extrinsic) motives, and interestingly, often tolerate extrinsic motives as long as the CSR initiatives are attributed to intrinsic motives as well (Sen et al. 2006). Indeed, this is consistent with the findings of Ellen, Webb, and Mohr (2006) that consumers respond more positively to CSR initiatives when they perceive both intrinsic and extrinsic motives. This growing tolerance of extrinsic motives indicates that as consumers learn more about CSR and its motivations, they are increasingly willing to adopt a "win-win" perspective: they often believe that CSR initiatives can and should serve both the needs of society and the bottom lines of business. As one of our focus group participants put it, "It's a two-way street."

Consumer-Company (C-C) Identification

Our research suggests that, given the appropriate efficacy and attributional beliefs, CSR can be extremely effective in bringing consumers pyschologically closer to the company, causing them to connect deeply with it. We conceptualize such a connection as consumer-company (C-C) identification (Bhattacharya and Sen 2003) and find it to be a fundamental driver of consumers' CSR-based prosocial behaviors toward a company.[2] Research on social identity (Tajfel and Turner 1985) and, more specifically, organizational identification (Bergami and Bagozzi 2000) suggests that individuals often identify with organizations they belong to (e.g., employees with employer organizations), incorporating favorable aspects of the organizational identity into their own identity to satisfy certain basic, higher-order self-related needs (Dutton, Dukerich, and Harquail 1994). These include the needs to know oneself (i.e., self-definition), to feel good about oneself (i.e., self-enhancement), and to feel special (i.e., self-distinctiveness). Although identification has been examined primarily in the context of formal organizational membership, we (Bhattacharya and Sen 2003; see Scott and Lane 2000) suggest that it can also occur in the absence of formal membership, as with the case of consumers and companies. In particular, due largely to the ascent of consumerism as the dominant force guiding the lives of many, as consumers learn more about and develop relationships with not just products but also the organization or people behind the products (McAlexander, Schouten, and Koenig 2002), they are drawn to identify, volitionally, with a select few such organizations (i.e., the companies), even though they are not formal members.

The basis for such identification, or consumers' perceived sense of overlap between their own identity and that of the company, are the company-related associations that make up its perceived identity. This identity is typically comprised of consumers' knowledge about two basic aspects of the company: its expertise in producing and delivering its products/services [corporate ability (CA) associations; e.g., industry leadership, technological innovation], and its activities with regard to important societal issues (i.e., CSR associations; Brown and Dacin 1997). In our research, we argue that consumers' identification with a company is more likely to be based on its CSR rather than on CA associations because CSR associations provide consumers with insight into its "value system," "soul," or "character" (Brown and Dacin 1997; Sen and Bhattacharya 2001). In other words, a company's character as revealed by its CSR actions is not only fundamental and relatively enduring but also often more distinctive by virtue of its idiosyncratic bases (e.g., sponsorship of social cause, environmentalism) than other CA-based aspects of company schema. Therefore, a company's CSR activities are likely to constitute the core defining characteristics of its corporate identity, triggering C-C identification. At the same time, however, a match between a company's CSR and CA activities (i.e., CSR-CA fit) will likely enhance the credibility of CSR activities, leading to a stronger belief that these CSR activities reflect the "soul" of the organization, and consequently, stronger C-C identification. On the contrary, a mismatch between CSR and CA activities will likely trigger extrinsic attributions and weaken the link between CSR and C-C identification.

BEHAVIORAL OUTCOMES

C-C identification aligns consumers' self interests with the interests of the company (Dutton et al. 1994), triggering a multitude of pro-company behaviors. Our research indicates that these behaviors range from short-term, transactional ones such as purchase, to longer-term, relational ones including consumer loyalty, resilience to negative information, and advocacy behaviors.

Purchase

Since consumption is the primary currency of C-C relationships, it is not surprising that consumers' positive reactions to a company's CSR are manifested through greater purchase. In fact, earlier research on the business case of CSR has focused primarily on the effect of CSR on product evaluations and purchase behavior (e.g., Brown and Dacin 1997; Sen and Bhattacharya 2001). Brown and Dacin (1997) argue that a company's CSR record provides a general context for consumers' product evaluation, and therefore, negative CSR associations will have a detrimental effect on product evaluations, whereas positive CSR associations can enhance product evaluations. Our early experimental research (Sen and Bhattacharya 2001) extends this basic finding by providing insight into the underlying process. Specifically, we find that a company's CSR activities promote C-C identification, which mediates CSR's influence on consumer purchase intention. Importantly, we also show that CSR's positive influence on consumers' company evaluation and purchase intention is moderated by several company-specific (e.g., fit between the company and the CSR issue) and consumer-specific (e.g., consumers' support of the specific CSR issue) factors. For example, a company's CSR actions produce a more positive effect on company evaluations and purchase intentions when the focal cause has the consumers' support and is in strategic, product-relevant domains (e.g., labor practices). This is corroborated in a more recent field study (Sen et al. 2006) wherein consumers who were aware of a large charitable gift by a company and supported child-related issues (i.e., the focal cause) to a greater extent expressed greater intention to purchase that company's products.

Loyalty

More recent research in the CSR area has shifted focus from CSR's influence on short-term purchase to its impact on long-term, more relational outcomes, including how CSR affects consumer loyalty. The importance of loyalty derives from its substantial impact on the company's long-term profit (Reichheld et al. 2000). In examining the link between CSR and consumer loyalty, we conceptualize the latter not merely as the tendency to purchase the same brand over time but as a deeper psychological "commitment to rebuy or repatronize a preferred product/service consistently in the future, thereby causing repetitive same-brand or same-brand–set purchasing, despite situational influences and marketing efforts having the potential to cause switching behavior" (Oliver 1999, p. 34). Our research suggests that a company's CSR activities enhance consumer loyalty.

Similarly, Lichtenstein, Drumwright, and Braig (2004) have found that consumers' accumulated dollar purchase (i.e., behavioral loyalty) from a grocery store is positively associated with their perceptions of that store's CSR engagement. In a field survey of three brands in the yogurt industry (Du et al. 2007), we found that consumers' CSR beliefs about a brand were positively associated with their affective loyalty (i.e., psychological commitment) to the brand. Similarly, in our investigation of the business outcomes of a corporate-sponsored dental health program (Du, Bhattacharya, and Sen 2008a), we found that beneficiaries as well as nonbeneficiaries who were aware of a corporate-sponsored dental hygiene program purchaseed the company's products more frequently (i.e., express behavioral loyalty) than those who were unaware of the program.

Resilience to Negative Information

Consumers' support for the company they identify with (recall that such identification is often driven by the company's CSR initiatives) often goes beyond routine consumption behavior. In particular, C-C identification can cause consumers to downplay any negative information they may receive about the company (or its products). For example, focus groups of Tom's of Maine customers (Chappell 1993) suggest that when customers share a company's values, their relationship with it is not tarnished by their disappointment over the performance of a single product.

Such resilience to negative information is likely because identification with a company causes people's interactions with it to be characterized by courtesy, altruism, and sportsmanship (Bergami and Bagozzi 2000). Accordingly, consumers are likely to make more charitable attributions regarding the company's intentions and responsibility when things go wrong and to be more forgiving of the company's mistakes if its culpability is established.

Such behavior is particularly evident in times of product-harm crises. Research by Klein and Dawar (2004) shows that when a product-harm crisis (i.e., well-publicized instances of defective or dangerous products) occurs, consumers are more likely to give a good corporate citizen the benefit of the doubt and attribute the crisis to sources external to the company. The researchers argue that even if positive CSR associations do not increase immediate profitability, they may be instrumental in reducing the risk of damage to company/brand evaluations in the event of a calamity (see also Peloza 2006). In this sense, CSR is like an insurance policy that is there when you need it.

Brand

Finally, when consumers identify with a company, they develop a vested interest in the success of the company and, because of their self-definition and self-enhancement drives, want to ensure that their affiliation with it is communicated in the most positive light possible (Ashforth and Mael 1989; Bhattacharya and Sen 2004). Thus, consumers' support for a company whose CSR activities engender identification is likely to be expressed through avenues other than just consumption (Scott and Lane 2000; Maignan and Ferrell 2004), such as initiating positive word of mouth about the company and its products among friends, families, colleagues, and important social others.

Such consumer-initiated word of mouth is highly valuable to a company because it is the most credible source of information and is closely linked to new customer acquisition (Wangenheim and Bayon 2007). Research has shown that customers' willingness to recommend a product or service to someone else correlates highly with a company's growth (Reichheld 2003). According to the consulting firm Satmetrix, Inc., a company's percentage of net promoters, that is, percentage of consumers who are most likely to recommend the company minus percentage of consumers who are least likely to recommend it, is the strongest predictor among all loyalty measures of a company's long-term growth (Satmetrix 2004).

The influence of CSR on consumer advocacy is evidenced in our research (Du et al. 2007); consumers' CSR beliefs about a brand are positively associated with their advocacy behavior toward the brand. Similarly, Du and colleagues (2008a) show that, in the context of a corporate-sponsored dental hygiene program, beneficiaries as well as nonbeneficiaries who are aware of the program are more likely to engage in such advocacy behaviors. In particular, given the popularity and vast reach of such Internet communication media as blogs, chatrooms, and online reviews, the power of CSR-triggered positive word of mouth has been magnified substantially. Indeed, companies such as Stonyfield Farm and Ben & Jerry's have benefited from consumer ambassadors who rave, in the virtual world, about their products and their social responsibility endeavors. For example, one consumer wrote enthusiastically about Stonyfield yogurt, "The yogurt tastes great and is organic too! . . . Stonyfield Farm not only produces some great tasting products, but the company has great values and culture" (Walker 2008).

CONTINGENCIES IN THE INPUT-OUTPUT LINK

Not all CSR initiatives are created equal. One of the most important lessons to emerge from our research is that the contribution of CSR to brand relationships is critically contingent on a host of initiative-, consumer-, and company-specific factors; one size does not fit all. Next we discuss some of the key contingent factors that have been examined by consumer research, including ours.

Initiative Factors

CSR Fit

Consumers often expect companies to sponsor only those social issues that have a logical association with their core corporate activities (Cone 2007; Haley 1996). In selecting a social initiative, therefore, companies need to consider fit, or synergy between the social cause and the company's business. Menon and Kahn (2003) suggest that CSR fit may result from common associations that the brand shares with the cause, such as product dimensions (e.g., herbal product brand sponsoring the protection of rain forests), affinity with specific target segments (e.g., *Self* magazine sponsoring prevention of breast cancer), or corporate image associations created by the brand's past conduct in a specific social domain (e.g., Ben & Jerry's and The Body Shop's activities in environment protection). Similarly, Varadarajan and Menon (1988, p. 65) argue that factors influencing a firm's choice of causes include the characteristics of its product offerings, brand image and positioning, and the characteristics of its served market. Much research points to the need for companies to choose CSR initiatives that are closely aligned with their business (Porter and Kramer 2006; Gourville and Rangan 2004); such CSR initiatives are likely to reap greater relationship benefits.

CSR fit likely moderates the influence of a CSR initiative on C-C relationship because it affects consumers' attributions of motives underlying a company's CSR activities (Menon and Kahn 2003; Simmons and Becker-Olsen 2006). According to the two-stage model of attributions (Gilbert 1989), consumers will first attribute CSR activities to dispositional motives (i.e., intrinsic motives), and then "correct" this inference, if they allocate sufficient processing capabilities and engage in more effortful elaboration, by considering alternative, contextual factors (e.g., competitive pressure, financial motivations). Low CSR fit will increase cognitive elaboration and make extrinsic motives more salient, thereby reducing the positive influence CSR has on C-C relationships. Not surprisingly, Simmons and Becker-Olsen (2006) find that compared to high-fit sponsorships, a company's low-fit social sponsorships lead to greater cognitive elaboration and less favorable attitude toward the sponsorship, and in turn have a less favorable effect on the firm's equity. Interestingly, however, Bloom and colleagues (2006; see also Hoeffler and Keller 2002) argue that under certain circumstances, the opposite can also happen; aligning with a low-fit cause might differentiate a company as being more sincere in its motive and thus increase the effectiveness of CSR in building relationships.

More generally, high fit can magnify the relationship rewards of a CSR initiative by facilitating the convergence of social and business interests. Specifically, according to Kotler and Lee (2004), a social initiative that leverages a company's business expertise (e.g., corporate social initiatives rather than, for example, corporate philanthropy) is likely to have maximal social impact. Since, to infer the company's motives, at least some consumers are likely to rely on their beliefs regarding whether or not the company is actually making a difference, maximal social impact will establish the credibility and authenticity of the company's engagement in CSR, ultimately resulting in stronger C-C relationships.

CSR Communication

More basically, the impact of CSR on C-C relationships will also depend on the extent to which such CSR is communicated to consumers. Since minimal benefits will accrue to companies if their target market is unaware of their CSR initiatives, companies need to work harder and smarter to communicate their CSR activities. Communicating CSR, however, is a very delicate matter. While consumers claim they want to know about the good deeds of the companies they buy from, they become leery of CSR motives when companies promote their CSR efforts.

In fact, Yoon and colleagues (2006) show that spending too much on CSR-related advertising can backfire because consumers infer extrinsic motives and react negatively to a company's CSR efforts. Perhaps the most credible CSR communication for a company is through news media coverage. Publications such as *Business Ethics,* or CSR ratings by independent organizations (e.g., *Fortune*) provide third-party, neutral reports about companies' CSR status and are perceived as more credible sources of CSR information. However, getting media cooperation is often difficult. On the other hand, corporate CSR advertising is more controllable but less credible. In addition to information sources, the credibility of CSR communication also derives from what is communicated. The communication of CSR will be perceived as more credible and trigger less skepticism if the company really owns the cause and communicates demonstrable concrete results. Thus, to be most effective in their CSR communications, companies need to convey aspects such as impact, consistency, and fit. CSR communication should also be factual and low-key, so as to avoid the impression of "bragging."

Company-Specific Factors

CSR Positioning

Given the widespread corporate engagement in CSR today, the influence of a company's CSR activities on consumer relationships will be contingent upon consumer reactions in the context of different CSR actions, particularly those taken by its competitors. For instance, companies vary in the extent to which they rely on their CSR activities to position themselves, relative to their competitors, in the minds of consumers. While many companies affiliate themselves with causes, some, such as Timberland, Ben & Jerry's, and the Whole Foods Market, go beyond just engaging in CSR to position themselves wholly in terms of CSR, becoming known as the socially responsible brand in a category.

In our research examining the moderating role of competitive positioning in CSR's influence on relationship benefits (Du et al. 2007), we argue that, because positioning on CSR reveals the "soul," or "character," of a company to a greater extent than positioning on more traditional platforms such as innovativeness or operational expertise, a CSR positioning strategy will be more uniquely associated with rarer, longer-term relational benefits, such as loyalty and advocacy. To test this, we contrasted the business returns of CSR initiatives undertaken by differently positioned brands in the same product category (i.e., Dannon, Yoplait, and Stonyfield Farm, the latter being the CSR brand in the yogurt category). We found that while the CSR initiatives of these brands all deliver short-term, transactional outcomes (e.g., greater purchase likelihood) and long-term, relational outcomes (e.g., greater identification, consumer loyalty, and advocacy behaviors), the CSR brand (i.e., Stonyfield) enjoyed superior relational outcomes (but not transactional outcomes) compared to the two mainstream brands (i.e., Dannon and Yoplait). Specifically, frequent buyers of Stonyfield Farm (i.e., the CSR brand) identify more with Stonyfield than frequent buyers of Dannon and Yoplait do with their respective brands. Similarly, frequent buyers of Stonyfield are also more loyal to the company, engage in more advocacy behaviors toward the brand than frequent buyers of Dannon or Yoplait to their respective brands. Furthermore, the positive relationships between consumers' CSR beliefs and these relational outcomes (i.e., C-C identification, loyalty, and advocacy) are stronger for Stonyfield than for Dannon and Yoplait. These findings indicated that the same CSR actions may elicit different reactions from consumers, depending on the extent to which these are viewed as isolated endeavors versus the very basis of the brand. Greater relationship rewards of CSR are likely to accrue to a brand that has successfully positioned itself along this dimension than to those who merely engage in CSR.

Reputation

A company's reputation is also an important factor in determining the effectiveness of CSR in building brand relationships. Conceptualized as "a collective representation of a firm's past actions and results that describes the firm's ability to deliver valued outcomes to multiple stakeholders" (Gardberg and Fombrun 2002), corporate reputation encompasses different dimensions, such as product quality, innovation, investment value, people management, and CSR. Reputation serves as a preexisting schema upon which consumers rely to interpret ambiguous information about the company (Fombrun and Shanley 1990), including a company's motives behind its CSR activities. We argue that one aspect of corporate reputation, a company's existing or prior CSR record, will be perceived as a highly diagnostic cue in consumers' interpretation of its CSR activities. For example, when Wal-Mart announced that it would invest $500 million a year in energy efficiency in an effort to become a "good steward for the environment," consumers were skeptical, considering this environmental initiative as a publicity stunt (Clark 2006). Yoon and colleagues (2006) have shown that companies with a negative reputation (e.g., a cigarette company) are likely to be suspected of harboring ulterior motives in their social initiatives, hence causing consumers to react negatively to such social initiatives. Interestingly, Yoon and colleagues (2006) further suggest that such a company will be able to overcome negative consumer reactions if its contribution to the CSR cause far exceeds its expenditure on CSR-related advertising. Similarly, findings from our research (Du et al. 2008a) indicate that when a company with a negative prior CSR record engages in a social initiative, consumers will refrain from making intrinsic attributions; this lack of intrinsic attributions, in turn, impedes such companies in reaping relationship benefits from their CSR investments.

Consumer Factors

CSR Support

One of the most important factors to moderate consumer reactions to a company's CSR efforts is the extent to which they support the focal issue of a CSR initiative (i.e., CSR support; Sen and Bhattacharya 2001). Since CSR support reflects consumers' personal needs and values, a CSR initiative that supports causes that consumers deem important or personally relevant will have maximal potential to build emotional connections with consumers. Our research (Sen and Bhattacharya 2001) shows that consumers will have greater identification with a company when its CSR efforts are in a domain they personally support. Similarly, based on findings from in-depth interviews with managers, Drumwright (1996) concluded that cause affinity among key constituents, including consumers, is a key factor that contributes to the success of a company's social campaigns.

Therefore, in choosing CSR activities, companies need to focus on social causes that their consumers care about. Such a notion is implicit in the opinion of CEOs worldwide: in a recent McKinsey survey (2007), CEOs assert that their company's consumers, as opposed to employees or other key stakeholder groups, are likely to have the greatest impact on the way they manage societal expectations over the next five years. More generally, linking back to our earlier discussion on CSR fit, a company's CSR activities that embody a high fit with not only its CA-related activities but also with the values and needs of its target consumers, will have the maximal potential to yield powerful relational outcomes.

Proximity to CSR

Related to but distinct from the notion of issue support is consumers' proximity to a company's CSR initiative. Proximity can range from a complete lack of awareness about a company's CSR activities (i.e., no proximity) to active participation, either as a beneficiary of the initiative or as a direct co-creator of the social outcomes (i.e., high proximity). Greater proximity is likely to not only facilitate the formation of CSR-related beliefs and outcomes but also influence the types of beliefs and relationship outcomes resulting from such initiatives. For instance, operationalizing proximity at three levels—beneficiaries of a CSR program, nonbeneficiaries who are aware of the program, and nonbeneficiaries who are unaware of the program—our research on consumer reactions to a corporate-sponsored dental care program targeted at children belonging to disadvantaged minority groups (Du et al. 2008a) shows that those with greatest proximity (i.e., the cause beneficiaries) demonstrate, naturally, the highest level of purchase as well as advocacy behaviors. Interestingly, nonbeneficiaries who are aware of the program also have greater purchase and advocacy behaviors relative to those who are unaware. Aside from the ability of the CSR initiative to build trust and a sense of reciprocity, this is due to the likelihood that greater proximity embeds a consumer more strongly and toward the center of the company-based social networks that typically develop around such initiatives (O'Hara, Beehr, and Colarelli 1994; Pratt 2000), making them more identified, and therefore more vested in the success of the company. This suggests that companies interested in building meaningful relationships with consumers might want to pick causes that actively involve at least their most valued consumers (e.g., in their local communities rather than at the national level; Hoeffler and Keller 2002), attempting over time to enable these consumers to co-create the CSR "product."

CONCLUSION

In this chapter, we review extant research on consumer reactions to corporate social responsibility to make the case that under certain initiative-, company-, and consumer-specific conditions, CSR can help companies bring consumers closer to their brands, engaging them in deep, meaningful, long-term relationships. This is because a company's actions in the CSR domain are particularly effective at revealing its values, "soul," or identity, increasing the likelihood that certain consumers will identify with it in their efforts to fulfill one or more higher-order self-related needs. Such identification causes consumers to feel deeply connected and committed to the company and its brands, spurring them to engage in a set of pro-company behaviors that go beyond mere purchase.

In our adoption of an identity-based perspective on the role of CSR in brand relationships, the ideas in this chapter dovetail with much of the other research contained in this book (e.g., Chapter 9) in implying that consumers often enter into strong brand relationships not for what the brand does for them at a functional level but because of what it stands for (i.e., its identity). In other words, CSR, among other things, infuses a brand with meanings that are valuable to consumers not in solving their everyday problems, as products are traditionally thought of as doing, but in their more fundamental quest for an enduring and affirming sense of their place in this world. Such meaning provision underlies CSR's ability to transform consumer-brand and consumer-company relationships from transactional, or exchange relationships to communal relationships (Aggarwal 2004; Chapter 2). As the global marketplace lurches tentatively but inexorably toward a brave new CSR world (*Economist* 2007; McKinsey 2007), it is in the very best interest of marketers to understand and harness the power of CSR in transforming people from mere consumers of their brands into passionate lifelong advocates.

NOTES

1. In this chapter, we use company and brand interchangeably.

2. The notion of C-C identification is related to but conceptually distinct from that of brand attachment, the focus of Chapter 17. While the authors of that chapter define attachment as "the strength of the bond connecting the consumer with a brand," we conceptualize identification more specifically as "consumers' perceived overlap between their own identity and that of the company." It is entirely plausible, of course, that CSR contributes to the development of brand/company attachment through identification. Exploring the precise relationship between identification and attachment would be a fruitful research endeavor.

REFERENCES

Aggarwal, Pankaj (2004). "The Effects of Brand Relationship Norms on Consumer Attitudes and Behavior," *Journal of Consumer Research,* 31 (September), 87–101.

Alsop, Ronald J. (2005). "Communicating Corporate Citizenship," *Leading Perspectives,* Summer, 4–5.

Ashforth, Blake E., and Fred Mael (1989). "Social Identity Theory and the Organization," *Academy of Management Review,* 14 (1), 20–39.

Bagozzi, Richard P. (1995). "Reflections on Relationship Marketing in Consumer Markets," *Journal of the Academy of Marketing Science,* 23 (4), 272–277.

Bergami, Massimo, and Richard P. Bagozzi (2000). "Self Categorization, Affective Commitment and Group Self-Esteem as Distinct Aspects of Social Identity in the Organization," *British Journal of Social Psychology,* 39 (4), 555–577.

Bhattacharya, C.B., and Sankar Sen (2003). "Consumer-Company Identification: A Framework for Understanding Consumers' Relationship with Companies," *Journal of Marketing,* 67 (April), 76–88.

———. (2004). "Doing Better at Doing Good: When, Why, and How Consumers Respond to Corporate Social Initiatives," *California Management Review,* 47 (1), 9–24.

Bloom, Paul N., Steve Hoeffler, Kevin Lane Keller, and Carlos Meza (2006). "How Social-Cause Marketing Affects Consumer Perceptions," *MIT Sloan Management Review,* 47 (2), 49–55.

Braum, Lutz (2002). "Involved Customers Lead to Loyalty Gains," *Marketing News,* 36 (2), 16.

Brown, Tom J., and Peter Dacin (1997). "The Company and the Product: Corporate Beliefs and Consumer Product Responses," *Journal of Marketing,* 61 (January), 68–84.

Chappell, Tom (1993). *The Soul of a Business: Managing for Profit and the Common Good.* Des Plaines, IL: Bantam.

Clark, Andrew (2006). "Is Wal-Mart Really Going Green?" Guardian.co.uk, November 6. Available at http://www.guardian.co.uk/environment/2006/nov/06/energy.supermarkets (accessed June 2008).

Cone (2007). "2007 Cause Evolution Survey." Available at http://www.coneinc.com/content1091 (accessed May 19, 2008).

Dawkins, Jenny (2004). "Corporate Responsibility: The Communication Challenge," *Journal of Communication Management,* 9 (2), 108–119.

DeWulf, Kristof, Gaby Odekerken-Schröder, and Dawn Iacobucci (2001). "Investments in Consumer Relationships: A Cross-Country and Cross-Industry Exploration," *Journal of Marketing,* 65 (October), 33–50.

Drumwright, Minette E. (1996). "Company Advertising with a Social Dimension: The Role of Noneconomic Criteria," *Journal of Marketing,* 60 (4), 71–87.

Du, Shuili, C.B. Bhattacharya, and Sankar Sen (2007). "Reaping Relationship Rewards from Corporate Social Responsibility: The Role of Competitive Positioning," *International Journal of Research in Marketing,* 24 (3), 224–241.

———. (2008a). "Strengthening Consumer Relationships through Corporate Social Responsibility." Working paper, Simmons College School of Management.

Du, Shuili, Sankar Sen, and C.B. Bhattacharya (2008b). "Exploring the Social and Business Returns of a Corporate Oral Health Initiative Aimed at Disadvantaged Hispanic Families," *Journal of Consumer Research,* 35 (3), 483–494.

Dutton, Jane E., Janet M. Dukerich, and Celia V. Harquail (1994). "Organizational Images and Member Identification," *Administrative Science Quarterly,* 39 (34), 239–263.

Economist (2007). "Global Business Barometer." economist.com. Available at http://www.economist.com/media/pdf/20080116CSRResults.pdf (accessed June 2008).

Ellen, Pam Scholder, Deborah J. Webb, and Lois A. Mohr (2006). "Building Corporate Associations: Consumer Attributions for Corporate Socially Responsible Program," *Journal of the Academy of Marketing Science,* 34 (2), 147–157.

Fombrun, Charles, and Mark Shanley (1990). "What's in a Name? Reputation Building and Corporate Strategy," *Academy of Management Journal,* 33 (2), 233–258.

Fournier, Susan, Susan Dobscha, David Glen Mick (1998). "Preventing the Premature Death of Relationship Marketing," *Harvard Business Review,* 76 (1), 42–51.

Gardberg, Naomi A., and Charles J. Fombrun (2002). "The Global Reputation Quotient Project, First Steps towards a Cross-Nationally Valid Measure of Corporate Reputation," *Corporate Reputation Review,* 4 (4), 303–308.

Gilbert, Daniel T. (1989). "Thinking Lightly About Others, Automatic Components of the Social Inference Process." In *Unintended Thought,* ed. James S. Uleman and John A. Bargh. New York, NY: Guilford Press, 189–211.

Goulder, Alvin W. (1960). "The Norm of Reciprocity: A Preliminary Statement," *American Sociological Review,* 25 (2), 161–178.

Gourville, John T., and V. Kasturi Rangan (2004). "Valuing the Cause Marketing Relationship," *California Management Review,* 47 (1), 38–57.

Haley, Eric (1996). "Exploring the Construct of Organization as Source: Consumers' Understanding of Organizational Sponsorship of Advocacy Advertising," *Journal of Advertising,* 25 (2), 19–36.

Hoeffler, Steve, and Kevin Lane Keller (2002). "Building Brand Equity through Corporate Societal Marketing," *Journal of Public Policy and Marketing,* 21 (1), 78–89.

Ioannou, Lori (2003). "Corporate America's Social Conscience," *Fortune.* Available at http://www.timeinc.net/fortune/services/sections/fortune/corp/2003_05csr.html (accessed May 2008).

Kinder, Lydenberg, and Domini Co. Inc. (1999). *Socrates: The Corporate Social Ratings Monitor.* Cambridge, MA: Kinder, Lydenberg, and Domini Co. Inc.

Klein, Jill, and Niraj Dawar (2004). "Corporate Social Responsibility and Consumers' Attributions and Brand Evaluations in a Product-Harm Crisis," *International Journal of Research in Marketing,* 21, 203–217.

Kotler, Philip, and Nancy Lee (2004). "Best of Breed," *Stanford Social Innovation Review,* Spring, 14–23.

———. (2005). *Corporate Social Responsibility: Doing the Most Good for Your Company and Your Cause.* Hoboken, NJ: John Wiley & Sons, Inc.

Lichtenstein, Donald R., Minette E. Drumwright, and Bridgette M. Braig (2004). "The Effects of Corporate Social Responsibility on Customer Donations to Corporate-Supported Nonprofits," *Journal of Marketing,* 68 (October), 16–32.

Maignan, Isabelle, and O.C. Ferrell (2004). "Corporate Social Responsibility and Marketing: An Integrative Framework," *Journal of the Academy of Marketing Science,* 32 (1), 3–19.

Marketing Science Institute (2006). *Research Priorities: 2006–2008 Guide to MSI Research Programs and Procedures.* Cambridge, MA: Marketing Science Institute.

Martin, Roger L. (2005). "Seek Validity, Not Reliability," *Harvard Business Review,* 83 (2), 23–24.

McAlexander, James H., John W. Schouten, and Harold F. Koenig (2002). "Building Brand Community," *Journal of Marketing,* 66 (January), 38–54.

McKinsey & Company (2007). *Shaping the New Rules of Competition: UN Global Compact Participant Mirror,* (July). Available at http://www.mckinsey.com/clientservice/ccsi/pdf/Shaping_the_new_rules.pdf.

Menon, Satya, and Barbara E. Kahn (2003). "Corporate Sponsorships of Philanthropic Activities: When Do They Impact Perception of Sponsor Brand?" *Journal of Consumer Psychology,* 13 (3), 316–327.

O'Hara, Kirk B., Terry A. Beehr, and Stephen M. Colarelli (1994). "Organizational Centrality: A Third Dimension of Intraoganizational Career Movement," *Journal of Applied Behavioral Science,* 30 (2), 198–216.

Oliver, Richard L. (1999). "Whence Consumer Loyalty?" *Journal of Marketing,* 63 (Special Issue), 33–44.

Palmatier, Robert W., Rajiv P. Dant, Dhruv Grewal, and Kenneth R. Evans (2006). "Factors Influencing the Effectiveness of Relationship Marketing: A Meta-Analysis," *Journal of Marketing,* 70 (October), 136–153.

Peloza, John (2006). "Using Corporate Social Responsibilities as Insurance for Financial Performance," *California Management Review,* 48 (2), 52–72.

Porter, Michael E., and Mark R. Kramer (2006). "Strategy and Society: The Link Between Competitive Advantage and Corporate Social Responsibility," *Harvard Business Review,* 84 (12), 78–92.

Pratt, Michael G. (2000). "The Good, the Bad, and the Ambivalent: Managing Identification among Amway Distributors," *Administrative Science Quarterly,* 45 (3), 456–93.

Reichheld, Frederick F. (2003). "The One Number You Need to Grow," *Harvard Business Review,* 81 (12), 46–54.

Reichheld, Frederick F., Robert G. Markey, and Christopher Hopton (2000). "The Loyalty Effect—The Relationship between Loyalty and Profits," *European Business Journal,* 12 (3), 134–139.

Reinartz, Werner, and V. Kumar (2002). "The Mismanagement of Customer Loyalty," *Harvard Business Review,* 80 (7), 86–94.

Satmetrix, Inc. (2004). "The Power behind a Single Number. Netpromoter: The New Standard for Measuring Customer Loyalty." Satmetrix Systems white paper. Available at http://www.satmetrix.com/pdfs/NetPromoterWPfinal.pdf (accessed June 2008).

Scott, Susanne G., and Vicki R. Lane (2000). "A Stakeholder Approach to Organizational Identity," *Academy of Management Review,* 25 (1), 43–62.

Sen, Sankar, and C.B. Bhattacharya (2001). "Does Doing Good Always Lead to Doing Better? Consumer Reactions to Corporate Social Responsibility," *Journal of Marketing Research,* 38 (May), 43–62.

Sen, Sankar, C.B. Bhattacharya, and Daniel Korschun (2006). "The Role of Corporate Social Responsibility in Strengthening Multiple Stakeholder Relationships: A Field Experiment," *Journal of the Academy of Marketing Science,* 34 (2), 158–166.

Simmons, Carolyn J., and Karen L. Becker-Olsen (2006). "Achieving Marketing Objectives through Social Sponsorships," *Journal of Marketing,* 70 (October), 154–169.

Smith, N. Craig (2003). "Corporate Social Responsibility: Whether or How?" *California Management Review,* 45 (4), 52–75.

Tajfel, Henri, and John C. Turner (1985). "The Social Identity Theory of Intergroup Behavior." In *Psychology of Intergroup Relations,* ed. Steven Worchel and William G. Austin. Chicago, IL: Nelson-Hall, 6–24.

Thomas, Jacquelyn S., Werner Reinartz, and V. Kumar (2004). "Getting the Most out of All Your Customers," *Harvard Business Review,* 82 (7/8), 116–123.

Varadarajan, P. Rajan, and Anil Menon (1988). "Cause-Related Marketing: A Coalignment of Marketing Strategy and Corporate Philanthropy," *Journal of Marketing,* 52 (July), 58–74.

Verhoef, Peter C. (2003). "Understanding the Effect of Customer Relationship Management Efforts on Customer Retention and Customer Share Development," *Journal of Marketing,* 67 (October), 30–45.

Walker, Lauren (2008). "A Stonyfield Farm Yogurt Review: Organic and Delicious," Associated Content, February 8. Available at http://www.associatedcontent.com/article/584769/ a_stonyfield_farms_yogurt_review_organic.html?cat=22 (accessed August 2008).

Wangenheim, Florian V., and Tomas Bayon (2007). "The Chain from Customer Satisfaction via Word-of-Mouth Referrals to New Customer Acquisition," *Journal of the Academy of Marketing Science,* 35 (2), 233–249.

Yoon, Yeosun, Zeynep Gurhan-Canli, and Norbert Schwarz (2006). "The Effect of Corporate Social Responsibility (CSR) Activities on Companies with Bad Reputations," *Journal of Consumer Psychology,* 16 (4), 377–390.

CHAPTER 11

ETHNICITY, RACE, AND BRAND CONNECTIONS

DAVID W. SCHUMANN, EDITH F. DAVIDSON, AND BRIDGET SATINOVER

For more than a century, companies in the United States have attempted to establish their brand in the eyes of an ethnic population; indeed, to form a connection with their brand. Since the end of World War II, we have seen a significant increase in market segmentation strategies that are based on ethnic group characteristics. This began with African Americans, followed by Hispanics, and recently Asians, the so-called model minority. Each of these groups represents a number of subgroups, each with an identified subculture. Sometimes, the attempted brand connections have been with a subgroup and other times with the overarching group.

The purpose of this chapter is to examine the development of ethnic/racial–group-based brand connections in the United States (the difference between the terms *ethnic* and *racial* will be addressed). We believe there are two major motivating sources of this race/ethnic brand-self connection: the marketer, who is attempting to establish a relationship between the brand and the individual with a focus on the individual's "race" through race-based target marketing, and the consumer, whose "ethnicity" may drawn him/her to certain brands, sometimes within identified product classes. Three major classifications of racial groups will be discussed: African American, Asian, and Hispanic.

ETHNICITY AND RACE

There is inconsistency on how the terms *ethnicity* and *race* are used by the general public as well as in academic literature. Historically, *race* has been used to refer to classifications based on biological differences. In the twentieth century, work by geneticists indicated that human beings were more alike than the concept of race indicated (Smedley and Smedley 2005). Current genetic data refutes the notion that races are genetically distinct human populations, as humans around the globe have been found to be 99.9 percent alike (Bonham, Warshauer-Baker, and Collins 2005; Smedley and Smedley 2005). Some scholars have discarded the word race as a category concept. However, the legacy of race is a socially constructed meaning that continues to be acted upon in many societies and is "inextricably intertwined with inequality in the distribution of wealth, power, privilege and prestige" (Spickard and Daniel 2004, p. 6).

The concept of race has been supplanted in some academic disciplines by the concept of ethnicity (Harrison 1995). *Ethnicity* provides a way to describe groups that focuses on culture and descent rather than on biology and the process of migration and adaptation. Some scholars feel that ethnicity is a less problematic concept than race since it is free of negative historical connotations (Spickard and Daniel 2004). Other scholars criticize this movement to replace race with ethnicity, because of the negative consequences associated with race (Harrison 1995). Still others believe that ethnicity may become a euphemism for race, another way of naturalizing differences (Ratcliffe 2004).

While the debate over the meaning and implications of these terms continues, from a marketing perspective the distinction between race and ethnicity may, in most cases, be less problematic. Davidson (2007) suggests that the question of race or ethnicity may be answered by first considering from whose perspective the researcher is exploring a phenomenon. In such cases, race refers to categorization to a geographically concentrated or phenotypically distinct group based solely on physical appearance. It is primarily this criterion that is used to lump together individuals from countries as varied as Japan, Pakistan, Taiwan, and India under the umbrella term *Asian American.* Ethnicity, on the other hand, refers to self-categorization based on ancestry or country of origin. In other words, race may be used when an etic perspective is utilized, ethnicity for an emic perspective (Davidson 2007). This terminology corresponds with that of other researchers who have noted, "Skin color, hair texture, nose width, and lip thickness have remained major markers of racial identity in the United States" (Smedley and Smedley 2005, p. 20); and "physical characteristics should never be included in a definition of ethnic identity" (Smedley and Smedley 2005, p. 18). This chapter incorporates this difference in describing race-based market targeting versus ethnic-based brand usage.

There are a number of examples of ethnic subcultures that exist within these large racial categories. For example, according to the U.S. Census, the label *Hispanic* may subsume individuals of Mexican, Puerto Rican, Central and South American, Cuban, and Dominican origin, as well as those of Spanish ancestry. The term African American refers to "people having origins in any of the Black racial groups of Africa but could include individuals from Nigeria or Haiti, South Africa or Jamaica." The federal government uses the term *Asian* to refer to "people having origins in any of the original peoples of the Far East, Southeast Asia, or the Indian subcontinent. It includes people who indicated their race or races as Asian Indian, Chinese, Filipino, Korean, Japanese, Vietnamese, or other Asian, or wrote in entries such as Burmese, Hmong, Pakistani, or Thai" (Reeves and Bennett 2003). One could argue that the U.S. Census has significantly reinforced these large racial categories.

RACE-BASED SEGMENTATION AND MARKET TARGETING

Focused marketing based on race dates back to the early twentieth century. As Gail Baker Woods notes in *Advertising and Marketing to the New Majority* (1995, citing Latham 1989), the person likely to be most often recognized as the first to target a product to African Americans was Madam C.J. Walker (who was African American). In 1900, Walker launched one of the first comprehensive, ethnic-focused, marketing campaigns for a new beauty care product that promised to remove the curl from blacks' hair. The promotional message as well as the product itself addressed both social and psychological needs stemming from the desire to assimilate into mainstream American culture. Walker advertised in newspapers including the *Pittsburgh Courier* and *New York Amsterdam News.*

Historically, three strategies have been employed by manufacturers and retailers to reach Hispanic, African American, and Asian consumers: primary market targeting, secondary market targeting, and subsumed market targeting.

A *primary market-targeting strategy* reflects products and brands that are developed and marketed to groups based on racial distinctions. Some types of products, such as cosmetics (e.g., Fashion Fair, Flori Roberts), pantyhose (e.g., Brown Sugar), and hair care products (e.g., Doo Gro, Carol's Daughter) seem to call for this type of differentiation. For other products, the rationale for segmenting along racial dimensions may be less obvious. In 1987, Hallmark introduced a line of cards, Mahogany, designed specifically for African Americans (hallmark.com). In 2003, the Sinceramente line was introduced by Hallmark to "mirror the values and perspectives" of Hispanic consumers" (hallmark.com 2008). In each of these examples, the manufacturer has developed an offering tailored for a particular group of people based on perceived racial traits, characteristics, personalities, or beliefs.

In retailing, Spiegel, Inc. and *Ebony* magazine teamed up in 1993 for a joint venture to produce a catalog, *E Style,* specializing in clothing for African-American women. Niche retailer Ashley Stewart has focused on targeting primarily African-American women since its inception in 1991 (Sokol 2003) and operates more than 200 stores, with its flagship store based in Harlem, New York. Ashley Stewart's ad campaigns feature primarily women in this demographic group. They also collaborated with the legendary singer Gladys Knight on promotional spots. These targeting efforts clearly extend beyond advertising into every area of their marketing mix. This is a key indicator of race-segmentation as a primary market targeting strategy.

In recognition of perceived racial differences, manufacturers typically choose to vary the messages communicated to minority audiences, but the product remains the same. This race-based segmentation practice is referred to as *secondary market targeting.* In 2004, Infiniti launched a media campaign with the goal of reaching African-American consumers. Entitled Infiniti in Black, the campaign tied the Infiniti brand with various African-American artists. The campaign was launched exclusively through African-American media, including *Essence, Ebony,* and *Black Enterprise* magazines as well as Black America Web, the Internet news and entertainment portal. Secondary market targeting uses cultural cues or adjusts the message to be culturally relevant for the targeted group (Brumbaugh 2002). In an effort to reach more Hispanic consumers, Hyundai initiated a campaign in 2008 with the tag line, "Descubrelo tu mismo" ("Discover it for yourself") (Wentz 2008). State Farm Insurance utilizes this strategy to reach African Americans, Hispanics, and Asians. In April 2007, State Farm kicked off the 50 Million Pound Challenge campaign to address the obesity epidemic that has disproportionately affected African Americans. The company's Chinese-American target campaign (2005) changed their well known tagline, "Like a good neighbor, State Farm is there" to "Having a good neighbor, there's peace every day." Manufacturers who use the secondary market targeting strategy utilize primarily segmented media and employ advertising firms that specialize in reaching specific minority audiences.

In the case of retailers utilizing this strategy, some variation may occur in store ambiance and product lines carried depending upon the demographic composition of the local markets. Even traditional big-box retailers are beginning to employ this strategy. In 2005, Home Depot created a line of paints to target Hispanics (Wentz 2007). Colores Origenes was originally developed to be sold in 400 stores in "heavily Hispanic" areas. The line exceeded expectations and eventually was rolled out to all Home Depot stores.

A *subsumed market targeting strategy* assumes that minority consumers will be reached utilizing the same products and messages used by the manufacturer or retailer to reach their broader target market. This type of market strategy, when used to expand into international markets, is often referred to as cross-market segmentation (Taylor 2008). The premise behind this strategy is that despite seemingly important demographic or cultural differences, people are basically more alike than they are different. This targeting strategy may include minority actors in advertising campaigns in which sponsorships or mediums may be selected to knowingly reach Hispanic, African-American, or Asian audiences. For example, Latina star Daisy Fuentes debuted her collection of clothing exclusively through Kohl's department store in 2004. In a press release issued at the time, a spokesperson noted that though the Fuentes apparel was expected to appeal to the Hispanic market, the alliance was not intended as a Hispanic marketing strategy because of Fuentes's broad appeal among Kohl's shoppers. In the subsumed market strategy, there is no variation in the message or the product. Though the message may be translated into other languages, the meaning remains the same.

RESEARCH ON RACE-BASED TARGET MARKET STRATEGIES AND BRAND CONNECTIONS

In his seminal work on marketing to minorities, Bullock noted, "Sellers would like to tailor their sales efforts to influence Negro consumers, but they do not know what kind of suit to make," (1961, p. 91). Though the terminology used to refer to minority groups has evolved since that statement was made, the research on targeting minorities may not have progressed as much. There is likely little optimism surrounding Hyundai's recent "Descubrelo tu mismo" campaign, which was created by the third Hispanic agency hired by the car company in as many years in an attempt to gain a foothold in this market. This raises the following questions: What is known about the determinants of a successful race-based targeting campaign and how do manufacturers and retailers build strong brand connections among minority consumers?

The changing demographics of the United States have obviously not been overlooked by researchers. This subject has garnered significant attention in advertising and marketing research. Over the past three decades there have been more than fifty articles focusing on minorities in advertisements published in advertising, communication, and marketing journals (this does not count a significant number of articles appearing before that time period, as well as multiple studies that have been reported in conference proceedings; see Davidson and Schumann 2005). The literature on minorities in advertising has addressed two primary concerns: the representation (number and nature) of each minority group in advertisements (e.g., Wilkes and Valencia 1989; Taylor, Lee, and Stern 1995) and the response to advertisements featuring minority groups among majority and minority audiences (e.g., Brumbaugh 2002; Whittler and Spira 2002; Green 1999). The first stream of research indicates that although progress has been made in terms of numerical representation for blacks, less progress has occurred for Hispanic and Asian representation using the proportionality criterion. Furthermore, the literature shows that advertising continues to promote stereotypical portrayals of all three groups. The second stream of literature has focused on the viewer's group membership and separates viewers into those who are in the minority actor's ethnic group and those outside of the minority actor's ethnic group, sometimes making comparisons between groups. This research has focused on how race is used by marketers to categorize and target minority groups. Collectively this research indicates that product-consistent advertisements featuring minorities facilitate purchase intentions for the minority group featured, while not deterring nonminority groups from purchasing the product.

As noted, ethnicity is defined in this chapter as self-categorization based on ancestry or country of origin (Davidson 2007). Consumer behavior research has examined how ethnicity influences product, brand, and retailer choice (e.g., Webster 1994, 1997; Chung and Fischer 1999; Bauer and Cunningham 1970; Donthu and Cherian 1994; Wyatt, Gelb, and Geiger-Oneto 2008). However, there is limited research indicating how this self-identification is manifested in ethnic minorities' experiences in retail environments, as well as research regarding specific brand selection and the effectiveness of race-based targeting campaigns.

PRODUCT AND BRAND CONNECTIONS AS INITIATED BY THE ETHNIC CONSUMER

The previous section noted the various ways in which racial groups have been segmented and targeted in an effort to establish and reinforce brand connections. This activity is initiated by the marketer in an effort to create more efficient means of marketing and delivering products based on the perceived similarities among a designated group. In this section we consider the consumer's identified ethnicity as a motivating factor in creating and reinforcing these connections. As such, we will examine the history of product (and brand) usage by ethnic groups in the United States. Note that we begin by describing product usage historically. Certain products at different times have been used more or less by one ethnic group when compared with white or other minority ethnic groups. Within the favored categories, certain brand favorites emerge.

The African-American Consumer in the United States

In the 1930s, a comprehensive study of Southern urban African Americans undertaken by Edwards (1932) estimated that, of the approximately 12 million blacks in the United

States, 75 percent lived in the South. Of those, about 10 percent lived in seventeen of the largest cities in the South. Edwards determined that most (70 percent and above) were classified as common labor or semiskilled labor, and that purchasing power of African Americans living in these cities was over $300 million, or approximately $340 per person annually. Edwards determined that 40 to 50 percent of purchases were made on food and clothing. For food, black consumers in common and semiskilled labor positions appeared to be very brand conscious, yet for clothing, they focused primarily on price. Edwards noted that those in professional and business occupations tended to be significantly more brand-oriented in their purchasing across the board. The study also found that African Americans appreciated advertising that included blacks, but only when portrayed appropriately. There was significant backlash (e.g., boycotts) when ads significantly demeaned black in their portrayals.

A study by the Research Corporation of America (Steele 1947) of the African-American market in three "northern" cities (Baltimore, Philadelphia, and Washington, D.C.) found that blacks favored several brands within certain product classes. The product classes included packaged coffee (Wilkins and Maxwell House), flour (Gold Medal), pancake or waffle mix (Aunt Jemima), bread (Wonder and Schmidt's), dog food (Red Heart for two of the cities), toothpaste (Colgate), alcoholic beverages (blended whiskey), cola drinks (Pepsi-Cola followed by Coca-Cola), and cigarettes (Camel). No brand differentiation was found for the categories of automobiles and laundry soap. The study did not compare these favored brands with those of white consumers. However, the choice of stores was very different for blacks versus whites during this time, which predates the civil rights movement and federal fairness legislation. Certain stores that demonstrated minimal discrimination were favored by African Americans. These included "layaway" stores targeting black consumers.

Friend and Kravis (1957) interpreted findings from the 1950–1951 Bureau of Labor Statistics (BLS) Cost of Living Survey (see also Alexis 1962). Compared to Caucasians, African Americans consumed more personal care items, clothing, alcoholic beverages, and transportation other than automobiles, and spent less on automobile expenses, recreation, and medical care. A division of regions in the United States reflected that blacks in the West and the North were significantly closer in their consumption patterns to those of whites, compared with those living in the South. This appears to be due to differences in income; Southern blacks earned significantly less than Southern whites when compared to both Western and Northern city populations of blacks and whites in the United States.

Bauer and Cunningham's (1970) report on the 1960–1961 BLS Cost of Living Survey found similar results comparing blacks and whites in the earlier study with the exception that no differences were found related to housing (when income was controlled). However, these researchers took issue with Friend and Kravis's (1957) analysis strategy regarding changes in spending over time, suggesting that differences in spending became minimal in terms of consumption expenditures in response to percentage change in after-tax income. In other words, as the income of blacks approaches that of whites, there are no real differences. The only consistent difference appears to be in spending for clothing and alcoholic beverages. Gibson (1969) discussed the many facets needed for consideration in targeting blacks. He cited a study collected by Brand Rating Index that identified thirty-one product categories in which product usage by blacks was higher than that of whites. Among the most apparent were canned evaporated milk, soft drinks, baby clothes, cloth and disposable diapers, laxatives, liquid and powdered starch, strained or junior baby food, canned pork and beans, bacon, and frankfurters. Maggard (1971) suggested that differences between whites and African Americans reflect the latter's tendency to over-consume certain products. He noted that blacks consumed 28 percent of all soda, 23 percent of all shoes, and 50 percent of all imported scotch whiskey.

Woods (1995) summarized two important studies of African-American consumer buying habits conducted by Deloitte and Touche trade retail and distribution services (1991) and the Target Market News (Smikle 2000). These studies reflected that in the early 1990s blacks composed 19 percent of the total health and beauty aids market and 34 percent of the hair care products market. At this time, blacks were found to be more likely than whites to purchase major items such as cars, stereo equipment, jewelry, and televisions. Blacks were also found to be heavy consumers of orange juice, soft drinks, compact discs, and cigarettes. They accounted for up to 25 percent of beer sales, 15 percent of all cola sales, and 9 percent of all domestic car purchases. This usage data has to be viewed in light of certain key statistics regarding African-American households. At this time 50 percent of African-American households were headed by a single mother and the number of people in these homes was higher than in white homes. Twenty-five percent of all college-aged African-American men were in prison, removing them from the earnings and spending figures within the household. By this time, 30 percent of all African Americans held white-collar jobs.

The Hispanic Consumer in the United States

Charting Hispanic consumption appeared to establish a foothold in the 1960s. A study published by the *Marketing News* (Soriano, 1965) generated a list of brands in product categories that New York metropolitan Hispanics (noted to make up 12 percent of the metropolitan population) used significantly more than non-Hispanics (New York Product Usage Study—NYMPHUS-II). These included canned fruit (Libby's), chocolate milk flavoring (Nestlé Quik), cooking/salad oil (Mazola), fruit-flavored drink (Hawaiian Punch), hot dogs (Oscar Meyer), ice cream, (Breyers), margarine (Parkay), packaged cookies (Almost Home), powdered drink (Tang), rice (Vitarroz), spaghetti sauce (Ragu), frozen vegetables (Green Giant), and cold remedies (CoTylenol).

In a study of the Miami Hispanic market in 1980, a study found a high index of Hispanic usage for certain product categories. These included baby food, alcoholic beverages (particularly malt liquor), fruit nectars and fruit drinks, canned spaghetti, hair conditioners and colorings, floor wax and cleaners, and pine oil disinfectants (as reported in *Advertising Age* 1981, and Segal and Sosa 1983). A national study of media conducted by Yankelovich, Skelly, and White (1984) as well as other authors writing at the time (e.g., Fones 1981; Guernica 1982), suggested a high degree of brand loyalty among Hispanics. However, Saegert, Hoover, and Hilger (1985) found minimal evidence to support claims of greater brand loyalty for Hispanics compared to non-Hispanics in the Southwest. Instead they found significant association with products and businesses that were familiar, as well as a focus on price consideration (see also Gillet and Scott 1975; Faber, O'Guinn, and McCarthy 1987). Penaloza and Gilly (1986), in an examination of Hispanic families, tied Hispanic consumption patterns to the relative youthfulness and size of Hispanic families. More concentrated use of baby-related products would be expected. Hoyer and Deshpande (1982) noted that conspicuous consumer behaviors among Hispanics were linked to values, self-identity, and family/cultural pride.

Mulhern, Williams, and Leone (1998) conducted a comprehensive study of Hispanic shopping and found that Hispanics were especially focused on price considerations when shopping in areas of Hispanic concentration, but overall did not differ on this dimension with non-Hispanics. Like Saegart and colleagues (1985), they did not find evidence for ethnic-specific brand loyalty. What they did find is that Hispanics are more likely to purchase private label brands than other shoppers. This reinforces Saegart's favorable finding regarding familiarity with products and businesses.

The Asian Consumer in the United States

Perhaps due to the lack of attention paid historically to the Asian market within the United States, only a few recent studies have discussed the behavior of this ethnic group as it relates to products or brands. However, each of these studies examined subcultures of the larger ethnic group. For example, in examining Chinese-Americans, Ownbey and Horridge (1997) found that this group is not brand loyal, enjoys shopping at shopping centers, bargain hunts at less expensive stores, and is highly store loyal. Comparing Korean immigrants with Americans, Lee and Um (1992) found that less acculturated Koreans maintain the collectivist influence of family in their evaluation of products.

Two important studies conducted by Kang and Kim (Kim and Kang 1995; Kang and Kim 1998) examined differences between three subcultures in their decision-making processes regarding the purchase of electronic goods and clothing for social occasions. These populations included the Chinese, Japanese, and Koreans, all in the United States. Both studies found ethnicity and acculturation effects. In both studies, Chinese respondents were found to rely on the opinions of family and relatives compared to either the Koreans or Japanese. In the clothing study, the Chinese and Koreans were more likely to rely on their same ethnic group friends compared to the Japanese respondents. Likewise, the Chinese and Korean respondent groups were similar when media influence was considered. When split into high and low acculturation groups, the low acculturation groups were found to be influenced more by television and radio than the high acculturation groups. However, for the Japanese groups, the opposite effect occurred. Finally, Chinese and Korean respondents were more likely to consider product-related appeals more important than their Japanese counterparts.

The literature reviewed here reflects significant differences that lie within the broader "Asian" category. These Asian ethnic group differences are likely to produce problems for marketers seeking to segment on ethnicity. Language, religion, culture, and values differ widely among Asian Americans. Both the business press (e.g., Fost 1990) and academic researchers (e.g., Schumann, Lee, and Watchravestingkan 2004) have argued that marketers and advertisers need to consider segmenting by nationality, rather than by these broad ethnic groups.

USE OF CULTURALLY SIGNIFICANT SYMBOLS AND MEANINGS

Ethnicity may be especially influential in the creation and maintenance of brand self-connections. Although there has long been recognition of this relationship among marketers, as noted earlier in this chapter, it does not appear that researchers have afforded it a great deal of attention. There has, however, been a significant stream of research related to brand self-connections and symbolism (see Escalas, 2004; Escalas and Bettman, 2005, etc.). These research endeavors address the issues related to the meanings of brands to the individuals who consume them. As long as ethnicity can be defined or considered within the realm of culture, one which defines its own symbolic categories, it should be recognized that ethnic cultures are likely to interpret and exhibit certain symbols as fundamental coordinates of meaning. These coordinates of meaning are representations of basic distinctions used by a culture to understand the phenomenal world (McCracken 1986). McCracken suggests that the most important categories devised by the general human community are those of class, status, gender, age, and occupation; whereas the most prominent distinctions of organizing the phenomenal world are categories of time, space, nature, and person. In short, "Each culture establishes its own special vision of the world, thus rendering the understandings and rules appropriate to one cultural context preposterously inappropriate in another" (p. 72).

Marketing practitioners have undoubtedly come to accept symbols as valid and useful in creating marketing advantage. As Levy (1959) noted, the "uneconomic man," is the consumer who no longer only assigns meaning to goods of practical matter, that is, goods that are essential to living, such as shelter, food, and clothing. Rather, this individual is one who buys things both for what they do and what they *mean,* as every commercial object has some symbolic character (Levy 1959). It is this symbolic character that we either associate with or reject as a reinforcement of our own self-concept. Levy's view of commercial goods as carriers of symbolic meaning has steadfastly survived in modern marketing thought, and researchers have continued to cultivate the topic. Holbrook and Hirschmann (1982) were pioneers in calling for more research into the meaning of experiential aspects of consumer behavior, realizing that reactions to less objective features of products, such as nonverbal cues and syntactic versus semantic characteristics of communication, were being overlooked in consumer research (e.g., styles of clothing, store lighting, or subtle color differences).

McCracken's (1986) model of meaning transfer has also helped intensify the study of symbols in consumer research. His model asserts that meanings of goods originate in what he calls the "culturally constituted world," moving into goods through the fashion system, word of mouth, reference groups, subcultures, influential personalities or celebrities, and the media. The model suggests that culturally constituted meanings consist of two elements: cultural principles (the ideals and human values that determine how cultural phenomena are organized, evaluated, and ranked) and cultural categories (the conceptual grids that divide the phenomenological world into smaller parcels). For example, the meaning of a brand may be transferred to the general public by associating a particular brand with the reference groups that most frequently use or display that brand.

Culturally Significant Symbols

"In consumer culture, ethnicity can be bought, sold, and worn like a loose garment," (Oswold 1999). Whether or not one subscribes to this opinion, this quote signifies that buying, wearing, or selling objective qualities of goods can reflect symbols of ethnicity. In her ethnographic study of one first-generation Haitian-American family residing in the United States, Oswold (1999) identifies the phenomenon she calls "culture swapping." She documents how members of this family employ brands and products as a means to shift back and forth between one cultural identity and another, attempting to negotiate relations between their home culture and the American culture. These findings are representative of writings by Ervin Goffman (1959) in his book, *The Presentation of Self in Everyday Life,* positing that individuals use symbols to create a "front," which is on display for others in order to establish one's social identity. In Goffman's view, our society is not a homogeneous creature, and thus we must act differently in different settings.

Symbols and signs carry meaning for particular groups of consumers, such as religious groups, ethnicities, subcultures, gender, and socioeconomic classes. One reason consumers value symbolic brand benefits is the notion that these benefits help consumers construct their self-identity or present themselves to others (Escalas 2004), such that products and brands can be viewed as extensions of the self (Belk 1976). Escalas and Bettman demonstrated that in order to assist themselves in constructing self-concepts, individuals often rely on reference groups and brand images that are representative of specific reference groups (Escalas and Bettman 2005). From this and Oswold's study, we extrapolate that the value individuals place on ethnic reference groups and the symbols associated with the ethnic group will affect the strength of their ethnic self-brand connections. Escalas and Bettman (2005) tested this assertion by comparing Hispanic and Asian consumers to white consumers. Their findings suggest that the ethnic group is a strong predictor of self-brand connection for brands whose images are aligned with the image of their ethnic ingroup.

Types of Ethnic-Brand Connections

Several sociology theorists have strongly posited that ethnic or religious groups hold a sacred set of symbols that act as unifying agents (Durkheim 1915) and depicted a sense of "ethnic honor" (Weber 1978). Berger and Luckmann (1966) considered these sets of symbols to comprise a "symbolic universe." Durkheim (1915) especially argued that these symbols permit a group to exist beyond a physical gathering. Clearly, the "fact that ethnic groups possess a unique symbolic universe is entrenched in the sociological literature; however, marketers have not considered the impact of ethnic symbols on consumers' behavior in-depth" (Rosenbaum 2005, p. 258). Only recently have consumer researchers begun to give primary attention to the ethnic implications of the importance of symbols in consumption. Rosenbaum (2005) explains why ethnic consumers are sensitized to a symbolic universe and, drawing upon Bitner's (1992) servicescape model, illustrates the approach/avoidance phenomenon of certain symbolic meanings. His research suggests that symbols encountered within a service experience elicit emotions and feelings that lead to either comfort (approach) or discomfort (avoidance) based on the meanings derived from the symbols.

Language may be the most freely exercised symbol of marketer-dominated ethnic brand connections by using slang or culturally representative words or catchphrases that speak directly to the group being targeted. This is especially evident when naming brands that signify ethnic heritage or culture. Some examples include Gerber Tropicals baby food (Hispanic) and Tazo Tea (Asian). Similarly, language serves as a strong symbol when presented in a native tongue, rather than in English. However, in some cultures, being able to respond to English advertisements is a credo of success and prestige. For Mexican consumers, brands such as Prada, TAG Heuer, BMW, and Chanel, who advertise in English, are especially popular among the social elites as they provide reminiscence of their European heritage (Vaezi 2005). Overcoming language barriers has been an essential task for marketers focusing on ethnic consumers, and several language faux pas have been the butt of jokes in marketing. In the 1920s, when Coca-Cola was entering the Chinese market, retailers used a set of Chinese symbols representing a close phonetic sound. Unfortunately, when put together the translation literally meant "bite the wax tadpole" (Little, 2007). Similarly, incorporating language and lingo that speak directly to English-speaking ethnic consumers offers a very specific mode of targeting. African-American consumers may be the group most prolifically targeted via language and lingo methods in mainstream media. Serving as anecdotal evidence is the fact that numerous books are dedicated to explaining "black talk" and "black lingo" and its continued force in nurturing the African language, which has been credited to the Black Church (Smitherman 1994). Mainstream media are rich with slang that originated among African Americans. The most popular of these may be the highly successful and award-winning Budweiser "Wassup" campaign (Watts and Orbe 2002).

Music genres are employed frequently, especially in connection with radio and television advertising. Latin, jazz, or hip-hop background music creates and reinforces associations between ethnic consumers and the brands being promoted, or to nonethnic consumers who wish to associate themselves with the referenced group. This strategy was historically employed primarily in ethnic-specific media, but now it is common in mainstream media. An example of this would be the recent combination of music genres with silhouetted dancers promoting iPods. Some of these advertisements feature artists such as Mary J. Blige and The Black Eyed Peas. Pepsi also frequently ventures into ethnic music and has recently used Shakira, a popular Latin artist, in Super Bowl commercials. Each of these examples could be found on network television stations, not solely on ethnically related cable stations.

Color schemes that present ethnically significant colors infer ethnic connections. Color schemes as symbols have been troubling to some marketers who have not understood their significance when targeting certain groups. For example, in Chinese culture, anything colored white, black, or blue symbolizes death. For Americans, the color white signifies purity and innocence and black represents death and mourning. For Chinese Americans, the interpreted meaning of these colors may depend heavily on their level of acculturation into mainstream Western culture.

Familial representation can also be highly symbolic, especially for more communal and family-oriented cultures such as Indians, Hispanics, and Asians. Also, roles of individuals within the family signify ethnically driven connections in the form of affiliation. For example, the well-known "Got Milk" campaign produced for the California Milk Processor Board was altered to meet the symbolic needs of Hispanic cultures, featuring the slogan "Generations" as an alternative. It was thought that the Got Milk campaign was not appealing to the Hispanic audience as many of the situations depicted in the ads were not part of the Hispanic cultural world, and that running out of milk signified the disgrace of a housewife who had failed her family (Maso-Fleishman 1997). The Generations campaign featured nurturing relationships between mothers, grandmothers, and daughters, highlighting family values and honoring women of the household. It is thought that the campaign was successful because of the image portrayed of the grandmother, who was seen as a mother archetype to whom viewers responded emotionally, yearning for the love and care that such women represented in their culture (Maso-Fleishman 1997).

Affiliation and representations of cultural origins and historical manifestations also play an important role in ethnic symbolism. In a multicountry study of Jewish symbolism, it was found that the three most commonly selected symbols of Jewish identification were Auschwitz, Israel, and Jerusalem (Cohen 2004), three places that almost none of the respondents had personal experience with, but that represented prominent historical manifestations of destruction, death, and rebirth (a common historical theme). Nancarrow and colleagues (2007) explored the opportunity for marketing to utilize national identity or country of origin for consumer groups, finding that some British consumers have "a hankering for Scottish 'products' motivated by nostalgia, romanticism, comfort seeking or a desire to differentiate" (p. 62). It is also reported that there is a "growing interest in genealogy and ancestral heritage" (Morgan, Pritchard, and Pride 2002), suggesting that even ethnic group members who do not have direct contact with their country of origin may identify with symbols of their homeland. The population of African Americans who have personal lived experiences or knowledge of their African descent is relatively small. However, a feeling of African heritage can be very strong. Asian Americans and Hispanic Americans, because of later immigration movements, have more recent contact with their cultural heritage and families may be comprised of first- or second-generation American-born citizens, as well as immigrant family members. In each case, the degree of acculturation to the American mainstream and the degree of cultural heritage may determine ethnic self-brand connections when symbols of cultural history are presented.

Finally, ethnic and cultural symbolism may not only take place in physical objective realms, as noted by Hirschman and Holbrook (1982), but also by experiences, behavior, and perceptions. In the Chinese culture, for example, it is not customary to use exaggerated hand gestures or for men to touch women in public, as these carry offensive connotations of disrespect. Gift giving is also treated differently than in many Western cultures, as presenting a gift in public may be embarrassing to the recipient in Chinese culture. In Japan, slurping noodles symbolizes enjoying food, and not doing so can be construed that the meal was not satisfying. Exhibiting symbols of ethnic behaviors can be readily found in marketing, including a McDonald's ad campaign that features young girls playing double-dutch (a typically African-American jump rope style).

CONSEQUENCES OF CREATING BRAND-SELF CONNECTIONS BASED ON RACE OR ETHNICITY

There are significant benefits that marketing segmentation strategies create that apply to ethnic groups. First, market segmentation provides the ability to match products and services to certain value drivers that define each ethnic segment. Previous literature has noted differences that exist between ethnic groups on numerous value dimensions (e.g., Rokeach 1973; Steenkamp, ter Hofstede, and Wedel 1999). Such values are often reflected in the message positioning of products. Second, market segmentation provides the ability to accurately target ethnic consumers who are most likely to be customers. This comes specifically in the form of targeted media and other promotional activities (e.g., point-of-sale) that create significant cost efficiencies. Third, market segmentation reinforces the need for product developers, manufacturers, and marketers to know the ethnic market by collecting accurate and timely data. Fourth, market segmentation encourages the more effective use of product distribution. By targeting ethnic groups and understanding the retailing locations where they shop, manufacturers can better forecast sales and thus minimize distribution costs. Finally, some might argue that market segmentation also inhibits undesirable markets from exposure to certain products by not targeting those groups.

The advantages of market segmentation strategies that incorporate ethnic groups are reflected in two key benefits to the individual groups. The first is the greater likelihood of the ethnic consumer receiving a product that has been designed especially to meet his or her unique needs. The second is significantly reduced costs that result from increased competition in the marketplace.

These benefits are important to both the marketer and consumer, but may not be without cost. For example, this adopted association of a specific brand to an ethnic group has not always been met with positive regard from the marketer who may feel that the adoption of their brand by one group may deter product adoption from other groups who wish to dissociate (White and Dahl 2007). This predicted negative reaction may serve to reinforce established stereotypes.

In *Breaking Up America,* James Turow (1997) reported on his years of interaction with the advertising, media, and marketing businesses:

. . . media were increasingly encouraging people to separate themselves into more and more specialized groups and to develop distinctive viewing, reading, and listening habits that stressed differences between their groups and others.

. . . marketers look for splits in the social fabric and then reinforce and extend the splits for their own ends.

The strategy of segmenting markets, whether intentional or not, potentially minimizes the exposure and knowledge of other groups in our society. It presents a "me" as owning certain products, doing certain activities, socializing with certain people, and a "they" as being different in their choice of products, activities, friends, and so on. It has been noted by the first author of this chapter that market segmentation can lead to a type of market segregation (Schumann 2003). Such restriction of information by individuals and groups is thought to lead to continued stereotyping and thus a potential prejudicial response against products/services that may be associated with specific groups. The degree to which market segmentation is harmful to society and perhaps provides a negative consequence that must be weighed against the significant positive outcomes (as noted above) is an empirical question and one that deserves further investigation.

A PATH FOR FUTURE RESEARCH

There is a long history of research that has attempted to better understand and detect changes in strategy, especially as it applies to targeted advertising and promotion. This research has taken two directions. The first occurs through content analysis of media strategy. The focus primarily has been on frequency and role portrayal. The second occurs through experimentation manipulating various ethnically related stimuli (e.g., models, language, and context). Continued research employing content analysis will provide historical markers as to how we are evolving in our portrayals and use of ethnic groups in advertising and promotion. Experimentation that examines response to ethnic-based advertising must continue.

Recent work in experimentation has sought to examine response from the target ethnic group, but also from the nontargeted groups (e.g., Appiah 2001; Brumbaugh 2002; Dimofte, Forehand, and Deshpande 2004; Forehand and Desphande 2001). This research needs to continue as it will determine over time the degree to which our stereotypes, both ingroup and outgroup, are acted upon. Indeed, the use of ethnic-based stimulus cues in advertising need to be better understood. Previous literature in social psychology reflects that such cues may automatically activate stereotypes (e.g., Devine 1989; Dovidio et al. 1997, 2002), but there remain questions as to when this activation of stereotypes results in a prejudicial response or some form of discrimination (e.g., brand boycott). Are there moderating factors involved? If such activation and resulting application (attitudinal and behavior response) occur, is it possible to desensitize the automatic prejudice response by providing a different format? For example, will the use of more mixed-group advertising and promotion diminish this activation? In advertising, these questions have yet to be explored.

CONCLUSIONS

There is an old adage that states, "race matters." This chapter suggests that for marketers in the United States, not only does race matter, but ethnicity does as well. Researchers are only beginning to understand how to effectively use race in targeting practices and how ethnicity influences brand connections. Retailers face an additional challenge. In social interactions, such as a retail exchange, race and ethnicity may exert reciprocal influences on each other as individuals perceived to be of different races interact with each other. We have suggested a program of research that may help to resolve some of these issues. It is likely that the changing demographics of the United States will continue to create challenges and opportunities for marketing researchers and practitioners.

REFERENCES

Advertising Age (1981*)*. Market Profile (April 6), s23–s24.

Alexis, Marcus (1962). "Some Negro-White Differences in Consumption," *American Journal of Economics and Sociology,* 21 (January), 11–28.

Appiah, Osei (2001). "Ethnic Identification on Adolescents' Evaluation of Advertisments," *Journal of Advertising Research,* 41 (5), 7–22.

Bauer, Raymond A., and Scott M. Cunningham (1970). "The Negro Market," *Journal of Advertising Research,* 10 (2), 4–13.

Belk, Russell W. (1976). "It's the Thought That Counts: A Signed Diagraph Analysis of Gift-Giving," *Journal of Consumer Research,* 3 (December), 155–162.

Berger, Peter, and Thomas Luckmann (1966). *The Social Construction of Reality: A Treatise in the Sociology of Knowledge.* Garden City, NY: Anchor Books.

Bitner, Mary Jo (1992). "Servicescapes: The Impact of Physical Surroundings on Customers and Employees," *Journal of Marketing,* 56 (April), 57–72.

Bonham, Vence L., Esther Warshauer-Baker, and Francis S. Collins (2005). "Race and Ethnicity in the Genome Era," *American Psychologist,* 60 (1), 9–15.

Brumbaugh, Anne M. (2002). "Source and Nonsource Cues in Advertising and Their Effects on the Activation of Cultural and Subcultural Knowledge on the Route to Persuasion," *Journal of Consumer Research,* 29 (September), 258–269.

Bullock, Henry A. (1961). "Consumer Motivations in Black and White, I & II," *Harvard Business Review,* 39 (May-June), 89–104; and (July-August), 111–124.

Chung, Ed, and Eileen Fischer (1999). "It's Who You Know: Intracultural Differences in Ethnic Product Consumption," *Journal of Consumer Marketing,* 16 (5), 482–501.

Cohen, Erik H. (2004). "Components and Symbols of Ethnic Identity: A Case Study in Informal Education and Identity Formation in Diaspora," *Applied Psychology: An International Review,* 53 (1), 87–112.

Davidson, Edith F. (2007). "Shopping While Black: Perceptions of Discrimination in Retail Settings." Published dissertation, University of Tennessee.

Davidson, Edith, and David W. Schumann (2005). "The Need for Transition in Minority Advertising Research: Recent Social Psychological Studies Provide New Direction." Proceedings for the American Association of Advertising Summer Conference.

Deloitte and Touche (1991). *Market Opportunities in Retail: Insight into Black American Consumers' Buying Habits,* January.

Devine, Patricia G. (1989). "Stereotypes and Prejudice: Their Automatic and Controlled Components," *Journal of Personality and Social Psychology,* 56, 1, 5–18.

Dimofte, Claudiu V., Mark R. Forehand, and Rohit Deshpande (2004). "Ad Schema Incongruity as Elicitor of Ethnic Self-Awareness and Differential Advertising Response," *Journal of Advertising,* 32 (4), 7–17.

Donthu, Naveen, and Joseph Cherian (1994). "Impact of Strength of Ethnic Identification on Hispanic Shopping Behavior," *Journal of Retailing,* 70 (4), 383–93.

Dovidio, John F., Kerry Kawakami, and Samuel L. Gaertner (2002). "Implicit and Explicit Prejudice and Interracial Interaction," *Journal of Personality and Social Psychology,* 82 (1) 62–68.

Dovidio, John F., Kerry Kawakami, Craig Johnson, Brenda Johnson, and Adaiah Howard (1997). "On the Nature of Prejudice: Automatic and Controlled Processes," *Journal of Experimental Social Psychology,* 33, 510–540.

Durkheim, Émile (1915 [repr. 1965]). *The Elementary Forms of the Religious Life,* trans. Joseph Ward Swain. New York, NY: The Free Press.

Edwards, Paul K. (1932). *The Southern Negro as a Consumer.* New York, NY: Prentice-Hall.

Escalas, Jennifer Edison (2004). "Narrative Processing: Building Consumer Connections to Brands," *Journal of Consumer Psychology,* 14 (1–2), 168–180.

Escalas, Jennifer Edson, and James R. Bettman (2005). "Self-Construal, Reference Groups, and Brand Meaning," *Journal of Consumer Research,* 32 (3), 378–389.

Faber, Ronald J., Thomas C. O'Guinn, and John A. McCarthy (1987). "Ethnicity, Acculturation and the Importance of Product Attributes," *Psychology & Marketing,* 4 (Summer), 121–34.

Fones, Michael (1981). "Two Worlds Together: Towns along the U.S.-Mexico Border Could Provide Marketing Edge," *Advertising Age,* 52 (15), S22.

Forehand, Mark R., and Rohit Deshpande (2001). "What We See Makes Us Who We Are: Priming Ethnic Self-awareness and Advertising Response," *Journal of Marketing Research,* 38 (August): 336–348.

Fost, Dan (1990). "California's Asian Market," *American Demographics,* 12 (10), 34.

Friend, Irvin, and Irving B. Kravis (1957). "New Light on the Consumer Market," *Harvard Business Review,* (January/February), 105.

Gibson, D. Parke (1969). *The $30 Billion Negro.* New York, NY: Macmillan Co.

Gillet, Richard A., and Peter C. Scott (1975). "Shopping Opinions of Mexican-American Consumers: A Comparative Analysis." In *AMA Educators' Conference Proceedings,* ed. Ronald C. Curhan. Chicago, IL: American Marketing Association.

Goffman, Erving (1959). *The Presentation of Self in Everyday Life.* Garden City, NY: Doubleday.

Green, Corliss (1999). "Ethnic Evaluations of Advertising: Interaction Effects of Strength of Ethnic Identification, Media Placement, and Degree of Racial Composition," *Journal of Advertising,* 28(1), 49–64.

Guernica, Antonio (1982). *Reaching the Hispanic Market Effectively.* New York, NY: McGraw-Hill.

"Hallmark Corporate Information/Hallmark Sinceramente Cards," Hallmark.com. Hallmark Corporation. http://corporate.hallmark.com/Product/Hallmark-Sinceramente. Accessed July 19, 2008.

Harrison, Faye (1995). "The Persistent Power of 'Race' in the Cultural and Political Economy of Racism," *Annual Review of Anthropology,* 24, 47–74.

Hirschman, Elizabeth C., and Morris B. Holbrook (1982). "Hedonic Consumption: Emerging Concepts, Methods, and Propositions," *Journal of Marketing,* 46 (Summer), 92–101.

Holbrook, Morris B., and Elizabeth C. Hirschmann (1982). "The Experiential Aspects of Consumption: Consumer Fantasies, Feelings and Fun," *Journal of Consumer Research,* 9 (September), 132–140.

Hoyer, Wayne D., and Rohit Deshpande (1982). "Cross-Cultural Influences on Buyer Behavior: The Impact of Hispanic Ethnicity." In *Educators' Conference Proceedings,* ed. B.J. Walker et al. Chicago, IL: American Marketing Association, 89–92.

Kang, Jikyeong, and Youn-Kyung Kim (1998). "Ethnicity and Acculturation: Influences on Asian American Consumers' Purchase Decision Making for Social Clothes," *Family and Consumer Sciences Research Journal,* 27 (1), 91–117.

Kim, Youn-Kyung, and Jikyeong Kang (1995). "The Shopping Patterns of Ethnic Consumer Groups in the United States," *Journal of Shopping Center Research,* 2 (1), 65–89.

Latham, Charles Jr. (1989) "Madam C.J. Walker and Company," *Traces,* Summer, 29–37.

Lee, Wai-Na, and Koog-Hyang Ro Um (1992). "Ethnicity and Consumer Product Evaluation: A Cross-Cultural Comparison of Korean Immigrants and Americans." In *Advances in Consumer Research* (vol. 19), ed. John F. Sherry and Brian Sternthal. Provo, UT: Association for Consumer Research, 429–436.

Levy, Sidney J. (1959). "Symbols for Sale," *Harvard Business Review,* 37 (July–August), 117–124.

Little, Elizabeth (2007) *Biting the Wax Tadpole.* New York, NY: Melville House.

Maggard, John P. (1971). "Negro Market-Fact or Fiction?" *California Management Review,* 14 (1), 71–80.

Maso-Fleishman, Roberta (1997). "The Grandmother: A Powerful Symbol for Hispanic Women," *Marketing News,* February 3, 13–14.

McCracken, Grant (1986). "Culture and Consumption: A Theoretical Account of the Structure and Movement of the Cultural Meaning of Consumer Goods," *Journal of Consumer Research,* 13 (1), 71–84.

Morgan, Nigel, Annette Pritchard, and Roger Pride (2002). "Marketing to the Welsh Diaspora: The Appeal to Hiraeth and Homecoming," *Journal of Vacation Marketing,* 9, (1), 69–80.

Mulhern, Francis J., Jerome D. Williams, and Robert P. Leone (1998). "Variability of Brand Price Elasticities Across Retail Stores: Ethnic, Income, and Brand Determinants," *Journal of Retailing,* 74 (3) 427–46.

Nancarrow, Clive, Julie Tinson, and Richard Webber (2007). "Roots of Marketing: The Marketing Research Opportunity," *International Journal of Market Research,* 49 (1), 47–69.

Oswold, Laura R. (1999). "Culture Swapping: Consumption and the Ethnogenesis of Middle-Class Haitian Immigrants," *Journal of Consumer Research,* 25 (March), 303–318.

Ownbey, Shiretta F., and Patricia E. Horridge (1997). "Acculturation Levels and Shopping Orientations of Asian-American Consumers," *Psychology & Marketing,* 14 (1), 1–18.

Penaloza, Lisa, and Mary C. Gilly (1986). "The Hispanic Family-Consumer Research Issues," *Psychology and Marketing,* 3 (Winter), 291–303.

Ratcliffe, Peter (2004). *Race, Ethnicity and Difference: Imagining the Inclusive Society.* New York, NY: Open University Press.

Reeves, Terrance and Claudette Bennett (2003). *The Asian and Pacific Islander Population in the United States: March 2002,* Current Population Reports, P20–540, U.S.Census Bureau, Washington, DC.

Rokeach, Milton (1973). *The Nature of Human Values.* New York: Free Press.

Rosenbaum, Mark S. (2005). "The Symbolic Servicescape: Your Kind Is Welcomed Here," *Journal of Consumer Behaviour,* 4 (4), 257–267

Saegert, Joel, Robert J. Hoover, and Marye T. Hilger (1985). "Characteristics of Mexican American Consumers," *Journal of Consumer Research,* 12 (June), 104–109.

Schumann, David W. (2003). "Media Factors That Contribute to a Restriction of Exposure to Diversity," In *The Psychology of Entertainment Media,* ed. L.J. Shrum. Mahwah, NJ: Lawrence Erlbaum.

Schumann, David W., Jinkook Lee, and Kittichai Watchravestingkan (2004). "The Importance of Sub-Group Differences within Asian Cultures," In *Diversity in Advertising,* ed. Jerome Williams, Wea-Na Lee, and Curt Haugtvedt. Hillsdale, NJ: Lawrence Erlbaum.

Segal, Madhav N., and Lionel Sosa (1983). "Marketing to the Hispanic Community," *California Management Review,* 26 (1), 120–34.

Smedley, Audrey, and Brian D. Smedley (2005). "Race as Biology Is Fiction, Racism as a Social Problem Is Real: Anthropological and Historical Perspectives on the Social Construction of Race," *American Psychologist,* 60 (1), 16–26.

Smikle, Ken (2000). *The Buying Power of Black America.* Chicago, IL: Target Market News.

Smitherman, Geneva (1994). *Black Talk.* New York, NY: Houghton Mifflin.

Sokol, David (2003). "The United Colors of Retailing," *Shopping Center World,* 32 (2) (February), 24–30.

Soriano, Elisa (1965). "Hispanic 'Dollar Votes' Can Impact Market Shares," *Marketing News,* September 13, 45–46.

Spickard, Paul, and G. Reginald Daniel (2004). *Racial Thinking in the United States: Uncompleted Independence.* Notre Dame, IN: Notre Dame Press, 103–123.

Steele, Edgar A. (1947). "Some Aspects of the Negro Market," *Journal of Marketing,* 11 (4), 399–401.

Steenkamp J.B.E.M., ter Hofstede, F., and Wedel, M. (1999). "A Cross-National Investigation into the Individual and National Cultural Antecedents of Consumer Innovativeness," *Journal of Marketing,* 63 (April), 55–69.

Taylor, Charles R. (2008). "Lifestyle Matters Everywhere: Marketers Need to Stop Targeting Consumers by Country and Instead Target Based on Habits, Likes, Dislikes, *Advertising Age,* May 19.

Taylor, Charles R., Ju Yung Lee, and Barbara B. Stern (1995). "Portrayals of African, Hispanic, and Asian Americans in Magazine Advertising," *American Behavioral Scientist,* 38 (4), 608–21.

Turow, James (1997). *Breaking up America: Advertisers and the New Media World.* Chicago, IL: University of Chicago Press.

Vaezi, Serge (2005). "Marketing to Mexican Consumers," *Brand Strategy* (March), 43–46.

Watts, Erick King, and Mark P. Orbe (2002). "The Spectacular Consumption of 'True' African American Culture: 'Wassup' with the Budweiser Guys?" *Critical Studies in Media Communication,* 19 (1), 1–20.

Weber, Max (1978) *Economy and Society: An Outline of Interpretive Sociology* (2 vols.), ed. Guenther Roth and Claus Wittich. Berkeley: University of California Press.

Webster, Cynthia (1994). "Effects of Hispanic Ethnic Identification on Marital Roles in the Purchase Decision Process" *Journal of Consumer Research,* 21, 319–331.

———. (1997). "Resource Theory in a Cultural Context: Linkages between Ethnic Identity, Gender Roles and Purchase Behavior," *Journal of Marketing Theory and Practice,* Winter, 1–5.

Wentz, Laurel (2007). "Home Depot Paint Line Connects with Hispanics," *Advertising Age,* 77 (27), 19.

———. (2008). "Hyundai Invites Consumers to 'Discover' the Brand," *Advertising Age,* 79 (9), 60.

White, Katherine, and Darren W. Dahl (2006). To Be or Not Be? The Influence of Dissociative Reference Groups on Consumer Preferences, *Journal of Consumer Psychology,* 16 (4), 404–416.

Whittler, Tommy E., and Joan Scattone Spira (2002). "Model's Race: A Peripheral Cue in Advertising Messages?" *Journal of Consumer Psychology,* 12 (4), 291–301.

Wilkes, Robert E., and Humberto Valencia (1989). "Hispanics and Blacks in Television Commercials," *Journal of Advertising,* 18 (March), 19–25.

Woods, Gail Baker (1995). *Advertising and Marketing to the New Majority.* Belmont, CA: Wadsworth Publishing Company.

Wyatt, Rosalind J., Betsy D. Gelb, and Stephanie Geiger-Oneto (2008). "How Social Insecurity and the Social Meaning of Advertising Reinforce Minority Consumers' Preference for National Brands," *Journal of Current Issues and Research in Advertising,* 30 (1), 61–70.

Yankelovich, Skelly, and White, Inc. (1984). *Spanish USA: A Study of the Hispanic Market.* New York, NY: Yankelovich, Skelly and White, Inc.

CHAPTER 12

CULTURAL VALUE DIMENSIONS AND BRANDS

Can a Global Brand Image Exist?

SUSAN FORQUER GUPTA, DOAN WINKEL, AND LAURA PERACCHIO

Consider the following scenario recounting Apple's branding campaign for the Mac. Apple launched advertising in the United States aimed at enticing consumers of PCs to buy a Mac. The Apple Mac brand was positioned as the underdog against all PCs and as "decidedly more fun and interesting to own" as well as more intuitive to use. Two known comedic personalities were chosen to represent a PC and a Mac in the advertising and to illustrate the differences between the two brands. "PC" was depicted as a business or work-oriented machine with connotations of efficiency and a seemingly negative quality of life. By contrast, "Mac" was portrayed as a play-oriented machine that connects to friends and family and allows for interpersonal interaction and relationship building. Numerous vignettes were designed to highlight the positive features of the Mac brand experience and the negative aspects of the PC brand experience. These Mac commercials developed a following in the United States and clearly differentiated the brand personality of the Apple as the preferred machine. The Mac was presented as the popular, cool, underdog brand versus the boring, rule-following, majority-preferred PC (Fowler, Steinberg, and Patrick 2007).

By contrast, when Apple launched much the same branding campaign for the Mac in Japan, problems arose. Although Apple had carefully selected a Japanese comedic team to portray "Mac" and "PC" and had toned down their rivalry, portraying them as a friendly duo with differing personalities, Japanese consumers reacted negatively. After viewing the ads, Japanese consumers described the Mac as sloppy and full of himself, and the PC as hardworking and adorable, hardly an interpretation that positively reinforced the Mac brand. Japanese consumers indicated that the PC's sacrifice for group conformity, work ethic, and pride in the organization were positive values, much more positive than the fun and approachable benefits offered by the Mac.

This scenario emphasizes and reinforces the importance of understanding national culture in portraying brands and developing consumers' relationships with brands. The base cultural values of the two countries, the United States and Japan, differ; therefore virtually the same ad content evokes very different responses from American and Japanese consumers. The positioning of the Mac as a better alternative to the majority-owned PC works well in American culture. Americans embrace the underdog and strive to be different. Japanese consumers embrace the majority and avoid being typed as the underdog and therefore do not desire a brand defined as such.

The objective of this chapter is to provide an understanding of the concept of national culture, as depicted in the Apple Mac scenario, and the potential role it may play in branding. National culture researchers have developed various measures of culture, including lists of values (Rokeach 1973); value hierarchies (Schwartz 1994); and value dimensions (Hofstede 1980, 2001). Much of cross-cultural marketing and management research has utilized the cultural value dimensions (CVDs) identified in the literature to explain cultural differences in behaviors, beliefs, and preferences (Hall 1976; Hofstede 1980, 1991, 2001; Schwartz 1994). We are only beginning to see national culture concepts introduced into marketing applications, including branding and consumer research. This chapter investigates the relevance and application of cultural value dimensions in understanding differences in branding and brand relationships across cultures. We present a discussion regarding how CVD theory can inform our understanding of how brand concepts are formed and how these concepts can differ across countries when the same brand communications, symbols, and references are employed.

THE NATURE OF THE CULTURE CONCEPT

Over the years, much research has focused on understanding culture, how it is acquired, how it changes, and what it impacts. Generally, it is agreed that culture is learned, shared, and used to adapt people to the natural and social environment. It is also manifested in social institutions, thought patterns or ideology, and material objects/technology (Herskovits 1947; LeVine 1982; Nanda 1987). Most researchers agree that culture is part of the environment created by humans, whether through technology or thought (Herskovits 1947; Triandis 1989, p. 122). That is, culture is nurture, not nature; it is social, not biological. Culture is created through the interaction of humans with their environment and with other humans.

Culture Is Learned

The process of learning one's culture is termed *enculturation*. Enculturation begins at birth and continues throughout our lives. Cultural learning occurs when people interact. Whether we term it behavior, ideas, or traditions, researchers seem to agree that initially parents have the highest degree of cultural transmission to their child. Culture is also transmitted to children by other individuals and sources including media, peer groups, nonparental relatives, siblings, other nonrelated individuals, and it is also transmitted from children to parents (Cavalli-Sforza et al. 1982; Boyd and Richerson 1980, 1982; Pulliam 1982; Ruyle 1973; Werren and Pulliam 1981).

Cultural learning, or transmission, is dynamic across time. We continue to build on our experiences throughout life with new experiences and interactions, adding to and supporting our previous cultural understandings or causing dissonance as disconfirming information is presented. "The difference between the nature of the enculturative experience in the early years of life and later, is that the range of conscious acceptance or rejection by an individual continuously increases as he grows older" (Herskovits 1947, p. 25). The adult only has to make *conscious* decisions of acceptance or rejection of ideas or behaviors when he or she is presented with a new situation. Therefore, it is enculturation that allows filtering of most behavior and perceptions of behavior to occur below the level of conscious thought. As a result, most individuals will implicitly evaluate the appropriateness of a particular behavior according to the connotations and meanings associated with the behavior in that context using their own cultural value system.

Culture Is an Adaptive System

As people are socialized, or enculturated, they are learning the behaviors accepted by their culture for adapting to the physical and social environment. These cultural behaviors, whether focused upon physiological needs or interpersonal interaction, are not necessarily the most efficient behavior for the task at hand. Each culturally adaptive behavior is just one of many possible solutions to the problem faced by those existing in that environment (Nanda 1987, p. 78). Individuals must learn to sort through an enormous amount of information in their environment. Adaptive behaviors and behavioral systems have developed over the centuries, allowing humans to function in their environment with a high level of effectiveness. These adaptive behaviors are passed from one person to the next as culture. What you believe, how you solve problems or make decisions, or even what you consider appropriate to consume, are shaped by your cultural value system.

Culture Varies

Within any culture, there is variation in any particular individual's behavior from accepted cultural norms. Some researchers have proposed that the variation between cultures is decreasing as intercultural communications increase. However, from a branding perspective it is important to be aware that, "World cultures as a whole are resisting homogenization, even as they eagerly embrace Western consumer goods and bureaucratic forms" (LeVine 1982, p. 80).

NATIONAL CULTURAL VALUES

One direction that culture research has taken is the identification of culture at the level of a nation in order to identify similarities and differences between national populations. Such research is particularly useful for understanding brands within and across cultures. Defining culture according to national borders is different from defining cultures ethnically or by religious or language groups (see Chapter 8 for an in-depth discussion of race and ethnicity). National culture encompasses multiple racial, ethnic, religious, economic, and political groups and subgroups. Thus, national culture embodies a variety of acceptable behaviors and beliefs. Defining culture at the level of nation captures the unique country-specific belief systems and behaviors that encompass shared history, governance, and economic systems and delineates the boundaries of expected behavior for a cultural group.

Clark (1990) provides a map for integrating national culture research into the marketing literature. He calls for the development of the national culture concept within marketing. According to Clark (1990), culture defined at the level of a nation, "can be viewed as a broader explanatory level or element in the psychological makeup of decision makers. As such, it can be expected to be related critically to all aspects of marketing decision-maker behavior, including problem identification, strategy formulation, and implementation." The important role of national culture is therefore ripe for investigation, in particular the way it informs consumer-brand relationships and brand meaning.

Measuring and Assessing National Culture

CVDs, or value orientations, are conceptualized as being universal in that they have meaning across national cultures, albeit with varying levels of salience in each. This characterization allows for the comparisons of cultures according to their relative positions on a particular value dimension. Researchers have developed various measures for assessing national culture (Hofstede 1980; Kluckhohn and Strodtbeck 1961; Rokeach 1973; Schwartz 1994; Trompenaars 1993). These measures include lists of values, value hierarchies, and value dimensions. Marketing researchers have employed CVDs to describe national cultural differences in behaviors, beliefs, and preferences

A literature review of branding and brand relationships reveals a growing interest in utilizing CVDs to inform our understanding of differing reactions to marketing and branding that have developed around the globe. The following sections discuss a selection of the studies that have found the cultural value dimensions informative in describing variations in brand constructs across national culture. Table 12.1 summarizes this literature review on branding and national culture.

CULTURAL VALUE DIMENSIONS AND BRANDING

Individualism/Collectivism and Branding

The cultural value dimension of individualism/collectivism has garnered research interest in many fields of inquiry including psychology, social psychology, anthropology, and sociology (Bochner 1994; Bochner and Hesketh 1994; Bond, Leung, and Wan 1982; Bond et al. 1982; Earley 1993; Gudykunst et al. 1992; Hofstede 1980, 1991; Hui and Triandis 1986; Hui and Villareal 1989; Schwartz 1997; Steenkamp 2001; Trompenaars 1993). According to Kagitcibaci (1987, p. 76), "Individualism and collectivism constitute probably the most important dimension(s) of cultural differences in social behavior."

Individualism/collectivism is important in understanding motivation. Individualistic cultures define the individual as an autonomous being, while collectivist cultures define the individual according to their position in a group. In national cultures with high indi-

Table 12.1

Review of Brand Literature Utilizing National Cultural Value Measures

Cultural Measures	Brand Construct	Study Outcome	Article Citation
Individualism/ Collectivism	Brand Image	The less individualistic a culture, the more amenable individuals will be to social brand image strategies	Roth, 1995
	Brand Credibility	Collectivists' value credible brands that reinforce group identity	Erdem, Swait, and Valenzuela, 2006
	Brand Loyalty	People scoring higher on individualism are more prone to brand loyalty	Lam, 2007
	Brand Name Value	Perceived brand name value is higher among individualistic cultures, which leads to higher customer loyalty	Malai and Speece, 2005
	Advertising and Brand Attitude	Individualistic societies (U.S.) are more accepting of advertisements for gambling, smoking, and drinking; American perceptions rely on informational value, Korean perceptions rely on trustworthiness and offensiveness aspects of ads and brands	An and Kim, 2007
		Hong Kong Chinese perceive less honesty and more forcefulness from a message source in an informational advertisement than do Anglo-Canadians; Individualism/collectivism cultural differences significantly impact consumers' attitude toward the brand	Toffoli and Laroche, 2002
Power Distance	Brand Image	The more power distance in a culture, the more amenable individuals will be to social brand image strategies	Roth, 1995
	Brand Loyalty	People scoring higher on power distance may be less prone to brand loyalty	Lam, 2007
Masculinity/ Femininity	Gender Roles in Advertising	In higher masculinity cultures, men are shown in more working and recreational roles, and women are shown in more decorative roles	Wiles, Wiles, and Tjernlund, 1995
	Consumer Involvement	Masculinity impacts the effect of consumer involvement on brand commitment (weaker) and brand experimentation (stronger)	Broderick, 2007
	Brand Loyalty	People scoring higher on masculinity may be more prone to brand loyalty	Lam, 2007
Uncertainty Avoidance	Brand Credibility	Higher uncertainty avoidance cultures value credible brands as they are viewed as having lower perceived risk and information costs	Erdem, Swait, and Valenzuela, 2006

	Brand Loyalty	People scoring higher on uncertainty avoidance are more prone to brand loyalty	Lam, 2007
	Consumer Involvement	Uncertainty avoidance impacts the effect of consumer involvement on brand commitment (stronger) and brand experimentation (weaker)	Broderick, 2007
Schwartz's Cultural Values	Brand Personality	Brands carry culturally common and national culture specific meaning; Japan (peacefulness) and U.S. (ruggedness) have culture-specific brand personality dimensions; Sincerity, competence, excitement, sophistication are common to both Japan and U.S.	Aaker, Benet-Martinez, and Garolera, 2001
		Brands carry culturally common and national culture-specific meaning; Japan (peacefulness) and U.S. (ruggedness) have culture-specific brand personality dimensions; Sincerity, competence, excitement, sophistication are common to both Japan and U.S.; Japan (passive likeableness and ascendancy) and U.S. (white collar and androgyny) have culture-specific brand personality dimensions; Trendiness, competence, sophistication, ruggedness, traditionalism are common to both Korea and U.S.	Sung and Tinkham, 2005
Specific vs. Diffuse	Brand Preference	Korean brands are more diffusive than U.S. brands	Jun and Lee, 2007
Analytic vs. Holistic Thinking Style	Brand Extension	Individuals with a holistic thinking style perceive higher levels of brand extension fit and evaluate brand extensions more favorably.	Monga and John, 2007, 2009
Independent vs. Interdependent Self	Brand Preference	Brand preference, as an indirect means of self-expression, is influenced by culture, because East Asian cultures see themselves as more interdependent, less independent than North American cultures	Aaker and Schmitt, 2001

vidualistic values, emphasis is placed on challenging work that allows for full use and development of individual skills, freedom to choose, and a high importance is placed on personal time. Collectivism, on the other hand, places value on identification with the group, its goals, and needs. In collectivist cultures, what is best for the group is best for the individual. High importance is placed on conformity, group processes, and relationships. A culture that supports highly individualistic values is more likely to place individuals in positions of power, set goals for individuals as opposed to groups, and view competition as a positive motivator. Cultures that support highly collectivistic values are more likely to use consensus decision making, set group goals, and view cooperation as a positive motivator.

In countries with highly individualistic cultures (e.g., European), brands that emphasize functional variety, novelty, and experiential needs are generally more effective than those that focus on social image strategies (Roth 1995). On the other hand, national cultures with low levels of individualism (e.g., Asian) are more amenable to social brand image strategies that emphasize group membership and affiliation benefits relative to sensory brand images (Roth 1995).

As an example of the importance of individualism/collectivism in branding and developing brand relationships, consider how the Philips HQ 803 razor brand was launched in Hong Kong. The Philips HQ 803 razor is a brand that taps into the strong need to fit in combined with a strong sensory appeal. The Philips brand razor was introduced in Hong Kong with a Web campaign complete with three female avatars who gave advice to young men on how to be accepted in society. The avatars were dressed in evening gowns and dispensed advice to men who wanted to make a good impression. "If you want to be a hit at that party, you can't go in with a beard. Who's going to want to talk to someone in a beard?" asks Victoria. Follow her advice, she says, and you can be "the star of the party." "Showing up for a job interview? Shave first," Jennifer says, "and you'll be far better off." Angelina writes, "Never forget that women never go for men with facial hair, so make sure you're clean-shaven before you step out the door on that first date." The advice is well aimed at a target audience of young men who are pampered by parents who often do not offer grooming advice, and as most of them do not have siblings, these young consumers have no brothers or sisters to rely upon for such advice (Cheng 2007).

Research has shown that the positive effect of brand credibility on choice is greater for consumers who rate higher on *collectivism*. Collectivists value credible brands that reinforce group identity (Erdem, Swait, and Valenzuela 2006). Consider, for example, the Nokia Communicator, a large cell phone/multimedia device with a strong brand image in Jakarta. Nicknamed "the Brick" due to its large size, it stands out as a visible status icon. It has sold well in Jakarta, including gold-plated versions, and has an official fan club with 30,000 members. It has become a popular and prestigious gift in business situations. The Nokia Communicator is the right price, enough to be considered expensive, but not so high as to be considered "wildly expensive." The size of the phone makes it obvious you own one, as it will not fit in a pocket and is usually worn in a belt harness. "Some folks carry two models—just because they can. Other politicians have two, so I have to have two," says Zulkieflimansyah, a member of parliament who alternates between his phones to answer calls and send messages (Wright 2007). Because the phone is visible, and the brand represents all the elements critical to the needs of a collectivistic society that views status symbols as an important part of defining group affiliation, the Brick is a huge success. This has not been the case in other markets where small, light phones that can be easily tucked away dominate.

Power Distance and Branding

The power distance dimension of CVD is based upon Hofstede's (1980) concept of power distance and is also similar in nature to Schwartz's egalitarianism/hierarchy dimension (1997). Hofstede (1991, p. 28) defines power distance as the extent to which the less powerful members of institutions and organizations within a country expect and accept that power is distributed unequally. Power distance encompasses more than just the power of an individual as ascribed by their status. It is broader and encompasses the equality of an individual and the degree to which the individual is defined solely by his or her position in an organization or society.

National cultures that are higher (vs. lower) in power distance attach more importance to brand names (e.g., Robinson 1996; Roth 1995). Research conducted by Lam (2007) suggests that individuals who score higher in power distance are less brand loyal and are more likely to switch brands in order to suit the whims of their power group, whereas individuals who score lower in power distance are not so influenced by high power groups and therefore purchase brands they like and develop greater brand loyalty.

Research has shown that in low power-distance cultures in which people are not focused on social roles and group affiliation (Germany, Netherlands), functional brands that de-emphasize the social, symbolic, sensory and experiential benefits of products are often preferred (Roth 1995). When the country's degree of power distance is high (China, France, Belgium), social and/or sensory needs should be emphasized, as these benefits are more effective in developing brands (Roth 1995). As an example of this concept, consider McDonald's branding campaign in China. McDonald's branding efforts have attempted to connect the Chinese belief in the strength-inducing properties of beef to its Quarter Pounder burger. Print ads show a woman's red shiny lips pursed over the picture of a Quarter Pounder. The burger chain's TV commercials are quite racy. In one spot, a man and a woman eat Quarter Pounders, and close-up shots of the woman's neck and mouth are interspersed with images of fireworks and spraying water. The actors suck their fingers. The voiceover says: "You can feel it. Thicker. You can taste it. Juicier" (Fairclough and Adamy 2006). Consistent with this high–power-distance culture, a strong combination of social and sensory needs are employed to build the brand image of McDonald's Quarter Pounder burger.

Masculinity/Femininity and Branding

The masculinity/femininity dimension (Hofstede 1980) was originally developed as a gender-based difference. However, the concept has become less gender-oriented over time and is closer in definition to the mastery/nurturance dimension (Schwartz 1994; Steenkamp 2001). National cultures that fall on the nurturance or feminine side of the continuum will value the relationship itself and consider it most important, while national cultures that fall on the mastery or masculinity side of the continuum will value the product of the relationship as it meets the goals or purpose that initiated the interaction. Translated into a business environment, national cultures that are feminine-based prefer to make decisions based on feelings and prefer social or relationship goals and rewards of appreciation. National cultures that are masculine-based prefer decision making based upon fact and prefer profit goals and monetary rewards. Therefore brands stressing positive social and relational outcomes will be preferred in feminine cultures, while masculine cultures will often prefer brand statements that purport functionality and efficiency and are supported by fact.

There is still a deep connection between gender roles and this CVD as shown in the research of Wiles, Wiles, and Tjernlund (1995). They found that the masculinity of a nation has a relationship to the roles of males and females portrayed in branding campaigns; greater role differences occur in the higher masculinity countries and lesser differences in roles occur in lower masculinity countries. Roles studied include working, family, recreational, and decorative roles. In higher masculinity societies, men are generally shown in more working and recreational roles while women are often depicted in more decorative roles.

Uncertainty Avoidance and Branding

Uncertainty avoidance addresses the comfort level of the individual or firm with ambiguous or uncertain situations. National cultures with higher uncertainty avoidance feel more threatened by uncertain or unknown situations than those cultures with lower uncertainty avoidance. These higher uncertainty-avoidance cultures shun ambiguity and, according to Hofstede (1991, 116), "People in such cultures look for a structure in their organizations, institutions, and relationships that makes events clearly interpretable and predictable." Higher uncertainty-avoidance national cultures value credible brands as they are viewed as having lower perceived risk and information costs (Erdem et al. 2006).

Power distance and uncertainty avoidance influence the focus of consumers' brand search activities, but not their tendencies to share brand-related opinions with others. The greater the uncertainty avoidance and power distance in a country, the smaller the proportion of consumers who search for brand information from impersonal and objective sources such as magazines or newspapers. Erdem and colleagues (2006) found that uncertainty avoidance reduces the effect of perceived risk and information costs on a brand's credibility and thus results in a more positive brand evaluation, positively influencing consumers' brand choice. Lam (2007) offers more confirmatory evidence that individuals scoring higher in uncertainty avoidance are more likely to exhibit stronger brand loyalty, likely because they have a lower risk-taking propensity and are therefore less willing to switch brands. Research by Broderick (2007) offers an explanation of uncertainty avoidance's impact on consumer involvement. She found that in higher uncertainty-avoidance national cultures, risk involvement results in a stronger effect on situational involvement and brand commitment, reducing the amount of brand experimentation.

Time Orientation and Branding

Time orientation is a very pervasive aspect of national culture and can affect the very fiber of a society and all of its dealings. In defining time orientation, we draw upon Hall's examination of monochratic and polychratic cultures (1976, 1987) and Hofstede and Bond's long-term time orientation (1988). Short-term–oriented cultures focus on the present and have little patience for the future. This translates into short-term goals and immediate gratification. Also, short-term–oriented cultures are usually more willing to accept change in any form as members maneuver to reach their short-term goals. For example, an individual might seek to adopt brands with strong brand identities that reflect the image they wish to project, augmenting the consumer's ability to immediately feel change has occurred. Weak or poorly defined brands would not afford the same benefit. In short-term–oriented cultures, brands promising convenience, quick results, and time saving are often preferred.

By contrast, long-term–oriented cultures look to the future and depend on the past. Long-term–oriented cultures connect past, present, and future into a continuous chain of events. As a result, respect of tradition is evident. Change is greeted in the context of the continuous flow of events from the past to the future and is either accepted or rejected based upon how critical it is to reach long-term goals. Long-term goals have priority, and rewards such as profit or praise can wait. Brands with image of tradition, taking time to produce the quality desired, and a focus on the process more than the result are preferred. Thus, time orientation has important implications for branding and developing brand relationships.

DIRECTIONS FOR FUTURE RESEARCH ON NATIONAL CULTURE AND BRANDING

Organizations entering foreign markets face a number of branding and marketing strategy decisions. A cross-cultural approach to branding should analyze cultural differences and similarities between the organization's home country culture and the host country culture and apply this information to managing the brand (Hsieh 2002). Consumers from different national cultures will likely evaluate brands differently based on cultural differences (Monga and John 2007). These differences are a critical obstacle that marketers must overcome in their attempts to communicate with global consumers to develop internationally accepted brands (Jun and Lee 2007) as culture strongly influences consumers' values, perceptions, and actions (e.g., Trompenaars 1994). There is a burgeoning literature investigating cultural dimensions in branding research, but it is in its infancy. There are several areas of research in branding that reflect focused and systematic investigation using measures of national culture to better understand the way culture informs consumers' understanding of brands.

BRAND PERSONALITY AND NATIONAL CULTURE

Brand personality is developed through consumers' direct and indirect contact with both product-related factors (e.g., packaging and other physical attributes) and non–product-related factors (e.g., celebrity endorsers, consumer's past experience, symbols) of the brand (D. Aaker 1996; J. Aaker 1997; Plummer 1985; Shank and Langmeyer 1994). A brand can hold a symbolic function for consumers, or it can play a self-expressive role (Keller 1993). Scholars have suggested that brand personality can develop emotional benefits (Ogilvy 1983), can increase consumer preference for and usage of a brand (Sirgy 1982), can differentiate brands (Plummer 1985; Biel 1992), and can be a foundation for building brand relationships (Fournier 1998; Sweeney and Brandon 2006). It has also been argued that brand personality can represent the beliefs and values of a specific culture (Aaker, Benet-Martinez, and Garolera 2001). Therefore, we suggest that there is a need for additional research that combines CVDs and brand personality and investigates the interaction of these factors.

Aaker (1997, p. 347) defined brand personality as "the set of human characteristics associated with a brand." Aaker investigated brand personality dimensions underlying 114 human personality traits used to describe 37 different brands. Using a factor analytical approachs, she identified 42 traits, 15 facets, and the following five core dimensions of brand personality: excitement (e.g., daring, spirited, imaginative, up-to-date), competence (e.g., reliable, intelligent, successful), ruggedness (e.g., outdoorsy, tough), sophistication (e.g., upper class, charming) and sincerity (e.g., down-to-earth, honest, wholesome, cheerful). This research revealed that these dimensions provided a comprehensive explanation of how American consumers perceive commercial brands across symbolic and utilitarian product and service categories, and thus brand personality has become a critical element of brand image and brand equity (Keller 1993). One drawback to Aaker's concept, however, is the focus on the positive brand attributes held by consumers without considering their negative brand-related associations (Bosnjak, Bochmann, and Hufschmidt 2007).

This foundational research provides a promising beginning, as cross-cultural researchers employing Aaker's (1997) approach found differences between national cultures in terms of the number of brand personality dimensions and their meaning (e.g., Aaker et al. 2001; Sung and Tinkham 2005). Aaker, Benet-Martinez, and Garolera (2001) examined the structure of symbolic and expressive attributes associated with commercial brands across several cultures including Japan and the United States. In comparing Japan and the United States, they found that both Japan (peacefulness) and the United States (ruggedness) had culture-specific dimensions, while sincerity, competence, excitement, and sophistication were common to both cultures. Sung and Tinkham (2005) examined the symbolic meaning of commercial brands across two cultures, Korea and the United States. They found that both Korea (passive likeableness and ascendancy) and the United States (white collar and androgyny) had culture-specific dimensions, while trendiness, competence, sophistication, ruggedness, and traditionalism were common to both national cultures.

Aaker, Benet-Martinez, and Garolera (2001) also investigated how brands represent cultural meaning, and using brand personality attributes found that brands do indeed carry culturally common and national culture–specific meaning. They found that embracing harmony-oriented value types is indicative of Japanese and Spanish national cultures more so than American culture. They suggested that various brand personality attributes, such as sincerity, excitement, and competence, matched with various national cultural values defined by Schwartz, such as conservatism, affective autonomy, and mastery needs, respectively.

Brand Preference and National Culture

Scholars researching branding and brand relationships have alluded to national culture's influence on brand preference. Aaker and Schmitt (2001) examined whether there is a national culture difference in self-expressive processes as reflected in brand preference. They suggest that since East Asian cultures see themselves as more interdependent and less independent than North American cultures, national culture has a significant impact on their findings indicating that brand preference is an indirect means of self-expression. Others have argued that national culture has a similar influence on brand communications. Applying Trompenaars and Hampden-Turner's (1998) specific versus diffuse cultural dimensions, Jun and Lee (2007) asserted that Korean brands are more diffusive, consisting of a less defined meaning than American brands. They found that logos used in Korea are more symbolic and abstract, which they argue is in line with a diffusive culture, where according to Trompenaars and Hampden-Turner, individuals generally dislike direct expression. Similar findings have emerged from research that investigates how national culture influences marketing communications, and therefore brands.

Brand Meaning and National Culture

Brand meaning is a broad construct that includes the physical attributes, functional characteristics, and personality of a brand (Plummer 1985), and "develops from the interchange among three environments: the marketing, individual, and social, as each environment contributes to a uniform way for consumers to identify and interact with a branded product" (Ligas and Cotte 1999, p. 610). Keller (2003) argues that companies should create brand meaning for their products by building a brand image that is strong, favorable, and unique and by identifying the salient characteristics of the brand and what the brand should stand for. Such development of brand meaning is often specific to a particular national culture.

Ligas and Cotte (1999) developed a framework for brand meaning creation, illustrating the relationships between the marketing, social, and individual environments and brand meaning. They argue that the meaning development process within each environment or national culture and the interactions of meaning between environments (or national cultures) depends on the individuals within each environment. Their basic premise is that in order to create brand meaning, meaning must be agreed upon between individuals within a particular environment in terms of the brand's physical attributes, its functional characteristics, and its personality. Research has shown that brands hold meaning for individuals as young as three or four years of age (Derscheid, Kwon, and Fang 1996; Haynes et al. 1993) and that incorporating these meanings into judgments could occur as early as late childhood, approximately ten to twelve years of age (Achenreiner and John 2003).

Brand meanings reflect the national culture environment in which they are embedded (Levy 1959) as they originate in a culturally constituted world (McCracken 1988). Therefore, the ability to transfer a brand and its meaning from one national culture to another is dependent upon the overlap of cultural symbols, contexts, and positions on the cultural value dimensions.

Brand Extensions and National Culture

Brand extensions have become a major focus of branding strategies aimed at fueling growth, improving competitive position, and increasing profits (Keller 1998). Brand extensions involve leveraging a well-known brand name in one category to launch a new product in a different category. For example, Arm & Hammer successfully leveraged its baking soda brand to launch new products in a variety of categories including oral care and laundry care. The goal of brand extension is to "capitalize on the brand image for the core product or service to efficiently inform consumers and retailers about the new product or service" (Keller 1993, p. 15). National culture influences consumer response to brand extensions. Monga and John (2007; also see Chapter 13 of this volume) found that East Asian consumers, who exhibit a more holistic style of thinking, perceive higher levels of brand extension fit and evaluate brand extensions more favorably than do Western consumers, who exhibit a more analytic style of thinking. For example, in India, Coca-Cola was able to extend their brand to popcorn as the Coca-Cola brand meaning was broad enough to include not only beverages but all items relating to movie entertainment. This same brand extension was not found to be viable among Western consumers who viewed the Coca-Cola brand more narrowly, negating the extension into the popcorn category.

Implications

The brand constructs reviewed here are those that have been studied in conjunction with cultural value dimensions. These studies begin to tap into the explanatory power of the CVDs but as a whole are unconnected and few in number. Additional studies investigating brand issues utilizing measures of national culture are needed. For example, in Chapter 6, Escalas and Bettman discuss reference group and celebrity endorsers and the role they play in establishing self-brand connections. Their work highlights the role of culture in defining reference groups and celebrity for a particular group. They found that brand images consistent with the images of an ingroup result in greater self-brand connections. If their work can be extended to imagery consistent with a national culture, researchers could explore the nature of brand connections within national culture. This and other research investigating branding and national culture should be pursued in the future.

CONCLUSION

The research discussed in this chapter provides evidence that consumers comprehend brands in the context of national culture and measures of national culture are useful in understanding branding. This suggests that it may not be possible to create a global brand image that resonates across all cultures with the same meaning because national cultural context varies. The research also provides evidence that there is a complex relationship between brands and culture. Meaning can be woven into a culture or built from existing image and belief systems within a culture. Understanding the ways in which national culture differences impact brand decisions and brand value increases a firm's ability to navigate the similarities and differences between markets.

It is important to recognize that research investigating the effect of national culture and cultural value dimensions on branding is in its infancy. There is a dearth of empirical research examining national culture and the cultural value dimensions. Much more research examining these concepts and their impact on branding is needed. While it is easy to see the need for expanding brand research to include the influence of national culture and CVDs, we caution that investigating these concepts is a difficult task. As Hans Magnus Enzensberger suggests, investigating "(national) culture is a little like dropping an Alka-Seltzer into a glass—you don't see it, but somehow it does something" (Glueck 1987). Our task as researchers is to build a conceptual understanding of national culture and its influence on brands by developing a lens through which we can view and appreciate the effect of national culture on brands.

REFERENCES

Aaker, David. A. (1996). *Building Strong Brands.* New York, NY: The Free Press.

Aaker, Jennifer L. (1997). "Dimensions of Brand Personality," *Journal of Marketing Research,* 34 (August), 347–356.

Aaker, Jennifer L., Veronica Benet-Martinez, and Jordi Garolera (2001). "Consumption Symbols as Carriers of Culture: A Study of Japanese and Spanish Brand Personality Constructs," *Journal of Personality and Social Psychology,* 81 (3), 492–508.

Aaker, Jennifer, and Bernd Schmitt (2001). "Culture-Dependent Assimilation and Differentiation of the Self," *Journal of Cross-Cultural Psychology,* 32 (September), 561–576.

Achenreiner, Gwen B., and Deborah R. John (2003). "The Meaning of Brand Names to Children: A Developmental Investigation," *Journal of Consumer Psychology,* 13 (3), 205–219.

An, Dauchun, and Sang H. Kim (2007). "A First Investigation into the Cross-Cultural Perceptions of Internet Advertising: A Comparison of Korean and American Attitudes," *Journal of International Consumer Marketing,* 20 (2), 49–65.

Biel, Alexander L. (1992). "Converting Brand Image into Equity." In *Brand Equity and Advertising: Advertising's Role in Building Strong Brands,* ed. David A. Aaker and Alexander L. Biel. Hillsdale, NJ: Lawrence Erlbaum, 67–81.

Bochner, Stephen (1994). "Cross-Cultural Differences in the Self-Concept: A Test of Hofstede's Individualism/Collectivism Distinction," *Journal of Cross-Cultural Psychology,* 25 (2), 273–283.

Bochner, Stephen, and Beryl Hesketh (1994). "Power Distance, Individualism/Collectivism, and Job Related Attitudes in a Culturally Diverse Work Group," *Journal of Cross-Cultural Psychology,* 25, 233–257.

Bond, Michael H., Kwok Leung, and K.C. Wan (1982). "How Does Cultural Collectivism Operate? The Impact of Task and Maintenance Contributions on Reward Allocation," *Journal of Cross-Cultural Psychology,* 13, 186–200.

Bosnjak, Michael, Valerie Bochmann, and Tanja Hufschmidt (2007). "Dimensions of Brand Personality Attributions: A Person-Centric Approach in the German Cultural Context," *Social Behavior and Personality,* 35 (3), 303–316.

Boyd, Robert, and Peter J. Richerson (1980). "Sociobiology, Culture, and Economic Theory," *Journal of Economic Behavior and Organization,* 1, 97–121.

Broderick, Amanda J. (2007), "A Cross-National Study of Individual-Cultural Nomological Network of Consumer Involvement," *Psychology and Marketing,* 24 (4), 343–374.

Cavalli-Sforza, L.L., Marcus W. Feldman, Kuang-ho Chen, and Sanford M. Dornbusch (1982). "Theory and Observation in Cultural Transmission," *Science* 218 (October), 19–27.

Cheng, Jonathan (2007). "Shaver's Cutting-Edge China Campaign Trio of Women Dispense Grooming Tips for Guys in Philips Web Effort," *Wall Street Journal,* May 4, B3.

Clark, Terry (1990). "International Marketing and National Character: A Review and Proposal for an Integrative Theory," *Journal of Marketing,* 54 (October), 66–79.

Derscheid, Linda E., Yoon-Hee Kwon, and Shi-Ruei Fang (1996). "Preschoolers Socialization as Consumers of Clothing and Recognition of Symbolism," *Perceptual and Motor Skills,* 82, 1171–1181.

Earley, P. Christopher (1993). "East Meets West Meets Mid-East: Further Explorations in Collectivistic versus Individualistic Work Groups," *Academy of Management Journal,* 36, 319–348.

Erdem, Tulin, Joffre Swait, and Ana Valenzuela (2006). "Brands as Signals: A Cross-Country Validation Study," *Journal of Marketing,* 70 (January), 34–49.

Fairclough, Gordon, and Janet Adamy (2006). "Sex, Skin, Fireworks, Licked Fingers—It's a Quarter Pounder Ad in China," *Wall Street Journal,* September 21, B1.

Fournier, Susan (1998). "Consumers and Their Brands: Developing Relationship Theory in Consumer Research," *Journal of Consumer Research,* 28, 343–416.

Fowler, Geoffrey A., Brian Steinberg, and Aaron O. Patrick (2007). "Mac and PC's Overseas Adventures: Globalizing Apple's Ads Meant Tweaking Characters, Clothing and Body Language" *Wall Street Journal,* March 1, B1.

Glueck, Grace. (1987, January 25). A Polemicist Who Aims At Political And Corporate Targets: [Review]. Review of Art, Hans Haacke. *New York Times* [Late Edition (east Coast)], p. A. 27. Retrieved February 17, 2009, from National Newspaper Abstracts (3) database. (Document ID: 956256241).

Gudykunst, William B., Ge Gao, Karen L. Schmidt, Tsukasa Nishida, Michael H. Bond, Kwok Leung, Georgette Wang, and Robert A. Barraclough. (1992). "The Influence of Individualism Collectivism, Self-Monitoring, and Predicted-Outcome Value on Communication in Ingroup and Outgroup Relationships," *Journal of Cross-Cultural Psychology,* 23 (2), 196–213.

Hall, Edward T. (1976). *Beyond Culture.* Garden City, NY: Doubleday.

Hall, Edward T., and Mildred R. Hall (1987). *Hidden Differences: Doing Business with the Japanese.* New York, NY: Doubleday.

Haynes, Janice, Diane C. Burts, Alice Dukes, and Rinn Cloud (1993). "Consumer Socialization of Preschoolers and Kindergartners as Related to Clothing Consumption," *Psychology and Marketing,* 10, 151–166.

Herskovits, Melville J. (1947). *Trinidad Village.* New York, NY: Knopf.

Hofstede, Geert (1980). *International Differences in Work-related Values.* Beverly Hills, CA: Sage.

——— (1991). *Culture and Organizations: Software of the Mind.* Beverly Hills, CA: Sage.

——— (2001). *Comparing Values, Behaviors, Institutions and Organizations Across Nations.* Beverly Hills, CA: Sage.

Hofstede, Geert, and Michael Harris Bond (1988). "The Confucius Connection: From Cultural Roots to Economic Growth," *Organizational Dynamics,* 16 (4), 4–21.

Hsieh, Ming. H. (2002). "Identifying Brand Image Dimensionality and Measuring the Degree of Brand Globalization: A Cross-National Study," *Journal of International Marketing,* 10, 46–67.

Hui, C.H., and Harry C. Triandis (1986). "Individualism-Collectivism: A Study of Cross-Cultural Researchers," *Journal of Cross-Cultural Psychology,* 17, 225–248.

Hui, C.H., and Marcelo J. Villareal (1989). "Individualism-Collectivism and Psychological Needs: Their Relationships in Two Cultures," *Journal of Cross-Cultural Psychology,* 20 (3), 310–323.

Jun, Jung W., and Hyung-Seok Lee (2007). "Cultural Differences in Brand Designs and Tagline Appeals," *International Marketing Review,* 24 (4), 474–491.

Kagitcibaci, Cigdem (Ed.) (1987). *Growth and Progress in Cross-Cultural Psychology.* Lisse, The Netherlands: Swets North America.

Keller, Kevin. L. (1993). "Conceptualizing, Measuring, and Managing Customer-Based Brand Equity," *Journal of Marketing,* 57, 1–22.

——— (1998). *Strategic Brand Management: Building, Measuring and Managing Brand Equity.* New York, NY: Prentice Hall.

——— (2003). "Brand Synthesis: The Multi-Dimensionality of Brand Knowledge," *Journal of Consumer Research,* 29 (4), 595–600.

Kluckhohn, Florence R., and Fred L. Strodtbeck (1961). *Variations in Value Orientations.* Evanston, IL: Row, Peterson.

Lam, Desmond (2007). "Cultural Influence on Proneness to Brand Loyalty," *Journal of International Consumer Marketing,* 19 (3), 7–21.

LeVine, Robert A. (1982). *Personality and Culture.* New York, NY: Aldine Publishing Company.

Levy, Sidney J. (1959). "Symbols for Sale," *Harvard Business Review,* 37 (4), 117–124.

Ligas, Mark, and June Cotte (1999). "The Process of Negotiating Brand Meaning: A Symbolic Interactionist Perspective," *Advances in Consumer Research,* 26, 609–614.

Malai, Veerapong, and Mark Speece (2005). "Cultural Impact on the Relationship Among Perceived Service Quality, Brand Name Value, and Customer Loyalty." *Journal of International Consumer Marketing* 17.4: 7–39.

McCracken, Grant (1988). *Culture and Consumption: New Approaches to the Symbolic Character of Consumer Goods and Activities.* Bloomington, IN: Indiana University Press.

Monga, Alokparna B., and Deborah R. John (2007). "Cultural Differences in Brand Extension Evaluation: The Influence of Analytic versus Holistic Thinking," *Journal of Consumer Research,* 33 (March), 529–536.

Monga, Alokparna B., and Deborah R. John (2009). "Understanding Cultural Differences in Brand Extension Evaluation: The Influence of Analytic Versus Holistic Thinking." In *Handbook of Brand Relationships,* ed. D. MacInnis, C.W. Park, and J Priester, Armonk, NY: M.E. Sharpe.

Nanda, Serena (1987) *Cultural Anthropology.* Belmont, CA: Wadsworth Publishing.

Ogilvy, David (1983). *Ogilvy on Advertising.* New York, NY: Random House.

Plummer, Joseph T. (1985). "How Personality Makes a Difference," *Journal of Advertising Research,* 24 (December-January), 27–31.

Pulliam, H.R. (1982). "A Social Learning Model of Conflict and Cooperation in Human Societies," *Human Ecology,* 10, 353–363.

Robinson, Chris (1996). "Asian Culture: The Marketing Consequences," *Journal of the Market Research Society,* 38 (1), 55–63.

Rokeach, Milton (1973). *The Nature of Human Values.* New York, NY: Free Press.

Roth, Martin S. (1995). "The Effects of Culture and Socioeconomics on the Performance of Global Image Strategies," *Journal of Marketing Research,* 32, 163–175.

Ruyle, Eugene E. (1973). "Genetic and Cultural Pools: Some Suggestions for a Unified Theory of Biocultural Evolution," *Human Ecology,* 1 (3), 201–215.

Schwartz, Shalom H. (1994). "Beyond Individualism/collectivism—New Cultural Dimensions of Values." In *Individualism and Collectivism: Theory, Method, and Applications* (vol. 18), ed. Uichol Kim et al. Thousand Oaks, CA: Sage.

——— (1997). "Values and Culture." In *Motivation and Culture,* ed. Donald Munro, John F. Schumaker, and Stuart C. Carr. New York, NY: Routledge.

Shank, Matthew D., and Lynn Langmeyer (1994). "Does Personality Influence Brand Image?" *Journal of Psychology,* 128 (2), 157–164.

Sirgy, M.J. (1982). "Self-Concept in Consumer Behavior: A Critical Review," *Journal of Consumer Research,* 9, 287–301.

Steenkamp, Jan-Benedict E.M. (2001). "The Role of National Culture in International Marketing Research," *International Marketing Review,* 18, 30–44.

Sung, Yongjun, and Spencer F. Tinkham (2005). "Brand Personality Structures in the United States and Korea: Common and Culture-Specific Factors," *Journal of Consumer Psychology,* 15 (4), 334–350.

Sweeney, Jillian C., and Carol Brandon (2006). "Brand Personality: Exploring the Potential to Move From Factor Analytical to Circumplex Models," *Psychology and Marketing,* 23 (August), 639–663.

Triandis, Harry C. (1989). "The Self and Social Behavior in Differing Cultural Contexts," *Psychology Review,* 96, 506–520.

Trompenaars, Fons (1993). *Riding the Waves of Culture.* London: Nicholas Brealy.

——— (1994). *Riding the Waves of Culture: Understanding Cultural Diversity in Business.* Chicago, IL: Irwin Professional Publishing.

Trompenaars, Fons, and Charles Hampden-Turner (1998). *Riding the Waves of Culture: Understanding Diversity in Global Business.* New York, NY: McGraw-Hill.

Werren, John H., and H. Ronald Pulliam (1981). "An Intergenerational Transmission Model for the Cultural Evolution of Helping Behavior," *Human Ecology,* 9 (4), 465–483.

Wiles, Judith A., Charles R. Wiles, and Anders Tjernlund (1995). "A Comparison of Gender Role Portrayals in Magazine Advertising: The Netherlands, Sweden and the USA," *European Journal of Marketing,* 29 (11), 35–49.

Wright, Tom (2007). "Ringing Up Sales in Indonesia Nokia's Bulky Smart Phones Find Niche Following There As Business Status Symbol," *Wall Street Journal,* May 22, B1.

CHAPTER 13

UNDERSTANDING CULTURAL DIFFERENCES IN BRAND EXTENSION EVALUATION

The Influence of Analytic versus Holistic Thinking

ALOKPARNA BASU MONGA AND DEBORAH ROEDDER JOHN

The increasing popularity of brand extensions over the last decade has ignited interest in understanding how consumers evaluate brand extensions. A number of factors have been identified that influence whether consumers will evaluate brand extensions in a favorable manner. Key among them is the degree to which a brand extension "fits" with the parent brand, which consumers judge in a variety of ways, including whether the extension is in a product category similar to other products produced by the parent brand, whether an attribute associated with the parent brand could be beneficial in the extension product category, whether prestige associated with the parent brand could transfer to the extension product category, and whether the parent brand has the requisite expertise to produce a product in the extension category (see Keller 2002). Brand extensions that are higher in perceived fit are typically evaluated more favorably than are those that are viewed as poor fits.

However, the vast majority of research has been conducted with American consumers, with little attention given to whether these findings apply to consumers around the world. To date, less than a handful of studies shed light on this issue, but they provide important insights into the way cross-cultural differences might emerge. One possibility is that brand extension response is driven by factors other than extension fit in other cultures, as suggested by a recent secondary analysis of eight brand extension studies conducted in the United States and abroad (Bottomley and Holden 2001). Han and Schmitt (1997) suggest a similar scenario, finding that U.S. consumers place more emphasis on brand extension fit than do consumers from Hong Kong, who rely on corporate reputation. A second possibility is that brand extension fit may be just as important in determining brand extension response in other cultures, but there may be differences in the way brand extension fit is assessed. This explanation is consistent with Monga and John (2007), who find that consumers from Eastern cultures take a more holistic view of brand extension fit, which allows them to see relationships between a brand extension and parent brand that does not occur to consumers from Western cultures. In the case of brand extensions that are distant from the parent brand, Easterners perceive a higher degree of brand extension fit and evaluate brand extensions more highly than Westerners do.

In this chapter, we explore cross-cultural differences in brand extension response in more detail. Specifically, we further examine the idea that brand extension response differs between cultures due to differences in the way that brand extension fit is judged. We base our research on cross-cultural psychology describing cultural differences in styles of thinking, with East Asian societies characterized by *holistic thinking* and Western societies characterized by *analytic thinking* (Nisbett et al. 2001). Holistic thinking involves an orientation to the context or field as a whole, whereas analytic thinking involves a detachment of the object from its context and a focus on attributes of the object. Our general prediction, in line with Monga and John (2007), is that styles of thinking influence the way in which consumers from Eastern versus Western cultures judge brand extension fit and arrive at brand extension evaluations.

We provide further support for styles of thinking as a major contributor to cultural differences in brand extension response in three studies. In study 1, we replicate Monga and John (2007), finding that Eastern consumers are more positive in their judgments of brand extension fit and evaluation than are Westerners. We find this pattern across multiple brand extensions that are very distant to moderately distant from their parent brands (Coke and Kodak). In addition, we provide evidence for styles of thinking as the mechanism for these differences, finding that the types of extension thoughts generated by Easterners (holistic) and Westerners (analytic) mediate the influence of culture on brand extension response. In the next two studies, we adopt novel approaches for examining brand extension evaluations across cultures. In study 2, we provide new evidence using a hypothetical parent brand (Excera), finding that Easterners (Westerners) provide more (less) positive evaluations of brand extensions distant from the parent brand. By using a hypothetical parent brand, we rule out alternative explanations for study 1 findings based on possible cross-cultural differences in parent brand knowledge/beliefs. In study 3, we take a different approach to studying the role of analytic and holistic thinking in cultural differences by comparing brand extension responses for Easterners, Westerners, and bicultural consumers. We find, as expected, that bicultural consumers fall midway between the two extremes, with brand extension responses that are more positive than those of Westerners but less positive than those of Easterners.

CONCEPTUAL BACKGROUND

Analytic and Holistic Processing

Nisbett and colleagues (2001) argued that there are cross-cultural differences in styles of thinking. Social differences between cultures are viewed as promoting certain cognitive processes more than others. Individuals in East Asian societies, embedded in many social relations, will have beliefs about focusing on the field and paying attention to relationships between objects. In contrast, individuals in Western societies, who have fewer social relations, will have beliefs that the world is discrete and discontinuous and that an object's behavior can be predicted using rules and properties. In this way, Eastern cultures promote holistic thinking, whereas Western societies promote analytic thinking. *Holistic thinking* is defined as "involving an orientation to the context or field as a whole, including attention to relationships between a focal object and the field, and a preference for explaining and predicting events on the basis of such relationships" (Nisbett et al. 2001, p. 293). *Analytic thought* "involves a detachment of the object from its context, a tendency to focus on attributes of the object to assign it to categories, and a preference for using rules about the categories to explain and predict the objects behavior" (Nisbett et al. 2001, p. 293). In our research, we focus on the greater ability of holistic thinkers (compared to analytic thinkers) to draw relationships between objects.

A considerable body of research supports this view. Since East Asians focus on relationships between an object and its environment, they have been shown to be more field dependent than Westerners (Ji, Peng, and Nisbett 2000). Masuda and Nisbett (2001) found that when exposed to scenes of fish and other animated objects, Japanese participants, compared to Americans, made more statements about background environment and relations between the fish and the environment. In another study, Chiu (1972) asked American and Chinese children to pick two objects that were most similar from a set of three objects and indicate why they went together. Americans adopted a style of thinking where objects were grouped based on category membership or attributes (e.g., a jeep and boat grouped together because both have motors). However, Chinese adopted a relational-contextual style of thinking, in which similarities were based on functional or thematic interdependence between objects (e.g., table and chair grouped together because you sit on the chair to eat at a table). As a result, Easterners often perceive stronger relationships between objects than Westerners, as illustrated in a study by Ji and colleagues (2000). When asked to judge the degree of association between pairs of arbitrary objects, Chinese students reported a higher degree of covariation than did Americans.

Cultural Differences in Brand Extension Evaluation

We propose that cultural differences in styles of thinking influence the way brand extensions are interpreted across cultures. Consider first the analytic style of thinking characteristic of Western societies. Analytic thinkers focus on an object's attributes and an object's category membership to draw inferences and make judgments. This style of thinking is consistent with research findings that (American) consumers often judge brand extension fit on the basis of product category similarity (e.g., is the extension in a product category similar to product categories associated with the parent brand?) and attribute transference across product categories (e.g., does the parent brand have an attribute that would be beneficial in the extension category?). Brand extensions that fail these tests, such as those in product categories too far away from those associated with the parent brand, are typically deemed to be a poor fit.

Now consider the holistic style of thinking that is characteristic of Eastern societies. Holistic thinkers possess an orientation to the context or field as a whole, and consider objects in terms of their relationship to the context and to other objects (Masuda and

Nisbett 2001). Because Easterners pay attention to context, they should be able to find relationships between brand extensions and parent brands that go beyond product category similarity and attribute transference across product categories. Given their focus on context, Easterners should more easily see relationships between a brand extension and parent brand based on usage context, such as complementarity of use. In addition, Easterners should be more likely to evaluate brand extensions in the context of the brand's overall reputation as well as their own feelings for the brand in general. This style of thinking is consistent with prior research showing that corporate brand reputation is more important in evaluating brand extensions for Eastern (Hong Kong) versus Western (U.S.) consumers (Han and Schmitt 1997). Although Western consumers use brand reputation and brand affect in evaluating extensions, these factors usually enter into the evaluation process only when the brand extension has passed the perceived fit test using other criteria, such as product category similarity. In sum, attention to context provides a basis for finding more connections between brand extensions and parent brands, which results in perceptions of better brand extension fit for consumers from Eastern cultures.

Thus, we propose that consumers from Eastern cultures will perceive a higher degree of brand extension fit than those from Western cultures, especially for extensions in product categories far from those associated with the parent brand. Brand extensions viewed as being far away from the domain of the parent brand could be viewed as a better fit if consumers were able to link them on a more holistic basis, which is a way of thinking that is more characteristic of Eastern consumers. As a consequence of cultural differences in perceptions of brand extension fit, we would expect to see concomitant differences in brand extension evaluations. We predict:

H_1: Consumers from Eastern cultures respond to brand extensions more favorably than consumers from Western cultures. Specifically,
   a. Easterners perceive a higher degree of brand extension fit
   b. Easterners evaluate brand extensions more favorably
H_2: Cultural differences in brand extension evaluation are mediated by styles of thinking. Specifically, brand extension thoughts (analytic vs. holistic) mediate the influence of culture on brand extension response.

STUDY 1

Overview

Hypotheses regarding cultural differences in brand extension fit and evaluations were tested by comparing a sample of consumers from the United States (Western culture) with one from India (Eastern culture) in a 2 (culture: Eastern, Western) × 3 (brand extension fit: very low fit, low fit, moderate fit) × 2 (brand replicates: Coke, Kodak) design. Experimental stimuli consisted of six brand extensions, with a Coke brand extension for each fit level and a Kodak brand extension for each fit level. Participants saw two of these extensions and were asked for their overall evaluation of the extension, thoughts about the extension, and perceptions of how the extension fit with the parent brand.

Sample

Fifty-seven participants were recruited for the U.S. sample (100 percent white American) from students enrolled in an Introductory Marketing class, who received course credit for their participation. Sixty-two participants were recruited for the Indian sample from the same university community using ads placed on Indian student organization Web sites and general notice boards in the university. Participants were required to be in the United States for less than three years to ensure that acculturation had not occurred to a marked degree.

Indian students residing in the United States were selected to minimize extraneous cultural differences between the Indian and U.S. subjects, such as differences in brand familiarity, brand advertising exposure, and brand breadth. Comparisons of Indian students in the United States to those residing in India have indicated similar responses to brand extensions (Monga and John 2004). Further, Indian populations have been found in prior research to have a holistic style of thinking consistent with the type of sample needed to test our hypotheses (Miller 1984; Shweder 1991).

Stimuli

Parent brands needed to be familiar and well liked among participants from both countries. We examined reports of the top brands in each country, explored Web sites for brands on both lists, and assessed brand familiarity, attitude, and brand associations in a pretest with Americans ($n = 29$) and Indians ($n = 35$) recruited from the same university population used in the main study. Based on this research, Coke and Kodak were selected as brands that were familiar and well-liked among American and Indian samples. We also examined whether different parent brand associations might be salient for the U.S. and Indian samples by coding the thoughts listed about each brand. Perceptions of Coke and Kodak were similar across cultures. For Kodak, the top two brand associations in both cultures were "films" and "positive affect/quality/excellence." For Coke, the most frequent mention for both cultures was "positive affect/liking/good taste."

Next, brand extensions for Coke and Kodak were selected. Hypothetical extensions were tested with a sample of U.S. students to identify extensions that would be considered a very low fit, low fit, and moderate fit to the parent brands from a Western perspective. Participants were asked to judge the perceived fit of several potential brand extensions on a 1 (inconsistent with brand) to 7 (consistent with brand) scale. Based on these ratings, each brand extension was categorized into one of three levels of fit: very low fit (fit ratings < 2), low fit (fit ratings between 2 and 4), and moderate fit (fit ratings between 4 and 6). Coke shampoo and Kodak shoes were chosen as very low fit extensions, Coke popcorn and Kodak filing cabinet were selected as low fit extensions, and Coke energy drink and Kodak greeting cards were chosen as moderate fit extensions.

Three sets of stimuli were developed using these brand extensions. Each set contained a brand extension for Coke and one for Kodak, each at a different fit level. Participants saw one of the following sets: (1) Coke shampoo and Kodak filing cabinet; (2) Coke popcorn and Kodak greeting cards, and (3) Coke energy drink and Kodak shoes. For each set, the order of presentation of brand extensions was counterbalanced.

Procedure and Measures

Participants were first asked to indicate their opinions of the focal parent brands on a seven-point scale (1 = poor and 7 = excellent). Then, participants were shown the name of the first brand extension and asked to give their evaluation of it on a seven-point scale (1 = poor and 7 = excellent). This was followed by an open-ended question about why they rated the brand extension in this manner: "Even though you have never tried this product, what went through your mind when you were deciding if it would be a good product or a bad product?" After evaluating the second brand extension in the same manner, participants evaluated the fit for both extensions on a scale ranging from 1 ("inconsistent with brand X") to 7 ("consistent with brand X"), similar to scales used in prior brand extension research (e.g., Loken and John 1993).

Next, participants completed two tests of analytic and holistic thinking, which served as manipulation checks to confirm different styles of thinking for our U.S. and Indian samples. Both measures were similar to the Embedded Figures Test (EFT; Witkin et al. 1971) that measures field dependence, which is one of the key indicators of holistic versus analytic thinking. In one test, participants were shown a black-and-white line drawing of a scene, which had line drawings of fourteen smaller objects (fish, needle) embedded in the scene. They were shown pictures of these fourteen objects and given five minutes to find as many objects as possible. For the second test of analytic-holistic thinking, we used a standard EFT measure (Horn 1962) that has been used in cross-cultural comparisons of cognitive style (Kühnen et al. 2001). The stimuli consisted of two columns containing forty geometrical patterns. The participant's task was to identify which one among a set of five simple figures was embedded within each geometrical pattern within a two-minute time limit. For both tests, we anticipated that the U.S. sample would find more objects because analytic processing is characterized by field independence, which makes finding embedded figures much easier and quicker.

Finally, participants were asked about their familiarity with brands included in the study on a four-point scale (1 = not at all familiar; 2 = somewhat familiar; 3 = familiar; 4 = extremely familiar). Participants then completed demographic questions about their nationality, years in the United States, language spoken at home, and ethnicity of their mother and father. These questions were used to screen students from the U.S. sample who were of a different nationality or bicultural.

Results

Manipulation Checks

Results for the analytic-holistic thinking tests were examined to confirm anticipated differences in processing style for the U.S. and Indian samples. For both tests, U.S. participants found more embedded objects than did Indian participants (Test 1: $M_{US} = 9.80$ and M_{India}

Table 13.1

Study 1: Means and Standard Deviations

Brand	Measure		Very low fit			Low fit			Moderate fit	
			U.S.	India		U.S.	India		U.S.	India
Coke	Extension fit	Shampoo	1.21	1.52	Popcorn	2.45	4.85	Energy drink	4.94	5.86
			(0.54)	(0.68)		(1.39)	(1.23)		(1.73)	(1.15)
	Extension evaluation	Shampoo	1.79	3.05	Popcorn	2.25	4.40	Energy drink	4.00	5.33
			(0.79)	(1.20)		(1.21)	(1.19)		(1.61)	(1.15)
Kodak	Extension fit	Shoes	1.11	2.62	Filing cabinet	2.89	3.95	Cards	5.20	6.15
			(0.32)	(1.86)		(1.70)	(1.69)		(1.32)	(0.88)
	Extension evaluation	Shoes	2.11	3.76	Filing cabinet	3.74	4.62	Cards	4.75	5.75
			(1.08)	(1.22)		(1.48)	(1.20)		(1.29)	(1.02)

Note: Standard deviations in parentheses.

= 7.66, $p < 0.01$; Test 2: $M_{US} = 14.39$ and $M_{India} = 10.80$, $p < 0.01$). Recalling that higher scores are indicative of analytic thinking, these results confirm that U.S. participants were more oriented toward analytical processing than were Indian participants.

Ratings of brand extension fit for the U.S. sample were examined to ensure that brand extensions included in the study represented the intended levels of fit (very low, low, moderate). Results confirmed that Coke shampoo ($M = 1.21$) and Kodak shoes ($M = 1.11$) were viewed as very low fit, Coke popcorn ($M = 2.45$) and Kodak filing cabinet ($M = 2.89$) were seen as low fit, and Coke energy drink ($M = 4.94$) and Kodak greeting cards ($M = 5.20$) were perceived as moderate fit extensions. In addition, perceptions were significantly different for the very low fit versus low fit extensions [Coke: $t(38) = 2.98$, $p < 0.01$; Kodak: $t(36) = 3.58$, $p < 0.01$] and the low fit versus moderate fit extensions [Coke: $t(37) = 2.98$, $p < 0.01$; Kodak: $t(38) = 2.98$, $p < 0.01$].

Brand Extension Fit

A 2 (culture: Eastern, Western) × 3 (brand extension fit: very low, low, moderate) analysis of variance was performed for each brand replicate (see Table 13.1 for means and standard deviations). Brand attitude and familiarity were included as covariates. As expected, a significant main effect of culture emerged for each analysis [Coke: $F(1, 111) = 27.82$, $p < 0.01$; Kodak: $F(1, 111) = 26.32$, $p < 0.01$]. In all cases, Indians perceived a higher degree of extension fit than did Americans. As expected, a significant main effect of brand extension fit also surfaced for each analysis [Coke: $F(2, 111) = 110.06$, $p < 0.01$; Kodak: $F(2, 111) = 75.24$, $p < 0.01$]. Extension fit perceptions rose as the manipulated levels of extension fit increased from very low to moderate levels.

Cultural differences were examined in more detail through a series of planned contrasts, with hypothesized differences between the U.S. and Indian sample being tested for each

Figure 13.1   **Study 1**

A. Brand Extension Fit Ratings

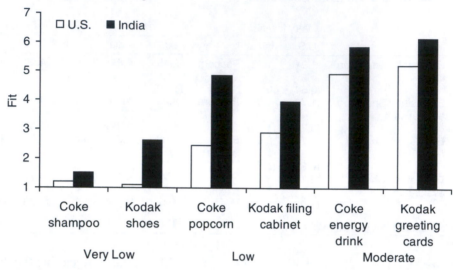

B. Brand Extension Evaluation Ratings

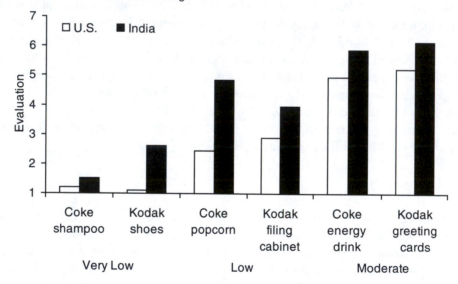

brand extension (see Figure 13.1). For Coke, contrasts indicated cultural differences in perceived extension fit for Coke popcorn [$F(1, 111) = 39.49, p < 0.01$] and Coke energy drink [$F(1, 111) = 5.27, p < 0.05$], but not Coke shampoo, although means were directionally consistent [$F(1, 111) = 0.65, p > 0.10$]. For Kodak, contrasts indicated cultural differences for Kodak shoes [$F(1, 111) = 17.16, p < 0.01$], Kodak filing cabinet [$F(1, 111) = 8.93, p < 0.01$], and Kodak greeting cards [$F(1, 111) = 5.39, p = 0.01$].

Brand Extension Evaluation

A 2 (culture: Eastern, Western) × 3 (brand extension fit: very low, low, moderate) analysis of variance was performed for each brand replicate (see Table 13.1 for means and standard deviations). Brand attitude and familiarity were included as covariates. As expected, a significant main effect of culture emerged for each analysis [Coke: $F(1, 111) = 65.08$, $p < .01$; Kodak: $F(1, 111) = 35.21$, $p < 0.01$]. In all cases, Indians rated the brand extensions more highly than did Americans. As expected, a significant main effect of brand extension fit also surfaced for each analysis [Coke: $F(2, 111) = 39.24$, $p < 0.01$; Kodak: $F(2, 111) = 37.81$, $p < 0.01$]. In all cases, brand extension evaluations rose as extension fit level increased from very low to moderate levels.

Cultural differences were examined in more detail through a series of planned contrasts, with hypothesized differences between the U.S. and Indian sample being tested for each individual brand extension (see Figure 13.1). For Coke, contrasts indicated cultural differences in brand extension evaluations for Coke shampoo [$F(1, 111) = 19.70$, $p < 0.01$], Coke popcorn [$F(1, 111) = 33.26$, $p < 0.01$], and Coke energy drink [$F(1, 111) = 16.61$, $p < 0.01$]. For Kodak, contrasts indicated cultural differences for Kodak shoes [$F(1, 111) = 27.63$, $p < 0.01$], Kodak filing cabinet [$F(1, 111) = 8.86$, $p < 0.01$], and Kodak greeting cards [$F(1, 111) = 7.20$, $p < 0.01$].

Mediation Analyses

As predicted, our findings show cultural differences in perceived brand extension fit, with Easterners perceiving a higher degree of brand extension fit than Westerners do. In developing our predictions, cultural styles of thinking were identified as the mechanism responsible for differences in perceived brand extension fit between Eastern and Western consumers. Holistic thinking was viewed as being more conducive to the discovery of relationships between brand extensions and parent brands, resulting in greater perceptions of fit among Easterners. Analytic thinking was viewed as being more constrained in providing a basis for relationships between brand extensions and parent brands, resulting in poorer perceptions of fit among Westerners.

A mediation analysis was conducted to test whether cultural differences in type of brand extension thoughts (analytic vs. holistic) are a mediator of cultural differences in perceptions of brand extension fit. To do so, we first analyzed the thoughts that participants expressed during the process of evaluating each brand extension. Consistent with our earlier discussion, responses were classified as analytic thought if they made reference to product category similarity (e.g., extension product category is similar to or different from ones associated with the parent brand) or attribute transference across product categories (e.g., parent brand has an attribute that would be beneficial or detrimental in the extension category). For example, responses that Coke popcorn was a bad idea because a "soft drink company making food does not make sense" (product category similarity) or that Coke popcorn would "taste bad because it would be Coke-flavored" (attribute transference) were classified as instances of analytic thought. Responses that made refer-

Table 13.2

Study 1: Type of Thinking as a Mediator of Culture's Effect on Brand Extension Fit

Brand Extension	Condition	Regression Equations
Coke	1	Culture (–.392**) influences type of thinking
	2	Culture (–0.288**) influences brand extension fit
	3	Type of thinking (0.303**) influences brand extension fit and decreases the influence of culture (–0.169) on brand extension fit
		Sobel's z = -2.67, *p* < .01
Kodak	1	Culture (–.213*) influences type of thinking
	2	Culture (–0.248**) influences brand extension fit
	3	Type of thinking (0.282**) influences brand extension fit and decreases the influence of culture (–0.188*) on brand extension fit
		Sobel's z = -1.90, *p* = .05

Note: Standardized beta weights for each predictor are shown in parentheses.
*p < .05; **p < .01; ***p < .001.

Table 13.3

Study 1: Brand Extension Fit as a Mediator of Culture's Effect on Brand Extension Evaluation

Brand Extension	Condition	Regression equations
Coke	1	Culture (–0.288**) influences brand extension fit
	2	Culture (–0.470***) influences brand extension evaluation
	3	Brand extension fit (0.678***) influences brand extension evaluation and decreases the influence of culture (–0.275**) on brand extension evaluation
		Sobel's z = -3.12, *p* < .01
Kodak	1	Culture (–0.248**) influences brand extension fit
	2	Culture (–0.343***) influences brand extension evaluation
	3	Brand extension fit (0.752**) influences brand extension evaluation and decreases the influence of culture (–0.156**) on brand extension evaluation
		Sobel's z = -2.71, *p* < .01

Note: Standardized beta weights for each predictor are shown in parentheses.
*p < .05; **p < .01; ***p < .001.

ence to usage complementarity, overall brand reputation, and overall brand affect were classified as holistic thoughts. For example, responses that Coke popcorn was a good idea because "Coke and Coke popcorn can be consumed together" (complementarity of use), because "Coke makes good products, so Coke popcorn would be good" (overall brand reputation), or because "I like Coke, so I will like Coke popcorn" (overall brand affect) were classified as instances of holistic thought. Two independent coders classified responses as analytic or holistic (inter-rater reliability = 90.2 percent), with disagreements resolved by discussion.

This data was then used to test whether analytic and holistic thinking mediated cultural differences in brand extension fit following Baron and Kenny's (1986) methods, which required running a series of three regressions for each brand. Evidence for mediation is obtained when regressions indicate that (1) the independent variable (culture) predicts the dependent variable (brand extension fit), (2) the independent variable (culture) predicts the mediator (type of thinking), and (3) when the dependent variable is regressed on the independent variable and the mediator, the mediator's effect remains significant, while that of the independent variable reduces in significance (partial mediation) or drops to nonsignificance (perfect mediation). Sobel's test, which provides a formal test of mediation, was also performed (Baron and Kenny 1986). The results, shown in Table 13.2, indicate that type of thinking is a perfect mediator for culture's influence on brand extension fit for Coke and a partial mediator for Kodak. A similar mediation analysis was conducted to test our proposition that cultural differences in brand extension evaluation are mediated by brand extension fit. The results, shown in Table 13.3, support our view. Brand extension fit was found to be a partial mediator for both Coke and Kodak.

Discussion

Our findings confirm the existence of cultural differences in brand extension evaluation. Across a wide variety of brand extensions, Easterners (Indians) perceived a higher degree of extension fit and provided more favorable extension evaluations than those of Westerners (Americans). Evidence regarding the process responsible for cultural differences also emerged. Specifically, brand extension thoughts generated by analytic and holistic thinkers aligned well with our definitions of analytic versus holistic thinking. Results of mediation analyses confirmed that differences in analytic versus holistic thinking mediated culture's influence on brand extension fit *and* that brand extension fit was a mediator of culture's influence on brand extension evaluation.

Thus, our findings support the view that cultural differences in styles of thinking lead to differences in the way that Eastern versus Western consumers respond to brand extensions. However, is it possible that other cultural differences could have contributed to these patterns of brand extension response? We examined several possibilities. First, we considered that there might be cultural differences in the level of consumer skepticism toward brand extensions in general, with Westerners being more skeptical and holding less favorable attitudes than Easterners. We explored this possibility by asking our study 1 participants to agree or disagree with the following statement: "Coke [Kodak] just wants to make money by putting their name on a lot of different products." Responses to this statement indicated a relatively low level of skepticism shared by Easterners and Westerners, reducing the viability of consumer skepticism as an alternative explanation for the less favorable brand extension evaluations on the part of Western consumers.

Second, we considered whether cultural differences in attitudes for the parent brand might have contributed to cultural differences in brand extension evaluations. More favorable attitudes toward a parent brand could easily result in more favorable evaluations of a brand extension. Despite careful pretests, our analyses uncovered several cases where

Western consumers held more favorable attitudes toward the parent brands in study 1. However, these favorable attitudes did not translate into more favorable evaluations of brand extensions. In fact, Westerners actually held less favorable attitudes toward the brand extensions.

Third, we considered whether different levels of brand knowledge and experience may have encouraged more scrutiny and less favorable extension evaluations from Western consumers. Although both Coke and Kodak are truly global brands, and were selected based on similar global rankings and consumer perceptions, we are unable to completely rule out the influence of this factor. Similarly, we are unable to rule out the possibility that specific brand associations may be more or less salient in one culture, providing the basis for perceptions of lower or higher extension fit.

To rule out alternative explanations related to parent brand attitudes, knowledge, and experience, we use a hypothetical parent brand in the next study to test our hypotheses of cultural differences in brand extension response. Using a hypothetical parent brand allows us to equalize brand information and experience across cultures. Thus, replicating findings from our first study with a hypothetical parent brand allows us to rule out alternative explanations based on cultural differences in parent brand attitudes, knowledge, or experience.

STUDY 2

Sample and Procedure

Cultural differences in brand extension response were tested in a 2 (culture: Eastern, Western) × 2 (brand extension replicate: filing cabinet, greeting card) between subjects design. Forty Indian and thirty-eight white American students were recruited from the same university population as before. Participants were first given information about a hypothetical brand (Excera), which was described as follows: "Excera is a manufacturer of high quality photo-films and cameras. Consumers describe the brand as being a leader in photography-related products." Participants were then asked to indicate their attitude toward Excera on a seven-point scale. Following this, they were asked to evaluate a brand extension—either Excera filing cabinet or Excera greeting card—that had been identified as low fitting by American standards in a pretest ($M_{\text{filing cabinet}} = 2.10$ and $M_{\text{greeting card}} = 3.3$). Low fit extensions were selected on the basis of findings from study 1, which indicated consistently strong cultural differences for these types of extensions. Next, participants completed an embedded figure test for analytic-holistic thinking, provided their perceptions of brand extension fit, and completed several demographic questions as per study 1.

Results

Manipulation Checks

First, results for the analytic-holistic thinking test were examined to confirm anticipated differences in processing style for the U.S. and Indian samples. As expected, the American sample found more embedded figures than did Indians [$M_{India} = 7.45$, $M_{US} = 9.66$; $F(1, 69) = 10.44$, $p < 0.01$], indicating a more analytic style of thinking for the American sample.

Second, attitudes toward the hypothetical parent brand (Excera) were examined to confirm that descriptions of the Excera brand provided to our participants evoked similar perceptions across cultures. For this purpose, a 2 (culture: Eastern, Western) × 2 (brand extension replicate: filing cabinet, greeting card) analysis of variance was performed on attitudes toward the hypothetical parent brand. As expected, none of the effects reached significance (p's > 0.10).

Brand Extension Fit

A 2 (culture: Eastern, Western) × 2 (brand extension replicate: filing cabinet, greeting card) analysis of variance was conducted for brand extension fit perceptions, showing a significant main effect of culture [$F(1, 74) = 9.20$, $p < 0.01$]. Planned contrasts indicated that Indian participants provided higher fit ratings than did Americans for both the filing cabinet [$M_{India} = 2.30$, $M_{US} = 1.79$; $F(1, 74) = 1.85$, $p = 0.08$] and greeting card extensions [$M_{India} = 4.20$, $M_{US} = 2.85$; $F(1, 74) = 8.08$, $p < 0.01$; see Figure 13.2].

Brand Extension Evaluations

A 2 (culture: Eastern, Western) × 2 (brand extension replicate: filing cabinet, greeting card) analysis of variance was conducted for brand extension evaluations, revealing a significant main effect of culture [$F(1, 74) = 9.74$, $p < 0.01$]. Planned contrasts indicated that Indian participants gave higher evaluations for both the filing cabinet [$M_{India} = 3.40$, $M_{US} = 2.75$; $F(1, 74) = 3.09$, $p < 0.05$] and greeting card extensions [$M_{India} = 4.60$, $M_{US} = 3.78$; $F(1, 74) = 5.28$, $p = 0.01$; see Figure 13.2].

Discussion

Our results replicate those reported for real brands in study 1. Easterners perceived higher brand extension fit and evaluated brand extensions more favorably than did Westerners. Given that parent brand attitudes, knowledge, and experience were equalized across cultures by using a hypothetical parent brand, cultural differences in brand extension response cannot be attributed to cultural differences in brand familiarity, attitude, or brand associations.

In the next study, we pursue further evidence for styles of thinking as the mechanism responsible for cultural differences in brand extension response by incorporating a bicultural sample of consumers. Specifically, we include a sample of Asian Americans, who have been described as being bicultural, possessing cultural values of an Eastern as well as a Western culture (Benet-Martinez et al. 2002; Hong et al. 2000) *and* lying between white Americans and Asians in terms of cultural values (Lau-Gesk 2003). Because Asian Americans have been exposed to both Eastern and Western cultures, we would expect

Figure 13.2 **Study 2**

A. Brand Extension Fit Ratings

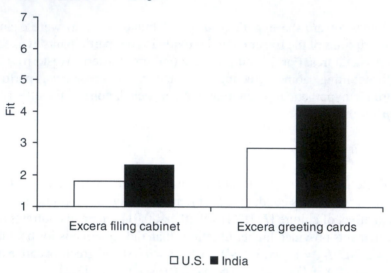

□ U.S. ■ India

B. Brand Extension Evaluation Ratings

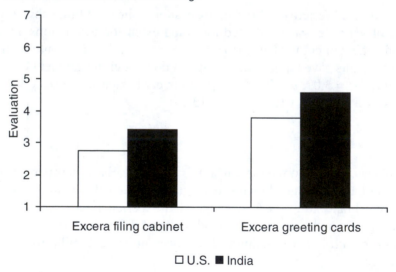

□ U.S. ■ India

their ability to engage in analytic and holistic thinking to lie between that of Westerners and Easterners (Norenzayan et al. 2002).

If analytic and holistic styles of thinking are responsible for cultural differences in brand extension responses, as we have argued, then Asian Americans should exhibit brand extension responses lying between those of Americans (analytic thinkers) and Indians (holistic thinkers). If other factors are responsible for the cultural differences we have observed—such as extraneous factors associated with living in an American consumer environment (e.g., advertising campaigns, retail environments)—then Asian Americans should respond to brand extensions in a manner similar to Americans. Consistent with our line of reasoning, we forward the following hypotheses:

H$_3$: Bicultural (Asian American) consumers will have perceptions of brand extension fit that are higher than those of Western (American) consumers, but lower than those of Eastern (Indian) consumers.

H$_4$: Bicultural (Asian American) consumers will have brand extension evaluations that are more favorable than those of Western (American) consumers, but less favorable than those of Eastern (Indian) consumers.

STUDY 3

Sample and Procedure

Thirty-nine AsianAmerican students were recruited from the same university as participants in prior studies. This sample had lived in the United States for an average of 17.42 years. Language ability associated with their Asian heritage (Hmong) averaged a 5.9 on a seven-point scale, indicating that although they had spent most of their lives in the United States, they did maintain their Asian culture through language. This is consistent with prior research showing that Hmong college students in the United States retain moderate levels of orientation to the Hmong culture in addition to endorsing American values (Tsai 2001).

The procedure followed that of study 1, with the following exception: Due to the data collection context, only one brand extension (Coke popcorn) was presented to participants for their evaluation. Responses to this extension were compared to those of the Indian and white American samples from study 1.

Results

Analytic-Holistic Thinking

As expected, a one-way analysis of variance indicated a significant main effect of culture [$F(2, 76) = 4.07$, $p < 0.05$], with Asian Americans falling between the Indian and American samples ($M_{US} = 10.35$, $M_{Asian American} = 9.46$, $M_{Indian} = 7.85$). Planned contrasts confirmed significant differences between Indians and Asian Americans [$F(1, 76) = 4.29$, $p < 0.05$] and also between Indians and Americans [$F(1, 76) = 7.83$, $p < 0.01$]. The difference between Americans and Asian Americans was directionally consistent with our hypothesis, reaching marginal significance [$F(1, 76) = 1.30$, $p = 0.12$].

Brand Extension Fit

A one-way analysis of variance revealed a significant main effect of culture [$F(2, 76) = 10.01$, $p < 0.01$]. Indians and Americans provided the most and least favorable fit ratings

Figure 13.3   **Study 3**

A. Brand Extension Fit Ratings

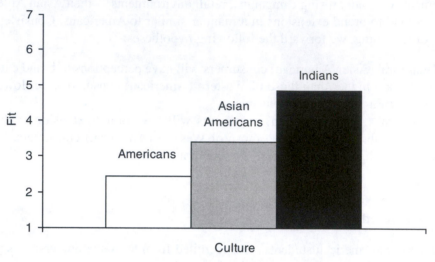

B. Brand Extension Evaluation Ratings

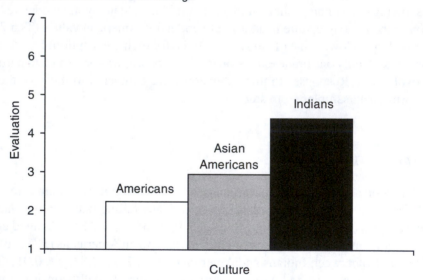

(M_{India} = 4.85, M_{US} = 2.45), with those from Asian Americans falling in between ($M_{\text{Asian American}}$ = 3.41). Planned contrasts indicated significant differences between Americans and Indians [$F(1, 76)$ = 19.65, $p < 0.01$], Americans and Asian Americans [$F(1, 76)$ = 4.16, $p < 0.05$], and Indians and Asian Americans [$F(1, 76)$ = 9.35, $p < 0.01$; see Figure 13.3].

Brand Extension Evaluation

A one-way analysis of variance revealed a significant main effect of culture [$F(2, 76)$ = 16.28, $p < 0.01$], with Indians and Americans providing the most and least favorable evaluations, respectively ($M_{US} = 2.25$ and $M_{Indian} = 4.40$). Evaluations from Asian Americans fell in between these extremes ($M_{Asian American} = 2.94$). Planned contrasts indicated significant differences between Americans and Indians [$F(1, 76) = 30.61$, $p < 0.01$], Americans and Asian Americans [$F(1, 76) = 4.33$, $p < 0.05$], and Indians and Asian Americans [$F(1, 76) = 18.41$, $p < 0.01$; see Figure 13.3]. Parent brand attitude did not differ among groups ($p > 0.10$).

Discussion

Results of this study provide further support regarding the influence of styles of thinking on cultural differences in brand extension responses. Brand extension fit and evaluations from a bicultural group (Asian Americans) fell midway between those of an Eastern (Indian) and Western (white American) sample. Asian Americans also fell midway between the Indian and American samples in terms of analytic-holistic styles of thinking. These findings strengthen our position by ruling out a number of alternative explanations for cultural differences in brand extension response observed in the first two studies. For example, Eastern (Indian) and Western (American) cultures vary in terms of the marketing environment, including differences in advertising practices, amount of brand extension activity, and type of brand extension activity. For these differences to be viable alternative explanations for cultural differences in brand extension response, one would expect to see little difference between Americans and Asian Americans, who have both lived their entire lives in the United States. However, our findings from study 3 show that Americans and Asian Americans have different responses to brand extensions, which we find to be related to analytic and holistic styles of thinking.

GENERAL DISCUSSION

Our research finds cultural differences in consumer response to brand extensions. Consumers from Western cultures, characterized by analytic thinking, have a more constrained view of brand extension fit than do consumers from Eastern cultures, characterized by holistic thinking. These differences in styles of thinking generally result in higher perceived brand extension fit and more favorable brand extension evaluations for Easterners than Westerners. These findings lend further support to the idea that styles of thinking are an important contributor to cultural differences in brand extension response, consistent with Monga and John (2007).

Further, our findings provide additional support that styles of thinking underlie cultural differences in brand extension response. In our first study, mediation analyses confirmed that differences in the type of brand extension thoughts (analytic vs. holistic) mediated the influence of culture on brand extension fit perceptions, which in turn mediated brand extension evaluations. Alternative explanations for cultural differences were also ruled out across these studies, including skepticism about brand extensions (study 1) and cultural differences in parent brand attitudes, beliefs, or experiences (study 2). In the last study, we also rule out alternative explanations based on cultural differences in the marketing environment. Despite living their entire lives in the United States, and being exposed to the same environment for advertising and brand extension activity, bicultural (Asian American) consumers exhibited brand extension responses different from Western (white American) consumers. Added together, results from all three studies provide additional evidence that styles of thinking are a driving factor in the way that consumers from Eastern versus Western cultures perceive and evaluate brand extensions.

Implications for Cross-Cultural Research

Our research adds to a sizable body of literature within consumer behavior reporting cultural differences. These findings suggest the usefulness of the styles of thinking framework compared to other frameworks for understanding the role of culture. Consider the individualism-collectivism framework, which distinguishes collectivist cultures, where individuals define themselves as interdependent members of a collective (e.g., family, coworkers), from individualistic cultures, where individuals stress autonomy and independence of the self (Triandis 1995). The analytic-holistic thinking framework and the individualism-collectivism framework have similar cultural antecedents—many versus few social relationships. Both frameworks predict that individualistic (analytic) cultures are less context-dependent than collectivist (holistic) cultures (Kühnen et al. 2001; Nisbett et al. 2001). However, the analytic-holistic thinking framework also predicts certain unique consequences. Compared to analytic thinkers, holistic thinkers (1) have a different notion of causes for events, (2) are more accepting of contradiction, (3) perceive events and the world to be always changing, and (4) are less likely to rely on categories and more on relations between objects (Nisbett et al. 2001; Choi, Koo, and Choi 2007). By drawing on this framework, we were able to offer insights about response to general information domains (that is, brand extensions), which would not have been possible with the individualism-collectivism framework.

Our results contribute to the set of growing findings in cross-cultural psychology and cross-cultural consumer behavior. All of the studies reported in this chapter make comparisons across different cultural groups (Americans vs. Indians). However, two important developments in the area of culture are worthy of mention. First, there is a growing recognition that culture is malleable and that aspects of culture can be situationally primed (Hong et al. 2000). Individuals can shift between different cultural styles of thinking depending on cues embedded in the environment. This suggests the possibility that priming analytic thinking in Easterners and holistic thinking in Westerners may result in significant shifts in the way these cultures evaluate brand extensions. Second, culture researchers have questioned whether labeling a country as analytic or holistic implies that all individuals within that country adopt an identical mode of thinking. For instance, Choi, Koo, and Choi (2007) demonstrate that analytic-holistic thinking can be conceptualized as an individual difference variable, resulting in substantial variations in styles of thinking within a single culture (Choi, Koo, and Choi 2007). This implies that brand extension responses may show significant variation within the United States or India. Further explorations are needed to better understand brand extensions responses within and across cultures.

Implications for Branding Research

Our findings also make an important contribution to the branding literature. Most studies in branding have used Americans participants to test their theories. Even the managerial literature has encouraged using similar branding strategies across cultures given the advantages of using standardized programs across the globe. Contrary to this view, our research suggests that culturally ingrained styles of thinking have important implications for responses to branding strategies. Our finding that Asian Americans responded more favorably to brand extensions than white Americans reflects the importance of taking into consideration the consumer's cultural background even while doing research within the United States.

Our findings also suggest that it may be worthwhile to examine the robustness of prior findings in branding research across cultures. Prior research has yielded a number of important findings about how consumers evaluate brand extensions depending on the nature of the extension (e.g., downward vs. upward stretch) and the parent brand (e.g., prestige vs. functional). Our findings suggest that these results may not generalize to consumers from other cultures. For example, the well-known finding that downward stretches of luxury brands may result in diluting a brand's reputation may not hold for consumers in Eastern cultures, who may perceive downward stretches as a relatively good fit to the luxury brand. Extending our research to other brand extension questions may shed new light on many issues related to cultural differences in consumer behavior.

ACKNOWLEDGMENT

This research was funded in part by an ACR-Sheth Dissertation Award for Cross-Cultural Research.

REFERENCES

Baron, Reuben M., and David A. Kenny (1986). "The Moderator-Mediator Distinction in Social Psychological Research: Conceptual, Strategic, and Statistical Considerations," *Journal of Personality and Social Psychology,* 51 (6), 1173–1182.

Benet-Martínez, Veronica, Janxin Leu, Fiona Lee, and Michael Morris (2002). "Negotiating Biculturalism: Cultural Frame-Switching in Biculturals with 'Oppositional' vs. 'Compatible' Cultural Identities," *Journal of Cross-Cultural Psychology,* 33 (5), 492–516.

Bottomley, Paul A., and Stephen J. Holden (2001). "Do We Really Know How Consumers Evaluate Brand Extensions?" *Journal of Marketing Research,* 38 (4), 494–500.

Chiu, Liang-Hwang (1972). "A Cross-cultural Comparison of Cognitive Styles in Chinese and American Children," *International Journal of Psychology,* 7, 235–242.

Choi, Inchol, MinKyung Koo, and Jong An Choi (2007). "Individual Differences in Analytic versus Holistic Thinking. *Personality and Social Psychology Bulletin,* 33 (5), 691–705.

Han, Jin K., and Bernd H. Schmitt (1997). "Product-category Dynamics and Corporate Identity in Brand Extensions: A Comparison of Hong Kong and U.S. Consumers," *Journal of International Marketing,* 5 (1), 77–92.

Hong, Ying-yi, Michael W. Morris, Chi-yue Chiu, and Veronica Benet-Martínez (2000). "Multicultural Minds: A Dynamic Constructivist Approach to Culture and Cognition," *American Psychologist,* 55 (7), 709–720.

Horn, Wolfgang (1962). *Leistungspreufsystem, L-P-S: Handanweisung fuer die Durchfuehrung, Auswertung und Interpretation* [A Performance Testing System: Manual for Administration, Scoring and Interpretation]. Goettingen, Germany: Verlag-Hogrefe.

Ji, Li-Jun, Kaiping Peng, and Richard E. Nisbett (2000). "Culture, Control and Perception of Relationships in the Environment," *Journal of Personality and Social Psychology,* 78 (5), 943–955.

Keller, Kevin L. (2002). *Branding and Brand Equity.* Cambridge, MA: Marketing Science Institute.

Kühnen, Ulrich, Bettina Hannover, Ute Roeder, Ahiq A Shah, Benjamin Schubert, Arnold Upmeyer, and Saliza Zakaria (2001). "Cross-cultural Variations in Identifying Embedded Figures," *Journal of Cross-cultural Psychology,* 32 (3), 365–371.

Lau-Gesk, Loraine (2003). "Activating Culture Through Persuasion Appeals: An Examination of the Bicultural Consumer," *Journal of Consumer Psychology,* 13 (3), 301–315.

Loken, Barbara, and Deborah Roedder John (1993). "Diluting Brand Beliefs: When do Brand Extensions Have a Negative Impact?" *Journal of Marketing,* 57 (3), 71–84.

Masuda, Takahiko, and Richard E. Nisbett (2001). "Attending Holistically Versus Analytically: Comparing Context Sensitivity of Japanese and Americans," *Journal of Personality and Social Psychology,* 81 (5), 922–934.

Miller, Joan (1984). "Culture and the Development of Everyday Social Explanation," *Journal of Personality and Social Psychology,* 46 (5), 961–978.

Monga, Alokparna Basu, and Deborah Roedder John (2004). "Consumer Responses to Brand Extensions: Does Culture Matter?" *Advances in Consumer Research,* 31, 216–219.

——— (2007). "Cultural Differences in Brand Extension Evaluation: The Influence of Analytic versus Holistic Thinking," *Journal of Consumer Research,* 33 (4), 529–36.

Nisbett, Richard E., Kaiping Peng, Incheol Choi, and Ara Norenzayan (2001). "Culture and Systems of Thought: Holistic Versus Analytic Cognition," *Psychological Review,* 108 (2), 291–310.

Norenzayan, Ara, Edward E. Smith, Beom Jun Kim, and Richard E. Nisbett (2002). "Cultural Preferences in Formal vs. Intuitive Reasoning," *Cognitive Science,* 26 (5), 653–684.

Shweder, Richard (1991). *Thinking Through Cultures: Expeditions in Cultural Psychology.* Cambridge, MA: Harvard University Press.

Triandis, Harry C. (1995). *Individualism and Collectivism.* Boulder, CO: Westview Press.

Tsai, Jeanne (2001). "Cultural Orientation of Hmong Young Adults," *Journal of Human Behavior in the Social Environment,* 3 (3/4), 99–114.

Witkin, Herman A., Phillip K. Oltman, Evelyn Ruskin, and Stephen A. Karp (1971). *Manual for the Embedded Figures Test.* Palo Alto, CA: Consulting Psychologist Press.

CHAPTER 14

LUXURY BRANDING

VANESSA M. PATRICK AND HENRIK HAGTVEDT

THE CHANGING FACE OF THE LUXURY MARKET AND THE EMERGENCE OF NEW LUXURY

The headline of a recent ad for Pegasus, a line of bathroom fittings by Home Depot, says, "Luxury is only for the privileged? What gave you that idea?" Today, the promise of the good life, the ultimate experience of luxurious living, is made to mass-market consumers by products in virtually every category. Silverstein and Fiske (2003) refer to this as the emerging "new luxury" market and describe it as a recent socioeconomic trend in which middle-market consumers trade up to "products and services which possess higher levels of quality, taste, and aspiration than [other] goods in the [same] category but are not so expensive as to be out of reach" (Silverstein and Fiske 2003, p. 1). Thus, the new luxury market is not restricted to conventional luxury goods such as diamonds, furs, and expensive cars (referred to by Silverstein and Fiske as "old luxury"), but may include any products at the top of their category, from sandwiches (e.g., Panera Bread) to body washes (e.g., Bath and Body Works). According to Silverstein and Fiske (2003), new luxury products are premium goods that connect with consumers on an emotional level.

With the emergence of the new luxury phenomenon, luxury branding is an increasingly important domain for research in marketing. Although there are some notable exceptions (e.g., Park, Milberg and Lawson 1991; Vigneron and Johnson 2004), the concept of luxury, the marketing of luxury products, and the management of luxury brands have for the most part been ignored in the extant literature. The central aim of this chapter is to present the current state of knowledge with regard to luxury branding and to identify gaps in this knowledge that pertain to (1) the conceptualization of luxury brands, (2) the understanding of how consumers relate to and process information about luxury brands, and (3) the identification of the benefits and risks inherent to managing the luxury brand concept.

In the remainder of the chapter, we first distinguish between the notions of new luxury and old luxury. Next we present a brief review of the state of the knowledge about the marketing of luxury products and brands. A great deal of this research investigates how a luxury brand should be managed from a marketer's point of view, a notion consistent with old luxury branding. Notably, however, some recent research has provided insight into the motivations driving luxury brand choice. After reviewing the relevant literature, we identify some critical gaps, with a focus on the reconceptualization of luxury brands,

Figure 14.1   **Diagrammatic Overview of Extant and Future Research on Luxury Branding**

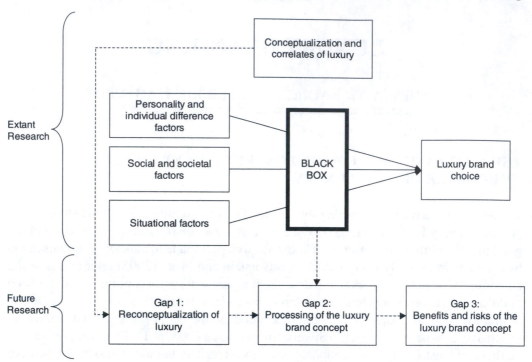

the need for an increased understanding of consumer processing of the luxury brand concept, and benefits and risks inherent to managing the luxury brand concept. Please see Figure 14.1 for a diagrammatic summary of extant and future research.

HOW DIFFERENT IS NEW LUXURY FROM OLD LUXURY?

Traditionally, underlying the consumption of luxury goods was the principle of rarity (Veblen 1899). However, Silverstein and Fiske (2003) identified a new type of luxury-goods consumer responsible for democratizing the luxury market (Tsai 2005). These middle-market consumers selectively trade up to "higher levels of quality, taste and aspiration." Indeed, these luxury brands have helped the middle class attain the perception of prosperity (Schwartz 2002). Not only is luxury being democratized, but the goods traditionally considered luxury are also changing. Traditional luxury categories, such as furs, watches, and jewelry, are being replaced by home appliances, fine dining, bath soap, and travel. Indeed, according to Danziger (2005), the old luxury was defined by product category, while the new luxury is independent of product category and is all about the experience.

The total market for luxury products and services in 2007 contributed to $321.9 billion in consumer spending (Unity Marketing 2008). Notably, this did not include the ever-expanding new luxury marketplace. Indeed, the emergence of new luxury in virtually every product category and the democratization of luxury (Tsai 2005), making the luxury experience accessible to more consumers, is viewed by many observers as a radical transformation of the luxury market. However, if the terms *old luxury* and *new luxury* are to facilitate understanding and discussion of this transformation rather than confuse the issue of what luxury really is, the relationship between the two concepts should be clarified. The latter concept is differentiated from the former concept in that it is not restricted to specific product categories. Further, the aspect of conspicuous consumption is less important for the latter concept, giving way to a more complete focus on experience, affect, and hedonism. Notwithstanding this trend in the marketplace, old luxury clearly exists alongside new luxury. Further, consumers' perceptions of old luxury inform their perceptions of new luxury, and the clear distinction between the two concepts is somewhat arbitrary. However, the distinction may nonetheless be useful for brand management in the current marketplace. While the old luxury market focused on the status and prestige of the brand, the new luxury market focuses on the pleasure and emotional connection the consumer has with the brand. In the old luxury market, brand management entailed managing the attributes, features, and image of the brand so as to convey the perception of luxury to consumers.

Notably, what constitutes luxury today is reflective of the changing nature of consumer needs, specifically the evolution of utilitarian or basic needs to hedonic or higher order needs. Many consumers no longer struggle to meet basic needs of survival, security, and comfort but strive toward enhancing their pleasure and broadening their life experiences. As the face of the luxury market rapidly changes, the issue of how luxury brands can and should be strategically and dynamically managed so they connect with consumers on an emotional level, ensuring that the consumer derives pleasure from the brand experience at each encounter, becomes an important issue to academic researchers and marketers.

REVIEW OF THE EXTANT LITERATURE ON LUXURY BRANDING

What Is a Luxury Brand?

Merriam-Webster's dictionary (2009) defines luxury as "a condition of abundance or great ease and comfort" or "something adding to pleasure or comfort but not absolutely necessary." This popular notion illustrates a clear link between the concept of luxury and the concept of hedonic consumption (Hirschman and Holbrook 1982). Indeed, Vigneron and Johnson (2004), citing Kapferer (1997), describe luxury products as those that provide extra pleasure and flatter all senses at once. They expand on this description to argue that psychological benefits, rather than functional benefits, are the main factor distinguishing luxury products from nonluxury products. Berry (1994) distinguishes luxury products from necessities by suggesting that necessities are utilitarian objects that help relieve the unpleasant state of discomfort while luxuries are seen as desirable objects that provide pleasure. Others have defined luxury products as those for which the ratio of functionality to price is low, but for which the ratio of intangible and situational utility to price is high (Nueno and Quelch 1998).

In this chapter, we put forward a consumer-focused definition of luxury brands that is reflective of current market trends and the emergence of new luxury. We conceptualize a luxury brand as one that is at the top of its category in terms of premiumness and connects with consumers on an emotional level, providing pleasure as a central benefit (Hagtvedt and Patrick 2008a). We suggest that this formulation of a luxury brand captures the prerequisite of premiumness for luxury but emphasizes the delivery of emotional benefits that constitute the primary benefit obtained by the consumer.

What Are the Correlates of Luxury Brands?

Extant research has investigated the different aspects of a brand that signal luxury to consumers. Although this research has largely examined what might be considered most relevant for old luxury, some of these brand correlates remain important for new luxury as well, although empirical research is needed to determine which ones they are.

Phau and Prendergast (2000) suggest that luxury brands are those that imply exclusivity, have a strong brand identity, have high brand awareness, and are perceived to be high quality. Indeed, other research systematically investigates the multidimensional nature of the luxury brand concept and suggests how these dimensions should be managed for creating lasting luxury brand value. Vigneron and Johnson (2004), for instance, propose five key dimensions of a luxury brand: perceived quality, perceived conspicuousness, perceived uniqueness, perceived extended self, and perceived hedonism. The first of these dimensions simply refers to the expectation that luxury brands should offer superior performance (Gentry et al. 2001). While an important source of revenue expansion for firms is increased purchase intent induced by increased perceptions of quality (Rust, Moorman, and Dickson 2002), luxury also implies premium pricing that could deter some consumers who might prefer a value-for-money proposition that connotes more quality per dollar spent. For the next three dimensions of luxury, a high price is, in fact, desirable. The concept of conspicuous consumption suggests that consumers purchase conspicuous goods because of their social signaling effect. These consumers thus achieve an enhanced level of status or prestige that sets them apart from others (Veblen 1899). Indeed, some research has even suggested that consumers' propensity to purchase a luxury brand is dependent on their susceptibility to interpersonal influence (Bearden and Etzel 1982). Perceived uniqueness or scarcity of the products adds to this social signaling effect, and firms sometimes incorporate this into brand strategies. For instance, Ferrari promised not to produce more than 4,300 vehicles despite a more than a two-year waiting list for its cars, and Christian Dior even sued supermarkets for carrying its products, fearing that wide availability could hurt its exclusive image (cited in Amaldoss and Jain 2005). The underlying assumption here is that luxury brands may serve to classify or distinguish consumers in relation to others. Consumers may also integrate the symbolic meaning of these brands into their own identity (Holt 1995). Belk's (1988) concept of extended self suggests that possessions may form part of a consumer's identity, and the construction of the self thus seems to be a factor in luxury consumption (Vigneron and Johnson 2004).

The last dimension, perceived hedonism, refers to the sensory gratification, as opposed to the social context, of luxury consumption. The hedonic aspect of luxury consumption thus refers to the intrinsic pleasure and emotional reward derived from the consumption experience itself (Hirschman and Holbrook 1982). This notion also is in line with Silverstein and Fiske's (2003) new luxury, that is, premium goods that connect with consumers on an emotional level, and it allows for luxury branding across a wide variety of product categories. After all, pleasure is not only a fundamental human drive (Higgins 1997), but it is universally applicable in that a consumer may be delighted and feel sensory and emotional gratification through the consumption of virtually any product category. Indeed, the "luxury fever" (Frank 1999) that has purportedly swept the nation is proposed to be not the pursuit of furs, diamonds, and cars, but of traditionally functional items like grills, washing machines, and lawnmowers. Further, although the rarity principle underlying conspicuous consumption (Dubois and Paternault 1995; Veblen 1899) may be counteracted by a high availability of products belonging to a luxury brand, there is no evident reason why consumers would be averse to sensory and emotional gratification in abundance.

Consumer Choice of Luxury Brands

Although research on luxury branding from a consumer's perspective is still at an early stage, some extant literature sheds light on motivations that drive consumers to choose luxury products and on conditions that facilitate choice of a luxury brand option. Early research motivated by economic theory has analyzed the consumption choices of affluent consumers (Dubois and Duquesne 1993; Dubois and Laurent 1994; Veblen 1899), the role of snobbery and conspicuousness in consumption choices (Leibenstein 1950), and the economic and political factors that drive luxury purchases (Vigneron and Johnson 2004). Other research has investigated consumer characteristics that predispose them to luxury consumption. Bearden and Etzel (1982) have shown that for consumers susceptible to interpersonal influence, approval from their reference group is a strong motivator for luxury brand choice. Dubois and Laurent (1994) suggest that individuals with high hedonistic and perfectionist motives are more likely to purchase luxury products, but feelings of guilt, on the other hand, dissuade consumers from making these purchases (Kivetz and Simonson 2002). Wong and Ahuvia (1998) illustrate that Asians and Westerners differ in their motivations to purchase status goods and luxury brands, implicating cultural differences as a driver of luxury consumption.

They assert that since East Asian culture is based on an interpersonal construal of self, Asians (vs. Westerners) tend to be influenced by group norms and goals, leading to a preference for public and visible possessions that communicate financial achievement. Conversely, Asians appear less likely than Westerners to display materialistic behavior based on personal tastes, traits, or goals. In a similar vein, Tsai (2005) discusses the differences between socially oriented and personally oriented consumers in terms of the luxury market, and also provides recommendations for enhancing luxury-brand purchase value for personally oriented consumers.

There are also scattered research findings that illuminate some situational factors that drive brand choice. Mandel, Petrova, and Cialdini (2006) demonstrate that when a depicted media personality is perceived to be similar and the media depiction is one of success (vs. failure) consumers tend to exhibit increased expectations of their own future wealth along with a preference for luxury brands. Chartrand and colleagues (2008) demonstrate that primed exposure to a premium/luxury concept (e.g., walking past Nordstrom) activates a prestige goal and results in an increased propensity to choose a luxury product (choice of a more expensive pair of socks). Kivetz and Simonson (2002) illustrate that when making a choice between a hedonic experience (going on a cruise) and a utilitarian one (saving for college), feelings of guilt often result in consumers choosing the latter. Interestingly, however, these researchers show that knowledge about these feelings of guilt results in individuals precommitting to luxury over necessities. These researchers show that people do prefer indulgent awards and that these awards are more effective than cash as an incentive to participate in a lottery, underscoring the appeal of luxury and its power to influence consumer behavior.

Dubois and Paternault (1995) discuss how the appeal of luxury can also change in a cycle of aspiration and consumption. These authors suggest that the luxury concept has "dream value." The paradox of luxury marketing is revealed through a regression analysis that shows that for luxury brands, awareness feeds the dream of owning the brand, but purchase makes the dream come true, thereby contributing to destroy it.

SUMMARY OF THE EXTANT LITERATURE AND IDENTIFICATION OF GAPS FOR FUTURE RESEARCH

Extant literature has focused a great deal on definitions and conceptualizations of the luxury brand and the correlates of luxury that connote luxury status. This was a reasonable approach since the purpose of the research was to enable better strategic decisions related to management of luxury brands and to determine the extent to which product features and attributes (like price or quality) determined luxury brand status. Early research also investigated the personality-related and social factors that drove luxury brand choice. Recent research in consumer behavior has begun to investigate the choice of a luxury brand as a dependent variable and the conditions under which this occurs. In this chapter, we identify three key sets of issues that represent gaps in the current knowledge: how luxury is conceptualized today, how consumers process luxury brand information, and what benefits and risks are associated with the luxury brand concept. These are pertinent today given the changing face of luxury in the marketplace and its emergence in diverse product categories.

First, we suggest a reconceptualization of what constitutes luxury in today's marketplace. We propose that luxury is pursued for its own sake and that the hedonic potential of luxury brands is what primarily distinguishes them from other brands within their category. We assert that the processing style and manner in which consumers respond to the luxury concept remains a "black box" even today. One might derive some insight into this black box from related research on hedonic consumer behavior, but an in-depth understanding of consumer response to the luxury brand concept is lacking in the current literature. Further, this understanding of consumer responses to luxury lends insight to a related issue of how managers can strategically and effectively manage luxury brands with a focus on the benefits and risks a luxury brand affords.

To summarize, we identify three key gaps in the literature and call for future research to illuminate these gaps:

1. To reconceptualize the luxury concept in the context of current market trends and conditions and to determine the source from which consumers derive value from luxury consumption.
2. To understand how luxury brands are evaluated, in other words, how consumers process luxury brand information.
3. To determine the benefits and risks of managing luxury brands and to provide insights to enable a more effective and strategic management of these brands.

Gap 1: Reconceptualizing Luxury Brands

It is assumed in marketing thought that the greater the benefits are that consumers derive, the more they are willing to pay. Thus, luxury brands have been able to command a premium price for the benefits of status, conspiciousness, and exclusivity. Indeed, extant research demonstrates that consumers view premium prices as indicators of higher quality (Quelch 1987; Garfein 1989; Arghavan and Zaichkowsky 2000; O'Cass and Frost 2002). Further, it is often said that luxury products often are purchased simply because they cost more, without providing additional direct utility over cheaper counterparts (Dubois and Duquesne 1993).

However, the real utility a consumer derives from a luxury product is largely psychological, and it is the psychological benefits that distinguish luxury products from nonluxury products and counterfeits (Arghavan and Zaichkowsky 2000). Increasingly, consumers are more willing to spend on luxury experiences, especially for holiday accommodations, home furnishings, food for dinner parties, restaurants, and so on, in other words, for hedonic experiences, status-related items, and products that are going to last a lifetime (Allsopp 2005). Given this, we conceptualize a luxury brand as one that is at the top of its category in terms of premiumness and connects with consumers on an emotional level, providing pleasure as a central benefit.

To better understand consumer response to luxury, we propose that the notion of luxury for its own sake should also be highlighted. Little or no research has been conducted or even proposed in this regard, but there is a growing stream of research in arts and aesthetics that may shed light on the subject. Dissanayake (1995) discusses art in relation to the concept of "making special" or "artifying," tied to religion and ritualistic behavior. In other words, humans have a drive, developed through the process of evolution, to make and experience the extraordinary, and this is what underlies our impulse for artistic creation and consumption. It seems reasonable to propose a parallel for the creation and consumption of luxury. Indeed, Kapferer (1997) refers to luxury as art applied to functional items. Similarly, Hagtvedt and Patrick (2008b) discuss the luxury perceptions inherent in the concept of art, noting that both are tied to a special kind of quest for excellence. Of course, this does not imply that luxury is the most salient or important aspect of art, but that an underlying drive that gives rise to both these expressions of human ingenuity stems from the same source, that is, the desire to experience the extraordinary.

Extant literature asserts that artworks, in the pure sense of the word, are valued in and of themselves and possess no utilitarian value (Hagtvedt and Patrick 2008b; Hirschman 1983). Indeed, it is argued that aesthetic experiences in general must be intrinsically motivated (Averill, Stanat, and More 1998). This intrinsic value is tied to the experience of the extraordinary for its own sake, and thus, following the above argument, pertains also to the concept of luxury. This insight further clarifies the role of hedonism in luxury consumption and exemplifies the relation to and relevance for research on luxury of several separate streams of research, such as those pertaining to arts, aesthetics, design, and hedonic products. Indeed, research in luxury might greatly benefit from the development of an overarching framework that captures the commonalities between these related areas.

Gap 2: Understanding Consumer Processing of the Luxury Brand Concept

Although there has not been much research that explicitly investigates the processing of luxury brand concepts, we can draw on the emerging stream of literature that investigates consumer responses to hedonic products as a starting point. Hedonic goods are multisensory and associated with fun, feelings, pleasure, excitement, and fantasy (Hirschman and Holbrook 1982). Previous research has suggested that hedonic products are evaluated by a different set of criteria (c.f. Yeung and Wyer 2004, 2005) and elicit a different set of consumption goals compared to functional products (Pham 1998).

We propose that luxury brands are also likely to be evaluated based on a different set of criteria than other brands. Given that a luxury brand is defined in terms of the emotional and hedonic benefits it delivers, the extent to which a luxury brand is able to meet affective expectations is more likely to influence evaluation than its performance along a series of attributes (c.f. Patrick, MacInnis, and Park 2007). Consequently, we might posit that if the brand delivers emotional gratification from consumption, the re-experience of this benefit may also be a key driver for repurchase as opposed to satisfaction in terms of specific performance criteria (Hagtvedt and Patrick 2008a). This notion has been supported in the literature in the context of hedonic products, in which Chitturi, Raghunathan, and Mahajan (2008) suggest that while functional products satisfy, hedonic products delight. We would argue that this experience of delight is likely to be a key driver of future purchase, not mere satisfaction, and re-experiencing emotional gratification becomes the consumption goal, not merely repurchase.

As Thomson, MacInnis, and Park (2005) point out, emotional attachment is indeed the tie that binds. Luxury brands constitute a unique context in which to examine some of the key findings in the attachment literature. We would argue that this is a category in which functionality and performance is less important than the emotional connection. The implications for brand loyalty within this category are also an important area for future investigation. Finally, recent research has emphasized the differential processing of brands among different populations, such as, for instance the holistic processing prevalent in Eastern societies versus the analytic processing prevalent in Western societies (Chapter 13). Future research may investigate other cross-cultural differences in the processing of the luxury brand concept.

Gap 3: Identifying the Benefits and Risks of the Luxury Brand Concept

Given the recent trends in the marketplace of "trading up" and the emergence of new luxury products in virtually every product category (Silverstein and Fiske 2003), a systematic understanding of the benefits and risks of the luxury brand concept as conceptualized here is needed. Based on the earlier discussion, the hedonic properties inherent in a luxury proposition represent benefits for the luxury brand that merit further investigation. After all, hedonic benefits are desirable in and of themselves, with the implications this has for brand and brand extension evaluations, attachment to the brand, purchase behavior, and so on. For instance, this aspect of hedonism implies that a luxury brand is inherently desirable, that luxury brand extensions may be judged on a less strictly rational basis than other brand extensions, that consumer attachment may be easier to achieve with luxury brands, and so on (see also Park, Milberg, and Lawson 1991). Indeed, the centrality of pleasure and emotional connection in the current conceptualization of luxury suggests that the feelings-as-information approach (Schwarz and Clore 1983) may be useful for the investigation of consumer responses to luxury branding (Hagtvedt and Patrick 2008a).

The management of a luxury brand portfolio is also an area in which a great deal of future research might be conducted. The issues of whether a brand line should extend within its category or extend across categories, and the overall impact of the brand on marketing-related criteria such as market share and shareholder value (see Park and Eisingerich 2008), are important for future investigation. Indeed, placing a monetary valuation on the emotional benefits delivered by a brand and translating this emotional brand value into a dollar value is important for future research.

It should also be noted, however, that there may be specific risks inherent in the luxury brand concept. Brand management entails, in part, maintaining consistency and positive brand associations in brand communication (Keller 1993; Park, Jaworski, and MacInnis 1986). The commitment to a specific brand concept entails providing brand cues consistent with that brand concept. For example, cues such as premium pricing and exclusive distribution may be considered consistent with a luxury brand concept (Amaldoss and Jain 2005; Silverstein and Fiske 2003). Further, cheap extensions may have an adverse impact on a parent luxury brand (Kirmani, Sood, and Bridges 1999). Research on brand dilution suggests that providing cues that are inconsistent with a brand concept decreases brand evaluation and consequently might have an impact on brand extendibility (Buchanan, Simmons, and Bickart 1999). In fact, even positively valued attributes, if they occur in a product in unexpected combinations, may lead to incoherence and uncertainty, which in turn may have an unfavorable influence on brand evaluation (Kayande et al. 2007).

Based on our assertion that hedonic associations are central to the luxury brand concept, a potential downside to this is that these perceptions are difficult to maintain and have to be carefully managed. Indeed, it seems reasonable that a luxury brand is sensitive to inconsistencies in brand cues, and that a disruption or interference of hedonic perceptions may cause unfavorable consumer evaluations and brand dilution. Further, inconsistencies in brand cues in extension categories are likely to have negative feedback effects on the parent brand.

Similarly, brand evaluation is enhanced by associating the brand with positive brand cues, while it is diminished by associating the brand with negative brand cues (Park et al. 1986). Several brand cues may influence how a brand is evaluated, for instance, advertising images, celebrity endorsement, product packaging, or word of mouth. In general, negative information about a product's attributes influences brand perceptions more than positive information does (Herr, Kardes, and Kim 1991) since consumers weigh negative information more heavily than positive information when forming overall brand attitudes (Herr et al. 1991). It seems reasonable that different brand concepts may be differentially sensitive to negative brand cues, and that consumers may be particularly sensitive to negative cues associated with the luxury brand concept, if the evaluation of this brand is based more on a general positive emotional connection than on specific performance criteria.

CONCLUSIONS

This chapter gives a brief introduction to recent research pertaining to luxury branding. Indeed, brevity is not difficult to achieve here, because only a few scholars have, as of yet, focused on this area. To better understand the domain of luxury, one might draw on previous research on prestige, conspicuous consumption, premium products, and so on, but luxury branding also merits a great deal of further attention. In this chapter, we have outlined some of the major issues in most immediate need of further research. Issues thus discussed pertain to the evaluation of luxury brands, processing of luxury brand information, and risks and benefits associated with luxury branding. Future research might also illuminate issues such as the possible moderating role of consumer goals on luxury brand evaluations and purchase intent, or the role of specific emotions in consumer response to luxury branding. Further, in line with recent literature (e.g., Silverstein and Fiske 2003), the current chapter emphasizes the democratization and changing face of the luxury market, with the notion that the luxury concept may apply to virtually any product category. However, future research may investigate whether new luxury and old luxury afford the same experience to consumers, and whether the inclusion of specific product types to a luxury brand may add to or detract from the favorable influence of a luxury brand proposition on, for instance, brand evaluation or purchase intent. Finally, while extant literature highlights cultural differences in the appeal of luxury (Wong and Ahuvia 1998), it seems clear that luxury also has universal appeals. Future research might disentangle cultural influences from biological predispositions in regard to luxury consumption, thus also providing insights for the strategic management of luxury brands across nations and cultures.

REFERENCES

Allsopp, Jamie (2005). "Premium Pricing: Understanding the Value of Premium," *Journal of Revenue and Pricing Management,* 4 (July), 185–194.

Amaldoss, Wilfred, and Sanjay Jain (2005). "Conspicuous Consumption and Sophisticated Thinking," *Management Science,* 51 (October), 1449–1466.

Arghavan, Nia, and Judy L. Zaichkowsky (2000). "Do Counterfeits Devalue the Ownership of Luxury Brands?" *Journal of Product and Brand Management,* 9 (7), 485–497.

Averill, James R., Petra Stanat, and Thomas A. More (1998). "Aesthetics and the Environment," *Review of General Psychology,* 2 (2), 153–174.

Bearden, William O., and Michael J. Etzel (1982). "Reference Group Influence on Product and Brand Purchase Decisions," *Journal of Consumer Research,* 9 (September), 183–194.

Belk, Russell W. (1988). "Possessions and the Extended Self," *Journal of Consumer Research,* 15 (September), 139–168.

Berry, Christopher J. (1994). *The Idea of Luxury: A Conceptual and Historical Investigation*, Cambridge, UK: Cambridge University Press.

Buchanan, Lauranne, Carolyn J. Simmons, and Barbara A. Bickart (1999). "Brand Equity Dilution: Retailer Display and Context Brand Effects," *Journal of Marketing Research,* 36 (August), 345–355.

Chartrand, Tanya L., Joel Huber, Baba Shiv, and Robin J. Tanner (2008). "Nonconscious Goals and Consumer Choice," *Journal of Consumer Research,* 35 (August), 189–201.

Chitturi, Ravindra, Rajagopal Raghunathan, and Vijay Mahajan (2008). "Delight by Design: The Role of Hedonic versus Utilitarian Benefits," *Journal of Marketing,* 72 (May), 48–63.

Danziger, Pamela N. (2005). *Let Them Eat Cake: Marketing Luxury to the Masses—As Well as the Classes.* Chicago, IL: Dearborn Trade Publishing.

Dissanayake, Ellen (1995). *Homo Aestheticus: Where Art Comes From and Why.* Seattle, WA: University of Washington Press.

Dubois, Bernard, and Patrick Duquesne (1993). "The Market for Luxury Goods: Income versus Culture," *European Journal of Marketing,* 27 (1), 35–44.

Dubois, Bernard, and Gilles Laurent (1994). "Attitudes Toward the Concept of Luxury: An Exploratory Analysis," *Asia-Pacific Advances in Consumer Research,* 1 (2), 273–278.

Dubois, Bernard, and Claire Paternault (1995). "Observations: Understanding the World of International Luxury Brands: The 'Dream Formula,'" *Journal of Advertising Research,* 35 (4), 69–76.

Frank, Robert H. (1999). *Luxury Fever.* New York, NY: The Free Press.

Garfein, Richard T. (1989). "Cross-Cultural Perspectives on the Dynamics of Prestige," *Journal of Services Marketing,* 3 (3), 17–33.

Gentry, James W., Sanjay Putrevu, Clifford Shultz, and S. Commuri (2001). "How Now Ralph Lauren? The Separation of Brand and Product in a Counterfeit Culture," *Advances in Consumer Research,* 28 (1), 258–265.

Hagtvedt, Henrik, and Vanessa M. Patrick (2008a). "The Broad Embrace of Luxury: Hedonic Potential as a Driver of Brand Extendibility." Working paper, University of Georgia.

——— (2008b). "Art Infusion: The Influence of Visual Art on the Perception and Evaluation of Consumer Products," *Journal of Marketing Research,* 45 (June), 379–389.

Herr, Paul M., Frank R. Kardes, and John Kim (1991). "Effects of Word-of-Mouth and Product-Attribute Information on Persuasion: An Accessibility-Diagnosticity Perspective," *Journal of Consumer Research,* 17 (March), 454–462.

Higgins, E. Tory (1997). "Beyond Pleasure and Pain," *American Psychologist,* 52 (December), 1280–1300.

Hirschman, Elizabeth C. (1983). "Aesthetics, Ideologies and the Limits of the Marketing Concept," *Journal of Marketing,* 47 (Summer), 45–55.

Hirschman, Elizabeth C., and Morris B. Holbrook (1982). "Hedonic Consumption: Emerging Concepts, Methods and Propositions," *Journal of Marketing,* 46 (Summer), 92–101.

Holt, Douglas B. (1995). "How Consumers Consume: A Typology of Consumption Practices," *Journal of Consumer Research,* 22 (June), 1–16.

Kapferer, Jean-Noel (1997). "Managing Luxury Brands," *Journal of Brand Management,* 4 (4), 251–260.

Kayande, Ujwal, John H. Roberts, Gary L. Lilien, and Duncan K.H. Fong (2007). "Mapping the Bounds of Incoherence: How Far Can You Go and How Does It Affect Your Brand?" *Marketing Science,* 26 (4), 504–513.

Keller, Kevin L. (1993). "Conceptualizing, Measuring, and Managing Customer-Based Brand Equity," *Journal of Marketing,* 57 (January), 1–22.

Kirmani, Amna, Sanjay Sood, and Sheri Bridges (1999). "The Ownership Effect in Consumer Responses to Brand Line Stretches," *Journal of Marketing,* 63 (1), 88–101.

Kivetz, Ran, and Itamar Simonson (2002). "Self-Control for the Righteous: Toward a Theory of Precommitment to Indulgence," *Journal of Consumer Research,* 29 (September), 199–217.

Leibenstein, Harvey (1950). "Bandwagon, Snob, and Veblen Effects in the Theory of Consumers' Demand," *Quarterly Journal of Economics,* 64 (May), 183–207.

Mandel, Naomi, Petia K. Petrova, and Robert B. Cialdini (2006). "Images of Success and the Preference for Luxury Brands," *Journal of Consumer Psychology,* 16 (1), 57–69.

Merriam-Webster (2009). "Luxury," available at http://www.merriam-webster.com/dictionary/luxury.

Nueno, Jose Luis, and John A. Quelch (1998). "The Mass Marketing of Luxury," *Business Horizons,* 41 (November/December), 61–68.

O'Cass, Aron, and Hmily Frost (2002). "Status Brands: Examining the Effects of Non-Product-Related Brand Associations on Status and Conspicuous Consumption," *Journal of Product and Brand Management,* 11 (2), 67–88.

Park, C. Whan, and Andreas B. Eisingerich (2008). "Managing a Brand's Extension Portfolio for Market Share Leadership and Shareholder Value." Working paper, University of Southern California.

Park, C. Whan, Bernard J. Jaworski, and Deborah J. MacInnis (1986). "Strategic Brand Concept-Image Management," *Journal of Marketing,* 50 (October), 135–145.

Park, C. Whan, Sandra Milberg, and Robert Lawson (1991). "Evaluation of Brand Extensions: The Role of Product Feature Similarity and Brand Concept Consistency," *Journal of Consumer Research,* 18 (September), 185–193.

Patrick, Vanessa M., Deborah J. MacInnis and C. Whan Park (2007). "Not as Happy as I Thought I'd Be: Affective Misforecasting and Product Evaluations," *Journal of Consumer Research,* 33 (4), 479–490.

Pham, Michel Tuan (1998). "Representativeness, Relevance, and the Use of Feelings in Decision Making," *Journal of Consumer Research,* 25 (September), 144–159.

Phau, Ian, and Gerard Prendergast (2000). "Consuming Luxury Brands: The Relevance of the 'Rarity Principle,'" *Journal of Brand Management,* 7 (5), 366–75.

Quelch, John A. (1987). "Marketing the Premium Product," *Business Horizons,* 30 (3), 38–45.

Rust, Roland T., Christine Moorman, and Peter R. Dickson (2002). "Getting Return on Quality: Revenue Expansion, Cost Reduction, or Both?" *Journal of Marketing,* 66 (October), 7–24.

Schwartz, John (2002). "Supersize American Dream: Expensive? I'll Take It," *The New York Times,* December 16, 8.

Schwarz, Norbert, and Gerald L. Clore (1983). "How Do I Feel About It? Informative Functions of Affective States." In *Affect, Cognition and Social Behavior,* ed. K. Fiedler and J.P. Forgas. Toronto, Ont.: Hogrefe International, 44–62.

Silverstein, Michael J., and Neil Fiske (2003). *Trading Up: The New American Luxury.* New York, NY: Portfolio Penguin Group.

Thomson, Matthew, Deborah J. MacInnis, and C. Whan Park (2005). "The Ties That Bind: Measuring the Strength of Consumers' Emotional Attachment to Brands," *Journal of Consumer Psychology,* 15(1), 77–91.

Tsai, Shu-pei (2005). "Impact of Personal Orientation on Luxury-Brand Purchase Value," *International Journal of Market Research,* 47 (4), 429–54.

Unity Marketing (2008). "Luxury Report 2008: Who Buys Luxury, What They Buy and Why They Buy." Available at http://www.unitymarketingonline.com/cms_luxury/luxury/Luxury_Report_2008.php.

Veblen, Thorstein (1899). *The Theory of the Leisure Class.* Boston, MA: Houghton Mifflin.

Vigneron, Franck, and Lester W. Johnson (2004). "Measuring Perceptions of Brand Luxury," *Brand Management,* 11 (July), 484–506.

Wong, Nancy Y., and Aaron C. Ahuvia (1998). "Personal Taste and Family Face: Luxury Consumption in Confucian and Western Societies," *Psychology and Marketing,* 15 (5), 423–441.

Yeung, Catherine W.M. and Robert S. Wyer Jr. (2004). "Affect, Appraisal, and Consumer Judgment," *Journal of Consumer Research,* 31 (September), 412–424.

——— (2005). "Does Loving a Brand Mean Loving Its Products? The Role of Brand-Elicited Affect in Brand Extension Evaluations," *Journal of Marketing Research,* 42 (November), 495–506.

PART IV

PSYCHOLOGICAL AND BEHAVIORAL EFFECTS OF STRONG BRAND RELATIONSHIPS

CHAPTER 15

ATTITUDES AS A BASIS FOR BRAND RELATIONSHIPS

The Roles of Elaboration, Metacognition, and Bias Correction

DUANE T. WEGENER, VANESSA SAWICKI, AND RICHARD E. PETTY

A CENTRAL ROLE FOR ATTITUDES IN BRAND RELATIONSHIPS

In a 1980s television ad, Brooke Shields made a famous and controversial declaration of dedication to her favorite brand of jeans, Calvin Klein. Although her statement that "nothing comes between me and my Calvins" can be taken as a double entendre, the statement most certainly also reflects her love of and commitment to her favorite jeans. This type of potentially close relationship is not limited to a model and her jeans; it may be that many consumers can identify with a strong preference for and even love of certain brands or products. In fact, this idea forms the basis for the current volume as well as a growing body of research.

Our chapter examines brand relationships from the perspective that a positive attitude toward the brand may form the core basis for that relationship. Attitudes have long played a central role in theories of relationships and relationship maintenance, even though the construct has often been called by other names. An attitude is one's overall evaluation of an object, person, or idea (e.g., Petty and Wegener 1998a). Therefore, evaluation of one's relationship partner or of the relationship itself certainly qualifies as an attitude. In the relationship domain, however, the more common label for an attitude toward the relationship is *relationship satisfaction*. That is, satisfaction is one's subjective evaluation of the relative positivity or negativity of outcomes of one's relationship (i.e., as they relate to one's general expectations, or comparison level, for relationships; Rusbult 1980). In the current chapter, we will use the terms *attitude* and *satisfaction* interchangeably, with each referring to a person's overall evaluation of the attitude object. Early in research on relationships, it was assumed that people would generally stay in satisfying relationships and leave relationships with which they were dissatisfied (Kelley and Thibaut 1978; Rusbult, 1983).[1]

However, evidence began to accumulate suggesting that people often stay in relationships even when satisfaction is low, and they also leave relationships that they find satisfying (Rusbult and Martz 1995). Such outcomes bear a resemblance to the literature on attitude-behavior relations. That is, in many studies, people's attitudes toward an object or a behavior failed to predict future behaviors; people might engage in favorable behaviors toward objects they disliked or engage in unfavorable behaviors toward objects they liked (e.g., Wicker 1969). These two literatures, on relationships and attitudes, dealt with this core issue of relations between evaluations and behaviors in some ways that were similar and in some ways that were different. We discuss these similarities and differences in the following sections.

The Measurement Approach

In the attitudes domain, a first approach to the attitude-behavior "problem" was to suggest that the problem was more a matter of inappropriate measurement than it was a lack of expected relations between psychological constructs. Fishbein and Ajzen (1974, 1975, 1977) championed this approach and suggested that many studies failing to show a substantial relation between attitudes and behavior were measuring the two constructs at different levels of specificity. There was little reason to expect, Fishbein and Ajzen suggested, that a general measure of attitude toward an object would strongly predict a specific behavior (i.e., a particular action toward the target in a particular context and at a particular time). Thus, for example, one could not expect that positive attitudes toward a particular brand of automobile would necessarily predict a particular automobile purchase (in a particular context at a particular time). However, if attitudes and behaviors are measured at the same level of correspondence (Ajzen and Fishbein 1977; later called compatibility, Ajzen 1988), then reasonably high levels of attitude-behavior consistency are generally obtained (Fishbein and Ajzen 1975). That is, although a particular purchase might not be predicted by a general attitude measure, an aggregation of all one's automobile purchases across many years might be predicted reasonably well. Similarly, a very specific attitude measure (specifying context and time) would be better at predicting a specific behavior. The late 1970s witnessed many direct demonstrations of higher correspondence (compatibility) in measures increasing attitude-behavior relations, both when specific attitudes predicted specific behaviors (e.g., Davidson and Jaccard 1979) and when more general (global) attitudes predicted general/aggregated behaviors (e.g., Weigel and Newman 1976).

On some level, measures of relationship satisfaction are naturally matched to the behavior in terms of the satisfaction measure referring specifically to the particular relationship toward which relationship-related behaviors would be directed. This fact is consistent with the generally strong relations between relationship satisfaction and commitment (Le and Agnew 2003). However, the notion of correspondence (compatibility) does suggest that a measure of general satisfaction with the relationship may be poor at predicting any specific relationship maintenance behavior (e.g., talking about a particular disagreement to seek consensus on the issue). The same general satisfaction measure might do a better job predicting an aggregate of many relationship-maintenance behaviors over time, however.

Theoretical Approaches

Multiple Predictors of Intentions

Beyond this measurement-based approach, attitude theories also took two theoretical approaches to the question of when and why attitudes predict behavior or fail to do so. One approach was to develop a theory of behavior prediction that included other variables. The two most prominent versions of this approach are the Theory of Reasoned Action (TRA; Fishbein and Ajzen 1975) and the Theory of Planned Behavior (TPB; Ajzen 1991). The TRA suggests that attitudes toward the behavior and subjective norms related to the behavior both influence behavior by first influencing intentions to perform the behavior, with intentions serving as the proximal cause of behavior. The TPB includes the same variables as the TRA but adds the person's perceived control over the behavior. The person's perceived control over the behavior can influence intentions (e.g., if the person cannot exert control over the behavior, he or she may not form intentions to perform the behavior). Also, perceived control can influence whether the person engages in behaviors that he or she intends to perform. Thus, this approach suggests that attitude-behavior relations might sometimes be weak because the normative (rather than attitudinal) factor provides a stronger influence on intentions or because some factor (such as lack of perceived behavioral control) has weakened the influence of intentions on behavior.[2]

The multiple-predictor approach is structurally similar to certain aspects of the Interdependence Theory/Investment Model approach that is common in the relationships literature (Kelley and Thibaut 1978; Rusbult 1983). That is, similar to the intention construct in the TRA and TPB (that mediates effects of attitudes on behavior), the proximal influence on relationship maintenance is hypothesized to be commitment to the relationship, with commitment including an intention to remain in the relationship (Arriaga and Agnew 2001). Satisfaction contributes to commitment (just as attitudes influence intentions), but does so alongside comparison level for alternatives (perceived benefits of being in other specific relationships) and investments (tangible and intangible benefits that one would lose if the relationship is dissolved). Thus, similar to the attitudes domain, satisfaction might fail to strongly predict relationship maintenance when alternatives are quite desirable (so that even satisfying relationships fail to engender commitment) or undesirable (so that even dissatisfying relationships seem like the best the person can get) or when investments in the relationship drive commitment (e.g., when large investments keep people in unsatisfying relationships).

The different predictors of intentions in attitude models and in relationship models provide interesting opportunities for integration across the two domains. For example, recent research suggests that subjective norms about one's relationship (i.e., what important others believe one should do about the relationship) predict relationship commitment above and beyond the traditional investment model variables (Etcheverry and Agnew 2004). Similarly, intentions to perform a variety of purchase behaviors may be predicted by the benefits people expect to receive from alternative brands (comparison level for alternatives; cf., Kardes et al. 1993; Nedungadi 1990), and costs they might accrue from switching to a new brand (investments).[3] In the investment model, satisfaction (attitude), comparison level for alternatives, and investments are typically correlated (Le and Agnew 2003). Thus, it is not surprising that in some consumer contexts, researchers might treat beliefs about how one brand compares with another as related to attitude toward the brand. However, at least within the relationships literature, it is clear that these are distinguishable constructs (see Rusbult, Martz, and Agnew 1998).

Attitude Strength as a Moderator

A second and more far-reaching approach to attitude-behavior consistency is to examine properties of attitudes that contribute to their strength, a component of which is the extent to which the attitude is capable of guiding future behavior (see Petty and Krosnick 1995). The idea behind this moderation approach is that it is often not enough that an attitude is positive toward a particular behavior. It may also be necessary that the attitude is strong enough to guide the behavior.

So even if consumers have a positive attitude toward a particular brand, they might not go out and buy the product. The stronger the attitude toward the brand, the more likely the attitude will last over time (until the point of purchase), will resist change (if attacked by an opposing brand's advertising), and will influence future thinking and behavior (see Petty, Haugtvedt, and Smith 1995; Fabrigar, MacDonald, and Wegener 2005). Many strength-related properties of attitudes have been studied (Wegener et al. 1995). For example, attitudes are stronger when the topic is of great importance to the person (Eaton and Visser 2008). So, if one can create a positive attitude toward a brand and the attitude is perceived as important to the person (e.g., because the brand supports the person's cherished values; cf., Holbrook et al. 2005), then this attitude may produce a lasting relationship with the brand (including repeated purchases, personal promotion of the brand, etc.). Thus, the goal of advertising should often be to facilitate development of strong attitudes that might create *true brand loyalty* (i.e., commitment to the brand), which can be contrasted from *spurious brand loyalty* (i.e., continued purchase by inertia, see Bloemer and Kasper 1995; cf., Chapter 3).

Some strength-related properties of an attitude may hold particular relevance for brand relationships. For example, the more *knowledge* one has about a brand, the more likely a positive attitude toward the brand will result in brand-supportive behaviors, such as purchases or publicizing the brand to others (cf., Davidson et al. 1985; Sujan, 1985). The more *accessible* an attitude is (i.e., the more quickly and easily the attitude comes to mind; Fazio 1995), the more likely the attitude will guide behaviors (e.g., Berger and Mitchell 1989; Fazio et al. 1982; for relations between accessibility and consumer behavior, see also Chapter 16). The more *certain* a person is in their attitude toward a product (Tormala and Rucker 2007), the more likely that attitude will guide consuming behavior. Certainty (confidence) will be discussed in greater detail in the subsequent section on metacognition as attitude certainty can serve as the mediator through which other variables (e.g., importance, knowledge, accessibility, etc.) exert their impact on behavior.

Some recent research on relationships shows that "strong" commitment (like strong attitudes) better predicts relationship persistence and maintenance (e.g., willingness to sacrifice, accommodative responses). That is, Etcheverry and Le (2005) found that commitment predicted relationship persistence and maintenance to a greater extent as commitment was reported more quickly in a reaction-time procedure (i.e., as relationship commitment was more accessible in memory (cf., Fazio et al. 1982). In a similar vein, it could well be that relationship commitment will better predict relationship stay-leave behaviors and maintenance when the commitment is based on higher levels of knowledge (perhaps associated with a longer time in the relationship), when the commitment is held with high certainty, or when the relationship is subjectively important to the person.

CREATING STRONG ATTITUDES: THE ELABORATION LIKELIHOOD MODEL

One factor that has much in common with many of the strength-related properties of attitudes is the extent to which people elaborate on the attitude object when forming or changing their attitudes. Elaboration is scrutiny of available attitude-relevant information in an attempt to assess the central merits of the attitude object. When people elaborate, they go beyond the information given to relate that information to existing knowledge they hold in memory (see Petty and Cacioppo 1986). Thus, when people elaborate, they gain knowledge from any new information presented, and they integrate that knowledge with previous knowledge. As a result of repeated activation and use of the attitude in processing, the attitude also becomes more accessible (see Kokkinaki and Lunt 1999; Priester and Petty 2003). Also, simply believing that one has thought carefully about the attitude object can increase one's confidence in an attitude (Barden and Petty 2008). Therefore, in part because of its many links with attitude strength, the amount of elaboration involved in attitude formation and change has become a central concern in research on persuasion (for links between elaboration and brand loyalty, see Bloemer and Kasper 1995).

A key theory that deals with the importance of elaboration is the Elaboration Likelihood Model (ELM; Petty 1977; Petty and Cacioppo 1986; Petty and Wegener 1999; see also Chaiken, Liberman, and Eagly 1989; MacInnis, Moorman, and Jaworski 1991). The ELM was developed, in part, to account for the fact that some attitudes are stronger than others (i.e., that some attitudes persist longer over time, better resist change, and provide greater influence on thinking and subsequent behavior; see Petty and Cacioppo 1986; Petty et al. 1995). In the following sections, we discuss general factors that influence how much people elaborate on available information and how specific persuasion variables can influence the valence of attitudes (and attitude strength) in different ways across different levels of elaboration.

The Elaboration Continuum

According to the ELM, people are motivated to hold accurate evaluations of attitude objects in their environment. Although this may be the default motivation, the extent to which people are willing and able to exert cognitive effort in reaching these reasonable views will vary across individuals, situations, and attitude objects. When people are motivated and able to work at evaluating the object, they will likely carefully scrutinize (elaborate on) information for its relevance to evaluation of the attitude object (e.g., tennis shoes, a vacation package, a restaurant). This scrutiny involves a careful assessment of the central merits of an attitude object, in order to reach a conclusion about the extent to which the object is good or bad.

The amount of elaboration is postulated as falling along a continuum ranging from minimal thought about product-relevant information to comprehensive elaboration and integration of all available product-relevant information. The high end of the continuum, involving complete elaboration, is referred to as the *central route* because the processing is in service of assessing the central merits of the attitude object. High levels of processing occur when motivation and ability to think are relatively high. Motivation can be high when the issue or object is important to the person (as when a product is personally relevant to the person, because the person is planning to make an imminent choice from that product class; Petty, Cacioppo, and Schumann 1983). Thus, one reason for important attitudes to be strong may be that those attitude objects receive high levels of elaboration (e.g., Blankenship and Wegener 2008; Holbrook et al. 2005; Petty and Cacioppo 1979). High levels of ability to think are present when people have the requisite knowledge to understand, interpret, and scrutinize available information (Ratneshwar and Chaiken 1991) as well as sufficient cognitive resources to be able to devote to the task of elaboration (e.g., an environment that lacks external distractions or other sources of divided attention, Petty, Wells, and Brock 1976).

At the low end of the elaboration continuum, people are said to follow the *peripheral route,* because, when elaborative processing is lacking, even factors quite peripheral to the central merits of the attitude object can influence attitudes. For example, if a restaurant is known as a place for great food, then attractiveness of the endorser in an advertisement is quite peripheral to the primary (central) qualities of the restaurant. Yet, when ad recipients lack motivation to process the ad carefully, attractiveness of the endorser can influence attitudes toward this type of restaurant (Shavitt et al. 1994; see also Petty et al. 1983).

According to the ELM, across different levels of elaboration, persuasion variables serve in different roles. The initial ELM research focused on four roles that variables can play. That is, a persuasion variable can serve as a cue when elaboration is low, can serve as an argument (i.e., information about the object's central merits) or can bias processing when elaboration is high, and can influence amount of processing when other factors in the persuasion setting do not constrain elaboration to be high or low (often with a baseline of relatively moderate elaboration). After describing these roles, we highlight a new (fifth) role that has been examined most recently.

Low Elaboration: Use of Persuasion Variables as Cues

When motivation or ability for processing is low, persuasion variables can influence attitudes by serving as a cue. In some cases, a variable may serve as a cue by simply becoming associated with the attitude object. For example, positive or negative affect might become associated with a brand or product through classical conditioning (e.g., Gorn 1982; Shimp, Stuart, and Engle 1991). This could occur when the mood state of the ad recipient colors evaluation of the product in the ad (e.g., Batra and Ray 1986; cf., Petty et al. 1993). Similarly, a variable such as mood can serve as part of a relatively simple decision rule or heuristic that suggests a certain attitude without the person having to process the merits of available information. One example of a decision rule that may be employed is the "How do I feel about it?" heuristic (Schwarz and Clore 1983; Cacioppo and Petty 1982). The idea behind this heuristic is that, when people are not thinking carefully about the attitude object (or when full scrutiny of all relevant information would be too costly to be worth the effort; Schwarz 1990), they may simply consult their feelings and assume that their current feelings reflect their reactions to the attitude object (when, in fact, their feelings may be attributable to the context surrounding the advertisement).

Many different persuasion factors have been studied in their role as cues (for reviews, see Petty and Wegener 1998a; Wegener and Carlston 2005). These factors include various source characteristics, such as expertise (e.g., Petty, Cacioppo, and Goldman 1981; Ratneshwar and Chaiken 1991), attractiveness (e.g., Kang and Herr 2006; Petty et al. 1983), and likeability (e.g., Chaiken 1980; Kahle and Homer 1985); message characteristics, such as length/sheer number of arguments (e.g., Petty and Cacioppo, 1984; see also Alba and Marmorstein1987); and contextual factors, such as audience support/consensus (Axsom, Yates, and Chaiken 1987).

From an attitude strength point of view, the downside of cue effects is that the attitudes that result from these processes do not tend to have lasting impact. A number of studies of persistence over time or resistance to counterpersuasion have compared low-elaboration cue effects of source characteristics or number of arguments with high-elaboration effects of message arguments, and high-elaboration argument effects produce stronger attitudes (e.g., Haugtvedt and Petty 1992; see Petty et al. 1995; Wegener et al. 2004). In recent research comparing low- and high-elaboration effects of the same variable (such as group membership in an impression-formation paradigm or numerical anchors), however, the high-elaboration effects continue to result in perceptions that last longer over time and better resist attempts at social influence (Blankenship et al. 2008; Wegener, Clark, and Petty 2006). This suggests that low-elaboration cue effects of a variable such as source expertise would also persist less over time or resist change less well than the same favorable attitudes produced by the high-elaboration (biased processing) effects of source expertise (see Chaiken and Maheswaran 1994).

High Elaboration: Persuasion Variables Scrutinized as Arguments and Biasing Processing of Available Information

When elaboration is high (i.e., with high motivation and ability to think), people scrutinize available information for its relevance to the attitude object's *central merits* (i.e., the primary qualities that determine whether the object or position is desirable or undesirable). When people are thinking carefully about the attitude object, people can consider many of the same persuasion variables that served as cues when elaboration was low (e.g., an expert source or their own positive mood). In contrast, however, when elaboration is higher, message recipients assess whether that variable constitutes a good reason to view the attitude object positively. In at least some cases, the variable itself is viewed as a central merit of the attitude object (i.e., as an argument for support of the object). For example, when evaluating the quality of a roller coaster or the quality of a potential dating partner, an individual's feelings may be viewed as highly relevant to the merits of choosing that roller coaster or that person. Similarly, a person's ethnicity or gender might be viewed as quite peripheral to some decisions about the person, but in other circumstances, the same qualities might be viewed as central and important (e.g., when choosing members of a committee where ethnic or gender balance is important).

Depending on the value of the given persuasion variable, the outcome of high-elaboration assessments of central merits might result in either favorable or unfavorable attitudes toward the attitude object. From an attitude strength position, however, the benefit of creating positive attitudes toward a brand through this route is that the positive attitudes should be stronger than those created by low-elaboration use of the variable as a cue (all else being equal).

Serving as a central merit of the attitude object is not the only high-elaboration way in which persuasion variables can influence attitudes, however. When people are thinking carefully, the persuasion variable can also bias the thoughts that come to mind. The use of the term *bias* should not necessarily be taken to denote less accuracy. In this instance, bias simply refers to a slanting of interpretation or emphasis to provide greater support for one of two or more equally plausible assessments of the attitude object. To be sure, biased interpretations cannot all be equally accurate. However, it would not necessarily be true that positive moods would always lead to judgments that are too positive or that negative moods would always lead to judgments that are too negative. There may be relative differences between the mood states that can be referred to as a mood-based bias in thinking (e.g., Petty et al. 1993), but locating which perceptions differ from a no-bias control would often require additional conditions that are not present in a particular study.

Some biases in processing may be primarily cognitive in nature. For example, the persuasion variable might simply activate a construct or idea that guides the processing. In one possible instance of this, Krosnick and Kinder (1990) showed that media coverage of the Iran-Contra affair in the 1980s influenced people's use of knowledge related to intervention in Central America when evaluating the performance of President Reagan (see also Sherman, Mackie, and Driscoll 1990; Yi 1990).

Other biases may be more motivational, however. For example, the person might want to maintain a positive self-view or might want to support an existing attitude. Of course, in each of these cases, it might often be that one's existing self-views or existing attitude might also activate knowledge that supports the existing view. This may make it difficult to argue clearly for a motivational rather than cognitive bias (cf., Clark 2005; Kunda 1990; Tetlock and Levi 1982). A number of variables common in consumer settings might bring about biases in processing that have both cognitive and motivational components. For example, the moods or emotions of message recipients might activate certain material in memory or might motivate efforts to manage the feelings (e.g., Isen

1987; Wegener, Petty, and Smith 1995). People might tend to agree with an expert message source because of knowledge that makes the person seem more likely to be correct or because of motives to identify with successful people (cf., Hovland, Janis, and Kelley 1953; DeBono and Harnish 1988). When one wishes to claim support for a motivational rather than cognitive explanation of the bias, it may be especially important to at least measure the presumed motives in order to support the motivational part of the bias (see Clark and Wegener 2008).

Biased processing is most likely to occur when product-relevant information is ambiguous or unclear (Chaiken and Maheswaran 1994; Ha and Hoch 1989). Therefore, manipulations of ambiguity of accompanying information might be one way to distinguish between high-elaboration effects that are due to biased processing and those that are due to the persuasion variable representing a central merit of the attitude object.

For both types of high-elaboration effects, the resulting attitudes should generally be stronger than effects of the same variables via their use as simple persuasion cues. This is because the high-elaboration attitudes should be more cognitively interconnected with existing knowledge, they should be more accessible in memory, and they should be associated with confidence and other perceptions that the attitude has merit (see Petty and Cacioppo 1986; Petty et al. 1995).

Moderate Background Levels of Elaboration: Persuasion Variables Influencing Amount of Information Processing

According to the ELM, a fourth role a variable can play is to affect how much people process attitude-relevant information when other factors in the persuasion setting do not constrain levels of motivation and ability to be especially high or low (i.e., when background elaboration likelihood is relatively moderate). For example, if a person is unsure whether processing available information is worth the effort, then additional variables in the persuasion setting might "tip the scales" to increase or decrease motivation to put effort into thinking about the brand or product.

A number of variables influence amount of processing when elaboration likelihood is moderate even though they serve as cues when motivation or ability is lacking and/or bias processing when elaboration likelihood is high. Some of the effects discovered so far are reasonably simple and "unidirectional." For example, messages that match rather than mismatch the functional basis of one's attitudes can increase message processing (e.g., Petty and Wegener 1998b). In many, if not most, cases, however, these effects are probably moderated by additional factors in the persuasion setting. Some examples of these higher-order effects include that high self-monitors (Snyder 1974) are more likely to process a message from an attractive (but nonexpert) source, whereas low self-monitors are more likely to process a message from an expert (but unattractive) source (DeBono and Harnish 1988). Also, although early research suggested that positive moods decreased processing of persuasive communications (e.g., Batra and Stayman 1990; Kuykendall and Keating 1990; Schwarz, Bless, and Bohner 1991), later research showed that positive mood can increase processing (if processing will help to maintain the positive state) or decrease processing (if processing will remove the positive state; see Wegener et al. 1995). Positive mood can also increase processing if the processing will help the message recipient maximize his or her long-term hedonic outcomes (i.e., if the processing serves long-term mood management; see Chen et al. 2005; Raghunathan and Trope 2002).

When a variable increases processing, this is more important from an attitude strength point of view than when the same variable increases favorability toward the attitude object through low-elaboration use as a cue. This is because the attitude resulting from the cue effect is likely to have less lasting impact than the attitude resulting from the higher level of processing. If the two attitudes are equally favorable after the message, then this would suggest that the attitude from the high-processing condition will be likely to last longer over time, to better resist attempts at change, and to have greater influence on future brand-relevant thinking and behavior.

Summary of Four Roles for Variables

According to the ELM, a given persuasion variable can influence attitudes in different ways across different levels of elaboration. Four potential roles were described: A variable can serve as a relatively simple cue when motivation or ability to think is lacking. A variable can influence motivation or ability to think, thereby influencing the extent of elaboration (especially if other factors in the persuasion setting do not constrain motivation or ability to be high or low). A variable can represent a central merit of the attitude object that is assessed when motivation and ability to think are high. Finally, a variable can bias the effortful processing that occurs when motivation and ability are high, especially if available information is open to alternative interpretations.

It is important to note that the same variable (e.g., source attractiveness, message recipient mood) could serve any of these different roles depending on the situation and could, therefore, ultimately lead to attitudes with different consequences over time. This does not mean that an attitude reached via the central route (high elaboration) is necessarily different in valence or is more extreme compared with an attitude reached via the peripheral route (low elaboration). High- and low-elaboration attitudes could be equally favorable or unfavorable toward the attitude object (e.g., the brand). The difference in consequences is that an attitude based on thorough elaboration of product-relevant information should persist over time, resist counterattack, and affect future thinking and behavior to a greater extent than an attitude based on only cursory thought about the product or brand. If so, then positive attitudes that come from low-elaboration cue effects are also less likely to result in the desired type of lasting and supportive brand relationship.

THE ROLE OF METACOGNITION IN PERSUASION AND ATTITUDE STRENGTH

Although ELM research originally focused on the four roles discussed previously (i.e., argument, cue, influence on amount of processing, and bias in processing), a fifth role for persuasion variables postulated by the ELM—affecting the structure of cognitions—has been investigated recently. Although variables might affect various structural aspects of thoughts such as their accessibility, much recent attention has been paid to metacognitive aspects of thoughts (i.e., thoughts about thoughts) that can influence the extent of attitude change and attitude strength. After describing research dealing with metacognitions about thoughts to a persuasive message, we turn to metacognitions about the attitude itself (see Petty et al. 2007).

Using an attitude toward the brand as an example, the attitude can be thought of as a primary cognition (e.g., "I like Brand X"). If so, then a metacognition reflects a second-ary cognition about the primary cognition (e.g., "I am sure that I like Brand X" or "it is undesirable to like Brand X"). A number of dimensions of metacognition parallel those for primary cognition. That is, a person can have thoughts about (1) the *target* of the thought (what the thought is perceived to be about), (2) the *origin* of the thought (from where the thought came), (3) the *valence* of the thought (whether the thought reflects something positive or negative about the target), and (4) the *amount* of thoughts (extent of thinking). In addition, some dimensions of metacognition go beyond these typical dimensions for primary thoughts (Petty et al. 2006). Two metacognitions that have received the most empirical attention are *evaluation* of a thought (whether it is a good thought to have) and *confidence* in thoughts (which can include confidence that one holds a particular thought, or confidence that a thought is correct or reasonable, see Petrocelli, Tormala, and Rucker 2007).

Before reviewing relevant work on metacognition, it is worth noting that the different types of metacognition are likely to be correlated in many settings. For example, thoughts whose origin is perceived to be the self are likely to be evaluated more favorably (Green-wald and Albert 1968; Wheeler, DeMarree, and Petty 2007) and perceptions that one has thought a lot about an issue can lead one to be more confident in the primary thoughts that arose from that processing (Barden and Petty 2008).

Effects of Confidence on Attitude Change

In addition to the four roles for variables in persuasion situations already reviewed, re-cent research has addressed a fifth role that variables can play to influence the extent of persuasion, that is affecting the confidence or doubt that people have in the thoughts they generate to the message. Most of this research has addressed the *self-validation hypothesis* (Petty, Briñol, and Tormala 2002), that increasing confidence in thoughts increases their impact on attitudes but increasing doubt in one's thoughts decreases their impact on at-titudes. Thus, when people are thinking positive thoughts, their attitudes should be more favorable to the extent that people hold the thoughts with confidence. But when people are thinking negative thoughts, their attitudes should be less favorable to the extent that people hold the thoughts with confidence. The reverse is true for doubt. Research supports the self-validation hypothesis regardless of whether the thought confidence is measured or manipulated by having people think about previous experiences of certainty or doubt or by telling people that their thoughts are similar or dissimilar to those listed by peers (Petty et al. 2002).

A number of traditional persuasion variables have also influenced thought confidence and, therefore, attitudes. For example, people hold their thoughts with more confidence when nodding their head up and down rather than shaking it side to side (Briñol and Petty 2003), when learning that a previous message came from an expert rather than nonexpert source (Briñol, Petty, and Tormala 2004), and when placed in a happy rather than sad mood following the message (Briñol, Petty, and Barden 2007). Consistent with the idea that metacognition is more likely when motivation and ability to think are high, the metacognitive effects of head nodding, source expertise, and mood were also shown to be more likely under conditions of high than of low elaboration.

The logic of self-validation may also help to explain certain persuasion effects that have previously been attributed to fluency. For example, Lee and Aaker (2004) showed that messages that matched individuals' promotion or prevention focus were viewed as easier to process and were more persuasive. It could be that the matching messages led to thoughts that were held with greater confidence than mismatching messages and this led to the greater persuasion (assuming that thoughts were generally favorable; see Petty et al. 2007, for additional discussion of this effect and of more general issues relating metacognition and persuasion processes).

Persuasion Variables and Attitude Confidence

A sense of certainty or uncertainty could presumably apply to almost any aspect of one's judgments or perceptions (Tormala and Rucker 2007). When certainty is applied to one's thoughts, it can affect the extent of persuasion. Despite a recent surge of studies on thought confidence, the majority of attention in social psychology has been to confidence in the validity of one's attitudes or perceptions of objects. For example, when one is not sufficiently certain that one's attitude is "correct," persuasion models predict, and research has shown, that message recipients can increase elaboration of available information (e.g., Chaiken et al. 1989; Petty et al. 2006; Tiedens and Linton 2001). Presumably, this increase in processing is aimed at increasing confidence in one's attitude (whether it means changing one's attitude to make it more defensible or gathering additional evidence to bolster one's current point of view). On the other hand, when people are already confident in their attitudes, it may not be necessary to engage in additional processing. Instead, the attitude held with certainty possesses a number of qualities associated with strong attitudes. That is, the attitude is likely to persist over time (Bassili 1996), to resist change (Tormala and Petty 2002), and to guide behavior (Berger and Mitchell 1989; Fazio and Zanna 1978).

Certainty in thoughts or attitudes can be influenced by many factors, including direct experience with the attitude object (Berger and Mitchell 1989; Fazio and Zanna 1981), repeated expression of the attitude (Holland, Verplanken, and van Knippenberg 2003), ease of generating attitude-consistent thoughts (Haddock et al. 1999; Tormala, Petty, and Briñol 2002), and consensual support for one's attitude (Visser and Mirabile 2004). Because persuasive messages can influence attitude valence and extremity, it should not be surprising that various qualities of persuasive messages and settings can also influence the certainty with which people hold their attitudes.

Effects on Confidence of Resistance Success and Resistance Failure

Traditional views of attitudes suggest that a message that does not change one's report of the attitude has had no effect. However, in a series of studies, Tormala and Petty have shown that the persuasive attempt might have important consequences even when message recipients seem to have completely resisted the claims of the persuasive message. For example, when people believe they have resisted strong arguments (Tormala and Petty 2002) or an expert source (Tormala and Petty 2004b), they are more certain of their attitudes. However, when people believe that they have resisted weak arguments or a nonexpert source, attitude certainty can actually decrease. These effects occur when message recipients consider the implications of their own resistance in the context of the qualities of the persuasive appeal. Also, when people believe that they have resisted in some flawed or illegitimate way, attitude certainty can decrease (Tormala, Clarkson, and Petty 2006; Tormala, Petty, and DeSensi in press). Consistent with the idea that metacognition is more likely to occur when motivation and ability to think are high, Tormala and Petty (2004a) showed that these effects of resistance on confidence were more likely when message recipients were high in need for cognition (Cacioppo and Petty 1982) or when the persuasive message was high in personal relevance (Petty and Cacioppo 1990).

Just as successful resistance can have implications for attitude certainty, so can failed attempts at resistance. Rucker and Petty (2004) asked research participants to find fault with a persuasive message (an ad for a pain reliever), but created arguments that were so strong that they were not vulnerable to counterarguments. Ad recipients who could not generate reasonable counterarguments when trying to do so were actually more convinced that their new (post-ad) attitude was valid compared with people who processed the message without the goal of counterarguing it.

Evaluation-Based Metacognition and Bias Correction

In many circumstances, people may come to view their thoughts or reactions as bad, unwanted, or inappropriate. When this happens, they may attempt to change or *correct* their thoughts or reactions, or they might try to limit effects of their reactions on subsequent judgments or behavior. For example, attempts to correct for the undue negative influences of an illegitimate source may play a role when people are more open to persuasion after resisting a minority source (Tormala et al. in press).

A number of theories have been developed to address attempts at bias correction (see Petty et al. 2007; Wegener and Petty 1997, 2001). According to the flexible correction model (FCM; Wegener and Petty 1997), attempts at bias correction are guided by perceivers' use of naïve theories of biases potentially at work (see also Petty and Wegener 1993; Strack 1992; Wilson and Brekke 1994). That is, corrections occur when perceivers are motivated and able to identify potential biases and correct for the perceived influences of those biases. According to the FCM, a given theory-based correction is likely to guide corrections to the extent that it is perceived to facilitate the perceiver's goal, is applicable to the time and setting, and is accessible in memory.

Similar to other types of metacognition, theory-based corrections are more likely to occur under high rather than low thinking conditions, all else being equal (e.g., DeSteno et al. 2000; Sczesny and Kühnen 2004). Over time, however, a particular correction might become well practiced and occur with less effort (cf., Glaser and Banaji 1999; Maddux et al. 2005).

Research guided by the FCM has shown that people correct their judgments in different directions when they hold opposite theories of bias, even when they are for different people perceiving the same context and target (Wegener and Petty 1995). People correct for perceived biases, even if there is no real bias (e.g., Wegener and Petty 1995). These corrections can then ironically create the opposite bias. One example of this type of effect is when people correct for perceived negativity toward the dislikeable source of a persuasive message. When the dislikeable source is encountered under high-elaboration conditions, little impact of source likeability is observed (as in Chaiken 1980). However, corrections for perceived negative influences of the dislikeable source can lead to more favorable attitudes than when the source was likeable (Petty, Wegener, and White 1998; see also Schul and Goren 1997).

Correction for perceived rather than real bias also means that people sometimes correct for one bias but leave others to influence their perceptions. For example, Sczesny and Kühnen (2004) found that people believe that gender can bias judgments of leadership qualities, but do not realize that physical features of masculine versus feminine appearance can have similar effects. Therefore, when encountering mock application materials that included photos, research participants corrected for gender but not for physical appearance when they had sufficient cognitive resources for corrections to occur. When cognitive load was high (and metacognitive activity should be reduced), research participants were more likely to hire male than female applicants and those with masculine rather than feminine appearance. However, when cognitive load was low (and corrections were more likely), research participants actually hired more female than male applicants, even though their preference for masculine rather than feminine applicants remained.

When forming or changing perceptions under high-thinking conditions, there could also be correction-related effects that parallel traditional ELM patterns. For example, initial perceptions that are formed in thoughtful ways might prove to be more resistant not only to external messages (e.g., Wegener et al. 2004) but also to more internal metacognitive analyses of whether corrections are needed. At times, high levels of initial thinking might make biases less likely to be identified as such and corrected (Petty and Wegener 1993). High levels of elaboration should lead to a great deal of integration of perceptions with existing knowledge (Petty and Cacioppo 1986). Depending on the type of knowledge related to the target, the highly integrated view of the target may seem justified by the existing information. If so, then people may view their opinions of the target as relatively appropriate and unbiased. Of course, this would undermine any perceived need to correct one's view of the target (see Wegener, Clark, and Petty 2006; see also Schul and Burnstein, 1985). High levels of integration could also spread the bias across many disparate perceptions, making identification of the bias more difficult.

SUMMARY

Brand relationships are likely to begin with positive attitudes toward the brand, and these relationships are likely to be maintained, at least in part, as a result of these positive attitudes being strong (i.e., persisting over time, resisting attempts at change, and guiding thoughts and behaviors related to the brand). This makes formation of strong positive attitudes a very important goal for communications about the brand. Much research in the area of attitudes has addressed features of attitudes that make them strong, and many of these features are tied to the amount of elaboration in which people engage when they receive attitude-relevant (in this case, brand-relevant) information.

The ELM specifies multiple roles for persuasion variables that operate across different levels of elaboration likelihood. A given persuasion variable may be able to act as a simple cue when elaboration likelihood is low or as a central merit of the attitude object (i.e., as an argument) when elaboration likelihood is high. The persuasion variable may also bias processing of brand-relevant information when elaboration likelihood is high and may affect the confidence in the thoughts generated. The biasing effect of variables is more likely when the variable precedes message processing, but an impact on thought confidence is more likely when the variable is salient following thought generation. Finally, variables can affect the level of elaboration likelihood when other background factors do not constrain elaboration likelihood to be high or low. From an attitude strength perspective, it would be the argument, biased processing, self-validation, and amount of processing roles that have the greatest potential for creating lasting brand relationships.

In addition to affecting thought confidence, recent research and theory on metacognition suggests how attitudes can be strengthened through metacognitive processes. A number of different metacognitions have been studied. Of greatest relevance to the current discussion, persuasion variables can influence how confident people are in their attitudes following a persuasive appeal, and these metacognitions can determine how strong or weak the resulting attitudes are. Finally, persuasion variables can also serve as biases that people wish to avoid. These corrections can sometimes reduce the judgmental impact of the perceived biases, but corrections for perceived biases that are not real can also ironically create the opposite bias.

NOTES

1. Similarly, consumer researchers sometimes talk about product satisfaction/dissatisfaction rather than product attitudes to describe effects of positive or negative behavioral experiences with the product or brand (e.g., Churchill and Surprenant 1982), and it is generally assumed that consumers will tend to stay with products with which they are satisfied and be motivated to switch when dissatisfied (e.g., Oliver 1980).

2. Other models of behavior prediction have also included other predictor variables, such as habits (see Chapter 3).

3. The concept of investment might also be related to some aspects of the concept of perceived behavioral control in the Theory of Planned Behavior (Ajzen 1991).

REFERENCES

Ajzen, Icek (1988). *Attitudes, Personality, and Behavior.* Chicago, IL: Dorsey.
——— (1991). "The Theory of Planned Behavior," *Organizational Behavior and Human Decision Processes,* 50, 179–211.
Ajzen, Icek, and Martin Fishbein (1977). "Attitude-Behavior Relations: A Theoretical Analysis and Review of Empirical Research," *Psychological Bulletin,* 84, 888–918.
Alba, Joseph M., and Howard Marmorstein (1987). "The Effects of Frequency Knowledge on Consumer Decision Making," *Journal of Consumer Research,* 14, 14–25.
Arriaga, Ximena B., and Christopher R. Agnew (2001). "Being Committed: Affective, Cognitive, and Conative Components of Relationship Commitment," *Personality and Social Psychology Bulletin,* 27 (9), 1190–1203.
Axsom, Danny, Suzanne M. Yates, and Shelly Chaiken (1987). "Audience Response as a Heuristic Cue in Persuasion," *Journal of Personality and Social Psychology,* 53, 30–40.
Barden, Jamie, and Richard E. Petty (2008). "The Mere Perception of Elaboration Creates Attitude Certainty: Exploring the Thoughtfulness Heuristic," *Journal of Personality and Social Psychology,* 95, 489–509.
Bassili, John N. (1996). "Meta-Judgmental Versus Operative Indexes of Psychological Attributes: The Case of Measures of Attitude Strength," *Journal of Personality and Social Psychology,* 7 (4), 637–653.
Batra, Rajeev, and Michael L. Ray (1986). "Situational Effects of Advertising Repetition: The Moderating Influence of Motivation, Ability, and Opportunity to Respond," *Journal of Consumer Research,* 12 (4), 432–445.
Batra, Rajeev, and Douglas M. Stayman (1990). "The Role of Mood in Advertising Effectiveness," *Journal of Consumer Research,* 17 (2), 203–214.
Berger, Ida E., and Andrew A. Mitchell (1989). "The Effect of Advertising on Attitude Accessibility, Attitude Confidence, and the Attitude-Behavior Relationship," *Journal of Consumer Research,* 16, 269–279.
Blankenship, Kevin L., and Duane T. Wegener (2008). "Opening the Mind to Close it: Considering a Message in Light of Important Values Increases Message Processing and Later Resistance to Change," *Journal of Personality and Social Psychology,* 94, 196–213.
Blankenship, Kevin L., Duane T. Wegener, Richard E. Petty, Brian T. Detweiler-Bedell, and Cheryl L. Macy (2008). "Elaboration and Consequences of Anchored Estimates: An Attitudinal Perspective on Numerical Anchoring," *Journal of Experimental Social Psychology,* 55 (6), 1465–1476.
Bloemer, José M.M., and Hans D.P. Kasper (1995). "The Complex Relationship between Consumer Satisfaction and Brand Loyalty," *Journal of Economic Psychology,* 16 (2), 311–329.
Briñol, Pablo, and Richard E. Petty (2003). "Overt Head Movements and Persuasion: A Self-Validation Analysis," *Journal of Personality and Social Psychology,* 84, 1123–1139.
Briñol, Pablo, Richard E. Petty, and Jamie Barden (2007). "Happiness versus Sadness as a Determinant of Thought Confidence in Persuasion: A Self-Validation Analysis," *Journal of Personality and Social Psychology,* 93, 712–727.
Briñol, Pablo, Richard E. Petty, and Zakary L. Tormala (2004). "The Self-Validation of Cognitive Responses to Advertisements," *Journal of Consumer Research,* 31, 559–573.
Cacioppo, John T., and Richard E. Petty (1982). "The Need for Cognition," *Journal of Personality and Social Psychology,* 42, 116–131.
Chaiken, Shelly (1980). "Heuristic Versus Systematic Information Processing in the Use of Source Versus Message Cues in Persuasion," *Journal of Personality and Social Psychology,* 39, 752–766.
Chaiken, Shelly, Akiva Liberman, and Alice H. Eagly (1989). "Heuristic and Systematic Information Processing within and beyond the Persuasive Context." In *Unintended Thought,* ed. J.S. Uleman and J.A. Bargh. New York, NY: Guilford, 214–246.

Chaiken, Shelly, and Durairaj Maheswaran (1994). "Heuristic Processing Can Bias Systematic Processing: Effects of Source Credibility, Argument Ambiguity, and Task Importance on Attitude Judgment," *Journal of Personality and Social Psychology,* 66, 460–473.

Chen, Zhansheng, Hyewook Jeong, Duane T. Wegener, Richard E. Petty, and Stephen M. Smith (2005). "Mood as a Conditional Resource: Long-Term Mood Management in Processing of Persuasive Communication," Paper presented at the 77th annual meeting of the Midwestern Psychological Association, Chicago, IL, May.

Churchill, Gilbert A., and Carol Surprenant (1982). "An Investigation into the Determinants of Customer Satisfaction," *Journal of Marketing Research,* 19 (4), 491–504.

Clark, Jason K. (2005). "Outcome Dependency and Impression Formation: Differentiating Biased from Objective Processing of Goal-Relevant Information," Unpublished master's thesis, Purdue University.

Clark, Jason K., and Duane T. Wegener (2008). "Unpacking Outcome Dependency: Differentiating Effects of Dependency and Outcome Desirability on the Processing of Goal-Relevant Information," *Journal of Experimental Social Psychology,* 44, 586–599.

Davidson, Andrew R., and James J. Jaccard (1979). "Variables that Moderate the Attitude-Behavior Relation: Results of a Longitudinal Survey," *Journal of Personality and Social Psychology,* 37, 1364–1376.

Davidson, Andrew R., Steven Yantis, Marel Norwood, and Daniel E. Montano (1985). "Amount of Information about the Attitude Object and Attitude-Behavior Consistency," *Journal of Personality and Social Psychology,* 49, 1184–1198.

DeBono, Kenneth G., and Richard J. Harnish (1988). "Source Expertise, Source Attractiveness, and the Processing of Persuasive Information: A Functional Approach," *Journal of Personality and Social Psychology,* 55, 541–546.

DeSteno, David, Richard E. Petty, Duane T. Wegener, and Derek D. Rucker (2000). "Beyond Valence in the Perception of Likelihood: The Role of Emotion Specificity," *Journal of Personality and Social Psychology,* 78, 397–416.

Eaton, Asia, and Penny Visser (2008). "Attitude Importance: Understanding the Causes and Consequences of Passionately Held Views," *Social and Personality Psychology Compass,* 2, 1719–1736.

Etcheverry, Paul E., and Christopher R. Agnew (2004). "Subjective Norms and the Prediction of Romantic Relationship State and Fate," *Personal Relationships,* 11, 409–428.

Etcheverry, Paul E., and Benjamin Le (2005). "Thinking about Commitment: Accessibility of Commitment and Prediction of Relationship Persistence, Accommodation, and Willingness to Sacrifice," *Personal Relationships,* 12 (1), 103–123.

Fabrigar, Leandre R., Tara MacDonald, and Duane T. Wegener (2005). "The Structure of Attitudes." In *The Handbook of Attitudes,* ed. D. Albarracin, B. Johnson, and M. Zanna. Mahwah, NJ: Lawrence Erlbaum, 79–124.

Fazio, Russell H. (1995). "Attitudes as Object-Evaluation Associations: Determinants, Consequences, and Correlates of Attitude Accessibility." In *Attitude Strength: Antecedents and Consequences,* ed. R.E. Petty and J.A. Krosnick. Mahwah, NJ: Lawrence Erlbaum, 247–282.

Fazio, Russell H., Jeaw-mei Chen, Elizabeth C. McDonel, and Steven J. Sherman (1982). "Attitude Accessibility, Attitude-Behavior Consistency, and the Strength of the Object-Evaluation," *Journal of Experimental Social Psychology,* 8 (4), 339–357.

Fazio, Russell H., and Mark P. Zanna (1978). "On the Predictive Validity of Attitudes: The Roles of Direct Experience and Confidence," *Journal of Personality,* 46 (2), 228–243.

——— (1981). "Direct Experience and Attitude-Behavior Consistency." In *Advances in Experimental Social Psychology* (vol. 14), ed. L. Berkowitz. San Diego, CA: Academic Press, 161–202.

Fishbein, Martin, and Icek Ajzen (1974). "Attitudes toward Objects as Predictors of Single and Multiple Behavioral Criteria," *Psychological Review,* 81, 59–74.

——— (1975). *Belief, Attitude, Intention, and Behavior: An Introduction to Theory and Research.* Reading, MA: Addison-Wesley.

——— (1977). "Attitude-behavior Relations: A Theoretical Analysis and Review of Empirical Research," *Psychological Bulletin,* 84 (5), 888–918.

Glaser, Jack, and Mahzarin R. Banaji (1999). "When Fair is Foul and Foul is Fair: Reverse Priming in Automatic Evaluation," *Journal of Personality and Social Psychology,* 77, 669–687.

Gorn, Gerald. J. (1982). "The Effects of Music in Advertising on Choice Behavior: A Classical Conditioning Approach," *Journal of Marketing,* 46, 94–101.

Greenwald, Anthony G., and R.D. Albert (1968). "Acceptance and Recall of Improvised Arguments," *Journal of Personality and Social Psychology,* 8, 31–34.

Ha, Young-Won, and Stephen J. Hoch (1989). "Ambiguity, Processing Strategy, and Advertising-Evidence Interactions," *Journal of Consumer Research,* 16, 354–360.

Haddock, Geoffrey, Alexander J. Rothman, Rolf Reber, and Norbert Schwarz (1999). "Forming Judgments of Attitude Certainty, Intensity, and Importance: The Role of Subjective Experiences," *Personality and Social Psychology Bulletin,* 25, 771–782.

Haugtvedt, Curtis P., and Richard E. Petty (1992). "Personality and Persuasion: Need for Cognition Moderates the Persistence and Resistance of Attitude Changes," *Journal of Personality and Social Psychology,* 63, 308–319.

Holbrook, Allison L., Matthew K. Berent, Jon A. Krosnick, Penny S. Visser, and David S. Boninger (2005). "Attitude Importance and the Accumulation of Attitude- Relevant Knowledge in Memory," *Journal of Personality and Social Psychology,* 88 (5), 749–769.

Holland, Rob W., Bas Verplanken, and Ad van Knippenberg (2003). "From Repetition to Conviction: Attitude Accessibility as a Determinant of Attitude Certainty," *Journal of Experimental Social Psychology,* 39, 594–601.

Hovland, Carl I., Irving L. Janis, and Harold H. Kelley (1953). *Communication and Persuasion: Psychological Studies of Opinion Change.* New Haven, CT: Yale University Press.

Isen, Alice M. (1987). "Positive Affect, Cognitive Processes, and Social Behavior." In *Advances in Experimental Social Psychology* (vol. 20), ed. L. Berkowitz. San Diego, CA: Academic Press, 203–253.

Kahle, Lynn R., and Pamela M. Homer (1985). "Physical Attractiveness of the Celebrity Endorser: A Social Adaptation Perspective," *Journal of Consumer Research,* 11, 954–961.

Kang, Yong-Soon, and Paul M. Herr (2006). "Beauty and the Beholder: Toward an Integrative Model of Communication Source Effects," *Journal of Consumer Research,* 33, 123–130.

Kardes, Frank R., Gurumurthy Kalyanaram, Murali Chandrashekaran, and Ronald J. Dornoff (1993). "Brand Retrieval, Consideration Set Composition, Consumer Choice, and the Pioneering Advantage," *Journal of Consumer Research,* 20, 62–75.

Kelley, Harold H., and John W. Thibaut (1978). *Interpersonal Relations: A Theory of Interdependence.* New York, NY: Wiley.

Kokkinaki, Flora, and Peter Lunt (1999). "The Effect of Advertising Message Involvement on Brand Attitude Accessibility," *Journal of Economic Psychology,* 20, 41–51.

Krosnick, Jon A., and Donald R. Kinder (1990). "Altering the Foundations of Support for the President through Priming," *American Political Science Review,* 84, 497–512.

Kunda, Ziva (1990). "The Case for Motivated Reasoning," *Psychological Bulletin,* 108, 480–498.

Kuykendall, David, and John P. Keating (1990). "Mood and Persuasion: Evidence for the Differential Influence of Positive and Negative States," *Psychology and Marketing,* 7 (1), 1–9.

Le, Benjamin, and Christopher R. Agnew (2003). "Commitment and its Theorized Determinants: A Meta–Analysis of the Investment Model," *Personal Relationships,* 10 (1), 37–57.

Lee, Angela Y., and Jennifer L. Aaker (2004). "Bringing the Frame into Focus: The Influence of Regulatory Fit on Processing Fluency and Persuasion," *Journal of Personality and Social Psychology,* 86, 205–218.

MacInnis, Deborah J., Christine Moorman, and Bernard J. Jaworski (1991). "Enhancing and Measuring Consumers' Motivation, Opportunity, and Ability to Process Brand Information from Ads," *Journal of Marketing,* 55, 32–53.

Maddux, William W., Jamie Barden, Marilynn B. Brewer, and Richard E. Petty (2005). "Saying No to Negativity: The Effects of Context and Motivation to Control Prejudice on Automatic Evaluative Responses," *Journal of Experimental Social Psychology,* 41, 19–35.

Nedungadi, Prakash (1990). "Recall and Consumer Consideration Sets: Influencing Choice without Altering Brand Evaluations," *Journal of Consumer Research,* 17, 263–276.

Oliver, Richard L. (1980). "A Cognitive Model of the Antecedents and Consequences of Satisfaction Decisions," *Journal of Marketing Research,* 17 (4), 460–469.

Petrocelli, John V., Zakary L. Tormala, and Derek D. Rucker (2007). "Unpacking Attitude Certainty: Attitude Clarity and Attitude Correctness," *Journal of Personality and Social Psychology,* 92, 30–41.

Petty, Richard E. (1977). *A Cognitive Response Analysis of the Temporal Persistence of Attitude Changes Induced by Persuasive Communications.* Doctoral dissertation, Ohio State University, Columbus, Ohio.

Petty, Richard E., Pablo Briñol, and Zakary L. Tormala (2002). "Thought Confidence as a Determinant of Persuasion: The Self-Validation Hypothesis," *Journal of Personality and Social Psychology,* 82, 722–741.

Petty, Richard E., Pablo Briñol, Zakary L. Tormala, and Duane T. Wegener (2007). "The Role of Meta-Cognition in Social Judgment." In *Social Psychology: Handbook of Basic Principles,* ed. E.T. Higgins and A.W. Kruglanski. New York, NY: Guilford Press, 254–284.

Petty, Richard E., and John T. Cacioppo (1979). "Issue Involvement Can Increase or Decrease Persuasion By Enhancing Message-Relevant Cognitive Responses," *Journal of Personality and Social Psychology,* 37 (10), 1915–1926.

——— (1984). "Motivational factors in Consumer Response to Advertisements." In *Human Motivation: Physiological, Behavioral, and Social Approaches,* ed. R. Geen, W. Beatty, and R. Arkin. Boston, MA: Allyn & Bacon, 418–454.

——— (1986). *Communication and Persuasion: Central and Peripheral Routes to Attitude Change.* New York, NY: Springer-Verlag.

——— (1990). "Involvement and Persuasion: Tradition Versus Integration," *Psychological Bulletin,* 107 (3), 367–374.

Petty, Richard E., John T. Cacioppo, and Rachel Goldman (1981). "Personal Involvement as a Determinant of Argument-Based Persuasion," *Journal of Personality and Social Psychology,* 41, 847–855.

Petty, Richard E., John T. Cacioppo, and David Schumann (1983). "Central and Peripheral Routes to Advertising Effectiveness: The Moderating Role of Involvement," *Journal of Consumer Research,* 10 (September), 135–145.

Petty, Richard E., Curtis P. Haugtvedt, and Stephen M. Smith (1995). "Elaboration as a Determinant of Attitude Strength." In *Attitude Strength: Antecedents and Consequences,* ed. R.E. Petty and J.A. Krosnick. Mahwah, NJ: Lawrence Erlbaum, 93–130.

Petty, Richard E. and Jon A. Krosnick (eds.) (1995). *Attitude Strength: Antecedents and Consequences.* Mahwah, NJ: Lawrence Erlbaum.

Petty, Richard E., David W. Schumann, Steven A. Richman, and Alan J. Strathman (1993). "Positive Mood and Persuasion: Different Roles for Affect under High- and Low-Elaboration Conditions," *Journal of Personality and Social Psychology,* 64 (1), 5–20.

Petty, Richard E., Zakary L. Tormala, Pablo Briñol, and W. Blair G. Jarvis (2006). "Implicit Ambivalence from Attitude Change: An Exploration of the PAST Model," *Journal of Personality and Social Psychology,* 90 (1), 21–41.

Petty, Richard E., and Duane T. Wegener (1993). "Flexible Correction Processes in Social Judgment: Correcting for Context-Induced Contrast," *Journal of Experimental Social Psychology,* 29 (March), 137–165.

——— (1998a). "Attitude Change: Multiple Roles for Persuasion Variables." In *The Handbook of Social Psychology,* ed. Daniel Gilbert, Susan Fiske, and Gardner Lindzey. New York, NY: McGraw-Hill, 323–390.

———— (1998b). "Matching versus Mismatching Attitude Functions: Implications for Scrutiny of Persuasive Messages," *Personality and Social Psychology Bulletin,* 24, 227–240.

———— (1999). "The Elaboration Likelihood Model: Current Status and Controversies." In *Dual-Process Theories in Social Psychology,* ed. S. Chaiken and Y. Trope. New York, NY: Guildford Press, 41–72.

Petty, Richard E., Duane T. Wegener, and Paul H. White (1998). "Flexible Correction Processes in Social Judgment: Implications for Persuasion," *Social Cognition,* 16 (1), 93–113.

Petty, Richard E., Gary L. Wells, and Timothy C. Brock (1976). "Distraction Can Enhance or Reduce Yielding to Propaganda: Thought Disruption Versus Effort Justification," *Journal of Personality and Social Psychology,* 34, 874–884.

Priester, Joseph R., and Richard E. Petty (2003). "The Influence of Spokesperson Trustworthiness on Message Elaboration, Attitude Strength, and Advertising Effectiveness," *Journal of Consumer Psychology,* 13 (4), 408–421.

Raghunathan, Rajagopal, and Yaacov Trope (2002). "Walking the Tightrope Between Feeling Good and Being Accurate: Mood as a Resource in Processing Persuasive Messages," *Journal of Personality and Social Psychology,* 83, 510–525.

Ratneshwar, S., and Shelly Chaiken (1991). "Comprehension's Role in Persuasion: The Case of Its Moderating Effect on the Persuasive Impact of Source Cues," *Journal of Consumer Psychology,* 18, 52–62.

Rucker, Derek D., and Richard E. Petty (2004). "When Resistance Is Futile: Consequences of Failed Counterarguing for Attitude Certainty. *Journal of Personality and Social Psychology,* 86, 219–235.

Rusbult, Caryl E. (1980). "Commitment and Satisfaction in Romantic Associations: A Test of the Investment Model," *Journal of Personality and Social Psychology,* 16, 172–186.

———— (1983). "A Longitudinal Test of the Investment Model: The Development (and Deterioration) of Satisfaction and Commitment in Heterosexual Involvements," *Journal of Personality and Social Psychology,* 45, 101–117.

Rusbult, Caryl E., and John M. Martz (1995). "Remaining in an Abusive Relationship: An Investment Model Analysis of Nonvoluntary Commitment," *Personality and Social Psychology Bulletin,* 21, 558–571.

Rusbult, Caryl E., John M. Martz, and Christopher R. Agnew (1998). "The Investment Model Scale: Measuring Commitment Level, Satisfaction Level, Quality of Alternatives, and Investment Size," *Personal Relationships,* 5, 357–391.

Schul, Yaacov, and Eugene Burnstein (1985). "When Discounting Fails: Conditions under which Individuals Use Discredited Information in Making a Judgment," *Journal of Personality and Social Psychology,* 49, 894–903.

Schul, Yaacov, and Harel Goren (1997). "When Strong Evidence has Less Impact than Weak Evidence: Bias, Adjustment, and Instructions to Ignore," *Social Cognition,* 15, 133–155.

Schwarz, Norbert (1990). "Feelings as Information: Informational and Motivational Functions of Affective States." In *Handbook of Motivation and Cognition: Foundations of Social Behavior* (vol. 2), ed. E.T. Higgins and R.M. Sorrentino. New York, NY: Guilford, 527–561.

Schwarz, Norbert, Herbert Bless, and Gerd Bohner (1991). "Mood and Persuasion: Affective States Influence the Processing of Persuasive Communications." In *Advances in Experimental Social Psychology* (vol. 24), ed. M.P. Zanna. San Diego, CA: Academic Press, 161–201.

Schwarz, Norbert, and Gerald L. Clore (1983). "Mood, Misattribution, and Judgments of Well-Being: Informative and Directive Functions of Affective States," *Journal of Personality and Social Psychology,* 45, 513–523.

Sczesny, Sabine, and Ulrich Kühnen (2004). "Meta-Cognition about Biological Sex and Gender-Stereotypic Physical Appearance: Consequences for the Assessment of Leadership Competence," *Personality and Social Psychology Bulletin,* 30, 13–21.

Shavitt, Sharon, Suzanne Swan, Tina M. Lowery, and Michaela Wänke (1994). "The Interaction of Endorser Attractiveness and Involvement in Persuasion Depends on the Goal that Guides Message Processing," *Journal of Consumer Psychology,* 3, 137–162.

Sherman, Steven J., Diane M. Mackie, and Denise M. Driscoll (1990). "Priming and the Differential Use of Dimensions in Evaluation," *Personality and Social Psychology Bulletin,* 16, 405–418.

Shimp, Terence A., Elnora W. Stuart, and Randall W. Engle (1991). "A Program of Classical Conditioning Experiments Testing Variations in the Conditioned Stimulus and Context," *Journal of Consumer Research,* 18, 1–12.

Snyder, Mark (1974). "The Self-Monitoring of Expressive Behavior," *Journal of Personality and Social Psychology,* 30, 526–537.

Strack, Fritz (1992). "The Different Routes to Social Judgments: Experiential Versus Informational Based Strategies." In *The Construction of Social Judgments,* ed. L.L. Martin and A. Tesser. Hillsdale, NJ: Lawrence Erlbaum, 249–275.

Sujan, Mita (1985). "Consumer Knowledge: Effects on Evaluation Strategies Mediating Consumer Judgments," *Journal of Consumer Research,* 12, 31–46.

Tetlock, Philip E., and Ariel Levi (1982). "Attribution Bias: On the Inconclusiveness of the Cognition-Motivation Debate," *Journal of Experimental and Social Psychology,* 18 (1), 68–88.

Tiedens, Larissa Z., and Susan Linton (2001). "Judgment under Emotional Certainty and Uncertainty: The Effects of Specific Emotions on Information Processing," *Journal of Personality and Social Psychology,* 81, 973–988.

Tormala, Zakary L., Joshua J. Clarkson, and Richard E. Petty (2006). "Resisting Persuasion by the Skin of One's Teeth: The Hidden Success of Resisted Persuasive Messages," *Journal of Personality and Social Psychology,* 91 (3), 423–435.

Tormala, Zakary L. and Richard E. Petty (2002). "What Doesn't Kill Me Makes Me Stronger: The Effects of Resisting Persuasion on Attitude Certainty," *Journal of Personality and Social Psychology,* 83, 1298–1313.

——— (2004a). "Resistance to Persuasion and Attitude Certainty: The Moderating Role of Elaboration," *Personality and Social Psychology Bulletin,* 30, 1446–1457.

——— (2004b). "Resisting Persuasion and Attitude Certainty: A Metacognitive Analysis." In *Resistance and Persuasion,* ed. E.S. Knowles and J.A. Linn. Mahwah, NJ: Lawrence Erlbaum, 65–82.

Tormala, Zakary L., Richard E. Petty, and Pablo Briñol (2002). "Ease of Retrieval Effects in Persuasion: The Roles of Elaboration and Thought-Confidence," *Personality and Social Psychology Bulletin,* 28, 1700–1712.

Tormala, Zakary L., Richard E. Petty, and Victoria L. DeSensi (in press). "Multiple Roles for Minority Sources in Persuasion and Resistance." In *Minority Influence and Innovation: Antecedents, Processes, and Consequences,* ed. R. Martin and M. Hewstone. London, UK: Psychology Press.

Tormala, Zakary L., and Derek D. Rucker (2007). "Attitude Certainty: A Review of Past Findings and Emerging Perspectives," *Social and Personality Psychology Compass,* 1, 469–492.

Visser, Penny S., and Robert R. Mirabile (2004). "Attitudes in the Social Context: The Impact of Social Network Composition on Individual-Level Attitude Strength," *Journal of Personality and Social Psychology,* 87, 779–795.

Wegener, Duane T., and Donal E. Carlston (2005). "Cognitive Processes in Attitude Formation and Change." In *The Handbook of Attitudes,* ed. D. Albarracin, B. Johnson, and M. Zanna. Mahwah, NJ: Lawrence Erlbaum, 493–542.

Wegener, Duane T., Jason K. Clark, and Richard E. Petty (2006). "Not All Stereotyping is Created Equal: Differential Consequences of Thoughtful Versus Non-Thoughtful Stereotyping," *Journal of Personality and Social Psychology,* 90, 42–59.

Wegener, Duane T., John Downing, Jon A. Krosnick, and Richard E. Petty (1995). "Measures and Manipulations of Strength-Related Properties of Attitudes: Current Practice and Future Directions." In *Attitude Strength: Antecedents and Consequences,* ed. R.E. Petty and J.A. Krosnick. Mahwah, NJ: Lawrence Erlbaum, 455–487.

Wegener, Duane T., and Richard E. Petty (1995). "Flexible Correction Process in Social Judgment: The Role of Naive Theories in Corrections for Perceived Bias," *Journal of Personality and Social Psychology,* 68 (March), 36–51.

———— (1997). "The Flexible Correction Model: The Role of Naive Theories of Bias in Bias Correction" In *Advances in Experimental Social Psychology* (vol. 29), ed. M. P. Zanna. Mahwah, NJ: Lawrence Erlbaum, 141–208.

———— (2001). "On the Use of Naive Theories of Bias to Remove or Avoid Bias: The Flexible Correction Model," *Advances in Consumer Research,* 28, 378–383.

Wegener, Duane T., Richard E. Petty, and Stephen M. Smith (1995). "Positive Mood can Increase or Decrease Message Scrutiny: The Hedonic Contingency View of Mood and Message Processing," *Journal of Personality and Social Psychology,* 69, 5–15.

Wegener, Duane T., Richard E. Petty, Natalie D. Smoak, and Leandre R. Fabrigar (2004). "Multiple Routes to Resisting Attitude Change." In *Resistance and Persuasion,* ed. E. Knowles and J. Linn. Mahwah, NJ: Lawrence Erlbaum, 13–38.

Weigel, Russell H., and Lee S. Newman (1976). "Increasing Attitude-Behavior Correspondence by Broadening the Scope of the Behavioral Measure," *Journal of Personality and Social Psychology,* 33, 793–802.

Wheeler, S. Christian, Kenneth G. DeMarree, and Richard E. Petty (2007). "Understanding the Role of the Self in Prime-to-Behavior Effects: The Active Self Account," *Personality and Social Psychology Review,* 11, 234–261.

Wicker, Alan W. (1969). "Attitudes Versus Actions: The Relationship of Verbal and Overt Behavioral Responses to Attitude Objects," *Journal of Social Issues,* 25, 41–78.

Wilson, Timothy D., and Nancy Brekke (1994). "Mental Contamination and Mental Correction: Unwanted Influences on Judgments and Evaluations," *Psychological Bulletin,* 116 (1), 117–142.

Yi, Youjae (1990). "The Effects of Contextual Priming in Print Advertisements," *Journal of Consumer Research,* 17 (September), 215–222.

CHAPTER 16

PUTTING CONTEXT EFFECTS IN CONTEXT

The Construction and Retrieval as Moderated by Attitude Strength (CARMAS) Model of Evaluative Judgment

DHANANJAY NAYAKANKUPPAM AND JOSEPH R. PRIESTER

Consider a brand manager contemplating that most ubiquitous of marketing decisions—resource allocation. Should resources be allocated toward advertising or end caps at the point of purchase? Recent debates about above- versus below-the-line spending suggest this is not a trivial issue; there is a fundamental difference in the implicit theories underlying decisions to go one way versus the other. A decision to invest in advertising likely suggests an underlying theory that consumers can be persuaded to form attitudes (or evaluative dispositions) and these brands and associated evaluations will be retrieved at the point of purchase to guide decisions. A decision to invest in point of purchase betrays an implicit theory that consumer evaluations are unreliable and memory for specific information needs to be prodded with contextual cues. There are, naturally, actual proposed theories in the academic literature reflecting these implicit notions and plenty of empirical evidence consistent with each position.

BACKGROUND

Evaluative Judgments as Constructions

> "All we assess in attitude measurement are evaluative judgments that respondents construct at the time they are asked, based on whatever happens to be accessible."
> *(Schwarz and Bohner 2001)*

> "An evaluation . . . represents a combination of numerous evaluations of various features of the object, rather than a solitary tag associated with the object representation."
> *(Ferguson and Bargh 2003)*

The above quotes illustrate the current zeitgeist that posits that evaluative judgments are the result of construction processes. When asked whether one likes or dislikes a product, place, person, idea, or thing, this perspective reasons that an individual constructs his or her answer based upon information that is salient at the time of response. Recent writing has not only championed the ubiquity of construction but has also suggested that all evaluative judgments are the result of such construction processes.

According to the contemporary construction perspective, peoples' evaluative judgments (i.e., how they feel toward target objects) depend upon how they are asked and what they are thinking about at the time of questioning, rather than being the result of retrieving an internally stored evaluation (see, for e.g., Bettman 1979; Bettman, Luce, and Payne, 1998; Bettman and Park 1980; Payne, Bettman, and Johnson 1992; Schwarz and Bohner 2001; Slovic 1995; Tesser 1978; Tversky, Sattath, and Slovic 1988; Wilson and Hodges 1992). These perspectives advance the notion that judgments and evaluations are the result of an active construction process. One consequence of such a process is that judgments ought to be highly sensitive to contextual information.

The evidence that context[1] can systematically influence evaluative judgments is vast. Subtle variations in how questions are worded, or the very order in which questions are posed, have been found to have profound influences on the report of evaluative judgments (see, e.g., Bishop 1987; Hippler, Schwarz, and Sudman, 1987; Schuman and Presser 1981; Schuman, Presser, and Ludwig 1981; Schwarz 1999; Schwarz and Sudman 1996; Strack and Martin 1987; Sudman, Bradburn, and Schwarz 1996; Tourangeau and Rasinski, 1988). Similarly, transient mood (Isen et al. 1978; Schwarz and Clore 1983; Schwarz et al. 1987), phenomenological experiences (Schwarz 1998; Schwarz and Clore 1983) and bodily sensations (Valins 1966; Wells and Petty 1980) at the time of providing evaluative responses influence such judgments. For example, the experienced ease or difficulty in retrieval of positive or negative information has been demonstrated to be the basis of judgments (Schwarz 1998; Schwarz et al. 1991; Strack, Martin, and Stepper 1988; Tversky and Kahneman 1973). For instance, bringing to mind three things one likes about one's spouse (a relatively easy task) results in more favorable subsequent evaluations of one's spouse, while bringing to mind twelve things one likes about one's spouse (a relatively difficult task) results in less favorable subsequent evaluations of one's spouse.

This bounty of evidence showing the influence of transient and contextual information on evaluative judgments has been used to infer that these judgments are constructed. It is argued that these variations cannot be the result of a retrieval process that accesses a stored prior reaction. Rather, the data suggests that, when asked, individuals construct their evaluative judgments based upon salient information.

Evaluative Judgments as Retrieved

The notion that evaluative judgments are the result of retrieving and using a stored evaluative tendency (i.e., an attitude) has a long tradition. In essence, the retrieval perspective argues that we come to store an evaluative disposition in memory as a ready guide to action should that target object be encountered again. As such, attitudes have historically been conceptualized as evaluations that are internally stored and relatively stable over time. Allport (1935) noted that attitudes "often persist throughout life in the way they were fixed in childhood or in youth" (p. 814; see also Cook and Flay 1978; Sherif and Cantril 1947, as well as Bennett 1975; Bishop, Hamilton, and McConahay 1980; Brown 1970; Marwell, Aiken, and Demerath 1987) and that attitudes are best thought of as a "mental or neural state of readiness" (see also Asch 1952; Eagly and Chaiken 1993).

There exist many findings consistent with such a perspective. One would expect a retrieved tendency to influence subsequent information processing, and research supports the notion that attitudes influence information processing in a manner consistent with that hypothesized by the retrieval perspective (e.g., Baumgardner et al. 1976; Lingle et al. 1979; Ahluwalia, Unnava, and Burnkrant 2001). Similarly, one would expect differential reactions to pro- versus counter-attitudinal stimuli, and extant findings are consistent with such a notion, be they the degree of counter arguing (Ahluwalia et al. 2000), the relative ratio of feelings to thoughts (Jewell and Unnava 2004) or neurological reactivity to positively and negatively evaluated stimuli (Cacioppo, Petty, and Geen 1989; Cacioppo et al. 1993; Cacioppo et al. 1994; Cacioppo, Crites, and Gardner 1996; Crites et al. 1995). In a related vein, attitudes have been shown to interfere with detection of changes in an attitude object (Fazio, Ledbetter, and Towles-Schwen 2000), a finding consistent with a retrieval perspective. Further, it has been shown that accessible attitudes ease the physiological stress associated with decision making (Fazio, Blascovich, and Driscoll 1992).

Difficulty in Testing

Although the two perspectives offer different explanations for the processes that generate evaluative judgments, empirically differentiating them has proven difficult. This difficulty results from the fact that while the two theories offer quite different process explanations, they generate similar empirical predictions, thereby rendering it difficult to test which of the two processes is at work. With additional plausible assumptions each perspective can be consistent with the data offered as support for the other perspective.

Consider, as an example, attitude accessibility. While Fazio and colleagues cite the effects of attitude accessibility as support for retrieval processes (see, for example, Fazio 1995, 1989), Schwarz and Bohner (2001) argue that latency data are mute as to which stage of the judgment process is responsible for producing a fast or slow response. Specifically, a fast latency might reflect retrieval of a highly accessible stored attitude, as Fazio and colleagues argue, or alternatively, the fast computation of a currently constructed judgment, facilitated by evaluatively consistent, rather than inconsistent, information coming to mind. In other words, a retrieved attitude is a sufficient, but not necessary, condition for fast evaluative responding.

Putting the boot on the other foot, the retrieval perspective can account for context sensitivity by arguing that the stored and retrieved attitude serves the purpose of an anchor. Contextual information is then integrated into the anchor in a manner similar to the anchoring and adjustment mechanism proposed by Kahneman and Tversky (1974). Thus, the stored attitude serves as a starting point and contextual information, if deemed relevant, might be integrated with the attitude to arrive at an evaluative judgment.

Moderation as a Resolution: Construction and Retrieval Moderated by the Attitude Strength (CARMAS) Model

A resolution to these seemingly mutually conflicting perspectives appears desirable. To such an end, we argue that a potentially more informative question to ask is not *if,* but *when,* evaluative judgments are the result of construction or retrieval processes. Thus, the crucial issue becomes finding theoretically compelling and a priori specifiable conditions governing when evaluative judgments are constructed and when they result from retrieval processes. In other words, we seek to find a theoretically informative moderator to the processes underlying evaluative judgments. We suggest that the attitude strength associated with an attitude is such a meaningful theoretical moderator.

Attitude Strength

Attitudes are indicative of the extent to which one likes or dislikes an attitude object and *attitude strength* is a measure of the extent to which one has come to such an attitude through relatively effortful, thoughtful or nonthoughtful, processes (see, for example, Petty and Wegener 1998). Krosnick and Petty (1995) review the empirical work on strength-related attributes and classify them into four categories: (1) aspects of the attitude itself, (2) aspects of the cognitive structure associated with the attitude and attitude object in memory, (3) subjective beliefs about the attitude and the attitude object, and (4) cognitive processes by which an attitude is formed. The fourth dimension is theoretically particularly interesting because it is the process by which the attitude is formed and it conceptually underlies and leads to the other constructs.

Elaboration

A key antecedent to attitude strength is elaboration. Attitude strength has been shown to result from relatively effortful cognitive elaboration or thinking about the central merits of an attitude object (Petty and Cacioppo 1986; Petty, Priester, and Wegener 1994; Petty and Wegener 1998). Elaboration is said to occur when individuals possess the motivation and ability to scrutinize information and is the process whereby an attitude is formed as a result of the thoughts (cognitive responses) that an individual has in response to an attitude object. When individuals lack the ability or the motivation to elaborate, it is still possible for them to form attitudes in response to information. However, attitudes formed under these conditions tend to be the result of relatively nonthoughtful associative and inference processes (Petty, Cacioppo, and Schumann 1983).

Elaboration is hypothesized to result in a change in the underlying cognitive structure associated with an attitude toward an attitude object. Specifically, elaboration is hypothesized to lead to a denser and highly interconnected associative network with a greater number of cognitive associations (Petty and Cacioppo 1986). These changes to the underlying cognitive structure that come about as a result of elaboration have been demonstrated to produce a number of consequences. Strong attitudes are more likely to possess greater accessibility (e.g., Priester and Petty 2003), persist over time (e.g., Haugtvedt and Petty 1992), resist counter-persuasive attempts (e.g., Haugtvedt and Wegener 1994), be considered prior to choice (Priester et al. 2004), and guide behavior (Cacioppo et al. 1986) than weak attitudes (see Fazio 1995; Petty, Haugtvedt, and Smith 1995).

Attitude Strength and Judgment

To understand the case for attitude strength as a moderator to construction and retrieval processes, it is helpful to consider the process involved in forming a judgment. When faced with a judgment situation, one needs to bring to mind information about the target object. It is generally accepted that the search is rarely exhaustive and is truncated relatively rapidly. The crucial questions in such a scenario become whether the attitude is one of the components brought to mind and if so, to what extent it influences judgment. Two critical factors that determine the influence of a piece of information on a subsequent judgment are its accessibility and diagnosticity. Thus, an attitude's influence on a judgment depends upon how accessible it is (i.e., does it come to mind) and how diagnostic (i.e., relevant) it is perceived to be to the judgment, compared to other information that is brought to mind.

As such, in a judgment situation, strong attitudes should enjoy certain advantages over weak attitudes. Strong attitudes, as a result of their greater accessibility, are more likely to be retrieved than weak attitudes. Furthermore, since they are based on effortful cognitive elaboration, and thus possess a richer associative network, they are more likely to be considered diagnostic or relevant than weak attitudes (see, for example, Menon, Raghubir, and Schwarz 1995). Thus, we hypothesize that strong attitudes are likely to be retrieved and considered diagnostic. As such, the evaluative judgment is hypothesized to be less susceptible to contextual influences. Weak attitudes are likely to be inaccessible, and even when they come to mind might be considered less diagnostic than other cues present in the context. An evaluative judgment is thus likely to be constructed on the basis of currently salient information and therefore should be more susceptible to contextual influences that render some elements of information more salient than others.

There are a number of testable hypotheses that can be developed from this position. The first is that attitude strength should moderate the contextual sensitivity of evaluative judgments. If, as we have argued, strong attitudes are more accessible and diagnostic, then there is less likelihood of contextual influence. This is precisely what we have found in a series of experiments.

Differential Context Sensitivity: Measured Attitude Strength

Prior research has revealed that individuals often use the accessibility of brands in memory as a cue to infer liking (Posovac, Sanbonmatsu, and Fazio 1997). We manipulated the context in which this accessibility was experienced so as to allow one to use, or call into question the diagnosticity of, the accessibility experience. Variation in liking as a function of this manipulation would entail evidence for the construction perspective. We further

Figure 16.1   **Diagnosticity of Recall: Predicted Category × Diagnosticity Interaction**

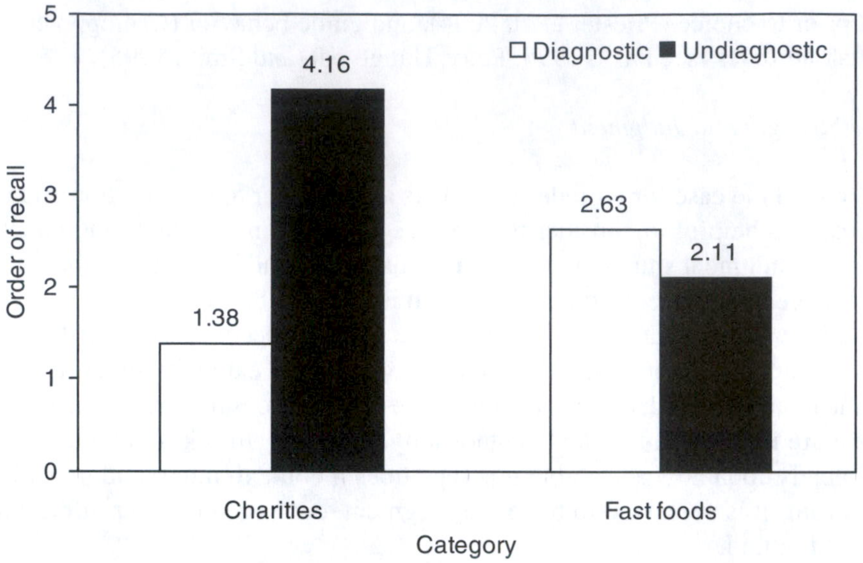

wanted to demonstrate that this influence of context would only emerge when attitudes were weakly held. Pretests had revealed that our student participants had stronger attitudes toward brands of fast foods (knew more about, had stronger preferences between brands, were more certain of their preferences, and had thought more about) than brands of charities. Thus, we conceptualized attitudes toward fast foods and charities as being strong and weak, respectively.

Thirty-six participants were asked to recall as many brands of fast foods (or charities) as they could. They were then asked to choose one of these brands. However, half the participants were told we were interested in their memory for brands, which allowed them to use ease of recall to infer a liking for earlier recalled brands. The other participants were told we were interested in how advertising might influence memory for brands, which served to taint any experienced ease of recall with the smell of bias; something might have come to mind easily because one had seen many ads for the same rather than because one liked it.

Analyses yielded a main effect for the diagnosticity of recall—$F(1, 31) = 4.82, p < 0.04$. Participants who were allowed to infer a liking from recall chose earlier recalled brands ($M = 2.00$) than participants whose recall experience was called into question ($M = 3.31$). This main effect was qualified by the predicted category × diagnosticity interaction, $F(1, 31) = 8.74, p < 0.01$. Figure 16.1 depicts this interaction. Participants choosing fast foods (strong attitudes) were immune to the contextual manipulation, $F < 1$. In contrast, for participants choosing charities (weak attitudes), a significant influence of the contextual cue emerged, $F(1, 15) = 7.29, p < 0.02$, with participants who were allowed to infer a liking from ease of recall choosing earlier recalled brands ($M = 1.38$) compared to participants for whom the recall experience was called into question ($M = 4.86$).

As predicted by the CARMAS theory, we find that a classic context effect (based upon ease of recall, which is arguably one of the most commonly used context effects in the literature), is moderated by attitude strength such that weak attitudes show large context effects while strong attitudes seem immune from contextual influence. The measured property of strength, however, allows for creative speculation about other correlated variables (such as fluency of construction). It thus becomes crucial to explore whether attitude strength moderates context influence, even when that attitude strength is manipulated, rather than measured, and the attitude object is novel, rather than familiar.

Differential Context Sensitivity: Manipulated Attitude Strength

Another experiment utilized only the charities category and experimentally manipulated attitude strength. Participants in the study were provided with an advertisement for a fictitious charity, designed with strong arguments as well as positive peripheral cues. Half the participants processed the advertisement under conditions designed to foster high elaboration (and result in strongly held positive attitudes) by asking them to pay attention to their thoughts and feelings, whereas the others processed the advertisement under conditions designed to constrain ability to elaborate (and result in weakly held positive attitudes) by asking them to count the number of polysyllabic words in the advertisement. Following manipulation checks and approximately 45 minutes later, participants were asked for the brand name of the charity and exposed to a manipulation of context similar to the previous study and were then asked to provide their intention to donate to the charity. Thus, intention to donate represents the indicator of the participants' evaluative judgment of the charity.

One hundred sixteen participants took part in the experiment for partial course credit. They were randomly assigned to one of four cells in a 2 (elaboration: high versus low) × 2 (context: ease of recall unambiguous versus ambiguous) between participants factorial experiment. A third factor was created based upon the ability of the participants to recall the name of the charity, resulting in an eight-cell design.

Manipulation checks showed that attitudes toward the charity did not differ as a function of elaboration, $F(1, 97) = 1.82, p < 0.2$, ($M_{\text{low elab}} = 2.7, M_{\text{high elab}} = 3.0$). Strength, however, did differ significantly across the elaboration conditions, $F(1, 106) = 11.8, p < 0.0008$, ($M_{\text{low elab}} = 5.42, M_{\text{high elab}} = 4.35$). In short, the elaboration manipulation created equally valenced attitudes, which differed on the underlying dimension of attitude strength.

Evaluative judgments reflected a main effect for recall, $F(1, 105) = 13.07, p < 0.001$, indicating that individuals who recalled the charity were more likely to consider donating to the charity. This main effect was qualified, however, by a higher order elaboration × context × recall interaction, $F(1, 105) = 6.51, p < 0.01$, which is represented in Figure 16.2.

This interaction was decomposed by examining the elaboration × context interactions separately for individuals who were able/not able to recall the name of the charity. Among those who recalled the name of the charity, a significant elaboration × context interaction emerged, $F(1, 61) = 3.98, p < 0.05$. As predicted, this interaction emerged

Figure 16.2   **Recall Effect: Higher Order Elaboration–Context–Recall Interaction**

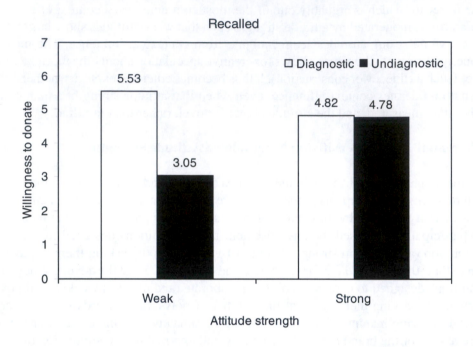

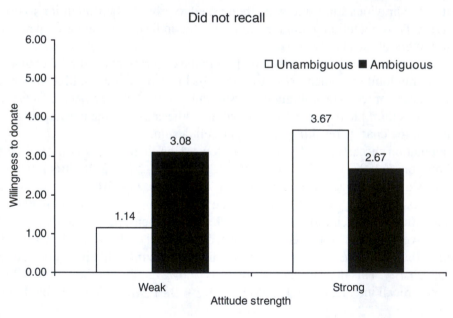

because context was more influential under conditions of low than high elaboration. When attitudes were weakly held, participants' intention to donate was significantly influenced by context, $F(1, 34) = 8.98$, $p < 0.005$ ($M_{\text{recall use allowed}} = 5.53$, $M_{\text{recall questioned}} = 3.05$). In contrast, manipulation of context did not influence evaluative judgments when attitudes were strongly held, $F < 1$ ($M_{\text{recall use allowed}} = 4.8$, $M_{\text{recall questioned}} = 4.8$).[2]

The results reveal that the evaluative judgments associated with weakly held attitudes were more influenced by the contextual manipulation than the evaluative judgments associated with strongly held attitudes. Since attitude strength has been manipulated and not measured, the contribution of experiment 2 lies in its ability to disconfirm alternative explanations associated with variables such as fluency of construction that might be correlated with a measured approach (e.g., product category as a proxy for strength).

Differential Context Sensitivity: An Individual Difference Approach

The results of the previous experiments are limited in that each focuses on a specific type of context effect related to the accessibility of a brand in a category. Finding that attitude strength moderates other context effects would be compelling and would indicate that this moderation is a robust finding. In addition, if attitude strength plays a key role in moderating which process guides judgment, it should be possible to observe such moderations with entirely different operationalizations of attitude strength. Such a utilization of maximally different indicators would provide convergent evidence for the notion that attitude strength moderates susceptibility to contextual evidence.

We conducted experiment 3 to this end. Considerable research of late has utilized individual differences as moderating variables to test theoretical frameworks (see Bagozzi 1994). In short, if the proposed notion that construction and retrieval are moderated by attitude strength is true, one would expect to find similar patterns of data emerging as a result of the inherent motivation some people have to indulge in elaborative and evaluative processes. Two constructs used in examining persuasive and evaluative phenomena are needed to evaluate (NTE; Jarvis and Petty 1996) and need for cognition (NCOG; Cacioppo and Petty 1982; Cacioppo et al. 1986). These two individual difference variables have been conceptualized to capture the fundamental motivation that people have to engage in elaborative and evaluative processes. NTE is an individual difference variable that measures the inherent motivation to arrive at an evaluative judgment. From our perspective, individuals high in the NTE are more likely to spontaneously evaluate a target entity and thus form an attitude for possible later retrieval. NCOG is an individual difference variable that measures an individual's inherent motivation to engage in elaboration. From our perspective, individuals high in NCOG are more likely to proceed through an elaborative process and form strong attitudes. Furthermore, we predict interactive influences since the individuals high in NCOG as well as NTE would be the most likely to spontaneously form strong attitudes.

Manipulation of Context Effect

Furthermore, we used a context effect that was not reliant on brand name recall. Specifically, it has been shown that the phenomenological sense of effort is often used as a cue to guide judgments (see Schwarz 1998), much as is suggested by the "availability" heuristic (Tversky and Kahneman 1973). Thus, we surmised that asking participants to list three reasons they liked a particular target object they were using should lead them

Figure 16.3 **Effect of Reason Condition**

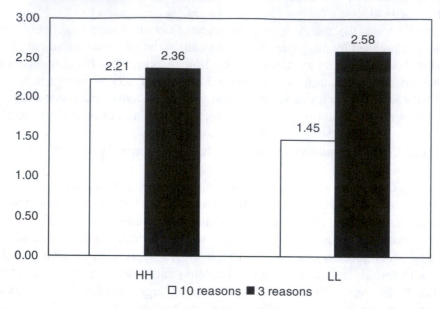

to like that object more, relative to those who were asked to list ten reasons they liked the object. Recall, however, that we hypothesize that attitude strength moderates this susceptibility to context—thus, the individual differences of NCOG and NTE, which moderate the likelihood of forming strong (versus weak) attitudes would moderate this susceptibility to context.

One hundred seventy-four participants took part in the experiment. The design of the study was a 2 [ease of recall: three reasons (easy) versus ten reasons (hard)] × need for cognition × need to evaluate, with the first factor manipulated between subjects and the second two factors measured between subjects. Participants in the study were seated at a desk and were provided with a pen that they used for approximately forty-five minutes to complete a series of booklets for unrelated experimental material. Subsequently, they encountered a booklet that asked them to list either three (or ten) things they liked about the pen and then asked them for their attitude toward the pen. Later on, in a supposedly unrelated booklet, they filled out the eighteen-item need for cognition scale and the sixteen-item need to evaluate scale.

Analyses yielded a significant main effect for the reason condition, $F(1,166) = 6.04$, $p = 0.01$. This main effect, reflected in Figure 16.3, indicated that participants who generated ten reasons they liked the pen came to like the pen less than the participants who generated three reasons ($M_{\text{ten}} = 1.88$, $M_{\text{three}} = 2.41$).

Interactive Effects of NCOG and NTE

As predicted, a significant, higher-order, three-way interaction between NCOG, NTE, and the reasons condition ($F[1, 166] = 5.51$, $p = 0.01$) emerged. We proceeded to test the focal hypothesis that the individual high in NCOG and NTE would be immune to contextual influence as compared to the individuals low in NCOG and NTE. Dichoto-mizing NTE and NCOG and comparing the susceptibility of evaluative judgments to the reasons condition of the high NCOG, NTE group against the low NCOG, NTE group. A marginal interaction emerged, $F(1, 106) = 2.44$, $p = 0.12$. The marginal interaction is perhaps not surprising given the great loss in statistical power. Planned contrasts revealed that the reasons condition did have an effect on the low NCOG, NTE group, $F(1, 58) = 7.38$, $p = 0.01$, ($M_{three} = 2.56$, $M_{ten} = 1.45$). That is, individuals who gener-ated three reasons for liking the pen came to like the pen much more than individuals who had generated ten reasons, demonstrating that these individuals utilized the ease of generating reasons to construct an evaluative judgment toward the pen. Importantly, the reasons condition did not have an influence on the high NCOG, NTE group, $F(1, 50) = 0.09$, $p = 0.76$, ($M_{three} = 1.70$, $M_{ten} = 1.67$). That is, individuals did not differ in terms of their evaluative judgments, regardless of whether they had generated three or ten reasons. The relative immunity of evaluations of participants high in NTE and NCOG suggests retrieval.[3]

The results thus provide converging evidence from a strikingly different perspective for the notion that attitudes differ in their susceptibility to context effects. Attitude strength appears to be a key, theoretical variable that influences the likelihood of an attitude be-ing retrieved at a later point in time, which thus governs the likelihood of an evaluative judgment being constructed.

Chronic Accessibility

While all this data is consistent with the notion of strong attitudes as more likely to be retrieved while weak attitudes are more likely to be constructed, there is one further sting in the tail. It could be argued that strong attitudes are associated with a wealth of chronically accessible information and that contextual information forms a relatively small part of the resulting mental representation. In contrast, when attitudes are weak, context is likely to form a much larger part of the mental representation. Thus, it is not that judgments associated with strong attitudes are immune to context, but rather that the context sensitivity is just harder to detect in light of the massive amount of chronically accessible information that makes up the bulk of the mental representation. Panel A and Panel B of Figure 16.4 show the chronic accessibility and the CARMAS perspectives respectively.

To examine this issue, we conducted two experiments that examined response times to render evaluative judgment and recognize attribute information. A crucial testable process difference between the two perspectives lies in what is actually brought to mind. The chronic accessibility perspective hypothesizes that it is information that is brought to mind, followed by a computation process wherein the information brought to mind (and other information rendered salient by context) is forged into an evaluative judgment. The CARMAS perspective makes the same prediction for weak attitudes but suggests that strong attitudes are stored as ready guides to action. All that comes to mind in this case is a stored evaluative component associated with the target object representation.

Figure 16.4   **Chronic Accessibility Perspective (A) versus the CARMAS Perspective (B)**

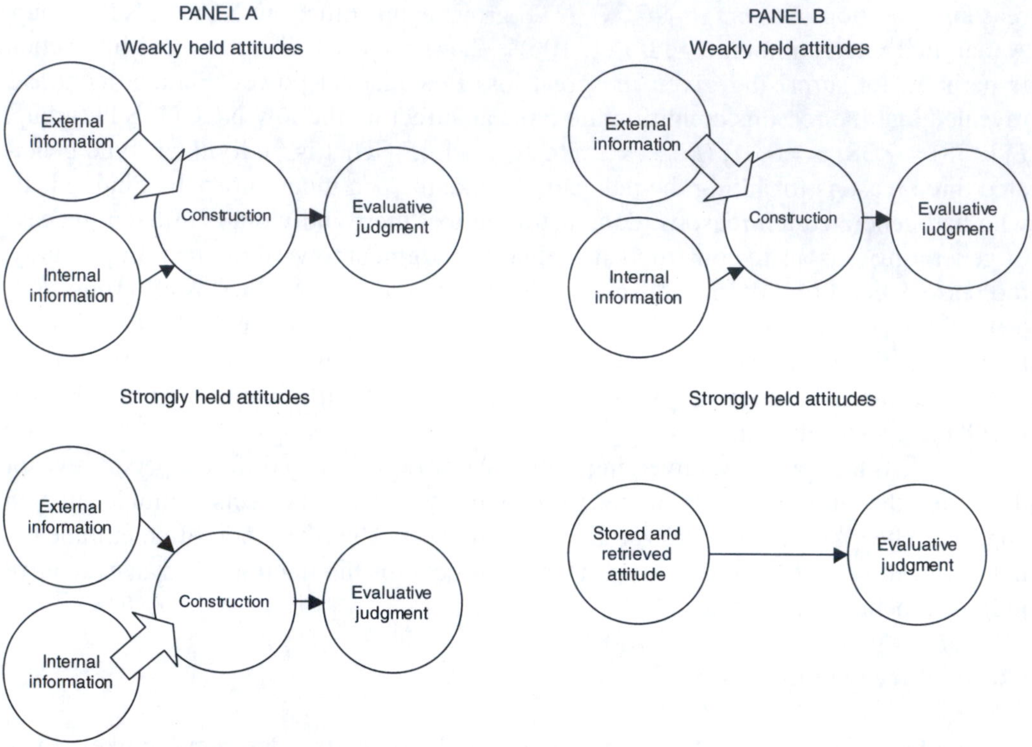

Specifically, the construction perspective would predict the following: Rendering an evaluative judgment would require bringing to mind information, which would thus be primed and available and would facilitate subsequent recognition of this information. Recognizing attribute information would serve to bring that information to mind, thus facilitating subsequent evaluative judgment; that is, information was already brought to mind and only a computation was left to be performed. Thus, the construction perspective would predict a mutual facilitation with evaluative judgments and attribute recognition facilitating each other; that is, either task will be quicker when performed second rather than first, and the second response will be quicker than the first. In contrast, the CARMAS model would predict an interaction by attitude strength—mutual facilitation for weak attitudes, but evaluative independence for strong attitudes. Specifically, the CARMAS model would suggest that strong attitudes, being formed for the purpose of action, would come to mind bereft of attribute information and would thus be faster, and independent of, attribute information (i.e., no mutual facilitation). Figure 16.5 graphs the predictions made by the chronic accessibility perspective and the predictions of the CARMAS perspective.[4]

In the first study, participants were exposed to the advertisement for the fictitious charity described earlier. In a follow-up study, they were exposed to a more terse ad-

Figure 16.5   **Predictions Made by (A) the Chronic Accessibility Perspective and (B) the CARMAS Perspective. (Solid lines represent attribute recognition followed by evaluative judgment; dashed lines indicate evaluative judgment followed by attribute recognition.)**

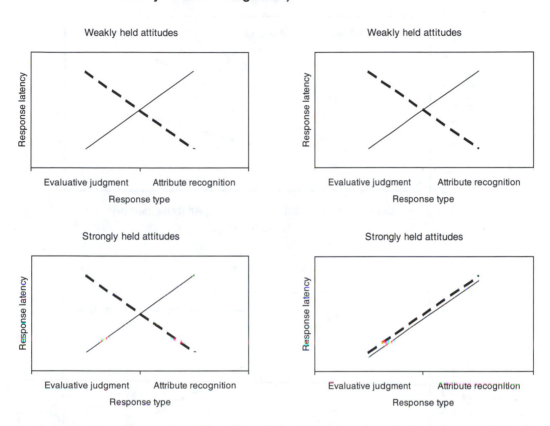

vertisement (smaller number of attributes) for a fictitious brand of toothpaste. In both studies, participants processed the ad under conditions that fostered high elaboration or provided a secondary cognitive load to reduce resources available for elaboration. They were then asked to render an evaluative judgment and recognize attribute information they had seen in the ad, but half the participants performed the attribute recognition first, while the other half performed the evaluative judgment first. The computer was used to track their response latencies to perform each task. The design of the studies was thus a 2 (attitude strength: high vs. low) × 2 (judgment task: evaluative judgment vs. attribute recognition) × 2 (order: evaluative judgment first vs. attribute recognition first) mixed factorial design with the first and third factor manipulated between participant and the second factor within.

Analyses yielded the three-way strength × order × judgment task interaction predicted by the CARMAS model in both studies. For the purpose of brevity, we only report the results of the second experiment. All lower-order effects were qualified by the significant, higher-order, three-way interaction, $F(1, 46) = 23.52$, $p < 0.0001$, which is graphed in Figure 16.6. Decomposing the three-way interaction across strong and weak attitudes

Figure 16.6   **Effect of Strong versus Weak Attitudes on Evaluative Judgment and Attribute Memory**

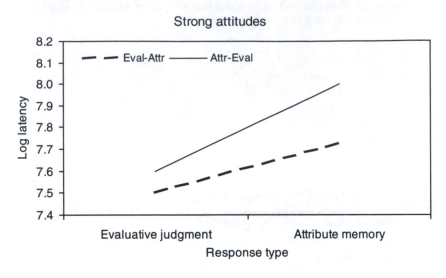

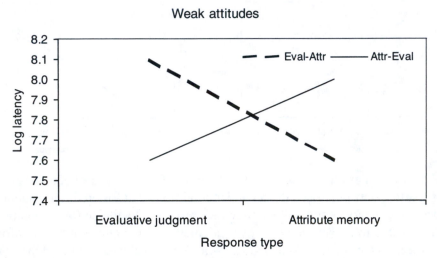

yielded a significant judgment task × order interaction for weak attitudes, $F(1, 23) = 46.95, p < 0.0001$. However, when attitudes were strongly held, this interaction was not significant ($F < 1$).

As can be seen in the figure, when attitudes were weak, performing one judgment task facilitated the other task (faster latency for a task when performed second rather than first), a pattern predicted by the chronic accessibility account as well as the CARMAS model. In contrast, when attitudes were strongly held, there was only a main effect for judgment task, with evaluative judgments being rendered significantly faster than attribute recognition, a pattern that is predicted by the CARMAS model and is at odds with the prediction of the chronic accessibility account.[5]

Figure 16.7 **Effect of Favorable Attitudes (Strong vs. Weak) on Likelihood of Consideration**

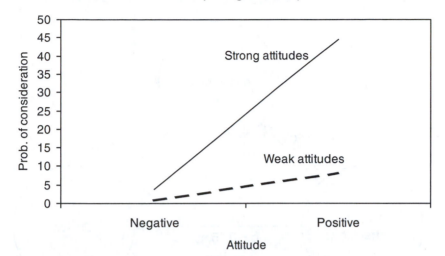

CARMAS IMPLICATIONS FOR CONSIDERATION SET SIZE

The CARMAS model of evaluative judgment has clear implications for consumer behavior. There is a long history in marketing of understanding choice as a series of steps, which includes a consideration set, that is, all of the possible brands and products considered prior to choice. If strongly held positive attitudes are more likely to be retrieved, this process should influence consideration as well as choice. Research we have conducted has explored the influence of attitude strength on consideration.

In a series of experiments, we (Priester et al. 2004) demonstrated that attitude strength had a strong moderating influence on the attitude-to-consideration link. Participants were asked to report attitudes and attitude strength toward various brands in the toothpaste category. In a subsequent stage, they were asked for their choice of toothpaste and to report a consideration set. Favorable attitudes increased the likelihood of consideration, which was particularly true for strongly held rather than weakly held attitudes. As only one example (see Figure 16.7), the following are the results of the first study (Priester et al. 2004) in the toothpaste category. The impact of strong attitudes is exceedingly powerful with almost a fourfold increase in the likelihood of consideration. Similarly, in an experiment in which attitude strength was manipulated, attitudes that resulted from elaboration (i.e., were strongly held) were more likely to be considered than attitudes that resulted from less thoughtful processes (i.e., were weakly held). In fact, in this experiment (as well as others) the influence of attitude strength on choice was fully mediated by consideration (see Figure 16.8); that is, it is because strongly liked brands are more likely to be included in a consideration set that such brands are subsequently chosen.

More recently, we have investigated another aspect to the influence of attitude strength on consideration set formation. Specifically, since consideration set formation is often characterized as a search for credible options, we surmised that the retrieval of a brand associated with high strength might serve as a signal for search truncation. If such were

Figure 16.8   **Effect of Attitude Strength on Choice When Mediated by Consideration**

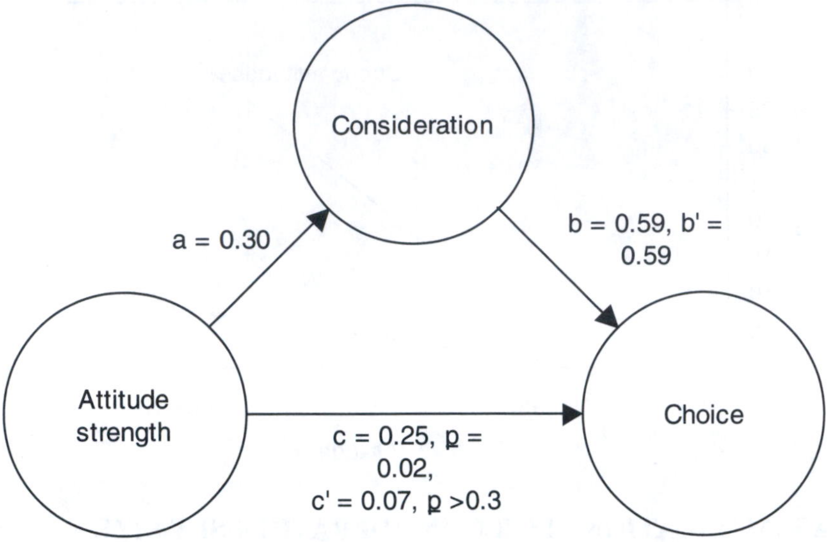

indeed the case, it would imply that strong attitudes might serve to constrain consideration set sizes. We went back to earlier data (from Priester et al. 2004) and examined the attitude strength of the chosen brand compared to the average attitude strength for other brands in the consideration set. The more extreme the strength of the chosen brand, compared to the strength of other alternatives in the consideration set, the smaller the consideration set sizes. This was true in the category of sodas, $F(1, 272) = 4.57, p < 0.03, B = -0.11$, as well as the category of toothpastes, $F(1, 293) = 10.94, p < 0.0001, B = -0.12$. Importantly, this effect of extremity of attitude strength emerged even when we controlled for extremity of attitude itself. Main effects emerged for attitude extremity, $F(1, 567) = 9.63, p < 0.002$, as well as strength extremity, $F(1, 567) = 18.44, p < 0.0001$.

In a second experiment, we manipulated the attitude strength toward three novel brands in three product categories. Subsequently, we had participants report consideration sets in the three categories. Lower-order effects were qualified by an elaboration × recall interaction, $F(1, 24) = 7.05, p < 0.01$. Participants who did not recall the advertised brand had similar consideration set sizes regardless of whether they were in the high elaboration ($M = 2.80$) or the low elaboration ($M = 2.79$) condition, $F < 1$. However, among the participants who did remember the advertised brand, high elaboration was associated with significantly smaller consideration set sizes ($M = 3.04$) than low elaboration ($M = 5.35$), $F(1, 24) = 9.75, p < 0.005$. This focal effect of smaller consideration set sizes among those high-elaboration participants (compared to low-elaboration participants) who remembered the advertised brand held true across all the categories: burgers ($M_{hi\text{-}elab} = 3.1, M_{lo\text{-}elab} = 5.3$), granola bars ($M_{hi\text{-}elab} = 1.0, M_{lo\text{-}elab} = 3.7$), and pizzas ($M_{hi\text{-}elab} = 4.6, M_{lo\text{-}elab} = 7.0$). There is obviously considerable theoretical and strategic power in understanding when a consideration set might comprise of two rather than eight alternatives.

Figure 16.9 **The Construction and Retrieval as Moderated by Attitude Strength (CARMAS) Model**

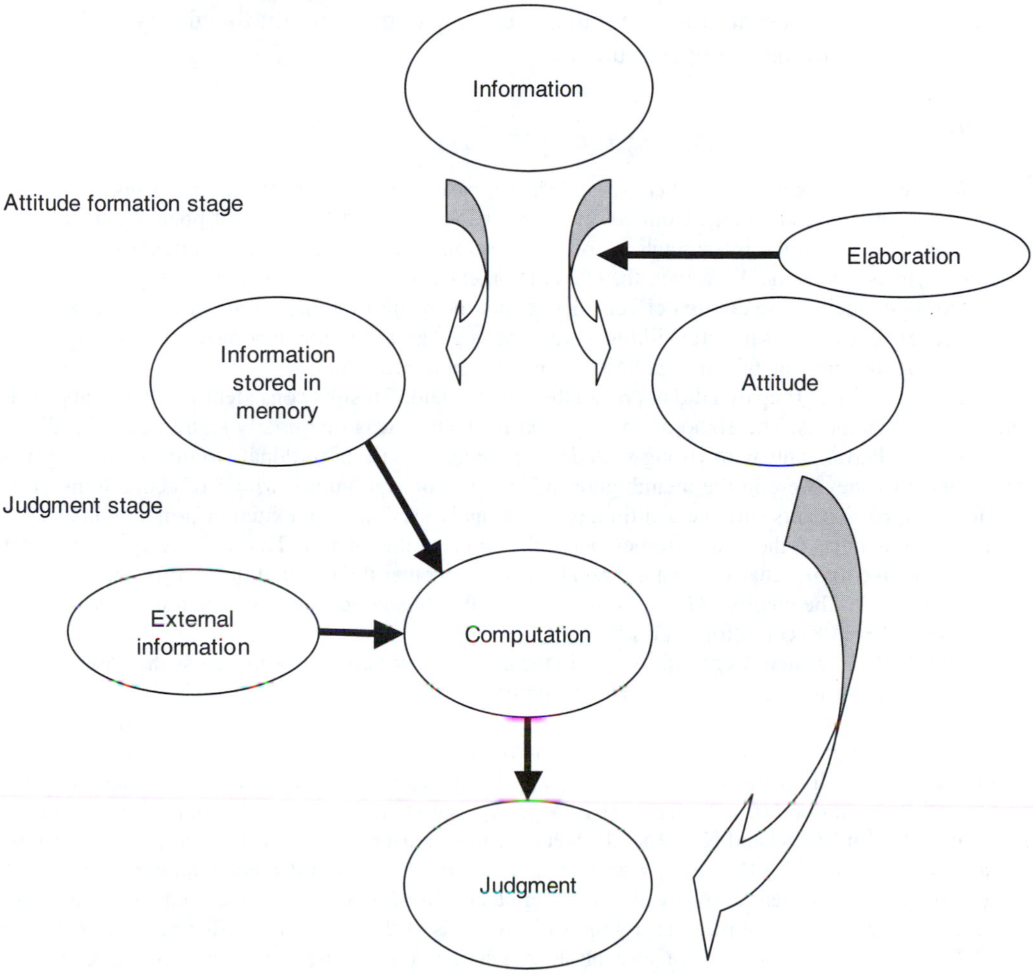

CONCLUSION

We have provided evidence that attitude strength moderates the susceptibility to contextual influence, such that while weak attitudes are particularly prone to context, strong attitudes appear to be immune to contextual influence. Figure 16.9 provides the essential concept of the CARMAS model. We consider attitudes as functional—they ease decision making. We distinguish between attitude formation/change from attitude expression. Attitude expression is a function of the ability to retrieve an attitude and a decision of whether the attitude is diagnostic to the task at hand. Strong attitudes enjoy advantages in such a situation. They are more accessible and, since they are based on cognitive elaboration, they are more likely to be considered diagnostic compared to other information in the context. Thus, strong attitudes enjoy relative immunity from context and have much greater influence on behavior.

In closing, we call you to cast your mind back to the resource allocation problem facing the brand manager posed at the start of this chapter. Resource allocation in light of the evidence we have presented is likely to be strongly contingent on the ability to develop strong attitudes among target consumers.

NOTES

1. We use the terms *context* and *context effects* for ease of exposition. We are referring to context effects on evaluative judgments. Context effects refer to a much wider range of phenomena and can result from changes in the interpretations of the question, interpretations of the target of judgment, response effects, and so on. However, the class of context effects most relevant for our purposes is on evaluations—namely those context effects that are not the result of a misinterpretation of the attitude object, but are due to shifts in actual liking toward the target as a function of some contextual cue since these bear on the question of retrieval versus construction of attitudes.

2. Analyses of the group that did not recall the charity yielded results consistent with the framework guiding the hypothesis. The elaboration × context interaction was marginally significant, $F(1, 37) = 2.61$, $p = 0.1$. Participants with strong attitudes were equally willing to donate to the charity, regardless of whether they were in the unambiguous ($M = 3.67$) or ambiguous ($M = 2.67$) conditions, ($F < 1$). However, participants with weak attitudes directionally used the contextual information in exactly the opposite manner to those who remembered the name of the charity. That is, they appear to have inferred a dislike for the charity from their inability to remember the name of the charity and were less likely to donate to the charity ($M = 1.14$) in the unambiguous condition than when they were in the ambiguous ($M = 3.08$) condition, $F(1, 19) = 2.1$, $p = 0.15$.

3. Could it be that there were differences in the ease of generating reasons across the various cells of the individual difference measures? That is, participants in the high NCOG, high NTE might have found it equally easy to generate three or ten reasons and the reason for no context effect is due to the manipulation working differentially across the individual difference variables. Analyses suggested this was not the case; individuals high in NCOG and NTE found generating three reasons easier than generating ten reasons, $F(1, 50) = 7.49$, $p = 0.01$, ($M_{ease\ for\ ten} = 4.86$, $M_{ease\ for\ three} = 6.97$). In similar fashion, individuals low in NCOG and NTE found generating three reasons easier than generating ten reasons, $F(1, 57) = 7.1$, $p = 0.01$, ($M_{ease\ for\ ten} = 4.78$, $M_{ease\ for\ three} = 6.81$). The difference between the ease of generating three versus ten reasons was not moderated by NCOG or NTE. Thus, even though the ease of generating reasons was similar across the various levels of the individual difference variables, the low NCOG, NTE participants were susceptible to a context effect based upon the ease of generating reasons, while the high NCOG, NTE participants were not. The former finding is consistent with the construction perspective. The latter finding is consistent with the retrieval perspective.

4. Note that there are two ways of examining these interactions. One could compare latencies for the first response versus the second response when an evaluative response (or attribute recognition) is performed first to examine facilitation effects. Another approach would be to examine the latency for evaluative responses (or attribute recognition) when performed first versus second. In fact, the latter might well be preferred in light of the fact that individuals are responding to the exact same question and thus variables such as differences in lengths of questions become irrelevant. However, we have elected to present analyses based on the former since that approach maps more closely onto the process we have outlined, namely how evaluative responses (or attribute recognition) facilitate each other. We would like to reassure readers who might prefer the second approach that analyses using that approach provide results consistent with the CARMAS perspective.

5. It is perhaps worth contrasting these results with results reported by Bassili and Roy (1998). Bassili and Roy asked individuals to evaluate a policy and then think of one of its consequences or think of one of the policy's consequences and then evaluate it. Thinking of a consequence of a policy facilitated

evaluative responses, regardless of whether the participant held strong or weak attitudes toward the policy. However, evaluating the policy facilitated thinking of consequences for participants with strong attitudes but not for participants with weak attitudes. There are a number of points worth making. First, thinking of consequences of a policy obviously could, but need not, map onto existing memory representations of attributes. Second, the results rely on a comparison of consequence (or evaluation) performed second and being compared to a control condition that performed a reading task first. The crucial latency data for the task performed first is not reported. Assuming the control condition task is similar to the baseline or performing-the-task-first latency, for the weak strength participants expressing an evaluation did not facilitate subsequent consequences, which would appear to go against the traditional construction perspective. Third, comparing the response latencies for expressing an evaluation in the control condition reveals no difference in response time across strong and weak attitude participants. The biggest paradox in the results reported in the paper (and acknowledged by the authors) is the fact that thinking of consequences took longer than evaluating the policy. This violates a key prerequisite for mediation—namely, that "judgments that take longer to arrive at cannot plausibly mediate or come prior to judgments that take a shorter time" (Smith and Miller 1983). A critical difference between the studies reported here and in the Bassili and Roy paper is that we measured or manipulated attitude strength first (an attitude formation stage) and examined facilitation effects (attitude expression stage) later. In contrast, Bassili and Roy performed these tasks in the reverse order (participants performed the latency task first and strength was measured later). It is perhaps plausible that participants' attitude strength might have changed as a function of performing the earlier task. Being asked to think of consequences of a policy plausibly is capable of prompting elaboration.

REFERENCES

Ahluwalia, Rohini, Robert E. Burnkrant, and H. Rao Unnava (2000). "Consumer Response to Negative Publicity: The Moderating Role of Commitment," *Journal of Marketing Research,* 37 (2), 203–215.

Ahluwalia, Rohini, H. Rao Unnava, and Robert E. Burnkrant (2001). "The Moderating Role of Commitment on the Spillover Effect of Marketing," *Journal of Marketing Research,* 38 (4), 458–471.

Allport, Gordon W. (1935). "Attitudes." In *Handbook of Social Psychology,* ed. C. Murchison. Worcester, MA: Clark University Press, 798–884.

Asch, Solomon E. (1952). *Social Psychology.* Oxford, UK: Oxford University Press.

Bagozzi, Richard P. (1994). "ACR Fellow Speech." In *Advances in Consumer Research* (vol. 21), ed. C.T. Allen and D.R. John. Vancouver, BC: Association for Consumer Research, 8–11.

Bassili, John N., and Jon A. Krosnick (2000). "Do Strength-related Attitude Properties Determine Susceptibility to Response Effects? New Evidence from Response Latency, Attitude Extremity, and Aggregate Indices," *Political Psychology,* 21 (1), 107–132.

Bassili, John N., and Jean-Paul Roy (1998). "On the Representation of Strong and Weak Attitudes About Policy in Memory." *Political Psychology,* 19, 669–681.

Baumgardner, Michael H., Michael R. Leippe, and Thomas M. Ostrom (1976). "The Role of Criterial Attributes in the Organization of Cognitive Representation." Paper presented at the Mid-Western Psychological Association, Chicago, IL, May.

Bennett, W.L. (1975). *The Political Mind and the Political Environment.* Lexington, MA: D.C. Heath.

Bettman, James R. (1979). *An Information Processing Theory of Consumer Choice.* Reading, MA: Addison-Wesley.

Bettman, James R., Mary F. Luce, and John W. Payne (1998). "Constructive Consumer Choice Processes." *Journal of Consumer Research,* 25(3), 187–217.

Bettman, James R., and Choong W. Park (1980). "Effects of Prior Knowledge and Experience and Phase of the Choice Process on Consumer Decision Processes: A Protocol Analysis," *Journal of Consumer Research,* 7 (12), 234–248.

Bishop, George F. (1987). "Experiments with the Middle Response Alternative in Survey Questions," *Public Opinion Quarterly,* 51, 220–232.

Bishop, George D., David L. Hamilton, and John B. McConahay (1980). "Attitudes and Nonattitudes in the Belief Systems of Mass Publics," *Journal of Social Psychology,* 110 (1), 53–64.

Brown, Steven R. (1970). "Consistency and the Persistence of Ideology," *Public Opinion Quarterly,* 34, 60–68.

Cacioppo, John T., Stephen L. Crites, Gary G. Berntson and Michael G. Coles (1993). "If Attitudes Affect How Stimuli are Processed, Should They Not Affect the Event Related Brain Potential?" *Psychological Science,* 4 (2), 108–112.

Cacioppo, John T., Stephen L. Crites, and Wendi L. Gardner (1996). "Attitudes to the right: Evaluative Processing Is Associated with Lateralized Late Positive Event-related Brain Potentials," *Personality and Social Psychology Bulletin,* 22 (12), 1205–1219.

Cacioppo, John T., Stephen L. Crites, Wendi L. Gardner, and Gary G. Berntson (1994). "A Late Positive Brain Potential that Varies as a Function of Trait Negativity and Extremity," *Journal of Personality and Social Psychology,* 67 (1), 115–125.

Cacioppo, John T., Richard E. Petty, and Thomas R. Geen (1989). "Attitude Structure and Function: From the Tripartite to the Homeostasis Model of Attitudes." In *Attitude Structure and Function,* ed. A.R. Pratkanis, S.J. Breckler, and Anthony G. Greenwald. Hillsdale, NJ: Lawrence Erlbaum, 275–309.

Cacioppo, John T., Richard E. Petty, Chuan Fend Kao, and Regina Rodriguez (1986). "Central and Peripheral Routes to Persuasion: An Individual Difference Perspective," *Journal of Personality and Social Psychology,* 51 (5), 1032–1043.

Cook, Thomas D., and Brain D. Flay (1978). "The Persistence of Experimentally Induced Attitude Change." In *Advances in Experimental Social Psychology* (vol. 11), ed. Leonard Berkowitz. San Diego, CA: Academic Press, 1–57.

Crites, Stephen L., John T. Cacioppo, Wendi L. Gardner, and Gary G. Berntson (1995). "A Late Positive Brain Potential that Varies as a Function of Attitude Registration Rather than Attitude Report," *Journal of Personality and Social Psychology,* 68 (6), 997–1013.

Eagly, Alice H., and Shelly Chaiken (1993). *The Psychology of Attitudes.* Fort Worth, TX: Harcourt Brace.

Fazio, Russell H. (1989). "On the Power and Functionality of Attitudes: The Role of Attitude Accessibility." In *Attitude Structure and Function,* ed. Anthony R. Pratkanis. et al. Hillsdale, NJ: Lawrence Erlbaum.

——— (1995). "Attitudes as Object-Evaluation Associations: Determinants, Consequences and Correlates of Attitude Accessibility." In *Attitude Strength: Antecedents and Consequences,* ed. Richard E. Petty and Jon Krosnick. Mahwah, NJ: Lawrence Erlbaum.

Fazio, Russell H., Jim Blascovich, and D.M. Driscoll (1992). "On the Functional Value of Attitudes: The Influence of Attitudes on the Ease and Quality of Decision Making," *Personality and Social Psychology Bulletin,* 18 (4), 388–401.

Fazio, Russell H., Janet E. Ledbetter, and Tamara Towles-Schwen (2000). "On the Costs of Accessible Attitudes: Detecting that the Attitude Object has Changed," *Journal of Perosnality and Social Psychology,* 78 (2), 197–210.

Ferguson, Melissa, and John Bargh (2003). "The Constructive Nature of Automatic Evaluation." In *The Psychology of Evaluation: Affective Processes in Cognition and Emotion,* ed. Jochen Musch and Karl Christoph Klauer. Mahwah, NJ: Lawrence Erlbaum, 169–188.

Haugtvedt, Curtis P., and Richard E. Petty (1992). "Personality and Persuasion: Need for Cognition Moderates the Persistence and Resistance of Attitude Change," *Journal of Personality and Social Psychology,* 63, 308–319.

Haugtvedt, Curtis P., and Duane T. Wegener (1994). "Message Order Effects in Persuasion—An Attitude Strength Perspective," *Journal of Consumer Research,* 21 (1), 205–237.

Hippler, Hans-J, Norbert Schwarz, and Seymour Sudman (1987). *Social Information Processing and Survey Methodology.* New York, NY: Springer-Verlag.

Isen, Alice M., Thomas E. Shalker, Margaret Clark, and Lynn Karp (1978). "Affect, Accessibility of Material in Memory, and Behavior: A Cognitive Loop?" *Journal of Personality and Social Psychology,* 36 (1), 1–12.

Jarvis, Blair W., and Richard E. Petty (1996). "The Need to Evaluate," *Journal of Personality and Social Psychology,* 70 (1), 172–194.

Jewell, Robert D., and H. Rao Unnava (2004). "Exploring Differences in Attitudes between Light and Heavy Brand Users," *Journal of Consumer Psychology,* 14 (1/2), 75–81.

Kahneman, Daniel, and Amos Tversky (1974). "Judgment under Uncertainty: Heuristics and Biases," *Science,* 185, 1124–1131.

Krosnick, Jon, and Richard E. Petty (1995). "Attitude Strength: An Overview." In *Attitude Strength: Antecedents and Consequences,* ed. Richard E. Petty and Jon Krosnick. Mahwah, NJ: Lawrence Erlbaum, 1–24.

Lingle, John H., Geva Nehemia, Thomas M. Ostrom, Michael R. Leippe, and Michale H. Baumgardner (1979). "Thematic Effects of Person Judgments on Impression Organization," *Journal of Personality and Social Psychology,* 37 (5), 674–687.

Marwell, Gerald, Michael T. Aiken, and N.J. Demerath (1987). "The Persistence of Political Attitudes Among 1960s Civil Rights Activists," *Public Opinion Quarterly,* 51 (3), 359–375.

Menon, Geeta, Priya Raghubir, and Norbert Schwarz (1995). "Behavioral Frequency Estimates: An Accessibility-Diagnosticity Framework," *Journal of Consumer Research,* 22 (2) (September), 212–228.

Payne, John W., James R. Bettman, and Eric J. Johnson (1992). "Behavioral Decision Research: A Constructive Processing Perspective," *Annual Review of Psychology,* 43, 87–131.

Petty, Richard E., and John T. Cacioppo (1986). "The Elaboration Likelihood Model of Persuasion." In *Advances in Experimental Social Psychology* (vol. 19), ed. Leonard Berkowitz. New York, NY: Academic Press.

Petty, Richard E., John T. Cacioppo, and David Schumann (1983). "Central and Peripheral Routes to Advertising Effectiveness: The Moderating Role of Involvement," *Journal of Consumer Research,* 10 (September), 135–145.

Petty, Richard E., Curtis P. Haugtvedt, and Stephen M. Smith (1995). "Elaboration as a Determinant of Attitude Strength: Creating Attitudes That Are Persistent, Resistant and Predictive of Behavior." In *Attitude Strength: Antecedents and Consequences,* ed. Richard E. Petty and Jon Krosnick. Hillsdale, NJ: Lawrence Erlbaum.

Petty, Richard E., Joseph R. Priester, and Duane T. Wegener (1994). "Cognitive Processes in Attitude Change." In *Handbook of Social Cognition,* ed. Robert S. Wyer and Thomas K. Srull. Hillsdale, NJ: Lawrence Erlbaum, 69–142.

Petty, Richard E., and Duane T. Wegener (1998). "Attitude Change: Multiple Roles for Persuasion Variables." In *Handbook of Social Psychology,* 4th ed. (vol. 1). Boston, MA: McGraw-Hill.

Posavac, Steven S., David M. Sanbonmatsu, and Russell H. Fazio (1997). "Considering the Best Choice: Effects of the Salience and Accessibility of Alternatives on Attitude-Decision Consistency," *Journal of Personality and Social Psychology,* 72 (2), 253–261.

Priester, Joseph R., Dhananjay Nayakankuppam, Monique A. Fleming, and John Godek (2004). "The A^2SC^2 Model: The Influence of Attitudes and Attitude Strength on Consideration and Choice," *Journal of Consumer Research,* 30 (4), 574–587.

Priester, Joseph R., and Richard E. Petty (2003). "When and Why Untrusted Endorsers Are More Effective than Trusted Endorsers: The Influence of Spokesperson Trustworthiness on Elaboration and Attitude Strength," *Journal of Consumer Psychology,* 13 (4), 408–421.

Schuman, Howard, and Stanley Presser (1981). *Questions and Answers in Attitude Surveys.* New York, NY: Academic Press.

Schuman, Howard, Stanley Presser, and Jacob Ludwig (1981). "Context Effects on Survey Responses to Questions about Abortion," *Public Opinion Quarterly,* 45 (2), 216–223.

Schwarz, Norbert (1998). "Accessible Content and Accessibility Experiences: The Interplay of Declarative and Experiential Information in Judgment," *Personality and Social Psychology Review,* Special Issue: *Metacognition.* 2 (2), 87–99.

———. (1999). "Self-Reports: How the Questions Shape the Answers," *American Psychologist,* 54 (2), 93–105.

Schwarz, Norbert, Herbert Bless, Fritz Strack, and Gisela Klumpp (1991). "Ease of Retrieval as Information: Another Look at the Availability Heuristic," *Journal of Personality and Social Psychology,* 61 (2), 195–202.

Schwarz, Norbert, and Gerd Bohner (2001). "The Construction of Attitudes." In *Blackwell Handbook of Social Psychology: Intraindividual Processes,* ed. Abraham Tesser and Norbert Schwarz. Oxford, UK: Blackwell, 436–457.

Schwarz, Norbert, and Gerald L. Clore (1983). "Mood, Misattribution, and Judgments of Well-Being: Informative and Directive Functions of Affective States," *Journal of Personality and Social Psychology,* 45 (3), 513–523.

Schwarz, Norbert, Fritz Strack, Detlev Kommer and Dirk Wagner (1987). Soccer, Rooms, and the Quality of Your Life: Mood Effects on Judgments of Satisfaction with Life in General and with Specific Life-Domains." *European Journal of Social Psychology,* 17, 69–79.

Schwarz, Norbert, and Seymour Sudman (1996). *Answering Questions: Methodology for Determining Cognitive and Communicative Processes in Survey Research.* San Francisco, CA: Jossey-Bass.

Sherif, Muzafer, and Hadley Cantril (1947). *The Psychology of Ego-Involvements: Social Attitudes and Identifications.* New York, NY: Wiley.

Slovic, Paul (1995). "The Construction of Preference," *American Psychologist,* 50 (5), 364–371.

Smith, Eliot, R., and Frederick D. Miller (1983). "Mediation Among Attributional Inferences and Comprehension Processes: Initial Findings and a General Method." *Journal of Personality and Social Psychology,* 44, 492–505.

Strack, Fritz, and Leonard L. Martin (1987). "Thinking, Judging and Communicating: A Process Account of Context Effects in Attitude Surveys." In *Social Information Processing and Survey Methodology,* ed. Hans J. Hippler, Norbert Schwarz, and Seymour Sudman. New York, NY: Springer-Verlag, 123–148.

Strack, Fritz, Leonard L. Martin, and Sabine Stepper (1988). "Inhibiting and Facilitating Conditions of the Human Smile: A Nonobtrusive Test of the Facial Feedback Hypothesis," *Journal of Personality and Social Psychology,* 54 (5), 768–777.

Sudman, Seymour, Norman M. Bradburn, and Norbert Schwarz (1996). *Thinking about Answers: The Application of Cognitive Processes to Survey Methodology.* San Francisco, CA: Jossey-Bass.

Tesser, Abraham (1978). "Self-generated Attitude Change." In *Advances in Experimental Social Psychology* (vol. 11), ed. Leonard Berkowitz. San Diego, CA: Academic Press, 289–338.

Tourangeau, Roger, and Kenneth A. Rasinski (1988). "Cognitive Processes Underlying Context Effects in Attitude Measurement," *Psychological Bulletin,* 103 (3), 299–314.

Tversky, Amos, and Daniel Kahneman (1973). "Availability: A Heuristic for Judging Frequency and Probability," *Cognitive Psychology,* 5 (2), 207–232.

Tversky, Amos, Shmuel Sattath and Paul Slovic (1988). "Contingent Weighting in Judgment and Choice." *Psychological Review,* 95, 371–384.

Valins, Stuart (1966). "Cognitive Effects of False Heart-Rate Feedback," *Journal of Personality and Social Psychology,* 4 (4), 400–408.

Wells, Gary L., and Richard E. Petty (1980). "The Effects of Overt Head Movements on Persuasion: Compatibility and Incompatibility of Responses," *Basic and Applied Social Psychology,* 1 (3), 219–230.

Wilson, Timothy D., and Sara D. Hodges (1992). "Attitudes as Temporary Constructions." In *The Construction of Social Judgment,* ed. Leonard Martin and Abraham Tesser. Hillsdale, NJ: Lawrence Erlbaum, 37–65.

CHAPTER 17

THE CONNECTION-PROMINENCE ATTACHMENT MODEL (CPAM)

A Conceptual and Methodological Exploration of Brand Attachment

C. WHAN PARK, JOSEPH R. PRIESTER,
DEBORAH J. MACINNIS, AND ZHONG WAN

Bowlby (1982), the pioneer of work on attachment, proposed that human infants are born with a repertoire of (attachment) behaviors designed by evolution to assure proximity to supportive others (attachment figures). This proximity provides a means of securing protection from physical and psychological threats. It also promotes affect regulation and healthy exploration (see also Mikulincer and Shaver 2005, and Berman and Sperling 1994 for the discussion). An individual's desire to become strongly attached to select entities is a basic motivation among humans that begins in infancy and extends through adulthood (Bowlby 1973; Ainsworth et al. 1978; Reis and Patrick 1996).

One of the most critical issues facing academic researchers and practitioners who study marketing is to understand the impact of consumers' attachment to a brand. Brand attachment is defined as the strength of the bond connecting the consumer with a brand. Attachment is critical as it impacts consumers' commitment to a brand (Fournier 1998; Thomson, MacInnis, and Park 2005; Pimentel and Reynolds 2004), that is, the extent to which they pledge to remain in a long-term relationship with the brand. Consumers who are strongly committed to a brand are not only less expensive to retain, they are less vulnerable to loss from competitive efforts and brand disasters. Moreover, committed consumers add strong revenue-enhancing capacities by their willingness to pay a price premium and their willingness to convert others to the brand (via positive word of mouth and brand advocacy).

Critical to future research on brand attachment is the existence of a valid and parsimonious measure of this construct. A valid measure would enable research on the determinants of brand attachment—particularly those that are fostered by marketing activities. A valid measure would also enable an assessment of the relationship between brand attachment and indicators of brand equity. Moreover, a parsimonious and valid measure would allow for tracking of brand attachment over time and the initiation of marketing activities designed to maximize attachment.

Despite the importance of the attachment construct, valid and reliable measures of brand attachment are scarce. Thomson and colleagues' (2005) measure of *emotional* attachment toward a brand has a number of desirable properties. However, because it is based solely on emotions linked to the brand, it may not fully tap key conceptual properties that comprise the attachment construct.

The goal of the present chapter is to develop a parsimonious, valid, and reliable measure of brand attachment and demonstrate its convergent, discriminant, and predictive validity. We first define attachment and suggest that two core elements represent the construct—brand-self connection and prominence of brand-relevant thoughts and feelings. In three studies we provide evidence supporting this two-factor structure of attachment. We also show that the proposed measure, the connection-prominence attachment model (CPAM), is empirically distinct from Thomson and colleagues' attachment measure, predicts commitment, and does so better than the Thomson et al. (2005) measure of attachment.

THEORY AND HYPOTHESES: CONCEPTUAL PROPERTIES OF THE ATTACHMENT CONSTRUCT (AND THE CPAM MEASURE)

Brand Attachment Definition and Indicator

We define brand attachment as the strength of the bond connecting the brand with the self. We propose that bond strength is revealed by two critical indicators: (1) brand-self connectedness and (2) the prominence of brand-relevant thoughts and feelings.

Brand-Self Connection

Consistent with prior research on attachment and work on self-expansion theory, attachment is reflected, in part, by the degree to which consumers view the brand as being part of or personally connected to themselves and reflecting who they are (see Escalas 2004; Escalas and Bettman 2005; Chaplin and Roedder John 2005). We view brand-self connections not as the number of brands to which the consumer is connected, but rather the strength of connectedness a consumer has to a given brand. The more the brand has been incorporated into one's sense of self and the greater the personal connection the consumer feels between the self and the brand, the stronger is their brand attachment.

We identify two indicators of brand-self connectedness. "Being part of oneself and reflecting who one is" relates to the self-identity basis of brand-self connectedness. "Being personally connected" reflects not self-identity per se, but rather personal meaningfulness. As Mittal (2006) implies, these are two different yet related bases of brand-self connectedness.

Prominence of Brand-Relevant Thoughts and Feelings

In addition to brand-self connectedness, attachment is also reflected by the prominence of brand-related thoughts and feelings in consumers' internal mental world. The prominence of brand-related thoughts and feelings (termed *brand prominence* for simplicity) is reflected by the ease with which brand-related thoughts and feelings are retrieved and the retrieval frequency of such thoughts and feelings. Thus, consumers' attachment to two brands with the same degree of brand-self connectedness will be greater for the brand that is more prominent in the consumer's mind. In this sense then, brand attachment is revealed by the strength of one's brand-self connectedness as well as the degree of brand prominence.

Including brand prominence an indicator of attachment is quite consistent with self-expansion theory. Because brands to which consumers are emotionally attached make consumers feel secure and good, brand-related thoughts and feelings should be prominent in times of emotional distress, as the brand offers the potential to ease negative feelings and facilitate coping with stress. Moreover, because the brand's resources are linked to those of the consumer, thoughts about the brand and the resources it brings to the consumer should make the brand salient in situations where consumers make decisions that involve resource availability and resource allocation. The fact that time is required to form strong attachments between a brand and the consumer suggests that consumers should have more knowledge about brands to which they are attached and have numerous consumption contexts where brand-self associations have developed. This depth of brand knowledge, the brand's linkage to autobiographical memories and active brand engagement (Keller 2003), should make the brand salient and cued whenever situations pertinent to the brand or its usage are cued. As evidence for the relevance of prominence as an indicator of attachment, prior research has established a relationship between attachment and activation of memory about attachment-relevant objects (Collins and Read 1994).

Although previous attachment research in psychology has focused on the relationship between attachment and memory retrieval as indicated by response latency (Collins and Read 1994), we extend this work by examining subjective judgments of prominence. We do so for several reasons. First, subjective assessments of prominence mirror brand-self connectedness and attachment, which are also subjective assessments. Second, because attachment is strongly linked with brand choice and usage, we anticipate that subjective judgments of prominence, more so than objective assessments of pure memory retrieval, influence brand purchase and usage. Third, objective assessments may, in fact, be inappropriate as they may fail to capture prominence. According to Schwarz (2004), consumers' reasoning behind their subjective experiences with the ease of recall and thought generation serve as a basis of judgment about the contents of the recalled declarative information, and can qualify the conclusions drawn from recalled content. Individuals subjectively experience, judge, and modify retrieved information. Finally, using subjective (vs. objective) assessments of prominence has practical value. Their ease of collection expands opportunities for studying attachment.

Note that, as indicated earlier, the two measures are more likely to differ in their relevance (memory versus behaviors). When and to what extent they are related and conditions under which one is more appropriate represents an interesting issue, though it is beyond the scope of the present study.

Importance of Both Indicators

Strong brand-self connections and prominent brand-related thoughts and feelings may be related. For example, a strong brand-self connection may allow for easier and more frequent retrieval of brand-related thoughts and feelings. However, we do not regard the two indicators as redundant. Instead we regard each as a critical indicator of attachment; both are necessary to fully capture the brand attachment construct.

As evidence, one may have some attachment to a brand from one's youth (e.g., GI Joe, Barbie) where the brand is strongly connected to the self ("part of me" and/or "personally connected") but where brand thoughts and feelings are not often accessed given the brand's linkage to a past self. Such attachment would be lower in degree than when brand thoughts and feelings are highly accessed through the brand's linkage to a present self (still collecting GI Joes or Barbie dolls). However, the fact that a brand reflects a past self need not imply that prominence is low. To the extent that the brand is prominent, even though linked to past self, attachment should be strong. One may also have some attachment to brands that are not strongly connected to one's sense of self, but whose ritualistic usage (e.g., preparing one's coffee with Coffee-Mate; getting dressed after putting on Johnson's baby powder) makes for a comforting consumption routine. This comfort would disintegrate were the brand not used or available. This attachment would, however, be far stronger if one also had a strong brand-self connection. Thus, we regard brand-self connectedness and prominence as sufficiently distinct to add uniquely to the assessment of the brand attachment construct; both are nonredundant indicators of attachment. This perspective assumes that the highest level of attachment is revealed when both dimensions are high (an assumption we test subsequently).

THE CPAM MODEL AND THE EMOTIONAL ATTACHMENT MEASURE

Measuring attachment based on the two components described (brand-self connection and prominence of thoughts and feelings) contrasts with Thomson, MacInnis and Park's (2005) ten-item measure of *emotional* attachment. The latter measure entails three attachment dimensions, each indicated by emotions linked to the brand. The first dimension (affection) is indicated by the items "affectionate," "loved," "friendly," and "peaceful." The second dimension (passion) is indicated by the items "passionate," "delighted," and "captivated." The third dimension (connection) is indicated by "connected," "bonded," and "attached." Although the ten-item measure has desirable psychometric properties and has been shown to meet several validation criteria, it reflects purely the affective responses linked to the attachment object.

Since brand attachment is described in terms of the *strength of the bond* connecting the brand with the consumer, and the bond is established with both cognitive and affective (emotional) bases, a measure based purely on the strength of the affective responses may not fully capture the cognitive and emotional bonds. While Thomson and colleagues' (2005) measure may provide an emotion-based indicator of brand-self connection (via the "connection" dimension), it would be better to measure the brand-self connection directly rather than indirectly through affective measures since it is possible that other factors (e.g., strong attitudes) may also lead to the similar emotion-based indicator. Finally, it does not tap the prominence component. While passion, intimacy, and connection may be indirectly associated with prominent thoughts and feelings, a more direct indicator of prominence may better tap the attachment construct.

Because both measures are designed to indicate the attachment construct, we anticipate that the Thomson (2005) measure will be strongly related to the CPAM measure. However, because the two measures tap different aspects of attachment we anticipate that they will be empirically discriminable. As such, we anticipate that

P_1: The proposed brand attachment measure (CPAM) is significantly related to but is distinctly different from Thomson and colleagues' (2005) measure of attachment.

We anticipate also that a valid measure would predict outcomes of attachment such as brand commitment. Before moving forward, it is important to distinguish commitment from attachment since the two constructs are sometimes confused in the literature.

ATTACHMENT AND COMMITMENT

We define commitment in a manner consistent with its usage in the emotional attachment literature (e.g., Levinger 1980; Rosenblatt 1977)—as a decision or pledge to maintain a long-term relationship with a brand into the future. Rather than being synonymous with attachment, we regard commitment as an outcome of attachment. Commitment is a psychological pledge regarding future behavior. Attachment is a characteristic of a relationship between a consumer and a brand. Attachment is a natural precursor to commitment (Rusbult et al. 1991).[1]

Thus, we anticipate that,

P_2: Evidence of the validity of the proposed measure of attachment (CPAM) would be shown by finding that it strongly predicts commitment and commitment-related behaviors.

P_3: Evidence of the validity of the proposed measure of attachment (CPAM) would be shown by finding that it predicts commitment better than Thomson and colleagues' (2005) emotions-based attachment measure.

STUDY 1: ITEM GENERATION AND SELECTION

Based on the conceptual definitions of brand attachment and commitment described earlier, the authors generated a set of items designed to tap the domain of the brand attachment and commitment constructs. All items were evaluated on eleven-point scales anchored by 0 (= "not at all") and 10 (= "completely").

Five items assessed brand-self connection (BSC): To what extent do you feel that (brand name) is part of you (BSC 1)? To what extent do you feel that you are personally connected to (brand name; BSC 2)? To what extent do you feel that you are emotionally bonded to (brand name; BSC 3)? To what extent is (brand name) part of you and who you are (BSC 4)? To what extent does (brand name) reflect the values you personally cherish (BSC 5)?

Five items assessed prominence of thoughts and feelings (PRO): To what extent are your thoughts and feelings toward (brand name) often automatic, coming to mind seemingly on their own (PRO 1)? To what extent does the word (brand name) automatically evoke many thoughts about the past, present, and future (PRO 2)? To what extent do your thoughts and feelings toward (brand name) come to mind so naturally and instantly that you don't have much control over them (PRO 3)? To what extent do you have many thoughts about (brand name; PRO 4)? To what extent do your thoughts and feelings toward (brand name) come to you naturally and instantly (PRO 5)?

Five items assessed brand commitment (BC): To what extent are you loyal to (brand name; BC 1)? To what extent are you committed to (brand name; BC 2)? To what extent have you made a pledge to yourself to use (brand name) in the future (BC 3)? To what extent do you feel an allegiance to (brand name; BC 4)? To what extent are you dedicated to (brand name; BC 5)? This commitment measure resembles the measure used by Beatty, Homer, and Kahle (1988).

Method

One hundred ninety-one undergraduate participants used the noted items to evaluate their attachment and commitment to three brands: Quaker Oats oatmeal, the Apple iPod, and their university. Participants evaluated all three brands.

Results

Exploratory factor analyses using oblique factor rotation were conducted for each brand. The results were consistent for all three brands. A three-factor solution provided the best fit [Root Mean Square Error Approximation (RMSEA) <0.08] and yielded meaningful factor structures (see Fabrigar et al. 1999). Means, standard deviations, and the factor loading for the factor analyses are presented in Tables 17.1 and 17.2. All of the items, save PRO 2 and PRO 4, loaded cleanly on their hypothesized factors supporting the discriminant validity of the brand attachment measure (P_2). PRO 2 and PRO 4 loaded equally on both brand-self connection and prominence of thoughts and feelings, and hence were dropped from further consideration.

While an eight-item scale (five items for brand-self connection and three items for prominence of thoughts and feelings) is not unusually long for academic use, we sought to make the scale as parsimonious as possible in order to maximize the scale's potential applicability to marketing practice. Hence, we selected two items designed to represent each of the two elements of brand attachment on both statistical grounds (strong factor

Table 17.1

Study 1: Means (and Standard Deviations)

	Quaker Oats	Apple iPod	University
Brand Self Connection 1	1.3 (2.2)	5.1 (2.9)	8.5 (1.5)
Brand Self Connection 2	1.2 (2.0)	4.7 (3.1)	8.5 (1.7)
Brand Self Connection 3	1.0 (1.8)	3.8 (3.2)	8.2 (2.1)
Brand Self Connection 4	0.8 (1.6)	4.1 (3.1)	8.2 (1.9)
Brand Self Connection 5	1.4 (2.2)	3.6 (3.0)	7.8 (2.1)
Prominence of thoughts and feelings 1	2.4 (3.1)	4.7 (3.2)	7.8 (2.0)
Prominence of thoughts and feelings 2	1.7 (2.4)	4.3 (3.1)	8.7 (1.5)
Prominence of thoughts and feelings 3	2.1 (2.9)	4.1 (3.2)	7.1 (2.7)
Prominence of thoughts and feelings 4	1.0 (1.5)	4.2 (2.9)	8.2 (1.6)
Prominence of thoughts and feelings 5	2.1 (2.9)	4.4 (3.2)	7.5 (2.2)
Commitment 1	1.2 (2.2)	4.9 (3.7)	9.0 (1.5)
Commitment 2	0.8 (1.8)	4.1 (3.5)	8.8 (1.8)
Commitment 3	0.8 (1.9)	3.9 (3.5)	8.0 (2.4)
Commitment 4	0.8 (1.8)	3.5 (3.4)	8.6 (2.0)
Commitment 5	0.9 (1.9)	3.5 (3.4)	8.7 (1.7)

Table 17.2

Factor Loadings, Study 1

	Oatmeal			iPod			University		
Factor	BSC	PRO	BC	BSC	PRO	BC	BSC	PRO	BC
BSC 1	.78	.16	.46	.79	.21	.37	.82	.28	.34
BSC 2	.82	.17	.46	.79	.24	.38	.73	.29	.41
BSC 3	.75	.24	.48	.74	.32	.41	.72	.30	.45
BSC 4	.69	.19	.56	.79	.28	.37	.77	.22	.44
BSC 5	.55	.24	.45	.57	.32	.37	.65	.31	.45
PRO 1	.14	.86	.18	.29	.81	.20	.24	.78	.29
PRO 2	.55	.48	.25	.60	.43	.23	.44	.47	.38
PRO 3	.13	.87	.20	.21	.86	.20	.17	.89	.18
PRO 4	.52	.35	.49	.47	.59	.31	.45	.54	.39
PRO 5	.22	.88	.13	.21	.87	.23	.23	.89	.15
BC 1	.50	.24	.65	.55	.25	.63	.43	.26	.76
BC 2	.49	.20	.78	.52	.23	.73	.45	.26	.78
BC 3	.34	.18	.80	.28	.28	.77	.33	.24	.70
BC 4	.38	.24	.83	.34	.26	.83	.33	.35	.65
BC 5	.48	.21	.75	.39	.21	.84	.59	.18	.72

loadings) and theoretical grounds (clear face validity). For brand-self connection these items were (1) "To what extent do you feel that you are personally connected to (brand name)?" and (2) "To what extent is (brand name) part of you and who you are?" for BSC. For prominence of thoughts and feelings the two items were (1) "To what extent are your thoughts and feelings toward (brand name) often automatic, coming to mind seemingly on their own?" and (2) "To what extent do your thoughts and feelings toward (brand name) come to you naturally and instantly?" for PRO. Three items were chosen for commitment given the same parsimony criterion: (1) "Are you loyal to (brand name)?" (2) Are you committed to (brand name)?" and (3) "Have you made a pledge to yourself to use (brand name) in the future?" Note that adopting this approach is more parsimonious and provides a more conservative test of propositions 1, 2, and 3.

We examined the change in alpha coefficient for reducing the total items loading on each factor compared to the more parsimonious approach. For brand-self connection, the alpha coefficients for the five-item approach were alpha = 0.950_{ats}, = 0.94_{iPod}, and = $0.95_{university}$; compared to the two-item approach using alpha = 0.920_{ats}, = 0.90_{iPod}, and = $0.86_{university}$. Thus, reducing the number of indicators provides a more parsimonious approach without significantly reducing the alpha coefficient for brand-self connection. Similar results were obtained for both prominence of brand-relevant thoughts and feelings and brand commitment. The alpha coefficients for the three-item approach for prominence of thought were alpha = 0.940_{ats}, = 0.94_{iPod}, and = $0.94_{university}$; compared to the two-item approach using alpha = 0.910_{ats}, = 0.90_{iPod}, and = $0.89_{university}$. The alpha coefficients for the five-item approach for brand commitment were alpha = 0.960_{ats}, = 0.95_{iPod}, and = $0.94_{university}$ compared to the three-item approach using alpha = 0.920_{ats}, = 0.91_{iPod}, and = $0.91_{university}$.

STUDY 2: PROMINENCE ITEM VALIDATION

Subjective and Objective Measures of Prominence of Brand-Related Thoughts and Feelings

This study was designed to examine the validity of the self-report measure of the prominence of brand-related thoughts and feelings. One might argue that there are differences in subjectivity perceptions of prominence (how often and quickly one believes thoughts come to mind) and objective experiences of prominence (how quickly thoughts actually do come to mind). Self-report measures of prominence may lack validity since respondents may not be aware of the extent to which thoughts and feelings about the brand are actually prominent in memory.

Method

One hundred and twenty-one participants were asked to complete two tasks. One assessed subjective prominence and the other assessed prominence using an objective (response latency) measure. Participants seated at computer workstations were told that they would be asked a series of questions. Their task was to respond to each question as quickly and as accurately as possible with a yes or no response. After a series of familiarity-building practice questions, respondents replied to the two-brand prominence items that emerged from the pretest as loading on the prominence factor (PRO 1 and PRO 5). Response latency to each item was measured. After completing the response latency task, participants completed the same questions using pencil and paper, with the modification that the questions were posed in such a way as to be answered on an eleven-point scale, anchored by 0 equal to "not at all" and 10 equal to "completely."

Results

Response latencies slower than two standard deviations than the mean response latency were deleted, resulting in data from 114 participants. Response latencies to the two prominence items were averaged, resulting in an average response latency for each participant. This average response latency was entered into a regression analysis with the eleven-point subjective prominence scale measure serving as the independent variable. A significant influence of prominence on response latency emerged: $b = -0.05$, $F(1, 112) = 9.43$, $p < 0.005$. The more that participants reported that thoughts and feelings came to mind automatically and naturally (i.e., subjective prominence), the faster they were able to provide responses (response latency) regarding the brand (i.e., objective prominence).[2] According to this result, the subjective measure of prominence is corroborated by its objective measure. It should be noted that the small size of the effect is most likely due to the nature of the response latency data collection, in that standard keyboards were used, thus significantly decreasing the sensitivity of the reaction time collection. What is noteworthy is that even given such reduced sensitivity, and hence power, the influence is still significant.

STUDY 3: TEST OF THE PROPOSITIONS

After having established the fundamental measurement properties, we turn to the issue of the two attachment models (one element versus two elements) and the testing of propositions. Specifically, study 3 was designed to determine whether the two-element (connection-prominence) model better fits the data than does a single-element model (see Figure 17.1). We also sought to test propositions 1–3. Thus, we anticipated that the CPAM measure of brand attachment would be significantly related to but distinguishable from Thomson and colleagues' measure of attachment (P_1); would be significantly predict commitment (P_2); and would do so better than the Thomson measure (P_3).

Method

Two hundred eighty participants completed a booklet that asked them to report their thoughts and feelings toward the Apple iPod. The iPod brand was chosen based on both its familiarity to the student population and the heterogeneity of preference and attachment. The test booklet contained the four items indicating the CPAM measure and Thomson's ten-item attachment scale. The four items designed to indicate brand-self connection and prominence of thoughts and feelings from study 1 were used to indicate the CPAM measure. Emotional attachment was represented by the ten-item Thomson (2005) measure.

Based on study 1, three items were used to indicate commitment: (1) "To what extent have you made a pledge to yourself to use the iPod in the future," (2) "To what extent are you committed to the iPod," and (3) "To what extent are you loyal to the iPod." Respondents used the same eleven-point scale described above.

Results

Test of the Two-Element Brand Attachment Model

A set of confirmatory factor analyses using the statistical package LISREL explored the notion that a two-factor model of brand-self connection and prominence of thoughts and feelings best represents the attachment construct compared to a single-factor model. To do so, we conducted two confirmatory factor analyses; one in which both factors were allowed to correlate $[r = 0.53; \chi^2 (3) = 32.09]$ and a second in which the two factors were forced to be perfectly correlated $[\chi^2 (4) = 616.10]$. Inspection of the change in χ^2 $[\Delta\chi^2 (1) = 584, p < 0.001]$ revealed that the first analysis better fit the data than the second. These analyses suggest that, although the two models are significantly correlated, they are not redundant. That is, these two models are consistent with the second-order factor structure.

Test of Proposition 1

A second set of models was conducted to test proposition. These models compared the second-order CPAM measure to the three-component Thomson measure. As in the previous analysis, we did so by conducting two confirmatory analyses, one in which both models were allowed to correlate $[r = .82, \chi^2 (78] = 2766)$ and a second in which the two factors were forced to be perfectly correlated $[\chi^2 (79) = 3232]$. Inspection of the change in χ^2 $[\Delta\chi^2 (1) = 466, p < .001]$, reveals that the difference between the two models is significant. Thus, these analyses support proposition, showing that the CPAM measure is related to but empirically distinct from Thomson and colleagues' attachment measure.

Test of Propositions 2 and 3

A third set of models explored the ability of the CPAM measure to predict commitment (P_2), and explored the relative ability of both the CPAM and Thomson's measure to predict commitment (P_3). Three models were estimated. The first estimates the ability of the CPAM measure to influence commitment. The second estimates the ability of the Thomson scale to influence commitment. The third estimates both the CPAM and emotional attachment measures on commitment.

The first model (see Figure 17.1A) fit well. The chi-square was not significant $[\chi^2 (11) = 12.92, p = 0.30]$ and the other fit statistics were excellent [Comparative Fit Index (CF) = 1, Standardized Root Mean Square Residual (SRMSR) = 0.026, Goodness of Fit Index (GFI) = 0.99]. The chi-square and resultant fit statistics suggest that the model satisfactorily fits the data. The results also showed that brand attachment significantly predicts commitment $(\chi = 0.56)$. These results support proposition 2.[3] The second model (see Figure 17.1B) examined the ability of the Thomson model to predict commitment. The model was significantly worse $[\chi^2 (61) = 279.94, p < 0.001]$ and the other fit statistics were not strong (CFI = 0.97, srmr = 0.050, GFI = 0.85), suggesting that model 1 is the

Figure 17.1   **Study 3: Test of P2 and P3**

Panel A. The Predictive Ability of the CPAM Measure for Commitment

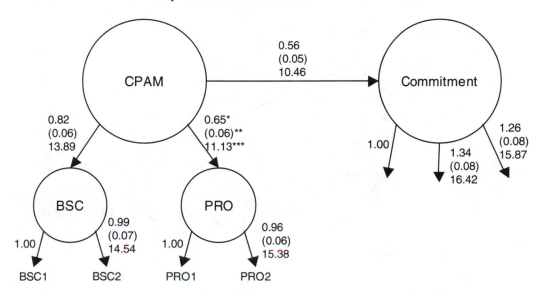

Panel B. The Predictive Ability of the Thomson and Colleagues' Measure for Commitment

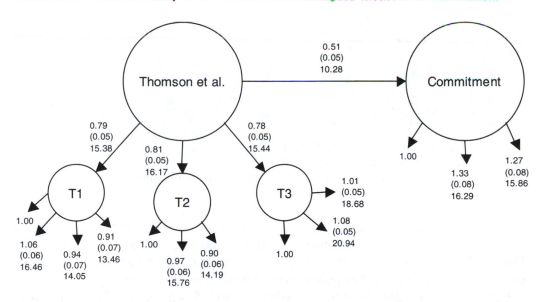

(continued)

Figure 17.1 *(continued)*

Panel C. The Simultaneous Comparison of the CPAM and Thomson and Colleagues' Measures for Commitment

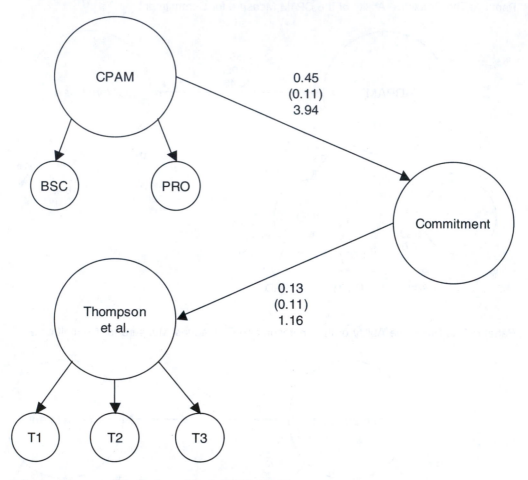

Source: Thomson, MacInnis, and Park (2005), 77–91.
*Parameter estimation; **Standard error; ***t-value.
Abbreviations: BSC, brand-self connection; CPAM, connection-prominence attachment model; PRO, prominence of thoughts and feelings.

superior model. Emotional attachment was a significant predictor of commitment ($\chi =$ 0.51), supporting the results of Thomson and colleagues (2005). The third model (see Figure 17.1C) estimated both the CPAM and Thomson (2005) attachment measures as predictors of commitment. The results showed that, when simultaneously estimated, the CPAM measure remains a significant predictor, $\chi = 0.45$, whereas the Thomson attachment measure becomes insignificant, $\chi = 0.13$. The differential ability of the CPAM (vs. Thomson et al.'s attachment measure) to predict commitment is significant, $z = 2.9$, p <0.01. These results support proposition 3.

Discussion

Study 3 supports propositions 1–3. The brand attachment measure is best represented by a two-factor structure incorporating brand-self connection and prominence of thought items as opposed to a single-factor structure, the measure is empirically discriminable from Thomson and colleagues' (2005) attachment measure (P_1), and it significantly predicts commitment (P_2) and does so better than Thomson and colleagues' emotional attachment measure (P_3).

GENERAL DISCUSSION

The development of a valid brand attachment scale that reflects the core properties of the brand attachment concept is important given the potential contributions of the attachment construct to marketing and consumer behavior. The present chapter has sought to develop a novel and valid measure of brand attachment. Brand attachment was defined as the strength of the bond connecting the brand with the self, and was conceptualized in terms of the degree of brand-self connection and the degree of the prominence of brand-related thoughts and feelings. The results of three studies support the validity of the two-element CPAM measure. Specifically, the measure is related to but discriminable from the attachment measure of Thomson and colleagues (2005); it is a significant predictor of commitment and predicts commitment better than the Thomson measure.

The existence of a valid and reliable measure of brand attachment allows us to test key hypotheses regarding other outcomes of brand attachment. For example, brand attachment may have strong impact on a brand's extendibility. High-attachment consumers are comparatively more motivated and able to categorize the extension as part of the parent brand because they simultaneously possess a desire to maintain a brand-self relationship and an enduring resistance to brand separation (Feeney and Noller 1996). Hence, compared to those with low attachment, high-attachment consumers may be more likely to view a brand extension as an opportunity to maintain and strengthen their relationship with the brand. This motivation makes them more likely to relate the extension to the parent brand and to accept it as part of the parent brand even though it may not fit well with the parent brand. Due to strong self-implications, a readiness to rely on the parent brand as a basis for categorization, the automatic retrieval of brand-related thoughts and feelings, and the greater motivation to categorize brand extensions with parent brands, strong brand attachment may predict the success of brand extension.

The existence of a measure of brand attachment also enables research on marketing factors that may foster attachment. Specifically, an attachment object becomes connected to the self when it is included as part of the consumer's self-concept. Aron and colleagues (2005) offer a motivational resource perspective that explains why some entities are included as part of the self-concept. As a relationship forms, an individual offers resources (social, knowledge, material, etc.) to the relationship partner. Over time, a cognitive reorganization takes place that links resources, the individual, and the relationship partner such that the partner's resources come to be seen as one's own. Through this resource/

self-other linkage, the partner's perspective and identity become linked to one's own. Brands, like people, can offer a number of resources (developed by marketers) to help consumers achieve desired goals (cf. Schultz, Kleine, and Kernan 1989). By examining consumer self-linkages, brand resources, and brand attachment changes over time, marketers may generate additional insights into the marketing variables that create brand-self linkages and hence foster brand attachment.

Finally, while the formation of attachment is important, equally interesting and important is the process of attachment termination. Monitoring attachment over time may provide clues to what factors trigger and mitigate attachment termination. A valid measure of brand attachment facilitates knowledge development on this topic.

NOTES

1. Exploratory factor analyses demonstrate that commitment loads on separate factors than brand attachment. See, for example, the results of study 1.

2. The CPAM was also found to be related to, but empirically discriminable from, commitment.

3. Note that this model focuses on the relative ability of each model to predict commitment. As such, the model fit indices are not as important as the gammas associated with each predictor. That is, we are not necessarily as concerned with how well the overall model fits as we are with the relative ability of each model to predict the criterion variable of commitment. Thus, whenever CPAM is compared to either the Thomson model or attitude strength, only the gammas and the test of the statistical difference between the two models being compared are reported. Overall model-fit indices, in these instances, are not reported.

REFERENCES

Ainsworth, Mary D.S., Mary C. Blehar, Everett Waters, and Sally Wall (1978). *Patterns of Attachment: A Psychological Study of the Strange Situation.* Hillsdale, NJ: Lawrence Erlbaum.

Aron, Arthur, Debra Mashek, Tracy McLaughlin-Volpe, Stephen Wright, Gary Lewandowski, and Elaine N. Aron (2005). "Including Close Others in the Cognitive Structure of the Self." In *Interpersonal Cognition,* ed. Mark W. Baldwin. New York, NY: Guilford Press, 206–232.

Beatty, Sharon E., Pamela Homer, and Lynn R. Kahle (1988). "The Involvement-Commitment Model: Theory and Implications," *Journal of Business Research,* 16 (2), 149–167.

Berman, William H., and Michael B. Sperling (1994). "The Structure and Function of Adult Attachment." In *Attachment in Adults: Clinical and Developmental Perspectives,* ed. Michael B. Sperling and William H. Berman. New York, NY: Guilford Press, 3–28.

Bowlby, John (1973). *Separation: Anxiety and Anger.* New York, NY: Basic Books.

———. (1982). *Attachment.* New York, NY: Basic Books.

Chaplin, Nguyen, and Deborah Roedder John (2005). "The Development of Self-Brand Connections in Children and Adolescents," *Journal of Consumer Research,* 32 (1), 119–129.

Collins, Nancy L., and Stephen J. Read (1994). "Cognitive Representation of Adult Attachment: The Structure and Function of Working Models." In *Attachment Processes in Adulthood,* ed. Kim Bartholomew and Daniel Perlman. London, UK: Jessica-Kingsley, 53–90.

Escalas, Jennifer E. (2004). "Narrative Processing: Building Consumer Connections to Brands," *Journal of Consumer Psychology,* 14 (1, 2), 168–179.

Escalas, Jennifer, and James R. Bettman (2005). "Self-Construal, Reference Groups, and Brand Meaning," *Journal of Consumer Research,* 32 (3), 378–389.

Fabrigar, Leandre R., Duane T. Wegener, Robert C. MacCallum, and Erin J. Strahan (1999). "Evaluating the Use of Exploratory Factor Analysis in Psychological Research," *Psychological Methods,* 4 (3), 272–299.

Feeney, Judith and Patricia Noller (1996). *Adult Attachment.* Beverly Hills, CA: Sage.

Fournier, Susan (1998). "Consumers and Their Brands: Developing Relationship Theory in Consumer Research," *Journal of Consumer Research,* 24 (March), 343–373.

Keller, Kevin Lane (2003). *Strategic Brand Management: Building, Measuring, and Managing Brand Equity,* 2nd ed. Upper Saddle River, NJ: Prentice Hall.

Levinger, George (1980). "Toward the Analysis of Close Relationships," *Journal of Experimental Social Psychology,* 16 (6), 510–544.

Mikulincer, Mario, and Phillip R. Shaver (2005). "Mental Representations of Attachment Security: Theoretical Foundation for a Positive Social Psychology." In *Interpersonal Cognition,* ed. Mark W. Baldwin. New York, NY: Guilford Press, 233–266.

Mittal, Banwari (2006). "I, Me and Mine: How Products Become Consumers' Extended Selves," *Journal of Consumer Behaviour,* 5 (6), 550–562.

Pimentel, Ronald W., and Kristy E. Reynolds (2004). "A Model for Consumer Devotion: Affective Commitment with Proactive Sustaining Behaviors," *Academy of Marketing Science Review,* no. 5.

Reis, Harry T., and Brian C. Patrick (1996). "Attachment and Intimacy: Component Processes." In *Social Psychology: Handbook of Basic Principles,* ed. E. Tory Higgins and Arie W. Kruglanski. New York, NY: Guilford Press, 523–563.

Rosenblatt, Paul C. (1977). "Needed Research on Commitment in Marriage." In *Close Relationships,* ed. George Levinger and Harold L. Raush. Amherst, MA: University of Massachusetts Press.

Rusbult, Caryl E., Julie Verette, Gregory A. Whitney, Linda F. Slovik, and Issac Lipkus (1991). "Accommodation Processes in Close Relationships: Theory and Preliminary Empirical Evidence," *Journal of Personality and Social Psychology,* 60 (1), 53–78.

Schultz, Susan E., Robert E. Kleine, and Jerome B. Kernan (1989). "These Are a Few of My Favorite Things: Toward an Explication of Attachment as a Consumer Behavior Construct," *Advances in Consumer Research,* 16 (1), 359–366.

Schwarz, Norbert (2004). "Metacognitive Experiences in Consumer Judgment and Decision Making," *Journal of Consumer Psychology,* 14 (4), 332–348.

Thomson, Matthew, Deborah J. MacInnis, and C. Whan Park (2005). "The Ties That Bind: Measuring the Strength of Consumers' Emotional Attachments to Brands," *Journal of Consumer Psychology,* 15 (1), 77–91.

CHAPTER 18

LOVE, DESIRE, AND IDENTITY

A Conditional Integration Theory of the Love of Things

AARON C. AHUVIA, RAJEEV BATRA, AND RICHARD P. BAGOZZI

The role of love in brand relationships has drawn increasing interest (Ahuvia 1992, 1993, 2005; Albert, Merunka, and Valette-Florence 2008; Carroll and Ahuvia 2006; Ji 2002; Kamat and Parulekar 2007; Keh, Pang, and Peng 2007; Shimp and Madden 1988; Whang et al. 2004; Yeung and Wyer 2005). While the primary focus of this chapter is on love in consumption, we also present a general theory of love that applies across a broad range of contexts, including interpersonal and person-object situations. By presenting a theory that is broad enough to cover many of the basic dynamics of love in person-object relationships, romantic interpersonal relationships, and family relationships, we do not mean to imply that all these types of love are identical. Past research has shown that even within romantic relationships there are many types of love (Lee 1988), so it would be foolish to deny the differences between a woman's love for her hobby and her love for her husband. But we focus here on developing a theory of love in consumption contexts that is also consistent with the research on love in interpersonal contexts. We leave a detailed exploration of the differences between these types of love to a separate project.

Some readers may question whether the concept of love is really applicable in person-object contexts. Skeptics might argue that when a consumer says "I love _____," whether it is football, wine, or whatever, they are simply using the term loosely, in the same way they might say "pass the chips, I'm starving" when in fact they aren't starving at all. This resistance to the idea that people can love things other than people comes in part from the view that love is sacred, and that by applying the term to things as prosaic as shoes, we cheapen and profane love's character (Ahuvia and Adelman 1993). Hence, examples of noninterpersonal love that have an elevated ethical or spiritual quality, such as love of God or love of country, rarely invoke the same skepticism as love of Gucci. Furthermore, we seldom hear the same skepticism expressed about the applicability of nonsacred psychological constructs such as hate to noninterpersonal settings.

While we sympathize with the idea that there is something special about love, considerable data suggests that love is nonetheless a psychological process that can be applied to people, ideas, activities, and objects. In exploring related topics, numerous consumer researchers have noted the presence of love in consumption (see Ahuvia 1993 for review). Working in psychology, Fehr and Russell (1991) asked respondents to list examples of love and found many examples, such as love of work, books, money, art, sports, honesty, animals, nature, pets, country, and others. In looking at romantic love, Marston, Hecht, and Roberts (1986) found that "many lovers employed no relational constructs in their definition of love, but rather used only physiological responses or behavioral actions. . . . (thus indicating) that love need not be conceived in strictly relational terms, even when love is reciprocated." Finally, although people might use terms such as "starving" or "love" loosely in many contexts, if you asked a person who said "pass the chips I'm starving" if he was literally starving, presumably he would be able to tell you that he was not. This chapter draws in part on data from a larger study that included directly relevant questions about what consumers mean when they say they love something. As will be shown, respondents were able to distinguish between situations where they truly loved something and where they were speaking hyperbolically. More than 70 percent of respondents reported truly loving at least one thing other than a person. This work draws on and integrates past research, but also includes original data from interviews with consumers. The original data were collected as part of a larger study, and other parts of these data have been published elsewhere (Ahuvia 2005). This interview data is used to generate and illustrate a theory of love at a very general level that holds across a wide variety of loved objects. Henceforth, we refer to this broad array of things people love including products, ideas, brands, nature, pets, activities, and so on as love objects (LOs). In this way our use of the term LO is different from the psychoanalytic concept of a love object, which generally refers to a person.

The theory presented here was generated using a constant comparative methodology in which the theoretical framework was compared to original findings and to findings from past research on interpersonal love and on consumer behavior. Because the research here emphasizes theory generation over theory testing, the hypotheses will not be presented prior to the discussion of the results.

After a discussion of research methodology, results are presented in which the incorporation of the LO into the lover's sense of identity is identified as the core of a larger psychological system of love. We then go on to explore the reasons why consumers want to incorporate objects or other people into their identity, and the processes by which this incorporation takes place.

DATA COLLECTION

Respondents were contacted through a snowball sampling procedure, which began with the first author asking personal contacts who fit the informant profile for a list of their acquaintances who might be willing to participate. The respondents were evenly split by gender (36 male and 33 female), predominantly white (white 56, black 10, Hispanic 2, other 1), ranging from 23 to 45 years of age ($M = 32$), and were well educated (post-college = 38, college = 27, high school or less = 5).

For all respondents, confidentially taped interviews were conducted over the phone and lasted between ten minutes and one hour, averaging twenty to thirty minutes. Respondents were asked, "If there is something you love, aside from people with whom you have a close personal relationship, what is it?" For each thing that they loved, respondents were

Figure 18.1 **Visual Representation of the Theory of the Love, Desire, and Identity Theory**

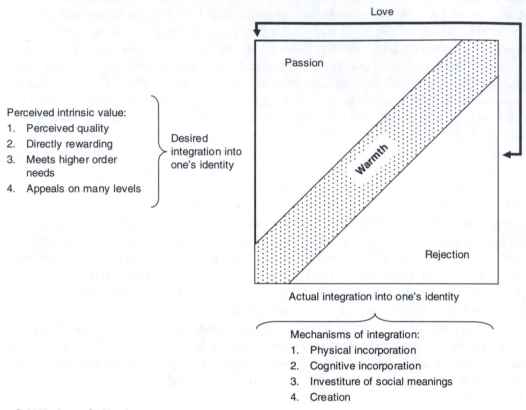

Perceived intrinsic value:
1. Perceived quality
2. Directly rewarding
3. Meets higher order needs
4. Appeals on many levels

Desired integration into one's identity

Love

Passion

Warmth

Rejection

Actual integration into one's identity

Mechanisms of integration:
1. Physical incorporation
2. Cognitive incorporation
3. Investiture of social meanings
4. Creation

© 2008, Aaron C. Ahuvia

asked a uniform set of questions addressing the depth of their feelings for the LO (love object), whether what they felt was love in the strictest sense of the word or if they were "just using the word loosely," and why they felt as they did. The interview continued until the respondent ran out of things that he or she loved.

Ten respondents (6 female, 4 male) were then selected for follow-up in-depth interviews in their homes lasting two to four hours. These respondents were selected based on the contents of their phone interviews, to allow for a more detailed investigation of key issues uncovered in the first set of interviews. These in-home interviews included a discussion of interpersonal love as well as a continued focus on LOs.

ANALYSIS AND RESULTS

Love was widespread among these respondents. Only two respondents claimed to not love anything aside from other people. Nor was the word *love* applied to objects only in a metaphorical sense. Even when respondents spoke in the strictest and most literal sense of the word, 72 percent still said that they loved something other than a person with whom they had a close personal relationship. Therefore, as the respondents define the domain of love, people love a wide variety of things beyond family, friends, and lovers (see Ahuvia 1992 for tables itemizing what people loved).

Results are presented as a system of emergent themes connected to form an integrated theory. Figure 18.1 presents a visual preview of this theory, which will serve as a road map for the subsequent discussion.

Integration of the Loved Object into the Self

In this chapter we use the terms *self* and *identity* interchangeably to refer to a person's conscious and nonconscious idea of whom and what they are. Although one's physical body and one's consciousness are seen by most people as important parts of their self-identity, the self generally extends far beyond these two elements. The notion that love involves an integration of the self and the LO, so that the LO becomes an important part of the lover's identity, has a long tradition in Western culture. In the interpersonal context, this notion dates back at least as far as Plato's Symposium, which refers to the myth that past humans had four arms, four legs, and two heads, but were split in two and now must search for their missing half. This tradition continues in studies that report that love is often experienced as a merging (Dion and Dion 1988; Murstein 1988; Tennov 1979), experimental studies that show that as a relationship becomes closer the other is increasingly merged with the self (Aron et al. 1991), and theories of love that in whole or in part see love as a merging of the lover and the beloved (Aron and Aron 1986; Aron et al. 1989; DeRivera 1984; Gonzales-Crussi 1988; Grant 1976; Hatfield 1982; Jeffries 1993; Kovecses 1991; Maslow 1970; Person 1988; Sperling 1985).

In consumer behavior literature, work on how products become part of consumers' identity has become a major theme of current research (Arnould and Thompson 2005, see also Chapter 4), and Ahuvia (2005) has shown that this process is particularly important to consumers' love of things. Thus, integration of an LO into the lover's identity may serve as a common psychological core, which can unite some streams of research on love in consumer behavior and interpersonal contexts.

Within the interviews, respondents commonly expressed the view that LOs were part of their selves and this view was systematically connected to the likelihood that these relationships would be considered real love. As one respondent said, LOs are "your identity, what you think of yourself, there's no separation. When you're talking about what you love . . . you are essentially talking about yourself" (female, graduate student, age 37). In total, fifteen respondents specifically talked about LOs as being part of them and 80 percent[1] of these respondents saw their relationships with these LOs as real love. In contrast, six respondents commented that the LO in question was not really part of themselves and none of these LOs were viewed as true love.

Four main themes characterized respondents' understandings of what it means for something to be part of the self. Things that are parts of the self (1) affect or change who you are, (2) express the self, (3) form physical extensions of the body, or (4) have a shared history with oneself. The idea that LOs are part of the self when they change an individual was the most central of these themes. This self-change can be focused on the public self by changing one's appearance, as in the woman who loved clothes shopping because "It's a way to become someone else, and start afresh" (female, public relations writer, 30). Conversely, one's private perspective can be changed.

> [Books] participate in making me up, or how would you say—they're part of me.
>   (Q: What do you mean when you say they're part of you?)
>   You incorporate them in such a way that it just adds on and on and on about how you would look at life, it's sort of expansive for myself. (female, unemployed, 37)

Second, self-expression is closely tied to self-extension in that we often "put a lot of ourselves" into that which we create. As a respondent said in describing his hand-painted model soldiers, "This is me, I did this" (male, freelance writer, 36). Creation is particularly important when the created object or event is primarily a form of self-expression rather than a response to pragmatic requirements or the demands of others.[2] As one respondent put it, dancing is "such a part of myself; it's a self-expression that's completely uninhibited and pure for myself" (female, actor, 26).

Third, some respondents also viewed LOs as a physical extension of the brain or body. This was particularly true for photo collections and journals that served as extensions of the respondents' memory and hence their life experiences. For example, one respondent reported loving photographs because "I like to be able to keep a record of that because my memory isn't that sharp" (female, salesperson, 30).

Finally, respondents tacitly recognized the concept of contamination (Belk 1988; Belk, Wallendorf, and Sherry 1989) when they expressed the idea that an LO becomes a part of the self by sharing an extensive history together. (As used here, the word *contamination* is a technical term that lacks the usual negative connotations and just means having something "rub off on you.") For example, one respondent explained that he loved his jeans because "they are so old and comfortable and part of me" (male, publishing, 24).

The four themes just mentioned—that objects become part of the self when they (1) affect or change who you are, (2) express the self, (3) form physical extensions of the body, or (4) have a shared history with you—reveal how respondents themselves understood the integration of LOs into their identity. But because a person's sense of self exists at both conscious and nonconscious levels, a person does not need to be overtly aware that an object is part of their identity for that to be the case. Self-relevant responses are one way to ascertain if an object is seen by someone as part of their identity, even if they are not consciously aware of that relationship. Self-relevant responses (shame, guilt, pride) occur in response to actions taken by the self but not when similar actions are taken by others (Roseman 1984) or in the case of responses like offense, when actions are directed at the self but not when similar actions are directed at others (Ortony, Clore, and Collins 1988). For example, if a stranger is insulted we may feel anger at the rude speaker, but we would only feel offense if we ourselves were the target of the barb. Hence, when respondents talked about being proud when their LOs were the focus of compliments, or insulted when their LOs were slighted, they were implicitly including these LOs in their selves. This was made explicit by a respondent's discussion of feeling "hurt" and "offended" when she felt her inherited antique furniture had been evaluated simply for its aesthetic properties.

> These are things that I love. If other people don't realize that they're not just pieces of furniture, then that's what hurts my feelings. . . . It felt like I wasn't being understood, because they're such an integral part of me (female, marketing manager, 35).

Evidence for seeing love as involving the integration of the LO into the lover's sense of identity also comes from projective techniques. When responding to projective questions that asked them to imagine what their LO would be like if it were a person, respondents tended to personify their LOs as a mirror image of themselves or their ideal selves. As a respondent said about his personification of political correctness, "it's male—cause that's me" (male, fund-raiser, 29). This mirroring of the self sometimes even occurred in situations where it seemed implausible. In an in-depth interview, one respondent projected both her plants and music as women who were thousands of years old. Yet she later said that she felt similar to them in this respect because "I feel as though I am a very old soul and so are they" (female, graduate student, 37). This was also common in the anthropomorphized projections of loved pets, supporting a similar finding by Hirschman (1994, pp. 620–621).

Since we construct our self in part through our choice of LOs, it follows that we would choose LOs that allow us to become the person we want to be. Hence respondents sometimes projected their LOs as their ideal self rather than their actual self. A freelance writer, who was living on a limited budget, personified his Macintosh computer as a Victorian gentleman "and also, a person who matches my tastes in all things. . . ." But "he would probably be a little more in the creature comforts . . . better meals." He then goes on to reflect, "I think I would have made a good Victorian gentleman. Yeah, someone who is hardworking and dedicated to what he does, but wants money to be beneath him. Yeah, really wish I was like that" (male, freelance writer, 36). This pattern of projecting one's self or one's ideal self into the personification of the object was entirely absent from respondents' projections of objects they felt neutral about.

Finally, evidence for the important role that integration of the LO into the self plays in love comes from the tests respondents used to determine if they truly loved something. "If possessions are viewed as part of self, it follows that an unintentional loss of possessions should be regarded as a loss or lessening of self" (Belk 1988). Since "loss of self" is traumatic, a good test of the degree to which an LO is part of the self is the extent to which it would be missed if it were lost. Similarly, one could also look at the degree to which someone would be willing to sacrifice to keep the LO from being lost. In light of this reasoning, it is interesting that the two most common tests that respondents used to judge if they really loved an item were "how much would I miss it" and "would I be willing to sacrifice for it." Respondents in the phone interviews mentioned nineteen times that they would greatly miss an LO if it were lost. Of those LOs, fourteen

(74 percent) were considered real love. In contrast, respondents mentioned nineteen times with reference to different LOs that they would not be greatly missed if lost. In this case only two (11 percent) were felt to be love in the literal sense of the word. A similar pattern was found when respondents talked about being willing to sacrifice for an LO. Respondents claimed five times that they would be willing to sacrifice for an LO, and in three of those cases (60 percent) that item was considered real love. But, in the four cases where respondents mentioned that they would not be willing to sacrifice for an LO, none of the relationships were seen as love in the strictest sense of the word. While an object's being part of the self is not the only reason one might sacrifice for it or miss it if it were lost, these feeling and behaviors are indicators of self-extension. In the context of the other evidence presented, it is plausible to conclude that when respondents were deciding if they loved something, their asking themselves if they would sacrifice for it or miss it if it were lost amounted to an introspective test of whether the LO was a part of themselves.

Conditional Integration: The Desired versus the Actual Level of Integration with the Loved Object

So far, we have seen through extant psychological literature that the merging of selves is a well-established construct in research on romantic love, and that possessions can also be incorporated into the self. The current research has integrated these findings by showing that the merging of self and other in love is not limited to the interpersonal domain, but is central to consumers' love of objects as well. This conclusion has been supported by evidence showing the importance of self-extension in respondents' understanding of love, as well as findings from projective techniques, self-relevant emotions, and anticipated feelings of loss.

Given this evidence, it might be tempting to simply equate love with the inclusion of the LO in the self. However, if love were synonymous with the LO being part of the self, how could we explain the respondents who had aspects of themselves that they did not love? For example, if self equals love, why did one of the in-depth interview respondents find it a constant struggle to maintain much love for herself at all?

Answering these questions requires a distinction between the desired level of integration (the vertical axis on Figure 18.1) and the actual level of integration (the horizontal axis on Figure 18.1). Love occurs when the desired level of integration is high and sets in motion a psychological process (described in the following section) by which the desired and the actual level of integration reach a psychological balance. This is why we label the theory of love presented here *conditional integration*. Integration of an object into a person's identity only constitutes love when that integration is highly desired. When people do not love themselves it simply means that there are aspects of themselves that they wish were not part of themselves (i.e., the actual level of integration is higher than the desired level). The relationship between the desired and the actual level of integration helps explain three other constructs related to love: passion, warmth, and rejection.

Passion, Warmth, and Rejection

Passion is sometimes experienced as "the urge to merge" (female, pastoral counselor, 30). Passion is the desire to invest mental and emotional energy in increasing or maintaining the extent to which an object is integrated into the self. The more the desired level of integration exceeds the actual level of integration the greater the passion will be. In some cases, when the integration of the LO into the consumers' identity is very high, it can take a great deal of mental and emotional investment just to maintain that high level of cathexis.

Warmth is an equilibrium condition that occurs when the actual level of integration approximately matches the desired level. Within the diagonal warmth region, the higher the level of integration, the more warmth is experienced (see Figure 18.1). Maintaining a high level of warmth requires mental, emotional, and physical energy. Just as friendships fade if neglected, respondents mentioned several hobbies and other formerly loved objects that had become less central to their selves through lack of involvement. It is possible that warmth is closely related to attachment, although a closer examination of the relationship between these two constructs is a topic for future research.

Rejection occurs in the situation when one desires a lower level of integration than is currently the case. When the actual level of integration is much higher than the desired level, rejection can become highly emotional and is termed "hate." Through rejection, objects are removed from the self. In Schouten's (1991) study of plastic surgery, he reported on a woman whose rejection of her nose was so strong that she did not consider it a part of her self. Because the interviews in our study focused on things the respondents loved, there was little discussion of rejection. However, this idea of rejection is logically consistent with what it would mean for an object to be an unwanted part of the self. Further research is needed to better understand this phenomenon and the process of person-object relationship dissolution in general.

Mechanism of Integration

The interviews conducted for this study revealed four basic mechanisms of integration: physical incorporation, cognitive incorporation, investiture of social meanings, and creation.

Physical incorporation occurs when the LO is seen as a literal or metaphoric element of the person's physical body (Belk 1988). Many respondents reported loving foods, which literally do become part of the body. But more often, physical incorporation operated through control. The distinction between self and other may arise in infancy through the realization that some objects defy direct control by the will, that is, the baby's hand moves by mental command but the rattle does not. Following this line of reasoning McClelland (1951) argues that when we can control an external object in the same way that we can control our own body, we come to see that object as part of the self. This can occur with physical objects, but it was most common among these respondents in gaining mastery over an activity such as athletics or the arts. In love, the direction of control is usually person over object, but this is not always the case. Food in particular was cited as an LO that respondents both controlled (e.g., cooking as creative expression) and were controlled by. Physical incorporation can also occur through "contamination" (Belk 1988), a more passive form of incorporation through close physical contact. Although contamination is an important mechanism by which objects such as clothing became part of the self, it played a fairly minor role in the examples of love uncovered in this study.

Cognitive incorporation involves learning about the LO (Sartre 1943), fantasizing about the LO (Campbell 1987; Stendhal 1947), or in some other way thinking about the LO (Aron et al. 1989) so as to strengthen its importance within one's self image. The desire to get to know the LO in a deep and intimate way is evident in the respondents' tendency to be experts in the area of their love. Along these lines, the following hyperbolic account of what it would mean to truly love books illustrates the importance of obsessive thought.

> If [my love of books] was real love I'd probably waste away. I'd probably never eat. I probably would never get up. I'd probably have a bed full of books and I don't think that's wholesome. You've got to eat, drink to survive. You can't just stay stuck with a book (male, office associate, 44).

Objects can also be integrated into a person's identity through the *investiture of social meanings.* On a social level, Lancaster and Foddy (1988) argue that the self is defined largely in terms of social roles that often contain role others (husband-wife, teacher-student, etc.), and that these role others can sometimes become part of the self (Markus and Kitayama 1991). Objects can also serve as role others, but in this case, the phrase "props for one's identity" might be more appropriate. For example, when a king is crowned, the crown invests authority in the king, and as such makes him who he is. We therefore call this *investiture,* in that objects invest their users with a social identity that then defines the self. Investiture is one of the most important mechanisms for self-extension in love. Virtually every LO contributed to the respondents' identities, if only inasmuch as loving music makes one a "music lover."

Purchase of a product facilitates all three mechanisms of incorporation discussed so far. Purchase allows greater access to the LO and hence can facilitate physical incorporation. Purchase also increases our thoughts about an object and our knowledge of that object, although for many consumers highly involved thinking about an object often precedes the purchase (Campbell 1987), and so it is possible for an object to become integrated into the self before the purchase takes place. And on a social level, the mere act of purchasing can increase the level of integration. To understand why, the following analysis looks more closely at what it means for something to be experienced as part of the self.

James (1890) divided the self into two main parts: the "I" and the "me." The I is the experiencing agent and the wellspring of volition and action. When you close your eyes and imagine an object, the I is that part of you which is "seeing" the object. It gets its name from the English grammar system in which we say "I did X" or "I prefer Y." The me consists of all the possessions of the I. It also gets its name because we say "my beliefs are part of me," "my memories are part of me," or "my books are part of me." That all of these things are *possessions* of the I is supported by the finding that when asked to name their most important possessions, people frequently list memories, abilities, and other intangible aspects of their selves (Hirschman and LaBarbera 1990). Furthermore, Prentice (1987) provided experimental evidence that possessions, attitudes, and values are all fundamentally similar at a psychological level. Because the me is connected to the I through the relationship of possession, the degree to which something is considered part of the self is a function of its level of subjectively felt ownership, the "mineness" of the thing (Rudmin 1991, 1993), as reflected in the romantic proposition, "Will you be mine?" This subjective sense of ownership is not the same as legal ownership. Many people feel a sense of ownership for a professional sports team but few people legally own one. Nonetheless, people generally feel a stronger sense of ownership for objects they have purchased. Therefore, simply by purchasing an object its "mineness" and hence its level of integration into the self can increase. Furthermore, owning an object increases the degree to which it invests us with a social identity.

Creation is the fourth mechanism of incorporation. Up to this point we have been following an implicit model in which love begins with encountering a desirable object outside of the self. This leads to passion, which in turn activates some combination of physical incorporation, cognitive incorporation, and investiture. These mechanisms continue to operate until the LO has been integrated into the self to the desired degree, and a state of warmth is achieved. This sequence of events explains why passion for an LO, whether a new car or a new lover, is generally highest at the beginning of the relationship. It is also of managerial importance to marketers, because it models the way the commercial products typically become loved and integrated into the self. But this is not the only possible way LOs become part of the self. Physical objects that are created by the respondents, and values or activities that are self-expressive for the respondents, are seen as emerging from the self and come into the world already a part of the self. In this way, self-enlargement follows a birth metaphor rather than a consumption "taking in" metaphor.

The ability of LOs to provide a means of self-expression was one of the stronger themes to emerge from the analysis, being mentioned by over half the respondents. Not surprisingly, activities such as cooking and making music figured prominently in these discussions. For example, one respondent talked about the experience of writing for her own pleasure.

> It's something that I feel constantly surprised and kind of tickled and delighted when I find the words and the expressions and the ideas I never knew I had and I certainly can't express verbally. I actually see it coming out on the page. I guess the reason I love it is not only a purging thing, a cathartic thing, it tickles a place inside me I don't think I knew I had before (female, social worker, 29).

In an extensive review of the literature on the self, Greenwald and Pratkanis (1984) concluded that "the self engenders strong feelings—ones often characterized by passionate warmth" (p. 151) and that "perhaps the most prominent feature of the self is the positive affect that is normally attached to one's own . . . attributes" (p. 166). It is not just that we like objects and therefore integrate them into our selves; the reverse is also true. We feel warmly about objects precisely because they are part of the self.

The Desired Level of Integration Equals Perceived Intrinsic Value

Several themes emerged from the data that can help explain why respondents desired to integrate an object into the self. Many of these are discussed in more detail elsewhere (Batra, Ahuvia, and Bagozzi 2008). These themes focus on (1) the perceived quality of the LO, (2) the directness with which the LO meets the lover's needs, (3) the relation of the LO to higher order versus lower order needs, and (4) the ability of the LO to appeal on many levels. Together, these themes support the interpretation that the desired level of integration is determined by the perceived intrinsic value of the object.

One of the most common themes to emerge from the data was the importance of *perceived quality,* that is, that the LO was, in one way or another, nothing short of magnificent. Since LOs provide us with valued experiences, the most desirable LOs would be the ones that were most capable of providing these experiences (i.e., the most excellent ones). It also seems that excellence in an LO is valued even beyond the instrumental benefits it brings us. Since LOs become part of the self, if we wish to be excellent people it makes sense that we should construct ourselves out of excellent building blocks. Compounding the tendency to love excellent things, there is also a tendency for people to endow the things they own or have created with a high level of perceived value that goes beyond what might objectively be warranted based simply on the quality of the object (Tom et al. 2007).

The things people loved were always *directly rewarding* to the consumer in some way. When the rewards for performing an action are (1) psychological states such as pleasure, happiness, a sense of accomplishment, existential meaning, and so on, and (2) perceived by the actor as the direct result of the action, the action is seen as intrinsically rewarding and the object that provides that reward is intrinsically valuable; that is, people talking about engaging in some activity "for the love of it" as opposed to seeing it as a means to another end. If a person works at a job she doesn't like to earn money to go skiing which she does enjoy, she might say that her job is financially rewarding but not loved, whereas skiing is intrinsically rewarding and hence loved.

The deepest and fullest experience of love was more strongly associated with LOs helping to meet *higher order needs* such as social connection, existential meaning, spirituality, personal accomplishment, or the expression of ethical values. As Person (1988) wrote, "love is an antidote not just to personal neediness, but to those existential anxieties that encompass our sense of the frailty and brevity of our life on earth. . . . It is the knowledge of our insignificance in the universe and, ultimately, the awareness of our own death that causes us to seek transcendence in soulful merger with a beloved" (p. 85). LOs met these higher order needs in a wide variety of ways. Gifts were often loved for the way they represented connections to other people, other LOs reflected political or religious commitments, loved products were also sometimes symbolically connected to significant personal achievements or the meaning of adulthood. When LOs only met lower order needs such as tasting good or being fun, respondents frequently talked about "enjoying" the LO but not truly loving it. Love represents an intimate and profound relationship dealing with deeply held values.

The previous discussion of LOs meeting higher order needs should not be read to imply that only sentimental, sacred, or existential values are related to love. If an LO can only provide one type of value, it is more likely to be loved if it relates to the lover in a deeply intimate way. But it is far better still if the LO can appeal on many levels by providing a wide variety of meanings and benefits. Generally speaking, for an LO to be considered real love it was not enough to be beautiful, or pleasurable, or spiritually meaningful, for example; rather, it had to be all three and hence "the perfect thing" (Mick and DeMoss 1990). The finding that true LOs appeal on many levels can also make sense of statements from the context of romantic love such as "you don't want me, you only want my body." This statement can present a minor puzzle because after all, one's body is surely "you." This puzzle is easily solved by realizing this statement really means "you only want one aspect of my self and not my entire self." Love in its fullest expression integrates our entire self with the totality of the other. As Simmel (1984; quoted in Bertilsson 1991) said, "as one who loves, I am a different person than I was before, for it is not one or the other of my 'aspects' or energies that loves but rather the entire person." Thus, LOs that appeal on many levels at once are more truly loved.

Caveat: Love Takes Place in the World

The discussion of love so far has focused on the respondents' internal psychological processes with regard to a specific LO. This may give the reader the false impression that love takes place between a person and an LO cut off from the rest of the world. For balance it is essential to understand at least the following point: LOs were simultaneously part of the respondents' selves and part of their intimate world. Along with seeing LOs as part of themselves, many respondents also spoke about LOs as being "part of their lives." This meant that an LO took up a lot of their time and energy. If it was an activity, they performed it frequently; if it was an object, they used it or thought about it regularly. Therefore, saying that an object is part of one's life implies that it is central to the world in which one lives. By loving, whether it is loving people, things, or activities, we are not only constructing the self but we are creating the world around us. By surrounding ourselves with loved objects and people we assure a level of harmony between the self and the environment through making self and parts of the environment one and the same.

CONCLUSION

The people and things we love are part of ourselves. We think about them the same way we think about ourselves, we act toward them as we act toward ourselves, we experience pride in their achievements and shame in their failures, our relationships with them help define our identity, and we take responsibility for their well-being. The conditional integration theory of love developed here can be seen as modeling two processes (see Figure 18.1). In the first case the LO is encountered as separate from the individual. This is common in commercial transactions where the object begins as a product or service being offered for sale. In these instances the desire to integrate the object into the self is a function of its perceived intrinsic value. Objects high in perceived intrinsic value elicit passion, which in turn activates social and psychological mechanisms for integrating the object into the self. As the object becomes integrated into the self, the passion cools and becomes warmth. The second case occurs when the LO is produced through personal creative activity. In this case it is already significantly integrated into the self upon completion. Once the LO has been created, the individual may increase or decrease its level of integration using the same mechanisms he or she would for an object he or she had purchased. But because the object is already part of the self, the individual may endow it with value that is higher than if the evaluation were made by a neutral party.

Love spans the somewhat artificial disciplinary boundary between consumer behavior and social science more broadly construed. Regrettably, the scope of this chapter did not allow for a discussion of this theory's implications for the models of romantic love on which it is based. However, this theory was constructed to be consistent not only with the data on love collected for this study, but also with the published data on interpersonal love.

This theory suggests that love has implications for managers regarding both initial and repeat purchases. Given the connection between love and impulse purchasing, in initial purchase situations marketers may desire for consumers to "fall in love" with their product. This might be accomplished by increasing the hedonic and symbolic value of the product. In repeat purchase situations consumers are likely to be extremely loyal to objects they love. If love is like interpersonal love, this loyalty may even lead to a strong cognitive bias to devalue alternative products so as not to be tempted to break the committed love relationship (Johnson and Rusbult 1989).

Artistic products that could be said to "come from the heart" of their producers (Hirschman 1983) had an easier time finding their way into the hearts of their consumers. The same was true for activities that facilitated creative self-expression, learning, or in other ways allowed the respondent to grow as a person or reflected their creative energies. This suggests that love may be a particularly important construct for marketers of extraordinary experiences (Arnould and Price 1993), social marketers, religion marketers, politicians, or others interested in promoting more profound ideas or activities [Deighton's (1994) suggestions for amplifying meaning and intensifying involvement in performances may be relevant here]. Love might also be a particularly relevant goal for product and service designers whose aesthetic output has a more personal feeling to it. Finally, it may also be a viable strategy to tie one's product into a loved object rather than make the product itself the direct focus of love (e.g., a current Nike ad campaign tries to tie Nike shoes into the love of running rather than talk about the love of shoes directly).

The study of consumer behavior has many missions, not the least of which is understanding those consumption experiences that play a significant role in the lives of consumers. Research on loved objects provides a spotlight for illuminating some of the most psychically significant consumption experiences. Love is an extreme experience, but not an aberrant one. By learning about love we learn more than isolated insights into consumer preferences. We learn an essential way in which people construct both the self and the intimate world.

NOTES

1. Percentages are used to contrast the frequency of responses within the sample. They are not intended to be generalized as survey data to a larger population.

2. This finding may be particularly limited to western individualistic culture. Markus and Kitayama (1991) found that defining true self-expression as the actualization of internal drives unencumbered by external social roles or other interpersonal considerations is largely a Western concept.

REFERENCES

Ahuvia, Aaron C. (1992). "For the Love of Money: Materialism and Product Love." In *Meaning, Measure, and Morality of Materialism,* ed. Floyd W. Rudmin and Marsha L. Richins. Provo, UT: The Association for Consumer Research, 188–198.

——— (1993). "I Love it! Towards a Unifying Theory of Love across Diverse Love Objects." Unpublished Ph.D. dissertation, Northwestern University, Kellogg School of Management.

——— (2005). "Beyond the Extended Self: Loved Objects and Consumers' Identity Narratives," *Journal of Consumer Research,* 32 (1), 171–184.

Ahuvia, Aaron C., and Mara B. Adelman (1993). "Market Metaphors for Meeting Mates." In *Research in Consumer Behavior: A Research Annual* no. 6, ed. Janeen Costa and Russell Belk. Greenwich, CT: JAI Press, 55–83.

Albert, Noel, Dwight Merunka, and Pierre Valette-Florence (2008). "When Consumers Love Their Brands: Exploring the Concept and Its Dimensions," *Journal of Business Research,* 61 (10), 1062–1075.

Arnould, Eric J., and Linda L. Price (1993). "River Magic: Extraordinary Experience and the Extended Service Encounter," *Journal of Consumer Research,* 20, 24–45.

Arnould, Eric, and Craig Thompson (2005). "Consumer Culture Theory (CCT): Twenty Years of Research," *Journal of Consumer Research,* 31 (March), 868–882.

Aron, Arthur, and Elaine N. Aron (1986). *Love as the Expansion of Self: Understanding Attraction and Satisfaction.* New York, NY: Hemisphere Publishing.

Aron, Arthur et al. (1991). "Close Relationships as Including Other in Self," *Journal of Personality and Social Psychology,* 60, 241–253.

Aron, Arthur, Donald G. Dutton, Elaine N. Aron, Adrienne Iverson(1989). "Experiences of Falling in Love," *Journal of Social and Personal Relationships,* 6, 243–257.

Batra, Rajeev, Aaron C. Ahuvia, and Rick Bagozzi (2008). "Brand Love: Its Nature and Consequences." Working paper.

Belk, Russell W. (1988). "Possessions and the Extended Self," *Journal of Consumer Research,* 15, 139–168.

Belk, Russell W., Melanie Wallendorf, and John F. Sherry Jr. (1989). "The Sacred and the Profane in Consumer Behavior: Theodicy or the Odyssey," *Journal of Consumer Research,* 16, 1–38.

Bertilsson, Margareta (1991). "Loves Labour Lost? A Sociological View." In *The Body: Social Process and Cultural Theory,* ed. Mike Featherstone, Mike Hepworth, and Brian S. Turner. London, UK: Sage, 297–324.

Campbell, Colin (1987). *The Romantic Ethic and the Spirit of Modern Consumerism.* Oxford, UK: Basil Blackwell.

Carroll, Barbara A., and Aaron C. Ahuvia (2006). "Some Antecedents and Outcomes of Brand Love," *Marketing Letters,* 17 (2), 79–89.

Deighton, John (1994). "Managing Services When the Service Is a Performance." In *Service Quality: New Directions in Theory and Practice,* ed. Richard Oliver and Roland Rust. Newbury Park, CA: Sage, 123–138.

DeRivera, Joseph (1984). "Development and the Full Range of Emotional Experience." In *Emotion in Adult Development,* ed. Carol Malatesta and Carol Izard. Beverly Hills, CA: Sage, 45–63.

Dion, Kenneth L., and Karen K. Dion (1988). "Romantic Love: Individual and Cultural Perspectives." In *The Psychology of Love,* ed. Robert J. Sternberg and Michael L. Barnes. New Haven, CT: Yale University Press, 264–289.

Fehr, Beverly, and James A. Russell (1991). "The Concept of Love Viewed from a Prototype Perspective," *Journal of Personality and Social Psychology,* 60, 425–438.

Gonzales-Crussi, Frank (1988). *On the Nature of Things Erotic.* New York, NY: Vintage Books.

Grant, Vernon (1976). *Falling in Love: The Psychology of the Romantic Emotion.* New York, NY: Springer.

Greenwald, A.G., and A.R. Pratkanis (1984). "The Self." In *Handbook of Social Cognition,* ed. R. Wyer and T. Srull. Hillsdale, NJ: Lawrence Erlbaum, 129–178.

Hatfield, Elaine (1982). "Passionate Love, Companionate Love, and Intimacy." In *Intimacy,* ed. Martin Fisher and George Stricker. New York, NY: Plenum, 267–292.

Hirschman, Elizabeth C. (1983). "Aesthetics, Ideologies and the Limits of the Marketing Concept," *Journal of Marketing,* 47, 45–55.

——— (1994). "Consumers and Their Animal Companions." *Journal of Consumer Research,* 20, 616–632.

Hirschman, Elizabeth C., and Priscilla A. LaBarbera (1990). "Dimensions of Possession Importance," *Psychology and Marketing,* 7, 215–233.

James, William (1890). *The Principles of Psychology.* New York, NY: Holt.

Jeffries, Vincent (1993). "Virtue and Attraction: Validation of a Measure of Love," *Journal of Social and Personal Relationships,* 10, 99–117.

Ji, Mindy F. (2002), "Children's Relationships with Brands: 'True Love' or 'One-night Stand'?" *Psychology and Marketing,* 19, 369.

Johnson, Dennis J., and Caryl E. Rusbult (1989). "Resisting Temptation: Devaluation of Alternative Partners as a Means of Maintaining Commitment in Close Relationships," *Journal of Personality and Social Psychology,* 57, 967–980.

Kamat, Vikram, and Ajit Arun Parulekar (2007). "Brand Love—The Precursor to Loyalty." Paper presented at the Advertising and Consumer Pscyhology Conference, New Frontiers in Branding: Attitudes, Attachments, and Relationships, Santa Monica, CA, June 7–9.

Keh, Hean Tat, Jun Pang, and Siqing Peng (2007). "Understanding and Measuring Brand Love." Paper presented at the Advertising and Consumer Psychology Conference, New Frontiers in Branding: Attitudes, Attachments, and Relationships, Santa Monica, CA, June 7–9.

Kovecses, Zoltan (1991). "A Linguist's Quest for Love," *Journal of Social and Personal Relationships,* 8, 77–97.

Lancaster, Sandra, and Margaret Foddy (1988). "Self Extensions: A Conceptualization," *Journal for the Theory of Social Behavior,* 18, 77–94.

Lee, John A. (1988). "Love Styles." In *The Psychology of Love,* ed. Robert J. Sternberg and Michael L. Barnes. New Haven, CT: Yale University Press, 38–67.

Markus, Hazel R., and Shinobu Kitayama (1991). "Culture and the Self: Implications for Cognition, Emotion, and Motivation," *Psychological Review,* 98, 224–253.

Marston, Peter J., Michael L. Hecht, and Tia Roberts (1986). "What is This Thing Called Love? The Subjective Experience and Communication of Romantic Love." Paper presented at the Annual Meeting of the Western Speech Communication Association, Tucson, AZ.

Maslow, Abraham H. (1970). *Motivation and Personality.* New York, NY: Harper and Row. (Orig. pub. 1954.)

McClelland, David (1951). *Personality.* New York, NY: Holt, Rinehart, and Winston.

Mick, David G., and Michelle DeMoss (1990). "Self-Gifts: Phenomenological Insights from Four Contexts," *Journal of Consumer Research,* 17, 322–331.

Murstein, Bernard I. (1988). "A Taxonomy of Love." In *The Psychology of Love,* ed. Robert J. Sternberg and Michael L. Barnes. New Haven, CT: Yale University Press, 13–37.

Ortony, Andrew, Gerald L. Clore, and Allan Collins (1988). *The Cognitive Structure of Emotions.* New York, NY: Cambridge University Press.

Person, Ethel S. (1988). *Dreams of Love and Fateful Encounters: The Power of Romantic Passion.* New York, NY: Penguin Books.

Prentice, Deborah A. (1987). "Psychological Correspondence of Possessions, Attitudes and Values," *Journal of Personality and Social Psychology,* 53, 993–1003.

Roseman, Ira J. (1984). "Cognitive Determinants of Emotion: A Structural Theory." In *Review of Personality and Social Psychology: Emotions, Relationships, and Health,* ed. Phillip Shaver. Beverly Hills, CA: Sage, 5, 11–36.

Rudmin, Floyd W. (1991). "Gender Differences in the Semantics of Ownership: Hazy Hints of a Feminist Theory of Property." In *Proceedings of the Conference on Gender in Consumer Behavior,* ed. Janeen A. Costa. Salt Lake City, UT: University of Utah Printing Service, 292–302.

———. (1993). "Dispossession for Semiotic Distance: The Objective Facts of Ownership in the Eye of White Fang." In *Flux, Complexity, and Illusion,* ed. Roberta Kevelson. New York, NY: Peter Lang, 391–406.

Sartre, Jean-Paul (1943). *Being and Nothingness: A Phenomenological Essay on Ontology.* New York, NY: Philosophical Library.

Schouten, John W. (1991). "Selves in Transition: Symbolic Consumption in Personal Rites of Passage and Identity Reconstruction," *Journal of Consumer Research,* 17, 412–425.

Shimp, Terrance A., and Thomas J. Madden (1988). "Consumer-Object Relations: A Conceptual Framework Based Analogously on Sternberg's Triangular Theory of Love," *Advances in Consumer Research,* 15, 163–168.

Simmel, Georg (1984). *On Women, Sexuality and Love,* trans. and ed. G. Oakes. New Haven, CT: Yale University Press.

Sperling, Michael B. (1985). Fusional Love Relations: The Developmental Origins of Desperate Love. Unpublished manuscript.

Stendhal (1947). *On Love.* Garden City, NY: Doubleday. (Orig. pub. 1822.)

Tennov, Dorothy (1979). *Love and Limerence.* New York, NY: Stein and Day.

Tom, Gail, Carolyn Nelson, Tamara Srzentic, and Ryan King (2007). "Mere Exposure and the Endowment Effect on Consumer Decision Making," *The Journal of Psychology,* 141(2), 117–125.

Whang, Yun-Oh, Jeff Allen, Niquelle Sahoury, and Haitao Zhang (2004). "Falling in Love with a Product: The Structure of a Romantic Consumer-Product Relationship," *Advances in Consumer Research,* 31, 320–327.

Yeung, Catherine, and Robert S. Wyer Jr. (2005). "Does Loving a Brand Mean Loving Its Products? The Role of Brand-Elicited Affect in Brand Extension Evaluations," *Journal of Marketing Research,* 42 (4), 495–506.

CHAPTER 19

CUSTOMER COPING IN RESPONSE TO RELATIONSHIP TRANSGRESSIONS

An Attachment Theoretic Approach

MARCEL PAULSSEN AND RICHARD P. BAGOZZI

In relationships, most partners eventually behave badly. Over the course of a relationship one or the other partner will at one point in time engage in such potentially destructive acts as yelling at a partner or being thoughtless in some way (Rusbult et al. 1991). Such potentially destructive acts violate the implicit or explicit rules guiding relationship evaluation and performance and are referred to generally as transgressions (Metts 1994). Relational transgressions of course occur not only in personal relationships but also in relationships between consumers and brands (Aaker, Fournier, and Brasel 2004). With increasing durations of relationships and increasing frequencies of interaction, the likelihood of transgressions grows (Grayson and Ambler 1999). Even though transgressions are inherent parts of consumer relationships, partners seem to adopt a "no transgression scenario" as their reference point (Aaker, Fournier, and Brasel 2004). How do consumers then react if a breach of expectations in a brand relationship occurs? Are they likely to exacerbate the problem and threaten the very existence of the brand relationship by reacting destructively, or are they more likely to protect the brand relationship by acting constructively?

Surprisingly few studies have investigated how consumers react to brand transgressions. Indeed, "work focusing on mistakes that companies or brands inevitably make has been rare in relationship research" (Fournier and Brasel 2002, p. 102). From a relationship perspective, transgressions are of pivotal relevance because people derive inferences and make conclusions about their relationship partners especially from negative acts when they occur. The high level of salience and diagnosticity of negative events provide the perceiver with a window into the dispositional qualities of the relationship partner and the status of the relationship (Fiske 1980; Ybarra and Stephan 1999). Inferences made in these critical "moments of truth" so to speak can threaten the relationship core and may be crucial for a person's willingness to continue in a relationship. Thus even though transgressions may vary in their severity and cause, they all have the potential to damage an existing relationship (Aaker, Fournier, and Brasel 2004). Understanding how consumers react to transgressions is therefore a crucial research question.

TRANSGRESSIONS IN MARKETING

Marketing relationship transgressions have been investigated in several research streams from different perspectives. Following Bitner, Booms, and Tetreault's (1990) seminal paper, a large stream of research has investigated transgressions by use of the critical incident technique (CIT). In the context of consumer-brand relationships, a negative critical incident corresponds to a relationship transgression. Especially relevant to our study is the fact that published CIT studies by definition assumed that collected incidents are indeed critical for a relationship but rarely assessed their impact on measures of relationship strength or behavioral response. Thus, CIT studies in marketing have not examined whether or to what extent transgressions are really related to the customer-firm relationship (see Edvardsson and Strandvik 2000).

A general view concerning the effects of transgressions for consumer relationships is that they are inherently damaging (Aaker, Fournier, and Brasel 2004; Gremler 2004). Several researchers, however, have proposed contingencies that moderate the destructive influence of transgression acts on consumer relationships. In this regard, Folkes (1984) investigated how consumers' attributions of transgressions impact satisfaction and subsequent behavioral response tendencies (e.g., Folkes 1984; Folkes, Koletsky, and Graham 1987; Tsiros, Mittal, and Ross 2004). The damaging effects of transgressions depend, in part, on how these transgressions are attributed by the consumer. Another stream of research examined the effects of recovery efforts following a relationship transgression (e.g., Maxham and Netemeyer 2002; Smith and Bolton 1998). The results of published studies on recovery efforts are somewhat equivocal (e.g., McCullough, Berry, and Yadav 2000). Nevertheless, there is evidence to support the conclusion that under certain conditions a highly satisfactory recovery following a relationship transgression can maintain or increase cumulative satisfaction and loyalty levels, even beyond their pretransgression values (e.g., Smith and Bolton 1998).

Another contingency factor that might moderate the damaging effect of transgressions on relationship outcomes is the personality of the consumer (e.g., Aaker, Fournier, and Brasel 2004; Maxham and Netemeyer 2002; Rusbult et al. 1991; Cupach 2000). The damaging effects of a transgression may depend on how consumers cope with the transgression (Rusbult et al. 1991). However, so far no study has elaborated on this individual difference perspective or investigated the impact of consumer characteristics on response tendencies to relational transgressions.

In the present study, we follow Aaker, Fournier, and Brasel's call (2004) to investigate consumer personality variables and identify relationship-relevant styles that may affect the interaction of consumers and brands. Prior research suggests the promise of adapting attachment theory, a theory from psychology that aims to explain behavior in personal relationships, in order to understand relationship heterogeneity in a consumption context (Thomson and Johnson 2002, 2006). Building on these studies, we employ an attachment theory approach to investigate individual differences in behavioral responses to relationship transgressions. To the best of our knowledge, no study has developed and tested a theoretical framework for investigating individual differences in coping with relational transgressions in a marketing context. Furthermore, we examine the cognitive and emotional processes that drive behavioral response tendencies. For relationship marketers, it is important to understand why some consumers exit their relationships with brands or suppliers when they encounter problems, whereas others engage in constructive problem solving (voice) or tolerate the problem (loyalty).

ATTACHMENT THEORY

Individuals enter relationships with a history of interpersonal experiences and a unique set of memories, beliefs, and expectations. The main tenet of attachment theory is that these memories, beliefs, and expectations influence how individuals think and feel about their relationships and how they behave in those relationships (Collins et al. 2006). Attachment theorists refer to the cognitive-affective representations of relationship experiences as internal working models of attachment. Working models are highly accessible, cognitive-affective representations of self and others that evolve through interactions with close relationship partners, so-called attachment figures (e.g., mother, father, teacher, partner, etc.) (Collins et al. 2006; Shaver, Collins, and Clark 1996). The working model of self includes beliefs about whether one is worthy of love and support, while the working model of others includes beliefs about whether the relationship partner will be trustworthy in fulfilling interpersonal needs (e.g., Gallo and Smith 2001). Organized representations of prior behavior and experience provide a frame of reference for comprehending and interpreting subsequent relational experiences, thereby guiding social interaction (Shaver, Collins, and Clark 1996). Working models may be initially formed during early interactions with primary caregivers, but they continue to evolve as individuals encounter new relationships throughout their lives (Bowlby 1988; Collins 1996). Once developed, these models are thought to operate largely outside of awareness in processes that shape perception, emotion, and behavior in attachment-relevant contexts (Collins et al. 2006). Even though Bowlby (1973, 1980, 1982) originally conceptualized attachment theory to characterize infant-parent emotional bonding, the theory has been extended to the study of adolescent and adult relationships and even to the study of broader social phenomena (Shaver and Mikulincer 2003).

Individual difference aspects of attachment theory have been developed by Ainsworth and colleagues (1978) who were the first to delineate three so-called attachment styles: secure, anxious, and avoidant. Different attachment styles or orientations result as a consequence of the quality of interactions with close relationship partners (Shaver and Mikulincer 2005). Positive interactions with available and responsive attachment figures in times of need foster an individual's sense of *attachment security.* Individuals who are securely attached possess what Waters, Rodrigues, and Ridgeway (1998) call "the secure base script." Due to positive expectations about the availability of others in threatening situations (termed the positive working model of other) and positive views of the self as competent, loved, and valued (called the positive working model of self), the secure base script consists of, among other things, increased confidence in the seeking of proximity and support as effective coping strategies. On the other hand, unavailable and unresponsive attachment figures in times of need induce *insecure attachment orientations,* either anxious or avoidant in nature. These so-called secondary attachment strategies (Main 1990) go along with more negative judgments of relationship others and can interfere with a whole range of life activities and, most importantly, relationship functioning (Mikulincer and Shaver 2003). Attachment orientations have been systematically related to relationship beliefs, partner perceptions, trust, commitment, support-seeking behaviors, conflict management and coping strategies, satisfaction, and relationship stability (see Mikulincer and Shaver 2003 and Shaver, Collins, and Clark 1996 for reviews).

Concerning the measurement and conceptualization of the attachment construct, a number of things are important to note. First, recent research suggests that a typological model of attachment styles may not adequately capture attachment organization (Fraley and Waller 1998; Shaver, Belsky, and Brennan 2000). Therefore, researchers in the attachment field have increasingly switched to dimensional measures of attachment orientation (Shaver and Mikulincer 2002a). Second, even though attachment orientations are often conceptualized as global orientations toward close relationships, theoretical reasons and empirical evidence clearly support the conclusion that people possess multiple attachment schemas. Early research on childhood attachment has shown that there is not always correspondence between a child's attachment to one parent and the other parent (Main and Weston 1981). Research has consistently shown that people can possess relation-specific attachment orientations organized around experiences with a specific partner that are not congruent with a global attachment orientation (Collins and Read 1994; Pierce and Lydon 2001). The current view is that specific and global attachment orientations are hierarchically organized. That is, models for specific relationships (e.g., with the mother) are nested within relationship-domain representations (e.g., parent-child relationships), which in turn are nested within more global models (e.g., global model of self and others) (Collins and Read 1994; Shaver and Mikulincer 2005). Therefore attachment researchers have proposed to develop different measures for different purposes and populations (e.g., special measures for consumer versus personal relationships; Shaver and Mikulincer 2002b).

CONCEPTUAL MODEL

The above-mentioned literature on transgressions in marketing and on attachment theory provides the building blocks for our individual difference perspective on consumer coping reactions to relational transgressions. Our approach rests on the premise that people form relationships with brands in much the same way in which they form relationships with each other (e.g., Aggarwal 2004; Fournier and Brasel 1998). Parallel patterns of results for the study of the effects of personal attachment and consumer attachment on measures of relationship quality and relationship strength in interpersonal and commercial settings are consistent with such relationship-theoretic translations (Thomson and Johnson 2002, 2006). Extending attachment theory specifically into the consumer setting, Fournier and Paulssen (2007) developed measures of secure consumer attachment. Two dimensions of secure consumer attachment were empirically validated: secure consumer attachment/ embrace of vulnerability (i.e., the consumer's ability, comfort, and willingness to rely on, trust in, and place himself or herself in a position of vulnerability regarding businesses and brands) and secure consumer attachment/drive for closeness (i.e., the desire to develop personal bonds with a business partner or its employees).

We confirmed that secure consumer attachment/embrace of vulnerability had a consistent and strong positive impact on satisfaction and trust in commercial relationships, and mediated effects on loyalty levels. The effects of secure consumer attachment/embrace of vulnerability persisted in a longitudinal study where the dependent relationship quality (satisfaction and trust) and loyalty constructs were measured twenty months after secure consumer attachment. Building on the cited studies that confirmed effects of attachment orientation on consumer-brand relationships, we investigated the process mechanisms that are responsible for the observed differences in relationship quality between securely and insecurely attached customers (Simpson, Rholes, and Nelligan 1992). Since only secure consumer attachment/embrace of vulnerability orientation had an impact on the quality and strength of consumer-brand relationships in prior research, we accordingly expect that only this facet of secure consumer attachment will influence consumer responses to relationship transgressions that might underlie these global effects.

How will consumers respond to transgressions in brand relationships? Based on Hirschman's (1970) exit-voice framework and later extensions of his response typology (e.g., Rusbult, Zembrodt and Gunn 1982; Rusbult and Zembrodt 1983), we propose that consumers will respond to relational transgressions in four ways: (1) exit: ending the relationship; (2) voice: actively working with the relationship partner to remedy problems; (3) loyalty: passively but optimistically waiting for conditions to improve, and (4) neglect: allowing the relationships to deteriorate (Geyskens and Steenkamp 2000; Ping 1993). These response strategies differ from each other on the dimension of constructiveness versus destructiveness and activity versus passivity. Voice and loyalty are constructive responses because their intention is to revive or maintain an existing relationship, while exit and neglect are destructive responses as they threaten the very existence of a relationship. The second dimension, activity/passivity, refers to the impact of the response on the problem itself, not the character of the behavior. Thus exit and voice are active behaviors with the goal to deal with a relationship transgression, whereas loyalty and neglect are more passive and diffuse behaviors (Geyskens and Steenkamp 2000; Rusbult et al. 1991).

Building on the findings across several studies in the adult attachment literature, we predict that secure attachment will be positively associated with constructive coping responses (Gaines et al. 1997; Mikulincer and Florian 1995; Scharfe and Bartholomew 1995; Simpson, Rholes, and Nelligan 1992). These predictions are consistent with hypothesized differences concerning regulatory strategies associated with secure attachment (i.e., the secure base script) vis-à-vis those associated with secondary attachment orientations. As a consequence of their positive working models of self and others, secure persons appraise relationship transgressions in less threatening terms than do insecure persons and cope with these events by relying on constructive responses, such as support-seeking strategies (Mikulincer and Florian 1995). Results of numerous studies in interpersonal relations also support the notion that a marked difference exists between secure and insecure attachment orientations concerning their corresponding behavioral response tendencies to transgressions. The differences between various insecure attachment orientations (anxious and avoidant orientations) are however less clear (Gaines et al. 1997, 1999, 2000; Mikulincer 1998; Scharfe and Bartholomew 1995). Building on these results and the social relationship analogy for consumer-brand relationships, we propose the following hypotheses:

H_1: Secure consumer attachment increases the likelihood of constructive coping responses (voice and loyalty) to a relationship transgression.

H_2: Secure consumer attachment decreases the likelihood of destructive coping responses (exit and neglect) to a relationship transgression.

Next, we develop hypotheses about the process mechanism underlying the proposed effects of consumer attachment on coping responses. A general framework for understanding the impact of working models of attachment on social perception processes, notably coping with transgressions, was developed by Collins and Read (1994). Working models of attachment, once activated through an attachment-relevant event such as a partner transgression, are proposed to shape cognitive and emotional response patterns. The outcome of these processes should determine a person's choice of coping strategies. That is, the impact of attachment orientation on behavior is largely mediated by the subjective interpretation of the situation (cognitive responses) and one's emotional reactions.

Given their importance for relationship functioning, attribution processes as mediating cognitive responses have been given much attention in the personal attachment literature (Collins 1996). The importance of attributions derives from their ability to shape subsequent action tendencies (Collins et al. 2006; Folkes, Koletsky, and Graham 1987). Adults with a secure attachment orientation possess working models consisting of positive self-images and optimistic expectations of others, and are thus likely to construe relationship experiences in favorable ways (Collins et al. 2006). Specifically, securely attached persons tend to appraise trust-violating episodes in their personal relationships as relatively unimportant and unrelated to a partner's personality (a stable cause) (Gaines et al. 2000; Mikulincer 1998). Insecure individuals, in contrast, are more likely to blame their partner for negative events and to attribute their partner's behavior to negative stable causes (Collins 1996; Collins et al. 2006; Gallo and Smith 2001). Taken together, research comparing insecure to secure individuals supports the conjecture that the former exhibit attribution biases that decrease the probability of attributing partner transgressions to stable causes. Thus

H_3: Secure consumer attachment decreases the attribution of stable causes to relationship transgressions.

Research in the consumption domain has investigated the impact of stability attributions solely on repurchase intentions and complaint behavior (e.g., Folkes 1984, 1988; Smith and Bolton 1998). The findings, although not unequivocal (Smith and Bolton 1998), indicate that a customer's stability attributions influence propensities to complain and intentions to repurchase (Curren and Folkes 1987; Folkes, Koletsky, and Graham 1987). In general the stability dimension seems to have special relevance for marketing relationships "because it signals whether the same problem (or success) can be expected in the future or whether the event was a fluke and, thus, is unlikely to be repeated in the future" (Oliver 1997, p. 277). If a relationship transgression is attributed to a stable cause, then the customer expects the same transgression to occur in the future, and this should increase the probability of destructive coping and decrease the probability of constructive coping. Hence,

H_4: Attribution of stable causes to relationship transgressions decreases the likelihood of constructive coping responses (voice and loyalty).

H_5: Attribution of stable causes to relationship transgressions increases the likelihood of destructive coping responses (exit and neglect).

Working models are conceptualized as cognitive-affective representations of self and others. These representations are activated by schema-triggered affect (Collins and Read 1994; Fiske and Pavelchak 1986). For example, less secure women have been found to experience more anger and distress toward their relationship partner in a conflict than secure women (Simpson, Rholes, and Phillips 1996). The positive working models of self and others that characterize secure attachment help people to positively appraise stressful encounters and buffer distress from relational transgressions (Collins 1996). Summarizing studies that investigated emotional reactions to a broad range of stressful events, Mikulincer and Florian (1998) concluded that secure attachment orientation leads to less intense emotional reactions compared to insecure attachment orientations (anxious and avoidant orientations). The unique impact of attachment orientations on emotional distress elicited through partner transgressions was confirmed, even after controlling for negative affectivity constructs such as depressed mood and self-esteem (Collins et al. 2006). Therefore

H_6: Secure consumer attachment decreases the degree of anger caused by relationship transgressions.

If a relationship partner's behavior induces negative emotions such as anger, then a behavioral response that punishes the partner is more likely to be selected (Collins and Read 1994). Negative emotional distress should therefore lead to behaviors that are likely to result in conflict and relationship distress (Collins 1996; Collins et al. 2006). As a consequence

H_7: Negative emotions caused by relationship transgressions decrease the likelihood of constructive coping responses (voice and loyalty).

H_8: Negative emotions caused by relationship transgressions increase the likelihood of destructive coping responses (exit and neglect).

Next we will test our model for relationship transgressions that occurred between customers and companies in the automotive industry in the characteristically high product-involvement levels and the prominence of relationship marketing activities and programs within that industry (Johnson et al. 1997).

OVERVIEW OF STUDY

Given the strong emphasis on relationship building in the automotive industry, understanding how customers react to transgressions, and particularly when customers are likely to exit or neglect a relationship, is highly relevant. In general, three possible research strategies can be used to investigate transgressions in consumer relationships: incident recall, simulation research, and experimental research. We chose incident recall because of its high face validity and ecological validity (Weiner 2000). In our study, we conducted extensive personal interviews and investigated transgressions in relationships between customers and their automotive dealerships.

Sample, Measures, and Procedures

Our empirical investigation was conducted with customers of retail outlets of a car manufacturer. Data collection took place in five different outlets of this manufacturer in a major metropolitan area. We drew a convenience sample of customers entering the dealerships by asking them to take part in a survey on customer satisfaction. A total of 203 face-to-face interviews were conducted. The interviews consisted of a fully structured portion followed by a semistructured portion using the critical incident technique (CIT).

In the structured portion, respondents were asked detailed satisfaction questions concerning the dealership and a specific car, as well as questions concerning personal and consumer attachment. The age distribution of the respondents was as follows: 20–29 years = 3.9 percent, 30–39 years = 16.7 percent, 40–49 years = 20.7 percent, 50–59 years = 20.2 percent, 60-plus years = 38.4 percent. Eighty-three percent of the customers were male. The age distribution is consistent with the luxury status of the brand. The semistructured portion of the interview followed the critical incidents procedure recommended by Bitner, Booms, and Tetreault (1990). Thus, the central question was: "Think of your experiences with your dealership. Can you remember particularly good or bad experiences during your contacts with the dealership?" Then respondents were asked to elaborate on any incident and to provide an accurate account of the situation. If necessary, the interviewers probed deeper with the following questions: "What happened exactly?"; "Who exactly did what?"; "Who or what was the subject of the incident?"; "When did the incident happen?"; and "What resulted that made you feel the interaction was satisfying (dissatisfying)?" (Bitner, Booms, and Tetreault 1990). There was no restriction on the length of the interview. The average duration of the verbatim incident descriptions was five and one-half minutes. For respondents who had experienced more than one negative critical incident, the most recent one was selected (e. g., Keaveney 1995).

Following the elaborate incident descriptions, respondents indicated the degree to which each incident made them experience various emotions, where scales from Richins (1997) were used to record responses. For negative incidents, we measured felt anger with three items: frustrated, angry, and irritated. Five-point response scales were used ("not at all," "a little," "moderately," "strongly," "very strongly") instead of Richins's (1997, p. 142) four-point scales in order to achieve greater variation. The attribution questions were asked in a semantic differential format paralleling their original formulations (Folkes, Koletzky, and Graham 1987; Russell 1982). After answering the attribution questions, respondents were asked again, using items from Ping's (1993) and Geyskens and Steenkamp's (2000) exit-voice scales, how they would react in case the same incident happened again.

Respondents were asked to think about their orientations in commercial relationships with brands/companies/suppliers in general. The introductory instructions read as follows: "Please think about important relationships with suppliers or companies for which you are a customer. For example, think about your relationship with your bank, your tax consultancy, your car brand, your phone and cable providers, or specialty shops that you frequent, and product brands that you use." This approach captures a general attachment orientation as is manifest within the broadly defined commercial relationship domain. Consumer attachment was measured prior to the critical incident questions. See Appendixes 19.1 and 19.2 for specific measures of attachment used in the study.

Results: Effects on Coping Responses

Of the 203 respondents who participated in the personal interviews, 102 reported having experienced a relationship transgression (negative incident). Overall, 175 negative critical incidents were recorded. On average, respondents reported 0.86 negative incidents and 49.75 percent did not report any negative incidents. Excluding customers from the analysis who did not answer all relevant questions, we obtained an effective sample size of 88 respondents. This sample size is problematic for estimation purposes, given the model complexity at hand. The number of estimated parameters would approach the sample size. In order to reduce model complexity, a partial aggregation model for both attributions and coping responses was used (Bagozzi and Heatherton 1994). Thus we calculated the means of items for each dimension and used these means as single indicators for the respective constructs. Cronbach's alpha for voice was borderline with a value of 0.60, but was considered acceptable, whereas the value for loyalty was clearly unacceptable (0.39). Thus loyalty was measured with a single item. Scale reliabilities for the remaining constructs were all equal or above the desired value of 0.70.

The hypothesized model depicted in Figure 19.1 was estimated with LISREL (Jöreskog and Sörbom 2001). The overall fit of the model was very good: $\chi^2(28) = 26.52$ (p = 0.54), RMSEA = 0.00, and CFI = 1.00. Due to our small sample size and the resulting low statistical power, we also reported effects with $p < 0.10$. Secure consumer attachment had, as proposed in hypothesis 3, a negative and significant effect on stability attribution (γ_{21} = –0.42, p < 0.05). Next we examined whether cognitive responses had an impact on coping strategies. Stability attributions increased exit ($\beta_{62} = 0.16$, p < 0.10) and neglect intentions ($\beta_{52} = 0.29$, p < 0.05), decreased loyalty intentions ($\beta_{42} = -0.26$, p < 0.05) and had no impact on voice ($\beta_{32} = -0.07$, p > 0.20). These results fully support hypothesis 5 and partially support hypothesis 4.

Secure attachment also had a negative effect ($\gamma_{11} = -0.29$, p < 0.06, t = –1.92) on experienced anger in relationship transgressions, confirming hypothesis 6. Next we assessed the impact of experienced anger in a relationship transgression on coping responses. The degree of experienced anger increased the likelihood of destructive coping in that it had a positive impact on exit ($\beta_{61} = 0.24$, p < 0.10) and neglect ($\beta_{51} = 0.26$, p < 0.05). Experienced anger also influenced constructive coping responses in that it negatively affected loyalty ($\beta_{41} = -0.21$, p < 0.10) but had no effect on voice intentions ($\beta_{31} = 0.13$, p > 0.10). We also tested for direct effects of secure consumer attachment in addition to the indirect effects and for direct effects only. None of these effects was significant at p < 0.10 (see Figure 19.2 for the model results). The explained variances in stability attributions and in

Figure 19.1 **Nomological Net of Transgression Responses in Consumer Relationships**

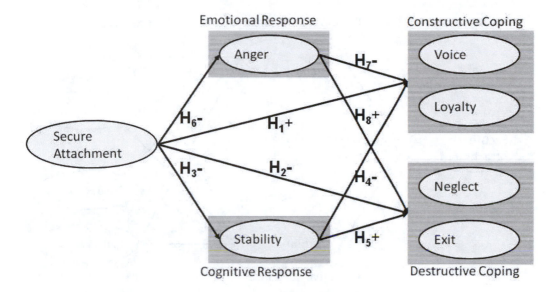

experienced anger following a relationship transgression were 17 percent and 7 percent, respectively. For coping responses, the explained variances were 9 percent for voice, 12 percent for loyalty, 8 percent for exit, and 15 percent for neglect. These values are not particularly high, but can to a high degree be attributed to attenuation through measurement error. We could correct for measurement error neither in attributions nor in coping responses in our partial aggregation model because of the relatively small sample size.

Discussion

Results of this study provide support for our conceptual model. Securely attached consumers develop an attribution bias that decreases the likelihood of destructive (exit, neglect) coping and increases the likelihood of constructive (loyalty) coping, in response to relationship transgressions. Furthermore, the study results also support the second proposed mechanism. Secure consumer attachment systematically affects emotional response patterns to relationship transgressions that in turn influence coping responses. Specifically, secure consumer attachment reduces the degree of anger experienced by respondents in response to a transgression. The degree of experienced anger again has a positive impact on destructive coping responses and a negative impact on loyalty. The direct effects of secure attachment on coping responses were not significant in this study. However, the significant paths from consumer attachment to cognitive and emotional responses, and from cognitive and emotional responses to coping support the proposed process mechanism. Results for voice were mixed. We did not find any direct or indirect effect of consumer attachment on voice. Again the low amount of statistical power might account for this. Further voice in our operationalization follows the conceptual model

Figure 19.2   **Model Results on Transgression Responses in Consumer Relationships**

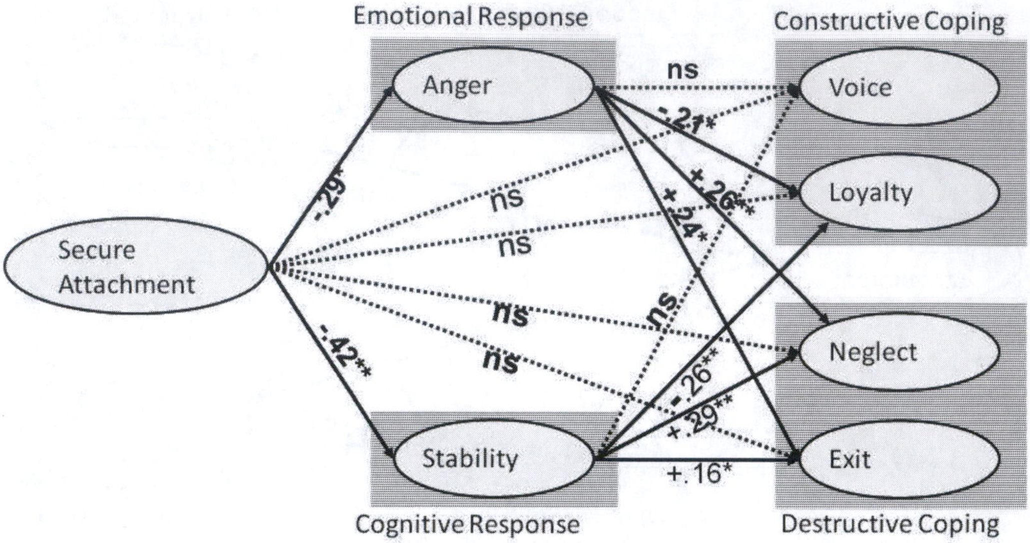

of constructive reaction. This type of reaction might be unlikely to occur in response to relationship transgressions—more common verbal reactions to complaints are negative word-of-mouth and complaining.

CONCLUSIONS

Our research was motivated by the following. First, there has been a lack of research concerned with the question of how consumers react to transgressions in commercial relationships (Fournier and Brasel 2002). Second, there have been calls to investigate consumer personality variables and identify relationship-relevant styles that may affect consumers' responses to relational transgressions (Aaker, Fournier, and Brasel 2004). Third, recent research (e.g., Thomson and Johnson 2002, 2006; Thomson 2006) has provided evidence that attachment theory could be a useful theoretical framework for identifying such relationship styles in the consumption context. The application of attachment theory to the study of consumer-brand relationships is still in its early stages. Previous research has demonstrated that secure personal attachment and secure consumer attachment are significant predictors of the nature and quality of relationships between consumers and their brands or companies (Thomson and Johnson 2002, 2006; Fournier and Paulssen 2007). So far, however, the process mechanisms underlying these effects have not been investigated. Therefore, a goal of this study was to shed light on those underlying process mechanisms.

Drawing from a general model proposed by Collins and Read (1994) for the personal relationship domain, we hypothesized that secure consumer attachment would be both directly and indirectly linked to cognitive and emotional response patterns that in turn drive behavioral responses to relationship transgressions in consumer-company relationships. The main hypothesis underlying this model was that consumers with different attachment orientations will explain and interpret relationship transgressions in a manner that is consistent with their beliefs and expectations about themselves and the companies with which they interact. Our study provided support for this hypothesis. Securely attached consumers tended to construe transgression experiences in ways that minimized their negative impact and limited their importance for broader issues of relationship stability. The patterns of results for both cognitive and emotional responses to transgressions were highly consistent with predictions. Results supported the conclusion that secure consumer attachment decreases stability attributions for relationship transgressions. Further results supported the conclusion that secure consumer attachment reduces the intensity of emotional reactions to relationship transgressions. The positive expectations that securely attached customers possess of companies and brands help them to positively interpret problematic interactions and buffer emotional distress from relational transgressions. These cognitive (attribution bias) and emotional (less intense negative emotions) response patterns of securely attached customers decrease the vulnerability of their relationships with companies to transgressions.

The confirmation of our model suggests parallel process mechanisms in relationships between consumers and brands/companies and personal relationships. Thus our results add to the growing body of research that provides empirical support for the contention that consumer-brand interactions function in ways similar to personal relationships (Aggarwal 2004; Aggarwal and Law 2005; Aggarwal and Zhang 2006; Fournier 1998; Price and Arnould 1999) and may thus be legitimately conceptualized as "relationships."

Managerial Implications

A key goal of relationship marketing is to build and maintain strong and stable relationships with customers. Companies invest considerable resources in various relationship marketing tactics in order to achieve this goal (De Wulf, Odekerken-Schröder, and Iacobucci 2001; Reinartz and Kumar 2003). However, previous research has found that there is considerable variability in consumers' predispositions to form strong and lasting relationships with companies and brands (Barnes 1997, 2001; Fournier 1998; Price and Arnould 1999). For relationship marketers, customer heterogeneity poses a problem, since investments in customers with no desire or disposition to form strong relationships are essentially lost and greatly diminish the effectiveness of relationship marketing programs (Dowling and Uncles 1997). The challenge for the relationship marketer lies in the identification of "right" customers, who are most likely to develop long-term relationships (Reinartz and Kumar 2000).

Securely attached consumers are likely to have more stable relationships because attribution biases and emotional response patterns predispose them to react more constructively (loyalty) and less destructively (exit, neglect) in response to relationship transgressions. They are thus less likely to exit or neglect their commercial relationships in response to relational transgressions. Customers who score high on secure consumer attachment are therefore "right" customers in the sense mentioned by Reinartz and Kumar (2000). They have predispositions to form strong and stable relationships with companies and brands and should be primary objects of relationship-marketing investments. One way to implement such a differentiated relationship marketing approach would be to include the items for secure consumer attachment in registration forms or the regular surveys of loyalty programs.

Limitations and Further Research

In order to investigate consumer response to relationship transgressions, we chose incident recall over two other approaches: simulation research and experimental manipulations (Weiner 2000). This approach was chosen for its high face validity and ecological validity, which is particularly important in studies of attribution (e.g., Forgas 1998). Further, incident recall allowed us to study real transgressions in existing and ongoing consumer-brand relationships. Our desire to study the effects of consumer attachment in real relationships stems from the fact that it is unclear whether the attachment system will be activated in scenarios or experiments (Collins et al. 2006). Yet a limitation of incident recall is that this method is subject to recall biases (Weiner 2000). We tried to minimize this concern by asking respondents to focus on the most recently experienced transgression (Keaveney 1995). Further, the alternatives (i.e., simulation research with scenarios or vignettes and experiments) also pose problems. Responses obtained by those methods do not mirror real-life reactions, and it is therefore unclear whether findings based on these approaches would generalize to authentic social interaction (Collins et al. 2006).

A next step to build on our research would be to investigate contingency conditions of our model. Does consumer attachment determine cognitive and emotional responses for all kinds of relationship transgressions in consumer-brand relationships? Collins (1996) proposed that some relationship events can be more relevant to attachment concerns and have a higher likelihood of activating the attachment system than others. Sample size issues (final N was 88) prevented us from testing separate models for incidents deemed to have a high relevance for attachment concerns (such as a break of a promise or not granting goodwill) versus those incidents deemed to have a lower relevance for attachment concerns (such as low speed of service).

Another area for further research would be to study transgression severity itself or even how interaction episodes are experienced and what determines whether a given interaction is perceived as a transgression by one customer but not another. A theoretical framework put forth in a recent paper by Rusbult and van Lange (2003) proposes that any given interaction situation is transformed into an effective situation that in turn drives behavior. The transformation of a given situation into an effective situation is determined by interpersonal dispositions (i.e., attachment orientation), social norms, and relationship-specific motives (i.e., commitment). Their framework marries two research areas that have started to receive increasing attention in relationship marketing: norms (Aggarwal 2004; Aggarwal and Law 2005; Aggarwal and Zhang 2006) and attachment (Thomson and Johnson 2002, 2006; Thomson 2006). Understanding why given interactions are severe transgressions for some but negligible encounters for others would be an exciting and challenging research topic.

Appendix 19.1

Constructs and Measures

Construct/Item	Construct Reliability/Factor Loadings	Mean	SD
Secure Consumer Attachment[a] (Embrace of Vulnerability)	**.75**		
It is easy for me to rely on my supplier.	.89	3.35	0.96
I have difficulties completely trusting my supplier. (recoded)	.53	3.14	1.13
I am comfortable relying on my supplier almost all the time.	.68	3.23	0.94
Stability	**.81**		
The cause of this problem is. . . .			
(1) Temporary ⟷ Permanent (7)		3.82	2.23
(1) Changing ⟷ Unchanging (7)		4.12	2.15
(1) Variable over time ⟷ Stable over time (7)		4.05	2.13
Experienced Anger[b]	**.87**		
How much did this incident make you feel angry?	.91	3.01	1.38
How much did this incident make you feel frustrated?	.71	3.03	1.17
How much did this incident make you feel irritated?	.86	3.57	1.20
Voice[a]	**.60**		
I would try to discuss the problem with my dealership.		3.99	1.30
I would try to solve the problem by suggestion changes to my dealership.		2.86	1.44
Loyalty[a]	—		
Problems with my dealership will usually fix themselves.		2.39	1.22
I will disregard the problem.	deleted	2.05	1.16
Exit[a]	**.85**		
I would consider ending the business relationship with my dealership.		2.18	1.19
I would look for a replacement dealership.		2.41	1.27
I would consider other dealerships in the near future.		2.94	1.31
Neglect[a]	**.78**		
I would only try to use the services that are absolutely necessary at my dealership.		2.63	1.43
I would let the relationship with my dealership die a slow death.		2.11	1.12

[a]Items measured with 5-point Likert scales ranging from: 1 = "does not at all apply" to 5 = "applies completely"; and

[b]Items measured with 5-point Likert scales ranging from: 1 = "does not at all apply" to 5 = "applies completely."

Appendix 19.2

Construct Intercorrelations

Scale name	1	2	3	4	5	6	7
1. Emotions (Anger)	1.00						
2. Stability	.02	1.00					
3. Voice	.14	−.07	1.00				
4. Loyalty	−.19	−.27	−.01	1.00			
5. Exit	.22	.19	−.23	−.35	1.00		
6. Neglect	.27	.31	−.27	−.28	.75	1.00	
7. Secure Consumer Attachment	−.23	−.41	−.03	.15	−.13	−.18	1.00

REFERENCES

Aaker, Jennifer, Susan Fournier, and Adam S. Brasel (2004). "When Good Brands Do Bad," *Journal of Consumer Research*, 31 (1), 1–16.

Aggarwal, Pankaj (2004). "The Effects of Brand Relationship Norms on Consumer Attitudes and Behavior," *Journal of Consumer Research*, 31 (1), 87–101.

Aggarwal, Pankaj, and Sharmistha Law (2005). "Role of Relationship Norms in Processing Brand Information," *Journal of Consumer Research*, 32 (December), 453–464.

Aggarwal, Pankaj, and Meng Zhang (2006). "The Moderating Effect of Relationship Norm Salience on Consumers' Loss Aversion," *Journal of Consumer Research*, 33 (December), 413–419.

Ainsworth, Mary D., Mary C. Blehar, Everett Waters, and Sally Wall (1978). *Patterns of Attachment: A Psychological Study of the Strange Situation*. Hillsdale, NJ: Lawrence Erlbaum.

Bagozzi, Richard P., and Todd F. Heatherton (1994). "A General Approach to Representing Multifaceted Personality Constructs: Application to State Self-Esteem," *Structural Equation Modeling*, 1 (1), 35–67.

Barnes, James G. (1997). "Closeness, Strength, and Satisfaction: Examining the Nature of Relationships between Providers of Financial Services and Their Retail Customers," *Psychology and Marketing*, 14 (8), 765–79.

——— (2001). *Secrets of Customer Relationship Management: It's All about How You Make Them Feel*. New York, NY: McGraw-Hill.

Bitner, Mary Jo, Bernard H. Booms, and Mary Stanfield Tetreault (1990). "The Service Encounter: Diagnosing Favorable and Unfavorable Incidents," *Journal of Marketing*, 54 (January), 71–84.

Bowlby, John (1973). *Separation: Anxiety, and Anger*. New York, NY: Basic Books.

——— (1980). *Loss: Sadness and Depression*. New York, NY: Basic Books.

——— (1982). *Attachment*. New York, NY: Basic Books.

——— (1988). *A Secure Base: Clinical Applications of Attachment Theory*. London, UK: Routledge.

Collins, Nancy L. (1996). "Working Models of Attachment: Implications for Explanation, Emotion, and Behavior," *Journal of Personality and Social Psychology*, 71, 810–832.

Collins, Nancy L., Maire B. Ford, AnaMarie C. Guichard, and Lisa M. Allard (2006). "Working Models of Attachment and Attribution Processes in Intimate Relationships," *Personality and Social Psychology Bulletin*, 32 (2), 201–219.

Collins, Nancy L., and Steven J. Read (1994). "Cognitive Representations of Attachment: The Structure and Function of Working Models." In *Advances in Personal Relationships*, ed. Kim Bartholomew and Daniel Perlman. London, UK: Jessica Kingsley, 53–59.

Cupach, William R. (2000). "Advancing Understanding about Relational Conflict," *Journal of Social and Personal Relationships*, 17 (August), 697–703.

Curren, Mary T., and Valerie S. Folkes (1987). "Attributional Influences on Consumers' Desires to Communicate about Products," *Psychology and Marketing*, 4 (Spring), 31–45.

De Wulf, K., Gaby Odekerken-Schröder, and Dawn Iacobucci (2001). "Investments in Consumer Relationships: A Cross-Country and Cross-Industry Exploration," *Journal of Marketing*, 65 (October), 33–5.

Dowling, Graham R., and Mark Uncles (1997). "Do Customer Loyalty Programs Really Work?" *Sloan Management Review*, 38 (Summer), 71–82.

Edvardsson, Bo, and Tore Strandvik (2000). "Is a Critical Incident Critical for a Customer Relationship?" *Managing Service Quality*, 10 (2), 82–91.

Fiske, Susan T. (1980). "Attention and Weight in Person Perception: The Impact of Negative and Extreme Behavior," *Journal of Personality and Social Psychology*, 38 (6), 889–906.

Fiske, Susan T., and Mark A. Pavelchak (1986). "Category-Based versus Piecemeal-Based Affective Responses: Developments in Schema-Triggered Affect." In *Handbook of Motivation and Cogni-*

tion: Foundations of Social Behavior, ed. Richard M. Sorrentino and Tony E. Higgins. New York, NY: Guilford Press, 167–203.

Folkes, Valerie S. (1984). "Consumer Reactions to Product Failure: An Attributional Approach," *Journal of Consumer Research,* 10 (4), 398–409.

——— (1988). "Recent Attribution Research in Consumer Behavior: A Review and New Directions," *Journal of Consumer Research,* 14 (4), 548–565.

Folkes, Valerie S., Susan Koletsky, and John L. Graham (1987). "A Field Study of Causal Inferences and Consumer Reaction: The View from the Airport," *Journal of Consumer Research,* 13 (4), 534–539.

Forgas, Joseph P. (1998) "On Being Happy and Mistaken: Mood Effects on the Fundamental Attribution Error," *Journal of Personality and Social Psychology,* 75 (2), 318–331.

Fournier, Susan (1998). "Consumers and Their Brands: Developing Relationship Theory in Consumer Research," *Journal of Consumer Research,* 24 (4), 343–373.

——— (2002). "Making Good of Doing Bad: Negotiating Transgressions in Consumer Product Relationships," *Advances in Consumer Research,* 29, 102–104.

Fournier, Susan, and Adam S. Brasel, and Marcel Paulssen (2007). "Attachment Security and the Strength of Commercial Relationships: A Longitudinal Study." Working paper, Boston University School of Management.

Fraley, R. Chris, and Niels G. Waller (1998). "Adult Attachment Patterns: A Test of the Typological Model." In *Attachment Theory and Close Relationships,* ed. Jeffrey A. Simpson and William S. Rholes. New York, NY: Guilford Press, 77–114.

Gaines, Stanley O., Jr., Cherlyn S. Granrose, Diana I. Rios, Ben F. Garcia, Mary S. Page Youn, Karlyn R. Farris, and Katrina L. Bledsoe (1999). "Patterns of Attachment and Responses to Accommodative Dilemmas among Interethnic/Interracial Couples," *Journal of Social and Personal Relationships,* 16, 277–287.

Gaines, Stanley O. Jr., Harry T. Reis, Shandra Summers, Caryl E. Rusbult, Chante L. Cox, Michael O. Wexler, William D. Marelich, and Gregory J. Kurland (1997). "Impact of Attachment Style on Reactions to Accommodative Dilemmas in Close Relationships," *Personal Relationships,* 4, 93–113.

Gaines, Stanley O. Jr., Cecile Work, Helena Johnson, Mary Sue Page Youn, and Kaycee Lai (2000). "Impact of Attachment Style and Self-Monitoring on Individuals' Responses to Accommodative Dilemmas across Relationship Types," *Journal of Social and Personal Relationships,* 17 (6) 767–789.

Gallo, Linda C., and Timothy W. Smith (2001). "Attachment Style in Marriage: Adjustment and Responses to Interaction," *Journal of Social and Personal Relationships,* 18 (2), 263–289.

Geyskens, Inge, and Jan-Benedict E.M. Steenkamp (2000). "Economic and Social Satisfaction: Measurement and Relevance to Marketing Channel Relationships," *Journal of Retailing,* 76 (1), 11–32.

Grayson, Kent, and Tim Ambler (1999). "The Dark Side of Long-Term Relationships in Marketing Services," *Journal of Marketing Research,* 36 (February), 132–141.

Gremler, Dwayne D. (2004). "The Critical Incident Technique in Service Research," *Journal of Service Research,* 7 (1), 65–89.

Hirschman, Albert O. (1970). *Exit, Voice, and Loyalty: Responses to Decline in Firms, Organizations, and States.* Cambridge, MA: Harvard University Press.

Johnson, Michael D., Andreas Herrmann, Frank Huber, and Anders Gustafsson (1997). "An Introduction to Quality, Satisfaction, and Loyalty—Implications for the Automotive Industry." In *Customer Retention in the Automotive Industry,* ed. Michael D Johnson, Andreas Herrmann, Frank Huber, and Anders Gustafsson. Wiesbaden, Germany: Gabler, 1–17.

Jöreskog, Karl, and Dag Sörbom (2001). *LISREL 8: User's Reference Guide.* Chicago, IL: Scientific Software International.

Keaveney, Susan (1995). "Customer Switching Behaviors in Service Industries: An Exploratory Study," *Journal of Marketing,* 59 (April), 71–82.

Main, Marry (1990). "Cross-Cultural Studies of Attachment Organization: Recent Studies, Changing Methodologies, and the Concept of Conditional Strategies," *Human Development,* 33, 48–61.

Main, Mary, and David Weston (1981). "The Quality of Toddler's Relationship to Mother and Father: Related to Conflict Behavior and the Readiness to Establish New Relationships," *Child Development,* 52, 932–940.

Maxham, James III, and Richard Netemeyer (2002). "A Longitudinal Study of Complaining Customers' Evaluations of Multiple Service Failures and Recovery Efforts," *Journal of Marketing,* 66 (October), 57–72.

McCollough, Michael A., Leonard L. Berry, and Manjit S. Yadav (2000). "An Empirical Investigation of Customer Satisfaction after Service Failure and Recovery," *Journal of Service Research,* 3 (November), 121–137.

Metts, Sandra (1994). "Relational Transgressions." In *The Dark Side of Interpersonal Communications,* ed. William R. Cupach and Brian Spitzberg. Hillsdale, NJ: Lawrence Erlbaum, 217–239.

Mikulincer, Mario (1998). "Attachment Working Models and a Sense of Trust: An Exploration of Interaction Goals and Affect Regulation," *Journal of Personality and Social Psychology,* 74 (5), 1209–1224.

Mikulincer, Mario, and Victor Florian (1995). "Appraisal and Coping with a Real-Life Stressful Situation: The Contribution of Attachment Styles," *Personality and Social Psychology Bulletin,* 21 (4), 406–414.

——— (1998). "The Relationship between Adult Attachment Styles and Emotional and Cognitive Reactions to Stressful Events." In *Attachment Theory in Close Relationships,* ed. Jeffrey A. Simpson and W. Steven Rholes. New York, NY: Guilford Press, 143–165.

Mikulincer, Mario, and Philipp R. Shaver (2003). "The Attachment Behavioral System in Adulthood: Activation, Psychodynamics, and Interpersonal Processes." In *Advances in Experimental Social Psychology,* ed. Marc. P. Zanna. New York, NY: Academic Press, 53–152.

Oliver, Richard L. (1997). *Satisfaction: A Behavioral Perspective on the Consumer.* New York, NY: Irwin/McGraw-Hill.

Pierce, Tamara, and John E. Lydon (2001). "Global and Specific Relational Models in the Experience of Social Interactions," *Journal of Personality and Social Psychology,* 80 (4), 613–631.

Ping, Robert A. (1993). "The Effects of Satisfaction and Structural Constraints on Retailer Exiting, Voice, Loyalty, Opportunism and Neglect," *Journal of Retailing,* 69 (3), 320–352.

Price, Linda L., and Eric J. Arnould (1999). "Commercial Friendships: Service Provider-Client Relationships in Context," *Journal of Marketing,* 63 (April), 38–56.

Reinartz, Werner J., and V. Kumar (2000). "On the Profitability of Long-Life Customers in a Noncontractual Setting: An Empirical Investigation and Implications for Marketing," *Journal of Marketing,* 64 (April), 17–35.

——— (2003). "The Impact of Customer Relationship Characteristics on Profitable Lifetime Duration," *Journal of Marketing,* 67 (January), 77–99.

Richins, Marsha L. (1997). "Measuring Emotions in the Consumption Experience," *The Journal of Consumer Research,* 24 (2), 127–146.

Rusbult, Caryl E., and Paul A.M. van Lange (2003). "Interdependence, Interaction and Relationships," *Annual Review of Psychology,* 54, 351–375.

Rusbult, Caryl E., Julie Verette, Gregory Whitney, Linda Slovik, and Issac Lipkus (1991). "Accommodation Processes in Close Relationships: Theory and Preliminary Research Evidence," *Journal of Personality and Social Psychology,* 60 (1), 53–78.

Rusbult, Caryl E., and Isabella M. Zembrodt (1983). "Responses to Dissatisfaction in Romantic Involvements: A Multidimensional Scaling Analysis," *Journal of Experimental Social Psychology,* 19, 274–293.

Rusbult, Caryl E., Isabella M. Zembrodt, and Lawanna K. Gunn (1982). "Exit, Voice, Loyalty, and Neglect: Responses to Dissatisfaction in Romantic Involvements," *Journal of Personality and Social Psychology,* 43, 1230–1242.

Russell, Dan (1982). "The Causal Dimension Scale: A Measure of How Individuals Perceive Causes," *Journal of Personality and Social Psychology,* 42 (6), 1137–1145.

Scharfe, Elaine, and Kim Bartholomew (1995). "Accomodation and Attachment Representations in Young Couples," *Journal of Social and Personal Relationships,* 12, 389–401.

Shaver, Philipp R., Jay Belsky, and Kelly A. Brennan (2000). "The Adult Attachment Interview and Self-Reports of Romantic Attachment: Associations Across Domains and Methods," *Personal Relationships,* 7 (1), 25–43.

Shaver, Philip R., Nancy Collins, and Catherine Clark. (1996). "Attachment Styles and Internal Working Models of Self and Relationship Partners." In *Knowledge Structures in Close Relationships: A Social Psychological Approach,* ed. Garth J.O. Fletcher and Julie Fitness. Mahwah, NJ: Lawrence Erlbaum, 25–61.

Shaver, Philip R., and Mario Mikulincer (2002a). "Attachment-Related Psychodynamics," *Attachment and Human Development,* 4, 133–161.

——— (2002b). "Dialogue on Adult Attachment: Diversity and Integration," *Attachment and Human Development,* 4, 243–257.

——— (2003). "The Psychodynamics of Social Judgments: An Attachment Theory Perspective." In *Social Judgments: Implicit and Explicit Processes,* ed. Joseph P. Forgas, Kipling D. Williams, and William von Hippel. Philadelphia, PA: Psychology Press, 85–114.

——— (2005). "Attachment Theory and Research: Core Concepts, Basic Principles, Conceptual Bridges." In *Social Psychology: Handbook of Basic Pronciples,* 2nd ed., ed. Arie Kruglanski and Tony E. Higgins. New York, NY: Guilford, 39–68.

Simpson, Jeffrey, William Rholes, and Julia Nelligan (1992). "Support Seeking and Support Giving within Couples in an Anxiety-Provoking Situation: The Role of Attachment Styles," *Journal of Personality and Social Psychology,* 62 (3), 434–446.

Simpson, Jeffrey, William Rholes, and Dede Phillips (1996). "Conflict in Close Relationships: An Attachment Perspective," *Journal of Personality and Social Psychology,* 71, 899–914.

Smith, Amy K., and Ruth N. Bolton (1998). "An Experimental Investigation of Customer Reactions to Service Failure and Recovery Encounters: Paradox or Peril," *Journal of Service Research,* 1 (1), 5–17.

Thomson, Matthew T. (2006). "Human Brands: Investigating Antecedents to Consumers' Strong Attachments to Celebrities," *Journal of Marketing,* 70 (July), 104–119.

Thomson, Matthew T., and Allison R. Johnson (2002). "Investigating the Role of Attachment Dimensions as Predictors of Satisfaction in Consumer-Brand Relationships." In *Advances in Consumer Research,* vol. 29, ed. Susan M. Broniarczyk and Kent Nakamoto. Valdosta, GA: Association for Consumer Research, 42.

——— (2006). "Marketplace and Personal Space: Investigating the Differential Effects of Attachment Style across Relationship Contexts," *Psychology and Marketing,* 23 (8), 711–726.

Tsiros, Michael, Vikas Mittal, and William T. Ross (2004). "The Role of Attributions in Customer Satisfaction: A Reexamination," *Journal of Consumer Research,* 31 (September), 476–483.

Waters, Harriet S., Lisa M. Rodrigues, and Doreen Ridgeway (1998). "Cognitive Underpinnings of Narrative Attachment Assessment," *Journal of Experimental Child Psychology,* 71, 211–234.

Weiner, Bernard (2000). "Attributional Thoughts about Consumer Behavior," *Journal of Consumer Research,* 27 (December), 382–387.

Ybarra, Oscar, and Walter G. Stephan (1999). "Attributional Orientation and the Prediction of Behavior: The Attribution-Prediction Bias," *Journal of Personality and Social Psychology,* 76 (5), 718–727.

PART V

CONCLUSIONS AND RESEARCH DIRECTIONS

CHAPTER 20

RESEARCH DIRECTIONS ON STRONG BRAND RELATIONSHIPS

C. WHAN PARK, DEBORAH J. MACINNIS, AND JOSEPH R. PRIESTER

Collectively, the chapters in this volume reveal numerous avenues for future research. Rather than merely summarizing the eloquently articulated research directions already described in previously, in this chapter we instead identify research issues pertaining to *strong* brand relationships. We emphasize this research domain over the nature and type of other relationships since strong brand relationships offer the greatest economic profit potential to companies; hence they matter to customers, meaning makers, and the companies that produce them. We focus on research issues pertinent to the construct of attachment, as we believe that attachment is a critical driver of strong brand relationships. We suggest that future empirical research is needed to (1) understand the conceptual properties of brand attachment relative to other brand relationship–oriented constructs, (2) understand *when* brand attachment would be most likely to develop, (3) *how* it affects customers' processing of brand information, brand-oriented behaviors, and the brand's market performance, (4) *why* it is desirable from the perspective of customers as well as a firm, and (5) what fosters its evolution, habitual processes, and termination.

Fournier (Chapter 1) accurately notes that brand relationships are multiplex phenomena, ranging across several dimensions and taking many forms. For example, Fournier (1998, Chapter 1) identified fifteen types of consumer-brand relationships. While these relationships are described along several dimensions including love (Chapter 18), commitment, intimacy, and passion, feelings of attachment lie at the "core of all strong brand relationships" (Fournier 1998, p. 363). Hence, one can ascertain that strong consumer-brand (and consumer-consumer) relationships, such as committed partnerships, best friendships, and secret affairs, are likely to be characterized by strong degrees of attachment; others, such as enslavements, arranged marriages, and marriages of convenience are likely to be characterized by low levels of attachment. The attachment construct may, thus, serve as a useful higher order construct that discriminates among the relationships identified by Fournier, the degree of love involved in brand relationships, and the norms that characterize those relationships (Chapter 2). Importantly, limited work has studied the relationship between attachment and strong brand relationships. However, the attachment measure articulated by Park et al. (Chapter 17) provides the potential for future work on this basic supposition.

Notably, despite the growing popularity of the attachment construct, its defining features remain elusive. As noted by Park et al. (Chapter 17), attachment is defined as *the strength of the bond connecting the brand with the self* and is revealed by *two critical* indicators: (1) brand-self connectedness and (2) the prominence of brand-relevant thoughts and feelings. Therefore, brand attachment is reflected by the brand-self connections identified in earlier chapters (e.g., Chapters 5, 6, 7, and 11). Although Priester and colleagues provided preliminary evidence that attachment is related to brand-self connections, additional work linking these two constructs is needed.

The motivations consumers have to engage in brand-self connections may be multifarious as suggested in Chapters 5, 6, 7, and 11, however these motivations may be articulated in terms of a higher form of motivation, as suggested by Aron et al.'s self-expansion theory (Aron et al. 2005, and also Chapter 6). They posit that individuals possess an inherent motivation for self-expansion; the desire to incorporate others into one's conception of "self." The more an entity is included in the self, the deeper the bond that develops between the individual and the other entity. Attachment develops over time as relationships between the individual and the entity evolve. Through time, a cognitive reorganization takes place such that the self expands to include the partner (Aron and Aron 1986). Individuals develop a positive feeling of oneness with the partner (Waugh and Fredrickson 2006; Aron and Aron 1996; Aron and Smollan 1992; Aron, Tudor and Nelson 1991) and tend to view the partner's resources as their own (Mittal 2006). Hence, an important future research issue concerns the extent to which attachment is linked to consumers' perceptions that the brand has served the purpose of self-expansion and that the brand's resources are seen as part of the consumers.

Attachment driven by self-expansion has several potential outcomes that foster a brand-self connection and relationship continuation. First, feelings of oneness are positive, offering the reward of emotional regulation. Second, by incorporating others into the self, one increases the resources, perspectives, and identities available to the self by including the partner's resources as one's own. These resources motivate relationship continuation because they increase the stock of resources possessed by the individual to achieve future goals. Third, by seeing the partner as "part of me," the individual treats the partner preferentially (Aron et al. 1991, 2005), offering resources of their own so as to foster relationship continuation. Fourth, attached individuals process information about the partner in a biased fashion (Aron et al. 1991), looking at their good points and downplaying their bad points. Fifth, because the relationship partner is seen as part of the self, the individual is more likely to make situational (as opposed to dispositional) attributions to explain relationship mishaps (Aron et al. 1991), which helps to smooth relationship transgressions (Waugh and Frederickson 2006). Future research should examine the relationship between brand attachment and positive feelings, feelings of oneness, preferential treatment of the brand, and the evocation of dispositional versus situational inferences about the brand. Whereas Paulssen and Bagozzi (Chapter 19) suggest that attachment style impacts brand forgiveness, future research should ask whether attachment strength also impacts such forgiveness.

BRAND ATTACHMENT AND BRAND ATTITUDE STRENGTH

Several chapters in this volume indicated the importance of having strong and positive brand attitudes toward brands (e.g., Chapters 15 and 16), since strong brand attitudes persist over time, are stored and accessed (vs. constructed), and resist persuasion attempts or change from brand disasters. Hence, strong brand attitudes can have important outcomes that are critical to the brand-building activities of marketers. Further research is needed to understand the relationship between strong positive brand attitudes and strong brand relationships (attachment).

Strong brand attitudes and brand attachment have similar properties and hence there is some reason to expect that they may elicit similar outcomes. First, like brand attachment, strong positive brand attitude is a psychological construct that references a brand. It also is linked to feelings of goodness and positive brand judgments. It is likely to have elements of prominence as it may be readily retrieved given the degree of processing that underlies it. Finally, both have implications for consumption behaviors relevant to marketing—for example, brand purchase, repeat purchase, and a willingness to recommend a brand.

However, strong brand attitudes and strong brand attachment may also be different. First, whereas attachment may be based on brand-self connections (Bowlby 1973, 1982; Collins 1996; Mikulincer et al. 2001; Park et al. Chapter 17) such connections do not seem necessary for strong positive brand attitudes. Instead, strong brand attitudes are based on thoughtful processes involving considerable analysis of a brand's merits. The formation of strong and favorable brand attitudes depends on high levels of motivation, ability, and opportunity to process information about a brand, and positive brand information. Thoughtful processing of this information leads to positive cognitive responses that support the brand's viability. Hence, brands for which attachment is strong may reflect attitude formation processes more similar to the identity-based processes described by Reed, Cohen, and Bhattacharjee (Chapter 7) than by the analytical attribute-based processes characterized by strong brand attitudes.

Second, the constructs may differ in the nature of affect they implicate. Whereas attachment implicates hot affect (Mikulincer et al. 2001), perhaps akin to feelings of love described by Ahuvia, Batra, and Bagozzi (Chapter 18), strong brand attitudes reflect evaluations and "cold affect" (Cohen and Areni 1991). Third, strong attachment is characterized by feelings of safety and emotional gratification (see Chapters 6 and 14), which are, in turn, engendered through feelings of intimacy and trust (Fournier 1998). These feelings are likely unnecessary for strong brand attitudes. The formation of strong attachments includes personalized brand experiences that are accumulated over time, stored as self-brand links in memory, and prominently represented in one's thoughts and feelings. Moreover, personalized self-brand linkages are not necessary for the development of strong positive attitudes (see, for example, Fazio 1995; Petty, Haugtvedt, and Smith 1995).

Beyond differentiating attachment from strong brand attitudes, future research might also focus on whether and when attachment and strong brand attitudes yield different psychological and behavioral outcomes. For example, will strong brand attitudes or brand attachment be more amenable to the development of habitual relationships (Chapter 3)? Or are habitual relationships independent of attachment and strong attitudes? Are brand relationships characterized by attachment better able than strong brand attitudes to predict behaviors that utilize considerable resources used by consumers (e.g., time resources such as involvement in brand communities, reputational resources such as willingness to spread favorable word of mouth, and monetary resources such as willingness to pay a price premium)? Would consumers be more likely to allocate such resources in support of the brand because they see their own resources as part of the brand?

BRAND ATTACHMENT AND BRAND COMMITMENT

Future research might also focus on the boundaries between attachment and brand commitment. We define commitment in a manner consistent with its usage in the attachment literature (e.g., Levinger 1980)—as a decision or pledge to maintain a long-term relationship with a brand into the future. Commitment is a psychological pledge regarding future behavior. Attachment is a characteristic of a relationship between a consumer and a brand. This definition also resonates with that found in a marketing context, where the construct has been primarily conceptualized in terms of intentions to remain loyal to (and hence maintain a relationship with) the brand in the future (Ahluwalia, Unnava and Burnkrant 2000). Finally, this definition is consistent with the definition proposed by Fournier (1998), who defines commitment as "the intention to behave in a manner supportive of relationship longevity" (p. 365).

Strong commitment derived from attachment to the brand is revealed by a set of commitment-related behaviors that promote relationship maintenance acts (Miller 1997; see Figure 20.1). Such behaviors include brand loyalty (Ahluwalia, Unnava and Burnkrant 2000), forgiveness of mishaps, and brand-advocating behaviors such as positive word of mouth and the derogation of alternatives (Miller 1997; Pimentel and Reynolds 2004; Finkel et al. 2002).

Although the two concepts seem similar, future research should verify whether commitment is synonymous with attachment or whether it is an outcome of attachment (see Figure 20.1). We hypothesize the latter. Brand attachment reflects a consumers' psychological state of mind (strong self-brand linkages and automatic retrieval of thoughts and feelings about the brand), while commitment reflects intention to engage in behaviors that maintain a brand relationship. Moreover, we propose that attachment is a more valuable destination for marketers than is commitment. Commitment may involve a pledge to stay in a relationship for a variety of reasons unrelated to attachment—hence, there are forms of commitment that are attachment-based and others that are not (what others have called affective-based commitment vs. normative and structural commitment; Johnson 1991). Individuals may be committed to a brand due to lack of competing alternatives or out of some sense of moral or contractual obligation to the company or its salespeople. Commitment formed through factors other than attachment may not be associated with strong forms of behavior such as willingness to pay a price premium. Commitment that is not based on attachment will not produce strong self-brand connections and prominent

Figure 20.1   **Antecedents and Outcomes of Brand Attachment Strength**

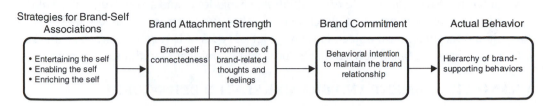

Strategies for Brand-Self Associations	Brand Attachment Strength		Brand Commitment	Actual Behavior
• Entertaining the self • Enabling the self • Enriching the self	Brand-self connectedness	Prominence of brand-related thoughts and feelings	Behavioral intention to maintain the brand relationship	Hierarchy of brand-supporting behaviors

thoughts and feelings about the brand. Attachment is a natural precursor to commitment (Rusbult et al. 1991). Strong attachment should predict a pledge to continue with a relationship and bring with that pledge the emotional energy that creates a satisfying long-term relationship.

BRAND ATTACHMENT AND BRAND INVOLVEMENT

Research might also differentiate brand attachment from "involvement." We expect that the constructs are related—consumers who are attached to an object are also likely to be involved with it. Hence involvement should be high for brands to which consumers are emotionally attached. However, emotional attachment is neither necessary nor sufficient for involvement. Consumers can be involved with brands for which they have developed little or no attachment. Furthermore, emotional attachments to brands are clearly relevant to the realm of emotions such as love (Chapter 18), whereas the concept of involvement arguably taps the realm of cognition. While involvement and attachment share a readiness to respond (Park and Mittal 1985), with involvement this readiness is linked to personal consequences and the desire to avoid risk, as well as extensive objective processing of information designed to reduce risk. In contrast, attachment is linked to the connection between the brand and the self and the motivated processing of information designed to retain this emotional bond.

BRAND ATTACHMENT AND BRAND LOVE

Brand attachment bears some similarity to the construct of love (Chapter 18). Undoubtedly, most of the prototypical features of love (e.g., trust, caring, honesty, and friendship; see Fehr 1993) are also typical of strong attachments. However, love is an emotion that characterizes the attachment bond, not the attachment bond itself. Thus, while one may feel love in the presence of the attachment object, attachment is more than this feeling. In addition, while attachment has both positive and negative valences, brand love only has positive valence. Conceptually, attachment may be understood either from the positively valenced relationship or from the negatively valenced relationship (e.g., obsessively antibrand relationship). It is a higher order construct than brand love. Brand love becomes highly similar only to the positively valenced brand attachment. Finally, there are many different types of love that differ among themselves in a number of critical dimensions

(Sternberg 1987; Fehr and Russell 1991). Examples include friendship love, familial love, maternal love, romantic love, infatuation, sexual love, and so on. Regardless of the type of love, we anticipate that attachment is reflective of strong connections between the self and the attachment object. However, not all types of love may share the same key characteristics (i.e., brand-self connectedness and prominence) with brand attachment.

BRAND ATTACHMENT AND BRAND-RELATED BEHAVIORS

An impressive array of research supports the relationship between attachment and social behaviors (see Mikulincer and Shaver 2005 for the discussion). Previous research on mother-child attachments has identified four distinctive behavioral indicators of attachment (Bowlby 1979; Hazan and Zeifman 1999): (1) proximity seeking (an infant's desire to be close to the mother), (2) secure-base behaviors (the willingness to explore unfamiliar environments when the mother is within close proximity), (3) safe haven (seeking security, protection, and comfort from the mother when the environment is threatening), and (4) separation distress (experiencing emotional and physical distress from real or threatened separation from the mother).

Building on these ideas, the attachment literature has developed a more general model of attachment and behaviors. Specifically, individuals avoid the danger of separation from the attachment object by adopting "hyperactivating attachment strategies" (Mikulincer and Shaver 2005; Berman and Sperling 1994). Such strategies involve increased vigilance to threat-related cues and a reduction in the threshold for detecting cues of the attachment figure's unavailability (Bowlby 1973). In a marketing context, such hyperactivating strategies are revealed by hoarding behavior to prevent product unavailability and hypervigilance to threats of the product being taken off the market (e.g., being replaced by a new brand). The 1985 New Coke fiasco illustrates the relationship between brand attachment and separation distress. Notably, additional research is needed to determine if consumer attachment to brands also reveals such hyperactivating strategies.

The human attachment literature also indicates that hyperactivating strategies can lead to self-defensive motivation revealed by cognitive closure and rigidity, the rejection of information that heightens ambiguity and challenges the validity of one's existing beliefs, derogation of members of other groups, and prejudice toward people who are different from oneself. In person-to-person contexts, individuals who are strongly attached to others are loyal to their partners (Drigotas and Rusbult 1992), and resist competing alternatives (Johnson and Rusbult 1989). In a marketing context, such behaviors would include counterarguing of competitive information that derogates the brand. It would involve derogating others who use competing brands and a rejection of what they stand for (e.g., Thompson, Rindfleisch, and Arsel 2006). Individuals who are strongly attached to others also forgive the mishaps of their partner (McCullough et al. 1998). Research should explore the relationship between the strength of one's brand attachment and these relationship-sustaining activities.

Considering a variety of behaviors consumers reveal toward a brand, one may understand them in the form of a hierarchy. Given the numerous behaviors that consumers can enact toward a brand, a critical question concerns the relationship between brand attachment strength and the various behaviors that comprise the hierarchy. Earlier, we noted that one's willingness to make sacrifices to maintain a relationship with the brand is an empirically supported discriminator of brand attachment strength. Willingness to sacrifice personal resources for the brand may be the basis on which attachment strength is linked to the behaviors within the hierarchy.

We articulate two dimensions of the sacrifices of personal resources. The first concerns consumers' willingness to sacrifice self-image resources for the brand. Self-image (or ego) resources refer to psychological resources cherished with respect to the self. They include self-pride and self-esteem. By publicly displaying, defending, advocating, or promoting their support for a brand, consumers are willing to face the risk of social ridicule, discredit, and social rejection. The second dimension is consumers' willingness to sacrifice scarce discretionary resources. To support a brand, consumers often make sacrifices of personal discretionary resources such as money, time, and energy. While the self-image resource dimension concerns others' judgments on one's self-image, the personal resource dimension refers to one's willingness to expend one's own discretionary resources for the brand.

Future research might investigate whether attachment is related to the self-image and/or personal discretionary resources the individual is willing to risk or expend for the brand. Specifically, when attachment is high, consumers may perceive the brand to be an extension of themselves. They may be defensive of attacks or criticisms against their brand and interpret such criticisms as personally threatening. Thus they may be willing to engage in behaviors on behalf of the brand, despite the potential self-image–related risks such behaviors may carry. These consumers may also be less cost-benefit oriented in their reactions to their brands. Thus personal sacrifices of time, money, and/or energy are more automatic.

Table 20.1 describes a potential relationship among brand attachment strength, the two dimensions of personal sacrifice, behavioral characteristics, and possible types of behaviors that future research might examine. Three levels of brand attachment strength (low, moderate, and high) are shown. At the low level, automatic retrieval of brand-self connections are unlikely given weak brand-self connectedness. Brand purchase, if engaged, is not linked to attachment. Rather, such behavior may be more adequately explained by evaluation-based mechanisms such as attitudes. Moreover, since consumers at a low level of brand attachment may be weak in their willingness to incur the loss of either self-image or personal discretionary resources, they may not engage in the types of strong brand-supporting behaviors described earlier (see Table 20.1).

At a moderate level of attachment, brand attitudes may also be strong. Such moderate attachment levels may be characterized by brand-supporting behaviors. Such behaviors may, however, arise from attachment, not attitudes, and may reflect a moderate degree of willingness to sacrifice self-image and/or personal discretionary resources. Thus, consumers at a moderate level of attachment may reveal behavioral characteristics linked to the sacrifices noted in Table 20.1. Moreover, consumers at this level of brand attachment may show brand loyalty (repeat purchase behavior) and other additional brand-supporting behaviors due to their motivation to maintain their relationship with the brand.

The first of the three forms of behavior may occur when consumers' willingness to sacrifice self-image resources is low but their willingness to sacrifice personal discretionary resources is moderate. Possible behaviors characterizing this form are paying price premium (money resource), postponing purchase when one's favorite brand is not available (time resource), and prolonging brand search when one's favorite brand is not easily located (energy resource).

The second form may occur when consumers' willingness to sacrifice self-image resources is moderate but their willingness to sacrifice personal discretionary resources is low. Possible behaviors belonging to this form include public display of a brand ownership, publicly defending a brand against criticisms, and recommending a brand to others.

The third form may occur when consumers are moderate in their willingness to sacrifice both self-image and personal discretionary resources. A possible behavior belonging to this form is consumers' participation in a brand community. Such behavior involves brand promotion and devotion of time, energy, and possibly money through community involvement (Muñiz and O'Guinn 2000).

The highest level of brand attachment may be characterized by an even greater willingness to sacrifice either or both resources. At this level, consumers also reveal stronger brand loyalty and more intense brand-supporting behaviors than is expected at the moderate level (Table 20.1). For example, a consumer would show greater consistency in repeat purchase behavior. Furthermore, brand community participation would be more intense. It is implicitly assumed that the sacrifice of both types of resources is linked to stronger brand attachment than is true when sacrifice of only one type of resource is present.

In conclusion, a brand's final destination is the highest level of brand attachment, in which consumers are willing to sacrifice both types of resources. When a brand reaches this level of brand attachment, it may enjoy not only a higher mind share (cognition-based), but also a higher heart share (affect-based) than brands with less attachment. Notably, while these ideas are provocative, they have yet to be empirically tested.

THE LIMITS OF MARKETING ACTIVITIES IN CREATING STRONG BRAND ATTACHMENT

Although strong brand attachment may be a critical destination point for marketers, future research should understand the limits of marketing activities in enabling such attachments. As O'Guinn and Muñiz (Chapter 10) point out, marketers are but one source of meaning makers that foster brand-self connections. Sen, Du, and Bhattacharya (Chapter 10) similarly note the limit of socially responsible corporate activities in fostering such connections, whereas Monga and John (Chapter 13) show that marketers lack full control over the meaning consumers in different cultures attach to brand extensions. Further research can investigate how reference groups, cultures, and subcultures—not to mention the other audiences described by O'Guinn and Muñiz—play a role in creating strong attachment.

Table 20.1

Brand Attachment and Behaviors

| Attachment | Types of Resource Sacrifice | | Brand Supporting Behaviors |
	Self-Image Resources	Personal Discretionary Resources	
Low	Low	Low	None
Moderate	Low	Moderate	Repeat purchase behavior accompanied with *paying a price premium, postponement of purchase, or prolonged brand search*
	Moderate	Low	Repeat purchase behavior accompanied with *public display, public defending of a brand, or recommendation to others*
	Moderate	Moderate	Repeat purchase behavior accompanied with *participation in the brand community*
High	Low/Moderate	High	Stronger repeat purchase behavior accompanied with *more willingness to pay a price premium, postpone purchase, or prolong brand search*
	High	Low/Moderate	Stronger repeat purchase behavior accompanied with *more willingness to display, defend, or recommend a brand to others*
	High	High	Stronger repeat purchase behavior accompanied with *more willingness to participate in the brand community*

WHAT CREATES BRAND ATTACHMENT?

Prior research on human attachment suggests that the desire to make strong attachments to particular human others serves a basic human need (Bowlby 1973; Ainsworth et al. 1978; Reis and Patrick 1996), beginning from a child's attachment to his or her mother (Bowlby 1982) and continuing through the adult stage with romantic relationships (Hazan and Shaver 1994), kinships, and friendships (Trinke and Bartholomew 1997; Weiss 1988). In the human infant, attachment forms when a primary caregiver is responsive to the needs of the human infant on a continuing and consistent basis. For an infant, such needs include comfort and sustenance, derived from food, sleep, sensory (oral, gustatory, tactile auditory, visual) gratification, and the lack of sensory and biological discomforts. They also include security derived from knowing who is and who is not part of one's group and can be relied on for care. As an infant grows, attachments enable the infant to differentiate the self from the primary caregiver, engage in exploration, and master independent experiences.

In an similar way, it is possible that brand attachments form when brands satisfy key aspects of the self: entertaining (pleasing or gratifying) the self (see Chapters 5 and 14); enriching the self (Chapters 4, 6, and 7); and enabling the self (Chapter 5). Thus, consumers may connect the brand to the self when it *pleases* the self by providing sensory, hedonic, or aesthetic pleasure. They become attached when the brand *enriches* the self by representing, defining, or expressing the actual or desired self or offering resources lacking in the individual. They may become attached when the brand solves problems or enables mastery experiences that help the individual achieve other goals relevant to the self. Research might also verify whether brands that foster connections on multiple dimensions create greater attachment than brands that emphasize only one.

WHY IS ATTACHMENT IMPORTANT TO BRAND EQUITY MANAGEMENT?

Future research should also explore relationships characterized by strong attachment with financial outcomes linked to the firm (e.g., brand equity). According to various brand metrics (Interbrand model, Ailawadi, Lehmann, and Neslin 2003), a brand's value to the company is typically affected by the brand's unit price, unit marketing costs (MC_t), and the number of units sold (Q). These three components are directly tied to and reflect the nature and intensity of customers' attachment and commitment to a brand.

It is possible that brand relationships characterized by strong attachment positively impact each of these components. The stronger the customers' attachment to the brand the higher the unit price that the brand can bear—that is, attachment may be related to customers' willingness to pay a price premium (Thomson et al. 2005; Van Lange et al. 1997). Strong attachments may also induce a devaluation of competing alternatives (Johnson and Rusbult 1989), a willingness to forgive the brand's mishaps (McCullough et al. 1998), and a willingness to inhibit impulses to react destructively to relationship mishaps. These intentions and behaviors may influence the stability of the Q component and reduce the costs of customer retention. Finally, strong attachments toward brands or individuals may impact trust of a partner, willingness to promote positive word of mouth, and a relative insensitivity to the reciprocity by one's partner (e.g., active marketing effort by a brand to reinforce or appreciate its customers' loyalty) (Thomson et al. 2005; Wieselquist et al. 1999). Such outcomes should impact the Q component and make the MC_t component more cost efficient.

Moreover, the positive impact of strong brand attachment may not be limited to its market share in its primary product class. It may also positively influence its need share (a share of the market among all the substitutable products), a wallet share (a share of all the yearly expenses consumers incur for their living), and even a stock investment portfolio share (a share of investment for the stocks of a firm that own a brand). These are empirical questions that need to be investigated. However, there are many compelling reasons that lead us to believe that the positive impact of strong brand attachment is not confined to the market share.

WHEN AND HOW DOES BRAND ATTACHMENT WEAKEN OR TERMINATE?

Several authors in this volume (e.g., Fournier, Reimann and Aron, Ahuvia et al., Tam et al., O'Guinn and Muñiz, and Aggarwal) point to a highly underexplored issue in the study of brand relationships (strong or otherwise); that is, just as we need additional research on how relationships form, we also need research on how they evolve, weaken, and terminate. While attachment formation processes are interesting and important, equally relevant is the process by which attachments weaken and terminate. Understanding such factors provides insight into how weakened bonds can be prevented. Indeed, Aggarwal (Chapter 2) identifies relevant issues that marketers can consider in preventing termination where relationships are deeper than a typical transaction-based relationship. Moreover, because attachments involve economic, time, and psychic costs (Kleine and Baker 2004) as well as a commitment of resources that could be invested elsewhere (Belk 1988), understanding how attachments can be weakened provides insight into how to avoid unhealthy attachment relationships. Hence, relevant research issues concern questions such as "Do relationships characterized by strong attachment evolve, weaken, and terminate differently from those characterized by weak relationships?" "Can relationships characterized by strong attachment evolve from love into hate under certain circumstances?" "What are those circumstances and how can they be prevented?" and "What is the role of various meaning makers in speeding or retarding attachment weakening or termination?"

Drigotas and Rusbult's (1992) dependence model provides a viable perspective on attachment termination. Using concepts from interdependence theory (Kelley and Thibaut 1978), the authors find that the decision to remain in or voluntarily end a relationship is strongly related to the degree of dependence on that relationship. According to the authors, an individual may sometimes remain in an unsatisfying relationship because it fulfills needs that cannot be gratified in alternative relationships (see also Berman and Sperling 1994). As such, the individual becomes dependent on the relationship partner despite the relationship's unsatisfactory nature. Levinger's (1979) cohesiveness model similarly argues that stay-leave decisions are influenced by relationship attractions and alternative attractions; the forces that drive one toward a relationship versus away from a relationship, respectively. When the brand loses its ability to gratify, enable, and enrich the self, attachments weaken and terminate, particularly when better options become available. The fact that individuals may stay in unsatisfying relationships underscores the importance of differentiating attachment from repeat purchase. Individuals may continue to purchase brands that fail to strongly provide highly satisfying levels of gratification, enrichment, or enabling outcomes simply because alternatives for more satisfying relationships are limited. However, as soon as better options become available, the individual will terminate the relationship with the brand.

While these models suggest that the opportunity for more satisfying relationships predicts relationship termination, attachment relationships may also terminate through processes that alter the appraisal of the attachment object. According to Mikulincer and Shaver (2005), when proximity seeking is appraised as failing to alleviate distress, attachment-deactivating strategies are adopted. The individual distances himself or herself from the attachment object and attempts to handle distress alone. Mikulincer and Shaver propose that attachment-deactivating strategies include (1) dismissing threat- and attachment-related cues, (2) suppressing threat- and attachment-related thoughts and emotions, and (3) repressing threat- and attachment-related memories. By adopting a self-reliant attitude that decreases dependence on others and discouraging acknowledgement of personal faults or weaknesses, one may in fact further reinforce these tendencies. One may adopt this type of coping strategy upon realizing the downside of maintaining strong attachment with the attachment figure. In a marketing context, such weakening may occur when the brand-self connection is no longer appreciated by consumers, due to the failure of the brand to sustain the connection (e.g., failure to provide gratification, enrichment, or enabling outcomes).

Attachments also weaken when the individual feels too close to the attachment object. Recent research indicates that the self (and its development) can be influenced detrimentally when others limit an individual's ability to control his or her environment or personal identity (Mashek and Sherman 2004; Aron et al. 2005). As a response to being unable to differentiate the self from the relationship partner, the individual begins a process of lowering attachment intensity. This idea resembles Deci and Ryan's (1991) self-determination theory, which holds that human beings have three primary innate psychological needs, one of which is interpersonal relatedness. Relatedness encompasses intimacy and other social involvement strivings, but with the qualification that interpersonal relations must be authentic (Reis and Patrick 1996). According to Deci and Ryan (1991), authentic bonds are possible only for people who approach social relations with a sense of their own autonomy. Basic needs for relatedness thus may not be fully satisfied through relationships that are controlling, suffocating, power-oriented, superficial, or constraining in a manner that limits partners' ability or willingness to express themselves openly and honestly.

In a marketing context, one might anticipate that when the ideology or values that characterize the brand impose undue burden on one's desire to expand the self, thus restricting rather than nurturing the development of the self, the individual may terminate the relationship with the attachment object.

These issues have interesting implications for the activities in which marketers must engage to sustain highly resource-infusive relationships over time. While brand attachment may be achieved through strategic considerations of the hedonic, symbolic, and functional resources offered by the brand, how the attachment was initially developed may influence its sustainability. Specifically, when attachment is developed through the tactical executions by creating strong, high-arousal emotions such as passion, attachment may be difficult to sustain over time. It may be more prudent for a brand to rely on the tactical decisions that develop consumers' attachment through moderate arousal emotions, such as warm and pleasant feelings (gratifying); feelings of competence and hopefulness that come from task enablement allowed by reliable and consistent performance-based trust (enabling); and feelings of inspiration, belongingness, or nostalgia from self-enrichment tactics. Although the development of attachment through these alternative emotional routes may take more time than attention-grabbing execution tactics that trigger strong and highly arousing emotions, they may be easier to sustain over time.

Another way to sustain strong attachment may be to continuously strengthen brand-self associations and connections through a creative mix of the three resource types over time. Such a strategy expands memory associations between a brand and self, allowing memory associations to accumulate and strengthen in the brand memory network. These stronger associations may enhance the brand's accessibility in memory, facilitating the automatic activation of brand-related thoughts and feelings.

Finally, sustaining attachment may require that the brand continuously improves its tangible product-specific benefits, independent of its specific resource-type positioning. No matter how great the resource type–based positioning and the execution tactics may be, it may not be sufficient for brand attachment to be sustained over time unless specific tangible product benefits continuously improve over time.

CONCLUSION

The ideas in this volume, and those articulated in this chapter, reveal that the study of brand relationships is rife with research potential. Much remains to be learned about the impact of myriad meaning makers on the meaning consumers attach to brands, the processes and motivators that link the brand with the self, the stability of these connections, both over context and across time, and their impact on the nature and type of relationships consumers develop with brands. So too is research on the psychological and behavioral outcomes linked to relationships characterized along various dimensions, types, and states of evolution. In sum, the ideas in this book merely scratch the surface of potential consumer and marketing insight to be gained from the study of brand relationships.

REFERENCES

Ahluwalia, R., Unnava, R. & Burnkrant, R. (2000). "Consumer Response to Negative Publicity: The Moderating Role of Commitment," *Journal of Marketing Research,* 37 (2), 203–215.

Ailawadi, Kusum L., Donald R. Lehmann, and Scott A. Neslin (2003). "Revenue Premium as an Outcome Measure of Brand Equity," *Journal of Marketing,* 67 (October), 1–17.

Ainsworth, M. D. S., Blehar, M. C., Waters, E., and Wall, S. (1978). *Patterns of Attachment: A Psychological Study of the Strange Situation.* Hillsdale, NJ: Lawrence Erlbaum.

Aron, Arthur, and Elaine N. Aron (1986). *Love and the Expansion of the Self: Understanding Attraction and Satisfaction.* New York, NY: Hemisphere Publishing.

Aron, Arthur, Debra Mashek, Tracy McLaughlin-Volpe, Stephen Wright, Gary Lewandowski, and Elaine N. Aron (2005). "Including Close Others in the Cognitive Structure of the Self." In *Interpersonal Cognition,* ed. Mark W. Baldwin. New York, NY: Guilford Press, 206–232.

Aron, Arthur, and Danny Smollan (1992). "Inclusion of Other in the Self Scale and the Structure of Interpersonal Closeness," *Journal of Personality and Social Psychology,* 63 (4), 596–612.

Aron, Arthur, Michael Tudor, and Greg Nelson (1991). "Close Relationships as Including Other in the Self," *Journal of Personality and Social Psychology,* 60 (2), 241–253.

Aron, Elaine N., and Arthur Aron (1996). "Love and Expansion of the Self: The State of the Model," *Personal Relationships,* 3 (1), 45–58.

Belk, R. W. (1988). "Possessions and the Extended Self." *Journal of Consumer Research,* 15, 139–168.

Berman, William H., and Michael B. Sperling (1994). "The Structure and Function of Adult Attachment." In *Attachment in Adults: Clinical and Developmental Perspectives,* ed. Michael B. Sperling and William H. Berman. New York, NY: Guilford Press, 3–28.

Bowlby, John (1973). *Separation: Anxiety and Anger.* New York, NY: Basic Books.

———. (1979). *The Making and Breaking of Affectional Bonds.* London, UK: Tavistock.

———. (1982). *Attachment.* New York, NY: Basic Books.

Cohen, J., and C. Areni (1991). "Affect and Consumer Behavior." In *Handbook of Consumer Behavior,* ed. T.S. Robertson and H.H. Kassarjian. Englewood Cliffs, NJ: Prentice-Hall, 188–240.

Collins, Nancy L. (1996). "Working Models of Attachment: Implications for Explanations, Emotion, and Behavior," *Journal of Personality and Social Psychology,* 71, 810–832.

Deci, Edward L., and Richard M. Ryan (1991). "A Motivational Approach to Self: Integration in Personality." In Richard Dienstbier (ed.), *Nebraska Symposium on Motivation: Perspectives on Motivation. Current Theories and Research in Motivation,* Lincoln, NE: University of Nebraska Press.

Drigotas, Stephen M., and Caryl Rusbult (1992). "Should I Stay or Should I Go: A Dependence Model of Break-ups," *Journal of Personality and Social Psychology,* 62 (1), 62–87.

Fazio, Russell H. (1995). "Attitudes as Object-Evaluation Associations: Determinants, Consequences, and Correlates of Attitude Accessibility." In *Attitude Strength: Antecedents and Consequences,* ed. Richard E. Petty and Jon A. Krosnick. Mahwah, NJ: Lawrence Erlbaum, 247–282.

Fehr, Beverly (1993). "How Do I Love Thee . . . ? Let Me Consult My Prototype." In *Individuals in Relationships,* ed. S. Duck. Newbury Park, CA: Sage, 87–120.

Fehr, Beverly, and James A. Russell (1991). "The Concept of Love Viewed from a Prototype Perspective," *Journal of Personality and Social Psychology,* 60, 425–438.

Finkel, Eli J., Caryl E. Rusbult, Madoka Kumashiro, and Peggy A. Hannon (2002). "Dealing With Betrayal in Close Relationships: Does Commitment Promote Forgiveness?" *Journal of Personality and Social Psychology,* 82 (6), 956–974.

Fournier, Susan (1998). "Consumers and Their Brands: Developing Relationship Theory in Consumer Research," *Journal of Consumer Research,* 24 (March), 343–373.

Hazan, Cindy, and D. Zeifman (1999). "Pair Bonds as Attachment: Evaluating the Evidence." In *Handbook of Attachment: Theory, Research, and Clinical Applications,* ed. J. Cassidy and P. Shaver. New York, NY: Guilford Press, 336–354.

Hazan, Cindy, and Phillip R. Shaver (1994). "Attachment as an Organizational Framework for Research on Close Relationships," *Psychological Inquiry,* 5, 1–22.

Johnson, Dennis J. (1991). "Commitment to Personal Relationships." In *Advances in Personal Relationships,* 3, ed. W.H. Jones and D.W. Perlman. London. UK: Jessica Kingsley, 117–143.

Johnson, Dennis J. and Caryl E. Rusbult (1989). "Resisting Temptation: Devaluation of Alternative Partners as a Means of Maintaining Commitment in Close Relationships," *Journal of Personality and Social Psychology,* 57 (6), 967–980.

Kelley, Harold, and John Thibaut (1978). *Interpersonal Relations: A Theory of Interdependence.* New York, NY: Wiley.

Kleine, Susan Schultz, and Stacey Menzel Baker (2004). "An Integrative Review of Material Possession Attachment," *Academy of Marketing Science Review,* 1, 1–35.

Levinger, George (1979). *Divorce and Separation: Context, Cues and Consequences.* New York, NY: Basic Books.

———. (1980). "Toward the Analysis of Close Relationships," *Journal of Experimental Social Psychology,* 16 (6), 510–544.

Mashek Debra J., and Michelle D. Sherman (2004). *Handbook of Closeness and Intimacy,* Mahwah, NJ: Lawrence Erlbaum.

McCullough, Michael E., K.C. Rachal, Steven J. Sandage, Everett L. Worthington Jr., Susan Wade Brown, and Terry L. Hight (1998). "Interpersonal Forgiving in Close Relationships, II: Theoretical Elaboration and Measurement," *Journal of Personality and Social Psychology,* 75, 1586–1603.

Mikulincer, Mario, Gilad Hirschberger, Orit Nachmias, and Omri Gillath (2001). "The Affective Component of the Secure Base Schema: Affective Priming with Representations of Attachment Security," *Journal of Personality and Social Psychology,* 81, 305–321.

Mikulincer, Mario, and Phillip R. Shaver (2005). "Mental Representations of Attachment Security: Theoretical Foundation for a Positive Social Psychology." In *Interpersonal Cognition,* ed. Mark W. Baldwin. New York, NY: Guilford Press, 233–266.

Miller, Rowland S. (1997). "Inattentive and Contented: Relationship Commitment and Attention to Alternatives," *Journal of Personality and Social Psychology,* 73 (4), 758–766.

Mittal, Banwari (2006). "I, Me and Mine: How Products Become Consumers' Extended Selves," *Journal of Consumer Behavior,* 5 (6), 550–562.

Muñiz, Albert M. Jr., and Thomas C. O'Guinn (2000). "Brand Community," *Journal of Consumer Research,* 27 (March), 412–432.

Park C. Whan, and Banwari Mittal. (1985). "A Theory of Involvement in Consumer Behavior: Problems and Issues." *Research in Consumer Behavior,* 23, 201–232.

Petty, Richard E., Curtis P. Haugtvedt, and Stephen M. Smith (1995). "Elaboration as a Determinant of Attitude Strength: Creating Attitudes That Are Persistent, Resistant, and Predictive of Behavior." In *Attitude Strength: Antecedents and Consequences,* ed. Richard E. Petty and Jon A. Krosnick. Mahwah, NJ: Lawrence Erlbaum, 93–130.

Pimentel, Ronald W., and Kristy E. Reynolds (2004). "A Model for Consumer Devotion: Affective Commitment with Proactive Sustaining Behaviors," *Academy of Marketing Science Review,* 5, 1–44.

Reis, Harry T., and Brian C. Patrick (1996). "Attachment and Intimacy: Component Processes." In *Social Psychology: Handbook of Basic Principles*, ed. E. Tory Higgins and Arie W. Kruglanski. New York, NY: Guilford Press, 523–563.

Rusbult, Caryl E., Julie Verette, Gregory A. Whitney, Linda F. Slovik, and Issac Lipkus (1991). "Accommodation Processes in Close Relationships: Theory and Preliminary Empirical Evidence," *Journal of Personality and Social Psychology,* 60 (1), 53–78.

Sternberg, Robert (1987). "Liking Versus Loving: A Comparative Evaluation of Theories." *Psychological Bulletin,* 102, 331–345.

Thompson, Craig, Aric Rindfleisch, and Zeynep Arsel (2006). "Emotional Branding and the Strategic Value of the Doppelgänger Brand Image," *Journal of Marketing,* 70 (January), 50–64.

Thomson, Matthew, Deborah J. MacInnis, and C. Whan Park (2005). "The Ties That Bind: Measuring the Strength of Consumers' Attachments to Brands," *Journal of Consumer Psychology,* 15 (1), 77–91.

Trinke, Shanna J., and Kim Bartholomew. (1997). "Hierarchies of Attachment Relationships in Young Adulthood." *Journal of Social and Personal Relationships,* 15, 603–625.

Van Lange, Paul A.M., Caryl E. Rusbult, Stephen M. Drigotas, Ximena B. Arriaga, Betty S. Witcher, and Chante L. Cox (1997). "Willingness to Sacrifice in Close Relationships," *Journal of Personality and Social Psychology,* 72 (6), 1373–1395.

Waugh, Christian E., and Barbara L. Fredrickson (2006). "Nice to Know You: Positive Emotions, Self-Other Overlap, and Complex Understanding in the Formation of a New Relationship," *The Journal of Positive Psychology,* 1 (2), 93–106.

Weiss, Robert S. (1988). Loss and Recovery. *Journal of Social Issues,* 44, 37–52.

Wieselquist, Jennifer, Caryl E. Rusbult, Craig A. Foster, and Christopher R. Agnew (1999). "Commitment, Pro-Relationship Behavior, and Trust in Close Relationships," *Journal of Personality and Social Psychology,* 77 (5), 942–966.

ABOUT THE EDITORS AND CONTRIBUTORS

Pankaj Aggarwal is an Associate Professor of Marketing in the Division of Management, University of Toronto, and at the Rotman School of Management, Ontario, Canada. He completed his PhD in Marketing from the Graduate School of Business, University of Chicago in 2002, examining the role of relationship norms in influencing consumer behavior and attitudes. He has published a number of papers in the *Journal of Consumer Research* examining diverse issues related to consumer-brand relationships. Recently, he has also taken an interest in the phenomenon of product and brand anthropomorphism and its influence on consumer behavior. He has MBA degrees from IIM Ahmedabad, India, and the University of Chicago. He worked for fourteen years in the advertising industry and was working as vice president of J. Walter Thompson, India, before deciding to pursue his doctorate.

Aaron C. Ahuvia is a Professor of Marketing at the Dearborn School of Management, University of Michigan (UM). He also holds an appointment at the UM Ann Arbor School of Art and Design and serves as a Faculty and Research Associate at George Washington University's Creative and Innovative Economy Center. He won the 2007 Distinguished Research Award, which is the University of Michigan–Dearborn's highest campus-wide award for scholarship, and the 2001 University of Michigan–Dearborn Faculty Member of the Year award for research, teaching, and service. He is the former vice president for academic affairs for the International Society for Quality of Life Studies, and former associate editor for the *Journal of Economic Psychology*. He has published more than thirty works including six papers that were republished in compilations or translations of classic research.

Arthur Aron is Professor of Psychology at the Department of Psychology at The State University of New York at Stony Brook. His research centers on the self-expansion model of motivation and cognition in personal relationships, employing methods including laboratory and field-intervention behavioral experiments, representative surveys, and neuroimaging. He serves on the editorial boards of *Psychological Science,* the *Journal of Personality and Social Psychology*, *Personal Relationships*, and *Journal of Personal and Social Relationships*, and is a fellow of the American Psychological Association, the Association for Psychological Science, the Society for Personality and Social Psychology, and the Society for the Psychological Study of Social Issues. He received the 2006

Distinguished Career Research Award from the International Association for Relationship Research.

Laurence Ashworth earned a PhD in Marketing from the University of British Columbia, Vancouver, and is currently Assistant Professor of Marketing at Queen's University in Kingston, Ontario. His general research interests concern social and affective influences on consumer judgment and decision making, with a particular interest in fairness, impression management, and affect. His work has appeared in the *Journal of Marketing, Journal of Consumer Research, Journal of Consumer Psychology,* and *Journal of Business Ethics.*

Richard P. Bagozzi is the Dwight F. Benton Professor of Marketing at the Ross School of Business, and Professor of Clinical, Social and Administrative Sciences at the College of Pharmacy, both at the University of Michigan. A graduate of the PhD program at Northwestern University, in recent years he has received honorary doctorates from University of Lausanne, Switzerland, and Antwerp University, Belgium. He does basic research in the theory of action and theory of mind, applying ideas derived thereof to research in consumer behavior, emotions, social identity, sales force behavior, organizational studies, health behavior, self-regulation, and structural equation models.

Rajeev Batra is the S.S. Kresge Professor of Marketing at the Ross School of Business at the University of Michigan. His research interests cover the creation and management of brand equity; the improvement of marketing communications productivity; emotional advertising; advertising repetition and budgeting, global branding, and marketing in emerging economies. He has almost fifty publications on these topics, including papers in the *Journal of Consumer Research, Journal of Marketing Research, Journal of Consumer Psychology, Journal of Marketing,* and others. He is also the co-author or co-editor of five books, including a textbook on Advertising Management. He is on the editorial boards of the *Journal of Consumer Psychology, the International Journal for Research in Marketing, Journal of Advertising Research, Journal of the Academy of Marketing Science,* and others.

James R. Bettman received his PhD from Yale University and is currently Burlington Industries Professor of Business Administration and Professor of Psychology and Neuroscience at Duke University. His research focuses on consumer decision making, emotion, and brands, and the self. His publications include *An Information Processing Theory of Consumer Choice; The Adaptive Decision Maker; Emotional Decisions: Tradeoff Difficulty and Coping in Consumer Choice,* and more than a hundred research papers. He has mentored more than thirty doctoral students in marketing, was co-editor of the *Journal of Consumer Research,* and is currently on the editorial boards of the *Journal of Consumer Research, Journal of Consumer Psychology,* and *Journal of Marketing Research.*

Amit Bhattacharjee is a Doctoral Candidate in the Marketing Department of The Wharton School, University of Pennsylvania, where he entered the doctoral program in the fall of 2007. Prior to joining the program, he received a BS (Economics) from The Wharton School, where he concentrated in Marketing with a minor in Psychology. His research interests include consumer self-expression through consumption behaviors and the impact of marketing actions on consumer and societal welfare.

C.B. Bhattacharya is the Everett Lord Distinguished Faculty Scholar and Professor of Marketing at the School of Management, Boston University. His research interest is in the area of marketing strategy innovation and stakeholder marketing. Specifically, he studies how companies can use levers such as corporate and brand identity, membership and brand communities, and corporate social responsibility to strengthen stakeholder relationships. He has served on the editorial review boards of the *Journal of Marketing* and *Corporate Reputation Review* and has published numerous articles in journals such as the *Journal of Marketing Research, Journal of Marketing, Journal of Applied Psychology,* and *Organization Science.*

Joel B. Cohen is Distinguished Service Professor Emeritus in the Marketing Department at the University of Florida. He has been a member of the University of Florida's Marketing Department since 1974, serving as chairman from 1974 to 1983. In 1972, he became the first elected president of the Association for Consumer Research and recently received a lifetime achievement award for distinguished service to the *Journal of Consumer Research.* Other editorial responsibilities included serving as editor of the *Journal of Public Policy and Marketing* from 2001 to 2006. He has published cutting-edge research on psychological factors and processes that influence judgment and decision making with a particular focus on both attitudes and affect. In addition to an extensive body of theoretical and empirical papers in leading journals, he has contributed authoritative chapters in the *Annual Review of Psychology, The Handbook of Consumer Behavior, Affect and Social Behavior, The Handbook of Consumer Psychology,* and *Do Emotions Help Or Hurt Decision Making,* among other volumes.

Peter Dacin is Kraft Professor of Marketing at Queen's University, Kingston, Ontario. He earned his PhD in Marketing from the University of Toronto. He has published on a variety of topic areas in marketing and his work has appeared in several journals, including the *Journal of Marketing, Journal of Consumer Research, Journal of Marketing Research,* and *Journal of the Academy of Marketing Science.*

Edith F. Davidson received her PhD from the University of Tennessee and is Assistant Professor of Marketing at Auburn University. Her primary research interest lies in marketing communications with diverse audiences, with an emphasis on understanding the social consequences and responsibilities associated with these targeting efforts. Secondary research interests include brand loyalty and dynamic retail encounters.

Shuili Du is Assistant Professor of Marketing, School of Management, Simmons College. She received her DBA in Marketing from the Boston University School of Management.

Her research interests primarily lie in understanding the effects of corporate social responsibility on consumers. Her research has appeared in the *Journal of Consumer Research, International Journal of Research in Marketing,* and *Marketing Science Report.* She has presented her research in leading academic forums such as the Advances in Consumer Research Conference, Society of Consumer Psychology Conference, and the INFORMS Marketing Science Conference.

Jennifer Edson Escalas received her PhD from Duke University and is Associate Professor at the Owen Graduate School of Management at Vanderbilt University. Her research explores how consumers use brands to express themselves and applies the concept of narrative processing to study how advertising affects consumers. She has published her research in the *Journal of Consumer Research, Journal of Consumer Psychology, Journal of Advertising,* and *Journal of Public Policy and Marketing.* She is a member of the *Journal of Consumer Research, Journal of Consumer Psychology,* and *Journal of the Academy of Marketing Science* editorial review boards. She is involved in the Association for Consumer Research (Advisory Council) and the Society for Consumer Psychology (Webmaster).

Monique A. Fleming is a Research Assistant Professor in the Psychology Department at the University of Southern California, where she has served on the faculty since 2005. She received a PhD in Social Psychology from Ohio State University after receiving a BA in Psychology from Stanford University. Her primary research area is in attitudes and persuasion, with a particular focus on the effects of important group memberships and prejudice on evaluative processes. She has also conducted research examining social cognition processes, judgmental bias and correction (particularly in a jury context), and the effects of having multiple versus few important group memberships on psychological well-being. She has published several articles and book chapters on these topics.

Susan Fournier is Associate Professor and Dean's Research Scholar at Boston University. Her research explores the creation and capturing of value through branding and relationship marketing. She has received best article awards for work published in the *Journal of Consumer Research, Journal of Marketing,* and *Journal of the Academy of Marketing Science.* She is a long-standing member of the editorial boards of the *Journal of Consumer Research, Journal of Relationship Marketing, Journal of Business-to-Business Marketing, and Marketing Theory,* the COO's Council at Irving Oil, and the Board of Advisors for Harley Owner's Group. She consults with a range of companies to inform on her teaching, case development, and research. Prior to joining BU, she served on the faculties of the Harvard Business School and the Tuck School of Business at Dartmouth, and held a VP/Director position at Young & Rubicam Advertising.

Susan Forquer Gupta is Assistant Professor of Marketing at Monmouth University, West Long Branch, New Jersey. She received her PhD from the University of Tennessee–

Knoxville, and MS and BS degrees from the University of Missouri–Columbia. Her research is focused on cross-cultural differences in managerial decision making, consumer decision making, culture measures, and cultural differences in branding in global markets. She has published articles in the *International Marketing Review, Journal of Business and Industrial Marketing,* and *Journal of Personal Selling and Sales Management.* She is currently serving as the President of Women in the Academy of International Business.

Henrik Hagtvedt is Assistant Professor of Marketing of Boston College. His primary research interests include imagery, the arts, aesthetics, design, and luxury. His research has appeared in the *Journal of Marketing Research, Journal of Consumer Psychology,* and *Empirical Studies of the Arts.* Prior to his doctoral studies, he studied painting at the Academy of Fine Arts in Florence, Italy, and worked full-time as an artist and exhibited internationally for several years. He also completed a Cand. Mag. degree in art history at the University of Oslo, Norway, before completing an MBA at the University of Georgia and entering the PhD program at the same institution.

Mindy F. Ji is a former Assistant Professor at Iowa State University. Her research interests include children and advertising, consumer-brand relationships, and habitual consumer behavior.

Deborah J. MacInnis is the Charles L. and Ramona I. Hilliard Professor of Business Administration at the Marshall School of Business, University of Southern California. Her research focuses on consumer behavior with an emphasis on emotion, persuasion, and branding. She is an associate editor for the *Journal of Consumer Research* and the *Journal of Consumer Psychology.* She has served on the editorial review boards of the top journals in marketing and consumer behavior. She won the Alpha Kappa Psi Award from the *Journal of Marketing* and the best article award from *Seoul National Journal* for her work on branding and management. She is also a recipient of the *Journal of Marketing's* Maynard Award and has been nominated for several other awards, including the Converse Award. She is a past president and past treasurer of the Association for Consumer Research and has received Marshall, USC, and national teaching awards.

Alokparna Basu Monga is Assistant Professor of Marketing at the Moore School of Business, University of South Carolina. She has a PhD in Marketing from the University of Minnesota and an MBA from Lancaster University, Lancaster, England. Her research interests focus on how consumers respond to branding activities as a function of their cultural orientation, analytic or holistic processing styles, and self-construal. Her research has appeared in or is forthcoming in the *Journal of Consumer Research, Journal of Marketing Research,* and *Journal of Consumer Psychology.* She is currently on the editorial review board for the *Journal of Consumer Psychology.* Her teaching interests include marketing strategy, international marketing, and brand management.

Albert M. Muñiz, Jr. is Associate Professor of Marketing at DePaul University. His research interests are in the sociological aspects of consumer behavior and branding, including consumer-generated content and value creation in consumption communities. He has researched extensively in the area of consumer brand communities for over a decade and his work has been published in the *Journal of Consumer Research, Journal of Advertising, Journal of Interactive Marketing* and *Journal of Strategic Marketing*. Professor Muñiz received his BS, MS and PhD from the University of Illinois, Urbana-Champaign. Before coming to DePaul, he taught at the University of California at Berkeley.

Dhananjay Nayakankuppam is an Associate Professor and Tippie Research Fellow at the Henry B. Tippie School of Business at the University of Iowa, where he has served on the faculty since 2001. He obtained his PhD in Marketing and MS in Psychology from the University of Michigan. Prior to that, he worked in advertising following an MBA. His research interests are in the area of evaluations and judgment. His inquiries in these areas have appeared in *Journal of Consumer Research, Journal of Consumer Psychology,* and *Marketing Science.*

Thomas C. O'Guinn is Professor of Marketing and Executive Director, Center for Brand and Product Management, University of Wisconsin–Madison. He has published widely, served on many editorial and advisory boards, and he studies the sociology of consumption. Of particular note in the context of this volume is his work on community, the social brand, integrated brand promotion and visual aspects of branding and design. He is a co-author of a leading text on *Integrated Brand Promotion*. He is currently leading a design/innovation initiative on the UW–Madison campus.

C. Whan Park is the Joseph A. DeBell Professor of Marketing and Director of the University of Southern California's Center for Global Branding. He has published numerous articles in leading marketing journals, such as *Journal of Marketing Research, Journal of Consumer Research, Journal of Marketing,* and *Journal of Consumer Psychology*. His current research is in the areas of brand attachment, branding strategy, and consumers' aesthetic experiences. He is an editorial board member of the *Journal of Marketing*. He is active in executive education nationally and around the world. He currently serves as editor of the *Journal of Consumer Psychology.*

Vanessa M. Patrick is an Associate Professor and Bauer Professor of Marketing at the C.T. Bauer College of Business at the University of Houston. She received her PhD from the University of Southern California, Los Angeles. Her research interests include the study of affect (mood and emotions), aesthetics and intertemporal issues in choice and consumption. Her research has appeared in the *Journal of Consumer Research, Journal of Marketing Research, Journal of Consumer Psychology, Journal of Retailing,* and *Empirical Studies of the Arts*. Prior to doing her PhD, she worked for several years in advertising and brand consultancy. She worked in account management and planning at

Ogilvy and Mather Advertising and J. Walter Thompson, and as a brand consultant and project manager at DMA, a London-based brand management consultancy.

Marcel Paulssen is Professor of Business Administration at HEC Geneva. His academic credentials include a BBA, a Master's degree in Management Science from the Stevens Institute of Technology, a Master's degree in Business Administration from the Technical University of Berlin, and a PhD in Marketing from the Technical University of Berlin. Prior to joining the faculty of Humboldt University in Berlin he gained more than four years of management experience in the area of strategic marketing with Matshushita and Daimler.

Laura Peracchio is a Professor of Marketing at the University of Wisconsin, Milwaukee. Her research focuses on persuasion, consumer decision making, language and culture, children's consumer behavior, and social marketing issues. She currently serves as an associate editor of the *Journal of Consumer Research,* and is a member of the editorial board of the *Journal of Consumer Psychology.* She has published widely in leading journals such as the *Journal of Consumer Psychology, Journal of Advertising, Journal of the Academy of Marketing Science, Journal of Consumer Research,* and *Journal of Marketing Research.* She has received research awards from the American Marketing Association, the Marketing Science Institute, and the *Journal of Consumer Research.*

Richard E. Petty is Distinguished University Professor of Psychology at Ohio State University. He received his BA from the University of Virginia and his PhD from Ohio State. His research focuses on the factors responsible for changes in beliefs, attitudes, and behaviors. He has published eight books and over 250 journal articles and chapters. Honors received include the Distinguished Scientific Contribution Awards from the Society for Personality and Social Psychology and the Society for Consumer Psychology, and service as president of SPSP and the Midwestern Psychological Association. He is past editor of the *Personality and Social Psychology Bulletin.*

Joseph R. Priester is Associate Professor of Marketing at the Marshall School of Business, University of Southern California. His research focuses on brand attachment, attitudes, and creativity. He is serving or has served as an associate editor for the *Journal of Consumer Research* and the *Journal of Consumer Psychology.* He is also a member of the editorial review board of the *Journal of the Academy of Marketing Science.* He is a past president of the Society for Consumer Psychology. He is also the recipient of the Marshall School Teaching Award.

Americus Reed II is Associate Professor in the Marketing Department of the Wharton School, University of Pennsylvania, where he has served on the faculty since 2000. He received a PhD (Consumer Behavior and Social Psychology) from the University of Florida's Warrington College of Business after receiving two Master's degrees in Organizational Behavior and Market Research Methods and a BBA in Strategy from Georgia

State University. His primary research and consulting areas are in brand equity, specifically identity-driven marketing—the study of creating and fostering "brand communities" that transcend the utilitarian aspects of products, connect to deep levels of emotional and social affiliation, and cultivate lifelong loyalty with consumers. In 2005, his academic work in this area received an honorable mention for the prestigious Robert Ferber Award for academic impact in the top scholarly outlet in consumer behavior. He has published several articles and book chapters on the topic.

Martin Reimann is a researcher at the University of Southern California and at Stanford University. He assesses consumers' decision making using measures in the following modalities: historical, psychometric, behavioral, and neural. He holds a PhD in Marketing from Technische Universität Bergakademie Freiberg (Germany). He edits two scholarly, peer-reviewed publications, the *Journal of Neuroscience, Psychology, and Economics* and *NeuroPsychoEconomics*.

Deborah Roedder John is the Curtis L. Carlson Chair and Professor of Marketing at the Carlson School of Management, University of Minnesota. She received her PhD in Marketing from Northwestern University. Her expertise lies in the area of consumer behavior, specializing in consumer branding and children's consumer behavior. She has published extensively and served on the editorial boards of premier marketing journals, including the *Journal of Marketing, Journal of Marketing Research,* and *Journal of Consumer Research.* She has also served as associate editor at the *Journal of Consumer Research* and president of the Association for Consumer Research.

Bridget Satinover received her MBA from the University of Tampa and is a doctoral student in Marketing at the University of Tennessee. Her research interests include marketing communications, media usage, social Internet behavior, interpersonal buying center dynamics, and other social psychological aspects of consumer behavior. Previous to pursuing her doctorate, she worked in the advertising and media industry.

Vanessa Sawicki is a doctoral student in the Psychological Sciences Department of Purdue University. Her broad research interests include attitudes and attitude change, attitude strength, and social cognition. More specifically, her current research examines strength-related properties of attitudes that influence the type and amount of information processing activity.

David W. Schumann received his PhD from the University of Missouri, is a consumer psychologist, and holds the William J. Taylor Professorship of Business in the Department of Marketing and Logistics at the University of Tennessee. His research interests center on issues concerning marketing communication strategy with specific focus on target segmentation, belief structures, attitude formation, persuasion, selective exposure, and prejudice reinforcement. He is a past president of the Society for Consumer Psychology and is a fellow of the American Psychological Association.

Sankar Sen is Professor of Marketing at the Zicklin School of Business, Baruch College, City University of New York. His research focuses on consumer decision making, corporate social responsibility, and social marketing. His research has appeared in the *California Management Review, MIT Sloan Management Review, Journal of Consumer Research, Journal of Marketing,* and *Journal of Marketing Research,* among other publications.

Leona Tam is an Assistant Professor of Marketing at Old Dominion University. Her research interests include habitual consumer behavior, consumer self-regulation, and consumer brand relationships.

Matthew Thomson earned his PhD in Marketing from the University of Southern California's Marshall School of Business. Before arriving at the University of Western Ontario, he worked at Queen's University in Kingston, Ontario. His research focuses generally on the interaction of marketing relationships, branding, and emotions, and recent projects have been published in the *Journal of Marketing* and the *Journal of Consumer Psychology.* Before his life in academia, he worked as an information management consultant to the Information, Privacy, and Ethics Commission of Alberta.

Doan Winkel is a doctoral candidate at the University of Wisconsin–Milwaukee. His major field of interest is Organizations, with a minor of Marketing. His research focuses on issues of diversity in entrepreneurship and in the broader workplace setting (specifically focusing on the work-family interface and emotional intelligence), as well as cross-cultural issues in marketing. He is a member of the Academy of Management, the Society for Industrial and Organizational Psychology, and the United States Association for Small Business and Entrepreneurship.

Zhong Wan is a doctoral candidate in Marketing at the Marshall School of Business, University of Southern California. Her primary research interests are consumer emotion, brand attachment, coping, and word-of-mouth communications. She is also interested in gender differences in consumer emotions and shopping behaviors. She was brought up in Beijing, China. She completed her BA degree in Marketing and worked as an executive assistant at Motorola (China) for a couple of years. She also received an MS degree in Retailing and Consumer Sciences from the University of Arizona.

Duane T. Wegener is Professor of Psychological Sciences at Purdue University. His research centers on the factors that influence the amount and nature of information processing in persuasion settings. He also actively studies biases in social judgments and attempts by social perceivers to remove or avoid those biases. He co-edits the Attitudes/ Social Cognition section of the *Social and Personality Psychology Compass*, and he is a past associate editor for the *Personality and Social Psychology Bulletin* and for *Basic and Applied Social Psychology.* He serves on the editorial boards of the *Journal of Personality and Social Psychology* and *Journal of Experimental Social Psychology* and is a fellow of the American Psychological Association, the Association for Psychological Science, and the Society for Personality and Social Psychology. He received the American Psychological Association Distinguished Scientific Award for an Early Career Contribution to Psychology (in Social Psychology) in 2001.

Wendy Wood is James B. Duke Professor of Psychology and Neuroscience at Duke University. Her research interests include the social psychology of gender, especially the evolutionary origins of gender differences, and habits and attitudes as determinants of behavior. She is a fellow of the American Psychological Association, a fellow of the Association for Psychological Science, and a founding member of the Society for Research Synthesis.

Name Index

Italic page references indicate tables and figures.

Subject Index

Italic page references indicate tables and figures.